ENCYCLOPEDIA OF
CONFLICTS
SINCE WORLD WAR II
SECOND EDITION

ENCYCLOPEDIA OF CONFLICTS
SINCE WORLD WAR II

SECOND EDITION

EDITED BY JAMES CIMENT

VOLUME ONE

SHARPE REFERENCE
an imprint of M.E. Sharpe, Inc.

SHARPE REFERENCE

Sharpe Reference is an imprint of M.E. Sharpe, Inc.

M.E. Sharpe, Inc.
80 Business Park Drive
Armonk, NY 10504

Library of Congress Cataloging-in-Publication Data

Encyclopedia of Conflicts Since World War II / James Ciment, editor. – 2nd ed.
p.   cm.
Includes bibliographical references and index.
ISBN-13: 978-0-7656-8005-1 (set : alk. paper)
ISBN-10: 0-7656-8005-X (set : alk. paper)
1. World politics—1945–1989—Encyclopedias.   2. World politics—1989—Encyclopedias.   3. Military history, Modern—20th century—Encyclopedias.   4. Military history, Modern—21st century—Encyclopedias.   I. Ciment, James.

D843.E46 2007
909.82'5—dc22   2006014011

Printed and bound in the United States of America

The paper used in this publication meets the minimum requirements of American National Standard for Information Sciences–Permanence of Paper for Printed Library Materials,
ANSI Z 39.48.1984.

(c) 10   9   8   7   6   5   4   3   2   1

Publisher: Myron E. Sharpe
Vice President and Editorial Director: Patricia Kolb
Vice President and Production Director: Carmen Chetti
Executive Editor and Manager of Reference: Todd Hallman
Senior Development Editor: Jeff Hacker
Project Manager: Wendy E. Muto
Program Coordinator: Cathleen Prisco
Editorial Assistant: Alison Morretta

Cover images, clockwise from top left, by Getty Images and the following:
Piero Pomponi; Sven Nackstrand; Marco Di Lauro;
Three Lions/Stringer; Jean-Philippe Ksiazek; STR/Stringer

CONTENTS

Volume 1

Roots of War

Conflicts

Africa, Sub-Saharan

Index

Volume 2

Index

Volume 3

Organizations, Alliances, Conventions, and Negotiations

Appendixes

Indexes

ALPHABETICAL LIST OF ENTRIES

Editor
James Ciment

Contributors

Fatimakhon Ahmedova
Khujand State University (Tajikistan)

William H. Alexander
Norfolk State University

Charles Allan
East Tennessee State University

Michael Andregg
University of St. Thomas

Daniel F. Cuthbertson
University of New Brunswick (Canada)

D. Elwood Dunn
University of the South

James Frusetta
American University (Bulgaria)

A.J.R. Groom
University of Kent (United Kingdom)

Aidan Hehir
University of Sheffield (United Kingdom)

Kenneth L. Hill
La Salle University

Adam Hornbuckle
Independent Scholar

Tim Jacoby
University of Manchester (United Kingdom)

Ravi Kalia
City College–City University of New York

John A. King Jr.
Ransom Everglades School

Keith A. Leitich
Independent Scholar

David MacMichael
Independent Scholar

Eric Markusen

Gordon H. McCormick
Naval Postgraduate School

Sean J. McLaughlin
University of Western Ontario (Canada)

Patit Paban Mishra
Sambalpur University (India)

Caryn E. Neumann
Ohio State University

Luke Nichter
Bowling Green State University

James D. Perry
Independent Scholar

Luke Perry
University of Massachusetts

Emin Poljarevic
Silk Road Studies Program/Central Asia-Caucasus Institute

Erika Quinn
California State University Sacramento

Kenneth Quinnell
Central Florida Community College

Peter Jacob Rainow
Independent Scholar

Julian Schofield
Concordia University (Canada)

Jeffrey A. Shantz
York University (Canada)

Carl Skutsch
Independent Scholar

Samuel Totten
University of Arkansas

Mark Ungar
Brooklyn College–City University of New York

Andrew J. Waskey
Dalton State College

Brandon Kirk Williams
University of Colorado

INTRODUCTION

The expression almost instantly became a cliché—that, after September 11, 2001, "everything had changed." And at least for the United States, it had.

Prior to that date, the country had been enjoying a post–Cold War decade of unparalleled global hegemony, declining defense expenditures, and a lowered overseas military profile. Aside from having its nose bloodied in Somalia in 1993 and suffering an assault on one of its destroyers—the USS *Cole*—in Yemen in 2000, the United States military had effectively been at peace since the end of the Gulf War in February 1991. The largest U.S. military commitment of the decade—as part of the North Atlantic Treaty Organization assault on Serbia in 1999—had come off without the death of a single American soldier.

Then came 9/11 and the deaths of nearly 3,000 Americans in New York, Washington, and Pennsylvania, the single deadliest day in the nation's history since the Civil War battle of Antietam. In the aftermath of that attack, President George W. Bush declared a "war on terrorism" and launched large-scale invasions of Afghanistan in 2001 and Iraq in 2003. As of 2006, more than 150,000 American troops were engaged in both theaters, and more than 2,500 soldiers had been killed. For the United States, then, 9/11 *had* changed everything.

But what of the rest of the world? For some countries—particularly those, like Great Britain, allied with the United States in the "war on terrorism"—there has been great change. They are now at war, whereas they were once at peace. Taking a still larger view of things, there is a growing feeling in the West and in much of the Islamic world—in both policy-making circles and among the public at large—that, to borrow from political scientist Samuel Huntington's now famous thesis, a "clash of civilizations" has begun. But, of course, this "clash" and others long predated 2001 (indeed, Huntington first presented his ideas in the early 1990s) and even the post–World War II era covered in this encyclopedia. For all their horror, then, the attacks on September 11 were more like a flare, illuminating to the American public a battlefield hitherto dimly seen.

In that light, September 11 changed little. Conflicts continue to rage around the world—some of them influenced by cultural clashes but most of them triggered by a host of factors, from economics to ethnicity to environmental breakdown to political ambition. Many are legacies of nineteenth-century colonialism, a few continue to reverberate with Cold War tensions, and some may indeed be attributable to clashes between global cultures.

What is indisputable—and indisputably disturbing—is how much new material needs to be included to bring this encyclopedia, just eight years old, up to date. The figures are distressing. Whereas the first edition contained articles on some 151 conflicts around the world, the new edition traces more than 175. In addition, almost 40 conflicts covered in the original edition have had to be substantially updated to keep track of continued fighting—though, in a few cases, the updates are happily concerned with reports of truces, treaties, and conflict resolution.

Like its predecessor, the second edition of the *Encyclopedia of Conflicts Since World War II* is comprehensive, covering every major and minor armed conflict—*inter*-state and *intra*-state—from 1945 through the middle of the first decade of the twenty-first century. That it takes approximately 1,400 pages to chronicle a mere sixty or so years of humanity's propensity to settle its differences through bloodshed is a sad indictment of both our species and the age in which we live. If, as American Civil War general William Tecumseh Sherman famously said, "War is hell," then these volumes serve as a travel guide to a netherworld of recent human creation.

From World War to Cold War

In 1945, the world emerged from a conflagration of epic proportions. With the broad exception of the Western Hemisphere, no part of the world lay untouched by World War II. Europe, Asia, North Africa, and the far-flung islands of the Pacific basin had all seen armies pass through and great battles fought. Much of the globe lay in ruins, devastated by bombing, artillery, street-fighting, and tank battles.

Humanity emerged from the war hungry, displaced, and shell-shocked.

What would happen next? There was hope. Fascism—in its German, Italian, and Japanese incarnations—had been crushed. A new United Nations offered an international dispute-resolution forum that seemed to offer more promise than had the doomed League of Nations established at the end of the century's first global conflict. There was an alliance, however shaky and uneasy, between the two emerging superpowers—the Soviet Union and the United States. For the peoples of Asia, Africa, and other colonized regions, the end of the war promised the possibility of independence, if only because the imperialist European powers (and Japan) had been left so wasted by the conflict. To paraphrase a popular World War II song, the lights appeared to be coming on all over the world

Sadly, they only flickered. The grand wartime alliance of the Soviet Union and the United States quickly disintegrated into a chilly standoff of distrust and blustering. The UN—enveloped in the smothering ideological confrontation between East and West—proved nearly as impotent in settling disputes as the League had.

The European powers, particularly France and Portugal, showed themselves unwilling to accept what British prime minister Harold Macmillan dubbed "the winds of change"—that is decolonization. Moreover, these stubborn colonial powers were joined by settler states such as Israel and South Africa, where the population of European origin—seen as alien by their non-European co-inhabitants, but lacking a native land to return to—attacked and came under attack repeatedly.

Even where the Europeans did depart, longstanding indigenous disputes—made worse by imperialist policy and practice—erupted with a vengeance. The nearly 1 million Muslims and Hindus slaughtered in the 1947 partition of the Indian subcontinent did not bode well for the postcolonial order, as was borne out by the seemingly endless conflicts that later engulfed Africa.

Finally, hanging over the collective head of humankind was a new weapon—tried and proved on Japan near the end of World War II—that finally made world-ending Armageddon, a portentous element in many of the world's great faiths, a distinct possibility. The mushroom cloud and the specter of World War III had come to haunt the world's imagination.

Many World Wars?

Some historians have argued, however, that World War III was not a specter but a reality, having taken the form of a Cold War between the superpowers that regularly turned hot on battlefields as far strewn in time and place as Greece (1947), Laos (early 1960s), and Nicaragua (1980s). In other words, World War III began within a few years of the close of World War II and continued through the collapse of the Soviet Union in 1991.

But what of the conflicts that have erupted in the wake of the Cold War? Despite ballyhooed predictions of history ending with the fall of Communism and the universal "triumph" of Western-style free-market economies and political democracy, fighting and dying continued on every continent. Had humanity entered a new phase of planetary warfare? And, finally, what of the fateful attacks on New York and Washington on that glorious blue-sky morning of September 11, 2001? Was that a portent of a new worldwide struggle to come? In short, has the post–World War II era merely been a series of evolving global conflicts? World Wars III, IV, and V, as it were.

A look at the evolution of war in the twentieth century might offers insights. The world wars of the first half of the twentieth century evolved from the largely static, European-based World War I to the mobile, semiglobal World War II. Moreover, the fronts of World War I—in France, Russia, and the Middle East—were hundreds of miles apart and largely involved the same adversaries. The fronts of World War II were thousands of miles apart and were fought by semi-related adversaries: primarily Germany and the Soviet Union in Eastern Europe; Britain, Germany, and the United States in Western Europe and North Africa; and the United States, Japan, and China in Asia and the Pacific.

The "world wars" of the second half of the twentieth century were transformed into truly global conflicts involving dozens of adversaries fighting along fronts entirely disconnected from one another. But World War II and the hypothetical World War III did have one thing in common: many of the adversaries were partly or fully integrated into grand alliances, even if the combatants fought their wars for a host of reasons unrelated to the power politics of the Cold War. As for the even more hypothetical World War IV, any hint of grand alliances and ideology seemed to have disappeared altogether. Conflicts in the wake of the Cold War appeared fought over entirely parochial issues.

The "war on terrorism"—"World War V" in the scheme of things suggested in this introduction—would appear at first to be a throwback to earlier conflicts, with the greatest alliance in world history—the nation-states of the world—pitted against an equally far-flung adversary, a shadowy global network of terrorists and perhaps a few "rogue" states that provide them sanctuary, weapons, and financing. Gone are the parochial concerns of the localized conflicts of the 1990s. In their place is a "clash of civilizations," or at least a global struggle between "civilization" and barbarism.

But the nature of the new battlefield bears out the twentieth-century pattern described above: from the static fronts of World War I to the disconnected global battlefields of the "war on terrorism." Now even the world capital of finance and the political capital of the world's only superpower were vulnerable to attack.

So what is new in all of this? Perhaps nothing. Perhaps the idea that the last hundred years of human history can be segmented into consecutive "world wars" is a flawed one. Rather than splitting history, it might be better to try lumping it together. Since the late fifteenth century, the capitalist order of Europe—and, later, a few of the more rapidly developing countries beyond its borders, such as the United States and Japan—has been gradually extending its grip over the rest of the world, while the rest of the world has mounted a mighty, though often futile, resistance. Might not the various "world wars" of the twentieth and early twenty-first centuries be seen as mere battles in a conflict half a millennium in the making? For all the madness of his methods, Osama bin Laden has made it quite clear that the presence of "infidels" (read: U.S. and European troops) on Islamic holy soil has been the prime motive for his terrorist attacks on the West.

This is, perhaps, too big a question for any single study to answer, especially one such as this—one that attempts to provide the details of dozens of conflicts that may or may not be manifestations of some grand, epochal war. Rather, the following articles attempt to define the differences among these many conflicts of the past sixty years, even as the accumulation of that detail hints at something bigger and more unifying.

Organization—How to Use This Encyclopedia

Encyclopedia of Conflicts Since World War II, Second Edition, is divided into three sections, plus two appendices, a bibliography, and specialized indexes.

Roots of War

The first section is called "Roots of War" and consists of eight entries outlining the major types of conflicts and the underlying causes of war in the post–World War II era. Each entry concludes with a bibliography.

"Cold War Confrontations" outlines how different historians interpret the roots of the Cold War in Europe and the developing world. In addition, it discusses how the superpower struggle manifested itself in various developing world conflicts. "Anticolonialism" reveals the ways in which many of the conflicts of the past fifty years remain a legacy of the European imperialist order of past centuries. "People's Wars" examines the means by which people of the developing world have struggled to overcome the legacy of the imperialist order in a world divided ideologically between East and West. "Coups" explains why violent internal power struggles—usually involving various groups of elites in developing world countries—have been so ubiquitous over the past fifty years. "Invasions and Border Disputes" provides an examination of international conflicts within the context of international law and geopolitical power struggles. "Ethnic and Religious Conflicts" explains why and how these long-standing internal divisions can sometimes become the battle lines of civil conflicts. "Terrorism: Global History Since the 1940s" discusses the means and ends of perhaps the most desperate of tactics in modern warfare. Finally, "International Arms Trade" offers a study of how the largely political neutral marketplace in weapons has served to exacerbate the conflicts of the post–World War II era.

Conflicts

By far the longest section of this encyclopedia, "Conflicts" consists of some 170 articles. The section is organized into regions: Africa, sub-Saharan; Americas; Asia, East and Southeast; Asia, South; Europe and the Former Soviet Union; Middle East and North Africa; Oceania. Within each section, conflicts involving multiple nations are arranged according to the most significant country involved in the conflict. Thus, Israel's several wars with neighboring Arab states are listed in the section Middle East and North Africa, under Israel. In conflicts involving two nations, the entry appears under the country that comes first in the alphabet. For example, the several conflicts between India and Pakistan are listed under India.

After listing the most important country involved in the conflict, the entry heading indicates the type of conflict and the participants in the conflict. The type of conflict category correlates with the "Roots of War" essays. For example, if a conflict is listed as a Cold War confrontation, the reader may turn to the appropriate essay in part 1 on this type of conflict to learn more about how that conflict fits into the larger context of the Cold War.

Each "Conflicts" entry concludes with two items: a "See also" heading that lists related entries within the "Conflicts" section, as well as in the "Roots of War" and "Organizations, Alliances, Conventions, and Negotiations" sections, and a bibliography listing books and articles for further reading.

Organizations, Alliances, Conventions, and Negotiations

This section deals with the ways various countries, regions, blocs of geographically and ideologically united or culturally related nations, or the international community as a whole have dealt with threats to security, resolved conflicts, maintained peace, and punished war criminals. In general, these efforts fall into two areas: collective security arrangements in the form of alliances and blocs, and conflict resolution and international tension reduction through the United Nations and international summits. This section consists of sixteen entries, arranged alphabetically. Each of the entries concludes with a bibliography listing articles and books for further reading.

Appendices

Biographies

This section consists of brief biographies of the most significant individuals involved in the conflicts and diplomacy of the post–World War II era.

Glossary

This section offers definitions of key organizations, groups, and terms involved in the conflicts and diplomacy of the post–World War II era. It also offers a handy reference guide to the many abbreviations and acronyms listed in the "Organizations, Alliances, Conventions, and Negotiations" and "Conflicts" entries.

Bibliographies

In addition to the bibliographies in the individual entries, a general bibliography is presented here, offering reading suggestions on the general history and theory of warfare, as well as individual conflicts.

Indexes

Encyclopedia of Conflicts Since World War II, Second Edition, contains three separate indexes: a general index, a biographical and organizational name index, and a geographical index.

ROOTS OF WAR

COLD WAR CONFRONTATIONS

The Cold War—a term coined by journalist and scholar Walter Lippmann in 1947—refers to the forty-five-year-long confrontation between the United States and the Soviet Union that began at the end of World War II and ended with the collapse of communism in Eastern Europe and the Soviet Union at the end of the 1980s and beginning of the 1990s.

Though appropriate for the time and poetic enough to last the ages, the term "Cold War" is something of a misnomer. Contrasted to a hot war—such as World War II—it implies a nonviolent confrontation between the two great superpowers of the post–World War II era. Where hot wars produce invasions, power politics, and the application of violence, the Cold War consisted of tense borders, ideological disputes, and an arms race—an unnerving and costly war, but essentially a bloodless one. Indeed, many American and Soviet apologists for the nuclear arms race that accompanied it say the Cold War kept the peace.

This is roughly true in Europe, where the Cold War began, but it is preposterous when applied to much of the rest of the world, particularly the developing world. There the Cold War turned hot. The Cold War only occasionally involved soldiers from the United States and the Soviet Union in significant numbers (Korea and Vietnam for the former; Afghanistan for the latter). Instead, the two superpowers armed their proxies, or substitutes, in Asia, Africa, and Latin America to do their fighting—and their dying—for them.

The Cold War is also a misleading term for a less direct reason: both the United States and the Soviet Union tended to interpret most civil and international conflicts as part of the great ideological struggle between East and West. Indeed, policymakers in both Washington and Moscow generally believed that their superpower opponent was behind every conflict. Both sides often failed to consider indigenous historical considerations in their assessment of why conflicts erupted and how conflicts could be resolved. Thus, in Vietnam, the United States ignored traditional Vietnamese nationalism, while the Soviet Union underplayed clan strife and Islamic fundamentalism before intervening in Afghanistan.

This entry attempts to define the Cold War in two ways. First, it examines the origins of the conflict—specifically, the different schools of thought concerning who started it and why. Second, it examines the Cold War in its effects—how it played itself out in the developing world. Indeed, after the initial, largely nonviolent confrontation over Europe in the late 1940s, the Cold War's real battlegrounds were in Asia, Africa, and Latin America. First, however, an account of the Cold War is required.

Origins

If the Cold War began shortly after World War II, its background can be found in the disaster of World War I. In March 1917, the czarist government of Russia collapsed, a victim of wartime shortages and antiwar sentiment as well as other, more long-term problems. The democratic government that replaced it insisted on keeping its wartime obligations to its allies, France and England. This intention inspired more unrest in Russian cities, leading to a second uprising, spearheaded by the Communist Bolsheviks under the leadership of Vladimir Lenin and implemented through local worker and peasant councils, known as "soviets." Promising "land, bread, and peace," the new Bolshevik government immediately pulled Russia (soon to be renamed the Soviet Union) out of World War I.

The revolution set off a civil war between Bolshevik and anti-Bolshevik, or "white" Russian, forces—bolstered by small contingents of troops from Britain, France, Japan, Czechoslovakia, and elsewhere. The civil war ravaged the country for two years and resulted in the total victory of Lenin and the Bolsheviks. The United States, among other nations, severed diplomatic relations with the new government in Moscow, not reestablishing them until 1933.

Meanwhile, within the Soviet Union, a struggle emerged following the death of Lenin in 1924 between advocates of world revolution and proponents of "socialism in a single country." The latter, led by Joseph Stalin, triumphed. Stalin industrialized the economy rapidly. He did this by collectivizing agriculture, starving out the independent peasantry, and centralizing economic decision-making. In the process, millions of people died, but the Soviet Union made rapid strides in creating an industrial infrastructure, an achievement admired by many in the West who were dismayed by capitalism's failure in the Great Depression.

Indeed, it was the Great Depression that helped propel the rise to power of National Socialism—or Nazism—in Germany in 1933. Advocating renewed militarism and German racial superiority, Nazi Germany quickly rearmed and began its expansionist crusade.

Nazism and Soviet Communism were bitterly opposed to each other, but for pragmatic reasons—each feared the other's power—they signed a nonaggression pact in August 1939. A month later, the Nazis invaded Poland, with the Soviets taking their own half of the defeated nation. England and France immediately declared war on Germany, and World War II began, with the Soviet Union largely neutral.

In June 1941, however, the Nazis tore up the nonaggression pact and sent a massive force into the Soviet Union in one of the greatest invasions in history. Within months, the Soviets had fallen back to the suburbs of Moscow, and it appeared as if the country might completely fall to the Nazis. Gradually, however, the Soviet Red Army halted the invasion and within eighteen months began to push the Germans back.

Meanwhile, following Japan's attack on Pearl Harbor on December 7, 1941, the United States entered the war. (Japan, Germany, and Italy had formed an alliance called "the Axis." After Pearl Harbor, Germany and Italy declared war on the United States.) An alliance was quickly established between the three main anti-Axis powers—Great Britain, the Soviet Union, and the United States. There were strains in the alliance, however. Stalin, in particular, was angry at what he perceived to be delays in Anglo-American plans to open a second front against Nazi Germany in Western Europe. Still, the alliance held through the end of the European war in May 1945. By that final year, when it was apparent that it was only a matter of time until Germany was defeated, questions began to present themselves concerning the postwar order. There were essentially three important areas of dispute: the fate of Germany, the fate of Eastern Europe, and the ongoing war with Japan.

In February 1945, the leaders of the three great powers—Soviet Premier Stalin, British Prime Minister Winston Churchill, and U.S. President Franklin Roosevelt—met at Yalta, in the Russian Crimea. There it was decided that Germany would be jointly occupied by the victors, East European nations would be permitted to decide their own destiny in popular elections (so long as they pursued a pro-Soviet foreign policy), and the Soviet Union would join the Anglo-American war against Japan ninety days after the surrender of Germany.

In July, the three powers met again at Potsdam, a suburb of Berlin, the former capital of the now-defeated Germany. There the three powers created a joint military administration (which also included France) for occupied Germany and agreed to move the borders of Poland westward. In midconference, however, the American delegation—headed by U.S. President Harry Truman, who had replaced Roosevelt upon the latter's death in April—received word that the atomic bomb had proved successful in tests in the New Mexico desert. The atomic bomb rendered Soviet help in the war against Japan unnecessary. By implication, this development undermined Britain and America's need to offer concessions to the Soviet Union over Eastern Europe—consisting largely of pro-Soviet regimes. After atomic bombs were dropped on Hiroshima (August 6) and Nagasaki (August 9), Japan surrendered and was occupied by the United States.

Post–World War II Crises

It did not take long for tensions to build between the former Allies. When the Soviet Union demanded access to the Dardanelles—linking the Black Sea to the Mediterranean—and Iran, with its oil reserves, the United States and Britain refused. Meanwhile, the Soviet Union refused to participate in the World Bank and International Monetary Fund, two institutions designed to revive the war-damaged capitalist economies of Europe and Asia. In Eastern Europe and the Balkans, tensions were highest. With the Red Army occupying all of the former and much of the latter (the main exceptions being much of Yugoslavia and Greece), there appeared to be little the Allies could do to demand free elections, short of launching World War III. In 1946, former British Prime Minister Churchill warned of a Soviet-imposed "iron curtain" falling across Eastern Europe.

In Greece, however, a civil war between pro-Western and Communist forces offered an opportunity.

Unresolved issues at the Potsdam Conference in July–August 1945—attended by (left to right) British Prime Minister Winston Churchill (later replaced by Clement Atlee), U.S. President Harry Truman, and Soviet leader Josef Stalin—foreshadowed the conflicts of the Cold War. *(Time Life Pictures/Getty Images)*

In 1947, the British government told Washington that it no longer had the resources to back the pro-Western elements there. This was part of an exhausted and war-ravaged Britain's overall retreat from much of the world, thus leaving the United States to assume the mantle of Western leadership. The U.S. administration responded with the Truman Doctrine, effectively promising U.S. aid to any country attempting to fight off a Communist insurgency. That same year, George Kennan, a State Department officer in America's Moscow embassy, enunciated a policy—known as the "containment" doctrine—that soon won the attention of the U.S. foreign policy establishment. The doctrine proposed that the Soviet Union's expansionist policies must be resisted by force if necessary, especially in those areas of vital interest to the United States.

Eastern Europe, it was soon decided, lay outside that area. Thus, while Stalin imposed pro-Soviet Communist regimes in these countries by force, the United States did little but complain. By the end of the 1940s, then, both Germany and Europe were divided into two spheres, with the western half of Germany and the continent (supported by the United States through the massive aid of the Marshall Plan) becoming democratic and capitalist and the eastern half (under the umbrella of the Soviet army) Communist. Both sides soon organized military blocs to protect themselves against attack by the other. In 1949, the United States established the North Atlantic Treaty Organization (NATO), followed six years later by the Warsaw Pact of Soviet-bloc countries. With the occasional confrontation over Berlin, the East-West confrontation in Europe soon settled into a status quo of peace, economic development, and nuclear tension (the Soviet Union having tested its own atomic bomb in 1949).

Shift to the Third World

By 1950, the battle lines between the capitalist and Communist worlds had shifted to Asia. In 1949, the

Communist Chinese had defeated the nationalists in a massive civil war. A year later, the Communist North Koreans invaded the non-Communist southern half of the peninsula. The United States—at the head of a United Nations force—rose to the latter's defense. The conflict became a three-year-long bloody stalemate following Communist China's entry into the war at the end of 1950. Meanwhile, in 1954, French colonial forces were defeated in Vietnam by Communist-led nationalists, leaving Vietnam divided between a Communist north and a non-Communist south.

Tensions between the Soviet Union and the United States eased a bit by the late 1950s. A more liberal Nikita Khrushchev had taken power in the Soviet Union following the death of Stalin in 1953. Khrushchev began to enunciate the doctrine of "peace-ful coexistence" with the West. Still, Khrushchev was determined to keep Eastern European countries in the Soviet orbit, sending an invasion force into wavering Hungary in 1956. The United States and the West refused to intervene, revealing to many in Eastern Europe that there was little chance the West would help them rid the region of Soviet control. The decision not to intervene was part of President Dwight Eisenhower's policy. After the war ended in Korea, he was not eager to engage U.S. forces in conflicts around the world. Instead, Eisenhower relied on covert action by the Central Intelligence Agency to overthrow developing world regimes deemed hostile to the West, while keeping the Soviets at bay through America's overwhelming nuclear superiority, which had been enhanced by the detonation of the first hydrogen bomb in 1953.

The 38th parallel divided the Korean peninsula between the communist North and democratic South in 1945, giving rise to the first major military confrontation of the Cold War era—the Korean War, from 1950 to 1953. *(STR/AFP/Getty Images)*

Increasingly, there was growing dissent to these policies in both the United States and the Soviet Union. In America, many politicians, including 1960 presidential candidate John F. Kennedy, believed that America must develop a more flexible response to the varied types of Communist threat—from nuclear blustering by the Soviet Union to the "brush-fire" insurgencies of Asia, Africa, and Latin America. In 1961, President Kennedy approved an Eisenhower-era plan to launch a CIA-backed invasion of Cuba, led by anti-Communist exiles. (Cuba had undergone a revolution in 1959 under the leadership of the Marxist-nationalist Fidel Castro.) The invasion failed disastrously. A year later, the Soviets began placing nuclear missiles on the island. Confronted by the United States, Khrushchev was forced down. The humiliation led to his overthrow two years later by Leonid Brezhnev and other hard-liners in the Kremlin who believed that the Soviet Union should pursue its interests in the developing world more forcefully.

Meanwhile, Kennedy—fearful of being branded soft on Communism by Republicans—began sending advisers to back the anticommunist regime in South Vietnam, under siege from indigenous Communist forces. Following Kennedy's assassination in 1963, his successor Lyndon Johnson escalated U.S. involvement. Eventually 550,000 U.S. troops were serving in Vietnam by 1968. The increasingly unpopular war led to Johnson's decision not to run for reelection and America's withdrawal in 1973. The rapid collapse of the South Vietnamese in 1975 embittered Americans toward direct involvement in international conflicts. This so-called Vietnam syndrome coincided with a period of Soviet expansionism. Having largely achieved nuclear parity with the United States by the mid-1970s, the Soviets embarked on a campaign to support Communist and pro-Communist regimes in Asia, Africa, and Latin America, largely through military aid and advisers. In Afghanistan, however, Moscow sent in tens of thousands of troops in 1979 to back the pro-Soviet regime there.

In the United States, political forces challenged the legacy of Vietnam. By the end of the Carter administration, the United States had started supporting anticommunist forces and governments from El Salvador to Afghanistan, while beginning a new arms build-up. This process was dramatically escalated during the presidency of Ronald Reagan, who also upped the level of anti-Soviet rhetoric.

By the mid-1980s, it was the Soviet Union's turn to feel the limits on its power. Bogged down in Afghanistan, the increasingly cumbersome centralized economy of the Soviet Union was going broke trying to match the latest arms build-up by the United States. Recognizing its plight, the ruling Politburo chose a young reformer named Mikhail Gorbachev to revamp the Soviet economy and ease tensions with the United States. Gorbachev quickly announced that as far as he was concerned, the arms race with the United States was no longer relevant, and he moved to develop closer relations with Washington. At the same time, he opened up political debate at home and made it clear to Eastern European governments that they could no longer expect Soviet aid in quelling domestic disturbances. This new doctrine allowed anticommunist sentiment to come into the open across Eastern Europe, leading to the collapse or total weakening of all Communist regimes there by the end of 1989. Soviet troops were soon withdrawn from the region, and the Warsaw Pact dissolved.

Beset by a collapsing economy at home and apparent political chaos, the Soviet army decided to step in, launching a military coup in August 1991. The rapid demise of the coup quickly led to the downfall of the Soviet Union. In December, Russian Federation President Boris Yeltsin officially dissolved the union, establishing the Commonwealth of Independent States in its place. With the Soviet Union gone and Eastern Europe no longer Communist, the Cold War had come to a sudden end.

Theories About Origins

Essentially, theories about the origins of the Cold War—at least, among scholars in the United States specifically and the West generally—fit into three general categories: orthodox, revisionist, and realist. To simplify—or rather, to oversimplify—the arguments of these three schools of thought, it can be said that orthodox theorists blame the Soviet Union for starting the Cold War, revisionist scholars say the United States was at fault, and the realists argue that both and neither powers were to blame. This latter group argues that the origins of the Cold War were fixed in misconceptions by both sides and driven by forces of history beyond the command of policymakers in both Washington and Moscow.

The orthodox theorists rose to predominance first. Largely products of the early years of the Cold

War themselves, the ideas of orthodox scholars reflected the thinking of policymakers in Washington and London. The revisionists came next, responding to U.S. hegemony overseas in the 1950s and 1960s, especially during the course of the Vietnam War. The realist school somewhat overlapped the revisionists, but generally came to the fore in the 1970s and 1980s, at a time when both the United States and the Soviet Union were aggressively pursuing their interests throughout the developing world.

Orthodox Theory

According to orthodox theorists, the United States was filled with good intentions as World War II came to a close. Hoping to build on the collective allied security principles of World War II, American policymakers wanted to rely on the newly created United Nations and its Security Council to resolve international tensions. Moreover, the United States was willing to forgo the advantage of its nuclear monopoly by turning over control of those weapons to an international monitoring agency. In Eastern Europe, says the orthodox school of thought, the United States was willing to meet the Soviet Union halfway. As long as there were free elections, Moscow could insist that the foreign policy of the democratic states be pro-Soviet. Finally, the United States was willing to help the Soviet Union and Eastern Europe recover from the devastation of World War II through the massive aid program known as the Marshall Plan. According to the orthodox school, America had reached an understanding on these points with the Soviets at Yalta—agreements that the Soviet Union either never intended to honor or refused to honor later.

For all these benign intentions, however, American policymakers were met by Soviet duplicity, intransigence, and aggression, say orthodox theorists. Rather than agreeing to collective security, the Soviet Union engaged in unilateral measures to ensure its national interests. It refused to allow free elections in Eastern Europe. It ignored American offers for an internationally monitored atomic bomb and embarked on a nuclear weapons program of its own. And it contemptuously dismissed the Marshall Plan as a clandestine American plot to undermine its Communist system. The Soviet Union, says the orthodox school, was also responsible for putting the Communists in power in China and giving the go-ahead to North Korea for its invasion of the south.

Differences of opinion existed, however, within the orthodox school when Soviet motivation was discussed. Extreme hard-liners—many of whom were exiles from the Soviet Union—claimed that Moscow was primarily driven by Marxist ideology, which called for a worldwide anticapitalist revolution. The implication of this interpretation was grim. Since any agreement would be torn up by the ideologically committed Soviets when it was convenient, negotiations with Moscow were worse than useless, they were dangerously naive. Moreover, the United States must adopt a policy of "liberating" Soviet-controlled countries or face an indefinite future of hostile aggression.

Others, especially the career diplomats and State Department officials such as Kennan, offered a less desperate view of Soviet motivations. Rather than being driven by ideological considerations, Moscow was merely trying to pursue its own national interests, just as the czarist government had done for centuries. Its efforts to dominate Eastern Europe were part of a centuries-old policy of using that territory to protect itself from aggressive Western European states, a fear aggravated by twin German invasions in World War I and World War II. By this reasoning, the United States could best deal with Soviet expansionism by meeting it with selective force, the so-called containment doctrine. Moreover, since Soviet aims were based on national self-interest, it was possible to negotiate with Moscow.

Revisionist Theory

Like the orthodox school of thought, revisionist theory has many variants, though all are united by several basic premises. First, the United States generally took the lead in provoking Cold War confrontations, whether by cutting off aid to the Soviet Union in the days following the end of World War II or making demands that ran counter to legitimate Soviet security interests in Eastern Europe. Secondly, the United States, with its overwhelming military and economic power in 1945, was, by necessity, the nation that should have offered conciliatory gestures. Third, the Soviet Union, having had much of its industrial infrastructure destroyed in the war and having lost some 8 percent of its population, was in a far weaker position than the United States and was motivated to take the actions it did out of fear.

According to what might be called the moderate school of revisionism, the United States—by making demands for democratic governments in Eastern Europe, the key security zone for a Soviet Union recently invaded via that region—provoked the Soviet Union into setting up puppet regimes in Poland and overthrowing the democratically elected government in Czechoslovakia. Moreover, the overall weakness of the Soviet Union during the 1940s and 1950s dictated a cautious foreign policy. For example, Stalin only acted in those parts of Eastern Europe where he felt that he had a right to do so. He quickly backed down in the face of Western protests in Iran and Turkey in 1946 and agreed not to intervene to help the Greek Communists in 1947. Thus, despite the ideological bravado and bombastic anti-Western rhetoric, the Soviet Union acted carefully abroad and stuck to the letter of the agreements it signed.

Most moderate revisionists blame the Truman administration for the origins and onset of the Cold War. Truman lacked the diplomatic finesse of Roosevelt. Instead of recognizing the Soviet Union's legitimate security concerns, Truman tried to bully Moscow. According to these revisionists, the dropping of two atomic bombs on Japan in 1945—despite evidence that Tokyo was about to surrender—was done to inform Moscow of U.S. possession of a nuclear arsenal and Washington's resolve to use those weapons. In other words, Truman practiced the age-old tactic of saber rattling to force the Soviet Union to back down, interpreted Soviet moves to defend itself as acts of aggression, precipitously cut off aid to a desperate former ally, and launched a war of rhetoric intended to rally world opinion against Moscow. All of these moves, then, forced the defensive and fearful Soviet Union to react.

More radical revisionists dismissed the moderate revisionist argument as too personality-based. It did not matter, they said, who was in charge of American foreign policy, since that policy was driven by political, economic, and ideological forces beyond the control of any administration. Specifically, they argued that in the wake of Britain's collapse, the United States took up the mantle of Western leadership. This meant maintaining the West's centuries-long hegemony over the rest of the world. Moreover, U.S. policymakers believed that a postwar depression could only be prevented through opening up the international marketplaces to U.S. products.

With the collapse of Nazism and Japanese imperialism in World War II, Soviet communism represented the only threat to Western hegemony, as witnessed by Moscow's successful efforts to reorient the economies of Eastern Europe away from the West. Indeed, this desire to keep Communism at bay—for fear of losing markets and Western control of the developing world, especially as the latter decolonized in the two decades following World War II—was the underlying motive behind American foreign policy throughout the Cold War. In effect, then, radical revisionists agreed with official Soviet theories on the origins of the Cold War. According to Moscow, America was driven not by a fear of the Soviet Union but a desire to capture world markets, since imperialist capitalism depended on ever-greater access to markets and resources. Communism, by this reckoning, threatened those markets and resources and had to be stopped. And since the Soviet Union generally supported Communist movements in those countries, it had to be contained.

Realist Theory

The realist school mixed elements of the revisionist and orthodox theorists in its own assessment of the causes of the Cold War. At the same time, it tried to mesh the actions of individuals with the forces of history. According to the realists, both sides hoped that wartime cooperation would continue after the war, though each expected this to happen on its own terms. The Soviets, pursuing what they considered their own legitimate security concerns in Eastern Europe, expected the United States to go along. Washington, fearful that a collapsing international economy would set off a major depression at home, expected the Soviets to accept U.S. hegemony in much of the world outside the immediate Soviet orbit. Neither wanted to precipitate a confrontation. But in taking steps to pursue their own interests, each forced the other to take countermeasures, thereby setting off a vicious cycle of fear and hostility on both sides. In short, the realists saw the Cold War confrontation as a new version of an old-fashioned balance-of-power struggle.

The realists also argued that internal politics in the United States and even the Soviet Union played a role in the Cold War confrontation. Because the Red Army occupied Eastern Europe toward the end of World War II, Roosevelt was forced to recognize Soviet hegemony there. He could not admit this to the country, however, especially since descendants of immigrants from that region were a key component of the New Deal coalition. Thus, when the reality of Soviet dominance became clear after the war, the American people felt that Roosevelt and the Democrats had betrayed the country, leading to a rise in anticommunist hysteria at home. At the same time, they also believed that the Soviets had gone back on their word and could not be trusted.

Other realists cited contradictions within the Communist system. They noted the great irony of the Cold War's ideological struggle: specifically, that those countries under Soviet control—namely, Eastern Europe—were the most hostile to Communism, while countries outside the Soviet orbit—including such countries as Italy, India, and Vietnam—were more amenable to Communism. In a sense, then, Soviet foreign policy was driven by an effort to survive in the face of a hostile capitalist West by maintaining control over a restive East European sphere of influence while projecting influence into those parts of the world that were sympathetic to Communism. Both of these policies served to further antagonize the West, leading to countermeasures that forced the Soviet Union into more aggressive action abroad.

Impact

The Cold War, as noted above, was driven in part by an ideological struggle between East and West. Part of this struggle, of course, involved the best means to organize human society—that is, via capitalist democracy or Communism. Aside from this basic split, however, there were many other underlying beliefs, beliefs that came to be accepted as unquestioned facts.

For Soviet leaders, there were several such truisms. One was that capitalism was doomed to collapse from its own contradictions. That is to say, that the exploitation of workers by capitalists was destined to intensify to a point in which the former would overthrow the latter. A second Soviet truism said that the only way this event could happen was through violent revolution. Third, capitalist powers, led by the United States, were determined to prevent this from happening by any means necessary. Since the Soviet Union offered a model for developing world countries to emulate—as well as concrete assistance to groups in those countries attempting to foment Communist revolution—the West felt compelled to contain Moscow, as part of its overall defense of capitalism worldwide.

Out of these beliefs gradually developed a Soviet policy in which virtually every nationalist rebellion or anti-Western government was seen as a potential Soviet ally, thereby deserving of help. Any movement fighting against a pro-Western government also fell into the same category. Thus, the Soviet Union found itself backing both legitimate Communist governments, as well as dictatorial governments that paid little more than lip service to the Communist cause.

This policy was mirrored by the United States, which also backed brutal dictatorships that were anticommunist. American policymakers had other truisms that were uniquely their own, leading to errors in policy. Such policy errors based on false truisms are not unique to the Cold War. For example, at the 1938 Munich conference, Britain and France acceded to Hitler's demands as a means of appeasing the German dictator and preventing war. Because they failed to do either, the Munich agreements offered powerful lessons to Western policymakers. Specifically, Munich confirmed the belief that bowing to a dictatorial government's demands only leads to further demands and eventually war. This experience offered a model for dealing with Soviet expansionism.

U.S. foreign policy during the Cold War was equally misguided. It assumed that all efforts to overthrow pro-Western governments were Communist in origin and that all of them were directed by Moscow. The depth of this belief can be measured by the fact that it persisted among many U.S. policymakers long after events revealed an increasingly hostile relationship between Moscow and Beijing—the two giants of the Communist world—in the early 1960s.

These truisms on both sides had fatal consequences. One, of course, was the arms race. Since both superpowers believed that the other was driven by ideology and self-interest to neutralize their antagonist, each side believed it had to defend itself by any means necessary. In a nuclear age, this meant building enough weapons to utterly destroy the other. This volatile situation, then, created enormous constituencies in both countries—the military elite in the Soviet Union and the military-industrial complex in the United States—that demanded more weapons to counter advances made by the other side. Ultimately, the arms race would distort the American economy and destroy the Soviet Union's.

More importantly for the purposes of this book, the truisms of the Cold War served to ensure that the United States and the Soviet Union involved themselves in many of the world's civil conflicts—conflicts that were often based on causes indigenous to each society. By offering money, weaponry, intelligence, military training, and, occasionally, advisers and soldiers, the United States and the Soviet Union exacerbated, extended, and exaggerated these conflicts. At the same time, the two sides cast the struggle in ideological terms, which made it impossible to seek out the true causes of the conflict. By setting up a kind of ideological force field, the Cold War confrontation deflected potential negotiations and peaceful solutions to many conflicts.

Many developing world countries tried to evade the implications of these Cold War truisms by advocating a middle course. In 1955, many of the leaders of the developing world met at Bandung, Indonesia, to establish the nonaligned group of nations. Somewhat successful in charting a third way for a number of developing countries, the movement faced enormous obstacles, perhaps the most important of which was the overall distrust in which Moscow and especially Washington held this movement. Much of the Cold War policy of both the Soviet Union and the United States was driven by one basic rule of thumb: those who are not with us are against us. Membership in the nonaligned movement—though widespread—was often rendered meaningless by Soviet and American policy of interference.

Of course, the Cold War had its ups and downs. From time to time, tensions between the Soviet Union and the United States eased, resulting in the occasional trade agreement and nuclear weapons limitation treaty, but it rarely served to limit U.S. or Soviet interventionism in developing world conflicts. Indeed, the mid-1970s, the period of warmest détente, or friendship, between Moscow and Washington, was marked by an escalation of U.S. and Soviet interference in the conflicts of Africa.

Thus, despite moves toward reconciliation on arms and trade or the easing of tensions along the heavily armed European divide, the Cold War never really lessened in the developing world. That should not seem too surprising since, with the advent of European peace in the late 1940s, it was the developing world—many of the countries newly independent—that served as a battleground between East and West and as the main prize sought by both sides. In that sense, the Cold War was little different than most of the major "hot wars" of the last several hundred years: it was a battle to control the vast resources and markets of the devel-

oping world. And like those hot wars, the Cold War could not end until one side was defeated.

Just as the two great struggles of the first half of the twentieth century—that is, World Wars I and II—left a legacy of troubled peace, so has the great Cold War confrontation. Many of the conflicts that punctuated the Cold War had origins that stretched to an era long before Yalta or even the Bolshevik revolution. It could be argued that the era of European imperialism planted the seeds for many of the bitterest and most long-lasting struggles of the post–World War II era, including the conflicts between Israel and Palestine, India and Pakistan, and even Vietnam. Clearly, the Cold War fueled the fury of these wars, although in the case of the first war, it started long before the Cold War began and has now outlasted it.

Yet, there are many other conflicts that, while rooted in the pre–Cold War era, were intensified so greatly by Soviet and American involvement that they can be said to be legacies of the Cold War. These conflicts include such long-simmering struggles as the one in Angola between the government and Jonas Savimbi's rebels (Savimbi was backed by the United States; the government by the Soviet Union) or the strife in Cambodia.

Moreover, the very collapse of the Communist order triggered a number of conflicts in that part of the world, most notably in the former Yugoslavia. The impact of the Cold War there is less certain. Clearly, Communism contained ethnic strife in the former Yugoslavia. Its repressive political system—whether it was triggered by Cold War fears or was an inherent part of Communism as it came to exist in Eastern Europe—prevented ethnic groups with both a long tradition of rivalry and a recent history of brutality (specifically, the struggle between fascist Croats and Communist Serbs during World War II) from cutting each other's throats. Whether the Communist system honestly reconciled these groups (if only temporarily), simply postponed the inevitable, or actually inflamed ethnic hatred by refusing to acknowledge it is uncertain.

One thing does seem certain, however. The legacy of the Cold War is bound to inspire as many competing scholarly theories as its origins.

James Ciment

Bibliography

Ball, Simon J. *The Cold War: An International History, 1947–1991.* New York: St. Martin's Press, 1998.

Clough, Michael. *Free at Last? U.S. Policy Toward Africa and the End of the Cold War.* New York: Council on Foreign Relations, 1992.

Crockatt, Richard. *The Fifty Years War: The United States and the Soviet Union in World Politics, 1941–1991.* New York: Routledge, 1994.

Day, Richard B. *Cold War Capitalism: The View from Moscow, 1945–1975.* Armonk, NY: M.E. Sharpe, 1995.

Hunter, Allen, ed. *Rethinking the Cold War.* Philadelphia: Temple University Press, 1998.

Judge, Edward H., and John W. Langdon. *A Hard and Bitter Peace: A Global History of the Cold War.* Englewood Cliffs, NJ: Prentice Hall, 1996.

LaFeber, Walter. *America, Russia and the Cold War, 1945–1990.* 6th ed. New York: McGraw-Hill, 1991.

Leffler, Melvyn, ed. *Origins of the Cold War: An International History.* New York: Routledge, 1994.

Rodman, Peter W. *More Precious than Peace: The Cold War and the Struggle for the Third World.* New York: Charles Scribner's Sons, 1994.

Young, John W. *Cold War Europe, 1945–1989: A Political History.* New York: Routledge, 1991.

ANTICOLONIALISM

Anticolonialism grew in response to European colonial expansion. Its origins can be traced to the West itself, although it ultimately found its strongest expression in Africa, Asia, and Latin America. Fueled by the maturing of commercial capitalism at home, and in pursuit of gold, God, and glory, Western Europeans in the fifteenth century began their great expansion overseas. What was different about commercial capitalism from earlier developments in the world was its inherently expansionist social order that stimulated the discovery of new lands overseas, the acquisitions of colonies globally, and the pursuit of economic theories and practices known as mercantilism. Simultaneously, Europe experienced the emergence of the scientific revolution, which, together with mercantilist theories, was to usher in the age of capitalist civilization.

Growing populations and increased output in agriculture, mining, fishing, and forestry stimulated economic growth in Europe, increasing the power and prestige of the European merchant class that was unmatched elsewhere in the world. In China, for example, merchants were regarded as socially inferior and suffered several political restrictions. Significantly, just when European merchants and their joint stock companies began to provide monarchs with the capital to launch overseas expeditions, the Chinese expeditions, which predated the European efforts, were suddenly halted by imperial fiat in 1433.

The resulting European global expansion between the sixteenth and nineteenth centuries led to the development of mercantilism, which by its inherent logic was aimed at enhancing and unifying the power of new monarchies. This result was to be achieved by amassing gold to pay for the cost of the recurring wars and the proliferating bureaucracies. Maintaining a favorable balance of trade became a preoccupation of every European monarchy and was to be achieved by granting royal charters of monopoly privileges to joint stock companies in colonizing or trading in specified overseas territories.

The logic of monopoly privileges to these trading companies meant that these privileges had to be defended at every cost to prevent unwanted competi-

tion, which inevitably subordinated the interests of colonies to those of European nations. Consequently, colonies were to provide markets for manufacturers, to supply raw materials that could not be produced at home, to support a merchant marine that would be valuable in wartime, and to engender a large colonial population that would provide manpower. All Western European nations followed these mercantilist practices, whether it was Portugal obtaining spices in the East Indies, Spain extracting gold and silver in the Americas, Holland developing a worldwide merchant marine, or Britain passing the Navigation Acts against Dutch trade and enforcing the British East India Company's tea monopoly, which culminated in the Boston Tea Party.

What distinguished this new mass trade in necessities from the earlier traditional trade in luxury goods was its unprecedented volume encompassing the globe and integrating countries and continents into the new international market economy in which each trading European nation was obligated to defend its monopoly. Defense of monopoly inevitably resulted in gaining political control of a colony. The Englishman W. W. Hunter best described the practice in the nineteenth century when he admitted that in the case of India the British, "true to our national character," had transformed themselves from "merchants" into "rulers."

Adam Smith, the astute Scottish economist of the late eighteenth century, perceived in his *The Wealth of Nations* the significance of the global trade when he noted that the overseas discoveries opened "a new and bottomless supply of customers for all European goods"—a market that encompassed "most of Asia, Africa and Americas." But he also noted the adverse effect of the global trade on the native populations:

By uniting, in some measure, the most distant parts of the world, by enabling them to relieve one another's wants, to increase one another's enjoyments, and to encourage one another's industry, their general tendency would seem to be beneficial. To the natives, however, both of the

East and West Indies, all the commercial benefits, which can have resulted from those events,
have been sunk and lost in the dreadful misfortunes which they have occasioned. . . . The savage injustice of the Europeans rendered an
event, which ought to have been beneficial to
all, ruinous and destructive to several of those
unfortunate countries.

In assigning "dreadful misfortunes" to the "savage
injustice of the Europeans," Adam Smith articulated
perhaps one of the earliest anticolonial sentiments and
opened a debate on the effects of colonialism that per-
sists to the present day. On the one hand, there are
those who have supported Smith's position, arguing
that Western colonization resulted in the deprivation
from which the third world still suffers. A more nu-
anced interpretation of this position has been provided by Edward Said, who in his polemical work
Orientalism (1978) argued that European literature
about the East could not be politically neutral because
of the authors' colonial relationship. On the other
hand, there are those who argue that pre-European
overseas societies were not "moral" utopias, and that
there was at least as much exploitation under native
rulers and elites as later under European administrators and businessmen. A more brazen interpretation of
this position has been provided by the Swiss-born
French architect Charles-Edouard Jeanneret (popularly known as Le Corbusier), who called Western colonization a "force morale" for development. A more
recent reassertion of this position was provided by
the American columnist Patrick Buchanan, who remarked that Africa would not have had railways and
all its other modern comforts were it not for European
rule.

The remarkable thing about Western expansion
after the fifteenth century is not that Europeans were
able to colonize such large territories globally; rather,
it is that Europeans in such small numbers were able
to control and govern such disparate peoples in far-
flung parts of the world for so long with relative ease.
It could not have been possible without the collaboration of the native populations in administering European rule in colonies. The Europeans were obliged
to educate at least enough natives to facilitate and
sustain the effective administration of the territories
recently brought under their vast new imperial umbrella. The alternative—training young Europeans to
become fluent enough in native languages to carry on
the daily chores of administrative collecting, spending, and punishing—was simply too expensive and
intellectually unappealing. The impact of Western
education, much like that of Christian missionary
preaching, proved, at best, a mixed blessing to European rule. The shrewd Scot, Mountstuart Elphin-
stone, had known how dangerous Western education
would prove to be when he had the courage to introduce it in Bombay in India; indeed, he called it "our
highroad back to Europe." Introduction of Western
education in colonies accelerated demands for the demise of European colonial rule by arming local elites
with the words with which to call for it.

Beginnings of Decolonization

Much of the European mystique and position had
been based on its historical establishment and control
of a world system. By the early twentieth century, the
fortunes of empire-building since the fifteenth century had given Europe influence in the hybrid New
World societies it had created and control over Africa
and much of Asia. Indeed, conscripts from the
colonies joined forces with the metropolitan states
during both world wars. But the wars weakened Europe just as they intensified the resolve of colonized
peoples to direct their own destinies. Many in the
colonies and beyond employed European socioeco-
nomic doctrines and different elements of nationalism to challenge the structures of dominance; the
postwar decades witnessed the self-assertion of the
non-European world at the expense of the imperial
systems.

At the end of World War I, U.S. President
Woodrow Wilson and Soviet Premier Vladimir Lenin
emerged as beacons of anticolonialism. In his Fourteen Points, Wilson's plan for a postwar order set the
principles for peace settlements, calling for "adjustment of all colonial claims," insisting that "the interests of the populations concerned must have equal
weight with the equitable claims of the government
whose title is to be determined." The United States
would be "intimate partners of all the governments
and peoples associated together against the Imperialists." Notwithstanding the fact that Wilson did not
have Asia and Africa in mind when he articulated
these positions to colonized peoples, they were still a
clarion call to independence and self-government.

Lenin had defined imperialism as "the highest
stage of capitalism," which he heartily condemned.

As leader of the Russian Revolution (1917) and heir to the Marxist doctrine advocating the end of oppression and the transformation of society, Lenin was poised to symbolize colonial struggles even though he paid little attention to the aspirations of the colonized in Asia and Africa. Lenin's Communism, however, provided both critical theory and an ideology that was amazingly adaptable to colonial assertion. The Soviet-led Communist International (Comintern, 1919–1943) offered a vehicle for the export of revolution, although the late twentieth-century events in Eastern Europe and the Soviet Union proved nationalism to be a far more powerful force than international Communism.

The process of decolonization transformed colonies into nations that were often geopolitical constructs at variance with the traditions and allegiances of the societies involved. That ambiguous force known as nationalism obviously played a consequential role in these designs. Decolonization created independent political units, but it did not end the "cross-fertilization" existing between the European states and their former colonies: migrations and cultural and economic movements have kept the ties alive. Sometimes these relationships have perpetuated conditions of dominance (economic, cultural, and so on) by former European colonial powers, a phenomenon referred to as "neocolonialism." When associated with earlier colonies (especially those in Latin America), these emergent states have been designated the "third world," a term that was coined after World War II to refer to countries that were not part of either NATO (the Western capitalist nations allied with the United States) or the Warsaw Pact (the Eastern Communist nations allied with the Soviet Union). The fortunes of third-world countries have run the gamut from positive nonalignment, founded in 1955 by Afro-Asian nations at the Bandung (Indonesia) Conference, to pawnship at the hands of the United States or the Soviet Union and their respective allies. China offered a different response to European influences, albeit a curious blend of Communist and capitalist principles, and a unique pattern of self-assertion against the Western world and the United States.

European society itself underwent major disruptions in the early part of the twentieth century that had startling repercussions for its global roles. The two world wars that emanated from traditional European power conflicts demonstrated the fragility of the European balance of power. While Europe's global dominance gradually came to be challenged by the United States and Japan, it became equally evident that, given the imperial system, a war among European states could scarcely be contained in that orbit. For the colonies, the wars displayed the vulnerabilities of the imperial powers, which during wartime were often forced to relax their controls over their charges. Hundreds of thousands of indigenes served in the war efforts under European banners and frequently on European battlefields. Many of those who remained in Europe after the wars became organizers of anticolonial movements.

Amid the turmoil of war, Europe actually consolidated its colonial holdings and refined its techniques of rule. Colonial officials were trained more seriously, and indigenous elites were increasingly incorporated into authority structures as policies of indirect rule ("association" or trusteeship) were employed. The empires of England and France expanded after World War I with the transfer of German territories in Africa and the Pacific and the acquisition of mandates over former Turkish subjects in the Middle East.

Europeans provided colonized peoples with examples—traditions of resistance and doctrines—which could be used to transcend local disparities of language, religion, and allegiance, and provided rallying points for common action. Such doctrines as socialism and nationalism were powerful ideologies, the effectiveness of which had been demonstrated in the European arena. Moreover, these ideologies were sufficiently flexible to allow for numerous interpretations, and they could be adapted to the needs of different societies. Nationalism and socialism were especially appropriate because of their popular appeals in the colonies. Religious kinship allegiances could be expanded to nationalistic fervor; forms of communalism and cooperation, important ingredients of socialism, were not alien to the colonized. Beyond these, populism suggested a folk orientation that could appeal to the primarily agrarian masses. But the element of modification is extremely important, for the colonized peoples had not shared in the experiences out of which the doctrines had originally emerged.

The challenge of employing European doctrines, even in modified forms, was complicated by the disparities between European societies and the non-European societies of their colonies. The latter were primarily agrarian societies with traditional economic structures; the inhabitants had little secular education, were often extremely religious, and were the victims of a situation where history and development had largely been frozen by colonialism. They confronted representatives of modern, industrial peoples rather confident of their historical roles. For pre-modern societies to adopt the expressions of modern societies, when in fact that very modernization had contributed much to the plight of colonized peoples, required considerable adjustment.

Decolonization and Third World Nationalism

"Westernized" elites were the vanguard of the liberation movements in colonial regions. The colonized elites often matured in European or Europeanized school systems, a long-standing practice that had increased in the early twentieth century. The elements and background of the European doctrines were familiar to the elites, and these doctrines included a long tradition of challenge to authority in European countries. Also, the elites and many others in each colony could make common cause through their use of a single language, albeit the one imposed by the colonizers.

After a decades-long nationalist struggle, India celebrated peaceful independence from Britain in August 1947. The partitioning of the subcontinent between India and Pakistan, however, proved highly volatile. *(Keystone/Getty Images)*

Given the arbitrariness that led to the establishment of many colonies, cutting across ethnic and linguistic divisions, one can only speculate whether colonized regions would have united in protesting their situation as effectively as they did had they not availed themselves of European doctrines. These doctrines—particularly, nationalism—had much value as organizing themes, which charismatic leaders could use to wield discipline and commitment. In the long run, though, it has been the practical needs of a movement rather than strict adherence to doctrinal subtleties that has determined its directions. The doctrines have been most important at the resistance and transitional stages; beyond this point, pragmatism has taken hold.

As a political ideology, nationalism is based on the premise that nationality (not territory) is the proper organizing principle for a state, and that therefore the existence of a nation is enough justification for the existence of a state that is to exercise sovereignty only over that nation. Thus, as it emerged in Europe by the middle of the nineteenth century, political nationalism signified the extension of representative democracy and popular sovereignty to the international system under the slogan "One nation, one state."

Imperial systems are always organized according to the territorial principle, and European empires were no exception. However, previous empires (including those of pre-nineteenth-century Europe) had to contend only with the resistance that normally meets conquest, but which, lacking in ideology as a rallying point, can be dealt with in a variety of ways. The new "imperialism" had to contend with what was essentially an anti-imperialist doctrine not amenable to "sensible modification." Nationalism holds that whether there is oppression or not, whether there are advantages or not, each nation must have separate statehood.

As long as the Great Powers held nationalism in check in Europe, it was also possible to rationalize imperial action. When self-determination for national groups became the ordering principle for post–World War I Europe, it became intellectually dishonest to defend colonial rule. The mandate system of the League of Nations acknowledged that territorial possessions would in time receive national independence.

There were other signs that the imperial armor had been seriously cracked. In 1931, the Statute of

Westminster, passed by the British parliament, recognized the extent of this process among white-settler colonies by granting independence and Commonwealth status to Australia, New Zealand, Canada, South Africa, and Newfoundland. And Egypt received nominal independence in 1922, in part due to agitation from the Wafd party.

The colonies were hit hard by the economic crisis of the 1930s. Prices for tropical raw materials declined, and colonies felt their vulnerability as the imperial powers became preoccupied with their own recovery. While many peasants migrated to urban areas, in general the output of the colonial peasant rose, reflecting a move toward self-sufficiency.

India, Indochina, and the Dutch East Indies are classic examples of the process of decolonization in Asia. These territories were pretty much within colonial orbits by 1870. The Dutch thrust into the East Indies (the fabled Spice Islands) dates from the seventeenth century, the British filled a power vacuum in India in the eighteenth, and France secured Indochina in the nineteenth. The impact of modernization affected the peoples of these lands in varying manners, but such elements as the construction of communications arteries and the use of a European language to facilitate contact among diverse linguistic groups did foster a tendency toward unification in each colony; yet World War II was the decisive historical juncture in the transition from colonial territory to independent state.

The Hindu religious renaissance of the nineteenth century had stirred national pride in India. The first Indian national congress met in 1885, and the idea of a self-governing dominion within the empire emerged around World War I. During the interwar period the nationalist movement grew under the leadership of Mohandas Gandhi, with his program of passive resistance (*satyagraha*—literally, to hold fast to truth) and home rule (*swaraj*), while at the same time Muslim factions agitated for a separate Muslim state where Muslims were a majority. Soon after World War II an Indian independence bill passed by the British parliament became law (August 1947) and gave rise to the Dominion of India and the Dominion of Pakistan.

The nationalist movement in the Dutch East Indies emerged in the early twentieth century, supported by the formation of a Communist party in the 1920s. The nationalists reacted to the Japanese occupation of the territory in March 1942, and at the close of the war, the Japanese finally offered them independence in 1945. The Dutch attempt to reclaim Indonesia resulted in years of fighting, but pressures from the United Nations and the United States led to independence at the end of 1949 under the leadership of Sukarno. The Dutch held on to New Guinea through several years of protracted hostilities until they finally surrendered the area in 1962. Most of the Dutch had been expelled, and the movement was complete.

Indochina offers a somewhat more complicated story, yet the process was similar. Nationalist uprisings began around 1908; Ho Chi Minh emerged as a charismatic leader, founding the Communist Party in 1931. Like Indonesia, Indochina was occupied by the Japanese (1941), and Japan also offered independence, with Tonkin, Annam, and Cochin China becoming the autonomous state of Vietnam under the emperor, Bao Dai. After a temporary Chinese-British occupation following the war, France attempted to resume its prewar colonial position and fought the nationalist Vietminh forces but was defeated in 1954. Later, the United States became embroiled in a protracted conflict in Vietnam. Finally, the states of Vietnam, Laos, and Cambodia emerged from French Indochina.

The Japanese takeover of most of Southeast Asia during World War II fatally weakened the position of the European colonial powers. Once Japan was defeated, independence in fact was a matter of time.

After World War II, there were only three independent states in Africa: Ethiopia, Liberia, and the Union of South Africa. Egypt, though technically independent since 1922, was still occupied by British troops. In 1945, the Sixth Pan-African Congress was held in Manchester, England. Significantly, unlike previous conferences, which had been organized by African Americans and West Indians, this one was dominated by Africans, who included Kwame Nkrumah, future president of Ghana, and Jomo Kenyatta, future president of Kenya. The congress, among other things, demanded complete independence for the colonial areas of black Africa. Nationalist revolts broke out in Madagascar, a French colony, in 1947, and in Kenya, a British colony with a large white-settler population, in 1952 (the Mau-Mau Rebellion). Two years later, in 1954, the Algerian war of independence began.

In 1957, the Gold Coast was granted its independence by England. Renamed Ghana, after the great medieval state in the savannah region, it was the first

Ghana's Kwame Nkrumah (left) and Kenya's Jomo Kenyatta (right), the first leaders of their respective independent nations, were at the forefront of the anticolonial movement in postwar Africa. *(Evening Standard/Getty Images)*

sub-Saharan African colony to gain its independence from a European colonial power. In 1960, a total of seventeen African colonies, including Nigeria, Somalia, Senegal, and Côte d'Ivoire (Ivory Coast), became independent. However, in southern Africa, Portugal resisted the trend toward independence by its colonies; war broke out in Angola in 1961, Guinea in 1963, and Mozambique in 1964.

In 1963, at the Pan-African Congress Conference meeting in Addis Ababa, Ethiopia, African leaders established the Organization of African Unity (OAU), now the African Union (AU). Since its founding, the OAU has successfully arbitrated a number of inter-African disputes. It also consistently opposed white minority rule in the Republic of South Africa. In June 1977, the last major European colony in Africa, Djibouti (the former French Somaliland and, later, the French Territory of the Ifar and Issas) became independent.

Following World War II, England, France, the Netherlands, and Portugal no longer had the will or the means to control vast colonial empires. Cold War realities demanded at least the rhetoric of decolonization from the European states. The Atlantic Charter and the United Nations Trustee Council endorsed self-government, and the United States, having fulfilled its promise of independence for the Philippines in 1946, actively supported the self-rule of India, Pakistan, and Indonesia. The paths of decolonization after 1945 were varied and often bumpy, with peaceful transfers of power in Ghana and Ceylon (modern Sri Lanka) matched by protracted colonial wars in Algeria, the Belgian Congo, and Angola.

Decolonization and the Cold War

The Cold War played an important role in shaping the world after 1945, but events in the 1990s marked a historical turning point. Communism collapsed almost everywhere by 1991, ending the Cold War and lifting the fear of global nuclear war. The Soviet Union, the last great colonial empire, dissolved into fledgling independent states, prompting Francis Fukuyama, a political analyst with the right-wing think tank Rand Corporation, to proclaim the "end of history." The 1990s also witnessed the dismantling of the apartheid system in South Africa. In 1994, a multiracial government headed by the African political activist Nelson Mandela replaced the minority white rule. (Southwest Africa, under United Nations guidance, made the transition to majority rule in 1990, as the country of Namibia.)

Neither World War II nor the collapse of the Soviet system and Communism really resulted in the end of history. The rise of ethnic and nationalist conflicts in Eastern Europe and the former Soviet Union have made some Western political analysts romanticize about the old Cold War rivalry. And the third world, made up principally of former colonies, continues to face severe economic challenges, even though since 1945 global economic productivity has expanded more rapidly than at any time in the past. Consequently, anticolonialism, which in the first half of the twentieth century was directed against European colonial rule, in the second half of the century came to be redirected against Western political dominance and disproportionate control of global economic resources. The countries of Asia, Africa, and Latin America maintained that they continued to be exploited by the Western states. Apart from being exploited in international trade and finance, these countries argued, they were being subjected to the "media imperialism" of the West. In fact, the controversy over the control of global resources and the international flow of information developed alongside a related north-south controversy: the demand for a New International Economic Order. Some third-world countries organized themselves in the "Group of Seventy-Seven" (named for the number of its original participants in 1964) in their efforts to gain economic leverage against the developed world and use the international forum of the United Nations and its many agencies to realize their demand for a fair share in world resources and communications, as these clearly affect their own economic and social development. Not surprisingly, Western countries, especially the United States, did not respond warmly.

Not all governments of the third world were hostile to the West, notwithstanding the political rhetoric used to gain popular support domestically. Third-world countries remained well aware of the West's power in encouraging economic and social development and in maintaining political peace. What the third-world governments complained about was the West's disproportionate control of global resources and its ethnocentric attitudes. The creation of a new world economic order in which the third world shared a proportionate representation would, in their view, eliminate the negative effects of the West's "predilection" for trivializing the developing countries.

Ravi Kalia and William H. Alexander

Bibliography

Chamberlain, Muriel Evelyn. *Decolonization: The Fall of the European Empires.* New York: B. Blackwell, 1985.

Childs, Peter. *An Introduction to Post-Colonial Theory.* New York: Prentice Hall, 1997.

Darwin, John. *Britain and Decolonisation: The Retreat from Empire in the Post-War World.* New York: St. Martin's Press, 1988.

Fanon, Frantz. *A Dying Colonialism.* New York: Grove Press, 1965.

Fredi, Frank. *Colonial Wars and the Politics of Third World Nationalism.* New York: I.B. Tauris, 1994.

Hintjens, Helen M. *Alternatives to Independence: Explorations in Post-Colonial Relations.* Brookfield, VT: Dartmouth Publishing, 1995.

James, Lawrence. *The Rise and Fall of the British Empire.* New York: St. Martin's Press, 1996.

Moore-Gilbert, B.J. *Postcolonial Theory: Contexts, Practices, Politics.* New York: Verso, 1997.

Said, Edward. *Orientalism.* New York: Vintage Books, 1978.

Smith, Adam. *An Inquiry into the Nature and Causes of the Wealth of Nations.* 1776. Reprint, Hartford, CT: Cooke & Hall, 1818.

Urquhart, Brian. *Decolonization and World Peace.* Austin: University of Texas Press, 1989.

Williams, Patrick, and Laura Chrisman, eds. *Colonial Discourse and Post-Colonial Theory: A Reader.* New York: Columbia University Press, 1994.

PEOPLE'S WARS

What is meant by the term "people's war"? The concept can be defined both narrowly and broadly. Defined narrowly, the term is used to denote the body of strategic thought on "protracted war" developed by Mao Zedong in the 1930s and 1940s, during the period of the Chinese Civil War and the struggle against the Japanese. This definition is firmly rooted in the larger Marxist-Leninist theory of class struggle. Defined broadly, the concept of people's war is used generically to denote any form of guerrilla conflict or popular insurrection, regardless of its ideological roots. By this definition, the opening and middle stages of the Chinese Communist struggle against the Nationalist (Kuomintang) regime was an example of a people's war, as was the Afghan campaign against the Marxist regime in Kabul in the 1980s and early 1990s.

The definition of people's war used in this entry takes a middle course. The term, on the one hand, will be used to describe a body of ideas on population-based conflict or insurgency that goes beyond the specific concept of operations developed by Mao. At the same time, we will retain the ideological meaning of the term by referring to those forms of "popular warfare" based on the concept of class struggle. Defining the concept in this manner distinguishes it, on the one hand, from the type of conflict waged in Afghanistan, which would represent a more generalized form of guerrilla warfare, as well as from the type of class-based revolutionary conflict envisioned by Lenin, which was based primarily on political rather than military forms of struggle. While the last act of revolutionary takeover, in Lenin's view, would be carried out by a popular insurrection, the months and years leading up to the insurrection would be characterized by careful, behind-the-scenes political work, designed to place the revolutionary party in a position to catalyze a final uprising and seize power when the historical moment was deemed to be propitious. It would not be characterized by a period of revolutionary *war*, per se, in which the outcome of the struggle would be decided by a military interaction.

Although the concept of people's war, for definitional purposes, can be usefully distinguished from the larger concept of guerrilla warfare, we should not lose sight of the fact that the first is merely an ideological subset of the second. The defining operational problem, in each case, is the same: overcoming the conventional military superiority of the state (or occupying power) through an asymmetrical campaign based on the support (and resources) of a constituent population. While the leadership of a people's war will attempt to draw support from among a revolutionary class (classically, the peasantry), the non-Marxist insurgency will define its natural constituency along different lines (e.g., ethnicity, communal affiliation, or regional identity). Where the first defines its popular base "horizontally" (according to class) across national or ethnic lines, the second defines its base of support "vertically" (according to some other group identifier) without regard to its class affiliation.

The underlying organizational tasks facing the leadership of a people's war are similar to those faced by that of any insurgency. We can define these as (1) *penetration*, which speaks to the revolutionary organization's need to "get inside" targeted social groupings as a prelude to "turning" them to the service of the organization's political and military objectives, (2) *transformation*, which speaks to the insurgency's need to consolidate its control over the targeted group and redirect some percentage of its resources to the organization's goals, and (3) *application*, which refers to the ways in which these resources are used to further develop an insurgent infrastructure, undermine the competing infrastructure of the state, and, ultimately, extend the insurgent's zone of control. Collectively, these tasks define the process of social mobilization. Every insurgent organization must address each of these operational tasks if it is to pose a viable challenge to the state. The manner in which it does so will define its theory of victory.

Revolutions and people's wars in the twentieth century have virtually all imitated or tried to imitate earlier revolutions. These successful cases of the past establish operational models that are adopted by latter-day revolutionaries who hope to repeat the success of those that preceded them by replicating their experience. While such cases have generally addressed the question of "why" one should revolt, as well as what revolutionary changes should be carried out in society at such time as one actually wins, the principal influence has been over *how* an armed revolt should be prosecuted in the first place. For those who come to the problem of overthrowing a standing regime with high ambition but little practical experience, a revolutionary paradigm offers an immediate (if often stylized) recipe for action.

The tradition of people's war, for its part, has been dominated by two original paradigms: the model of protracted conflict developed by Mao Zedong in China and the *foco* concept of guerrilla warfare developed by Ernesto "Che" Guevara in Latin America. Most revolutionary insurgencies since the end of World War II have sought either to apply or adapt and refine one or the other of these concepts of operation to local circumstances. The concept of protracted conflict developed by Mao is designed to be carried out by a "low-profile" organization carrying out a "bottom-up" approach to insurgency. By contrast, the theory of insurgency developed by Che Guevara is designed to be prosecuted by a "high-profile" organization from the "top down." In key respects, these two models represent operational opposites, and they represent the outer limits of the concept of people's war.

Chinese Model of People's War

Mao's assessment of the operational problem facing the Chinese Communist Party during its early struggles in the 1920s and 1930s rested on two essential considerations that bear on the general study of people's war. The first of these was his assessment of the standing government's overwhelming material advantage over the Communist Party. The second was the government's equally apparent political weakness. Deposing the old regime, in Mao's view, would require the party to overcome its material weaknesses by exploiting the opportunities provided by its comparative political advantage. As Mao observed at the time, "All guerrilla units start from nothing and grow." At the outset of this type of struggle, the standing regime represents a force in being. The guerrilla, by contrast, represents a force in development. The latter begins with little more than an idea. The guerrilla's one opening under these circumstances, according to the theory of class conflict, is provided by the inherent frailty of the regime's political base and the corresponding weakness of its institutional presence through-

Mao Zedong (left), seen with Zhou Enlai on the Long March of 1935, brought his Chinese Communist Party to power in a highly strategic and protracted people's war that began in the countryside and grew into a nationwide insurgency. *(Keystone/Getty Images)*

out the countryside. Exploiting this opening, Mao argued, will permit a guerrilla force to bridge the gap between its grand ends and limited means over the course of the struggle.

Time, Space, and Initiative

The strategy designed by Mao to square the circle between ends and means rested on the calculated use of time and space. Buying time, Mao argued, was essential if the regime's strengths were to be turned into weaknesses and the guerrilla weaknesses were to be turned into strengths. The struggle, in its most abstract form, was envisioned to be an institutional contest between the developing architecture of the "new state" on the one hand and the declining institutions of the "old state" on the other. Building the new and dismantling the old, Mao recognized, would be a protracted undertaking. As this process unfolds, however, the relative balance between the guerrilla and the government would gradually shift. This shift, furthermore, could be expected to take on a dynamic quality over time. Guerrilla successes, he argued, would tend to be self-reinforcing, just as the regime's growing record of failure would tend to lead to the further erosion of the state and its administrative organs. While this process would ebb and flow, over the long run the decline of the state could be expected to accelerate, eventually at an increasing rate. The guerrillas' principal operational challenge, in this view, was not to end the war quickly, but to keep it going.

Unlimited time, in this strategy, required unlimited space. Space, in Mao's view, would provide the guerrillas with the room for maneuvers to buy the time necessary to win. All space, in this sense, is not created equal. For practical purposes, a distinction was made between territory that, in the opening stages of the engagement, was under the effective control of the regime, and that which was not. If the guerrillas' evaluation of the political environment facing each side was accurate, the regime's administrative control throughout the countryside would be imperfect. To survive their weak beginning, the guerrillas would open the struggle in those areas of the country in which the regime was weak and avoid making a stand in those areas of comparative regime strength. In pursuing such a strategy, the insurgency would give itself the best opportunity to gain the time it required to establish an institutional counterweight to the state. Revolutionary organization, in turn, would further extend the guerrillas' ability to establish effective spatial control.

These ideas formed the basis of Mao's concept of protracted war. According to this formula, the war will evolve via the dual mechanisms of "destruction and construction"—through the step-by-step destruction of the state and the associated construction of the new counterstate. The two, in Mao's view, are mutually dependent and must proceed in tandem. The erosion of the government's administrative architecture at the margin of its control will open additional opportunities for the insurgents to expand their own institutional presence, just as the organization's earlier (if still limited) institutional base provided the springboard to open its campaign against the state in the first place. This can be expected to take on an iterative quality over time, as each new advance by the guerrillas lays the groundwork for the next. The speed with which this campaign unfolds will be regulated by the strength of the state (which will tend to increase as the opposition pushes forward from the periphery to the state's center of gravity),

the nature of the government's counterstrategy, the level of local resistance to the guerrillas' efforts to establish their own institutional presence, and the natural time limits associated with building an alternative set of political and military forms.

Expressed in geographical terms, this progression is intended to result in a slow extension of guerrilla authority from peripheral areas of the countryside (or political margin), where state control will be comparatively weak, toward the cities (or political center) of the country, where the position of the regime is traditionally much stronger. This process can be described as one of protracted encirclement, in which the urban regions of the country are encircled and eventually detached from the interior. The dynamic quality of this strategy is manifest in several ways. First, it calls for the guerrillas to push into areas of marginal control, even as they are being pulled into these areas by the political vacuum created by the retreat of the state. Second, as the opposition gains ground, it will naturally acquire the means to gain strength by gradually expanding its base of popular support. The inverse process, meanwhile, is occurring with the state, which is losing ground in a contest for territorial control with the guerrillas. The result, in theory, is a compound shift in the relative balance of advantage as the guerrillas become absolutely stronger and the regime grows absolutely weaker at a more or less equivalent rate.

The nature of this encirclement strategy is somewhat different from that which typically characterizes Western military thought. For Mao, encirclement is not achieved by means of development, but through a process of "strategic convergence." Encirclement in the first sense, as one commentator noted some years ago, refers to a process of "eccentric maneuver," in which the attacking force advances from a single point to surround and strike at the enemy's flanks. In the Maoist system, by contrast, encirclement has taken on a more subtle cast. It is not a single action, but a complex "concentric maneuver" in which semi-autonomous forces converge on their target from multiple points in a protracted series of coordinated moves. Such an approach, if successful, will complicate the task facing the regime, which will be forced to counteract the guerrillas on multiple fronts, while simplifying the task facing the insurgents, who will be able to reduce their profile (and hence their vulnerability) to the enemy by not placing all of their eggs in a single (easily targeted) basket.

The Evolution of the Armed Struggle

A centerpiece of this strategy is the development of a series of rural bases from which the insurgents will attempt to extend their areas of control. "Political mobilization," Mao observed, is a fundamental condition for winning the war. Mobilization, in turn, will only be translated into effective insurgent support if it results in the creation of a network of strategic areas that are able to service the guerrillas' material needs. The base area, in this sense, provides a "protective shell" that provides the guerrillas with the opportunity "to organize, equip, and train." It is formed by bringing a large number of points of influence together under a common administrative center. This process is achieved by establishing a local military advantage, displacing (or neutralizing) the residual presence of the old regime, and creating an alternative set of governing and administrative institutions. This progression, once again, is a dynamic one. According to Abimael Guzman, one of Mao's recent imitators, "Base development, the [concomitant] development of [a] popular guerrilla army, and the resulting extension of the people's war [can be expected to take on a] momentum of their own, leading to the greater unfolding of the revolutionary situation." One thing leads to the next.

In developing this view, Mao clearly distinguished between "guerrilla bases" and "guerrilla zones." The guerrilla base, as we have suggested, is a region that has already been incorporated into the emerging insurgent regime. While Mao acknowledged that there could be different types of bases, depending upon their location and relative vulnerability to government attack, each represents a guerrilla "stronghold." Such strongholds can be distinguished from guerrilla zones, which Mao defined as areas in which the insurgents were able to operate with relative freedom, but where the state still retained a meaningful political and military presence. The guerrilla zone, in this sense, is considered to be an area of transition (contested ground). The final conquest of the zone, according to Mao, will be achieved by using the established basing system as a springboard to converge on any remaining state presence within the target area. Bases, in this view, effectively "encircle" guerrilla zones, which, once captured, will be absorbed into an expanded base area.

The revolution, in Mao's concept, will unfold in a series of stages, moving from the "strategic defensive," through a period of "strategic equilibrium," on to the "strategic offensive." The initial defensive stage of the conflict can be characterized as a period of "preparation." The insurgents' overriding objective during this phase is to establish a secure political base in the interior from which they can subsequently branch out and expand their range of operations. This is a period of high vulnerability. As on a water course, the guerrillas must find their own level. Decisive battles, head-on engagements, and areas of regime strength must all be avoided as the opposition gradually lays down its roots. This view was summarized nicely by Mao in his argument that the "first principle of war is to preserve oneself, and destroy the enemy." The insurgents' primary concern during the defensive stage of the struggle, in this view, must be to preserve their core organization, from which the means to destroy the enemy will eventually develop. By the end of this period, much of the countryside will have been transformed into a political checkerboard. While the regime will still enjoy effective control at the center, large areas of the countryside will have been brought under guerrilla influence.

The second stage of the conflict, strategic equilibrium, will be reached when the insurgents feel they have achieved "equivalence" with the incumbent regime. Mao referred to this stage as a period of "stalemate." If the initial defensive struggle can be described as a period of preparation, this phase of the war can be characterized as one of "consolidation." While the overriding concern during phase one was to establish an initial series of base areas, the primary operational objective in stage two will be to geographically connect these bases in an effort to consolidate and further extend the guerrillas' zone of control. Over time, the regime's remaining positions of influence in the interior are to be restricted, isolated, and gradually disconnected from the center. The checkerboard or "jigsaw" pattern of influence that characterized the end of phase one will evolve into an increasingly continuous pattern of guerrilla control by the end of phase two. At the conclusion of this period, the regime will find itself forced into a defensive posture, preoccupied with hanging on to what it has and decreasingly able to move offensively against the guerrillas.

In Maoist parlance, the final phase of a people's war is the period of "annihilation." It might also be thought of as a period of "exploitation," in which the institutional groundwork laid during the preparatory and consolidative phases of the struggle are brought to fruition. The guerrillas will enter this stage poised to transition to the strategic offensive. The early pattern of territorial dispersion made necessary by the weakness of the guerrillas will have been transformed over time into a pattern of territorial control in which the insurgents will have surrounded all but the most important points of regime influence. This development, in Mao's view, should be matched by a reorganization of significant elements of the guerrilla "army," which can now be gradually reformed into units capable of carrying out fluid but increasingly conventional operations. Guerrilla warfare, according to Mao, is not a strategy of choice but of necessity, imposed by the initial material weakness of the opposition. Once the balance of advantage in the conflict has swung to the opposition, the guerrillas are in a position to come out of the shadows and confront the regime on its own terms.

Cuban Model of People's War

The Cuban model of people's war, codified by Che Guevara, was based on a highly stylized (and often inaccurate) interpretation of the Cuban insurrection (1956–1959). The baseline document outlining the key features of this model was written by Che Guevara and published by the Cuban Ministry of the Armed Forces in 1960 under the title *Guerrilla Warfare*. It was Che Guevara's first and most influential book. Guevara opened the monograph with the following observation: "The victory of the Cuban people over the Batista dictatorship . . . showed plainly the capacity of the people to free themselves by means of guerrilla warfare from a government that oppresses them." Three "fundamental lessons," he argued, could be drawn from this experience: First, that "popular forces can win a war against the army"; second, that "it is not necessary to wait until all conditions for making [a] revolution exist, the insurrection can create them"; and, third, that "in underdeveloped America the countryside is the basic area of fighting." The model of action that emerged from these "lessons" would shape or otherwise influence revolutionary efforts over the next thirty years.

Guevara's concept of operations was developed without reference to Mao's earlier writings on protracted war or a close understanding of the experiences of the Chinese Revolution. Guevara and Fidel Castro both claimed to have only been introduced to

The Communist guerrilla leader Che Guevara—seen here at a decisive battle in the Cuban revolution in late 1958—codified a new paradigm of the people's war that he believed could be successfully prosecuted throughout Latin America. *(Keystone/Getty Images)*

Mao's work in 1958, after the key features of the Cuban insurrection were already well defined. In their view and the view of others, this lack of knowledge proved to be fortuitous, freeing them from the temptation to apply revolutionary lessons from a time and place that may have little to do with the particular challenges (and opportunities) faced by the Cuban guerrillas. The "university of experience," in Guevara's view, was a more useful instructor "than a million volumes of books." This perspective was echoed by Régis Debray, one of the chief interpreters of the Cuban insurrection, who suggested that it was a "stroke of good fortune that Fidel had not read the writings of Mao Zedong before disembarking on the coast of Oriente: he could thus invent, on the spot and out of his own experience, principles of a military doctrine in conformity with the terrain."

Where Mao's concept of protracted conflict may have been an appropriate model for the Far East, the new doctrine of people's war that emerged from the experience of the Cuban insurrection, it was argued, was the model of choice for the unique circumstances found in Latin America. "Revolutionaries in Latin America," Debray observed, were "reading Fidel's speeches and Che Guevara's writings with eyes that have already read Mao on the anti-Japanese war, Vo Nguyen Giap, and certain texts of Lenin—and they think they recognize the latter in the former." This, he argued, was both a distorted and dangerous "superimposition." The popular struggle in Latin America, according to Debray, possessed "highly special and profoundly distinct conditions of development, which [could] only be discovered through a particular experience." Prior "theoretical works on people's war," accordingly, could "do as much harm as good." While such writings, he suggested, "have been called the grammar books of the war, . . . a foreign language is learned faster in a country where it is spoken than at home studying a language manual." The Cuban experience, in short, was believed to offer a new paradigm for action.

The Foco

The central instrument in Guevara's theory was the guerrilla *foco*, or guerrilla band. In Guevara's view, the foco was the nucleus of the insurrection. It would consist of a handful of dedicated men who would "jump-start" the campaign to overthrow the standing government through the power of example. Over time, Guevara envisioned, the foco would naturally begin to attract recruits. As this occurred, it would slowly grow until it reached some maximum (optimal) size, which Guevara defined as somewhere between thirty and fifty men. At this point, it would split in two, each foco working independently of the other to attract a following in different regions of the country. Over time, as this budding process continued, the number of operational guerrilla bands would grow until the insurgents would eventually become a force to be reckoned with in the countryside. In Guevara's view, this process was similar to that of a beehive "when at a given moment it releases a new queen, who goes to another region with a part of the swarm." The "mother hive," in this case, "with the most notable guerrilla chief will stay in the less dangerous places, while the new columns will penetrate other enemy territory [and repeat the earlier] cycle."

Guevara's concept of operations, to be sure, shared certain features with the theory of protracted war formulated by Mao. First and foremost was the assumption that the guerrillas' natural base of support would be found among the peasantry. It followed, in turn, that the natural locus of the insurgency should also be in the countryside. While Guevara, at least in theory, did not completely dismiss the supporting role that could be played by an urban underground, he clearly relegated the struggle in the cities to a subordinate position. The insurrection would turn on the rural guerrilla. Those who, "following dogma," still believed that a revolutionary action could only be carried out by urban workers, underrated, in his view, both the revolutionary sentiment of the peasantry on the one hand and the difficulties associated with operating in an urban environment on the other. "Illegal workers' movements," Guevara argued, faced "enormous dangers" (which were not similarly faced by their rural counterparts) because of their greater proximity to the regime's center of influence. To offset this greater risk, "They must function secretly without arms." The rural guerrilla, by contrast, is able to operate "beyond the reach of the oppressive forces," and is thus able to sidestep the state's opening advantage.

Like Mao, Guevara also believed that the insurgent struggle would evolve in stages. The first stage of the conflict was the "nomadic" phase, in which the initial guerrilla nucleus must continually remain on the move in order to survive. As the foco's relationship with the peasantry began to stabilize, the guerrillas would move into the second, "semi-nomadic" phase, in which the guerrillas, while still retaining a high level of fluidity, would be able to establish the first permanent base areas. The final phase of the conflict, Guevara argued, was the stage of "suburban guerrilla warfare." In language reminiscent of Mao, Guevara wrote that this stage would finally enable the guerrillas to "encircle fortified bases," engage in "mass action," and confront the army in open battle and win. "The enemy will fall," he suggested, when "the process of partial victories becomes transformed into final victories, that is to say, when the [army] is brought to accept the battle in conditions imposed by the guerrilla band; there he is annihilated and his surrender compelled." This, in turn, would ultimately result in an uprising of popular sentiment against the standing regime, sweeping it from power.

The Heroic Guerrilla

While Guevara's writings on people's war share certain similarities to those of Mao, the strategic theory that underlies this work is, in the end, quite distinct. First, in contrast to Mao, Guevara gave primacy to what he referred to as the "subjective" rather than "objective" conditions for victory. A successful insurrection, in this view, did not require that the peasantry be already primed to revolt; the conditions for revolution could often be engineered by the guerrilla band. While Guevara gave at least passing reference to the necessary preconditions for revolution in his initial discussion of the problem in *Guerrilla Warfare*, this caveat was increasingly relaxed over time. Guerrilla conflicts, he argued in a later article, could be successfully prosecuted throughout Latin America. Once set in motion, the revolution would "make itself." While the "initial conditions" did not exist everywhere in the orthodox sense of the term, the desire for revolutionary change lay just below the surface of the popular consciousness. It was only necessary to define, release, and finally channel these sentiments.

In contrast to Mao, Guevara's theory of victory ultimately relied heavily on the spontaneity of the insurgent's natural allies to provide the guerrilla foco with the critical mass it required to win. Guevara assumed that Latin-American society was in an inherently unstable state. The task facing the guerrilla nucleus was to aggravate the tension that he believed defined every Latin-American society, kick out the props that held up the old regime, and stand back while the target government was overcome in a popular uprising. Once set in motion, the guerrillas would not so much control this event as ride it into power. What was required under these circumstances was not a grassroots, step-by-step program of local contact, indoctrination, and organization, but an action-oriented program designed to capture the popular imagination and inspire the peasantry "from above." The foco's operational challenge, in this respect, was to sharpen and accelerate the natural process of social polarization, raise the peasants' political consciousness, and embolden them to join the revolution.

While the Chinese model of people's war considered political organization to be a necessary precondition for social mobilization, the Cuban model argued that a high-profile "guerrilla outbreak" could be used to effectively bypass the organizational requirement and proceed directly to mobilization. The basis of the insurgency, in the first case, rests with the vitality of the guerrillas' interlocking, village-based associations. Collectively, these represent an institutional counterweight to the state and the foundation of the insurgency's political and military position. The basis of the insurgency, in the second case, rests squarely on the shoulders of the guerrilla combatant and, through him, the guerrilla foco. Success or failure in this case depends on the power of their example. The guerrilla, for his part, must be a "fighter-teacher," who "need know little more than what is required of a good man or soldier." The guerrilla foco, for its part, must be an "armed nucleus," able to employ its limited resources to move its would-be followers to action. Creating this effect would not depend on organization, but on courage, discipline, and a willingness to act.

As this discussion suggests, the Cuban model placed great importance on the psychological dimensions of a guerrilla conflict. The guerrilla combatant, we are told, must never lose faith. He must "see reasons for a favorable decision even in moments when the analysis of the adverse and favorable conditions does not show an appreciable positive balance." It is particularly important to continually generate the impression of impending victory. This can be achieved initially in small ways that have big effects. A small guerrilla force can enhance its offensive punch, for example, by "striking like a tornado" to "sow panic" within the enemy's ranks. The cumulative effects of small victories won in such a fashion can, in turn, have higher-order effects on the general morale (and, hence, effectiveness) of the regime's military and political base, imbuing them with a sense of imminent doom. As these perceptions begin to take hold, the "objective conditions" of the conflict will gradually begin to shift to the insurgents' advantage, making it increasingly easy to sustain this momentum over time. The guerrillas will win when the enemy has finally come to believe that its own defeat is inevitable.

The theory of guerrilla warfare advanced by Che Guevara, in the end, had an uneven relationship to the underlying dynamics of the Cuban insurrection. Many aspects of the Cuban experience that proved to be critical to the ultimate success of the July 26 revolutionary movement were either left out or significantly downplayed in Guevara's concept of operations. Several of these should be noted here. First and foremost, perhaps, was Guevara's increasingly unrealistic view of the "revolutionary readiness" of Latin American society. As noted above, Guevara gave little attention to the particular preconditions that must exist to bring to fruition even the best-laid plan to seize power in a popular insurgency. Revolution for Che Guevara could effectively be created out of whole cloth. What was of critical importance was not the particular state of society, or even the competing institutional strength of the opposition, but the courage, fortitude, and determination of the guerrilla fighter. Winning, in his view, boiled down to an act of will. Weak, preexisting objective conditions could be offset by the individual guerrilla's grim refusal to accept defeat.

Second, in focusing on the *rural* guerrilla, Guevara ignored the decisive role played by the urban underground during the Cuban insurrection. The latter provided significant assistance to Fidel's rural operations. During the early days of the war, in particular, support from the July 26 movement's preexisting urban networks was critical to the very survival of the rural foco. Throughout the course of the war, the actions of the urban underground—often carried out in a coordinated and simultaneous manner across the country—served as a major source of distraction, providing the guerrillas with the breathing space they required to stay in the game. The army was continually faced with the need to divide its efforts between the countryside and the cities, which made it difficult to concentrate on finding, fixing, and finally destroying Fidel's small group of rural combatants. In these and other ways, the cities proved to be a key variable in the outcome of the war. Despite this fact, the role of the urban underground was effectively dismissed in Guevara's writings in favor of his naturally heroic country cousin.

Finally, as much as Guevara appreciated the inherently dynamic, interactive nature of warfare, in attempting to generalize from the Cuban experience he imposed a post facto order and associated determinism on the course of the Cuban insurrection that it did not possess. Under the best of circumstances, combat is an uncertain process. There is often a high level of uncertainty surrounding the thousands of individual events that might make up a battle, and the hundreds of battles that might make up a war, which will often prove to be decisive in determining who is left standing at the end of the day. This was certainly the case in the Cuban insurrection, where, except for happy chance, the guerrillas could have been defeated on any number of occasions during the course of the struggle. As the Duke of Wellington said of the Battle of Waterloo, "it was a close run thing." And yet, the problematic character of the conflict (and guerrilla warfare in general) is missing in Guevara's interpretive mode.

The inherent uncertainty surrounding the problem of revolutionary action, in this case, is effectively replaced by a discussion of the guerrilla's fighting spirit. The guerrilla, in Guevara's view, will dominate events because of his superior determination.

The limits of this last assumption were demonstrated once and for all in Guevara's final action in Bolivia (1966–1967), where he was captured and killed attempting to put his theory into practice. The dramatic nature of his defeat proved to be the death knell for his model of guerrilla warfare. While the heroic quality of his death served to inspire those who came after him, subsequent guerrilla operations in Latin America would be defined by their efforts to correct the weaknesses inherent in his voluntarist theory of people's war.

Summary

The Chinese and Cuban models of people's war represent competing views of the structure and dynamics of guerrilla warfare. While both theories acknowledge that the underlying basis of revolutionary change ultimately rests on long-run historical forces, the operational guidance given to revolutionary hopefuls attempting to tap into and harness these forces, in each case, is distinct. For the Maoist, it is ultimately a problem of organization, which, in this sense, means building a grassroots, village-based alternative to the state. It follows that the chief measure of performance—which in this case is provided not by the scope or intensity of one's military actions, but by the scope, depth, and vitality of one's organizational forms. The guerrilla's ability to pose a political and military challenge to the state is believed to be a byproduct of his slowly developing institutional base. There is nothing "willful," in this view, about revolutionary outcomes. Strength of character and a pure heart are not considered to be effective substitutes for building an institutional counterweight to the state.

The opposite point of view, in many respects, defines the Cuban model of insurgency. Guerrilla actions, in this theory, are not a manifestation of popular support but the source of such support in the first place. The target population, in this respect, is not "organized" but "impressed." Popular mobilization is less an iterative *process* than a catalytic *event*, in which the insurgents' natural constituency, spurred by the dramatic character of guerrilla actions, discovers its revolutionary identity and joins the rebellion.

This shift, as noted, is expected to occur with little or no organizational investment by the insurgents. It will occur not as a result of a prior shift in local control, but in the wake of a general change in the sentiment of the revolutionary class. The guerrillas' primary task, then, is not institutional but psychological. Their goal is to capture the popular imagination in the expectation of generating a popular uprising against the state. Will, rather than numbers, can be expected to carry the day.

These two models of people's war, then, can be defined by a simple dichotomy. The Chinese model represents a bottom-up, low-profile approach to guerrilla conflict. For the low-profile challenger, insurgency is considered to be an institutional contest. The conflict will be pursued by undermining the institutional architecture of the state and replacing it with the guerrillas' own institutional alternative. Popular support is mobilized at the grassroots level (from the bottom up) in a staged process of organization building. The Cuban model, by contrast, can be defined as a top-down, high-profile approach to insurgency. For the high-profile challenger, a guerrilla conflict will not be prosecuted by undermining the state's institutional forms, but by attacking its perceptual foundations. The regime will not be slowly dismantled and replaced, but effectively taken by storm (from the top down) in a psychological convergence of popular sentiment away from the old regime and in favor of the opposition. The guerrilla's operational challenge is, first, to provide the spark that sets the conflict in motion and, second, to serve as a conduit to channel the population's revolutionary sentiments.

Gordon H. McCormick

Bibliography

Boorman, Scott A. *The Protracted Game: A Wei-chi Interpretation of Maoist Revolutionary Strategy.* London: Oxford University Press, 1969.

Childs, Matt D. "An Historical Critique of the Emergence and Evolution of Ernesto Che Guevara's *Foco* Theory." *Journal of Latin American Studies* (October 1995).

Connor, Walker. *The National Question in Marxist-Leninist Theory and Strategy.* Princeton, NJ: Princeton University Press, 1984.

Debray, Régis. *Revolution in the Revolution?* Westport, CT: Greenwood Press, 1980.

Dunn, John. *Modern Revolutions.* Cambridge: Cambridge University Press, 1972.

Guevara, Che. *Guerrilla Warfare.* Lincoln: University of Nebraska Press, 1985.

———. "Guerrilla Warfare: A Method." In *Venceremos! The Speeches and Writings of Ernesto (Che) Guevara*, ed. John Gerassi. New York: Macmillan, 1968.

———. "Interview with Laura Berquist" (No. 1). In *Che: Selected Works of Ernesto Guevara*, ed. Rolando E. Bonachea and Nelson P. Valdés. Cambridge, MA: MIT Press, 1969.

Guzman, Abimael. "Interview." *El Diario*, July 24, 1988.

Johnson, Chalmers. *Autopsy on People's War.* Berkeley: University of California Press, 1973.

Katzenbach, Edward L., Jr., and Gene Hanrahan. "The Revolutionary Strategy of Mao Tse-tung." *Political Science Quarterly* (September 1955).

Mao Zedong (Mao Tse-tung). "Guerrilla Warfare." In *Mao Tse-tung on Guerrilla Warfare*, trans. and ed. Samuel B. Griffith II. Baltimore: Nautical and Aviation Publishing Company of America, 1992.

———. "On Protracted War." In *Selected Military Writings of Mao Tse-tung.* Beijing: Foreign Languages Press, 1967.

———. "Problems of Strategy in Guerrilla War Against Japan." In *Selected Military Writings of Mao Tse-tung.* Beijing: Foreign Languages Press, 1967.

McCormick, Gordon H. "Che Guevara's Revolutionary Odyssey." *Queen's Quarterly* (Summer 1998).

———. *Peruvian Maoism: The Shining Path and the Theory of People's War.* Santa Monica, CA: RAND, 1992.

———. *Sharp Dressed Men: Peru's Tupac Amaru Revolutionary Movement.* Santa Monica, CA: RAND, 1993.

Tucker, Robert C. *The Marxian Revolutionary Idea.* New York: W.W. Norton, 1969.

COUPS

The most common form of change in government since World War II has been the coup d'état. A coup is a quick, violent, and illegal overthrow of a government by a faction of the armed forces or other powerful sector in society. There are many specific kinds of coups. One type, a *putsch*, occurs during or immediately following a war, in which a segment of the military forms an alternative leadership as a first step toward creating a new government. Other unconstitutional changes are not considered coups, such as a "palace revolution" in which government insiders manipulate or replace the leader. The practice goes as far back as government itself, ever since Absalom conspired with leaders of ancient Israel's tribes to try to depose his father, King David.

Such overthrows began to be called "coups d'état" in the late seventeenth century, as the rise of the modern state and its professional militaries—along with the nationalist tumult set in motion by the French Revolution—made them both feasible and common. Latin America's first century of independence, for example, was characterized by frequent coups, often in the form of the *pronunciamiento*, in which the military used its constitutional position as the defender of the national interest to conduct a ritualized process of consultations prior to bringing down a weak government. The proliferation of new nations and ideologies in the twentieth century—combined with the superpower rivalry of the Cold War—led to an exponential increase in coups around the world after 1945. Nearly every Latin American country, and a majority of African and Asian countries, suffered successful and unsuccessful overthrows in this era. There were an estimated 380 successful coups and coup attempts between 1945 and 1967. There were at least 50 successful and 150 unsuccessful coups in Africa alone between 1955 and 1985.

Causes

Although coups are usually facilitated by external support and internal upheaval, the need for secret planning precludes inclusion in the planning by large sectors of the armed forces or population. All that is needed by a small group of plotters is the existence of a state bureaucratic apparatus. When that bureaucracy is filled with people who are linked to the political leaders through ethnic or other loyalties, as in countries such as imperial China and contemporary Saudi Arabia, clandestine infiltration and sudden action are exceedingly difficult. But in the political development of most countries, fewer state employees are connected with the leaders, the state bureaucracy becomes the foundation of governmental control and societal interaction, and the military and police forces become more hierarchal and professional. Under such conditions, it is far easier to have a sudden seizure of the state and removal of the government officials who run it.

Coups themselves encourage further coups, since each one sets a legal and political precedent that weakens civilian rule and makes its overthrow even more legitimate and practical. Constitutional executives under the threat of a coup feel pressed to maintain popular support through patronage and rash short-term policies, which end up undermining both the government and popular support for democracy. When combined with ethnic, political, or other societal divisions, such patterns lead to what political scientist Samuel Huntington calls "praetorian politics," in which every sector becomes more mobilized, less willing to compromise with other groups, and more likely to clamor for the "ultimate" resolution to domestic ruptures: a coup. In the process, the framework of democracy—accountable state agencies, meaningful elections, and a rule of law—becomes even more debilitated. Legitimization also comes through official or de facto recognition by other countries. The Wilson-Tobar Doctrine prohibits international recognition of a regime that seizes power by force, at least until it has demonstrated public support. This and related international standards, however, are not legally binding and in any case are obviated by the fact that states give de facto recognition to new governments by simply *not* making any declarations.

Although modern political developments have made coups common, the causes of each coup are rooted primarily in the particular conditions of the country in which it takes place. A country's own political, economic, and social conditions often lead to demands for a change in government, and the existence of a state structure, combined with meddling from other countries, makes a coup the easiest and quickest way to fulfill such demands. An understanding of coups in the post–World War II era, therefore, requires a look not just at American and Soviet actions, but at their underlying national and regional causes and at the motives of those carrying them out.

Most generally, coups are caused by the inability of political parties and governments to enact effective policy and to keep societal divisions in check. Most coups, in fact, occur in the wake of an economic downturn or a bout of political conflict, as manifest social discontent and waves of mobilization compel the military and its allies to intervene. Many coup leaders cite economic mismanagement and fault the deposed government's inability to control spending, maintain citizens' standard of living, or avoid painful austerity measures. An economic decline not only undermines the government's legitimacy, but undercuts support from key sectors such as the middle class. Such scenarios are often rooted in "relative deprivation," which is the difference between the population's expectations of entitlements and its capabilities to attain them. When those capabilities decrease or the expectations increase without a corresponding change in the other, the result is often mass protest in the forms of strikes, looting, and rebellion. When the military also suffers from relative deprivation, the likelihood of a coup increases dramatically.

The frequency and causes of coups are also determined by regional characteristics. Latin America has the longest tradition of coups, rooted in a history of civil strife, political instability, the military's institutional and legal power, and, since the beginning of the twentieth century, the battle against socialism and Communism. In East Asia, agitation by Communist and nationalist forces during the Cold War was one of the main causes of that region's coups. In the Middle East, independence and Cold War geopolitics brought out the deep-seated tensions between traditional and modernizing sectors, which coups tried to reconcile, often in the name of Islam and pan-Arabism. Even greater levels of economic underdevelopment and institutional weakness in sub-Saharan Africa combined with ethnic rivalry and the chaos of decolonization to give that region the greatest frequency of coups in the post–World War II period.

Motives and Justifications

Underlying and often contradicting the causes of a coup, however, are its motives and justifications. Motives are the coup-makers' specific judgments, assessments, and personal and collective ambitions. While causes set the stage for a coup, motives make it happen. Ethnic and class differences cause coups, for example, but only when the military and its allies deem them serious enough. Amid Africa's prevalent ethnic strife, some successfully integrated militaries have launched coups in an attempt to control violence in society. Other armed forces mirror their societies' ethnic division, spurring coups when one group seizes power in its rivalry with the others. Only about one-third of Africa's armies have a stable ethnic balance, in fact, and threats to a particular ethnic group were at least one of the causes in most of the continent's coups. Class interests are another motive of coup-makers. Most military officers come from the middle classes—mainly from the middle and upper-middle classes in Asia and Latin America and mainly from the lower-middle classes in Africa and Asia—and so often represent and speak for the interests of those classes.

Justifications, which are usually but not necessarily in line with the motives, are public stances designed to maximize political support for the coup leaders. Divulged in the new government's first public statements, justifications usually focus on the actions of the previous government, such as overcentralizing power, suppressing political opposition, indulging in nepotism, curtailing constitutional rights, fomenting ethnic rivalry, mismanaging the economy, or inviting condemnation by the international community. Most new leaders point to the specific shortfalls of their predecessors, who they claim are incompetent, too greedy, or too absorbed in personal rivalries to run a government that promotes the nation's interests. In all too many cases, the difference between justifications and motives becomes clear as the new regime repeats practices it had criticized.

Another common set of justifications is the military's self-proclaimed responsibility to act on behalf of the "national interest" in times of internal disorder, threats to national institutions, or foreign intervention. Such justifications usually mask motives of resentment against the government's interference in military affairs, its unwillingness to cooperate with the military, or its tarnishing of the military's honor.

It is often the process of asserting that control, rather than the control itself, that breeds coup plots. A government asserting little control is unlikely to be offensive to the military, and most governments that already have control are capable of preventing coups altogether. A government makes itself vulnerable by trying to alter recruitment and dismissal policies, change training and education, or place its own officials in the military's top ranks. Another provocative move by the government is to establish security forces separate from the military, such as presidential or party militias. Prior to his 1971 coup in Uganda, for example, Major General Idi Amin criticized President Milton Obote for establishing an elite security force. Even military "professionalism" does not inoculate governments against coups. While some argue that the professional military's national loyalty, social responsibility, and attention to procedure make them less disposed to coups, others counter that such assumptions all hinge on the military's "principle of civil supremacy" and point to the many "professional" armies that have launched coups.

Even though it is carried out by a small group, a coup does not necessarily imply any political orientation. While most coups since 1945 have been headed by conservative elements against leftist or moderate governments, many other coup-makers have been leftist or progressive aiming to remove oligarchies that block needed reform and they often align themselves with workers and peasants. Coup-makers' ideology, in fact, is often formed in opposition to that of the existing government. According to Huntington, "In the world of oligarchy, the soldier is a radical; in the middle-class world he is a participant and arbiter; as the mass-society looms on the horizon he becomes the conservative guardian of the existing order." In Venezuela, for example, the military intervened on behalf of the progressive Acción Democrática Party in 1945 and 1958, but against it in 1948.

While coup leaders often portray their action as a temporary measure to restore order, democracy, or the "legitimate" government, they often have a long-term agenda that is revealed gradually and "requires" them to stay in power in order to carry it out. The 1968 coup in Peru, for example, enacted a radically new and extensive economic program, including renationalization of key industries. Such long-term maintenance of power is supported through violent repression or legitimizing means such as new constitutions or elections or, in most cases, a combination

of the two. Augusto Pinochet in Chile (1973–1989) and Sani Abacha in Nigeria (1993–1998) were two presidents who used such a combination.

Sometimes junior officers are the ones who carry out a coup, overriding superiors who are regarded as part of the existing government. While most older officers gained their positions through traditional routes and were perhaps trained by the colonial power, junior officers often are educated with a very different set of principles and suffer from inadequate or irregularly paid salaries. Without some involvement by top military leaders, though, such attempts usually fall short—intentionally or unintentionally— of a complete takeover. Junior officers arrested their superiors in Ethiopia but did not attempt to bring down the government in 1964, for example, while in Venezuela junior officials were responsible for two failed coup attempts in 1992. On the other hand, a coup based solely on the personal ambitions or grievances of a top military officer is rare. Even in extreme examples of personal ambition, such as Jean Bedel Bokassa's takeover of the Central African Republic on December 31, 1965, the coup leader must be able to exploit some flaw in the government and to convince other officers to help depose it.

Coups and the Cold War

Since 1945, all of these causes and motives played themselves out in a world where the Cold War between the United States and the Soviet Union pervaded nearly every country and had at least some connection to nearly every coup. Rarely did the superpowers intervene directly; instead, they armed and encouraged military factions or revolutionary groups, bringing a country's own political polarizations to the boiling point and providing a justification for the government's overthrow. Coups were also set off by regional "contagions," in which military factions acted out of fear of being pulled into neighbors' moves into the Communist or Western camp.

For the Soviet Union, coups were often the best way to install Communist or otherwise friendly regimes. With the Red Army occupying Eastern and Central Europe at the end of World War II, coups were unnecessary in countries, such as Poland and Hungary, or in countries with strong indigenous Communist movements, such as Yugoslavia and Albania. But in Czechoslovakia, despite the fact that the Communists won a larger share of the vote than any other party in the postwar elections, the 1948 coup was needed to give them complete power.

Because the Soviet Union had weak ideological links to the third world and little to offer it in terms of long-term economic development, coups were also the usual way that pro-Soviet governments came into power in Asia, Africa, and Latin America. Prior to the 1960s, the Soviets optimistically predicted that decolonization and rejection of the West would alone bring about pro-Soviet coups around the world. By the time of the fall of Premier Nikita Khrushchev, however, this optimism had been deflated by reality. There had been thirteen pro-Soviet coups, but many of them were unstable or more closely connected with religious or other ideologies than with Soviet Communism. (Such coups include those in Egypt in 1952; Iraq in 1958 and 1968; Syria in 1966; Peru and Republic of Congo-Brazzaville in 1968; Somalia, Sudan, and Libya in 1969; Benin in 1972; Ethiopia in 1974 and 1977; South Yemen and Afghanistan in 1978; Grenada in 1979; and Suriname in 1980.) Many of them were short-lived and soon fell to pro-Western forces.

While they still continued to encourage coups among military factions, the Soviets broadened their strategy by also promoting "vanguard" parties that would bolster Marxist governments' defenses against military plots. This approach had several notable successes, in countries such as Angola, Mozambique, and South Yemen. With generous military assistance and the provision of Cuban, East German, or Soviet advisers to "protect" these governments, chances of a countercoup were minimized. In many countries the presence of Cubans was less offensive and imperialistic than that of Russians. Cuban advisers helped put down coup attempts against pro-Soviet presidents Massamba-Debat of Congo-Brazzaville in 1966 and Agostinho Neto of Angola in 1977. (In some cases, however, Cuban and Soviet interests diverged, as in Grenada in 1983, when a radical Marxist pro-USSR faction overthrew President Maurice Bishop, a close ally of Cuba. In other cases, East German advisers helped prevent coups, such as the 1980 attempt against pro-Soviet Libyan leader Muammar Qaddafi.)

The United States was more successful in encouraging, engineering, or suppressing coups. (Coups in Africa that replaced pro-Soviet governments with pro-American ones include those in Algeria in 1965, Ghana in 1966, Mali in 1968, Sudan in 1971, and Equatorial Guinea in 1979.) While it never formulated an explicit policy on coups, U.S. action could be divided into two approaches. In the first, the United States directly fomented and organized coups by military factions or armed opposition groups in countries of vital geopolitical importance. In 1953, the United States and Great Britain feared a turn toward Communism in Iran under that country's popular nationalist prime minister, Mohammed Mossadegh. It then carried out an elaborate plan in which the hereditary shah of Iran replaced Mossadegh during demonstrations whipped up in the capital of Teheran. A year later, the U.S. Central Intelligence Agency used similar tactics to oust reformist President Jacobo Arbenz of Guatemala, orchestrating a fake invasion that forced the army and the population to lose faith in Arbenz and force him out. In 1963, as Vietnam became a central concern of U.S. foreign policy, the Kennedy administration worked with disgruntled military factions to overthrow the increasingly corrupt and repressive South Vietnamese regime of Ngo Dinh Diem.

As its operations came under more criticism and became a liability for its allies, the United States tried to avoid direct participation in coups, relying instead on economic aid and covert action. This new approach had mixed success. It supported successful coups against João Goulart in Brazil in 1964 and against Cambodian Prince Norodom Sihanouk in 1970 and helped stave off coups against friendly regimes in Egypt and the Dominican Republic. But it failed in Iran in 1979 and in Libya during the 1980s, resulting in anti-American revolutions and coups.

The United States and the Soviet Union, though, were not the only powers using coups as an instrument of foreign policy. Eager to maintain influence in their former colonies and to ensure supplies of raw materials, Great Britain and France used military assistance and economic aid to encourage or suppress coups throughout Africa and Asia. If circumstances called for it, they did not flinch from direct intervention. The British were becoming annoyed with Ugandan President Milton Obote, for example, and inexplicably delayed his flight back from a 1971 Commonwealth meeting while Idi Amin was seizing power in Uganda; then Britain quickly recognized the Amin government. Unlike other powers, France has been unapologetic about using its military to help out its friends. It has been on the scene during unstable times in Benin, Burundi, Zaire, Togo, Chad, and

Congo-Brazzaville. Though France's exact role is often unclear, on some occasions French troops prevented coups, such as the February 1964 effort to save Gabon President Léon M'Ba.

Most coups from the end of World War II to the late 1980s, in sum, were the result both of internal conflicts and weaknesses and of external Cold War politics. Three case studies, each from a different region, demonstrate how a particular set of causes and motives combined with international politics to lead to coups.

Argentina, 1976

An ever-growing Communist menace aggravated Latin America's predilection toward coups, especially after the Cuban Revolution in 1959. While countries such as Mexico and Colombia escaped this pattern, a rash of coups that hit Central and South America brought in regimes far more durable than those in the past. Chile had been South America's most demo-

cratic country, for example, until the 1973 coup supported by the United States brought on seventeen repressive years of military rule. But the most brutal military regime in the region was the one that seized power in Argentina in 1976. Carried out against a weak civilian government unable to suppress leftist guerrillas, the coup seemed at first to be caused by Cold War politics, but it was rooted in a national history of civil strife and authoritarianism that extended back to the colonial era.

After declaring independence in 1816, Argentina plunged into sixty years of civil war between the Unitarians of the powerful Buenos Aires province and the Federalists from outlying provinces. The violence was brought under control only by the increasing power of the military and the executive. A series of coups beginning in 1828 eventually led to the rule of Juan Manuel de Rosas, who used a populist appeal to create a highly centralized, paternalistic, and repressive state that maintained continuing dominance over the economy by an agricultural and industrial oligarchy.

Argentinian soldiers stand guard at Government House in Buenos Aires after the March 1976 coup that overthrew President Isabel Perón. *(Keystone/Getty Images)*

Political strife reemerged at the turn of the twentieth century amid growing immigration and trade union activism. In 1912, a progressive government introduced democratic and electoral reforms, which were continued through the 1920s under President Hipólito Yrigoyen of the Radical Party. Yrigoyen's democratic policies and his own concentration of power rankled conservatives, who supported his overthrow by the military in 1930. The Supreme Court ruled the new regime legal and put in place a vehicle that would justify military coups over the course of the next fifty years. The military regime repealed the democratic reforms, carried out widespread arrests, dismissed judges, and annulled local elections. Amid worsening economic problems, a military faction called the Group of United Officers (GOU) overthrew it in 1943. Disunity in that junta led to the rise of General Juan Perón, who quickly came to dominate a divided society that could not accept its own diversity. As president, Perón purged the judiciary, created a monopolistic government-backed union, and enacted a constitution that gave him authority to impose a "state of internal war."

The military faction that overthrew Perón in 1955 promised a timely return to "the rule of law" and "an authentic democracy." With the Peronists banned, fresh elections brought in two weak Radical presidencies, but the party's stint in power was abruptly ended in June 1966 by the "Argentine Revolution," a military junta that made no pretense of being "provisional." It promptly dissolved Congress and the Supreme Court, prohibited political activity, awarded itself full executive and legislative authority, governed by decree, and demoted the constitution to third place behind the "Revolutionary Objectives" and the "Statute of the Argentine Revolution." Growing internal violence by armed groups such as the left-wing pro-Peronist *Montoneros* guerrillas led to even harsher measures, such as the creation of special courts for insurrectionists.

The exiled Perón returned to power in 1973, but his government was riven both by factionalism and unrealistic popular expectations. Upon his death in 1974, Perón was succeeded by his widow and vice president, Isabel. Her incompetent government was no match for the increasing leftist violence, and two years later it was overthrown by a military junta that ruled the country for the next seven years. As before, the Supreme Court recognized the new regime by citing the need to end internal instability, which the regime did by dismantling the constitution, subjecting civilians to military tribunals, and "disappearing" nearly 30,000 people suspected of sympathizing with leftist parties. So while the battle with Communism was the declared motive and justification for the 1976 coup, its main causes were historical patterns of military rule, internal violence, and political division.

Ghana, 1966

While Latin America already had a long history of coups by 1945, the many newly independent nations of Africa hoped to have a different start. Most hope was pinned on countries with buoyant economies and highly developed political structures, such as Ghana. But the 1966 coup that overthrew Ghanaian President Kwame Nkrumah revealed that Cold War Africa was not immune to coups.

When Ghana became the first sub-Saharan African colony to gain independence in 1957, Nkrumah's Convention People's Party (CPP) had already become the dominant political force during the 1951–1957 period of internal self-government. Although many traditional leaders did not accept the CPP and although distrust continued among the country's main ethnic groups, Nkrumah's charisma and anticolonial populism succeeded in uniting the country. The CPP distributed patronage widely, and the Ghanaian military was thoroughly steeped in the British apolitical tradition. The immense expectations accompanying independence, however, generated increasing political pressure and opposition from all sides, including regional movements, the Muslim minority, and farmers who complained that their cocoa crop was subsidizing the poorer southern regions. National institutions were too fragile to accommodate these divisions, and political organizations began resorting to violence and electoral fraud.

Nkrumah began restricting regional governments, deporting political leaders, enacting preventive detention laws, and stepping up anti-Western rhetoric. As the regime became more personalistic and corrupt, it lost touch with the people and its own grassroots base. The 1960 parliamentary elections were suspended, and a 1964 referendum officially made the country a one-party state. On the economic front, the president began instituting a policy of "socialism from above," with measures such as agricultural collectivization. Although these policies

Workers in the streets of Accra, Ghana, cheer the overthrow of President Kwame Nkrumah—the populist liberator turned "great devil"—in a February 1966 military coup. *(AFP/Getty Images)*

increased state controls and strengthened the CPP, they soon collapsed into runaway unemployment and inflation. Along with a fall in cocoa prices, this failure obliged the government to turn to loans and aid from the Communist bloc.

Nkrumah's pan-African interventions in countries such as Democratic Republic of the Congo (formerly Zaire) further harmed the Ghanian economy and raised the ire of the 14,000-man military. The armed forces had a strong personal affinity with the British, which had educated, trained, and equipped them, and so reacted strongly when Nkrumah began purchasing arms from the Soviet Union and sending recruits there for training. Antagonism deepened when the president formed a Russian-trained presi-

dential guard, cut the military's budget, neglected to implement military plans, and increased his interference in activities ranging from officer selection to troop exercises. Confident that it would have Western support, a group of military officers overthrew the Nkrumah regime on February 24, 1966, during a presidential trip to Beijing and Hanoi.

Iraq, 1963

Coups in the Middle East were rooted less in institutional or economic weakness than in tension between supporters of tradition and advocates of modernization. As one of the most economically and politically developed Arab states with a pivotal role in the superpower rivalry in the region, Iraq illustrated how this tension interacted with Cold War politics. As a British mandate after World War I, the country adopted Western democratic institutions such as a parliament, judiciary, and civil service. This transplant was eased through the leadership of King Faisal I, who was trusted by both the modernizing elite and traditional sectors. After becoming independent in 1932, however, Iraq's system of government fell apart. Faisal died unexpectedly in 1933, generating a period of upheaval in which the army constantly replaced unpopular governments or took power itself. This praetorian pattern was halted only with the revolution of 1958. A new generation of intellectuals and professionals, disparaged by the elite, had begun to grow in importance and numbers. They allied with a growing number of military officers who were also becoming convinced that progress required a radical change in leadership and policy. These "Free Officers" created a Central Organization in the mid-1950s and were bound with the intellectuals by nationalism and Ba'athism, a pan-Arabist movement begun in Syria in 1940. On July 14, 1958, Brigadier Abd al-Karim Qasim, leader of the Free Officers, successfully overthrew the government and killed the royal family.

Qasim, however, continued old practices of centralization and repression. He aligned the country with the Soviet Union. His military forays included staking old claims to neighboring Kuwait and beginning an internal war with the Kurds, embarrassing his Soviet allies.

Meanwhile, the Free Officers split into pro-Communist and pro-Ba'athist factions, adding to the growing assertiveness by both the Communist and Ba'athist parties. On February 8, 1963, an army faction supported by the Ba'athists overthrew Qasim, once again trying to stop the cycle of praetorianism with an appeal to Islam and Arab nationalism.

Mark Ungar

Bibliography

Andrews, William George. *The Politics of the Coup d'Etat: Five Case Studies.* New York: Van Nostrand Reinhold, 1969.

Ciria, Alberto. *Parties and Power in Modern Argentina (1940–1946).* Buenos Aires: Editorial Universitaria de Buenos Aires, 1964.

David, Steven R. *Third World Coups d'Etat and International Security.* Baltimore: Johns Hopkins University Press, 1987.

Farcau, Bruce W. *The Coup: Tactics in the Seizure of Power.* Westport, CT: Praeger, 1994.

Finer, S.E. *The Man on Horseback.* London: Pall Mall Press, 1962.

Gurr, Ted Robert. *Why Men Rebel.* Princeton, NJ: Princeton University Press, 1970.

Huntington, Samuel. *Political Order in Changing Societies.* New Haven, CT: Yale University Press, 1968.

Kraus, John. "Ghana, 1966." In *The Politics of the Coup d'Etat,* ed. William G. Andrews and Uri Ra'anan. New York: Van Nostrand Reinhold, 1969.

Luttwak, Edward. *Coup d'Etat: A Practical Handbook.* New York: Knopf, 1969.

Malaparte, Curzio. *Coup d'Etat: The Technique of Revolution.* New York: E.P. Dutton, 1932.

Nordlinger, Eric. *Soldiers in Politics.* Englewood Cliffs, NJ: Prentice-Hall, 1977.

O'Kane, Rosemary H.T. *The Likelihood of Coups.* Brookfield, VT: Avebury, 1987.

Tullock, Gordon. *The Social Dilemma: The Economics of War and Revolution.* Blacksburg, VA: University Publications, 1974.

Wheatcroft, Andrew. *The World Atlas of Revolution.* New York: Simon and Schuster, 1983.

Woddis, Jack. *Armies and Politics.* New York: International, 1978.

INVASIONS AND BORDER DISPUTES

The twentieth century saw more change in warfare than did the previous 3,000 years. One obvious change was the development of weapons of mass destruction. Early in the century, most casualties in a war were military personnel, but by the end of the period, most casualties were civilians. Less obvious has been the transition from interstate wars to intrastate wars, from conflicts between countries to conflicts *within* countries. In recent years, almost all wars have been civil wars between factions within a nation-state.

The latter change highlights an often-overlooked dimension of war, its legal status. Initially, invasions are almost always illegal unless preceded by a formal declaration of war (a rarity after World War II). That legal status can change overnight when treaties are signed, or almost imperceptibly as the world becomes accustomed to what once was a tragic crime. For example, the invasion of Tibet by the forces of Communist China in October 1950 was widely condemned. But decades of patient diplomacy have done little to change this "fact on the ground," and on the maps published around the world. Tibetan partisans point out grotesque conditions that continue, resulting in very high death rates for ethnic Tibetans who are being slowly replaced by Han Chinese. Most of the capitals of the world observe discreetly, however, because their calculations favor the government in Beijing.

Technical students of war sometimes refer to border disputes as "irredentist" disputes. More narrowly, irredenta refer to territories historically or ethnically related to one political unit, but presently subject to another. There are many. A global history of wars and of mass migrations of refugees fleeing war or persecution has left many irredenta that can serve as flashpoints for future war. Other than its use here, the term "irredentist" will be replaced with the word "border."

Border Disputes Versus General Roots of War

The causes of "invasions and border disputes" are not significantly different from the causes of wars in general, except for the fact that disputes over borders can reflect especially arcane bits of history. For example, most people know that the Persian Gulf War of 1990–1991 between Iraq, Kuwait, and the United States and its allies began with an invasion of Kuwait by Iraq on August 2, 1990. Almost everyone knows that control of oil supplies was more important than details of the border. Very few people in the Western world, however, know the seminal role played seventy-three years earlier by Sir Percy Cox. Cox was a British diplomat based in Baghdad who drew the line between what would become Iraq and Kuwait, as part of the Sykes-Picot agreement of 1916 between Britain and France. He deliberately separated one tiny village, which became Kuwait City, and a large area of oil-rich desert from what would become modern Iraq. This was more than merely an expression of the principle of divide and rule as applied by the British in controlling oil supplies in the region. The British were also concerned about Turkey, which was then an ally of Germany and Austria in their war against Britain, France, and other Allied Powers. Cox was also trying to balance British and French "spheres of influence" among the dozens of tribes and clans in the region. The Iraq-Kuwait border, drawn for reasons long forgotten and past, served as the flashpoint for the first Gulf War in 1991.

Several wars in Africa late in the twentieth century reflect similar echoes of colonial mapmakers who carved up African lands according to European concerns and were relatively indifferent to local ethnic geography. For example, Sudan suffered about 1 million dead in a long-running civil war between fundamentalist Islamic Arabs in the North, who controlled the central government, and animist or Christian Nubians and other black Africans in the South. The central political issue was the Arabs' move to impose strict Sharia (Islamic law) on the whole nation. This would not have been an issue if colonial mapmakers had not created a cultural artifact called "Sudan," which puts very different peoples into the same formal nation-state.

The general causes of war include: competition for resources and power, population pressure, corruption of governance, authoritarian politics and militant religions, inequalities of wealth within and between nations, the hubris and demagoguery of scapegoating politicians, and the desire of people to find an enemy to blame all for their problems. The lack of effective "international conflict resolution systems" is another important root of organized, armed conflict in the modern world. By contrast, the United States has managed to control most local violence. Who could imagine, for example, Minnesota going to war with North Dakota over rights to the Red River water? Killing a neighbor because of a disagreement regarding city boundaries is considered murder all around the world. But Iraq's Saddam Hussein started an eight-year war that killed about a million people in September 1980, when he asserted a historic claim to the Shatt al-Arab waterway, which divides Iraq from Iran. No higher authority existed to restrain him, and the international community did not have the intelligence or the will to stop him.

Another great complication for those who study why wars start is called "transmutability of cause," which means that causes can shift and blend so that no one can say for sure which cause for a particular war was the "most important." For example, one could say that Iraqi leader Saddam Hussein's later invasion of Kuwait was motivated by historic border disputes (as he did) and recent insults like Kuwait poaching oil from across the border by slant drilling (which it was). Or one could say that history played little part and that the war was a simple struggle over oil or money. The point is that no one can find a truly "objective" way to determine which of these, or twenty other putative causes of that war, was the most important.

Invasions are easier to discern precisely because of borders: One group using the force of arms crosses a common border and moves into someone else's territory. But even then, the question of who was the aggressor can be difficult to answer because provocations often precede the invasion—for example, intelligence organizations may stage bogus events to precipitate a crisis. The dark art of psychological operations, in which propaganda is used to play with the minds of the enemy, and covert action were much enhanced by the Cold War between the superpowers, which led to interventions nearly everywhere on earth.

The Cold War and Its Aftermath

The Cold War between the United States and the Soviet Union thoroughly dominated the period from 1947 to 1991, when the Soviet Union disintegrated into fifteen independent states. Many wars in third world locales resulted from the very conscious decision of the superpowers to do everything possible to avoid nuclear warfare. The reasoning was that regular combat forces of the United States and the Soviet Union should never fight each other publicly, lest their own populations insist on full-scale nuclear war. Instead, the fierce contest between capitalism and Communism was fought by proxy wars around the world as the United States and the Soviet Union took opposite sides in scores of local disputes. About sixty countries around the world attracted major covert operations during the Cold War, many with large-scale lethal consequences. Everywhere the CIA was, the KGB (Soviet intelligence) was there also. Some of these wars would have occurred in any event, because many arguments had local roots. Other proxy wars would never have occurred without the "assistance" of the superpowers, which were eager to play out their competition on foreign soils without engaging their own combat units. But almost all of the proxy wars and many civil wars that attracted support by the superpowers went on longer and were far more lethal than otherwise would have been possible because of the relatively unlimited supplies of small arms and financial support available to those who would be clients of the superpowers.

As the Cold War came to an end, Soviet/Russian aid for previous clients declined rapidly in their many proxy wars with U.S. interests. The reduction of aid and the end of superpower hostility led to eventual resolution of several civil wars. Examples include El Salvador, Guatemala, Mozambique, and, ultimately, Angola. In Angola, peace was achieved with UN help, between the central government in Luanda (formerly sponsored by the Soviets) and the Union for the Total Independence of Angola (UNITA), the main insurgent group backed by the United States. Soon afterward, however, UNITA's Jonas Savimbi began the war again when he lost the UN-sponsored election. That war continued until his death in 2002.

One thing that the Cold War almost always accomplished was a massive transfusion of weapons and political money into combat zones around the world. For example, Mohammed Siad Barre of Somalia in northeast Africa played off the United States and the Soviet Union, alternately accepting support from each. When he left the scene in 1991, the money was gone, and vast stocks of light arms were available for the many militias that arose to continue fighting over the borders. An abortive peacekeeping effort by the United Nations in 1992–1994 managed to save many people from starvation but utterly failed to stop the fighting and was ultimately driven out of the capital city, Mogadishu. For years afterward, no recognizable central government existed in Somalia.

These connections do not mean that border wars stopped with the end of the Cold War. In fact, shortly after the breakup of the Soviet Union, several small wars began at the edges of its own empire. In Moldova, between 830 and 930 persons died in a brief but fierce dispute in 1991 and 1992. In the Ingush Republic, about 350 died when Slavic North Ossetians battled Muslim Ingush over who would rule. In Georgia, latent ethnic tensions between dominant Georgians and minority Abkhazians in one area and South Ossetians in another led to a three-front civil war from 1989 to 1994. In Tajikistan, at least 20,000 people died during another civil war over succession to power. And in Azerbaijan, ethnic Armenians in a disputed enclave called Nagorno-Karabakh joined forces with Armenians from the homeland (formerly another Soviet republic, now an independent state) to battle the Azeris over this territory. Approximately 20,000 people died there from 1991 to 1994.

The greatest casualties, however, occurred in Chechnya, where an invasion by Russian troops on December 11, 1994, led to a minimum of 40,000 dead, including several thousand Russian troops. Chechnya, unlike the other war sites, had never been recognized as one of the Soviet republics, which theoretically retained some independence. Although Chechens were fiercely independent, their land had been considered part of Russia ever since it was overrun by czarist troops in the nineteenth century. The Chechens declared independence in 1991, under the leadership of former Soviet air force general Dzhokhar Dudayev. In the war that followed, the two sides described it in completely different terms. To the Russians it was a civil war within territorial Russia. To the Chechens, the Russians had invaded independent Chechnya. As a practical matter, the Russian side of the argument carried the day because other national governments had refused to recognize Chechnya as an independent state.

Why Latin America Is Different

Although there are many theories on this, the most likely is that Latin America has been so thoroughly dominated by the United States, its patron to the north, that many disputes have been suppressed, or at least settled short of large-scale, lethal conflict. So the armies of this region have turned to persecuting their own peoples, in the name of stability and order, rather than planning invasions of their neighbors, which all know would be quickly, and if need be ruthlessly, suppressed by the United States. Certainly a long history of "gunboat diplomacy" in this area, familiar to every Latin American if not to every North American, would support that point of view.

In the post–World War II period, examples of that "diplomacy" in the Caribbean and Central America include the Bay of Pigs invasion of Cuba (1961) and the secret war that followed, armed intervention in the Dominican Republic (1965), invasions of Granada (1983) and Panama (1989), and the long "secret" war against Nicaragua, staged from Honduras and Costa Rica (1982–1990). Other civil wars in Central America, like in El Salvador and Guatemala, involved the superpowers, but while some involved invasions and borders (especially the "contra" war in Nicaragua), they were mainly local disputes between rich and poor enflamed by the Cold War competition between superpowers using third-world battlegrounds.

The dirty war in Argentina (1976–1979) and its analogs in Uruguay, Bolivia, Chile, Brazil, and elsewhere, while killing many thousands of people, often innocent ones, reflected the same forces and very seldom involved crossing borders. This leaves five cases with other dynamics or unambiguous border crossings by armed forces: the "secret war" between America and Cuba known to spies as Operation Mongoose during the mid-1960s (preceded by the invasion of the Bay of Pigs); the "soccer war" of 1969 between El Salvador and Honduras; the semiannual border "war" between Ecuador and Peru, which killed few but grew more serious with global competition for resources; the Falklands war of 1982 between Argentina and Britain; and the invasion of Panama by U.S. forces on December 20, 1989.

Operation Mongoose in Cuba is unknown to most North Americans but very well known to Cubans. It was a covert war carried out by the U.S. Central Intelligence Agency after the Cuban missile crisis of October 1962. In that crisis, begun when the United States revealed evidence of Soviet nuclear missiles in Cuba, the superpowers came close to nuclear holocaust. The crisis was resolved when the Soviets agreed to remove the missiles. In return, President John F. Kennedy promised never to invade Cuba again. However, the CIA was determined to proceed with covert paramilitary operations, using expatriate Cubans based mainly in Miami and the Florida Keys. The CIA's Miami station became its largest station in the world. Hundreds of Cuban enemies of Fidel Castro were trained in paramilitary commando tactics and armed with various weapons. Besides blowing up oil installations and attempting many times to assassinate Castro (twenty-eight tries, according to Cuba), many unconventional attacks were launched, including the use of biological weapons against Cuban crops and pigs.

The "soccer war" between Honduras and El Salvador in 1969 was simpler, but no less bizarre. The nominal cause of this brief war was a disputed call in a soccer game. But this war began for another, more fundamental reason. That problem was illegal immigration from desperately crowded and poor El Salvador into much less crowded but no less poor Honduras. Honduras expelled about 11,000 Salvadoran "settlers" (of between 200,000 and 300,000 estimated in that country). El Salvador's army invaded Honduras to protect the remaining settlers. Honduras responded to protect its territory. Both claimed to be protecting the honor of World Cup soccer, and about 5,000 people died. The Organization of American States intervened diplomatically; the regional powers and common sense stopped the fighting.

The war between Peru and Ecuador had deep historical roots. The countries had disputed the location of a jungle border since its creation in 1821. From that time until the late twentieth century, there was nothing really to fight about since the jungle is extremely dense, waterlogged, and virtually uninhabited. Still, for many years border clashes between the respective forces have occurred over three disputed areas during the few months when travel of any kind is practical there. These skirmishes became more severe as oil companies explored the region. Oil—or other valuable substances—might one day give a real purpose to the yearly battles.

Similarly, the dispute between Great Britain, which claims the Falkland Islands, and Argentina, which calls them the Islas Malvinas, had endured for almost 150 years. These barren rocks in the South Atlantic were home to about 2,000 people and 50,000 sheep. The Falkland Islands War (which the British won) is illustrative of "scapegoating," the so-called "Simmel effect," so named for an Austrian sociologist who first formulated it in print. Simply put, foreign wars distract from domestic discontent. Argentine President Leopoldo Galtieri was losing domestic support prior to an election, due partly to the fact that he was being blamed for bad economic times and many dead Argentines after the dirty war from 1976 to 1979, when about 15,000, mostly young people, died at the hands of secret police. Galtieri sought support in a time-honored way, by resurrecting an ancient land claim to the Malvinas (as Argentines called the Falklands) and making it a cause of the people. The Argentine navy and army invaded the islands, whose virtually unarmed people promptly surrendered.

The residents did, however, call London and beg for help. Britain's Prime Minister Margaret Thatcher was facing political opposition of her own. The "Iron Lady" of Britain was already known for her strong will, and she commanded a powerful military force with genuine global experience. British nuclear submarines sank an Argentine troop ship, resulting in the largest casualties of the conflict. Britain won the war, and Thatcher was reelected, while Galtieri was not. About 1,000 people died in this political exercise.

The invasion of Panama by U.S. forces in the early morning of December 20, 1989, was called Operation Just Cause. No one will ever know the true number of casualties. The official U.S. count was 516 Panamanian and 24 American deaths, while local estimates ran to at least 4,000. Almost a year after the event, American news organizations documented several mass graves, which the Pentagon had denied existed, leading to an estimate of 1,500 killed in the invasion. The nominal causes of the war were the need to remove dictator Manuel Noriega, to stop drug running through Panama, to safeguard American citizens there, and to "restore democracy." Other than disobedience by Noriega, none of these official "just causes" was likely a real cause of this war.

Far more important was the desire to reassert American control over Panamanian politics and to send an unambiguous message to Nicaragua, which was facing an election in two months that could end the long-running contra war, which was also being backed by the United States. Noriega was later convicted in U.S. courts of drug trafficking. This was the same Manuel Noriega who had been recruited from a military academy by the U.S. Central Intelligence Agency at the age of seventeen. The problem was that he was becoming uncontrollable, building an independent base of support among the poor and the defense forces in Panama, and had refused to allow Panama to become a staging area for the U.S.-backed contras. (Nicaragua's more compliant neighbors, Honduras and Costa Rica, had agreed.) So Noriega was removed, by force of arms. His Panamanian defense forces were decimated, and his base of support among the poor was warned by the complete destruction of a neighborhood called Chorrillo.

All that said, Latin America experienced fewer wars than any other major third world region thanks in part to the watchful eye of its powerful northern neighbor. The danger remains, however, that the dominance of the United States may one day incite a reaction in the region that even its great power cannot control.

Colonial Maps and African Conflicts

In the twentieth century, Africa, by contrast, had more wars than any other continent and more bloodshed by most counts. Most of these conflicts have not been invasions from without or disputes over recognized borders, but civil wars among factions within the nation-states. The great majority resulted from the great decolonization of Africa following World War II. Many of those retreats by Western powers were preceded by wars of national liberation. The list of wars includes: Algeria (4 wars), Angola (2), Burundi (2), Cameroon, Chad (2), Congo (then Zaire, now the Democratic Republic of Congo, 4 wars), Ethiopia (2), Ghana (2), Guinea-Bissau, Kenya (2), Liberia (2), Libya, Madagascar, Morocco, Mozambique (2), Namibia, Nigeria (4), Rwanda (3), Sierra Leone (1), Somalia (1), South Africa (2), Sudan (2), Tunisia, Uganda (4), Western Sahara (1), Zambia (1), and Zimbabwe (formerly Rhodesia, 3). At least 15 million people have died in these wars or by related famine, as in Sudan, where denial of food was used as a weapon against the south.

The most obvious problem in Africa is the history of colonization and all that it has represented. An equally important problem later was the tendency of some African leaders to blame all problems on their former colonial masters. Other causes for the high level of conflict included widespread inexperience in large-scale government and poverty. The old problem of maps—in which the correlation between political boundaries and the distribution of ethnic groups is very poor—remains a big problem. Many of the borders were drawn up by colonial Europeans

without much interest in ethnic variations, yet in a region as ethnically diverse as Africa, they would likely not have succeeded in drawing perfectly logical boundaries. For example, Nigeria alone has about 400 linguistic groups, including three very large tribes dominant in their respective areas, and a dozen other major tribes. To further complicate matters, there are deep disputes among Muslims, Christians, and animist, or nature-based, religious groups.

So, colonial history and mixed ethnicity are pervasive in Africa, as well as poverty and meddling by the superpowers. What else applies to Africa?

1. A long history of armed nomadic groups, relatively indifferent to geopolitical boundaries.
2. A short history of governance by Western methods, which led both to hatred of elites and also to inflated expectations when elections finally came, soon to be dashed by corrupt practices that are inevitable even in advanced Western democracies.
3. Crushing debts to international institutions, some of which sincerely tried to help during the postcolonial period, but did not do so effectively, others of which clearly set out to create banker-managed capitalism via debt.
4. Very high birth rates, which, aside from the obvious contribution to competition for resources, also result in skewed age distributions where half the population is under the age of twenty, sometimes under fifteen years old.

In many African states, huge numbers of teenage males in desperate poverty with low confidence and even lower prospects for employment watch very wealthy elites gain government appointments and company jobs for their clans while excluding others. Add plenty of arms left over from the Cold War, and you have a very explosive mix. Add an AIDS epidemic that has infected huge fractions of young adults, and you have the kind of despair that leads to conflicts of every sort.

A single example will illustrate this. Rwanda had the bloodiest war on earth in 1994, when between 500,000 and 1,000,000 mostly ethnic Tutsi were slaughtered with small arms and machetes by the majority Hutu in a period of about three months. Rwanda also had a long colonial history in which the Belgians manipulated the region's ethnic differences, the French manipulated economic and military interests, and complex internal politics made moderate Hutu in the political elite the primary target for the

Hutu special forces when the killing began. Ironically, a Tutsi-led army based in Uganda (the Rwandan Patriotic Front) ultimately won this war and drove the hard-line Hutu out. Rwanda also had the highest birth rate in Africa when the killing began, yielding a growth rate of 3.8 percent per year. At that rate, the population would double in just over eighteen years, with half the population under the age of fifteen. Under these circumstances, even an extremely fertile country like Rwanda will become deforested, and crowded, and any ethnic conflicts that existed before will be further enflamed as places to hide, or even places to make a living, become scarce.

The history of African conflicts after World War II is not complete without mention of its most notable successes. In 1980 very few observers would have predicted that South Africans would successfully end their brutal civil war among nine tribal and linguistic groups (two white, seven black) to forge a multiethnic nation with a relatively wealthy and stable economy. Also, Tanzania has avoided most of these problems and certainly war, due largely to enlightened leadership and industrious peoples.

Asian Agonies

Any discussion of Asia and war properly begins with China, the imperial power of its region since World War II. As soon as that war concluded, China was convulsed by its own civil war, between the Communist forces of Mao Zedong and the Nationalist forces of Chiang Kai-shek. By 1949, Mao and his Communist troops had gained control of the country, and the defeated Nationalists had fled to the island of Taiwan. In the next forty years, China was involved in invasions or border disputes with at least five countries: Tibet (1950–1951); Korea (1950–1953); India (1962); the Soviet Union (1969); and Vietnam (1979 and 1987).

There is no doubt that the invasion of Tibet was a disaster for that thinly populated country with a history of prior wars with and domination by China. After the invasion, the land of Buddhist temples and its people was slowly absorbed into China. Tibet's remoteness from Western capitals made the invasion an "internal affair," as the Chinese claimed, but protests continue around the world.

Korea, unlike Tibet, was much closer to Western interests. After World War II it was partitioned, with the north dominated by Soviets and the south dominated by Americans. Just who crossed the border first

in 1950 is a matter of dispute, but there is no doubt the north soon invaded the south with a huge Soviet-supplied army. President Harry Truman gained United Nations support to defend South Korea, and a long contest between capitalism and Communism began. When U.S. and South Korean troops invaded the North and neared the Chinese border, the Chinese got involved. Massive attacks by China almost pushed the Americans into the sea, but increased Western support allowed them to gain the upper hand. The war ended in a stalemate with the line between North and South Korea very near the border before the fighting began. About 3 million people died in that conflict.

The vast second Indochina war between North Vietnam, which received support from China, and South Vietnam, which was heavily subsidized by the United States (1962–1973), also spread to neighboring Cambodia and Laos, where North Vietnamese regular forces and special U.S. forces fought a clandestine battle. In the war, more bombs were dropped than were used in all of World War II. The aggregate death toll was estimated to be at least 2 million Vietnamese, 58,000 to 60,000 Americans (depending on the status of 2,000 still missing), and uncounted numbers of Cambodians and Laotians caught in the crossfire. It is likely that at least 3 million people died as a direct or indirect result of this war.

Even as North Vietnam took full control of the country in 1975, civil war was raging in Cambodia (1975–1998). Radical Communist Pol Pot, supported by the Chinese, took power in 1975 as leader of the Khmer Rouge, then killed or "caused to die" roughly a million of his fellow Cambodians. In 1978, Vietnam invaded Cambodia, allegedly to stop the slaughter and at least to stop the waves of refugees into destitute Vietnam, and installed a client of their own named Hun Sen. The civil war continued for many years between these two groups and another "royal" faction. That conflict ended with the death of Pol Pot in 1998, and the virtual elimination of the Khmer Rouge.

In 1975, Indonesia was consolidating power under Suharto, who had deposed his predecessor (Sukarno) ten years earlier at a cost of about 650,000 lives. Indonesia is a vast nation encompassing hundreds of islands. While the world's attention in Southeast Asia was on ending the Vietnam War, Suharto decided to remove a minor irritant by invading and annexing the free half of the island of Timor. The island had been divided for almost 500 years between Dutch and Portuguese colonists. But the age of colonies was over.

Indonesia already controlled the western half. Suharto thought the East Timorese would surrender quickly and that no one would care. He was right that few cared, and he got permission from U.S. President Gerald Ford and Secretary of State Henry Kissinger just days before the invasion. He was wrong about resistance. By the time the Indonesian army was finished, about one-third of East Timor's population of 600,000 were dead. The slaughter gained the world's attention, and Indonesia was forced to withdraw from the region. East Timor voted for independence as a nation, and with the help of United Nations peacekeepers achieved independence in 2002.

Many smaller ethnic groups on smaller islands in Indonesia, the Philippines, Malaysia, and elsewhere in the world have been overwhelmed by central governments that considered themselves not as invaders but as peacekeepers, bringing the rule of national government to "rural areas." Such was the fate of many minority populations in this world. Either they accepted the terms and definitions of the central government with the bigger guns, or they passed the way of indigenous peoples of many places and times, including the Iroquois long gone from North America and the Yanomami of Brazil, who are rapidly disappearing today.

India and Pakistan have fought three wars since they were born by partition of Britain's south Asian colony in 1947. Most of the blood was shed over a small piece of territory that began as a "princely state" called Kashmir. In the original partition, regions with a majority of Muslims became part of Pakistan and those with a majority of Hindus part of India. As inevitably occurs with such partitions, there were some places where two faiths were mixed quite thoroughly and where the residents' loyalty to their local ruler was stronger than to either emerging nation.

Although Pakistani and Indian populations differ ethnically, religiously, and culturally, they compete for the same natural resources. Who controls fertile ground can be the difference between life and death when harvests are slim. The two countries have many causes for friction, some extending back centuries or millennia and some much more recent, including the seemingly endless border dispute over Kashmir. The rest of the world took special note of the rivalry in 1998, however, when both India and Pakistan began substantial tests of nuclear weapons. Neighboring China has had nuclear weapons and border disputes of its own (it seized some Himalayan territory from

India in 1962), and China's contested province of Tibet lies right on India's border.

The Balkans

World War I nominally began when a militant Serb in Sarajevo named Gavrilo Princip murdered Austrian archduke and heir to the throne, Franz Ferdinand, on June 28, 1914. Within a few weeks, all of Europe was at war. Before the war ended, one-tenth of all young European men were dead.

During World War II, the Nazis involved themselves in Balkan disputes. They supported the Croatian faction there, whose Ustashe security force helped kill Chetnik Serbs, Bosnian Muslims, and Communist partisans of many ethnicities led by Josip Broz Tito. About a million died in these conflicts, setting the stage for the largest war in Europe during the post–World War II period, when the newly formed state of Yugoslavia disintegrated during three wars.

Field Marshal Josip Broz Tito became the dictatorial ruler of Yugoslavia, which was Communist but genuinely independent. A Croatian Catholic by birth, he married a Serbian woman, and having led the dominant partisans during the downfall of Nazi Germany, he was in a position to establish the Yugoslav

Josip Broz (Marshal Tito), the leader of the Yugoslav resistance during World War II and Communist head of state until 1980, succeeded in quelling longstanding ethnic rancor. His death and the demise of Communist rule opened a new era of fragmentation in the Balkans. *(John Phillips/Time Life Pictures/Getty Images)*

Republic and to stifle ethnic dissent during his time. The ethnic peace he had imposed began to unravel shortly after his death, with mysterious but calculated hate campaigns dominated by the Serbs and a former Communist official named Slobodan Milosevic. Tensions grew, especially between the prosperous north (the Yugoslav republics of Slovenia and Croatia) and the poorer, but militarily stronger, south (Serbia and smaller republics that it dominated). Slovenia, Croatia, Bosnia, and Macedonia seceded, leaving the old Yugoslavia so reduced that it was soon renamed Serbia and Montenegro. Serbia's autonomous region of Kosovo became the scene of further ethnic struggle as the majority population (ethnically Albanian) demanded independence from its Serbian masters. The United States intervened in this dispute and in 1999 bombed Serbian positions in Kosovo and in the rest of Serbia. Eventually Milosevic, the Serb leader, was ousted and was later tried for war crimes. In the meantime, Kosovo remained under UN supervision.

One can tease out the historic roots of this conflict forever. Devotion to historic grievances and excessive nationalism were the main causes. But there are many others, including leaders more interested in power than in governing, religious differences (Yugoslavia had large populations of Roman Catholic and Orthodox Christians and Muslims), and broader world trends. With the dissolution of the Soviet Union in 1991, the idea of national or ethnic independence was in the air in Eastern Europe.

The Balkans are a region where civilizations collide, cultures mix, and the permutations of conflict are complex. Some of the issues tie the region to large populations in other parts of the world, increasing the risk that small conflicts will escalate into large ones, as occurred at the beginning of World War I. Another area with an unparalleled history of armed conflict is the Middle East.

The Middle East

Judaism, Christianity, and Islam all converge in present-day Israel. Paradoxically, faithful followers of all these religions are working hard for peace in the midst of bitter conflict, but the entire area remains one big dispute over borders. Every square centimeter is claimed by at least two parties, and there have been many invasions there since World War II.

Views about responsibility for these conflicts are highly polarized. Of the six wars involving Israel, hard-liners among both Arab and Jewish populations blame everyone on the other side. Parallel realities among polarized enemies like this can result in cycles of war without apparent end. And cycles of revenge provide many opportunities for each side to blame the "other" still again.

Israel was established in 1948 by the declining colonial powers in the Middle East and the recently organized United Nations as a homeland for Jews who had survived the Holocaust in Europe in which millions had been killed. On the day the British left the newly created state, members of the Arab League invaded. When the Israeli Jews won the first rounds of the 1948–1949 war, they killed some Palestinians and expelled many more (about 700,000), who became a new refugee population. Many Palestinians stayed, however, making up about 20 percent of Israel's population.

In 1956, when Egypt attempted to nationalize its biggest resource, the Suez Canal, taking it from a British-French company, Israel joined Britain and France in seeking a military assault against the Egyptians, but the action was countermanded after widespread disapproval from other powers, including the United States. In 1967, in response to a direct threat along the length of Israel's territory, the Israelis started what came to be known as the Six-Day War by bombing Egyptian air bases at dawn (they felt that war was inevitable, and called the bombings a "pre-emptive strike"). As in many crises, this one had been preceded by a long period of mutual animosity in which each side provoked the other. The 1967 war resulted in substantial territorial losses to all Arab states involved: Israel occupied Egypt's Sinai Peninsula; the West Bank and East Jerusalem, which had been under the rule of Jordan; and Syria's Golan Heights.

Egypt's President Nasser began a long series of small border skirmishes along the Suez Canal, which came to be known as the War of Attrition and lasted until 1970. In 1973, still another war began on the Jewish holiday of Yom Kippur. This time, according to the United Nations, Egypt and Syria began the hostilities. Fighting was intense for several weeks, until the threatened use of "clandestine" nuclear weapons helped American and Soviet Union diplomatic efforts to broker another UN cease-fire. This time Israel suffered the major losses, including 6,000 dead and economic costs of nearly $7 billion, equal to Israel's annual GNP, and eventually led to the Camp David

Palestinian leader Yasir Arafat holds up a map of the West Bank during Israel's construction of a security barrier in 2003. Territorial disputes in the Middle East have ancient roots. *(Hussein Hussein/PPO via Getty Images)*

Accords involving U.S. President Jimmy Carter, Egypt's Anwar Sadat, and Israel's Menachem Begin.

Meanwhile, the rest of the Middle East was also not peaceful. In 1974, Turkey's army invaded the island of Cyprus, not far from the Israeli and Syrian coasts, in a dispute between Turkish and Greek Cypriots. The invasion divided the island into separate ethnic sectors, which remain to this day. To the world, it was not very important (and nuclear weapons were not threatened). But to the Cypriots, it divided a beautiful and prosperous island into two bitter enclaves, each much poorer by far.

During this time, and continuing to this day, there were also large numbers of armed actions involving ethnic Kurds seeking independence from the four countries their historic territories straddle: Turkey, Iran, Iraq, and Syria. To the Kurds, this land was "Kurdistan," but no other nation recognizes such a state. Thus the wars and skirmishes do not count as border wars, even though each of the four named countries has sent troops past national boundaries in pursuit of Kurdish rebels. Turkey, in particular, killed thousands of Kurds across its border in Iraq.

In 1982, the Israelis invaded Lebanon in a bid to rid themselves of continued attacks by Palestinian terrorists The Israelis had been provoked by many rocket attacks from Lebanese positions and commando raids across their border—hundreds of episodes over thirty-six years. Israeli armored divisions drove all the way to Beirut, Lebanon's capital, occupying a third of the country along the way, and did indeed destroy the Palestinian governmental structures there. Of course, the Palestinian people still had no permanent land and continued to harbor bitter grudges. So despite the ten-mile buffer strip in southern Lebanon, and despite a virtually permanent UN presence feeding Palestinian refugees there, commando raids across the Israeli border and terrorist bombings continued, as did Israeli bombing raids and artillery attacks on Palestinians in Lebanon. In response to Israeli incursions, neighboring Syria occupied Lebanon's Bekaa Valley in 1982, with a mandate from the Arab League to restore order and protect what was left from the Israelis. Once again, in 2006, Israel invaded Lebanon, partly to halt rocket attacks on its territory launched by the Shiite militia Hezbollah.

Recall the eternal causes of wars: competition for resources and power, population pressure, authoritarian political systems and militant religions, corruption of governance, inequalities of wealth within and between nations, the lack of effective international conflict resolution systems, the hubris of political leaders and especially demagogic leaders who thrive on the hatred of others, and the folly of the people who follow them. One can find all these elements in both the Balkans and the Middle East.

Michael Andregg

Bibliography

Anderson, Malcolm. *Frontiers: Territory and State Formation in the Modern World.* New York: Blackwell, 1996.

Boggs, Samuel Whittemore. *International Boundaries: A Study of Boundary Functions and Problems.* New York: AMS Press, 1966.

Prescott, J.R.V. *The Geography of Frontiers and Boundaries.* Chicago: Aldine, 1965.

Schofield, Clive H., ed. *Global Boundaries.* New York: Routledge, 1994.

Wilson, Thomas, and Hastings Donnan, eds. *Border Identities: Nation and State at International Frontiers.* New York: Cambridge University Press, 1998.

ETHNIC AND RELIGIOUS CONFLICTS

While interethnic competition, some with religious overtones, can be traced to biblical times, it has been a prominent characteristic of the post–World War II era. More than 300 of these struggles have occurred since the end of the war. Only with the end of the Cold War did the international community recognize how pervasive such ethnic disputes had become. Communal conflicts devastated the former Yugoslavia, threatened or even overwhelmed the stability of most of the former republics of the Soviet Union, brought about state collapse in a variety of African countries, exacerbated historic disputes in the Middle East and Southeast Asia, and even threatened violence in some Western industrialized countries. Together, such conflicts have serious implications for international peace and security.

The domestic instabilities and collapses have spawned a sharp rise in refugees and the internally displaced and have triggered some fifty episodes of genocide or mass murder directed at more than seventy ethnic and religious minorities, resulting in between 12 million and 25 million civilian fatalities. Such developments are accompanied by a proliferation of both conventional and nuclear arms. This consequence was dramatically underscored in May 1998 when India and Pakistan expressed their rivalry by competitive tests of nuclear weapons.

Perhaps a natural outcome of these unsettling facts is the alarmist interpretation that some analysts have advanced, such as post–Cold War "global chaos," unrestrained "international disorder," and global "pandemonium." Professor Samuel Huntington even promoted a thesis of "cleavage among civilizations," asserting that a "cultural" curtain has replaced the "iron" curtain that previously divided the world, and that religion (a crucial component of culture) provides new fuel for conflict as it inspires intolerance and irreconcilable images of "identity" and loyalty.

Yet ethno-religious conflicts are not necessarily the harbingers of global chaos, for most seem amenable to some form of management or resolution. Most minorities, often the subject of ethno-political conflicts, have sought "voice" or "access" within existing societies, not "exit" or adjustment of international borders. Thus, in the midst of an alarming number of ethnic and religious conflicts stands the hope that such communal conflicts may be limited or ended by some form of political settlement.

Defining the Problem

What is an ethnic group? What is a religious group? How do they become politically salient within or beyond the nation-state? What is it that gives rise to groups' protests and rebellions or their demands for voice, access within, or exit from the societies of which they are a part? Answers to these questions may help understand the ethno-religious conflicts since the end of World War II, and especially since the end of the Cold War in 1991.

Max Weber, the great German sociologist, defines an ethnic group as a people holding "a subjective belief in their common descent." There is a "presumed," "artificial," "accidental" identity that may be associated with such characteristics as physical appearance, customs, common memories, language, religion, and so on. Many scholars are in agreement about these "ethnic criteria," loose as they are, and point out that the strength of ethnic groups lies in the bonds of culture and not in those of association.

Questions remain regarding the context of those "bonds of culture" and how one might explain the religious component. Usually, conflict is occasioned by the recognition of discrimination and politically channeled collective grievance within a society, as well as the authorities' resistance to such demands. Ethnic conflicts are thus "conflicts in groups that define themselves using ethnic or national criteria," and on this basis claims on behalf of collective group interests are made against political actors, including the state.

Ethnic conflicts also bear a correlation with religious belief in that ethnicity's subjective belief in a common descent carries with it a "sacred" focus of group attention, the idea of a "chosen people," a "providential mission." Although religion can often be a force for peace and harmony, espousing universalistic ideals that accept all people's rights, it can also be a

Weapons captured in a 2003 raid against ETA, the militant Basque separatist organization, are displayed in the northern Spanish city of Bilbao. Basques were granted home rule in 1980, but ethnonationalist violence has continued. *(Rafa Rivas/AFP/Getty Images)*

catalyst for "holy wars." When religious groups adopt particularistic and intolerant outlooks, they become a potential source of conflict and war. Often religious and ethnic solidarity are joined. Arab Muslims in the Middle East or Irish Protestant and Roman Catholic Christians in Northern Ireland are communal groups that define themselves in terms of both ethnic and religious beliefs. Their religious differences reinforce and add a special intensity to ethnic conflicts.

A study by Ted Robert Gurr suggests that religious cleavages are contributing factors to communal conflicts but seldom the root cause. He found that only eight of forty-nine militant minority sects studied were defined solely or mainly by religious beliefs. The Shiites of Lebanon and Iraq have goals of political recognition, not faith propagation, and the sectarian minorities represented by Catholics in Northern Ireland and Turks in Germany have clear political (not religious) agendas, as do the Kurds and Palestinians of the Middle East.

It has been suggested that coexisting with (or existing within) most or all modern states are five important politically active ethnic groups: *ethnonationalists* (independent identities seeking to reestab-lish their own state); *indigenous peoples* (primarily concerned with protecting their traditional lands, resources, and culture); *communal contenders* (one among a number of culturally distinct groups in plural societies that compete for a share of political power); *ethno-classes* (desirous of equal rights and opportunities to overcome effects of discrimination resulting from their immigration and minority status); and *militant sects* (politicized minority peoples defined wholly or substantially by religious beliefs).

Ethno-nationalists include Corsicans and Bretons in France, Basques in Spain, French Canadians, Palestinians and Kurds in the Middle East, Slovenes, Latvians, and Armenians. Since 1991, more than a dozen new ethno-nationalities have emerged within the former states of the Soviet Union and Yugoslavia. Usually equipped with an organized leadership and occupying substantial territory, these groups or movements may straddle internationally recognized borders, and thus their activities spill over such borders with consequences for international peace and security.

Indigenous peoples are descendants of the original inhabitants of conquered or colonized regions. A major impetus for their development of a common identity of purpose is their being discriminated against and exploited by peoples with advanced technology. Examples of indigenous peoples include the natives of the Americas (36 million or 5 percent of the population of the Western Hemisphere, though in Bolivia, Guatemala, and Peru they constitute one-half of the populations), the Aborigines of Australia, the Maori of New Zealand, and the Masai of East Africa. For a long time, these groups resisted discrimination in uncoordinated uprisings. The League of Nations was petitioned, with little effect, by a number of North American indigenes and the Maori of New Zealand. Since the creation of the United Nations, however, a number of measures have been taken to address the problems of indigenous peoples. They include the creation in 1975 of a World Council of Indigenous Peoples, a non-governmental organization that provides a forum for discussion, publicity, and concerted planning; the 1992 UN-sponsored conference in Brazil, which issued an Indigenous Peoples Earth Charter, a document that outlines a comprehensive set of cul-

tural and environmental demands; and the UN Working Group on Indigenous Populations, which assembles 200 groups at annual meetings in Geneva, Switzerland. The latter has prepared a draft Universal Declaration of Indigenous Rights, which many hope will become a part of the corpus of international law.

Communal contenders are ethnic groups within national societies more interested in acquiring access to power than in instigating exit from the state. Such contenders include the Maronite Christians and the Druze, Sunni, and Shiite Muslims of Lebanon, the South Sudanese, and the Igbos of Nigeria. The context for struggle involving this group is usually an arrangement where government political power is based on a coalition among traditional or modern leaders of ethnic groups. Failure to establish or maintain multiethnic coalitions or otherwise manage cleavage conflicts may lead to wars of secession such as the Biafran attempt to secede from Nigeria in the late 1960s and the recent conflict in the Sudan, which essentially pitted two culturally and religiously dissimilar groups, one

The Golden Temple in Amritsar, India, the chief Sikh shrine, has been the site of sporadic violence between militant separatists and government forces. Here, the wounded are carried out after Indian Army troops opened fire during a May 1988 siege on the temple complex. (*Pablo Bartholomew/Getty Images News*)

having the advantage of control of the government. The distinction between communal contenders and ethno-nationalists is not a rigid one, for a communal group, once interested in secession, may be persuaded to enter a power-sharing arrangement at the political center. Settlement efforts in the Sudan have this in view, as did the restoration in the 1960s of the breakaway province of Katanga to the central government of the Democratic Republic of Congo, when Moise Tshombe, the secessionist leader, assumed the premiership of the Congo republic.

Ethno-classes are ethnic groups that resemble classes. They are ethnically and culturally distinct minorities, often descendants of slaves and immigrants, whose circumstances led them to specialize in distinctive economic activities, usually of low status. Ethno-classes in advanced industrial societies include the Muslim minority in France, people of color in Britain and the United States, Koreans in Japan, and blacks in some nine countries of Latin America. In developing countries, ethno-classes at times are economically advantaged but politically restricted. They include merchants and professionals, such as the Chinese minorities in many countries of Southeast Asia, Indians in East Africa, and Lebanese in much of West Africa.

Militant sects are religiously defined politicized minority peoples and include Islamic minorities in societies dominated by other religious traditions, such as Turks in Germany, Muslim Albanians in the former Yugoslavia, Arabs in Israel, and Malay Muslims in Thailand. They also include the warring Sunni, Shiite, and Druze in Lebanon, the Shiite in Iraq and Saudi Arabia, and the Kashmiris and Sikhs in India. Some non-Muslim groups include the Jews of Argentina, the Copts of Egypt, and the Baha'is of Iran.

Whether categorized or characterized as national peoples (ethno-nationalists or indigenous peoples), or minority peoples (ethno-classes, communal contenders, or militant sects), these groups share a perception about something that sets them apart from other groups. Cultural, economic, and political differentials between a group and others tend to reinforce identification.

Historical Context of Conflicts

Citizenship is an element of identity that can reinforce or compete against other elements such as race, ethnicity, religion, region, class, and so forth. As nation-states gain control of their citizens, many show a growing intolerance to other identity elements. Some

scholars suggest that other elements of modernization such as development of a market economy and the communications revolution may encourage such intolerance.

Historically, ethnic groups, nations, empires, and other large-scale social organizations (Islam, Christendom) have coexisted, but since the seventeenth century, the state has been the dominant form of social organization. The state has been defined by the territory it controls, its sovereignty, and its ability to claim the allegiance of its subjects/citizens.

Prevailing ideologies and political movements within state systems dramatically influence ethnic conflict. In the 1920s and 1930s, anti-Semitic doctrines in Germany and other European countries promoted ethnic polarization. They competed with Communist doctrines in the Soviet Union and elsewhere, which emphasized a common interest of all national (even international) Communist peoples and minimized the significance of ethnic and other particularistic identities.

In the 1940s and 1950s, anticolonial sentiments found expression in nationalist movements in Asia, Africa, and the Caribbean to challenge European colonial domination. Such sentiments, in time, resulted in a marked increase in the number of states claiming exclusive loyalties of diverse peoples. For a while, then, nationalists succeeded in uniting ethnic groups to end colonial rule and to consolidate their newly won independence. Later, they began to have their own problems with local minorities. During the Cold War (1945–1991), the United States and the Soviet Union helped new states to consolidate and enforce national unity, often to speed up "economic development."

By the late 1960s and early 1970s, decolonization was all but completed, but politicized ethnic consciousness soon reemerged in a number of states such as the Democratic Republic of Congo, Nigeria, and Sudan. More recently, a new kind of resistance to the monopolistic state system has left few world regions unaffected and has led to an increasing number of movements for ethnic autonomy.

In emulating the industrialized states of Europe and North America, newer states began to subordinate the interests and relative autonomy of ethnic minorities in the name of pursuing national goals of consolidation or expansion. State-building came to mean policies of assimilating national and minority peoples, curbing their historical autonomy, and extracting their material and human resources for the state. The building of Communist states in Eastern Europe after

1945 followed this pattern. There were exceptions. For example, overseas Chinese in Southeast Asia were able to share power and prosperity at the center of the several developing states. Elsewhere, as in parts of Africa, the reach of state power was limited, which enabled some groups to retain de facto local autonomy.

The state-building process was accompanied by development of the market economy and a revolution in communications technology. Colonial imperialism grafted large populations of colonized peoples onto the global capitalist economic system primarily assigning to them the role of providing raw material and being consumers of finished products. The communications revolution reduced distance, removed isolation, and disseminated information on such a scale that human relations were irrevocably changed. These developments deeply affected the old-fashioned state system premised on the notions of state sovereignty and the subordination of national and minority peoples.

Two competing trends can be seen in the treatment of national and minority peoples. One is the reemergence of xenophobia, as seen in Germany, France, and Britain, as well as in movements demanding ethnic purity in the newly independent states of the former Soviet Union and Yugoslavia. The second trend is the rise of oppressive leaders who defend existing state borders at all costs, disregarding historically justified claims for internal autonomy or independence by national peoples, such as Kurds and Southern Sudanese. Ironically, the leaders of former Asian and African colonies were willing to fight to maintain existing boundaries that had been drawn arbitrarily by colonial authorities, sometimes to purposely divide ethnic and or religious groups.

It appears that world leaders have become more willing to reconsider the balance between the old norms of sovereignty and territorial integrity against the long ignored rights of ethnic and religious groups. This new attitude is often expressed as seeking to balance nations' rights with peoples' or human rights. It can be seen in such regional groups as the Conference on Security and Cooperation in Europe, and the Mechanism for Conflict Resolution and Management of the Organization of African Unity.

Regional Manifestations of Conflicts

Employing the term "ethno-religious" to encompass all categories of conflicts among national and minority peoples, how have the various regional manifestations

informed our understanding of the phenomenon? Sub-Saharan Africa is the region most associated with the phenomenon of ethno-religious conflict, especially in its negative and intractable forms. Often it is equated with racial conflict. Anthropologists have challenged the idea that ethnicity is an essentialist and apolitical concept, insisting that the concept is relative, linked to socially defined and publicly expressed ideas about culture and political identities that are changeable.

Thus the debate about the nature of ethnicity in Africa has been between the primordialists—ethnicity as an immutable set of emotionally charged biological, cultural, linguistic, and religious givens that are the primary source of identity—and the situationalists—ethnicity as an almost totally flexible set of identities, which vary depending on rational calculation of material, political, and other types of advantages, and which are often stimulated by political mobilization led by actors whose primary identities and motives are nonethnic. A middle interpretation maintains that ethnicity is a shared cultural identity that may be energized in response to political, class, and economic interests or circumstances, or alternatively weakened depending on the same set of circumstances.

Since 1945, all types of ethno-religious conflicts have occurred in Africa, but the group called *communal contenders* has been the most common instigator. This prevailing form of conflict stems from competition over political and economic power in unstable, multiethnic coalitions, either within single governing parties or among officers in a military regime.

All types of politicized communal groups exist in Africa. Examples of the more intense and violent ethno-religious conflicts involve ethno-nationalist groups, ethno-classes, and militant sects. Some have been long term (in Burundi, Rwanda, Chad, Ethiopia, Sudan, apartheid South Africa), and others have been relatively short term (civil wars in Angola, Liberia, Nigeria, Uganda, Congo/Zaire).

In terms of their impact on international relations, communal contentions in the following African countries stand out: Sudan, Ethiopia, Mozambique, Angola, Liberia, Somalia, Western Sahara, Rwanda, and Burundi, among others. All tend to sustain the situationist position that politicized communal contention over political power-sharing and economic distribution issues is the prevalent form of politically relevant ethnicity in Africa, not the primordialist intractability of the Western media.

Eastern Europe and Russia constitute the third-largest concentration of politicized communal groups after Africa and Asia. This region has perhaps received more world attention than others, a fact that once prompted former UN Secretary-General Boutros Boutros Ghali to lament that the "rich man's war" in Bosnia received far greater attention than the "poor man's war" in Somalia.

Where most countries of Western Europe are nearly culturally homogeneous, those in Eastern Europe and Russia are culturally and ethnically heterogeneous multinational states. Before the breakup of the Soviet Union and Yugoslavia, the two together accounted for thirty-two ethnic groups, or 35 percent of the region's population. The ideology of Marxist-Leninism managed to contain the cultural and ethnic tensions implicit in aggrieved situations of such diversity. With its demise, a dramatic change occurred in ethnic relations and the status of minorities in this region.

Three of the federated, multinational states of the region—the Soviet Union, Yugoslavia, and Czechoslovakia—disintegrated because their constituent republics exercised their constitutional rights of secession from the political union. As if that were not enough, at least two of the successor sets of states—the former Yugoslavia, now known as Serbia and Montenegro, and the Russian Federation—are now themselves at risk of massive disruption in social relations and have each, in fact, experienced civil wars. The original state of Yugoslavia was dismembered into five sovereign states—Croatia, Slovenia, Macedonia, Bosnia-Herzegovina, and Serbia and Montenegro. But ethnopolitical divisions within each of the new units, particularly Bosnia and Croatia, have occasioned wars accompanied by "ethnic cleansing," or genocide, on such a scale that the world community, though reluctantly and belatedly, was drawn into the conflicts to resolve or at least contain them. The efforts continued with new violence in the Serbian province of Kosovo, where ethnic Albanians asserted their identity in response to overbearing Serbian nationalism.

The Russian Federation was challenged by a long and violent rebellion in Chechnya, which resulted not only in brutal fighting and the destruction of the Chechen capital, but also in terrorist attacks outside Chechnya, on a theater in Moscow and a school in Beslan, among others. Other ethnic battles consumed the newly independent states of Armenia and Azerbaijan over the fate of an Armenian enclave in Azerbaijan named Nagorno-Karabakh.

Still, many newly independent nations, free from the shadow of the former Soviet central government, have provided freedom and opportunity to subject nations and national ethnic groups. Peoples formerly disadvantaged and aggrieved became governing majorities and sought to redefine themselves and their relations with one another peacefully.

North Africa and the Middle East together have thirty-one politicized minorities comprising 28.8 percent of the total population. Kurds and Palestinians are the most numerous among those who lost out in the twentieth-century process of state formation. There are also the Saharawis (who continue to resist incorporation by Morocco), the Berbers of North Africa, and the Azeris of Iran.

Since World War II, North Africa and the Middle East have seen the most significant rebellions and disruptions of any other world region. The Palestinians in Israeli-occupied territories represent a dispersed group seeking greater autonomy and independence. They are, in fact, a national people dispersed throughout the world, with politically active segments in Jordan, Israel, Lebanon, the West Bank and Gaza, and Jerusalem. The bilaterally negotiated Oslo Accords of September 1993 led to the creation of a Palestinian Authority in the West Bank and Gaza, but a number of intractable issues remained outstanding between the Palestinians and the government of Israel.

The Kurds were also a dispersed national people, but their situation differed from the Palestinians' in that they were a non-Arab, mostly Sunni Muslim, people. Their territory, which they call "Kurdistan," contains 21 million Kurds and stretches across part of four independent states—Turkey, Iran, Iraq, and Syria. They number 10 million in Turkey alone. In each of these countries, the governments view the Kurds as a threat to national unity and civil peace.

Relations among communal groups in North Africa and the Middle East are shaped in a fundamental way by Islamic doctrine and practice. Where shari'ah, or Islamic law, reigns supreme, there is no separation of state and religion. The perennial tension between secular forces and pious Muslims is a result of the inability of modernizers to reduce a religious culture to a personalized path to salvation. With the rise of the Islamic Salvation Front in Algeria, Muslim modernizers faced increasing challenges. On this account, the ethno-religious conflicts in this region have no easy answers. If religious revivalists eventually achieved electoral victories in Algeria, Jordan, and Egypt, could they build modern states based on Islamic principles? Or was modernity incompatible with Islamic principles? How compatible was the ever-increasing separation among ethnic or national groups with the doctrinally prescribed unity of the religious community?

Minorities in Western democracies and Japan, from a global perspective, are distinct from those in other world regions because they usually express their grievances through protest as opposed to rebellion, and the responses of their governments tend generally to accommodate their interests, not to enforce their subordination or incorporation. But seemingly intractable problems remain in Northern Ireland and Canada's Quebec.

These regions have the smallest number of minority populations (twenty-four groups or 84 million people), including ethno-classes of African, Islamic, and Asian origin in Western Europe and the United States. In these countries, one also finds the indigenous rights movements. In France, Spain, Italy, Britain, and Canada, ethno-national demands have generally been resolved or managed by resource and autonomy concessions.

Northern Ireland has not been amenable to this approach because it remains at odds both with its own state (Great Britain) and with the Irish Republic, which occupies most of the land area of Ireland. A middle course for genuine power-sharing between the Catholic and Protestant contenders was being worked out, but deep resentments and dangers remain.

Quebec nationalism within the Canadian federal system was another remaining challenge. A near vote on secession in 1995 seriously threatened national unity and resulted in a political impasse. While there was little potential for violence, a resolution to the impasse could produce negotiated sovereignty for Quebec and thus lend further credence to the principle of the rights of peoples to exit sovereign states.

In world regions as varied as Eastern Europe and Russia, sub-Saharan Africa, North Africa, the Middle East, and the Western democracies, ethno-religious conflicts have played themselves out with devastating effects for an increasingly large number of national and minority peoples.

Challenge of International Response

As indicated at the outset, a major characteristic of the past half-century has been a growing realization of the coexistence of the state with ethno-religious and other groups. Where once states claimed exclusive rights over their citizens, now competing identities challenge such rights. The nature of the challenge is itself a subject of controversy, since the international order recognizes the sovereign state and its exclusive prerogatives. Challenge to the state is tantamount to challenge to the international order, and the ethno-religious challengers are deemed to have no independent status in the international system.

Yet these culturally bounded groups are quite capable, given the often fierce loyalties of their members, of presenting the international community with major humanitarian disasters—including genocide, "ethnic cleansing," huge internal and external displacements of civilian populations, and the death of millions of the most vulnerable in societies around the world. There is no world region that has been free of such conflicts, and a new wave was unleashed in the aftermath of the Cold War. Some of these conflicts were joined to geopolitical rivalries and border disputes, further complicating their resolutions.

It bears repeating that a primary factor in the political saliency of ethno-religious identity is unequal treatment by the larger society or national government. Nevertheless, such an ethnic grievance must be mobilized, and the mobilization process may involve movement from ethnic disadvantage to grievance, to protest, or to rebellion. There are often many factors involved, including the "demonstration effect," or groups emulating others; "cessation of suppression," or sudden liberation, as occurred in Eastern Europe and Russia; and the availability of "ethnic entrepreneurs" who provide leadership. But the most crucial of the factors is the response of the state to these manifestations of mobilization. Does it cultivate loyalty by granting access, does it coerce loyalty, or does it negotiate exit?

Once mobilized, ethno-religious grievances raise a number of questions for the state and the international order, the principal one being how to address contradictory principles that coexist in international law—on one hand, the principles of sovereignty, territorial integrity, and noninterference, and, on the other hand, the right of outsiders to intervene in domestic jurisdictions in cases of serious violations of human rights and humanitarian principles.

One strategy requires a careful balance in preserving minority rights and the legitimate claims of the state. The UN Agenda for Peace, formulated by Secretary-General Boutros Boutros Ghali on June 17, 1992, outlined four types of responses to ethno-religious conflicts: preventive diplomacy (creative measures to preempt conflict); peacemaking (international action for peaceful settlement); peacekeeping (use of military personnel in noncombatant roles, such as monitoring cease-fires); and post-conflict peace-building (international action to address root causes of conflict such as economic despair, social injustice, and political oppression).

Another strategy for conflict resolution is to allow secession of the aggrieved group from the larger government. Traditionalists point out that widespread use of this option could increase pressures on largely heterogeneous states to give corresponding rights to their own minorities. Put simply, the question is how to balance the rights of states already established with the rights of groups currently in contention.

The way forward for all types of ethno-religious conflicts is not to attempt a reconstruction of the state system so that territorial boundaries are more closely aligned to ethnic borders. That direction would simply raise the kind of complex issues that successor states to the Soviet Union and Yugoslavia have grappled with. Rather, the way forward is to acknowledge and strengthen ethno-religious groups within the existing state system by the devolution of authority, among other measures. Scholar Elise Boulding contends that devolution of authority to leaders of ethno-religious groups would concentrate attention on the process of problem-solving rather than on the problems themselves.

For the international community, the challenge is to develop and strengthen norms for the protection of collective rights within the emerging international system. Such protected rights should include the "rights to individual and collective existence and to cultural self-expression without fear of political repression" or other forms of reprisal. Such rights should be accompanied by the pledge of the state or regime to refrain from imposing of ethno-religious standards or agendas on other peoples.

Unless the international community upholds such obligations and otherwise develops human rights and humanitarian law, as well as equips itself with some measure of political will to address ethno-religious conflicts, everyone will lose as these conflicts threaten peace and security everywhere.

D. Elwood Dunn

Bibliography

Allen, T., and J. Eade. "Anthropological Approaches to Ethnicity and Conflict in Europe and Beyond." *International Journal on Minority and Group Rights* 4 (1997): 217–46.

Boulding, Elise. "Ethnicity and New Constitutive Orders: An Approach to Peace in the Twenty-First Century." Paper prepared for a Festschrift (Memorial Conference) for Kinhide Mushakoji, 1990. See Gurr, "Communal Conflicts."

Crocker, Chester A., and Fen Osler Hampson, with Pamela Aall, eds. *Managing Global Chaos: Sources of and Responses to International Conflicts.* Washington, DC: U.S. Institute of Peace Press, 1996.

Gurr, Ted Robert. "Communal Conflicts and Global Security." *Current History* 94, no. 592 (May 1995): 212–17.

———. *Minorities at Risk: A Global View of Ethnopolitical Conflicts.* Washington, DC: U.S. Institute of Peace Press, 1993.

Gurr, Ted Robert, and Barbara Harff. *Ethnic Conflict in World Politics.* Boulder, CO: Westview Press, 1994.

Huntington, Samuel P. *The Clash of Civilizations and the Remaking of World Order.* New York: Simon and Schuster, 1996.

Kegley, Charles W., Jr., and Eugene Wittkopf. *World Politics: Trends and Transformations.* 6th ed. New York: St. Martin's Press, 1997.

Moynihan, Daniel Patrick. *Pandaemonium: Ethnicity in International Politics.* New York: Oxford University Press, 1993.

Smith, Anne-Marie. "Advances in Understanding International Peacemaking." USIP Publication, n.d.

United Nations. *An Agenda for Peace: Preventive Diplomacy, Peacemaking and Peace-keeping.* Report of the Secretary-General (Boutros Boutros Ghali) pursuant to the statement adopted by the Summit Meeting of the Security Council on January 31, 1992. New York, 1992.

TERRORISM: Global History Since the 1940s

The horrors of terrorism were brought home to Americans on September 11, 2001, when hijacked airliners were flown into the World Trade Center in New York City and into the Pentagon in Washington, D.C. Although terrorism and the "war on terror" dominated political discourse in the United States and American foreign policy after that day, the shock and fear of terrorism had become familiar to people in many parts of the world long before 2001.

In the years after 9/11, Western nations soon found themselves divided over the best response to the rise of Islamic terrorism. Most of America's traditional allies supported the Bush administration's initiative to attack Afghanistan, which provided safe haven for those who helped plan and finance the 9/11 attacks. But many of those same nations rejected the administration's preemptive military strike against the "rogue state" of Iraq in early 2003. Years after these conflicts began, it was still difficult to measure progress in the suppression of modern terrorism, given its nebulous character. Islamic militants struck again on March 11, 2004, when they bombed a commuter railway in Madrid, killing 190 and injuring more than 1,800. On July 7, 2005, another cell carried out coordinated attacks on the London Underground, killing 56 and injuring 700. These fresh attacks indicated that Islamic terrorism remained a potent and unpredictable force.

Defining Terrorism

There is no internationally accepted definition of terrorism because of the difficulty of separating a "pure" terrorist act from a legitimate act of war committed by "freedom fighters." The most widely accepted academic definition is provided by UN expert A.P. Schmid, who argues that terrorism is employed by semi-clandestine individuals, groups, or state actors largely for personal, criminal, or political reasons. Terrorists choose their targets at random—often deliberately killing innocent civilians—to draw attention to their demands, inspire anxiety in the targeted population, and intimidate or coerce their opponent

into submission. Their most common methods are car bombings in crowded areas or against symbolic targets (e.g., police or army facilities, foreign banks or companies), targeted assassination, hostage-taking, and airplane hijacking.

Terrorists rarely consider themselves as such, preferring to adopt the mantle of freedom fighters forced to adopt unconventional tactics to counter the overwhelming conventional strength of their opponents. They seldom work for national governments but occasionally find common cause with a rogue regime willing to sponsor them. President George W. Bush singled out Iran, Iraq, and North Korea as the "Axis of Evil" in his January 29, 2002, State of the Union address in an allusion to the Axis powers in World War II—Nazi Germany, Italy, and Japan. The United States also accused Sudan, Libya, Syria, and Cuba of sponsoring terrorism in recent years, but Sudan and Libya had publicly renounced terrorism, and evidence of terrorist acts sponsored by Cuba was sparse.

Terrorism can be divided into four broad categories: political terrorism, state terrorism, state-sponsored terrorism, and criminal terrorism. The primary aim of *political terrorism* is to force the enemy state to comply with the terrorists' political demands by instilling fear in its populace or by provoking it into taking countermeasures that undermine its own core values and damage its institutions. Political terrorists almost always cite long-standing historical grievances or unfinished business from past conflicts as justification for their actions.

State terrorism is a government strategy designed to intimidate the regime's own citizenry through political purges, persecution of certain elements in society, mass starvation, and the like. This form of terrorism was perfected by Nazi Germany and Josef Stalin's Soviet Union.

State-sponsored terrorism is a form of proxy war in which a state actor clandestinely employs third-party terrorist organizations or separatists to strike out against a rival state. Muammar Qaddafi's Libya, for example, based its foreign policy in the 1970s and 1980s on a mix of pan-Islamic, Arab nationalist, and socialist ideologies. Qaddafi is widely believed to have financed and harbored a variety of international and domestic terrorists, including those responsible for the 1988 bombing of Pan Am Flight 103 over Lockerbie, Scotland.

Finally, criminal terrorism is designed to bring monetary or commercial gain rather than to further a political goal and can include kidnapping, extortion, and racketeering.

Historical Background

The terms "terrorism" and "terrorist" have their roots in the Jacobin Reign of Terror in early post-revolutionary France (1793–1794), in which successive government leaders and their closest associates were executed or driven into exile. Long before the invention of the term, however, terrorism was a facet of world politics. One early instance of terrorism was the activity of two Jewish sects, the Zealots and Sicarii, during the first century C.E. in present-day Palestine. The Zealots and Sicarii launched brazen daytime attacks on the Roman officials who governed the province, on soldiers, and on Jewish moderates, seemingly at random, a tactic to provoke fear and escalate Jewish-Roman tension. The groups succeeded in inspiring a widespread revolt among the Jews against Judea's Roman occupiers, but the Romans crushed the rebellion, pursuing the leaders of the insurgency to the death. About a thousand Sicarii were trapped at Masada and chose mass suicide rather than being captured by the victorious Romans.

From the eleventh to the thirteenth centuries C.E., the Assassins, a Shi'ite Ismaili Muslim sect, combined equal doses of religious fanaticism and political extremism in terrorizing Persia, Iraq, and Syria. Feared for their secrecy, golden daggers, and suicidal attacks on Christians and Sunni Muslims alike, the group reputedly used hashish before launching a raid and became known as the *hashashin*, or hashish eaters.

With the onset of European colonialism from the eighteenth century on, various local groups targeted their imperial rulers in India, Indonesia, and the Philippines with terrorist tactics, but most were small and accomplished little to disrupt imperial rule.

In nineteenth- and early-twentieth century Rus-sia, anarchist and populist revolutionaries employed terrorist methods in their battle against the authoritarian czarist regime. The Narodnaya Volya (People's Will), a socialist movement that emerged in the 1870s, launched a campaign of terror against government bureaucrats who abused their authority. Its members used primitive dynamite bombs to great effect—one of its suicide bombers succeeded in assassinating Czar Alexander II in 1881. The attack proved to be the group's greatest triumph, since the government's subsequent security crackdown resulted in the arrest of its leadership, permanently crippling the organization.

The assassination of Austrian Archduke Franz Ferdinand by the Bosnian Serb nationalist Gavrilo Princip in Sarajevo on June 28, 1914, was undoubtedly the most far-reaching single act of terrorism ever committed. The killing prompted Austria to take harsh countermeasures against neighboring Serbia, which it blamed for the assassination. Russia intervened on behalf of the Serbs, and soon the local dispute between Austria-Hungary and Serbia spiraled out of control. Germany, France, and Britain mobilized in support of their respective alliance partners, leading to the outbreak of World War I. More than 15 million people were killed in four years of fighting.

Terrorism Since World War II

After World War II, terrorism grew in intensity and frequency. In many cases, the peoples in colonial empires grew restive and sought to overthrow their weakened European masters, seeking independence and greater economic opportunity. Other terrorist groups were minority groups in multi-ethnic states who were similarly seeking greater autonomy or independence and expanded economic choices. Still other terrorists were driven by their belief in radical Communism, seeking to reform corrupt traditional regimes and redistribute political power and economic resources.

Frustrated by the lack of rights accorded their countrymen, national liberation movements throughout the Middle East and Africa began to take up arms against European colonial rule beginning in the 1940s, frequently adopting terrorist tactics when avenues to peaceful change appeared closed. Britain, France, and other colonial powers had been seriously damaged during the war and had spent most of their military and economic resources. Often they had little choice but to yield to political and terrorist pressures and abandon their colonies.

Algeria

The bloodiest terrorist campaign against colonial rule took place in Algeria from 1954 to 1962. North African Arabs living under French rule were inspired by France's defeat in Indochina by Viet Minh guerrilla fighters in 1954 and soon after began to escalate their own respective independence campaigns. While the socialist government of French premier Pierre Mendes-France chose to concede autonomy for Morocco and Tunisia, both French protectorates, it refused to countenance self-determination for Algeria, which had a large French settler population and constitutional links to metropolitan France. Recognizing that French authorities had no intention of relinquishing control, the Front de Libération Nationale (FLN) and other Algerian independence groups launched a series of attacks against symbols of French rule in November 1954. The FLN initially took care to target only military, economic, and governmental facilities, but one local commander ordered the massacre of French civilians at Phillipeville in August 1955. Infuriated by the slaughter of 123 Europeans—including women, children, and the elderly—the French army, police, and settler gangs responded with brutal reprisals against Muslims, killing as many as 12,000. Radicalized, the FLN responded with regular bombings against civilian targets, while the French army used increasingly brutal methods of torture and killed Muslims indiscriminately. After eight years of violent guerrilla warfare, France was exhausted and humiliated. It finally granted a shattered Algeria its independence in 1962.

Israel/Palestine

The British faced similar difficulties as their empire began to crumble, especially in Palestine, where the ascendant forces of Arab nationalism and Zionism had been struggling against one another since the late nineteenth century. Britain assumed a League of Nations mandate to govern Palestine in 1918, at the end of World War I, and it tried vainly to balance competing claims by Jews and Arabs. Soon the British government was under attack by discontented members of both camps. Two ultra-radicals in the Jewish

Lehi underground, Eliyahu Hakim and Eliyahu Bet-Zuri, assassinated Lord Moyne, the British minister of state for the Middle East, in Cairo on November 6, 1944, after he sought to ban Jewish immigration to Palestine. In the fall of 1946, Jewish militants in the Irgun blew up the King David Hotel, which was serving as the British military and police headquarters, killing 92 people, mostly civilians.

Soon after the bombing, Britain announced that it would withdraw from its mandate responsibilities and pull out of Palestine by 1948. The United Nations developed a new partition plan for Palestine, but on May 14, 1948, the Jewish community declared the establishment of the independent state of Israel. Palestinian Arabs attacked the new government, but Israel won a quick victory in its "War of Independence."

These events set the stage for one of the bitterest and longest conflicts of the postwar era. Palestinians and their Arab allies in neighboring states sought to reverse the *Nakba* (catastrophe) of 1948, which forced the exodus of roughly 700,000 Arabs from Israeli territory. Israel, surrounded by enemies but supported by the United States and countries in Western Europe, took active measures to defend itself.

The first two decades of the conflict were marked by sporadic, small-scale Palestinian border raids and attacks on Israeli settlements. This period of relative tranquility was broken by Israel's resounding victory over Egypt, Syria, and Jordan in the Six Days' War of 1967, during which it occupied the Gaza Strip, the Sinai Peninsula (formerly under Egyptian control), the West Bank (protected by neighboring Jordan), and the Golan Heights (formerly controlled by Syria). With the defeat of Israel's neighbors, the Palestinians formed the Palestine Liberation Organization (PLO) and affiliated groups to continue their struggle against the Jewish state via guerrilla warfare and terrorism.

Early acts of Palestinian terrorism were geared toward drawing international attention to the plight of Arabs living under Israeli occupation and to secure the release of Palestinian prisoners. Unlike much later terrorism in the Arab Muslim world, these acts, which ranged from plane hijackings to targeted attacks on Israeli civilians, were motivated largely by a secular brand of nationalism. In fact, Luttif "Issa" Afif, the leader of the PLO-affiliated Black September group that captured and killed 11 Israeli athletes at the 1972 Munich Olympics, was born to a Jewish mother and a Christian father.

A German official negotiates with one of the Black September terrorists holding nine Israeli athletes hostage at the 1972 Olympic Games in Munich. This and other atrocities by Palestinian terrorists brought international attention to their cause. *(Keystone/Getty Images)*

Cooler heads within the Palestinian camp considered terrorism as a means to force negotiations with Israel, leading to establishment of a Palestinian state. After years of struggle, the 1993 Oslo Peace Accords between Israel and Palestine did establish the PLO as a political organization with which Israel was to negotiate. So many Palestinians had been radicalized by decades of conflict, however, that the PLO found it increasingly difficult to restrain their nonsecular rivals, such as Hamas and Hezbollah, which continued to practice terrorism.

Terrorist acts from the 1960s to the present have succeeded in focusing the world's eyes on the Palestinian struggle, though mostly in a negative light. The steady barrage of suicide bombings beginning in the mid-1990s in Israel and the occupied territories expressed the frustration and misery of young Palestinians, but they did little to facilitate a comprehensive regional settlement. While there was a tactical logic to suicide bombings, they helped create a pow-

erful response by Israeli hard-liners, who blocked a full withdrawal from the West Bank and discouraged serious negotiations with Palestinian leaders. Thus, the vicious cycle continued.

Western Europe

In the 1960s and 1970s, various separatist movements in Europe adopted violent terrorist tactics, often couching their struggle in Marxist-Leninist terms. Most of these movements petered out over the two decades after 1980. The main exception was the Basque separatist movement Euskadi Ta Askatasuna (ETA). ETA launched a wave of robberies, car bombings, kidnappings, and politically motivated assassinations across the Basque country of northern Spain and in the Spanish capital, Madrid, in the mid-1960s in response to three decades of government attempts to suppress Basque culture and language. More recently, however, the vast majority of Basques demonstrated their rejection of violence after Spain transformed itself into a model European state. Even though it had lost broad support, however, ETA refused to renounce terrorism as a means of achieving its goals. The Spanish government made major concessions, providing regional autonomy for the Basque territory, but remained unable to negotiate a final settlement with ETA. ETA attacks claimed well over 800 victims over 40 years. The victims included judges, journalists, businessmen, police officers, and politicians. In 1973, ETA attacks reached their height with the assassination of Spanish Prime Minister Luis Carrero Blanco.

Meanwhile in Ireland, sectarian violence between Catholic Republicans and Protestant Unionists in Northern Ireland during the late 1960s brought the establishment of the Irish Republican Army (IRA). The dispute had roots dating back to British settlement in Ireland in the seventeenth century and to the settlement after the Irish Civil War in the early 1920s. At that time, most of Ireland became independent, but the smaller northern region traditionally dominated by Protestants remained under the control of Britain.

Approximately 1,700 civilians and British soldiers and police were killed during the "Troubles," as Provisional IRA (PIRA) militants learned to use car bombings, pub bombings, targeted assassinations, and sniping to deadly effect. In one of its most spectacular operations, it nearly succeeded in assassinating British Prime Minister Margaret Thatcher in October 1984 during a Conservative Party conference at the Grand Hotel in the British seaside resort of Brighton.

After twenty-five years of terrorism, however, most PIRA militants recognized that their tactics had done little to secure a British withdrawal and chose to accept peace and negotiation with London. The Provisional IRA agreed to a cease-fire in 1997 and officially announced the end of its armed campaign in July 2005. That left only two small factions, the Real IRA and the Continuity IRA, as the sole remaining practitioners of political terrorism within the Irish Republican movement.

Left-Wing Terrorism

Revolutionary leftist terrorist groups took up arms in various countries across the globe beginning in the mid-1960s as a violent effort to reform capitalist society. The first of these was the Fuerzas Armadas Revolucionarias de Colombia (FARC) in Colombia in 1964. Founded as a Marxist-Leninist militia dedicated to protecting Colombia's poor, FARC was increasingly associated with Colombian drug producers and was often accused of becoming a drug cartel hiding behind a façade of revolutionary Communism. Peace talks between the government and FARC from 1998 to 2002 failed to yield any lasting results, leading FARC to resume its campaign of bombings, kidnapping for ransom, extortion, and guerrilla warfare. The United States provided millions of dollars in military aid to the Colombian government to crush FARC, but little real progress was made. FARC continued to control roughly a third of the country's territory, and about 3,500 Colombians were killed each year in the crossfire between the army and rival militias of the right and left.

Other Communist terrorist groups formed in the late 1960s and early 1970s, but all were considerably smaller and less successful. The Red Army Faction (RAF, also known as the Baader-Meinhof Gang) in Germany, the Red Brigades in Italy, and the Japanese Red Army in Japan all shared the same goal: the overthrow of their capitalist national governments and the establishment of revolutionary leftist regimes. Many of their members received weapons training in the Middle East and North Africa—frequently alongside Palestinian terrorists—and targeted NATO or U.S. military installations, industrialists, the conservative press, and politicians.

Although the Red Brigades and the Japanese Red Army both made headlines—the former kidnapped and murdered former Italian prime minister Aldo Moro in 1978 and the latter attacked Lod Airport in Tel Aviv with machine guns and grenades in 1972 as an act of solidarity with their Palestinian counterparts—arrests of key members took their toll on both organizations. Their activities dropped off sharply by the 1980s, and both were effectively neutralized by the end of the decade. The RAF, meanwhile, had received substantial support from the Stasi, East Germany's secret police for its terrorist activities in West Germany. Thus, when Germany was reunified in 1990, the RAF was defused; it announced its dissolution in 1998.

Rise of Extremist Islamic Terrorism

Modern Islamic terrorism has its philosophical roots in the writings of Egyptian literary critic Sayyid Qutb

(1906–1966), but almost certainly it would not have become the political force that it has without a widespread sense of humiliation in an Arab Muslim world that found itself seemingly powerless to resist Israeli and American military incursions.

Qutb wrote several highly influential works on the Koran that earned him the status of modern Islam's most notable theorist before his execution by Egyptian authorities in 1966. Qutb spent two years in the United States in the late 1940s and became deeply hostile to Western mores and "modernity" (capitalism, individualism, promiscuity, and decadence), which he saw as threats to Islamic values. Osama bin Laden and his al-Qaeda followers share Qutb's perception that Islam is under a two-pronged attack from the West: first, the external military challenge in Iraq, Palestine, Kashmir, Chechnya, and elsewhere; and second, the spread of Western values that challenge traditional notions of Islam. Al-Qaeda and its allies believe that this tide can be reversed only through jihad (holy war) against Islam's domestic and foreign enemies.

Some Islamic terror groups dedicated themselves to achieving local goals, such as the overthrow of a single national government and its replacement with an Islamic state—notably the al-Aqsa Martyrs Brigade, Hezbollah, and Hamas in Palestine/Israel; Abu Sayyaf Group (ASG) in the Philippines; the Armed Islamic Group (Groupe Islamique Armée, or GIA) in Algeria; Asbat al-Ansar in Lebanon; and Gama'a al-Islamiyya in Egypt. Others, like al-Qaeda, embrace a more global vision. In broad terms, international Islamic terrorist groups share several or all of the following key aims: the destruction of the state of Israel, a rollback of American influence in key Middle Eastern governments, the elimination of Western military bases in Islamic countries, the overthrow of secular Western-backed regimes in the Muslim world, and the creation of a pan-Islamic caliphate from Morocco to the Philippines.

Al-Qaeda emerged as a force during the ten-year war in Afghanistan against the Soviet Union (1979–1989). Muslim guerrillas from outside Afghanistan, the international mujahideen, were lined up against Soviet efforts to establish a regime friendly to Soviet Communism. The United States and Saudi Arabia provided financial aid for the guerrilla forces, and Pakistan provided logistical support. Aiming to "bleed the Soviet Union white," the Reagan administration in the United States backed the most fanatical Muslims in Afghanistan because they would refuse

peace negotiations with Moscow and prolong the conflict as long as possible. During the resulting battles, Osama bin Laden and his collaborators learned how to finance and run logistics for a large international terrorist organization. He also came to believe that a small band of dedicated *mujahideen* could defeat and topple a superpower if they set their minds to it.

Bin Laden and other leaders were driven to action against the United States by the events of the first Persian Gulf War (1990–1991). Bin Laden was infuriated when his native country, Saudi Arabia, invited U.S. troops to take up positions on its soil to counter the threat of an Iraqi invasion. Bin Laden believed it was blasphemous to invite Western nonbelievers into a nation that was home to Islam's holiest cites, and he was further angered when American forces did not leave Saudi Arabia at the end of the conflict. He was exiled from Saudi Arabia in 1992 for his strident attacks against the Saudi government and began organizing the nucleus of al-Qaeda in Sudan. As an heir to a huge Saudi fortune, he provided the financial resources. Bin Laden's followers, mostly former mujahideen, saw action fighting with Bosnian Muslims in the mid-1990s, then returned to Afghanistan at the invitation of its hard-line Islamic Taliban regime at the end of the decade.

Al-Qaeda camps in Afghanistan became the control center for a series of attacks on American military targets and embassies in Asia and Africa during the late 1990s, ultimately culminating in bin Laden's plan to use hijacked planes as missiles to attack the World Trade Center in New York and targets in Washington. After the successful strike on September 11, 2001, the United States and several Western allies invaded Afghanistan, seeking to put al-Qaeda out of business and unseat the country's Islamist government. They succeeded in overthrowing the government but were less successful in pursuing al-Qaeda. Clashes between al-Qaeda remnants and allied forces continued along the mountainous frontier with Pakistan for years.

After the United States also invaded Iraq in 2003, an al-Qaeda offshoot run by Jordanian Abu Musab al-Zarqawi carried out devastating suicide bombings in Iraq and played a major role in assisting local insurgents fighting against occupying coalition forces and the provisional government. The kidnapping and execution of foreigners, in addition to suicide and car bombings, became a staple of daily life in post-invasion Iraq.

Efforts to Combat Terrorism

Democratic governments in the West, preoccupied with their Cold War rivalry with the Soviet bloc, proved to be ill equipped to deal with modern terrorism. After the kidnapping and murder of Israeli Olympic athletes in Germany in 1972, some governments began to take counterterrorist measures. These included the creation of SWAT-type units, improved intelligence gathering, and tightened security measures for likely terrorist targets (such as transportation hubs, government buildings, and financial centers). A series of antihijacking conventions was instituted to increase international cooperation after a wave of political skyjackings in the late 1960s and 1970s.

After September 11, 2001, the United States reorganized its agencies to create a new Department of Homeland Security (although the major intelligence agencies, including the CIA and FBI, were not part of the department). It was not yet clear what practical effects this reorganization would have on U.S. success in counteracting terrorist groups.

Threats of terrorism from Muslims created special concerns in Europe, where many countries had substantial populations of Muslims who were guest workers or descendants of former colonies. Most countries were not eager to assimilate Muslims as full citizens. They tightened immigration regulations to discourage increased immigration and insisted on strict standards for Muslims who sought permanent resident status. They hoped that these steps would decrease the pool of future homegrown terrorists.

The attacks of September 11, 2001—the deadliest ever on U.S. soil—made antiterrorism the centerpiece of American foreign policy and made homeland security the focus of domestic policy. *(AFP/Getty Images)*

At the same time, intelligence and law enforcement agencies in the United States, with the cooperation of Israel, Russia, and Western Europe, adopted an aggressive strategy of preempting terrorists by capturing or killing them before they could act. The antiterrorist sponsors have been accused of holding suspected terrorists without charges for months or years, operating secret detention centers, and using torture to obtain key information about future plots. Such policies have raised heated debate over the conflict between curbing terrorism and preserving civil liberties.

The most drastic countermeasure to Islamic terrorism is military intervention. Although the United States enjoyed near universal support from its Western allies for the 2001 invasion of Afghanistan, many traditional U.S. allies did not support the 2003 invasion of Iraq, also justified as part of the war on terror. Several smaller countries that did support the invasion later withdrew their forces. Many Europeans felt that the alleged links between Saddam Hussein's regime in Iraq and Islamist terrorism were tenuous at best. They warned that a second war with a major Arab state in the Middle East could actually increase the likelihood of further terrorist attacks. Spain and Britain, both strong backers of the war in 2003, were victims of major terrorist bombings in the following two years.

Conclusion

The transformation of some terrorist groups into responsible political organizations provides faint hope that today's terrorists organizations may choose to lay down their arms and pursue their aims through peaceful negotiation. However, the ultimate success of other terrorists (including Israeli groups in the 1940s and the FLN in Algeria in the 1950s and 1960s) may still provide hope to future terrorists. It seemed unlikely that the fanatics in al-Qaeda and similar organizations would relent until they are either destroyed or accomplish their goals.

It also appeared that Iraq itself would fill Afghanistan's former role as a terrorist training ground, providing a new generation of terrorists with the opportunity to hone their deadly craft. To defeat modern Islamic terrorism, the United States and its allies would need to deal carefully both with the Arab Muslim world and with their own respective Muslim minorities. Improved intelligence and military capabilities, most experts agree, must be accompanied by a measured political strategy if they are to be effective.

Sean J. McLaughlin

Bibliography

Chomsky, Noam. *Pirates & Emperors: International Terrorism in the Real World.* New York: Claremont Research and Publications, 1986.

Crenshaw, Martha, and John Pimlott, eds. *Encyclopedia of World Terrorism.* Armonk, NY: M.E. Sharpe, 1997.

Laqueur, Walter. *The New Terrorism: Fanaticism and the Arms of Mass Destruction.* New York: Oxford University Press, 1999.

Mamdani, Mahmood. *Good Muslim, Bad Muslim: America, the Cold War, and the Roots of Terror.* New York: Pantheon Books, 2004.

Milton-Edwards, Beverley, and Peter Hinchcliffe. *Conflicts in the Middle East Since 1945.* New York: Routledge, 2004.

Poland, James M. *Understanding Terrorism: Groups, Strategies, and Responses.* Englewood Cliffs, NJ: Prentice Hall, 1988.

Sageman, Marc. *Understanding Terror Networks.* Philadelphia: University of Pennsylvania Press, 2004.

Schanzer, Jonathan. *Al-Qaeda's Armies: Middle East Affiliate Groups & the Next Generation of Terror.* New York: Specialist Press International, 2005.

Schmid, Alex P., Albert J. Jongman, et al. *Political Terrorism: A New Guide to Actors, Authors, Concepts, Data Bases, Theories, and Literature.* Amsterdam: North-Holland Publishing, 1988.

Yapp, M.E. *The Near East Since the First World War: A History to 1995.* New York: Longman, 1996.

INTERNATIONAL ARMS TRADE

The massive international arms trade has been as much a hallmark of the post–World War II period as the wars it spawned and aggravated, though the commerce in weapons has origins before the war. In the 1930s, for example, a congressional investigation cited the "merchants of war"—that is, U.S. weapons suppliers—as the significant culprits in drawing the United States into World War I. By supplying arms to belligerents, Congress argued, the United States inevitably joined their ranks, forced to defend the arms trade by going to war.

The result was the so-called cash-and-carry legislation that required combatants engaged in World War II before the United States joined the fighting to pay in advance for their supplies—including arms—and pick them up in their own ships from U.S. ports. Like later efforts to curb U.S. arms sales abroad, however, the legislation ultimately proved futile.

The arms trade in the decades after World War II—especially after 1970—put all earlier weapons trafficking in the shade, and the United States was not the only country involved. Today, arms sales are a major export of most industrialized countries and a host of industrializing ones. Moreover, the market for arms has spread to all corners of the globe.

Quantity

Statistics on the sale of arms are tricky to assess, due to varying kinds of measurements and a lack of verification in many instances, but it is clear that the volume of arms sales and arms transfers (those delivered as part of military aid packages) is enormous. According to the Congressional Research Service, it was estimated that some $33 billion in international arms orders went through in 1996. Four years earlier, in 1992, the total reached $42 billion, because Persian Gulf countries were replacing armaments destroyed in the first Gulf War (1991).

Between 1945 and 1960, international arms sales were relatively small. The United States, for example, sold just $500 million worth of weapons annually during these years. This relatively low figure was due to several causes. First, large parts of the third world were still colonized, and thus not a market for arms. And those countries in Asia and Latin America that were independent were generally too impoverished to purchase much in the way of weapons overseas.

Thus, much of the market for weapons was in the Western bloc of nations dominated by the United States and in the Soviet bloc, which included Eastern Europe and the Balkans. Many of the countries in these regions had arms industries of their own. Indeed, the United States and, to a lesser extent, the Soviet Union actively rebuilt the arms industries of Germany and other former Axis powers, despite wartime agreements not to do so.

The dynamics of the early Cold War also worked to limit arms sales. During the 1940s and 1950s, neither the United States nor the Soviet Union saw the third world—those countries not aligned with either nation—as a significant battleground for their ideological struggle and made few efforts to arm them. In the 1960s, both sides shifted strategies and began to arm regimes that would carry on "proxy wars" directly or indirectly supported by the superpowers.

It was the events of the 1970s that produced the great rise in international arms sales. In the wake of its Vietnam debacle, the United States embarked on what was called the Nixon Doctrine, a policy of setting up regional powers to act as surrogates for the United States. This doctrine involved beefing up the armories of these various third world countries. At the same time, one group of countries had grown enormously wealthy and became major customers for arms. The quadrupling of oil prices made it possible for states rich in hydrocarbon resources to arm rapidly. Thus, between 1971 and 1975, U.S. arms sales alone climbed from about $1.4 billion annually to nearly $16 billion. Other industrialized countries, in both the East and West, showed similar gains.

Indeed, by the mid-1970s, international arms sales were becoming a significant political issue in the United States, Britain, and several other Western democracies. In the United States, presidential candidate Jimmy Carter made the reduction of arms sales a key plank in his foreign policy platform. When he took office in 1977, he offered plans to limit arms sales significantly. The policy was strongly opposed, however, especially by defense industries, and the final bill was riddled with loopholes and exceptions. It slowed the upward trend in sales but did not reverse it. In 1980, Carter's last year in office, foreign military orders still amounted to some $16 billion.

The Reagan years witnessed a quantum increase in U.S. arms sales, matched by similar increases in other industrialized countries. Indeed, not only did the Reagan administration remove the limitations on weapons sales and transfers enacted during the Carter presidency, but policymakers actively moved to streamline the process, offering new financial arrangements and subverting congressional oversight in ways both legal and illegal (in the case of Iran and the contras of Nicaragua). By 1982, U.S. arms sales totaled more than $22 billion.

The Soviet Union was also seeking to bolster its allies' military capacities—and its own balance of payments—in the competition with U.S. efforts. In 1973, the Soviet Union delivered some $5.3 billion in weapons overseas; by 1982, the total was nearly $11 billion. European arms exporters increased their sales from roughly $5 billion in 1974 to $13 billion in 1982. In addition, by the 1980s several major industrializing countries, including Brazil, China, and Israel, had become major producers of armaments.

Under presidents George H.W. Bush and Bill Clinton, the U.S. government took an even more active role in the sale of arms. Both administrations made the promotion of world trade—including arms sales—a major component of their foreign policy, with U.S. arms sales reaching a historic peak in the early 1990s.

This new pro-trade policy further increased competition from other countries with arms to sell. At the same time, the dissolution of the Soviet Union and the end of the Cold War left a vast arms manufacturing capacity both in the West and the former Communist bloc. Russia, in particular, desperately used arms sales to bring in much-needed foreign exchange in the 1990s. Still, a lowering of tensions in the weapons-buying Middle East and economic downturns in many third world countries led to a slackening demand in the arms business and a decline in arms orders and deliveries.

Quality

Just as there has been a general upward trend in the quantity of weapons offered in the international arms market, so too have the variety and sophistication of available weapons increased in recent decades. Essentially, there are two kinds of arms transfers: those involving weapons and weapons systems, and those including the technology to manufacture weapons. The latter can include licensing agreements, coproduction deals, or, more rarely, the supply of turnkey factories.

Throughout the 1960s, most arms exports consisted of weaponry, most of it rather unsophisticated or considered obsolete by the selling nation. For example, most of the military aircraft sold by the United States in this period were hand-me-downs from its own military services. By the early 1970s, increased quantity was being matched by increased complexity, as wealthier and more sophisticated buyers in both the West and among the nonaligned nations demanded newer equipment of more recent vintage. Thus, by the late 1970s and early 1980s—despite the Carter administration's effort to withhold weapons systems that would upset regional balances of power—the United States was selling arms that were only slightly less advanced than those used by its own military services. These included such near top-of-the-line items as F-15 and F-16 fighters, M-60 tanks, and Sidewinder air-to-air missiles. The Reagan administration shifted from a policy constrained by fears of a local arms race to a view that appropriate weapons for export by the United States meant anything that, in the words of expert Michael Klare, produced a "net contribution to enhanced deterrence and defense."

This naturally created a spiral in the sophistication of weapons sold by other suppliers, since the United States not only led the world in its volume of arms sales but in the quality of the weapons it sold as well. For reasons of geopolitical competition, the Soviet Union was forced to respond by upscaling the weapons it exported, to maintain the balance of power between its surrogates and those of the United States. This became especially critical after the 1967 Arab-Israeli war, when the U.S. weapons systems used by Israel proved to be superior to Eastern bloc systems used by Arab forces.

For the big four European arms suppliers (France, Britain, Italy, and Germany), economic competition was more important than the Cold War rivalry. To win a share of the most lucrative markets—particularly in the Middle East—the European arms industry increased the sophistication and improved the quality of weapons it offered. Between 1975 and 1982, for example, the Soviet Union sold more than 3,000 supersonic aircraft to nonaligned nations, along with more than 18,000 surface-to-air (SAM) missiles. The former included such items as late-model MiG 23s and 25s. The big four European arms suppliers also sold about 500 such aircraft and nearly 3,000 missiles.

This tendency toward high-end items only increased in the 1990s after the end of the Cold War. With oversized arms industries in much of the industrialized world, the pressure to stay afloat economically forced manufacturers to market their cutting-edge technology aggressively. Moreover, national governments in the West and in the former Communist bloc were actively engaged in promoting the most sophisticated wares of their arms industries, largely for economic and domestic political reasons—that is, to maintain high employment at home.

These "big-ticket items" gain most of the publicity in discussions of the arms trade. The vast bulk of arms sales, however, receive little attention. They involve small arms, useful for both military and policing purposes, including handguns, rifles, grenades, and land mines; counterinsurgency gear, including jeeps, trucks, helicopters, and light attack planes; and riot control equipment, including tear gas, handcuffs, armored cars, and truncheons. In the late 1970s, the United States exported over 50,000 rifles, 600,000 tear-gas grenades, and 55 million rounds of small-arms ammunition to the police forces of nonaligned nations. For rough comparison, between 1975 and 1982, the Soviet Union and Europe provided more than 1,200 light aircraft, some 2,800 helicopters, and nearly 17,000 armored cars to military and police forces of nonaligned nations.

In addition, sales of goods classified in the so-called "gray areas" increased. These included items that could be used for civilian or military/police purposes, such as jeeps, trucks, transport planes, communications gear, and computers. Such items were sold even to countries under arms embargoes, since they could be classified as material for civilian use. During the 1970s and 1980s, for example, a number of American and European companies sold such equipment to the embargoed apartheid regime in South Africa.

During the post–World War II era, the United States led the world not only in the sale of weapons, but also in the sale of weapons-making technology. Until the early 1970s, it arranged most of the licensing

and coproduction deals with its allies in NATO and with Australia and Japan. The Soviet Union generally shared its arms-making expertise with its Warsaw Pact allies and China. By the late 1970s, however, the same forces pushing arms manufacturers to offer more complex weapons systems were leading to more technology transfers.

Still, most such U.S. transfers involved countries with historical ties to the United States or great strategic significance. Thus, in 1978, the United States had just eight technology transfer programs with four countries: Taiwan, South Korea, the Philippines, and Turkey. Several other countries, including Argentina, Brazil, and Israel, had licensing agreements with U.S. arms suppliers. Under the Reagan administration, licensing for weapons-making technology changed dramatically. By 1982, Egypt, Pakistan, Saudi Arabia, Singapore, and Thailand also had such licensing agreements.

The agreements covered increasingly sophisticated weapons. For example, South Korea was coproducing F-15 fighter jets. In general, European arms manufacturers were more circumspect in their technology transfers, largely for economic reasons. They did not want to give up their technology edge. As for the Soviet Union, most of its third-world buyers were not technologically advanced enough to use such technology transfer. More advanced industrializing countries tended to prefer the higher-quality weaponry of the United States and Europe.

Finally, many of these technology deals involved the temporary assignment of technicians from the supplying nations. In deals with the United States and Europe, these were usually civilians from private companies; in deals with the Soviet Union, the technicians were usually military personnel. At the same time, both Western and Soviet firms and countries welcomed students and technical workers from friendly third-world nations. Those who worked for arms manufacturers could take their knowledge and skills back to their native countries, where they could help develop arms production facilities.

Of course, not all of the spread of arms-making technology transfers originated with the United States or the Soviet blocs. A number of nonaligned countries developed their own arms-manufacturing capacity, especially those that were embargoed by the United States and the Soviets because of war, political isolation, or egregious human rights violations. Thus the so-called pariah states—Israel, Taiwan, and South

Africa—developed their own arms industries in the 1970s, sharing technology among themselves. At the same time, both India and Pakistan, locked in a strategic struggle and embargoed during their several wars, made it national policy to develop their own arms-making capacities.

Nor is the problem of technology transfers strictly confined to sophisticated weapons systems. In recent years, there has been a growing international awareness of the destructive capacity of land mines and small arms, both decidedly low-tech items. It is estimated that no fewer than fifty countries have the capacity to produce small arms, while two dozen or so can make land mines.

Who's Selling and Why

As noted above, the six most important arms-supplying countries for most of the post–World War II era were the United States, the Soviet Union, and the big four European countries—France, Britain, Germany, and Italy. These main suppliers were supplemented by Japan, Sweden, Czechoslovakia, and several other European countries. In more recent years, a number of industrializing countries joined the ranks of major arms suppliers. The most important of these included Brazil, China, Israel, and South Africa.

Still, the United States remained the number-one arms exporter through the entire period in both the quality and cost of weapons. Between 1974 and 1982, for example, the United States signed arms agreements with third-world countries that amounted to more than $82 billion, the big four European sellers contracted for roughly $65 billion among them, and the Soviet Union made deals for about $70 billion. The total world market for arms-export orders in those years was roughly $260 billion. Thus, the United States controlled about a third of the business, while Europe and the Soviet Union accounted for roughly 25 percent each. These numbers did not

A salesman for a U.S. defense contractor shows an air-to-surface missile system to potential buyers at the Dubai Air Show. The United States accounts for more than 40 percent of global weapons sales. *(Barry Iverson/Time Life Pictures/Getty Images)*

change significantly in the 1990s. In 1996, the United States accounted for about 35 percent (more than $12 billion) of all arms orders, while Russia's share had fallen to about 15 percent (roughly $5 billion).

The United States had a variety of motives for selling arms abroad, which changed over time and varied from customer to customer. During the Cold War, political and strategic imperatives tended to predominate. These included the need to support U.S. allies and share military burdens—particularly in the wake of the Vietnam War; to gain political influence and leverage; to block successes by the Soviet bloc; to gain access to bases and to political and military elites; and to bolster friendly regimes against internal unrest. A final factor that tended to make political and strategic factors paramount over economic ones—especially during the first thirty years of the Cold War—was that the business of arms sales was rather small, accounting for a tiny proportion—about 1 percent in the 1950s and 1960s—of all U.S. exports.

For the Soviet Union, the motivations were roughly similar to those of the United States, though Moscow had a few idiosyncratic reasons of its own for promoting the sale of arms, including a desire to establish secure borders. Thus, the Soviet Union made a major point of selling arms to friendly countries on its periphery, first in Eastern Europe and later in Asia, including long-term agreements with India and Iraq. In addition, Moscow used arms sales and transfers to compete with China and win the allegiance of leftist regimes among nonaligned nations.

For the big four European powers, strategic considerations were also important, but they remained secondary to economic ones, even at the height of the Cold War. To bolster their influence in regions they considered to be in their traditional sphere of influence, France and Britain in particular sold weapons to former colonies in Africa and the Middle East. Finally, as mentioned earlier, the pariah states such as Israel, South Africa, and Taiwan sold arms of their own manufacture as a way to shore up support in a hostile world.

In the post–Cold War era, economic considerations tended to outweigh other factors in the promotion of arms sales abroad. Of course, strategic matters still matter, and it is sometimes difficult to separate economic from strategic considerations, since the bolstering of friendly regimes can have a direct economic impact on the arms-selling country.

In addition, the arms industry—largely a creation of the Cold War in the United States and the Soviet Union—had gained economic imperatives of its own. In both the United States and the Soviet Union, offsetting some of the huge costs of weapons development at home drove the governments to share the burden with allies by selling them the improved weapons. Since manufacturing costs tend to go down with increased output, selling abroad was a way to lower the costs of new weapons. In other cases, the superpowers subsidized the cost of new weapons by selling off the old. When they wrote technology transfer agreements, they could even share the cost of research and development.

Even during the Cold War, the arms manufacturers were driven in part by economic factors. For example, at the end of the Vietnam War, the U.S. military demand for armaments dropped rapidly. Arms manufacturers were forced to look abroad to keep their factories running and their profits up. The U.S. government itself had an interest in keeping employment high, especially because the end of the war occurred during a recession. Thus, political leaders agreed to allow companies to sell their arms abroad.

For the United States—as well as the Europeans and even the Soviet Union—there were foreign economic considerations in the promotion of arms exports in the 1970s and 1980s. Specifically, all their economies faced increasing balance-of-payments crises, due in part to the spiraling cost of oil in the West and the stagnation of the agricultural sector in the Soviet Union. Thus, the governments in all of these countries used arms sales to win back some of the money they were paying to oil-producing or grain-exporting countries. In the case of the United States, the transaction was direct, since it effectively financed oil purchases through the sale of armaments to the oil-producing states of the Persian Gulf.

After the end of the Cold War, other economic factors came into play. Both for the United States and more critically for the former Soviet Union, the end of the Cold War brought a crisis in the arms business, with declining domestic demand. Not surprisingly, both Moscow and Washington have moved from permitting and indirectly encouraging arms sales to working actively with arms manufacturers as part of the normal governmental policy of promoting exports. The administrations of George H.W. Bush and Bill Clinton—both especially assiduous in developing cooperative relations with exporters or potential exporters—had few qualms about extending this new relationship to encompass arms manufacturers.

Indeed, it can be argued that political and strategic factors have at times been harnessed to economic considerations. Some experts, for example, contended that the first Gulf War (1991) represented, at least in part, a way to show off new weapons systems to potential buyers around the world. Later, in the Clinton administration's sale of more sophisticated arms sales to Latin America, there was evidence that the needs of the domestic arms industry were an important consideration. The Clinton administration was heavily criticized for its sales of certain technologies with military capabilities to China. The public position of the administration was that it did not know about these deals or that the deals did not involve critical technologies, but some observers detected a hidden message: If America does not offer this technology, someone else will, thus winning the economic and political benefits of doing so.

Who's Buying and Why

During the first thirty or so years of the post–World War II era, as noted above, most arms purchases were made by the industrialized countries of Europe, as well as Japan. Beginning in the 1970s, however, a variety of factors came into play that encouraged many non-aligned nations to increase their arms purchases. The most important were the countries of the Middle East, especially those rich in petroleum resources and, with the hike in oil prices of those years, awash in petrodollars. These included Iraq (buying largely from the Soviet Union and Europe), the Persian Gulf Arab countries (making purchases mostly from the United States and Britain), and, above all, the shah's Iran (buying almost exclusively from the United States).

Between 1976 and 1980, Saudi Arabia purchased roughly $5 billion in weapons on the international market: 40 percent from the United States, 20 percent from Britain, and another 20 percent from France and West Germany combined. At the same time, Iraq bought nearly $8 billion in weapons, 60 percent of which came from the Soviet Union. Iran, however, outbid them all, with weapons purchases well in excess of $8 billion, 75 percent of which were made in the United States.

Moreover, the so-called frontline states—those facing the enormous power of the Israeli Defense Forces—purchased large quantities of arms in the late 1970s, when tensions with Israel remained high. Between 1976 and 1980, Syria, for example, bought some $6.6 billion in arms, roughly 80 percent of which was from the Soviet Union and much of which was intended to replace equipment destroyed in the 1973 Arab-Israel War and Syria's incursions into Lebanon in the late 1970s.

Even when the price of oil declined, countries of the Middle East continued to make large purchases. The volatile political climate, regional rivalries, and near-constant state of war in the region ensured a steady demand, which arms-supplying countries— eager to balance their oil payments—actively filled. This steady trend could be observed over the course of the 1990s. While arms sales to the region peaked in the year after the first Gulf War—as nations in the region replenished their depleted arsenals—they declined only very slowly in the following years. In 1990, before the war, the Persian Gulf countries purchased $37.2 billion in arms; after the Gulf War in 1992, they bought $42.2 billion in arms. As late as 1996, however, Saudi Arabia alone purchased $5.2 billion, making it the largest arms importer in the world.

In the 1980s, increasing purchases on the other side of Asia enhanced the market for weapons in the Middle East. During these years, the industrializing countries of East Asia—the so-called tiger economies— found themselves increasingly able to purchase weapons and pay for them through exports. At the same time, they sought to bolster their own defense capacities, largely to counter the overwhelming power of China. Thus, Taiwan, South Korea (which, of course, also faced a well-armed foe in North Korea), Singapore, and later Malaysia, Thailand, and especially Indonesia hiked their defense purchases dramatically in the 1980s. The latter purchased some $1.5 billion in arms between 1984 and 1993, over one-third of which was from the United States.

Finally, these rapidly developing counties had a variety of reasons to buy weapons on the international arms market. First, and most importantly, were legitimate defense concerns, either against an external foe or, in the case of unpopular regimes, against domestic opposition. Other factors included a desire to project an image of strength abroad for reasons of national pride or to gain concessions in disputes about territory, offshore resources, and the like. Internally, some military leaders needed weapons purchases to gain the upper hand in their struggle with other national elites.

Economic factors came into play as well. The more developed countries sought weapons or weapons technology to study and emulate as they developed their own weapons development capacities. More countries—especially in East Asia—demanded technology transfers as a precondition for arms sales, a stipulation that supplier governments—eager to bolster their own defense industries—were increasingly willing to meet.

Impact

Arms-supplying nations consistently argued that their sales of weapons do not contribute to armed conflict. Rather, they said, the sales helped promote regional and global security by providing effective deterrence, regional balances of power, and the means for governments to stabilize disruptive and subversive domestic elements. The confidence that arms sellers have in these arguments are called into question by their own warnings that arms sales by rival suppliers threaten instability. Thus, throughout the Cold War, the United States and the Soviet Union exchanged charges that the other was undoing carefully nurtured balances of power in various regions of the world.

Washington accused the Soviet Union of fomenting unrest and subversion by providing arms to left-wing insurgents and belligerent leftist countries. At the same time, Moscow said that the United States was supporting regressive and unpopular regimes by providing them with the military and police supplies they needed to remain in power. In the 1980s, Moscow added the charge that the United States itself was fomenting subversion by supplying weapons to anticommunist insurgents in Afghanistan, Angola, Nicaragua, and elsewhere.

More recently, there was a shift in rhetoric among arms-supplying countries. No longer did they accuse each other of fomenting conflict by selling weapons abroad. Instead, the criticisms involved the sophistication of arms, particularly so-called weapons of mass destruction (chemical, biological, and nuclear weapons) and vehicles (particularly missiles) by which to deliver them. In recent years, various members of the U.S. government charged China, France, Russia, and even Israel of selling inappropriate military technology to countries the United States considered dangerous, such as Iran. Meanwhile, other countries contended that the United States set a double standard, selling arms to Turkey and Indonesia—which used them to invade Cyprus and East Timor, respectively, in 1974—while condemning sales to Iran in the 1980s.

Aside from the charges hurled at each other by the arms-supplying nations, there remain the simple numbers of wars and human rights violations involving governments that have made substantial purchases of arms in the international marketplace. The United States—as the largest supplier of arms—found itself with the dubious distinction of having its weapons involved in more wars than any other arms-exporting nation. Among the fifty or so ongoing conflicts in developing nations and former socialist bloc states in the early 1990s, U.S. weapons were involved in some forty-five, or 90 percent, of them. In more than half the wars, the United States continued to provide arms after the wars had begun. Moreover, in many countries with ongoing insurgencies—such as Israel, Egypt, Somalia, Indonesia, and Mexico—the United States remained the largest supplier of counterinsurgency or riot control weaponry and equipment.

The damage done by the arms trade is not confined to periods of war. Though the international community acted to ban the sale of antipersonnel land mines, there remain some 50 to 70 million scattered across current and former war zones around the globe. In places like Angola and Cambodia, it was estimated that these mines produced a new death or crippling injury every day. Small arms, too, continue to haunt countries long after the war is over. It was estimated in the late 1990s that there were some 75 million assault rifles in circulation around the world. This means they can be had readily and cheaply, for as little as $6 in places like Mozambique. Just as the end of a war means an abundance of weapons, it also means an abundance of demobilized soldiers and guerrillas, a recipe for banditry in many parts of the developing world, particularly in Africa.

Finally, it is important to note the consequences of arms sales for the arms-supplying countries themselves. First, there is the boomerang effect, in which the weapons sold are used against the countries that have supplied them. In the case of the United States, in four recent military missions—Panama, Iraq, Somalia, and Haiti—its troops have faced an enemy armed with U.S. weapons. A second consequence is called "blowback." This involves national action that later contributes to injure that same nation. For example, during the Soviet war with Afghanistan (1979–1988), the United States helped train and arm Islamist militants in Afghanistan to fight Soviet forces. Later terrorist attacks on U.S. embassies in Africa and on New York's World Trade Center in 1993 were carried out by terrorists trained and formerly armed by the Central Intelligence Agency in Afghanistan. In 2001, after the attacks of September 11, U.S. troops found themselves in Afghanistan in combat against some of these same people.

There are also large costs—both direct and indirect—to the taxpayers of arms-supplying countries. First, governments pay enormous subsidies to arms manufacturers, often in the form of military aid to friendly countries, which allows them to purchase the weapons with taxpayer money. The governments may also offer low-interest loans and credits to arms customers and sponsor promotional activities on behalf of arms manufacturers. In the United States in 1995, for instance, it is estimated that these subsidies amounted to some $7.6 billion, nearly half the total value of the weapons exported. Indirect costs can be even higher. As weapons suppliers offer more sophisticated systems to other countries, a vicious cycle is perpetuated. Because the United States and other large arms-producing countries try to keep the most advanced weapons for their own use, selling ever more sophisticated weapons creates strong pressures for developing ever newer and more expensive weapons for the domestic military.

Efforts at Control

With most arms sales in the period from 1945 to 1977 confined to Western and Eastern blocs in the Cold War, there was little concern about controlling the international trade in weaponry. The proliferation of sales to the countries of the Middle East—and especially Iran—in the mid-1970s, however, brought the issue to the fore, at least in the United States. As noted above, presidential candidate Jimmy Carter voiced serious concerns about U.S. involvement in the international arms trade during his 1976 campaign and sought to limit arms sales during his term of office. He imposed specific controls on arms sales. These limits included a total ceiling on U.S. sales based on 1977 levels, a ban against modifying advanced systems for export purposes, the prohibition on co-production deals, an end to governmental promotion of arms sales, a linkage between human rights and arms sales, and efforts at multilateral negotiations among the major arms-supplying countries both in the West and the Communist bloc.

Carter's efforts, however, were hamstrung from the beginning in several ways. First, they contained many exemptions, exceptions, and waiver possibilities. NATO and ANZUS (Australia and New Zealand) countries, as well as Japan and Israel, were never included. Second, the rules allowed the president to waive these limitations in "exceptional circumstances." Thus, under a variety of domestic and foreign pressures, Carter increasingly used waivers to allow arms sales in individual cases. In addition, Carter's political opponents criticized the administration's arms sales limitations as being detrimental to the projection of U.S. power and interests abroad.

Paradoxically, even Carter's own peacemaking efforts—in the Camp David Accords between Egypt and Israel in 1979—required him to provide more military aid to these two countries. Ultimately, however, the fact remained that as long as other countries were willing to sell arms to undesirable customers, a unilateral set of limitations by the United States remained unfeasible. Thus, arms orders approved by Washington increased from $8.8 billion in 1977 to $11.7 billion in 1978, and included such controversial deals as the sale of 200 modern jet aircraft to three Middle Eastern countries.

As noted above, the Reagan years witnessed a near-total disregard for limitations of any kind. Indeed, the new administration actively promoted arms sales as a means of shoring up U.S. power abroad and fighting Communism. With the United States taking the lead, international arms sales soared in the 1980s and early 1990s, once again provoking efforts to establish some kind of controls on the sale of weapons abroad. These initiatives, however, were largely aimed at the two extremes of the trade. First were attempts to create treaties limiting the transfer of technologies required to construct weapons of mass destruction—including chemical, biological, and nuclear weapons—and their delivery systems. The effectiveness of these treaties has been limited. For example, India developed much of its nuclear weapons manufacturing capacity on its own, while Pakistan received help from China, Libya, and European suppliers. Pakistan's nuclear experts also proved eager to pass their knowledge and designs to other countries eager to develop nuclear capabilities.

At the same time, there was a concerted effort to limit the international trade in small arms. In 1997, most of the international community signed a treaty banning the production, sale, and use of antipersonnel land mines. (The United States, citing its needs to defend South Korea, refused to sign.)

The push to set international limits on the trade in small arms, especially assault rifles, was stymied by several factors. First, domestic lobbying groups including the National Rifle Association in the United States pressured politicians and negotiators not to sign any treaties that limit the domestic sales of small arms.

Second, advocates faced serious logistical problems in limiting the international trade in small arms. Trade of big-ticket items such as aircraft, tanks, and missiles can be policed with the help of inspections and reconnaissance; by contrast, it is virtually impossible to police the trade in small arms. This has led to talk of designing small arms with built-in obsolescence devices or designing ammunition that scars weapons, thus demobilizing them after a certain period of use. Still, the fact that small arms—as well as land mines—can be manufactured cheaply and easily with low-tech equipment means that limitations on international sales may be difficult, if not impossible, to sustain. Advocates for control answer that any limitation is worth the effort, since it is bound to dry up some of the lethal supply.

James Ciment

Bibliography

Boutwell, Jeffrey, Michael Klare, and Laura Reed. *Lethal Commerce: The Global Trade in Small Arms and Light Weapons.* Cambridge, MA: American Academy of Arts and Sciences, 1995.

Grimmett, Richard. *Conventional Arms Transfers to the Third World, 1986–1993.* Washington, DC: Congressional Research Service, 1994.

Hartung, William. *And Weapons for All.* New York: HarperCollins, 1995.

———. *US Weapons at War.* New York: World Policy Institute, 1995.

Klare, Michael. *American Arms Supermarket.* Austin: University of Texas Press, 1984.

Klare, Michael, and Peter Kornbluh. *Low Intensity Warfare: Counterinsurgency, Proinsurgency, and Antiterrorism in the 1980s.* New York: Hill and Wang, 1988.

Rana, Swadesh. *Small Arms and Intrastate Conflicts.* New York: United Nations Centre for Disarmament Affairs, 1995.

Sampson, Anthony. *The Arms Bazaar.* New York: Viking Press, 1977.

Sennott, Charles. "Armed for Profit: The Selling of U.S. Weapons—A Special Report." *Boston Globe*, February 11, 1996, supplement.

U.S. Arms Control and Disarmament Agency. *World Military Expenditures and Arms Transfers, 1990.* Washington, DC: U.S. General Printing Office, 1990.

CONFLICTS

AFRICA, SUB-SAHARAN

Sub-Saharan Africa

Countries in Sub-Saharan Africa that have experienced conflict on their own soil since World War II

ANGOLA: War of National Liberation, 1961–1974

TYPE OF CONFLICT: Anticolonial
PARTICIPANT: Portugal

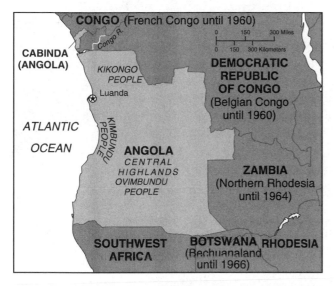

Angola, one of the first territories to be incorporated into a European empire, had been a Portuguese colony since the late fifteenth century when explorers looking for an all-sea route to India and China established trading posts and forts near the mouth of the Congo River and the present-day capital of Luanda. Nevertheless, Portuguese efforts to penetrate and establish hegemony over the interior of the colony were sporadic and largely ineffectual until the twentieth century.

That is not to say, however, that the Portuguese soldiers, traders, and settlements did not have an impact far outweighing their limited numbers and limited geographical penetration. Many of the settlers took Angolan wives, gradually establishing a population of mixed Afro-Portuguese in Angola. This group of people established themselves as a class of commercial intermediaries between the European traders of the coast and the African nations of the interior. These creoles spoke Portuguese, but blended European and African customs to create a unique culture that would

eventually become dominant among Angola's elite. Later, these creoles would play the leading role in their nation's struggle for independence from Portugal in the mid-twentieth century.

The Afro-Portuguese defended their position by balancing the interests of the Europeans and the Africans, preventing either from coming into contact with one another or growing too powerful. This balancing act allowed them to maintain their role as the irreplaceable middlemen of Angolan trade, including its most lucrative commodity, human beings. It has been estimated that fully 12 million Africans from lands south of the equator were forcibly shipped to the Americas, and the bulk of these were captured in or transported through Angolan territory.

But several factors in the late nineteenth century undermined the position of the Afro-Portuguese. The outlawing of the international slave trade eliminated a valuable commodity. The Berlin Congress, which divided Africa into European colonies, forced Portugal to begin asserting its claims for territory by demonstrable efforts to suppress indigenous peoples. And finally, the presence of the British in the interior of southern Africa led to new trading patterns and competitors.

The Afro-Portuguese in the cities faced their own problems. By the turn of the century, more and more impoverished whites were emigrating to Angola, many encouraged by the government. Lisbon hoped to solve several problems through immigration to Africa. First, it hoped to relieve population pressures in Portugal, then one of the most crowded and poorest countries in Europe. Second, the government hoped to provide a white bulwark in the colonies as a defense against both rebellious Africans and covetous Europeans in neighboring colonies. Third, it hoped that new

KEY DATES

Late 1400s–early 1500s	Portuguese begin to settle in Angola and engage in the slave trade.
Late 1950s–early 1960s	France and Britain grant independence to almost all of their colonies in Africa.
1960	Rioting breaks out among farmers in Malange Province over falling prices for their crops set by the government; some 7,000 protesters are killed; police arrest nationalist leader Agostinho Neto.
1961	Large-scale rioting breaks out against police brutality in Luanda in February; Kikongo people, led by the Union of the Peoples of Northern Angola (later the National Liberation Front in Angola, FNLA, its Portuguese acronym), rise up in rebellion in March; some 20,000 Kikongo are killed; fighting breaks out in October between the FNLA and another rebel group, the Popular Movement for the Liberation of Angola (MPLA).
1966	Jonas Savimbi, a leader among the Ovimbundu people of the southern part of the country, organizes the Union for the Total Independence of Angola (UNITA).
1974	Portuguese dictator Marcello Caetano is overthrown by left-wing, anticolonialist military officers in the Carnation Revolution; the new government announces it will immediately pull out of Portugal's African colonies.
1975	Heavy fighting breaks out between the FMLN and the MPLA; each is trying to take control of the capital before the Portuguese officially pull out; UNITA launches an offensive against the MPLA in August; MPLA is largely victorious in both struggles, taking control of the capital and becoming the ruling party upon Angola's formal independence on November 11.

farmers would raise valuable tropical products that would bring revenue to the treasuries of both Angola and Portugal.

The policy largely failed. The farmers, usually the least educated and least successful in Portugal, could not make a go of it in the harsh wilds of Angola. Most drifted to Luanda or to the provincial capitals, where they increasingly competed with the Afro-Portuguese for civil service and commercial positions. They pressured the government to defend their own interests with a series of racist edicts, favoring whites over Africans and creoles.

The situation intensified after dictator Antonio Salazar rose to power in Portugal in the 1920s. Like Mussolini in Italy, the fascistic Salazar was eager to revive a glorious national past. He hoped to accomplish this by building what was called a Lusotropical (Luso is the adjective for Portuguese) empire in Africa, Asia, and even Brazil. Settlement of white farmers in Angola was again encouraged, but this time with better effect. Better roads, more capital, and more effective medicines against tropical disease allowed many white farmers to succeed. Most important, Portugal's neutral status in World War II put it in an ideal situation to produce and sell critical tropical products to both the Allies and Axis powers. Angola flourished, and more white settlers poured in, though most of them still ended up in the cities.

The decades following the end of World War II saw much of the same, but at an even more accelerated pace. In the great capitalist expansion of the 1950s and 1960s, Angola's products—including cotton, coffee, ivory, diamonds, gold, and increasingly oil—were in high demand. By the early 1970s, several hundred thousand whites—mostly Portuguese, but also Spanish and Italian—lived in Angola. Many remained poor, living in conditions little better than the creoles and often competing for the same jobs.

At the same time, however, the winds of decolonization were sweeping across sub-Saharan Africa, beginning in Ghana in 1957 and spreading to virtually the entire continent from the Congo River basin north. Soon only southern Africa remained under white control, including the two settler republics of Rhodesia and South Africa and the Portuguese colonies of Mozambique and Angola. Portugal had several reasons for resisting the so-called winds of change in Africa. For one, large parts of the population in Angola and Mozambique wanted to remain under Portuguese rule. They even helped to develop a rationale for continuing occupation in an age of decolonization. The Portuguese, it was argued, had developed a nonracial form of cooperation with the Africans, unlike the racist apartheid regimes in South Africa and Rhodesia. The races socialized, worked, and married together, creating a unique Lusotropical civilization.

There was a kernel of truth to these assertions. The Portuguese did not seem quite so obsessed with maintaining the separation between the races; there was a far more relaxed social atmosphere in Angola and Mozambique than in neighboring Rhodesia and South Africa. But this kernel of truth was wrapped in layers of hypocrisy. Angolan society was stratified by race, with white colonists in near total control of the political and commercial scene. For Africans and creoles, there was more than just poverty to bear; there was a repressive police state designed to break any attempts to organize or demonstrate for improved economic conditions or true political equality.

The more important reason for Portugal to hold on to its African colonies was that they were immensely profitable. Portugal, unlike France and Britain, the two other colonial powers in Africa, did not have the means to compete in the international marketplace. They knew that if they lost political control of their colonies, they could not maintain their economic control against the encroachments of other Europeans and South African whites. France and Britain would develop a kind of neocolonialist system based on economic control in their former African possessions, but Portugal did not have the resources to do the same.

Angolan Society

In the early 1960s, on the eve of the national liberation struggle in Angola, it was a complex society. Stratified by race and class, it had a small elite of administrators, businesspeople, and planters. Beneath the elite was a middle class of professionals, retailers, and civil servants, largely white but including the occasional *assimilado*, the official designation for the Afro-Portuguese and other educated and acculturated Africans. Beneath the middle class were the masses of workers in the cities, largely black, and farmers in the countryside.

This group, representing the vast majority of Angolans, was itself divided by ethnicity and economics. The indigenous African people of Angola were divided into three major ethnic and linguistic groups: the Ovimbundu in the south and central parts of the country, the Kimbundu along the coast, and the Kikongo in the northeast. Moreover, each of these different peoples played a different role in the country's economy and was, in turn, shaped by that role. Many of the Ovimbundu worked for the cotton planters of the Central Highlands, but others had migrated or been transported to the north to work on the coffee plantations. This move put them into a fierce rivalry with the Kikongo, who resented their access to jobs and who held them in contempt for being under the thumb of white planters. Meanwhile, the Kimbundu of the coast dominated the African neighborhoods of the major cities and were increasingly resented by the Kikongo and Ovimbundu for their street-smart ways and their control of the job market in the port cities.

War for Independence

In the late nineteenth century, Portugal was forced to assert strong administrative control over its African colonies because of the aggressive forays of Belgium into the Congo. In a similar manner, the beginnings of the movement resisting Portuguese rule in Angola in the 1950s can be traced to the sudden decolonization of the Belgian Congo. In 1959, Belgium agreed to a four-year decolonization plan, but then abruptly changed its mind, giving the Congo independence in 1960. Ill prepared, the country was immediately embroiled in a multisided struggle for power between right- and left-wing elements, as well as separatists in different provinces of the vast new country.

The conflict in the Congo worried the authorities in Angola since the two shared a border more than 1,000 miles long. More ominous was the large Kikongo population in the Congo, many of whom drifted back to their homes in Angola after the Belgian-owned plantations where they worked closed down. Even before the war, the Kikongo had taken the lead in pushing for autonomy. Under the leadership of Holden Roberto, they formed the Union of the Peoples of Northern Angola (UPNA, later the UPA) in 1957, a largely ethnic-based, rural organization. With a leadership largely made up of small commercial farmers and small-time urban entrepreneurs, the organization took on a strongly anticommunist ideology.

Meanwhile the Kimbundu people in Angola were also getting organized, having formed the Popular Movement for the Liberation of Angola (MPLA, its Portuguese acronym), under the leadership of an *assimilado* doctor named Agostinho Neto. Like Neto himself, the MPLA was cosmopolitan in outlook and socialist in its political orientation, quite unlike the UPNA. In June 1960, colonial police arrested Neto, setting off riots in Luanda that resulted in the deaths of several unarmed demonstrators. Then, in an entirely separate incident, thousands of Kimbundu cotton farmers in the Malange province 400 miles southeast of Luanda began an armed uprising (the arms were machetes) over falling prices. They destroyed colonial livestock and property before being brutally suppressed by soldiers. It is estimated that some 7,000 farmers were killed. The incident, so distant from the capital, went largely unnoticed.

Then, in February 1961, hundreds of African residents of Luanda, angered at police brutality and arbitrary arrests in the city, stormed the prisons, freeing dozens of militants along with petty criminals. While the MPLA claimed credit, most historians believe it was a spontaneous affair. In either case, the uprising fueled a violent reaction among the city's whites, who brutally killed hundreds of unarmed blacks in retaliation. This particular incident officially marked the beginning of the war of liberation and is celebrated today as Angola's major national holiday. A month later, the Kikongo of the north rose up under the loose control of the UPNA, now renamed the National Liberation Front of Angola (FNLA). Again, the Portuguese forces reacted brutally, killing some 20,000. These repressive measures were largely effective against the FNLA. Within a couple of years, the organization was limited to ineffective raids across the border from its sanctuary in the now-independent Congo.

Even more destructive for the cause of Angolan independence was the growing animosity between the rightist, rural, Kikongo-based FNLA and the socialist, urban, and cosmopolitan MPLA. Indeed, as early as October 1961, FNLA partisans were attacking MPLA guerrillas, a harbinger of much worse to come. Soon afterward, MPLA cadres were evicted from the Congo by its right-wing dictator, Joseph Mobutu (later Mobutu Sese Seko), and were forced into Congo-Brazzaville, which shared no border with Angola proper. This made it difficult for MPLA to attack inside Angola. Despite these setbacks, the MPLA, with its more left-wing politics and nontribal inclusiveness, attracted the lion's share of recruits to the rebel cause.

Finally, in 1966, part of the MPLA relocated to Zambia, on Angola's eastern border. Once again it was within striking distance of colonial forces. Unfortunately for the MPLA, however, the move to Zambia also put the organization into conflict with yet another rebel movement, that of Jonas Savimbi's Union for the Total Independence of Angola (UNITA). Savimbi, once a leader in Roberto's FNLA, had left that organization because of its timidity and its ethnic exclusiveness. Savimbi was a well-educated and highly ambitious Ovimbundu man who felt that his own career and the interests of his people were better served by their own organization. He formed UNITA in 1966. From the beginning, the MPLA had suspicions about the organization. They claimed it was really a front set up by the Portuguese, to engage the MPLA in battle and keep the Ovimbundu in line. (These accusations were later corroborated.)

Meanwhile, the Portuguese military began employing the anti-guerrilla strategy developed by the United States, which was also its main weapons provider. All the tactics used in Vietnam were copied on a smaller scale in Angola, including search-and-destroy missions, helicopter-aided mobility, the establishment of village militias, and even the use of napalm to deny the rebel forces jungle cover. Ovimbundu peasants were herded into relocation camps to keep them from providing aid to the rebels. Because of the vast reaches of the country and the relatively small areas in which the Portuguese planters and urban population lived, the army was able to keep the guerrilla war largely out of sight and out of mind. But the effort was costly, both in financial and political terms.

Independence and Internecine Fighting

Trying to suppress rebellions in several of its colonies—Angola, Guinea-Bissau, Cape Verde Islands, and Mozambique—put too much of a strain on Portugal. In February 1974, a group of centrist and left-wing military officers overthrew the dictatorship of Marcello Caetano, the man who had acceded to power after Salazar's death in 1968. For a time, the new government, under the leadership of war hero Antonio de Spinola, tried to find a way to maintain some kind of political union with the colonies. But in October, Spinola was forced out by officers who immediately declared their intention to free Portugal's colonies.

The news caught the different rebel groups and the colonial leadership in Angola by surprise. The MPLA, its Luanda and eastern factions locked in a power struggle, were suspicious. The FNLA, backed by Zaire and China, believed it was in the best position to assume power. It welcomed negotiations with Lisbon, as did the more isolated UNITA in the southeast. Meanwhile, the whites of Angola were, not surprisingly, filled with trepidation about the events unfolding in Lisbon. Riots, largely instigated by whites, broke out in the capital. The whites talked about a unilateral declaration of independence, much as Rhodesian whites had done when Britain talked of black rule there in 1965.

Arms began to flow into the country as the Portuguese prepared to pull out. The FNLA was supplied with weapons by China and, oddly, by the CIA as

The Soviet-backed Popular Movement for the Liberation of Angola (MPLA) prevailed over rival nationalist groups and took the reins of power after the withdrawal of Portuguese colonial forces in 1975. *(Library of Congress, POS 6—U.S., no. 739)*

well. This case of strange bedfellows can be explained by Beijing and Washington's mutual suspicions of the Soviet-backed and armed MPLA. By November 1974, when representatives of the three rebel groups met with Portuguese officials in the Lisbon suburb of Alvor, Angola was slipping into a foreign-aided civil war. While the Alvor accords promised elections following Angola's formal independence on November 11, 1975, few observers believed the situation would be solved off the battlefield.

In March 1975, the well-armed FNLA in the northeast marched on Luanda, hoping to capture the strategic junction at Caxito just north of the city. In response, the Soviets and Cubans began a major arms shipment to the MPLA. The fighting escalated through the summer, causing the vast majority of Portuguese colonists to flee, though not before vengefully destroying whatever property they could not take with them. In mid-September came the inevitable showdown between the FNLA and the MPLA. Utilizing rather ineffective but terrifying World War II–vintage Soviet rocket launchers—popularly known as "Stalin's Organs"—the MPLA routed the FNLA. Roberto's advisers from the U.S. Central Intelligence Agency (CIA) advised him to retreat and regroup, but the FNLA leader insisted on pushing on toward Luanda. The FNLA forces arrived in the suburbs of the capital on the eve of independence but were again turned back by MPLA and Cuban forces, this time for good.

Meanwhile, the war was heating up in southern Angola. By August, UNITA had formed a strategic alliance with the government of South Africa, the latter fearing an Angola ruled by the socialist and militantly anti-apartheid MPLA. On October 16, the South African Defense Forces (SADF) invaded Angola in order to back UNITA's push on Luanda, only to be pushed back by a Cuban and MPLA counteroffensive in mid-November. The SADF soon retreated to South African–controlled Namibia, Angola's neighbor to the south.

By the end of the year, the MPLA was in firm control of most of the country. The FNLA, having pulled back to Zaire, largely collapsed, especially after the U.S. Congress passed a law forbidding CIA intervention in Angola, and Beijing decided it needed to find a way to work with the victorious MPLA government. UNITA was a different story. A more effective strategist and leader than Roberto, Savimbi led the remnants of his forces on a "long march" into the bush of southern Angola, determined to fight another day.

James Ciment

See also: Anticolonialism; Angola: Struggle over Cabinda, 1960– ; Angola: First War with UNITA, 1975–1992; Angola: Second War with UNITA, 1992–2002; Congo, Democratic Republic of the: Post-Independence Wars, 1960–1965; Guinea-Bissau: War of National Liberation, 1962–1974; Mozambique: War of National Liberation, 1961–1974.

Bibliography

Bender, Gerald. *Angola Under the Portuguese: The Myth and the Reality.* Berkeley: University of California Press, 1978.

Ciment, James. *Angola and Mozambique: Postcolonial Wars in Southern Africa.* New York: Facts on File, 1997.

Davidson, Basil. *In the Eye of the Storm: Angola's People.* Garden City, NY: Doubleday, 1972.

Marcum, John. *The Angolan Revolution.* Volume 1, *The Anatomy of an Explosion.* Cambridge, MA: MIT Press, 1969.

———. *The Angolan Revolution.* Volume 2, *Exile Politics and Guerrilla Warfare.* Cambridge, MA: MIT Press, 1978.

Minter, William, ed. *Operation Timber: Pages from the Savimbi Dossier.* Trenton, NJ: Africa World Press, 1988.

Stockwell, John. *In Search of Enemies: A CIA Story.* New York: W.W. Norton, 1978.

ANGOLA: Struggle over Cabinda, 1960–

TYPE OF CONFLICT: Separatist
PARTICIPANT: Portugal

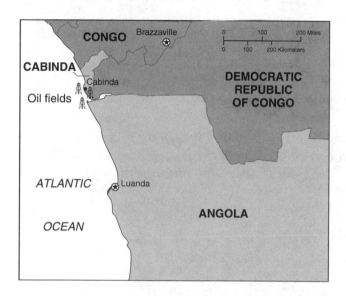

The enclave of Cabinda, a province of Angola since that country's independence in 1975, has been a site of often intense conflict since the 1960s, first involving Cabindan struggles for independence against the Portuguese colonizers and, later, similar struggles against the Angolan government. Prior to Angolan independence in 1975, Cabinda, a small, oil-rich territory separated from the rest of Angola by the Democratic Republic of Congo, was listed by the Organization of African Unity as a country to be liberated.

Cabinda's first independence movement, the Movement for the Liberation of the Enclave of Cabinda (MLEC from its acronym in Portuguese) was founded in 1960 at the time armed struggle was launched throughout Angola against Portuguese rule. In 1963, MLEC merged with two other groups, the Committee for Action and Union of Cabinda (CAUNC) and the Maiombe Alliance (ALLIAMA), to form the Front for the Liberation of the Cabinda Enclave (FLEC), which has continued in various forms up to the present. Over the years, FLEC would engage in guerrilla warfare first against the Portuguese and later against Angolan troops. It also supported the occasional kidnapping of oil industry officials.

In 1974, a new government in Portugal took steps to grant Angola's independence, setting up talks in Alvor, a seaside town along the Portuguese coast. These negotiations for independence included three Angolan nationalist groups but excluded FLEC. Article 3 of the Alvor Accord of 1975 affirmed Cabinda's status as a province of Angola. Soon afterward, Cabindan independence forces began a guerrilla struggle against the Angolan government. The violent conflict in Cabinda continued even as Angola carried out a series of peace conferences and negotiations with other dissident groups in the country but continued to ignore and exclude the Cabindan dissidents in FLEC.

Upon the withdrawal of Portuguese troops from Cabinda, forces from the Popular Movement for the Liberation of Angola (MPLA), which has formed Angola's government since independence, gained control of the province. Since then, various Cabindan separatist forces have fought with the Angolan government for control. In the three decades of struggle, almost 30,000 people have lost their lives.

Oil

Cabinda is critical to Angola's economic development since the province is the source of more than half of Angola's oil production, which totals approximately 1 million barrels per day. Oil revenues make up more than 40 percent of Angola's gross national product and provide the funding for more than 80 percent of Angola's national budget.

A key point of contention for Cabinda separatists is the way the Angolan government spends the revenues it receives from Cabinda's plentiful oil. Cabindans point out that they bear the negative impacts of the oil industry on its environment and society but receive a very small fraction—only about 10 percent—of the revenues. There is also little indication that the

83

KEY DATES

1960	The Movement for the Liberation of the Enclave of Cabinda (MLEC, its Portuguese acronym) is formed to fight for independence against Portuguese colonizers.
1963	MLEC joins with two other Cabinda liberation organizations to form the Front for the Liberation of the Cabinda Enclave (FLEC).
1974	Portugal signs the Alvor Accord with three Angolan liberation organizations but not FLEC; accords call for Cabinda to be included in an independent Angola, which comes to be the following year.
1975–2002	Intermittent fighting occurs between the Angolan government and FLEC militants.
2002	Having reached a peace accord with its main internal enemy—the Union for the Total Independence of Angola (UNITA)—the Angolan government conducts a major sweep of Cabinda, defeating FLEC militarily.
2003	Negotiations begin between the Angolan government and Cabinda independence advocates.
2004–2005	While some refugees return to Cabinda from neighboring Republic of Congo, the UN issues a report saying the enclave is still unsafe for political dissidents owing to the presence of large numbers of Angolan military personnel.

oil companies contribute to the humanitarian and social development needs in the province.

Cabinda suffers from shortages of food and farming materials as well as a lack of educational and employment opportunities. The oil companies employ thousands of people, but most of them work and live outside the territory. Cabindans charge that they are exploited both by the companies and by the Angolan government.

The situation for Cabinda was especially difficult in the 1990s. In 1992, troops of the dissident UNITA party occupied the diamond mines in southern Angola, which were the country's other major source of income. This occupation increased the government's dependence on oil revenues, prompting it to step up efforts to control activities in Cabinda and vanquish the Cabindan insurgents. A large-scale sweep of Cabinda by Angolan forces in 2002 destroyed the main bases of FLEC's two main factions and forced many independence fighters to give up the guerrilla struggle. FLEC's leaders went into exile and in 2003 began negotiations with Angolan authorities. At the same time, the Angolan army continued to maintain a strong military presence in Cabinda.

Human rights groups and observers in Cabinda reported numerous atrocities, including rape, abuse, torture, and illegal detentions, carried out against the local population by the Angolan army. A 2004 report by Human Rights Watch also documented cases of arbitrary arrest, military interference with civilians' freedom of movement, and extra-judicial executions. The Angolan government did not begin the process of forming a national human rights institution until January 2005. Even then, citizen groups complained that public participation was still not allowed.

In February 2005, a delegation of Cabindan refugees made a brief visit to their former home and determined that it was unsafe for them to return because of the presence of Angolan military forces in civilian areas. The United Nations High Commission on Refugees (UNHCR) did not have a permanent presence in Cabinda because of the continuation of conflict and because the primitive conditions restricted their access to necessary resources. The presence of land mines, along with impassable roads and bridges destroyed by fighting, made the movement of refugees unsafe and slowed the delivery of food to those who still lived there.

Despite these unpromising conditions, more than 100 refugees returned to the province in September 2005 from the Republic of Congo-Brazzaville. This was the first repatriation of refugees to Cabinda in more than two years. Those who returned were a small percentage of those who had been stranded in Congo-Brazzaville, and a similarly large number of refugees are living in the Democratic Republic of Congo. In addition to the great number of refugees outside of Cabinda, at least 25,000 internally displaced persons were within the province itself.

Many Cabindans, while still desiring independence, would settle for autonomy within Angola. Their main demand is a fairer return on the contribution of their oil to the Angolan economy. In addition, civil society groups demand the end of human rights violations by the Angolan army, improved rights for oil workers, and better living conditions.

Negotiations

In the peace negotiations with the Angolan government, the Cabindan Dialogue Forum, which includes FLEC and various Cabindan citizen groups, represents Cabinda. The negotiations proceeded with great difficulty and the prospects for peaceful resolution seemed dim. Fighting continued.

Cabinda's importance to the Angolan economy became even greater in 2005, when Angola's state-owned oil company Sonangol announced that it would soon begin explorations for additional oil in Cabinda itself. It is believed that new onshore oil reserves will prove even greater that those in the substantial offshore fields already developed.

Pro-independence forces were strongly opposed to any onshore oil development under Angolan direction. They cite the history of political and environmental damage within the province and continued concerns for local autonomy and self-determination as reasons for their opposition. It seemed likely that the prospect of new oil reserves in Cabinda would harden the positions of both the secessionist forces and the Angolan government. Already, in response to the Sonangol announcement, younger militants had promised to form a more radical and violent guerrilla force than the greatly diminished FLEC.

Jeffrey A. Shantz

See also: Invasions and Border Disputes; Angola: War of National Liberation, 1961–1974; Angola: First War with UNITA, 1975–1992; Angola: Second War with UNITA, 1992–2002; Congo, Democratic Republic of the: Post-Independence Wars, 1960–1965.

Bibliography

Ciment, James. *Angola and Mozambique: Postcolonial Wars in Southern Africa.* New York: Facts on File, 1997.

Porto, João Gomes, and Imogen Parsons. *Sustaining the Peace in Angola: An Overview of Current Demobilisation, Disarmament and Reintegration.* Pretoria, South Africa: Institute for Security Studies, 2003.

ANGOLA: First War with UNITA, 1975–1992

TYPE OF CONFLICT: Cold War Confrontation; Ethnic and Religious
PARTICIPANTS: Congo (Zaire); Cuba; South Africa; Soviet Union; United States

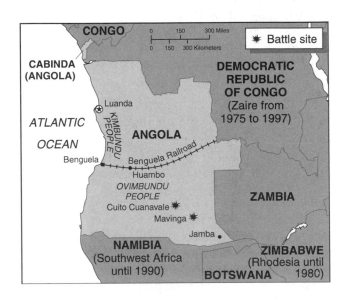

On November 11, 1975, Angola held what may be the strangest independence day in African history. As Portuguese Admiral Leonel Cardoso lowered his country's flag over the capital city of Luanda, artillery could be heard in the background. While the left-wing Popular Movement for the Liberation of Angola (MPLA, its Portuguese acronym) took the reins of power, a rival group, the National Front for the Liberation of Angola (FNLA), backed by the U.S. Central Intelligence Agency (CIA), was marching on the city. Meanwhile, in the southern provincial capital of Huambo, a third liberation force, the South African–assisted Union for the Total Independence of Angola (UNITA), was conducting its own independence celebration and getting ready to launch a military drive on the capital hundreds of miles to the north.

Within a few months, however, MPLA forces, backed by Soviet arms and augmented by Cuban troops, would crush both the FNLA and the UNITA in battle, sending the former into oblivion and the latter on its famous "long march" into the southern Angolan bush, to prepare for yet another round of fighting.

In the capital, the leadership of the MPLA moved on its political enemies. Both UNITA and the FNLA were outlawed, and what few supporters remained in Luanda were rounded up. Some thirteen FNLA mercenaries, mostly Americans and Britons, were convicted of various crimes, and four were executed. Even dissidents within the MPLA felt the postwar wrath. Two top advisers to President Agostinho Neto were arrested for organizing opposition within the party.

Meanwhile, the MPLA tried to establish its international credentials. Strong-arming neighboring Zaire and Zambia, both dependent on Angolan railroads and ports for the bulk of their international trade, Angola won agreements that neither country would sponsor rebel movements within the country. While leaning toward the socialist bloc countries—for both ideological and military reasons—the MPLA government also tried to reach out to the West, knowing that only the big oil companies could provide the expertise and capital necessary to fully exploit the country's vast reserves.

MPLA spokespersons refused to see any contradiction in establishing a socialist government even as they opened up the country to capitalist investment. This contradiction was made possible by the general political tenor of the times. The socialist bloc was confident and assertive, having defeated the United States in Southeast Asia and having taken power in Angola, Ethiopia, and Mozambique in Africa. At the same time, both the South African government under Prime Minister John Vorster and the U.S. government under President Jimmy Carter were in periods of foreign policy retrenchment, both having been burned in Angola by backing a losing side.

Despite this auspicious beginning, the MPLA began making mistakes in its administration of the Angolan economy. Rather than attempting true land reform, the government continued the hated agricultural policies of the earlier Portuguese colonists,

KEY DATES

1975   As independence approaches, various rebel forces—including the Popular Movement for the Liberation of Angola (MPLA, its Portuguese acronym), the National Liberation Front of Angola (FNLA), and the Union for the Total Independence of Angola (UNITA) battle for control of the country; the MPLA wins the conflict; when Portugal grants independence, the MPLA takes power in Luanda; the FNLA largely disbands while UNITA retreats to rural areas in southern and central Angola.

1977   An attempted coup by top MPLA official Nito Alves is crushed.

1981   With accession of anticommunist Ronald Reagan to the U.S. presidency, South Africa feels emboldened to increase its attacks on the leftist MPLA government.

1983   South Africa launches Operation Askari, working with UNITA forces to put Jonas Savimbi in power; the offensive fails but causes high casualties.

1984   A cease-fire is signed in Lusaka, Zambia, between UNITA, MPLA, the Southwest African People's Organization (SWAPO), and South Africa.

1987   Battle of Cuito Carnevale results in major Cuban-backed MPLA victory over South Africa and UNITA.

1989   Moderate F.W. de Klerk becomes president in South Africa, replacing hawkish P.W. Botha; de Klerk vows to reach a peace settlement for interconnected conflicts in Southwest Africa and Angola; South Africa pulls out of Southwest Africa, which is renamed Namibia, the following year.

1991   Under the aegis of the Soviet Union, the United States, and Portugal, UNITA and MPLA sign Bicesse Accords, agreeing to a cease-fire, a demobilization of UNITA, and national elections.

1992   National elections result in an MPLA victory; Savimbi, whose forces do not fully demobilize, charges fraud and vows to continue fighting.

forcing small farmers to sell their crops at below-market rates to government purchasing boards. To guarantee stability in the countryside, the government often used holdovers from colonial times, many of them chieftains and labor bosses who had worked with the Portuguese. And on top of all this, the MPLA laid down an enormous bureaucracy to institute a centralized, command economy on the lines of its mentors, the Soviet Union and Cuba.

This combination of blunders sparked a coup in 1977 among more radical members of the MPLA including Nito Alves, who had been put in charge of

organizing Luanda's citizens into *poder popular* (people's power) committees during the late stages of the national liberation war. The coup was easily crushed and the committees were hounded out of existence, but their repression left a residual bitterness among the Angolans and killed any possibility of a diplomatic opening to the United States or South Africa.

Rise of UNITA

Following his defeat in 1975, UNITA leader Jonas Savimbi maintained a low profile in a redoubt hidden

UNITA leader Jonas Savimbi retreated to southeastern Angola after his defeat by the leftist MPLA in 1975 and launched a U.S.-backed guerrilla war that did not end—or at least pause—until the Bicesse Accords of 1991. *(Selwyn Tait/Time Life Pictures/Getty Images)*

in the southern Angolan bush, an area the Portuguese had aptly named "the land at the end of the earth." His main backer, South Africa, had largely abandoned him, and a potential backer, the U.S. government, was legally mandated by an act of Congress to stay out of Angolan affairs. Still, by 1977, Savimbi felt confident enough to begin launching hit-and-run attacks on isolated MPLA outposts and infrastructure targets, the latter mostly confined to the Benguela rail line between the Atlantic port of that name and the copper belt of Zambia. By 1980, however, UNITA had grown significantly, both in numbers and in military potential, and was now capable of hitting the railroad at almost any point along its 700-mile length in Angola.

How UNITA grew so fast is a matter of some controversy. Its supporters say that it appealed to disenchanted farmers of the Ovimbundu tribe, who were upset by the government's agricultural policies, which included the consolidation of villages into farming cooperatives under the control of bureaucrats from Luanda and local chieftains, many of them quite unpopular. Savimbi himself was an Ovimbundu, and UNITA offered his fellow tribesmen a way to fight back.

The organization's opponents say that UNITA's forces improved only after South African Defense Minister P.W. Botha staged a right-wing "coup."

Botha had made support of anticommunist rebel movements in southern Africa a key part of his strategic defense of the apartheid regime. The policy, known as "total strategy," was intended to make surrounding countries ungovernable and to portray black majority rule as incapable of bringing peace and prosperity. At the same time, he hoped to strong-arm the new independent black states into giving up any support for the African National Congress (ANC), which was fighting for an end to apartheid in South Africa.

Then in 1980, conservative Ronald Reagan defeated Jimmy Carter for the U.S. presidency. Botha in South Africa now felt he had a kindred spirit in Washington. So, too, did Savimbi, who was quoted as saying that Reagan's election was "the best news since the beginning of the war." Indeed, the assistant secretary of state for African affairs, Chester Crocker, outlined his "constructive engagement" policy toward South Africa and insisted on a new linkage of southern African issues. Specifically, he urged that South Africa agree to pull out of its illegal colony in Namibia only when Cuban troops left Angola.

South Africa Invades

With the green light on in Washington, South Africa stepped up its support for UNITA dramatically. In 1981 alone, the South African Defense Forces (SADF) conducted over 1,000 bombing missions and fifty ground assaults, including the massive Operation Protea, in which a 5,000-man force occupied the southern Angolan province of Cunene for several weeks. The declared rationale was to eliminate Southwest African People's Organization (SWAPO) forces, which were fighting for the liberation of Namibia from South Africa. Eventually, Angolan forces, with Cuban support, halted the South African advance sixty-five miles north of the Namibian border.

UNITA, now a well-armed and formidable force of its own, had stolen the MPLA government's authority in much of southern Angola, as well as in the Ovimbundu homeland in the central highlands. Still, it was always at a disadvantage, because the MPLA had an enormous war chest paid for by its substantial oil revenues. The MPLA had more soldiers, more arms, and virtually total control of the skies, except when South African forces invaded, as they did once more with Operation Askari at the end of 1983. Initially, Askari was not meant to be a mere attack on southern Angola, as Protea had been, but an all-out invasion intended to put Savimbi and UNITA in power in Luanda. But when military satellites revealed the extent of the South African buildup, the Soviet Union, a supporter of the Angola government, issued stern warnings to South Africa, forcing it to scale back its plans.

With anti-apartheid sentiment growing in the United States in the election year 1984, the Reagan administration temporarily backtracked, pushing negotiations on all parties to the conflict. An accord signed in the Zambian capital of Lusaka included a cease-fire and assurances that neither UNITA nor SWAPO would take advantage of a SADF pullback from southern Angola. But South Africa had no intention of honoring its word, a fact made plain when a group of South African commandos were captured while attempting to blow up oil facilities in the Angolan enclave of Cabinda far to the north.

On the eve of Angola's tenth anniversary of independence, both UNITA and the MPLA were growing weary. The MPLA was alarmed at the SADF's capacity to attack anywhere in the country, and UNITA was worried, for a time at least, that the Lusaka accord might mean an end to South African aid. Rather than encouraging peace, this mutual weariness led to increasingly brutal tactics by both sides. Savimbi's aim was to make Angola ungovernable. To do this, UNITA engaged in a reign of terror, murder, and destruction. Its combatants attacked and destroyed cooperative farms and forcibly recruited villagers to serve as porters, servants, farmers, and soldiers in the UNITA cause.

For its part, the MPLA considered almost any Ovimbundu person to be a potential supporter of UNITA. This thinking led to mass arrests and confinement of thousands of Ovimbundu peasants in camps that bore a striking resemblance to the fenced-in, prison-like strategic hamlets Portugal set up during Angola's war of independence. Thus, UNITA was not always required to forcibly recruit new soldiers; MPLA tactics did much of this work.

Nor did war weariness encourage any of the warring parties to scale back their operations. Indeed, 1986 represented a watershed in the war, as UNITA, the MPLA, and their respective allies prepared for what they all saw as the decisive showdown in the now almost decade-long conflict. The flood burst the following year in the great land battles of Mavinga and Cuito Cuanavale, the largest military engagements in the history of sub-Saharan Africa.

The precipitating event was the result of the MPLA's military edge over UNITA. Having installed air defense systems capable of keeping the South African air force out of Angolan skies, the MPLA had been ruthlessly tracking down and bombing UNITA forces. Fearing defeat, Savimbi appealed to South Africa, which then launched a massive 10,000-man assault first on the town of Mavinga, then on the fortified city of Cuito late in 1987. With supplies running low, the MPLA turned to its patron, Cuba, which came to its aid with some 50,000 troops. A successful Cuban-MPLA assault on the SADF's rear placed the South Africans in dire straits, pummeled by the Angolan air force and unable to retreat. Fearful of a mass surrender, and facing increasing protests at home, the South African government agreed to pull out of Angola and sit down to negotiate an end to its war in Angola.

End of the War

The defeat was not just a watershed moment in Angolan history, but also for South Africa itself. Many students of apartheid believe that the defeat in Angola represented a critical blow to both the "total strategy" policy and the Botha administration. Within two years of the Cuito defeat, a new and more conciliatory South African government under F.W. de Klerk had legalized the African National Congress (ANC) and set the country on the road to racial reconciliation. South Africa also agreed to free Namibia before the Cubans pulled out of Angola, one of the sticking points in earlier negotiations. Indeed, Namibia held elections in 1989 and 1990, leading to independence and the victory of SWAPO as the country's ruling party. Cuba lived up to its word and pulled its troops out of Angola by the May 1991 deadline in the accords, which were signed in New York in 1988.

Savimbi was distraught as a result of these developments, and by the knowledge that the Reagan administration was coming to an end. But when George Bush was elected president in 1988, Savimbi was assured of American support. Bush had been director of the CIA during that agency's earlier foray into Angola in 1975. In addition, the congressional act banning aid to the parties in the Angola conflict had expired in 1986.

In 1989 and 1990, both the war and the negotiations to end the war sputtered on. The U.S. government, taking up the slack left by the departing South Africans, pumped millions into UNITA coffers, sending in biweekly flights with supplies to UNITA's headquarters at Jamba, in southeastern Angola, from bases in Zaire. Even though the Soviet Union was in collapse and its Cuban allies were scheduled to leave Angola, they provided handsome support for the MPLA government. The Soviets not only provided much-needed weapons, but also rescheduled some $2 billion in loans owed to Moscow.

Still, both the military and political situations had changed dramatically since the signing of the New York Accords. Gone were the days of major land battles. Instead, the war returned to the course it had taken in the early 1980s, in which the MPLA and UNITA engaged in guerrilla attacks and counterattacks, with the civilian population caught in the middle. Meanwhile, the departure of the Cubans and South Africans had pulled the ideological rug out from under the feet of both parties to the conflict. With Havana gone and the Cold War ebbing, Savimbi could no longer portray himself as the bulwark against the spread of Communism in southern Africa. And with South Africa's withdrawal, the MPLA lost its most compelling rationale for all-out war against UNITA. Thus, both sides were more willing to negotiate, even if talks served as a cover for their continuing efforts to settle their struggle for power on the battlefield.

In June 1989, Zairean dictator Mobutu Sese Seko invited both sides to talk at his presidential compound in Gbadolite. Mobutu, however, proved himself a disingenuous intermediary by promising mutually exclusive things to the MPLA and UNITA, telling one that Savimbi would go into exile and the other that he would be guaranteed a role in a government of national reconciliation. Not surprisingly, the talks went nowhere and both sides dug in their heels. Many in Luanda felt that Savimbi had been South Africa's puppet and, with aid from Pretoria drying up, he could be easily defeated. For his part, Savimbi ruthlessly purged his ranks of leaders favoring conciliation, including his chief lieutenant Tito Chingunji.

Meanwhile, UNITA was coming under increasing fire from human rights organizations, which accused it, among other things, of using food relief as a weapon. Since 1990, it had blocked UN convoys from delivering much-needed foodstuffs to Angolan peasants, who were suffering both from disruptions caused by the war and from the extended drought that hit southern Africa in the late 1980s and early 1990s.

As 1990 drew to a close, both the war and the talking—the latter, this time, under the aegis of the Portuguese—accelerated. In December, the MPLA launched its long-expected assault on Jamba. But instead of defending his headquarters, Savimbi outflanked the government forces and took his army to the north and east. It was a clever tactical move. Without the support of the SADF, Savimbi knew he could not beat the MPLA in a head-on conflict. Instead, he adopted a more mobile strategy, employing hit-and-run tactics. In addition, he sought to entrench himself in the diamond-mining areas near the country's northeastern frontier with Zaire, thereby assuring himself of a steady source of revenues and access to U.S. arms.

By spring 1991, the war had again stalemated, with neither side able to deliver the knockout blow against the other. This situation, however, benefited Savimbi who, by the oldest rule of guerrilla warfare, simply had to survive in order to win, which is exactly the way he liked it. The UNITA leader had always made it clear that he did not like to negotiate from a position of weakness. In May, the two sides finally signed onto a deal that seemed to promise an end to hostilities. Under the so-called Bicesse Accords, named after the Portuguese resort town where they were signed, both sides agreed to an in-place cease-fire within one month, a UN-monitored election and demobilization of both forces, a joint commission to draw up a new constitution—overseen by the three Bicesse guarantors: the Soviet Union, the United States, and Portugal—and an integrated 50,000-man army.

The treaty did not come a moment too soon. In the fifteen years since independence, war had engulfed the country and brought appalling losses in its wake. Some 100,000 Angolans had died in battle, while another 700,000 died from disease and malnutrition directly related to the war. Approximately 30 percent of the nation's 10 million citizens had been displaced and over 6 million land mines laid, leaving Angola—together with Cambodia—as a world leader in amputees. It is estimated that between them, the MPLA and UNITA spent $10 billion prosecuting the war, with a further $2 billion pumped in by both the Soviet Union and South Africa, and with several hundred million provided by the United States. Cuba had committed no fewer than 100,000 troops over that same period of time. It was, by all accounts, the bloodiest war in the history of southern Africa.

Participants

Despite its claims to being the most inclusive of Angola's three major political movements of the pre-independence period, the MPLA had a leadership largely composed of urban intellectuals. Both Neto and Jose Eduardo dos Santos—who became president in 1979 and held the office for more than thirty-five years—held advanced degrees. A further contradiction in the makeup of the party was its factionalism. While the leaders shared similar backgrounds, the infighting among them was often intense. Both Daniel Chipenda and Nito Alves, among the leading figures in the movement before independence, were ruthlessly purged when their radical politics ran afoul of the bureaucratic and centralized dictates of Neto and dos Santos.

The MPLA was heavily criticized on several counts, and not just by supporters of UNITA. First, its urban leadership, many say, failed to understand the needs of the vast majority of Angolans who remained in the countryside. Its push to communalize holdings offended many tradition-bound farmers, while its support of purchasing boards run by local strongmen seemed too akin to Portuguese practices. Finally, its army—often forcibly recruited, poorly trained, and underpaid—tended to act like an army of occupation rather than as a defender against rebel attacks.

In several ways, UNITA has been the mirror opposite of the MPLA. Where the MPLA liked to portray itself as an inclusive party representing all Angolans, Savimbi did little to dispute the charges that UNITA was nothing more than an Ovimbundu political and military front. Yet while the MPLA leadership remained in Luanda, almost entirely out of touch with the Angolan peasantry, Savimbi remained in the bush and sought to retain a close rapport with the peasant farmers in his area of control.

At the same time, however, UNITA was largely the creation and tool of Savimbi's own thinking and ambition. Savimbi was a very effective military and political leader, resurrecting an almost totally destroyed or outnumbered force on at least two occasions through his ruthless and charismatic leadership. A chameleon-like political figure, Savimbi espoused a

cross section of doctrines and won accolades from an odd cross section of admirers that, over the years, included such disparate figures as Ronald Reagan and Mao Zedong.

Issues and Tactics

Like many civil conflicts, the post-independence war in Angola was sparked by one set of issues but became bogged down in other disagreements as it continued on for fifteen years. As a self-proclaimed Marxist-Leninist organization, the MPLA instituted a bureaucratic centralized state, with forced communalization of the countryside, state-run agricultural purchasing boards, single-party politics, and a repressive political apparatus. In essence, the MPLA tried to create a Soviet-bloc–style state in a country whose economy, outside of a few key sectors, was dominated by subsistence farmers.

This is what Savimbi and UNITA said they were fighting against. Savimbi made it clear that he believed that a free market economy and a nonintrusive state were what Angolans wanted and needed. His rhetoric included frequent references to the use of Angolans as guinea pigs in a misguided experiment to impose a command-style economy on a people with a free enterprise tradition. But his chameleon-like ways often made his criticisms seem suspect. Having once trained in mainland China, Savimbi began his career as a Maoist believer in peasant revolution. When the Cold War heated up, he changed his tune, emphasizing his anticommunist credentials. And when the Cold War ended, he reworked himself once again, this time as a defender of democracy.

As the war continued, however, new issues came to the fore. Most important among these was foreign involvement. By appealing for aid from South Africa, Savimbi lost credibility with many Angolans and with leaders throughout Africa. At the same time, the MPLA constantly charged that UNITA was a mere tool of reactionary white regimes, in both Pretoria and Washington, determined to prevent the establishment of a truly revolutionary state in southern Africa. UNITA countered with charges that the MPLA was little more than a tool of Soviet expansionists and their Cuban allies.

Because of its length, intensity, and wide array of outside interests, the MPLA war with UNITA saw virtually every tactic of modern warfare employed during the fifteen years from independence to cease-fire. They included guerrilla warfare in the bush as well as house-to-house urban fighting. There were great land battles and lengthy sieges. Aside from the massive amount of weaponry employed, the only constant during the war was the suffering of the civilian population caught in the middle.

Both sides also engaged in egregious human rights violations, not as a by-product of the war but as a conscious tactic to win. Aiming to overthrow the MPLA government, UNITA tried to undermine the government's authority in the countryside by destroying infrastructure and murdering civilians, both tactics aimed at showing the peasantry that the government could not effectively defend them. As for the MPLA's forces, their mission to uproot a largely Ovimbundu army in Ovimbundu territory led to a military mind-set in which every Ovimbundu-speaking person was a potential enemy.

Negotiations

The long post-independence war between the MPLA and UNITA saw no fewer than four separate attempts to find a negotiated settlement. The first were the 1984 Lusaka Accords. A complete failure, the accords were meant to disengage South African, Cuban, and Angolan forces in the southern part of the country. They lasted less than six months, when the MPLA government discovered that both South Africa and UNITA were engaging in illegal sabotage. The second set of negotiations in 1988 led to the only permanently successful agreement of the war. With the New York Accords, both South Africa and Cuba agreed to pull their forces out of Namibia and Angola, respectively, with the former country being granted independence. Both Cuba and South Africa lived up to the letter and spirit of the accords in full.

The final two sets of negotiations—those conducted under Zairean aegis in 1989 and those held in Portugal in 1991—concerned the two Angolan antagonists. The Zairean talks utterly failed, undermined by the mutually exclusive promises Mobutu made to each side. The Bicesse Accords of 1991—with the United States, the Soviet Union, and Portugal as guarantors—was nominally more successful, though it, too, would prove temporary. With its strict deadline and demobilization deadlines, the Bicesse Accords did not allow enough time for the tensions between the two sides—built up over years of bitter and bloody fighting—to subside sufficiently to conduct such delicate procedures. They, too, would break down, leading to a second and even fiercer war between the MPLA and UNITA.

James Ciment

See also: Cold War Confrontations; Ethnic and Religious Conflicts; Angola: War of National Liberation, 1961–1974; Angola: Struggle over Cabinda, 1960– ; Angola: Second War with UNITA, 1992–2002; Congo, Democratic Republic of the: Post-Independence Wars, 1960–1965; Namibia: War of National Liberation, 1966–1990; South Africa: Anti-Apartheid Struggle, 1948–1994.

Bibliography

Bridgland, Fred. *Jonas Savimbi: A Key to Africa.* Edinburgh: Mainstream, 1986.

Ciment, James. *Angola and Mozambique: Postcolonial Wars in Southern Africa.* New York: Facts on File, 1997.

Minter, William. *Apartheid's Contras: An Inquiry into the Roots of War in Angola and Mozambique.* London: Zed Books, 1994.

Ohlson, Thomas, and Stephen Stedman. *The New Is Not Yet Born: Conflict Resolution in Southern Africa.* Washington, DC: Brookings Institution, 1994.

Saul, John. *Recolonization and Resistance in Southern Africa in the 1990s.* Trenton, NJ: Africa World Press, 1993.

Seidman, Ann. *The Roots of Crisis in Southern Africa.* Trenton, NJ: Africa World Press, 1985.

Spikes, Daniel. *Angola and the Politics of Intervention.* Jefferson, NC: McFarland, 1993.

Vines, Alex. *Angola and Mozambique: The Aftermath of Conflict.* Washington, DC: Research Institute for the Study of Conflict and Terrorism, 1995.

ANGOLA: Second War with UNITA, 1992–2002

TYPE OF CONFLICT: Ethnic and Religious
PARTICIPANT: Democratic Republic of Congo

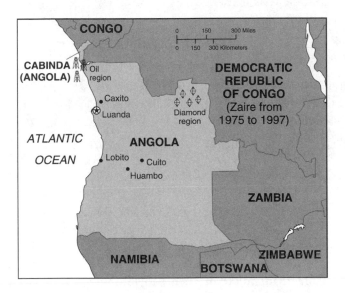

With the Bicesse Accords of May 1991, the first post-independence war between the Popular Movement for the Liberation of Angola (MPLA, its Portuguese acronym) government in Angola and the U.S.-supported rebel forces of the National Union for the Total Independence of Angola (UNITA) came to a gradual end, though sporadic fighting between the two groups continued through 1992. Under the Bicesse Accords, named after the Portuguese resort town where the accords were signed, both sides agreed to the following: an in-place cease-fire within one month, national elections by September 1992, and the demobilization of both forces and their integration into a 50,000-man national military force by the same time. A multinational UN force was supposed to monitor all these activities.

The problems began here. The United Nations committed neither the money, the personnel, nor the guidance on the complicated and sensitive procedures required. The UN budgeted about $130 million and dispatched 500 peacekeepers and election monitors to disengage and demobilize two large and hostile armies scattered over a terrain twice the size of Texas, while simultaneously registering millions of voters, albeit with the help of both government and UNITA officials, and setting up some 6,000 polling stations.

Mistaken assumptions and expectations compounded these massive logistical problems. Like most outside observers, and indeed like most Angolans, the UN force expected UNITA leader Jonas Savimbi to win the elections handily, given the rotten shape of the Angolan economy and the widespread criticisms of the MPLA that UN officials were hearing from the Angolan people. Thus, when journalists and human rights activists pointed out the egregious campaign irregularities and intimidation of voters occurring in the zones under UNITA control, the United Nations turned a blind eye, since it expected Savimbi to win anyway. In addition, UN peacekeepers largely ignored the fact that only the Angolan army was effectively demobilizing, while UNITA was merely handing over its most out-of-date weapons, keeping its more modern armaments and best-trained men in reserve in bush camps.

The UN was not wholly at fault. Fearful of infringements on its sovereignty—not a surprising attitude given its experience with foreign interference since independence—the MPLA insisted on keeping the UN force as small as possible and giving it minimal freedom of action. For example, UN monitors could do nothing to stop violations of the Bicesse Accords; they could only take notes and make their reports.

Electoral predictions, however, did not turn out as anyone expected. Instead of awarding a landslide victory to UNITA, Angolan voters—fearing the harsh, ethnically charged rhetoric coming from the UNITA camp—chose the MPLA. As campaign graffiti on the walls of Luanda put it: "The MPLA steals; UNITA

KEY DATES

1992	Union for the Total Independence of Angola (UNITA, its Portuguese acronym) leader Jonas Savimbi loses the election for the presidency; claiming fraud, he vows to continue fighting.
1993–1994	Using oil revenues, the Popular Movement for the Liberation of Angola (MPLA) purchases $3.5 billion in new weaponry, goes on the offensive against UNITA forces in northeastern Angola; new talks between MPLA and UNITA begin in Lusaka, Zambia.
1994	MPLA and UNITA sign the Lusaka Accords, calling for UNITA demobilization and national elections.
1995–1998	Even as fighting continues, the UN begins setting up demobilization camps throughout the country.
2002	Government forces kill Savimbi on February 22 during a military offensive; representatives of UNITA and the government meet to sign a peace agreement on April 4.
2003	UN peacekeepers wind up their observation mission in February.

kills." Voters evidently preferred thieves to murderers and gave the MPLA 129 out of 220 seats in the national assembly. They also opted for MPLA leader Jose dos Santos over Jonas Savimbi as president. UNITA garnered only 70 seats, with the vast majority of its votes coming from the areas under its own control.

The troubles began on September 30, 1992, the second and final day of voting. Both sides had suspicions about voter fraud and intimidation. But UNITA was particularly upset that MPLA-controlled radio and TV announced the government party's victory even before the polls had closed. Adding to the problem, neither the Angolan parties nor the United Nations had thought much about what would happen after the elections. That is to say, all parties were so concerned with the electoral process itself that they did not concern themselves with questions about what kind of government would exist after the elections and what role the opposition would play in that government.

War Begins Again

Within days, angry rhetoric had degenerated into violence. As UNITA troops began to drift out of the demobilization camps, others in the south launched their first attack against government-controlled towns in mid-October. At the same time, riots broke out in the capital. Both government troops and civilians began to attack UNITA supporters, ultimately killing more than 1,000 of them, including UNITA vice president Jeremias Chitunda, who was gunned down as he tried to flee the city. Savimbi, meanwhile, fled Huambo, the provincial capital and Ovimbundu stronghold. His return to the bush portended ominous things, given his past record of regrouping and retaliation.

At first it seemed that Savimbi had made a gross error in judgment. Usually an astute reader of the American political scene, the UNITA leader had banked on support from past patron President George H.W. Bush, whom he expected to win the American elections that were being held just over a month after those in Angola. But Bush lost to Democrat Bill Clinton, who made it clear that the United States would not continue to support a movement it considered a relic of the Cold War, especially when it apparently refused to play by the rules of the electoral game.

Even though UNITA now lacked a superpower patron, it still had the advantage over the MPLA on the battlefield, which had effectively demobilized in the months leading up to the election. By the middle

A UNITA soldier oversees local *garimpeiros* (miners) searching for diamonds along a river in northern Angola. UNITA used the profits from diamond mining to buy weapons for its ongoing civil war with the ruling MPLA. *(Piero Pomponi/Getty Images News)*

of November, UNITA forces were on the offensive, having captured some 57 of Angola's 164 official municipalities, including 3 provincial capitals, in both the north and the south of the country, as well as the port of Lobito in the south. A brief government offensive stalled in December, and Savimbi, sensing the tide was going with UNITA, kept the military pressure on.

Using his resources from diamond-mining interests in his stronghold in the northeast of Angola, Savimbi went on a buying spree in the international arms market, importing some $100 million in weapons from Israel and the South African homeland of Bophutswana. Caxito, a major hydroelectric station, was captured, leaving the capital of Luanda without electricity and water. But Savimbi's main targets were the central highlands cities of Huambo and Cuito, both of which came under lengthy and bloody sieges through much of 1993. After nearly two months of fighting,

both fell to the rebels. Thousands of civilians fled Huambo, but UNITA forces executed many who remained, including wounded civilians and soldiers in the town's hospital.

It took some six months for the MPLA forces to get back on their feet, aided by more than $3.5 billion in weapons purchased with oil revenues in late 1993 and early 1994. Reorganized and rearmed, the Angolan army went on the offensive, sweeping UNITA forces away from the coast and into the interior. Both Huambo and Cuito came under heavy aerial and artillery bombardment, which killed thousands of civilians. Huambo returned to government control in January 1994 and, after months of block-to-block fighting, so did Cuito. With both armies poorly provisioned, soldiers and rebels alike took turns hijacking UN food convoys and seizing food drops from the air.

As he had done after his defeat in 1975, Savimbi took the still substantial remnants of his army deep into the Angolan bush, though this time he headquartered himself in the east and northeast, which were the source of his diamond revenues and were close to airfields in neighboring Zaire (later renamed the Democratic Republic of the Congo). Despite international sanctions, Savimbi appeared to have little trouble in securing the weapons he needed on the international arms market and getting them to his troops over the porous border with Zaire. Indeed, the Zairean dictator Mobutu Sese Seko turned a blind eye to planes transshipping arms through his country to UNITA. By the end of 1993, when a new round of talks between the MPLA and UNITA began in the Zambian capital of Lusaka, the war seemed to be returning to a familiar stalemate.

Negotiators at Lusaka, under the aegis of the UN, were far more careful, patient, and sober than they had been at Bicesse three years earlier. Having learned their lesson the hard way, all sides were willing to take their time in hammering out a set of accords that would work. It took them nearly a year. The Lusaka Accords of November 1994, though similar in content to those of Bicesse, were far more flexible in terms of implementation. Gone were the strict deadlines for demobilization and elections. Instead, all sides agreed to let these processes move forward under their own momentum. And this time, the United Nations committed the necessary resources, including over $1 billion and several thousand peacekeepers.

From 1995 to 1998, the United Nations set up demobilization camps throughout the country. While the UN proclaimed it was making progress, both sides of the conflict continued to engage in sporadic armed confrontations. In addition, UN peacekeepers and monitors were attacked in several incidents. The worst of these occurred in late 1998 and early 1999 when UNITA forces shot down two UN transport planes. In February 1999, the Angolan government ejected the UN after the international organization attempted to negotiate with UNITA to protect its UN observers in UNITA-controlled territory. The government, arguing that Savimbi and his UNITA organization were terrorists and war criminals, said the UN's actions were inappropriate. In November 1999, the government also rejected a UN effort at peace negotiations.

Luanda's hard line on the UN reflected the government's belief that it was gaining the upper hand in the conflict with UNITA. Although well manned and well armed—from stores kept hidden after the 1991 peace agreement and through purchases on the international arms market—UNITA was becoming increasingly isolated by the late 1990s, as its three main sponsors either disappeared or cut off support: the apartheid regime in South Africa had given up power in 1994; the United States no longer saw the need for supporting an anticommunist guerrilla movement since the Cold War had come to an end in the early 1990s; and the Mobutu regime in Zaire had collapsed in 1998 in the face of a rebel movement led by Laurent Kabila. Indeed, the MPLA government had sent troops into Zaire to support the rebels, who renamed their country the Democratic Republic of Congo.

Savimbi's Death, and Peace

Still, the fighting remained intense through 2000 and 2001. The major government breakthrough came in early 2002. On February 22, 2002, government forces killed Savimbi during fighting in the eastern province of Moxico. As the government had made such announcements before, many of the Angolans and much of the world remained skeptical until the body was shown on national television a few days later. As UNITA had always been a tightly hierarchical rebel force, with the charismatic Savimbi as its indispensable leader, his death was catastrophic for the organization. Already reeling from major government offenses, and no longer enjoying access to the international arms market through air bases in the former Zaire, UNITA sought to arrange a ceasefire with the Angolan military.

Meeting in the Angolan parliament building in Luanda on April 4, 2002, UNITA chief of staff General Geraldo Abreu Kamorteiro and General Armando Da Cruz Neto, head of Angola's armed forces, signed the peace agreement that ended more than a quarter century of civil war in Angola. The agreement called for the total demobilization of UNITA forces under UN aegis and their integration into the Angolan army and police. By August, UNITA's military wing had officially disbanded, and in February 2003 the UN wrapped up its observation mission. Meanwhile, UNITA turned itself into a political party, led by Isaias Samakuva, the organization's former unofficial "ambassador" to Europe.

Almost continuous fighting in the country since 1961—when the armed struggle against Portuguese colonizers began—left an awful legacy of over 1.5 million dead and 3 million displaced. Much of the nation's infrastructure lay in ruins, and the country had been seeded with anywhere between 1.5 million and 6 million land mines, most of them still in the ground. Because of frequent land mine injuries, Angola had perhaps the highest number of amputees in the world. On the positive side, most observers say the country was unlikely to return to war. Moreover, the resource-rich country had the potential for an economic renaissance, especially when oil prices rose steeply beginning in 2005.

James Ciment

See also: Ethnic and Religious Conflicts; Angola: Struggle over Cabinda, 1960– ; Angola: First War with UNITA, 1975–1992; Congo, Democratic Republic of: Kabila Uprising, 1996–1997; Congo, Democratic Republic of: Invasions and Internal Strife, 1998.

Bibliography

Bayer, Tom. *Angola. Presidential and Legislative Elections, September 29–30, 1992. Report on the IFES Observation Mission.* Washington, DC: IFES, 1993.

Human Rights Watch/Africa. *Angola: Arms Trade and Violations of the Laws of War Since the 1992 Elections.* New York: Human Rights Watch/Africa, 1994.

Knudsen, Christine, and I. William Zartman. "The Large Small War in Angola." *Annals of the American Association of Political and Social Sciences* (September 1995).

Pearce, Justin. *An Outbreak of Peace: Angola's Situation of Confusion.* Claremont, South Africa: D. Philip, 2005.

Pereira, Anthony. "The Neglected Tragedy: The Return to War in Angola." *Journal of African Studies* (Winter 1994): 76–90.

BURKINA FASO: Coups, 1966–1987

TYPE OF CONFLICT: Coups, Left and Right

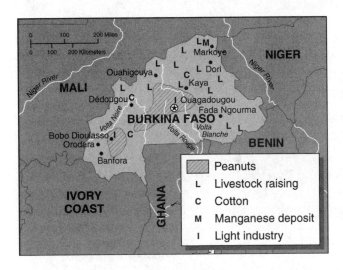

Burkina Faso, originally known as Upper Volta, was a part of French West Africa until 1960. It is a landlocked nation of 105,870 square miles with a population estimated at 14 million in 2005. The capital, Ouagadougou, has about 650,000 people. Burkina Faso is bordered on the north and west by Mali, on the east by Niger, and on the south by, from east to west, Benin, Togo, Ghana, and Côte d'Ivoire. Desperately poor, with an estimated per capita national income of only about $170 a year, the country is heavily dependent on remittances that migrant workers send home to their families.

About 85 percent of the people practice subsistence agriculture. National policy has been to encourage food self-sufficiency, and the main crops are maize, sorghum, and millet, with some rice and sugar. Some cotton is grown and exported. The northern and northeastern parts of the country are typical Sahel semi-desert suitable only for very limited cattle grazing. Further south are savannas, also subject to frequent drought and creeping desertification. Commercial agriculture is only possible in the country's three river valleys. There is some mining, principally for gold. Manufacturing employs less than 1.5 percent of the labor force.

The official language is French, although a large number of tribal languages are in common use. The majority of people practice animist (traditional) religions; about one-quarter of the population is Muslim and 10 percent Christian, principally Roman Catholic. The literacy rate is not much more than 10 percent. Life expectancy is only about forty-two years for men and forty-eight for women.

Historical Background

During the colonial era, France used Burkina Faso chiefly as a labor reserve. Beginning in 1919, the French authorities instituted a system of forced labor—which lasted until 1946—under which village chiefs were required to provide a quota of men to work for specific periods to ensure a flow of workers to other parts of France's African empire. While the majority of the population was used as semi-slave labor, France did, after 1946, educate a small elite, groomed to take over government after independence and to be amenable to continuing informal French control.

Upper Volta became independent on August 5, 1960. The first president, Maurice Yameogo, was surrounded by French advisers. Widespread dissatisfaction with government corruption and the obvious enrichment of Yameogo and his cronies served as the excuse for a military coup in 1966 headed by Colonel Sangoule Lamizana. Lamizana held power for fourteen years, periodically allowing limited political activity and then clamping down when he deemed things to be getting out of hand. Notably, in a country with almost no industry or industrial workers, labor unions headed by French-educated left-wing intellectuals were the most active of Lamizana's opponents. In fact, the overwhelming majority of union members were civil servants.

Nevertheless, it was not workers or bureaucrats but another military coup led by Colonel Saye Zerbo that ousted Lamizana in November 1980. Zerbo ruled through a thirty-one-member Military Committee for Recovering National Progress (CMRPN), among whose members were reform-minded, even

KEY DATES

1960	Burkino Faso, then known as Upper Volta, wins independence from France.
1966	Protesting corruption in civilian government, Colonel Sangoule Lamizana seizes power in the country's first military coup.
1980	Colonel Saye Zerbo ousts Lamizana in coup; Zerbo establishes the Military Committee for Recovering National Progress (CMRPN, its French acronym) as the governing body; CMRPN is made up of reform-minded military officers, including Thomas Sankara and Blaise Compaore.
1982	Zerbo is ousted in a coup by Major Jean-Baptiste Ouedraogo, who names Sankara prime minister in a leftist government, angering France.
1983	The French support an effort by Zerbo allies to seize Sankara, Campaore, and other revolutionary leaders; Campaore escapes and frees Sankara; in August, Sankara and Campaore seize power in a coup.
1984	Sankara establishes the National Revolutionary Council, launches anticorruption campaign, promotes national agricultural self-sufficiency, and changes the country's name to Burkina Faso.
1984–1987	Sankara's anticorruption campaign and land reform policies upset powerful interests in the country.
1987	Campaore seizes power; Sankara is murdered.

radical, young officers including future presidents Thomas Sankara and Blaise Compaore. Sankara acted as minister of information and gained local fame for such populist gestures as riding his bicycle to work and refusing the usual ministerial perks.

In November 1982, Zerbo, in turn, was ousted and replaced by Major Jean-Baptiste Ouedraogo, who named Sankara prime minister. Sankara dissolved the CMRPN and brought civilians, notably the Marxist-Leninist union leader Souman Toure, into the government. Evidently this turn to the left disturbed French security officials. In May 1983, French president François Mitterrand's adviser on African affairs, Guy Penne, arrived unannounced in Ouagadougou. Shortly afterward, allies of Zerbo seized Sankara, Compaore, and two other revolutionary officers. Compaore escaped, succeeded in gaining control of the country's major military base, and freed Sankara and the other two officers. In August, Sankara and Compaore led yet another coup and forced Ouedraogo's resignation.

The Sankara Years

Sankara, although pronouncing himself a Marxist-Leninist on taking power at the head of the National Revolutionary Council (CNR, its French acronym), was basically a populist reformer with a genuine hatred of corruption. He considered it wrong, in a country where the vast majority were desperately poor, that anyone, no matter how the wealth was gained, could be rich. He assumed, in most cases correctly, that the wealthy of Upper Volta had not earned their wealth honestly. His anti-corruption campaign took particular aim at civil servants. He was determined that they not set themselves up as a well-remunerated educated elite, lording it over the illiterate masses. To show he meant business, he organized Popular Revolutionary Tribunals (TPR) to conduct show trials of the corrupt. Zerbo and other high officials were subsequently convicted by these courts.

Sankara cracked down on the bureaucracy. For example, in 1984, Sankara prohibited the wearing of expensive foreign clothing by civil servants, making them wear clothing made of Burkinade cotton, woven and tailored locally. He also prohibited any civil servant, regardless of rank, from using any automobile larger than a Renault 5. These restrictions resulted in bitter enmity from the civil servants, which would later contribute to his downfall.

A brilliant public speaker and self-publicist, Sankara not only endeared himself to the masses of Upper Volta, which he renamed Burkina Faso (Land of Incorruptible Men) in August 1984, he quickly became something of a cult figure among nationalistic young people throughout Africa. At the same time, he was feared and loathed by Africa's "big men," the postcolonial dictators who flaunted their new wealth while their countries remained impoverished.

Sankara's economic policy stressed food self-sufficiency. Key to this was developing new water resources, and a system of reservoirs was begun. More immediately, he ordered cutbacks on cotton production, ending the government incentives paid to cotton growers and requiring that more of the fertile land along the country's rivers be turned over to food production. He also severely limited imports of luxury foods. Real progress was made against tremendous odds as Burkina Faso was almost able to eliminate food imports in 1985. After that, however, population growth, desertification, and a resumption of cotton exporting resulted in huge food deficits.

Another Sankara economic objective was to develop major manganese deposits in the north. However, the only rail line in the country ran south from Ouagadougou to Côte d'Ivoire, and the investment required to reach the deposits caused foreign investors to shy away.

Sankara's social programs emphasized health care and education. Here again he was frustrated. It proved easy to build schools and clinics in the villages but almost impossible to staff them with qualified teachers and health care workers. A number of Cuban doctors provided assistance, but there were never enough.

Throughout, Sankara preached self-sufficiency. He was outspoken in his denunciations of foreign aid missions. Typically, he was offended by the contrast between the living standards of foreign aid mission employees and those of the people they were ostensibly assisting. He believed that far too great a percentage of foreign aid benefited the aid workers and the local elites they employed. In an address to the UN General Assembly shortly after taking power, he said: "Few other countries have been inundated with all types of aid as mine has been. This aid is supposed to favor development. You will look in vain for any signs of anything connected with development."

In turning to countries such as Cuba, China, and Libya for guidance and assistance while publicly denouncing French imperialism, Sankara made numerous foreign enemies. The United States drastically reduced its economic assistance to show its displeasure.

By 1987, Sankara's personal popularity was still high among poor citizens, who were grateful that he had passed a tax relief program and granted women the right to own property. Nevertheless, he had clearly lost most of his support in the military and the civil service. His puritanical intolerance for corruption offended the ambitious, and land reform angered the rich landowners; even the Marxist-Leninists were outraged. They hoped to act as a revolutionary vanguard, but instead were being sent off to work on village construction projects. In May 1987, a major tax fraud investigation led to the closure of many small businesses. In the same month, civil service trade union officials, who had led protests against job cutbacks and other austerity measures, were arrested for "counter-revolutionary activities."

On October 15, 1987, Sankara, age thirty-seven, was murdered, probably by order of Blaise Compaore, his one-time comrade. Thirteen members of the CNR died with him.

After Sankara

Compaore, announcing establishment of a new Popular Front (FP), dissolved the CNR and denounced Sankara, even while declaring he would continue to pursue his revolutionary objectives. It soon became clear, however, that the age of reform was over. Among Compaore's first acts was to accept a gift of a fleet of armored Alfa Romeo cars from Libya's Muammar Qaddafi.

The traditional left was pacified by emphasizing top-down control of local development work instead of Sankara's insistence on local control and involvement. The traditional right—village chiefs in the rural areas and businessmen in the cities—were quietly notified that their freedom of action had been restored. Foreign powers, offended by Sankara's often strident anti-imperialist rhetoric, also found Compaore much friendlier. Although retaining ties to Libya, Burkina Faso reestablished relations with Israel and broke relations with China to recognize Taiwan. Finally, in a gesture to the memory of Sankara, in 1991, Compaore raised a memorial tomb to the former leader in Ouagadougou.

David MacMichael

See also: Coups; Ivory Coast: Civil Disorder Since 1999.

Bibliography

Baxter, Joan, and Keith Somerville. "Burkina Faso." In *Benin, the Congo, Burkina Faso*, ed. Bogdan Szajkowski. London and New York: Pinter, 1989.

BURUNDI: Ethnic Strife Since 1962

TYPE OF CONFLICT: Ethnic and Religious

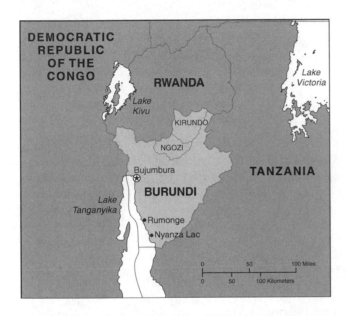

Burundi, like its next-door neighbor Rwanda, has been wracked by genocidal conflict between the two dominant ethnic groups, the Tutsi and the Hutu. In Rwanda, at least half a million Tutsi died in a genocidal slaughter in 1994. Burundi's mass killings came earlier: one in 1972, in which more than 100,000 Hutu were killed, and another in 1988, in which tens of thousands of Hutu were killed. Since 1988, ethnic warfare in Burundi has smoldered on, with the death toll approaching 200,000.

Journalists blamed the killings on inevitable ethnic strife between "ancestral enemies," but this explanation was overly facile. Most African countries have an ethnic mixture at least as complex as that of Burundi, yet they have managed to avoid the internecine murders that plagued both Burundi and Rwanda. Furthermore, it was impossible to accurately characterize Hutu and Tutsi as ancestral enemies. The roots of their animosity did lie in the past, but they were tangled.

Historical Background

In the 1930s, about 14 percent of the indigenous populations of Burundi were Tutsi, 85 percent were Hutu, and Twa pygmies made up the remaining 1 percent. These figures do not take into account the sizable immigrant community in Burundi. The origins of the two ethnic groups is unclear, but oral legend suggests that the Hutu may have arrived first, displacing the original Twa pygmies, and were in turn followed by the Tutsi immigrants from the north. The first reliable historical accounts come from European invaders in the nineteenth century. They found that the Tutsi in Rwanda had forced the Hutu into a subsidiary economic and political position, with Tutsi kings, chiefs, and their families dominating a Hutu peasant class. In Burundi, the situation was more complex. Tutsi tended to dominate, but Hutu chiefs still survived, and a powerful Hutu clan might have substantially more prestige and wealth than a poor Tutsi clan. Furthermore, a third class of princes, Ganwa, arose and were viewed as separate from both Hutu and Tutsi.

Despite the ethnic and class divisions between Tutsi and Hutu, their history saw substantial intermingling; Hutu and Tutsi married, merged languages and culture, yet never quite merged into one ethnic group. The Tutsi remained dominant, but it was possible for a Hutu through marriage or clan membership to be accepted as Tutsi and for a Tutsi who had suffered misfortune to sink down to Hutu status. The designations "Tutsi" and "Hutu" became as much caste or class categories as ethnic labels. The situation was also complicated by the Ganwa princely caste. The Ganwa appealed to both Tutsi and Hutu for support, and political conflict was based on Ganwa rivalries, not ethnic divisions.

The Germans, who ruled Burundi and Rwanda from 1897 to 1916, accentuated the existing differences between Tutsi and Hutu. Viewing Rwanda through the lens of nineteenth-century European prejudices, the Germans saw the Tutsi, who tended to be taller and more "European" in appearance than their Hutu neighbors, as obviously superior and deserving

KEY DATES

1962 Burundi gains independence from Belgium on July 1 under Tutsi rule.

1965 A Tutsi refugee from neighboring Rwanda assassinates the Hutu prime minister of Burundi in January; in May elections, Hutu win, but King Mwambutsa IV appoints a Tutsi prime minister; Hutu military officers attempt to overthrow the government in October.

1966 The Tutsi-controlled military overthrows the monarchy and establishes a republic; over the next six years, the Tutsi purge the Hutu from the army.

1972 Uprising by the Hutu in the south leads to a crackdown by the Tutsi government, resulting in roughly 100,000 Hutu deaths.

1988 Hutu in the northern part of the country rise up against the Tutsi government; hundreds of Tutsi are killed; Tutsi retaliation leads to reprisals in which 15,000 Hutu are killed; the military leader of Burundi, Pierre Buyoya, attempts to calm the situation by bringing more Hutu into government.

1993 After five years of Hutu–Tutsi clashes, elections are held in June, and Hutu candidate Melchior Ndadaye becomes president; in October, Tutsi military units seize the presidential palace and kill Ndadaye; a coalition government selects Hutu Cyprien Ntaryamira as president.

1994 Ntaryamira and Rwandan President Juvenal Habyarimana are killed when their plane is shot down in Rwanda, leading to Hutu genocide of over half a million Tutsi in Rwanda and an influx of 200,000 Tutsi refugees into Burundi; in October, Hutu and Tutsi politicians form a coalition government with a Hutu president and Tutsi prime minister.

1996 Tutsi military officers topple the coalition government and establish a military dictatorship.

2003 Hutu rebels sign a cease-fire with the government of Burundi, but sporadic fighting continues.

2005 Hutu parties win national elections but with guarantees for minority Tutsi representation.

---

of their higher status. The Germans seemed not to recognize that intermarriage and class mobility had already blurred physical differences between the two groups, making it very difficult to reliably identify a Tutsi or a Hutu from appearance alone. Prompted by their racial misreading of Rwandan society, the Germans favored the Tutsi ruling class, using them as their colonial puppets and proxies. The Tutsi were labeled a superior race descended from Ethiopian invaders, while the Hutu were categorized as an inferior Bantu people.

The Belgians, who took over Rwanda after World War I, went even further and issued identity cards that officially identified the ethnicity of each Rwandan as either Tutsi or Hutu. This policy exacerbated tensions between the two groups. Some Tutsis used their status to oppress Hutus, which naturally increased Hutu resentment.

Independence

Under pressure from the United Nations, the Belgians agreed to grant Burundi and Rwanda their independence in 1962. The government was to be a constitutional monarchy, with the traditional Burundi royal clan providing the kings. In the years leading up to independence, two main political parties were created. The first was the Union pour le Progrès National (UPRONA). UPRONA, led by Prince Louis Rwagasore—a member of the Ganwa class and the eldest son of Burundi's king, Mwambutsa IV—was a progressive nationalist party that advocated uniting all sections of society under a single banner. Its rival was the Parti Démocrate Chrétien (PDC), a more conservative party with strong ties to the Belgian administration.

The Belgian colonial administration favored the PDC over UPRONA, but Rwagasore was extremely popular among both Hutu and Tutsi. In the pre-independence election held in September 1961, his party won fifty-eight out of sixty-four seats in the vote for a new assembly. Two weeks later, on October 13, Rwagasore was shot by a Greek assassin who had been hired by the PDC. There was strong evidence that the Belgian authorities had some connection to the assassination. They had thought that Rwagasore and UPRONA were too radical and suspected them of having Communist sympathies—a completely erroneous belief.

On July 1, 1962, Burundi achieved a peaceful transition to independence. But without the unifying force of Rwagasore, politics in Burundi became increasingly polarized. King Mwambutsa IV attempted to give positions in his government to both Tutsi and Hutu, but both resented what they felt was favoritism for the other.

Polarization between the Hutu and Tutsi of Burundi was increased by a revolution in neighboring Rwanda, where ethnic divisions had always been much more important. Chafing under Tutsi domination, the Hutu of Rwanda had created an avowedly ethnic party, the Parti du Mouvement de l'Emancipation du Peuple Hutu (PARMEHUTU). PARMEHUTU led a 1961 revolution that ended the Tutsi control of the country and went on to eliminate Tutsi from almost all positions of importance.

In Burundi, many Hutu looked at events in Rwanda with envy. Hutu politicians began to campaign on a populist platform that advocated an end to Tutsi control in Burundi. Similarly, Tutsi in Burundi saw the Rwanda revolution as a sign that their own power might be in danger—their fears fanned by an influx of Tutsi refugees from Rwanda. Tutsis reacted by attacking all Hutu parties that they perceived as ethnically based. Thus, although Burundi had not had the same kind of ethnic polarization as Rwanda did, events in Rwanda pushed Hutu and Tutsi into becoming more like their neighbors, thereby helping to fulfill their own prophecies of ethnic conflict. UPRONA, the party that had unified Burundi, began to lose its Hutu supporters and become a Tutsi-dominated party.

Martin Ndayahoze, a moderate Hutu army officer, described the way in which unscrupulous politicians used ethnicity to gain power: "If they are Tutsi, they denounce a Hutu peril which must be countered. If they are Hutu, they unveil a Tutsi apartheid which must be combated." Ndayahoze was killed by Tutsi in 1972.

Tutsi Take Control

In January 1965 tensions were increased in Burundi when a Tutsi refugee from Rwanda assassinated the Hutu prime minister. In new elections held in May 1965, the Hutu won a victory, but then were incensed when King Mwambutsa IV chose a Tutsi prime minister. Hutu officers within the army and police reacted in October by attempting to overthrow the government. Their attempt was suppressed, and the Tutsi victors took advantage of their success to seize many of the leading Hutu politicians and military officers and have them executed.

The attempted coup and its suppression led to upheaval in Burundi's countryside. Through October and November, roving bands of Hutu attacked Tutsi homes and in turn were targeted by Tutsi troops and paramilitary political gangs, who also attacked innocent Hutu civilians. The Hutu, their leadership gone, received the worst of the violence; thousands were killed, many of them soldiers in the army slaughtered by their own commanders.

In 1966 the now completely Tutsi-controlled army overthrew the monarchy—King Mwambutsa IV had fled the country during the failed October 1965 coup—and declared Burundi a republic. The new government was completely dominated by Tutsi officers and politicians, one of whom, Michel Micombero, was chosen to be president. The monarchy, which had given Hutu and Tutsi a shared symbol of unity and authority, was gone.

1972 Massacre

From 1966 to 1972, Tutsi officers steadily purged the Hutu from the army. Some Hutu were included in the National Revolutionary Council (NRC), which ruled the country, and although the NRC denied that it was an ethnically based party, it was clear that part of their agenda was to make sure that Hutu had no more than a token presence at the highest levels of government. This Tutsi elitism inspired unrest among most Hutu, who felt that they were living under a system of ethnic apartheid.

The animosities between Tutsi and Hutu fed off each other. When Hutu radicals accused the Tutsi of ethnic elitism, the Tutsi denounced the Hutu for practicing ethnic politics and then further tightened their grip on power. Extremists on both sides gained support by becoming even more extreme. Tutsi-Hutu hatreds, while having some historical roots, were largely manufactured by opportunistic politicians.

Hutu fear and hatred escalated into violence in late April 1972 with an uprising in the southern part of Burundi, traditionally a region dominated by the Hutu. In what was probably a planned uprising, Hutu seized armories in several southern towns, including Rumonge and Nyanza-Lac, and started killing any Tutsi they could find (as well as some Hutu who refused to join their rebellion). Two or three thousand Tutsi died during the week-long revolt.

The Tutsi government, led by President Micombero, responded to the Hutu rebellion with a coordinated attack on the entire Hutu elite. In May, while Tutsi troops were crushing the rebels, Hutu elsewhere who had not taken part in the uprising were rounded up and executed. Even Hutu who had helped fight against the rebels, as many had, were arrested and killed.

The Tutsi carrying out these attacks came from the army and the Jeunesse Nationaliste Rwagasore (JNR), a Tutsi UPRONA youth group (by this time UPRONA was an exclusively Tutsi party). The murders were carried out with guns, clubs, and machetes. Those Tutsi who protested against the killings risked being killed themselves.

Although any Hutu was vulnerable during the massacres, the Tutsi particularly targeted the educated classes. Teachers at all levels were killed, as were their students, including those in primary school. Tutsi students helped the executioners find their victims by making lists of their Hutu classmates. A U.S. embassy report read, "Trucks ply the road to the airport every night with a fresh contribution [of bodies] to the mass grave."

Over the course of May and June the Tutsi killed at least 100,000 Hutu. This number amounted to about 2 percent of the Hutu population but included almost every educated Hutu. The Tutsi extremists of President Micombero's government had succeeded in wiping out those Hutu who would have been best able to resist Tutsi control. The massacres left behind a legacy of hatred that would haunt Burundi.

The Tutsi State

In 1976, Micombero was overthrown by Jean-Baptiste Bagaza, another Tutsi officer and a cousin of Micombero's. Bagaza attempted to maintain Tutsi power through strict bureaucratic controls placed on society. Education was restricted so that Hutu, still the vast majority of the population, were only a minority in secondary schools. Churches and missionaries were restricted because Bagaza and the Tutsi suspected them of being sources of dangerous ideas among the Hutu. Bagaza also attempted, with limited success, to force farmers to live in villages so that a closer watch could be kept upon them. In an attempt to eradicate Hutu "tribalism," Bagaza also forbade all mention of ethnicity, in public or in private. This policy maintained Tutsi control without ever admitting that there were any such groups as Tutsi or Hutu.

Officially, anyone was allowed to be a part of Burundi's government, but in practice it was almost completely managed by Tutsi. Most government ministers were Tutsi, and the thirty-member military council that ran the country was entirely Tutsi.

Bagaza's policies were unpopular among both Hutu and Tutsi. His regime was handicapped by its nature: It was difficult to lead a system that enforced apartheid while never admitting that apartheid existed. Extremist Tutsi wanted more limitations put on the Hutu. Hutu and moderate Tutsi wanted the government to attempt reconciliation and reintegration of the two ethnicities.

In 1987, Bagaza was overthrown by another coup led by a Tutsi army officer, Pierre Buyoya.

Buyoya's Regime

Buyoya, who ruled from 1987 to 1993, attempted to institute a more flexible approach to the problem of Hutu-Tutsi relations. He permitted greater freedom of speech and allowed ethnic terms to be discussed openly again. Many political prisoners, mostly Hutu, were also released. Buyoya argued that Tutsi and Hutu had to cooperate for Burundi to prosper. Finally, Buyoya ended the restrictions on religion that the previous regime had imposed. However, beyond a few superficialities, Buyoya's regime was not substantially different from that of Bagaza before him. Tutsi still dominated the army, the civil service, and the judiciary.

In August 1988, frustrated by what they perceived as a lack of change—especially after their hopes had been raised by Buyoya's promises—Hutu in the northern provinces of Ngozi and Kirundo rose up and killed hundreds of Tutsi. This uprising, unlike the one in 1972, seemed to have been completely unplanned. The Hutus who revolted suspected that extremist Tutsi were planning another massacre and staged a preemptive strike. The Hutu fears were not completely groundless. Many ethnic clashes had occurred in the early part of 1988, often initiated by Tutsi extremists, and Tutsi army units had seemed suspiciously active in the two provinces.

The murders of the Tutsi were carried out with great brutality, and the Tutsi reaction was even more brutal. Some 15,000 Hutu were killed in the reprisals that followed. Unlike 1972, this Tutsi response did not seem to be organized from the center; rather, it was a combined action from individual Tutsi commanders.

Buyoya's response to the 1988 massacres was unusual for Burundi. Rather than clamp down harder on the Hutu, Buyoya accelerated his liberalization policies. Buyoya brought a number of Hutu into his government and appointed a Hutu as prime minister. He also created a commission composed of an equal number of Hutu and Tutsi members to investigate the massacres. Buyoya's decision to open his government was probably caused in part by foreign pressure: international opinion was extremely critical of the Tutsi policies, and Buyoya risked a loss in foreign aid payments if he did not moderate Tutsi practices.

Ethnic friction continued in the early 1990s, with the occasional flare-up of violence. Buyoya, however, continued to move Burundi toward more openness. Under his guidance, Hutu gradually took over a majority of cabinet posts in the government. Finally, in June 1993, Buyoya allowed an open presidential election to be held. It was won by the Hutu candidate, Melchior Ndadaye, with 65 percent of the vote (Buyoya received 33 percent). Ndadaye's party, the Front pour la Démocratie au Burundi (FRODEBU), also won a majority of the seats in Burundi's legislature.

Chaos in Rwanda and Burundi

Ndadaye served as president for four months. Although the Hutu dominated the government, the Tutsi still controlled the army, and extremist officers resented Ndadaye's attempts to bring Hutu into the army. In October 1993, Tutsi army units seized the presidential palace and executed Ndadaye and other government leaders. The leaders of this coup were not backed by the rest of the army and were either put under arrest or forced to flee the country, but the damage caused by the coup was severe.

Ethnic violence by fearful Hutu and extremist Tutsi continued through 1993 and into 1994. The government was put back together with the ministers who were still alive. Moderates in the two major parties, the Hutu-dominated FRODEBU and the Tutsi-controlled UPRONA, put together a governing coalition in an effort to restore order. The coalition government picked a Hutu president, Cyprien Ntaryamira, and a Tutsi prime minister, Anatole Kanyenkiko. Their attempts to end the violence were handicapped by the Tutsi-controlled army's reluctance to search for those within its ranks who had helped the October 1993 attempted coup. The Hutu suspected, probably correctly, that the army was protecting some of its own commanders who had been involved in the coup attempt. Hutu in the countryside remained afraid of another Tutsi-led genocidal slaughter. The reaction of peasants in the villages was to target each other. Hundreds were killed every week.

In a further attempt to calm the situation, the president of Rwanda, Juvenal Habyarimana, and Burundi's president, Ntaryamira, both Hutu, met in an international summit in Tanzania. On their return, their plane was shot down above the Kigali airport in Rwanda. Who assassinated the two presidents has not been discovered as of early 2006. It was assumed by many that Hutu extremists in Rwanda had decided that the two men must die in order to prevent further reconciliation between Hutu and Tutsi. If the assassins were Hutu, where they acquired the

Burundian soldiers check the papers of Hutu leaving the country for Zaire in 1995. The growing number of Hutu exiles in Zaire raised an armed force that slipped back across the border to carry out guerrilla attacks against the entrenched Tutsi. *(Alexander Joe/AFP/Getty Images)*

equipment to shoot down a jet airliner was unknown. An April 6, 1994, report by the French paper *Le Figaro* claimed that French officers admitted having sold the missiles to the Hutu as part of a general policy of supporting Rwanda's Hutu-controlled government. A retired French minister responded by suggesting that the United States had been responsible. This seemed unlikely, particularly as other sources had proved that France continued to supply the Hutu with arms even after some of their anti-Tutsi intentions had become clear.

In Rwanda, the double assassination was the trigger for a wave of violence that killed at least half a million Tutsi. In Burundi, the government, now shared between Tutsi and Hutu, was able to prevent any large-scale violence from breaking out. Small-scale violence, however, continued.

Violence and Breakdown

In October 1994, the government—again a coalition between FRODEBU and UPRONA—appointed another Hutu, Sylvestre Ntibantunganya, as president; the Tutsi Kanyenkiko continued on as prime minister. Although it was clear that some elements among both Tutsi and Hutu desired an end to the bloodshed between the two ethnic groups, extremists on both sides remained eager to undercut their efforts.

Particularly troublesome was the influx of some 200,000 Hutu refugees from Rwanda. In July 1994 a Tutsi-led army defeated the Hutu government of Rwanda, and hundreds of thousands of Hutu fled, fearing reprisals. The violence in Rwanda had been greater than in Burundi, and the refugees helped to raise Burundi Hutu fears—and may have contributed directly to violence in Burundi. Assassinations of government officials and murders of civilians of both ethnicities continued, with women and children being prime targets.

Hutu in exile in Zaire organized an armed militia to fight against the Tutsi army. The guerrilla group, Force pour la Défense de la Démocratie (FDD), which was the military wing of the extremist Hutu Conseil National pour la Défense de la Démocratie (CNDD), slipped its men across the border to attack Tutsi villagers. The Tutsi army responded with campaigns against the Hutu-occupied suburbs of Bujumbura, Burundi's capital. By 1996, Burundi was becoming segregated, with the larger towns and Bujumbura becoming all Tutsi, while the countryside was transformed into Hutu-only territory.

In July 1996, the Tutsi army toppled Ntibantunganya's government (Ntibantunganya fled to the American embassy) and replaced it with a military dictatorship led, again, by Pierre Buyoya. The world, tired of the killing in Burundi, responded with economic sanctions against the country, but Buyoya refused to step down. The Hutu-dominated party, FRODEBU, now excluded from the government, became more radical and militant. Some of its members joined the CNDD in calling for an armed struggle against the Tutsi.

Possible Return to Peace

In August 2000, most of the political parties of Burundi agreed to an end to hostilities and a gradual return to democracy. The two holdouts were the Hutu party CNDD-FDD and the extremist Hutu Forces of National Liberation (FNL). However, the CNDD-FDD finally signed a cease-fire with Buyoya's government in 2003. Domitien Ndayizeye, the leader of FRODEBU, the Tutsi party, became president of Burundi in late 2003.

The radical FNL continued to refuse integration into the peace process and rejected the return to democracy. In August 2004, the FNL killed 152 Tutsi refugees from the Congo who had been staying at a camp in western Burundi. The government attempted to arrest the heads of the FNL and legally classified the FNL as a terrorist organization. The FNL embarked on a campaign of armed rebellion, chiefly in the countryside surrounding the capital. In 2005 the government concluded a cease-fire with the FNL, but hostilities did not entirely end.

Long-awaited national elections were held in the summer of 2005 and were won by the Hutu CNDD-FDD. The head of the group was Pierre Nkurunziza, who was overwhelmingly elected president by the country's CNDD-FDD–dominated parliament. However, Tutsis received guaranteed numbers of governmental positions and significant control of the army. President Nkurunziza took office on August 26, 2005, in a ceremony attended by eight African heads of state, including the presidents of South Africa and Kenya.

Nkurunziza said that his priorities were restoring law and order to the country and preventing further ethnic conflict. As the son of a Hutu father and a Tutsi mother, he seemed well suited to achieve that end, according to observers. Without law and order, he argued, the international aid that was essential to the economy could not be used effectively. The government also hoped to reestablish Burundi's now moribund cash crops of tea and coffee, a key to its longer-term prospects. In regards to Burundi's ethnic woes, Hutu extremists (as embodied by the FNL) remained opposed to the political settlement and considered the current government to be imposed by outside international forces. Some experts suggested that the FNL was seeking a general amnesty before it would sign any agreement to end its rebellion. In any case, the FNL reminded Burundi of its power in August 2005 by bombing a market in Bujumbura one day before Nkurunziza's inauguration.

Carl Skutsch and Charles Allan

See also: Ethnic and Religious Conflicts; Congo, Democratic Republic of: Kabila Uprising, 1996–1997; Congo, Democratic Republic of: Invasions and Internal Strife, 1998; Rwanda: Civil War and Genocide Since 1991.

Bibliography

Chrétien, Jean-Pierre. Trans. Scott Straus. *The Great Lakes of Africa: Two Thousand Years of History.* New York: Zone Books, 2003.

Eggers, Ellen K. *Historical Dictionary of Burundi.* Lanham, MD: Scarecrow Press, 1997.

Lemarchand, René. *Burundi: Ethnic Conflict and Genocide.* Washington, DC: Woodrow Wilson Center, 1996.

CENTRAL AFRICAN REPUBLIC:
Coups Since 1966

TYPE OF CONFLICT: Coups, Left and Right
PARTICIPANT: France

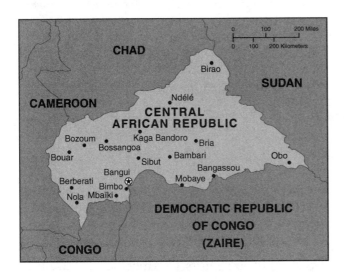

The Central African Republic (CAR), formerly part of French Equatorial Africa, has a land area of 240,500 square miles and a population estimated at 3.9 million. On the south it shares a 2,200-mile border with the Republic of Congo and the Democratic Republic of Congo (formerly Zaire), on the north a 1,400-mile border with Chad, and on the east one of equal length with Sudan; on the west it has a short border with Cameroon. As its name implies, the nation lies almost in the center of Africa. The capital is Bangui, with a population of about 700,000.

Subsistence agriculture is the major economic activity. Coffee, cotton, and tobacco are grown for export. The major earner of foreign exchange is diamond mining. There is some lumbering, but the country's primitive road network and distance from large markets limits this enterprise. This remoteness may be an economic blessing because the combination of a relatively small population and the difficult access to natural resources has allowed the preservation of great areas of rain forest and animal life.

National leaders see ecotourism as a potential industry and have adopted a strong policy to preserve the environment.

The CAR has about thirty different tribal groups, but, unusual for Africa, only one tribal language, Sango, is used by almost the whole population. Life expectancy is low—forty-eight years for men and about fifty-three for women—and AIDS is widespread.

Very important for any consideration of the Central African Republic is that it is the main African base for the former colonial power, France. During World War II, Bangui was the headquarters for General Jacques-Philippe LeClerc's Free French forces. Today, France maintains about 1,200 elite troops in the country. For military reasons, France has considerable influence over CAR affairs and a strong interest in seeing that order is maintained.

Historical Background

The area of Bangui apparently had an advanced Neolithic culture and was later part of several important medieval African kingdoms. During the sixteenth, seventeenth, and eighteenth centuries, the area and its inhabitants suffered from the depredations of slave raiders attacking from Chad and Sudan. In 1889, France established the town of Bangui and, in 1907, formally set up the colony of Oubangui-Chari (later the CAR) as part of French Equatorial Africa. French rule was harsh, and the exploited native plantation workers rose continually in revolt.

World War II produced great changes in French Equatorial Africa. Many local men were recruited into the French military and fought with distinction in campaigns in North Africa and Syria. To ensure their loyalty, General Charles de Gaulle convened a conference at Brazzaville in 1944 at which plans were

KEY DATES

1960	The Central African Republic gains its independence from France.
1965	General Jean Bedel Bokassa seizes power in a military coup.
1976	Bokassa declares an end to the republic and announces the formation of the Central African Empire, with himself as emperor.
1979	Responding to continuing repression by Bokassa, France sends paratroopers to oust the emperor, revive the republic, and place David Dacko in power.
1981	Dacko's government is overthrown in a military coup led by General André Kolingba.
1993	Elections return the country to civilian rule with Ange-Félix Patasse voted in as president.
1996–1998	Several army mutinies prompt France to send in troops; they are soon replaced by a peacekeeping force of African nations, and finally UN troops.
2003	A military coup led by Kolingba overthrows the unpopular Patasse regime.
2005	The country returns to civilian rule following the election of François Bozize as president.

made to abolish the worst features of colonial rule. These plans were incorporated in the French constitution of 1946, which granted limited voting rights and representation in the French National Assembly to the inhabitants of French Equatorial Africa (now consisting of Gabon, the CAR, the Republic of Congo, and part of Cameroon).

The first native African deputy from French Equatorial Africa was Barthelmy Boganda, who was also the first such person ever ordained as a Catholic priest. Boganda, very much a francophile (he married a French woman after leaving the priesthood), returned to French Equatorial Africa from service in Paris disillusioned. The French people, he had learned, had little interest in the well-being of Africans. Back in his native Ubangi region of French Equatorial Africa in 1949, he began grassroots organizing. His Movement for the Social Evolution of Black Africa (MESAN, its French acronym) worked for full political and social equality between whites and blacks. Eventually, he looked to create a single

nation within the French Commonwealth, including all the former colonies of French Equatorial Africa. By the 1950s, Boganda had become the leading native political figure in the region and a hero to black Africans everywhere.

In 1958, de Gaulle, back in power after resigning in 1946, established the Fifth French Republic, whose constitution provided for the free association of autonomous republics, with France, of course, as the senior partner. Boganda went to Paris to seek de Gaulle's endorsement of his plan for a United States of Latin Africa, which, besides the states of French Equatorial Africa, would include Rwanda, Burundi, the Belgian Congo, Angola, and Cameroon. De Gaulle was cool to the idea, as were the leaders of the other colonies of French Equatorial Africa, who were not eager to give up their local power. Boganda had to accept the situation. In December 1958, he proclaimed the constitution for an independent Central African Republic, with elections scheduled for April 1959. Boganda died in a suspicious plane crash shortly before the election, however, and the CAR began life without its recognized leader.

Boganda's chief aide and obvious successor, Abel Goumba, seemed positioned to become the first president of the CAR. However, Paris and the local French residents saw him as too nationalistic and radical. Through judicious bribery, they persuaded the interim assembly to select a young cousin of Boganda's, David Dacko, who was suspected by many of having engineered the crash that killed Boganda. Dacko, backed by the money of French commercial interests, rapidly made himself dictator. His period of rule has been described as an orgy of corruption. By 1965, Dacko's combination of political authoritarianism and economic incompetence had brought the country to bankruptcy and the edge of revolt. His French backers, fearful of a left-wing revolution or the accession of the independent Abel Goumba (whom Dacko had imprisoned for two years), ordered Dacko to step down and arranged for a staged coup on New Year's Day 1966 that would replace him with the commander of the gendarmerie, Jean Izamo, a man they considered safe.

Emperor Bokassa

Left out of the calculations was the commander of the army, Colonel Jean Bedel Bokassa. A World War II veteran who had become a lieutenant in the French army in Vietnam and was supposedly a nephew of Boganda, Bokassa learned of the plot. He feared that the CAR army, which numbered only about 3,000, would be displaced by the gendarmerie and that Izamo planned to have him assassinated. On New Year's Eve, he invited Izamo to army headquarters and arrested him. Meanwhile, he had his troops seize the airport to prevent the landing of any French forces. Dacko, seemingly unaware, was busy packing and getting ready to be "surprised" by Izamo. Instead, he was captured by Bokassa and, early in the morning of January 1, turned the government over to him. Bokassa declared that he acted to save Dacko's life from Izamo, who was acting for Communist China. The embarrassed French accepted the situation in silence.

Early on, Bokassa was popular. The removal of Dacko was welcome, and both Bokassa and his chief assistant, Captain Alexandre Banza, represented the Mbakas, a large tribal group that had been excluded from the Dacko government. France soon learned that it had little to fear from Bokassa, who actually

Self-proclaimed emperor Jean-Bedel Bokassa of the Central African Republic spent an estimated one-third of the national budget on a lavish coronation ceremony in December 1977. *(Pierre Guillaud/AFP/Getty Images)*

asked for and received a contingent of French paratroopers to serve as his personal security guard. Throughout his regime, monetary and technical assistance from France rose steadily.

Banza, promoted to lieutenant colonel, led an anticorruption campaign that discomfited entrenched interests and made him unpopular with his brother officers, who expected to profit from an army-run regime. Bokassa eased him out of office after a year and, in 1969, had him executed for plotting against the government. By 1967, it was clear that the promised elections would not take place and the government had been turned into the private business of Bokassa and his clique, with the 4,000-member civil service essentially functioning as his employees. There was little protest. French interests were served; the bureaucracy, or some of it, was able to enjoy a European lifestyle; and the majority of the population was almost entirely unaffected by what went on in Bangui's dingy corridors of power.

In 1972, Bokassa declared himself president for life. In March 1975, French President Valéry Giscard d'Estaing apparently endorsed the arrangement when he honored Bokassa with a state visit. The two reportedly developed a personal friendship.

However, cracks in Bokassa's personal regime were already visible. Between late 1974 and early 1976, a series of coup attempts were staged by dissatisfied elements in the military and the bureaucracy. Bokassa, who was showing signs of psychotic behavior, responded on December 4, 1976, by proclaiming the establishment of the Central African Empire with himself as the emperor, and his wife, Catherine, as empress. A year later, he spent one-third of the national budget on an elaborate coronation ceremony, duplicating the expenditure the following year with the celebration of his anniversary on the throne. This created a serious financial situation by the end of 1978, as the regime found itself unable to pay government salaries or, just as important, student stipends. These stipends served as a sort of general welfare system for much of the population; for some families, student support was their largest source of cash income.

In January 1979, Bokassa compounded his difficulties by ordering that all students in secondary schools had to purchase and wear a school uniform made in a factory owned by the Empress Catherine. This produced genuine popular demonstrations. Students in the streets cried, "Down with the uniforms," and "Down with Bokassa," and began looting stores. Police and military units killed as many as 200 demonstrators. The emperor went on the radio to pronounce the whole thing a Libyan and Soviet plot, but he also revoked the school uniform decree.

France quickly provided enough cash to pay the student stipends and civil salaries. This move did not end the affair, however. University students and faculty denounced Bokassa's wealth. The army occupied the university in April and began a roundup of students suspected of disloyalty. Bokassa took part personally in the torture and killing of at least 100 young people and had them secretly buried in a mass grave. When Amnesty International published the shocking news, the French public was outraged, and even Giscard was embarrassed. Some way had to be found to get rid of Bokassa. Like Dacko before him, he was pressured to resign. Unlike Dacko, he refused.

Finally, on September 20, 1979, French paratroopers landed again in Bangui, this time "to reestablish the Republic." Bokassa was conveniently in Libya, avoiding the embarrassment of being arrested by the French. The paratroopers brought with them former president Dacko, the same man they had covertly ousted in 1966, who incidentally had been serving most recently as Bokassa's personal counselor. Almost the first act of the French occupiers was to remove the CAR national archives to Paris, since they might reveal the sometimes close relationship between Bokassa and Valéry Giscard d'Estaing. Bokassa himself was denied asylum in France but was received "out of Christian charity" by President Félix Houphouët-Boigny of Côte d'Ivoire.

Dacko in Power

Dacko was immediately provided with the equivalent of $17 million in French francs. French troops remained to protect him from the attempts of Goumba, who had never taken part in the Bokassa government and had organized a popular political movement in Bangui, and Ange-Félix Patasse, a populist who had developed a following among students and the unemployed. Patasse had been imprisoned several times by Bokassa.

Throughout 1980, Dacko showed his usual ineptness. There were show trials and executions of some of Bokassa's intimates (widely believed to have been carried out to prevent them from revealing what they knew about Dacko's own involvement with the former emperor).

In December 1980, a new constitution was issued, providing for a multiparty system, protections for human rights, and a six-year term for a president, who had the power to appoint a prime minister. Voters approved this in a February 1981 referendum. In the subsequent presidential election, Patasse was undoubtedly the winner. However, Dacko, again with at least the tacit blessing of the Giscard government in Paris, was found to have gained just over 50 percent of the vote. But the results were disputed, and Patasse's supporters rioted, giving Dacko the opportunity to declare a state of emergency and to announce the indefinite postponement of legislative elections. With the electoral defeat of Giscard in the French elections in May 1981, Dacko became desperate and resorted to even more dictatorial measures, declaring that the CAR would not be ready for democracy for another ten years. Patasse was arrested, and Goumba had to flee the country.

More Coups

The assumption of the French presidency by François Mitterrand spelled the end for Dacko. Another coup was arranged. This time, French-trained General André Kolingba, formerly the CAR's ambassador in West Germany and Canada, carried out the charade. He asked for and received Dacko's resignation on September 1, 1981, the day after Patasse, released from arrest, returned to Bangui, where he received a joyful welcome.

Kolingba's attempts to impose a regime of fiscal austerity soon brought the usual complaints from those elements accustomed to dining well at the public trough. On March 3, 1982, he barely suppressed a military coup attempt. As rioting broke out in Bangui, Patasse claimed that he was the legitimate president and that Kolingba should step down. Kolingba's response was to postpone any further elections until at least 1985. Patasse had to take asylum in the French embassy. In August, when Abel Goumba, who had been appointed head of the national university, enlisted French support for a more rapid return to constitutional rule, Kolingba had him tried and sentenced to prison for trying to destabilize the country. France disapproved, but short of withdrawing all financial support and seeing the country turn to Libya, it had to go along. The subsidies continued. In 1983, Paris even permitted Bokassa, who retained French citizenship, to come live in France, where he had enormous properties. In 1986, Bokassa returned to the CAR, where he was promptly imprisoned for life.

Under pressure to legitimize his rule, in May 1986, Kolingba created his own political party, the Central African Democratic Assembly, and promulgated a one-party constitution under which he was elected president for a six-year term. This device stalled serious demands for political change for four years. In 1990, a difficult year economically, his attempts to institute austerity measures and job cuts had the predictable result of producing strikes, demonstrations, and calls for political reform.

Elections

In March 1991, Kolingba agreed that the elections scheduled for October 1992 would be open to opposition parties. However, he refused to meet with the opposition to plan for them and then caused a crisis in mid-1992, when he canceled the scheduled elections, possibly on the advice of his cousin, Mobutu Sese Seko, the dictator of the Democratic Republic of the Congo (Zaire), and certainly in defiance of French pressure to move forward.

He may also have looked for support from the new conservative government that replaced Mitterrand in the spring of 1993, but Paris made it clear that there would be consequences if the process did not move forward quickly. The first round of elections was held on August 22, 1993, with four main parties competing: Patasse and the Central African People's Movement (MLPC), Goumba and the Concert of Democratic Forces (CDF), Dacko as an independent, and Kolingba now heading the Patriotic Front for Progress (FPP). Kolingba used the advantages of incumbency freely, flying around the country in the presidential helicopter and using strong-arm squads to harass opposition meetings. However, when the electoral commission issued the preliminary results on August 28, Kolingba was in fourth place, with a humiliating 11 percent. Immediately, he issued decrees prohibiting further publication of results unless they were certified by a supreme court judge. The opposition candidates threatened civil war if the results were not published immediately.

Again, it was French action that was decisive. All French financial aid was suspended immediately. Kolingba's French military security detail was withdrawn, as was his French doctor and, worst of all, his helicopter pilot. Mitterrand, still in office, telephoned personally to warn of worse to come. Kolingba withdrew his decree. The second round of voting went smoothly, and Patasse won the runoff over Goumba, 53.5 percent to 46.5 percent. Parliamentary elections also gave Patasse's MLPC the largest number of seats, with Goumba's CFD coming in second.

The transfer of power went smoothly, with Patasse naming a multiparty cabinet. Kolingba did not go altogether quietly. On September 1, he gave amnesty to all prisoners in the country's jails, including former emperor Bokassa, who had returned to the CAR in 1987. In addition, he decreed himself a generous pension and numerous other presidential perks. This caused some outrage because civil servants had not been paid for ten months.

In 1996–1997, the Patasse government experienced three mutinies, as soldiers engaged in rioting and looting over unpaid wages and discrimination against military officers from different ethnic groups.

French forces put down the uprisings and, fearing a return to fighting upon their withdrawal, were replaced by an African peacekeeping force composed of members of French-speaking African countries. That force occupied Bangui until 1998, when a UN peacekeeping mission took over.

The CAR's overall economic situation did not change greatly during the Patasse presidency. However, despite the occasional intensity of partisan battles in the parliament and cabinet, there was no reversion to authoritarian or one-man rule. One sign of mellowing was the return of Catherine Bokassa, the former empress, in late 1995, shortly after her husband suffered a brain hemorrhage and was allowed to return to France to die.

Despite President Patasse's popular anti-French rhetoric, he established civil relations with the conservative Chirac administration in Paris. In fact, the most serious threat to his presidency was an army mutiny in June 1996 that was put down by French troops.

Continuing unrest in the country prevented national elections from being held in August 1998, and the balloting in 1999 saw Patasse claim a second six-year term in the face of charges of electoral fraud. The Patasse government was plagued by the combined effects of the economic damage caused by the civil unrest, energy crises, and government mismanagement. The departure of the last of the UN forces in 2000 set the stage for a March 2001 coup attempt involving military forces led by Kolingba. The attempt was defeated by forces loyal to Patasse with the assistance of troops from Libya and a Congolese rebel movement (Movement for the Liberation of the Congo), following several days of heavy fighting.

In 2003, François Bozize led a successful coup against the widely unpopular Patasse, who was not in the country at the time. Patasse went into exile in Togo. Bozize and Patasse had a long history of rivalry. Not only had Bozize lost the presidential election to Patasse during the CAR's first democratic elections in 1993, but he was also the former chief of staff of the armed forces who had been fired by Patasse. Bozize had also been linked to an unsuccessful coup attempt in 2001. Between November 2001 and mid-2002, forces supporting Bozize had clashed sporadically with CAR forces along the border with Chad, the country to which Bozize had fled. Following the 2003 coup, Bozize declared himself president, dissolved the National Assembly, and suspended the constitution. He also pledged to work toward national reconciliation and to improve the country's human rights record. In December 2004, the country's new constitution was accepted through a referendum. Bozize also lived up to his commitment to restore democratic rule in the CAR and ran as an independent.

The elections of May 2005 ended two years of military rule. Bozize received more than 64 percent of votes in the second round of balloting against his challenger, former prime minister Martin Ziguele. Bozize immediately called for national unity and pledged a period of security for the coup-weary country. Despite his earlier promises, the human rights record of the Central African Republic remained troubling. Reports continued to cite instances of arbitrary detention, torture, and even extrajudicial killings. Journalists were also threatened for publishing articles critical of the government.

The prospects for continued peace in the CAR were tempered by the easy availability of illegal weapons throughout the country, a legacy of years of conflict. Armed groups remained active in the northern regions, and fighting caused thousands of civilians to flee into neighboring Chad. In addition, the diamond industries of the CAR remained a target for unscrupulous developers and corrupt government officials alike.

David MacMichael and Jeffrey A. Shantz

See also: Coups; Congo, Republic of: Civil Conflict, 1997.

Bibliography

Economic Intelligence Unit (EIU). Reports, 1993–1998. London: Economic Intelligence Unit, 1998.

Kalck, Pierre. *Historical Dictionary of the Central African Republic.* 3rd ed. Metuchen, NJ: Scarecrow Press, 2005.

O'Toole, Thomas. *The Central African Republic: The Continent's Hidden Heart.* Boulder, CO: Westview Press, 1986.

CHAD: Civil Wars, 1960s–1990s

TYPE OF CONFLICT: Ethnic and Religious
PARTICIPANTS: France; Libya

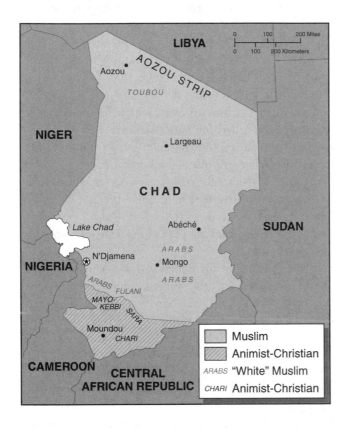

In many ways, Chad resembles its better-known neighbor of Sudan. The north was settled by a mix of nomadic peoples, some of them Arabs but mostly Muslims. The south was settled by black Africans in prehistoric times who focused on agricultural pursuits and were either animists or, later, Christians. After Chad's independence from France in 1960, its civil wars, like those of Sudan, were rooted in these north-south divisions.

There are also significant differences between the two countries. In Chad, the black south is more populous and powerful and has dominated much of the country's postwar history. Chad is also far poorer than Sudan. With much of its land consisting of the southern reaches of the Sahara Desert, and without any railroads or an effective river network for transportation,

Chad has remained one of the most backward countries in the world—and one of the most thinly populated, with 9.8 million people (according to a 2005 estimate) scattered across nearly 500,000 square miles.

Historical Background

Chad became a colony of France in 1913 after French expeditions and military forays into its territory that began in 1890. The borders defined by the colonial government bore no relation to any regional ethnic groupings. Indeed Chad had more than a dozen major ethnic groups and languages, with over 100 subgroups. This would later make post-independence governance difficult.

In 1958, France granted Chad autonomy, helped it to organize a political system based on the French model, and granted it full independence in August 1960. Unlike many other colonial powers, France maintained close ties with its ex-colonies, and Chad signed treaties that kept it within France's economic orbit. It also provided for French military aid upon request by the Chadian government.

François (N'Garta) Tombalbaye, a trade union leader from the black south, was chosen as Chad's first president. In 1963, Tombalbaye outlawed all parties but his own Parti Progressiste Tchadien (PPT), turning the country into a one-party personal dictatorship. He justified his actions by claiming that he was simply preempting a Muslim coup that was being planned. Dozens of Muslims were arrested and charged with conspiring against the state. Both northern Muslims and southerners were originally part of Tombalbaye's government, but after 1963 he gradually eliminated the northerners, packing his cabinet with his cronies. The conflict between north and south may have been inevitable, but Tombalbaye's actions started the open struggle between the two regions.

114

KEY DATES

1960	Chad wins its independence from France.
1965	Rebellion breaks out in the Muslim northern part of the country, led by the National Liberation Front of Chad (FROLINAT, its French acronym).
1968–1972	French forces arrive in the country to help the government put down a FROLINAT uprising; by 1972, FROLINAT is largely defeated, and the French troops leave.
1973	Libyan forces occupy the disputed Aozou strip in the north.
1975–1982	President François (N'Garta) Tombalbaye is overthrown in a military coup; over the next seven years, control of the government alternates between civilians and the military; in 1982, Hissène Habré seizes power.
1987–1988	Habré defeats his rival, Goukouni Oueddei, and Libya and Chad reach a peace agreement.
1990	Idriss Deby, a former supporter of Habré's, launches an attack from Sudan and seizes power.
1994	Libya withdraws its last troops from Aozou.
1998–2003	The Chadian government battles rebels of the Movement for Justice and Democracy (MDJT) in the north of the country.

Wars Begin

In 1965, a full-scale revolt broke out in the Muslim north. The rebel Front de Libération Nationale du Tchad (FROLINAT) was originally based in Sudan but transferred its base of operations to the southern deserts of Libya after 1971, when Libya's ruler, Muammar Qaddafi, provided them with support. Many of the rebels belonged to the Toubou ethnic group, whose members lived on both sides of the Libyan-Chad border. Although FROLINAT was a coalition of groups and accepted soldiers from a variety of ethnicities and religions, its primary focus was on freeing the Muslim north from the control of the Tombalbaye regime.

Under increasing pressure from the rebels, Tombalbaye turned to France for support. French troops began arriving in 1968, and by 1972 FROLINAT had been turned back (although not destroyed). French troops were withdrawn from the country, motivated in part by a diplomatic disagreement between Paris and Tombalbaye, who accused the French of interfering in Chad's domestic affairs.

With the French gone, Libya was emboldened in 1973 to send forces into northern Chad to occupy a strip of land surrounding the oasis of Aozou. Many Libyans, including Qaddafi, had long claimed that much of northern Chad rightfully belonged to them. Libya continued to supply FROLINAT with weapons and supplies, a task now made easier by Libya's base at Aozou.

Power Struggles

In April 1975, Tombalbaye was overthrown and killed during a military coup led by southern officers, and General Félix Malloum was chosen to lead the country. Over the next seven years, Chad was involved in a complex dance of civil war and coalition government. At first, the security of Malloum's government was aided by divisions within FROLINAT's ranks. Hissène Habré, who had led FROLINAT, was expelled from the alliance because he objected to Libya's annexation of the Aozou strip. Habré formed his own faction, Forces Armées du Nord (FAN), and took up arms against FROLINAT and its new leader, Goukouni Oueddei.

In 1978, Habré and Malloum, through French mediation, formed an alliance and agreed to share power. But by February 1979, fighting had broken out between their two armies in the capital of N'Djamena, which gave Goukouni, leading the FROLINAT faction known as the Forces Armées Populaires (FAP), the opportunity to gain ground against the distracted government troops. By 1979, FAP had 4,000 soldiers in the field—almost as many as the Chadian army; it was also better trained and led.

Chad broke into provincial fiefdoms, each leader and army controlling its own sector of the country. Libya and France, which stationed troops in N'Djamena, occasionally interfered in the ongoing political and military struggles. Although north-south issues were still important, the struggle was largely driven by individual strongmen and their regional supporters.

In April 1979, the four major armies of Chad negotiated another settlement. The two FROLINAT factions (Goukouni's FAP and Habré's FAN), together with the former government's army (the Forces Armées Tchadiennes, or FAT, now led by Colonel Wadal Kamougue), and still another Muslim resistance group (Abubakar Abdelrahmane's Mouvement Populaire pour la Libération du Tchad, or MPLT) combined to form an unwieldy coalition government. Goukouni was made president, and the other leaders took positions in his cabinet.

The coalition government gave Chad the ability to respond to a new threat from Libya, which was attempting to use its base at Aozou to move more deeply into Chad. From April to June 1979, the FROLINAT and FAT armies were able to hold back Libya from expanding into more territory.

However, the four-way alliance did not last out the year. Fighting broke out between the factions, some of which were again supplied with arms and training by Libya's Qaddafi. By 1980, Goukouni's FAP had gained possession of N'Djamena, and in December of that year, he requested and received the support of Libyan troops in stabilizing his control over the country. In January 1981, Goukouni and

Qaddafi signed an agreement that would merge Chad and Libya into one country. Both France and elements within Goukouni's FROLINAT faction objected strongly to this merger. Skirmishing broke out between the Libyans and some rebel groups, and Goukouni, thinking himself firmly in command, asked the Libyans to withdraw, which they did in November 1981. A peacekeeping force from the Organization of African Unity (OAU) helped to supervise the withdrawal in 1981 and 1982.

The withdrawal of Libyan troops opened the way for Habré and FAN to lead a counteroffensive from bases in neighboring Sudan. FAN scored its first small successes in January 1982, and by June it had reached the outskirts of N'Djamena. Goukouni fled to Algeria, and Habré became Chad's new president.

Habré Regime

Hissène Habré attempted to establish a regime that would end the fighting that had plagued the country. His government included members of many former opposition parties and a substantial number of southerners, even though Habré was a northern Muslim.

Habré's success was short-lived. Goukouni, again supported by Libyan troops, attacked from the north in the spring of 1983, and the fighting continued. The use of Libyan troops brought a counter-commitment of American supplies and 3,000 French troops to the Habré government. Both the French and the Libyans were reluctant to face each other, so a stalemate line was established along the sixteenth parallel in northern Chad. Habré's government forces were aided in their northern war by a merger of his FAN faction with elements of FAT, called Forces Armées Nationales Tchadiennes (FANT).

While Habré fought Goukouni's Libyan-backed northern invasion, he also faced a rebellion by southerners in late 1984. The government's suppression of this revolt included brutal attacks against the civilian population, which alienated those southerners who had considered supporting Habré.

In 1984, France and Libya both agreed to withdraw their forces from Chad. However, Libya did not abide by the agreement, leaving some 4,000 troops behind in the Aozou strip. These forces continued to support Goukouni's efforts to defeat Habré. In 1987, France began supplying limited air support to the

In the mid-1980s, FANT troops supporting Chadian President Hissène Habré conducted a scorched-earth campaign against guerrillas in the southern part of the country that razed villages and forced thousands of civilians to flee the country. *(Joel Robine/AFP/Getty Images)*

Habré government, supplemented by American aid. Neither the Americans nor the French wished to see Qaddafi increase his power in the region.

By 1987, Habré had defeated Goukouni (who again fled to Algeria) and pushed Libya out of all of northern Chad but the oasis of Aozou itself. In 1988, Chad and Libya agreed to a cease-fire and reestablished diplomatic relations.

Deby and the MPS

Habré's regime was still plagued by opponents. Goukouni continued to try to gather support against him from outside the country. In April 1989, Habré claimed to have suppressed a mutiny by two former supporters. One of these, Idriss Deby, fled to Sudan with his followers. In March 1990, Deby's army, the Mouvement Patriotique du Salut (MPS), invaded Chad, but, with French support, Habré was able to force Deby's troops back into Sudan.

In November 1990, Deby again launched an attack from Sudan. It was clear that he had received additional support from Libya and Sudan. France, unwilling to get involved in an intra-Chad dispute, stood by. Units of Habré's FANT army began to desert to Deby's MPS. By the end of November, Deby's forces had reached N'Djamena and seized the city. Habré fled to Cameroon.

Over the next five years, Deby solidified his control over Chad. From 1991 to 1992, his government withstood attacks from former supporters of Habré, and attacks by various small southern factions continued as late as April 1998. Gradually, however, Deby was able to bring a large part of the country's political establishment over to his side, and the fighting gradually died down.

In early 1994, Libya withdrew from the Aozou strip, ending one of Chad's long-standing trouble spots. Deby won Chad's first multiparty presidential elections in June 1996, defeating 1975 coup leader

General Komougue, and his MPS party won 63 of 125 seats in the January 1997 legislative elections. However, both the legislative and presidential elections were marked by serious irregularities, according to international observers.

In 1997, the newly elected government signed peace agreements with several insurgent groups and cut off their bases in neighboring Cameroon and the Central African Republic. Hopes for a lasting peace were shattered once again, however, when one of the groups renewed its fighting against the government, finally surrendering the following year. In the intervening months, several hundred civilians in the south were killed.

Between 1998 and 2003, the government battled forces of the Chadian Movement for Justice and Democracy (MDJT) under former defense minister Youssouf Togoimi, who had external support from Sudan. The fighting, primarily in the mountains and deserts of the northern Tibesti region, killed hundreds of civilians along with government and rebel forces. Under a formal peace agreement signed in 2002, many MDJT fighters became part of the Chadian army, but a small core continued a low-level armed struggle into 2003.

Meanwhile, oil had been discovered in Chad and was being developed by an international consortium led by U.S.-based Exxon-Mobil. Revenue from the oil promised relief for Chad's impoverished citizens, but the promise was slow to be fulfilled. At the same time, oil development threatened ecological damage and renewed fighting between Chad's many ethnic and political factions, each of which threatened to demand control over some of the funds coming from oil exports.

In May 2001, Deby won a victory in the presidential elections, but only after six opposition leaders were arrested. During the announcement of election results, another opposition member was killed. Because of widespread unrest, legislative elections were postponed until the spring of 2002. Labor unions and opposition leaders called for demonstrations, including general strikes, but did not succeed in shaking Deby's hold on power.

Analysis

Although Chad's wars were largely the result of long-standing antagonisms between north and south, they were greatly exacerbated by struggle between indi-

vidual power-hungry leaders. Ethnic and religious differences made it possible for leaders to rally support for their cause; pride and a desire for power prevented them from compromising. Finally, the fighting was complicated by Libyan territorial claims on the Aozou strip, which led Qaddafi to support first one faction, then another.

In the end, Libya's role may actually have helped heal the north-south divisions. Most Chadian factions—even those receiving aid from the Libyan government—opposed any territorial concessions by Chad to the Libyans. The opposition to a threatening neighbor motivated Chadian factions to settle differences among themselves and unite under a single administration. Muslims in the north and Christians in the south could both agree that they did not want Libya interfering in their affairs.

Deby's victory also confirmed the importance of the Muslim north in Chadian politics. Despite being outnumbered by southerners, northerners were successful in establishing themselves in a position of power—even if they were forced to include southerners in a coalition government.

Still, observers remained concerned that Chad's long, open borders left it vulnerable to incursions from forces based in neighboring countries. As conflict grew in Sudan's province of Darfur, small-scale skirmishes began with Sudanese militias that occasionally crossed into Chad. In March 2004, the Salafist Group for Preaching and Combat (GSPC), an accused terrorist group based in Algeria, briefly entered Chad. Such incidents and lingering concerns within Chad led the government to join the Pan Sahel Initiative (PSI), whose member nations provide military assistance to each other to address terrorist operations and illegal border crossings.

Carl Skutsch and Jeffrey A. Shantz

See also: Ethnic and Religious Conflicts; Chad: War with Libya, 1986–1987.

Bibliography

Decalo, Samuel. *Historical Dictionary of Chad.* Lanham, MD: Scarecrow Press, 1997.

Nolutshungu, Sam C. *Limits of Anarchy: Intervention and State Formation in Chad.* Charlottesville: University Press of Virginia, 1996.

Thompson, Virginia McLean. *Conflict in Chad.* Berkeley: University of California Press, Institute of International Studies, 1981.

CHAD: War with Libya, 1986–1987

TYPE OF CONFLICT: Invasions and Border Disputes
PARTICIPANTS: France; Libya

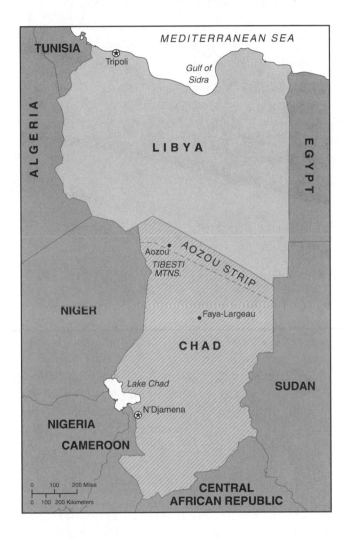

The conflict between Chad and Libya began before either was an independent nation. The French had conquered Chad in 1913; the Italians had completed their conquest of Libya in the late 1920s. At that point the two colonial powers negotiated a possible border change between their two territories. The colonial borders in Africa had always been arbitrary, cutting across geographic and ethnic boundaries. As the northern third of Chad included a sizable Arab and Muslim population, it was reasonable that France might be willing to turn over a portion of northern Chad to the Italians in Libya, which was almost completely inhabited by Muslims. Pierre Laval and Benito Mussolini drew up a Franco-Italian treaty in 1935 that would have given a northern strip of Chad to Italy, but the treaty was never ratified by the French Chamber of Deputies and never took effect. World War II intervened, in which France and Italy fought on opposite sides. When Libya became independent in 1951, some Libyans pointed to the Franco-Italian treaty and argued that the northern strip of Chad should rightfully be their territory. This was the first cause of conflict between Chad and Libya.

In 1966, a Muslim group in northern Chad, the Front de Libération Nationale du Tchad (FROLINAT, its French acronym), led a rebellion against Chad's government, gaining some sympathy from Muslims across the border in Libya. Then in 1969, Muammar Qaddafi took over the Libyan government in a coup. Almost immediately, he began support for FROLINAT in northern Chad. After 1971, the rebels received military supplies and the use of bases in southern Libya. This was the beginning of Libya's involvement with Chad.

Proxy War and the Aozou Strip

For two years Libya aided FROLINAT's offensives, which had some success against Chad's government forces. Libya's help was counterbalanced by French aid to Chad's army, which had helped defeat FROLINAT attacks, but in 1972, French troops withdrew from Chad. This retreat gave Qaddafi the opportunity to move directly into northern Chad. In 1973, his troops invaded Chad and occupied the "Aozou strip"—the strip of land on the Libya-Chad border centered on the Aozou oasis, which Libya claimed as its own, based on the unratified 1935 treaty.

From 1973 on, Libya continued to support FROLINAT forces, but whether FROLINAT succeeded or

KEY DATES

1965   Rebellion, supported by Libya, breaks out in the Muslim northern part of the country, led by the National Liberation Front of Chad (FROLINAT, its French acronym).

1972   Aided by French troops, the Chadian government defeats FROLINAT, but Libyan forces maintain occupation of the Aozou strip, a Chadian territory on the border with Libya.

1984   France and Libya agree to pull troops out of Libya, but Libyan President Muammar Qaddafi keeps 4,000 troops in the Aozou strip.

1986   Libyan-backed opposition leader Goukouni Oueddei invades the country trying to overthrow the government; a small contingent of French forces and planes aid the Chadian government; Qaddafi has Goukouni arrested, and Goukouni's troops switch sides and join the Chadian government forces.

1987   With his troops isolated in Aozou, Qaddafi agrees to a cease-fire.

1988   The last Libyan troops leave Aozou.

1994   The International Court of Justice determines that Libya has no legitimate claim to the Aozou strip.

not, Qaddafi clearly intended to keep the Aozou strip. The occupation of Aozou may have been part of larger Libyan territorial goals. Unofficial maps published in Libya in 1976 showed an expanded Libya that included large sections of Chad, Niger, and Algeria. Not all FROLINAT forces were pleased with the annexation of Aozou, however. One faction led by Hissène Habré joined forces with the Chad government in protest against Libya's actions.

In 1979, both FROLINAT factions were able to come to an agreement with the southern government forces and create a new coalition government, led by FROLINAT leader Goukouni Oueddei. One of the few things the coalition government could agree on was that the Libyan annexation of the Aozou strip was invalid.

Libyan Skirmishes

Libya responded to this turnabout by FROLINAT and its new allies by staging a series of ground and air raids into central Chad during April and May 1979. In June 1979, these raids escalated into an invasion by a 2,500-man army. The Libyans attacked using several motorized columns supported by French-made Mirage fighters, but Chadian forces—mostly Toubou tribesmen fighting under the FROLINAT banner—were able to repel the Libyans in a series of desert skirmishes in and around the Tibesti Mountains. The Libyans made it as far as Faya-Largeau in north-central Chad before being turned back. The Chad forces captured a number of Libyan prisoners in a series of ambushes, but although the Libyans retreated, they were still able to maintain control of the Aozou strip.

This first direct clash between Libya and Chad demonstrated the problems of military conflict in the Sahara region. Libya's ability to supply and advance its forces was handicapped by the rough desert terrain, the Tibesti Mountains lining Chad's northern border, and the familiarity of Chad tribesmen with their own backyard. With few roads or villages, the Libyans were forced to hop from one oasis to another in a kind of leapfrog campaign, and each hop left them more vulnerable to ambushes and supply line interdiction. The deeper they penetrated into Chad, the harder it was to keep their troops supplied.

Libyan Intervention

Libya's troops had withdrawn from all of Chad except the Aozou strip, but they continued to interfere with Chad's internal affairs by supporting different factions within Chad's coalition government. By March 1980, the government had broken down and Qaddafi was again helping FROLINAT leader Goukouni—now president of Chad—in his struggle against Habré, his defense minister. Libya invaded, and by December 1980, Libyan tanks were in N'Djamena, Chad's capital, fighting with Habré's forces.

Habré was defeated and forced to withdraw to eastern Chad. In January 1981, Qaddafi and Goukouni announced that their two countries would work toward complete unity. This was too much for France, which still had troops stationed at the N'Djamena airport, as well as for many FROLINAT rebels. Responding to the general outcry, Goukouni requested that Libya withdraw the 10,000 troops that it had stationed in Chad. By October 1981, the Libyans had departed—except, of course, from the Aozou strip.

In another of Chad's reversals, Goukouni was forced out of N'Djamena by troops loyal to Habré in June of 1982. Habré would remain Chad's president until 1990. Goukouni returned to his patron, Qaddafi, who again began providing Goukouni's faction with supplies and bases in the Aozou strip.

The increased Libyan presence in the Aozou region, combined with the use of Libyan bombers to hit Habré's troops, disturbed both France and the United States. America began supplying weapons to Habré's government, while France moved 3,000 soldiers to Chad in August 1983. The French established a defensive line at the sixteenth parallel (which divided Chad almost evenly between north and south), and Libya, which did not wish a direct confrontation with French troops, kept its 6,000 soldiers north of that line.

In late 1984, the French and Libyans agreed to withdraw both their armies from Chad. The French were completely withdrawn by November, but Qaddafi kept at least 4,000 soldiers in occupation of the Aozou strip.

Open War with Chad

In February 1986, the fighting, which had continued to smolder, broke out again when Goukouni's forces, with Libyan support, invaded Chad. France responded to the attack by providing a small contingent of fighter-bombers to shield Habré's government troops. Goukouni's forces had some limited success. In October 1986, however, Goukouni and Libya's Qaddafi had a falling out and Qaddafi tried to hold Goukouni under house arrest in Tripoli. Goukouni's forces in northern Chad defected, once more establishing friendly relations with the Chad government and giving up their invasion.

Without any Chad proxies in the north, Libya's troops were on their own. The war became an open struggle between Chad's President Habré and his FROLINAT allies, on one side, and the Libyans, on the other. By January 1987, Habré had succeeded in recapturing the northern administrative center of Fada. Qaddafi responded by sending 9,000 more troops into northern Chad, raising the total Libyan presence to at least 14,000. From January to April, the Chad army inflicted a series of defeats on its Libyan counterpart. The Libyans were much better equipped, being supplied with Russian tanks and missile launchers, but their soldiers were far less enthusiastic. Many were university students given short training courses and then shipped to the front. The Chad troops facing them were experienced desert fighters who were eager to push Libya out of their country.

The Chad army also outmaneuvered the Libyans, using hit-and-run tactics to keep the larger Libyan force off balance. Chad soldiers in Toyota trucks would bounce past slow-moving Libyan tanks and then open fire from either side with antitank weapons mounted in the backs of their trucks. As much as possible, the Chad army avoided attacking large Libyan garrisons, instead focusing on their supply lines. When the Libyans came out to chase the Chad troops away, they were ambushed in the desert.

By April 1998, the Libyans had been pushed completely out of all but the Aozou strip. They had lost more than 3,600 troops, along with 14 planes, 150 tanks, and more than 500 other vehicles. In August, Habré's forces captured Aozou itself, but it was soon retaken by Libya. Chad responded with a raid against an airbase in Libya itself on September 6, 1987, destroying a number of planes and killing at least a thousand troops.

On September 11, 1987, Qaddafi agreed to a cease-fire.

Epilogue

Although the Aozou strip remained under Libyan control, Qaddafi had clearly lost his eagerness to hold it at all costs. Diplomatic relations resumed between the two nations in October 1988. Negotiations over the Aozou strip continued during 1989 and 1990, with no agreement being reached.

In December 1990, the political situation changed when forces led by Idris Deby overthrew Chad's President Habré. Deby had used Sudan as his base of operations but had received supplies from Libya.

In 1994, the International Court of Justice ruled that Libya had no claim to the Aozou strip. Although Qaddafi had said he would abide by the court's ruling, he was at first reluctant to withdraw. Negotiations between Deby and Qaddafi—whose relations remained fairly good after 1990—finally convinced the latter to withdraw from the strip in May 1994.

Libya's territorial ambitions drew it into a confused civil war in Chad. As long as the various factions in Chad continued to fight each other, Qaddafi was able to maintain this control over much of northern Chad. Once the Chad factions united against Qaddafi, his position became extremely difficult.

Chad's defeat of Libya rested on three foundations: limited American and French support, which provided Chad with some air cover as well as critically needed antitank weapons; motivated troops who used innovative hit-and-run tactics; and the rugged Sahara terrain, which handicapped Libyan logistical efforts and gave a particular advantage to the local Chad tribesmen operating in their own backyard.

Carl Skutsch

See also: Invasions and Border Disputes; Chad: Civil Wars, 1960s–1990s.

Bibliography

Deeb, Mary-Jane. *Libya's Foreign Policy in North Africa.* Boulder, CO: Westview Press, 1991.

Nolutshungu, Sam C. *Limits of Anarchy: Intervention and State Formation in Chad.* Charlottesville: University Press of Virginia, 1996.

Wright, John. *Libya: A Modern History.* Baltimore: Johns Hopkins University Press, 1982.

COMOROS: Coups, 1980s

TYPE OF CONFLICT: Coups
PARTICIPANT: France

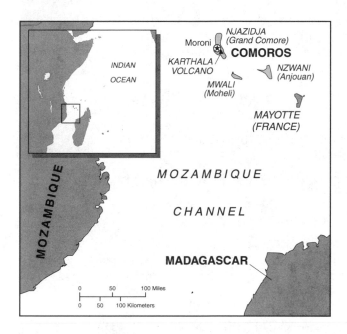

The Comoros, a small archipelago of four islands in the Indian Ocean, lie across the northern end of the Mozambique Channel between Mozambique and Madagascar. Three of the islands, Grand Comore (also known as Njazidja), Anjouan (Nzwani), and Moheli (Mwali), make up the Federal Islamic Republic of the Comoros. The fourth island of the group, Mayotte, is a French overseas territory with representation in the French National Assembly. The Federal Islamic Republic claims Mayotte, under the name of Mahore, as part of its territory. The capital, Moroni, is located on Grand Comore.

The three islands of the Federal Islamic Republic, with a number of small islets, cover an area of 833 square miles and have a population of about 675,000 people. Almost an equal number of Comoro islanders have settled in Madagascar and Mozambique, a result of the population pressure that makes the Comoros one of the most densely populated nations on earth, with about 800 people per square mile. The islands' economy is essentially based in subsistence agriculture, but

soils are poor despite the islands' volcanic character, and constant overcultivation has eroded and exhausted the soil, making the Comoros highly dependent on imports of basic foods. Exports are almost entirely spices and scent essences, primarily to France. Poverty is pervasive; malnutrition and consequent poor health are widespread. Medical services are few and poor. Education is rudimentary, and illiteracy nearly universal.

Ethnically, the people of the Comoros are of mixed Arab and West African stock, the latter descended from slaves brought to the islands in the eighteenth and nineteenth centuries. They are almost entirely Muslim. The language is a dialect of Swahili.

Historical Background

The Comoros have figured in world history three times. The first was during the period of European discovery and colonization between the fifteenth and eighteenth centuries. The Portuguese controlled most of the southwest coast of Africa, and Dutch, English, and French ships found the Comoros, then independent, a convenient stopping place for fresh water and repairs where they did not have to pay fees to Portugal. Later, as Europeans established plantations on other Indian Ocean islands, including Mauritius and Reunion, the petty sultans who ruled in the Comoros established slave markets. Slavery on the Comoros was not finally abolished until 1889. The islands also became a base for European pirates who preyed on the ships of the Dutch and British East India Companies.

During the nineteenth-century scramble for African colonies, the Comoros again attracted European attention. Until then, Western nations, mainly Britain and France, had managed relations with the Comoros by making informal agreements with one or more of about fifty Comoran sultans. France was the first to take a more active role, establishing a presence

KEY DATES

1974	In a plebiscite, residents of the Comoro Islands vote to become independent of colonial power France; only residents of Mayotte vote to stay part of France.
1975	With the exception of Mayotte, the Comoros become independent of France.
1977	Comoro residents in Madagascar are massacred, sending 17,000 refugees back to the islands; the Karthala volcano erupts on the island of Njazadija, killing 2,000 and making another 20,000 homeless.
1978	French mercenaries overthrow the government of the Comoros, putting Ahmed Abdullah in charge of the country.
1979	The National Assembly declares the Comoros a one-party government.
1987	Under pressure from France, Abdullah agrees to multiparty elections.
1990	Multiparty elections lead to a change in government.
1995	Taki Abdulkasim, the loser of the 1990 elections, hires French mercenaries to overthrow the government of Mohammed Djohar, but the coup fails.
1999	The government is overthrown in a military coup.
2001–2002	National elections in the Comoros lead to more autonomy for different islands; local elections lead to rejection of secessionist parties.

on the island of Mayotte in 1843. In the 1880s, France gained direct control over neighboring Madagascar. After England and Germany expressed interest in the Comoros, the French in Mayotte took possession of the remaining islands in 1886. They made the Comoros part of their colony of Madagascar in 1912.

British forces landed in the Comoros in July 1942, during World War II, and took control from the French Vichy government. They turned the islands over to the administration of the Free French government of Charles de Gaulle, then operating in exile. After the war, France granted independence to its African colonies but strove to maintain its political and economic influence and prevent any Soviet or Chinese inroads. In 1947, the Comoros were separated from Madagascar and became a French overseas territory with administrative autonomy and the right to elect one senator and one deputy to the French legislature in Paris. The islands gained internal self-government in 1961, electing a Chamber of Deputies, which in turn elected a territorial president.

In 1975, following a December 1974 plebiscite, the Comoros became independent and were admitted to the United Nations. Only Mayotte voted to retain its ties with France, which then stationed a detachment of foreign legionnaires on the island to prevent the Comoro government at Moroni from forcibly annexing it. When the Comoros broke diplomatic relations with France in the dispute over Mayotte, France withdrew all of its nationals, including doctors, technicians, administrators, and teachers, from the main islands, forcing schools and hospitals to close. France also ended its financial aid, which had amounted to three-quarters of Comoro government revenues. The rift with France and the resulting loss of skilled workers and government revenue set the scene for the Comoros' stormy political future.

Era of Coups

The territorial president of the Comoros under the 1961 arrangement was Ahmed Abdullah, a wealthy vanilla exporter who was elected president of the new country in 1975. Despite his generally pro-French sentiments and conservative political beliefs, Abdullah was a nationalist and was determined to bring Mayotte into the Islamic Republic. His pursuit of this goal had caused him to lose favor in Paris, and he had barely taken office when he was overthrown in a coup led by Ali Soileh, which appeared to have French approval and assistance. Soileh, a French-educated agronomist, was eager to modernize the country. French aid was not restored, however, and Soileh appealed to the world community for help. In a short time, both the Soviet Union and China sent aid missions, as did the Organization of African Unity (OAU), the Arab League, and francophone countries such as Belgium, Switzerland, Canada, and even Haiti. Naturally, the Chinese and Soviet presence at a time of great Western fear about Communist influence in Africa raised concerns not only in France but also in Great Britain, the United States, and South Africa.

Concern grew when Soileh began a radical restructuring of the traditional island society. Tanzanians were brought in to organize a defense force, and a state company was set up to handle imports and exports. The elaborate marriage and funeral ceremonies that absorbed families' savings were banned, and the legal powers of the Muslim clergy were restricted. As a sign of liberation, women were prohibited from wearing the veil.

The pace of Soileh's revolution quickened in 1977 after the Comoros were hit by two disasters. Comorans on Madagascar were massacred by the regime of President Didier Ratsiraka, and some 17,000 refugees flooded back home, all needing emergency assistance. Then, in April, the Karthala Volcano on Grand Comore erupted, killing 2,000 people, rendering another 20,000 homeless, and destroying the island's agriculture.

Faced with these emergencies, Soileh and his youthful supporters attempted a complete reordering of society on a survival basis. As a symbol of new beginnings, the government archives were burned. Central government was temporarily abandoned, and the country was reorganized into thirty-four *moudiryias*, or communes of about 10,000 people, each grouped into seven prefectures. Each moudiryia, under its own judge, was to concentrate on subsistence agriculture, education, and security. A rudimentary national government with a council of state and a national assembly was established at the end of the year, and yet another plebiscite approved the new constitution declaring the Comoros a secular democratic republic.

A five-year plan addressed the country's urgent problems, principally food. A modest land reform program brought unused private land into cultivation, but the emphasis was on helping peasant farmers produce more and not on any social restructuring. Soileh's program was modeled on Julius Nyerere's Tanzania. Not surprisingly, this intrusion of government into traditional peasant farming and marketing practices prompted growing opposition, and armed resistance flared on the islands of Anjouan and Moheli.

Ahmed Abdullah was in exile in Paris and in contact with French government officials, who were unhappy with affairs in the Comoros. Abdullah struck a deal with the conservative French government of the day, which would help him return to power in exchange for his promise not to press the issue of incorporating Mayotte. Robert Denard, a French mercenary soldier with close ties to French intelligence and a long record of involvement in Africa, agreed to recruit an invasion force for a reported payment of $2 million. On the night of May 12, 1978, Denard, with fifty French mercenaries, slipped ashore and captured Soileh. Co-conspirator Ahmed Abdullah immediately took power, proclaimed the Federal Islamic Republic, and abolished Soileh's reforms. France recognized the new government and restored diplomatic relations. Three weeks later, Soileh was shot and killed while "attempting to escape."

With Denard at his side, Abdullah moved quickly to consolidate power. In October, he was elected president under a new constitution, and in January 1979, the national assembly declared a one-party government. Soileh's former ministers were executed without trial. Even three years later, France had to exert pressure on Abdullah to release 300 remaining political prisoners or bring them to trial.

The OAU, angered by Abdullah's use of European mercenaries to overthrow the Comoro government, expelled the Comoros from the organization. French economic and military assistance was restored on a limited basis, but there was widespread corruption. Abdullah and Denard, with the assistance of a Pakistani financier, organized a company that monopolized the import and export trade. Denard himself held a post in the Comoros embassy in Paris for a time. In short, the Comoros had returned to semicolonial status.

Throughout the 1980s, Abdullah cemented his political control over the government even though his actual policies were to a large degree controlled by Paris. In 1987, at the urging of the French socialist government of François Mitterrand, Abdullah authorized multiparty elections on Grand Comore. When it became clear that the vote was rigged, the opposition rioted, and Abdullah called on French and South African mercenaries to quell the unrest. Several

hundred opponents were arrested. In 1989, Abdullah called a vote on constitutional amendments that would allow him to run for a third six-year term. Rioting again broke out, followed by more arrests.

At this point, Denard realized that Abdullah's growing unpopularity threatened his own profitable arrangements. The presidential guard, which he controlled, assassinated Abdullah, and when the chief justice of the supreme court, Mohammed Djohar, attempted a constitutional accession to the office of president, Denard and his mercenaries overthrew him too, killing some twenty-seven members of the Comoran army.

Denard had gone too far. French paratroopers landed in December, arrested Denard and his men, and deported them to South Africa. Djohar took office with the promise that the French military presence would remain for two more years.

French paratroopers intervened in the Comoros to end the September 1995 coup by forces under mercenary leader Robert Denard. Mohamed Djohar was restored as president, if only briefly. (Alexander Joe/AFP/Getty Images)

After Abdullah

In January 1990, France supervised new multiparty elections. Djohar and his Comoros Union for Progress Party defeated Mohammed Taki Abdulkasim and the Union for Comoran Democracy, but once again a mercenary coup was attempted. In August 1995, Taki hired another French soldier of fortune, Max Veillard, to organize an invasion, but this one failed. Veillard was captured and sent to France for trial; Taki Abdulkasim was imprisoned.

With the end of the Cold War in the early 1990s, the strategic significance of the Comoros, never great, declined even further. The economic situation of the islands steadily worsened, as population pressures caused further environmental deterioration, and foreign assistance diminished. As a result, political instability continued.

It was something of a surprise in September 1995 when the disgraced mercenary Denard reappeared at the head of another mercenary band, defeated the Comoran army, unseated Djohar, and made Taki Abdulkasim president once again. The French quickly sent a force of 900 paratroopers, captured Denard and his men, and imprisoned them in France. Taki Abdulkasim, however, stayed on as president, and in 1996 he extended his authority with a new constitution that also made Islam the basis for the nation's laws.

Secession Struggle

Taki's authoritarian rule and the continuing economic malaise in the country set off months of protests in Anjouan and Moheli, which culminated in declarations of secession by both islands in August 1997. The secessionists had long resented the concentration of political and economic power in Grand Comore, and their stated goal was to gain reunion with France. The French government refused to support the secessionists, however.

In September, troops from Grand Comore landed on Anjouan but were routed by the secessionists.

In 1998, Taki died of natural causes. Aging politician Tadjidine Ben Said Massounde took over as acting president until new elections could be held. Massounde moved to quell unrest in Anjouan and Moheli by meeting with secessionist representatives in Madagascar and offering greater autonomy to the two islands. The secessionists asked for time to consult with their citizens, but the request for a delay was interpreted as a rejection of the offer. In the capital of Moroni, people of Anjouan origin were attacked and beaten in the streets.

Massounde's inability to resolve the secession led to his overthrow in a military coup in April 1999. The new regime backed dissident military leaders on Anjouan, and in 2001 they seized power, intending to rejoin the island to the Comoros. Fighting continued in Anjouan, but negotiations began at the same time. In December 2001, voters on all three islands voted for a constitution allowing increased island autonomy but would keep the country together. In April 2002, pro-integrationist leaders won election on each island.

Tensions eased throughout the Comoros, and secessionist impulses quieted. In November 2005, however, Mount Karthala erupted again, forcing thousands of residents of Grand Comore to flee the stricken area. This new disaster was seen as another potentially disruptive force on the Comoros polity.

David MacMichael and James Ciment

See also: Coups; Madagascar: Independence Movement and Coups, 1947–2002.

Bibliography

Day, Alan J., ed. *Border and Territorial Disputes.* 2nd ed. Essex, UK: Longman Group, Keesing's Reference Publications, 1987.

Economic Intelligence Unit. *Comoros: Country Profile.* London: Economist Intelligence Unit, 2003.

Newitt, Malyn. *The Comoro Islands: Struggle Against Dependency in the Indian Ocean.* Boulder, CO: Westview Press, 1984.

CONGO, DEMOCRATIC REPUBLIC OF THE:
Post-Independence Wars, 1960–1965

TYPE OF CONFLICT: Cold War Confrontation; Ethnic and Religious
PARTICIPANTS: Belgium; France

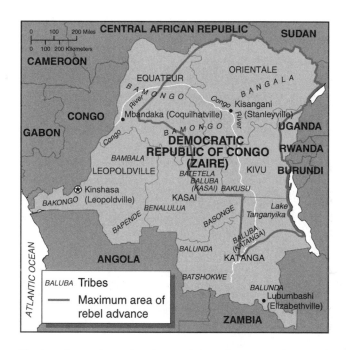

By its sheer size, the Congo* has dominated the affairs of central Africa since it was carved out of the region as the personal fiefdom of Belgium's King Leopold II in the late nineteenth century. Indeed, it was Leopold's move into the Congo River basin that triggered the Berlin Conference of 1884–1885, at which various European governments divided the continent up among themselves, without even a nod to the territorial lines established by the Africans themselves over hundreds of years.

Then, during the great African decolonization year of 1960, disputes within the Congo triggered the first great Cold War confrontation on the continent

and set off the war of national liberation in neighboring Portuguese Angola. In addition, the post-independence rebellion of the Katangese in the southeast part of the country (now called Shaba) represented the first great separatist movement in postcolonial, sub-Saharan African history.

After several years of fighting—which witnessed, among other things, the first major UN peacekeeping effort on the continent—an army officer named Joseph Mobutu (later Mobutu Sese Seko) emerged as the nation's strongman. His corrupt and dictatorial regime, supported by the United States as a bulwark against Communism, represented the quintessential example of African governmental mismanagement and repressiveness for three decades.

Historical Background

The Congo River basin, which comprises most of present-day DRC, was first inhabited by forest-dwelling pygmies tens of thousands of years ago. During the great Bantu migrations of the first millennium C.E., the Pygmy people were pushed deeper into the rain forests and became a tiny minority of the people inhabiting the region. Upon the eve of European penetration of Africa in the 1500s, the region was inhabited largely by Bantus, but with significant minorities of Sudanese and Nilotic peoples in the north and northeast. There are still some 200 distinct linguistic groups in the country today.

*The Democratic Republic of Congo (DRC) has changed names several times in its history. Dubbed the Republic of the Congo upon independence, its name was changed to the Democratic Republic of the Congo in 1964, the Republic of Zaire in 1971, and back to the Democratic Republic of Congo in 1997. Adding to the confusion, its neighbor to the west—the former French Congo—is now officially known as the Republic of Congo. To simplify things, the name Congo—or the initials DRC—will be used throughout this entry. The Republic of Congo will be referred to as Congo-Brazzaville, after its capital.

KEY DATES

1960   On June 30, Congo wins its independence from Belgian colonizers, with leftist Patrice Lumumba as head of state; civil strife breaks out between ethnic groups on the following day, particularly in the breakaway province of Shaba (Katanga) under Moises Tshombe; Belgium sends in paratroopers to protect its citizens in the country; Lumumba asks for Soviet help in driving the Belgians out on July 14; on October 11, military chief Joseph Mobutu issues an order to arrest Lumumba; Lumumba is captured on December 1.

1961   Lumumba is transferred from the capital to hostile Katanga on January 18; the UN demands his release after delegates note that he has been beaten in a Katanga prison; on February 12, government announces Lumumba has been killed trying to escape; the UN later claims he was assassinated, while Soviets imply the U.S. Central Intelligence Agency was involved in Lumumba's transfer to Katanga and certain death; the slaying of Lumumba sets off demonstrations around much of the country; on April 24, Mobutu has Tshombe arrested; Tshombe reneges on promise to integrate his forces into the national army; in early September, the UN agrees to conduct its first aggressive action putting down the rebellion in Katanga; in the middle of September, UN Secretary-General Dag Hammarskjöld flies to Katanga, where he dies in a plane crash; the Congolese army invades Katanga on October 30.

1962   By January, rebellions in both Katanga and the eastern provinces of Congo have been suppressed.

1964   Followers of the late Lumumba rise up in rebellion but are quickly put down by Mobutu, who is now head of state.

1965   Mobutu dismisses Tshombe from the cabinet; with rising unrest in the Congolese capital of Kinshasa, Mobutu calls out the military to quell protests.

1966   Mobutu outlaws all political parties and assumes absolute power.

1997   Mobutu is driven from power by a rebellion led by former Lumumba follower Laurent Kabila.

The first known state in the region was the Luba Kingdom, which lay in what is now Shaba province and dated back to the sixteenth century C.E. Later states to emerge included the Kuba, the Kongo, and the Lunda kingdoms, all products of the eighteenth century, though the latter two were largely situated in what is now Angola.

Belgium's presence in the Congo dates back to 1876, when King Leopold II organized the Association Internationale du Congo, which began setting up a series of trading posts along the Congo River. Leopold's expanding territorial ambitions triggered alarm in other European capitals, resulting in the Berlin Congress in 1884–1885. For the next twenty years, Leopold's territory—dubbed the Free State of Congo—became increasingly notorious for its brutal economic exploitation of native peoples. An indigenous police force under the direction of European officers forced local peoples to tap the region's numerous wild rubber trees. Thousands were killed when they could not fulfill their quotas.

Conditions became so bad that the international community—largely Britain and the United States—interceded, forcing Leopold to turn the colony over to the Belgian government in 1908, whereupon the region was named the Belgian Congo. While the worst of the atrocities came to an end, Brussels hardly offered an enlightened regime. There was little economic development, and political institutions remained completely under European control until shortly after World War II, when a consultative body—made up largely of white civil servants and missionaries—served to represent African interests.

The lack of official outlets for political expression forced the growing number of Congolese nationalists to set up underground independence organizations of varying ideological slants. The largest of these was the Alliance des Ba-Kongo (ABAKO), founded in the 1950s. In response to the growing unrest—particularly among the small educated elite and urban masses in the capital Leopoldville (now Kinshasa)—the Belgians established a series of councils in the territory's three largest cities, designed to (very) gradually develop indigenous representative institutions and eventually lead to independence. Still, real decision-making power lay in the Colonial Ministry in Brussels, which exercised its authority through governors and governor-generals in each of the colony's six provinces.

This arrangement—an unsatisfactory one from the African perspective—was put to the test in January 1959, when an ABAKO-sponsored demonstration in the capital was attacked by police, resulting in the deaths of some fifty Africans. Brussels responded first with an offer to extend indigenous government up to the provincial level and then, in October, announced the establishment of a central Congolese government, albeit under Belgian aegis. This, too, fell far short of African expectations, prompting the convening of the Brussels Round Table Conference in January 1960.

At the conference, representatives of the Belgian government and various Congolese nationalist groups—as well as a number of ethnic-based organizations—hammered out an agreement calling for a four-year transitional government, with Africans gaining increasing control over the colony until independence was achieved. Fearing the possibility of a protracted war, facing growing public disenchantment, and believing that it could still maintain its economic interests in the region even after an independent Congo was established, the Belgian government changed its mind shortly after the conference ended, announcing it would grant total freedom to the Congo on June 30, less than five months away.

Independence day found the Congo almost totally unprepared for self-government. Because the Belgians had kept a tight rein on the colonial administration, there were few African civil servants, except at the lowest levels. Belgium expected its civil servants to remain for some years, but most of them, caught up in the ethnic violence that broke out shortly after independence, fled the country. This was also true of the security forces. The Force Publique was officered exclusively by whites, most of whom also fled after independence.

Nor were there any real broad-based political parties, with national recognition, in the Congo. Instead, the new country's political scene was divided up into a host of ethnically based parties mostly led by uneducated leaders. While primary education was widespread—about half the population was literate, high for Africa at the time—only 25,000 Congolese had achieved a secondary education by 1960. The first university in the country had opened only six years before.

Lumumba Regime

With its vast size, hundreds of ethnic groups, arbitrary borders, and a history almost completely lacking in participatory government, the Congo was a nation in name only on independence day, as had already been made clear at the Brussels Conference earlier in the year. There, the various aspirants for national power—Joseph Kasavubu and ABAKO; Moise Tshombe's Katanga Province Conakat Party; the National Progress Party's Paul Bolya; Albert Kalonji, leader of the more conservative elements in the Congolese National Movement (MNC, its French acronym); and Patrice Lumumba, head of the latter's radical African nationalist wing—could not agree on the kind of state they wanted.

Both Kalonji and Lumumba, the latter recently freed from a Belgian prison, insisted on a centralized republic. But the other three wanted a federal state, with the provincial governments retaining most of the power. They also disagreed about the nature of the relationship between the Congo and its former colonial overlord, Belgium. Tshombe and Bolya wanted close political and economic ties, while the MNC and ABAKO wanted the Congo to go its own way, unfettered by ties to Brussels. In the May 1960 elections for the Congo's first National Assembly, no party received anything close to a majority, though Lumumba's faction won the largest group of seats, 36 out of 137. On June 24, Lumumba was confirmed by the assembly as the nation's first premier, or prime minister, while Kasavubu was chosen as president. A week later, Belgium's King Baudouin came to the Congo to declare it independent on June 30, 1960.

Civil strife broke out the very next day in the capital and several other cities, when members of two ethnic groups clashed. Lumumba, warning citizens "that the liberty we have just received does not mean license," sent in troops and imposed a nighttime curfew that ended independence day celebrations. New and more serious problems arose that very same week, when enlisted men mutinied against the continued presence of white officers and demanded promotions. The army was turned over to the command of a Congolese noncommissioned officer, sparking a sudden mass exodus of the Congo's remaining European inhabitants, who represented most of the new country's skilled and educated classes.

Problem of Katanga

To protect its fleeing citizens and crush the mutiny, Belgium sent 800 paratroopers into Elizabethville, capital of Katanga province, after Congolese soldiers had attacked Europeans. The intervention was welcomed by both Kasavubu and Tshombe, the former worried about the exodus of Europeans and the latter hoping to secure Katangese independence from the Congo. Indeed, Tshombe declared Katanga independent on July 11, 1960, denouncing the government in Leopoldville as communistic, and refused to allow a plane carrying Lumumba and Kasavubu to land in Elizabethville.

Worried that his own mutinous troops were incapable of controlling the growing violence in the country, Lumumba appealed to the United Nations for peacekeeping troops. The Security Council was called into special session in mid-July and, despite accusations by the Soviet Union that Belgium and the West were seeking to undermine the sovereignty of the Congo, agreed to dispatch a force, largely made up of

African nationals and supplied by the United States and other Western countries, which began to arrive in the Congo within a few days. Belgian officials agreed to pull out their forces, once the UN force had achieved order, adding that their own troops would confine their activities to protecting Belgian nationals. But the Belgian troops, increasingly being augmented by air, continued to attack Congolese troops, prompting a warning from Lumumba that he would seek assistance in preserving Congolese sovereignty from any source. Belgium, meanwhile, insisted that it had a right to protect its interests in the country.

Lumumba's warning was a veiled threat that he would ask the Soviet Union for assistance, a threat that became more real on July 14, when Lumumba said he would call in Soviet troops if the Belgians did not leave in seventy-two hours. Premier Nikita Khrushchev responded positively, despite the fact that the Congolese Senate officially annulled Lumumba's request. Meanwhile, the UN Security Council issued a warning to Belgium to pull out of the Congo and insisted that all other outside powers refrain from intervening. The American ambassador to the United Nations, Henry Cabot Lodge, added his own warning, which constituted a less than subtle threat that the United States would react to any Soviet involvement.

In late July, Lumumba toured a series of Western capitals, asking them to put pressure on Belgium to withdraw, before flying on to UN headquarters. While he was unable to win a firm UN commitment to oust the Belgians, he did get UN Secretary-General Dag Hammarskjöld's commitment to send UN technicians and security experts to help the Lumumba government. Hammarskjöld also promised to visit both Belgium and the Congo to try and resolve the dispute. Failing to win a firm commitment from Brussels to withdraw, Hammarskjöld arrived in Leopoldville, where he dispatched Undersecretary Ralph Bunche to Katanga.

Tshombe, however, was in no mood to cooperate. From his base in Elizabethville, he warned Hammarskjöld that UN forces would meet armed resistance and then issued an order for full mobilization of all able-bodied men in the province. When Bunche arrived in Elizabethville, Tshombe refused to meet with him and forced a plane carrying UN technicians to leave the moment it landed. At this point, Hammarskjöld canceled UN plans to send troops to Katanga but then backed off when Lumumba, ordering his own mobilization of troops, warned he would

Moise Tshombe, who led the secession of Katanga Province from the newly independent Democratic Republic of the Congo in July 1960, awards medals to his troops. The Katangan rebellion was quelled in 1963, but Tshombe went on to become president of the Congo. *(Terrence Spencer/Time Life Pictures/Getty Images)*

send forces into Katanga if the United Nations would not.

That prompted a reassessment of the situation by the Security Council, which once again ordered UN troops to Katanga, with the strict caveat that they not try to block or support the separatist movement. This decision prompted many of Lumumba's supporters, both inside the Congo and out, to conclude that the United Nations was not serving the interests of a member state. Indeed, many critics argued that the United Nations was caving in to U.S. pressure that it do as little as possible to support Lumumba's left-wing government. With Hammarskjöld in the lead, the first UN troops—an advance contingent from the secretary-general's native Sweden—arrived in Katanga on August 12. Within the week, the UN forces had secured the province, and the Belgian troops had returned to a nearby base.

Lumumba was angry, however. He denounced the use of white UN troops rather than African ones to secure Katanga, and he accused the secretary-general of plotting with Tshombe, an accusation that Hammarskjöld called "unfounded and unjustified." Lumumba then warned the United Nations to work with Congolese forces to disarm and occupy Katanga. When Hammarskjöld said he had to go to the Security Council for further instructions, Lumumba declared he had "lost confidence" in the secretary-general. The council, however, backed Hammarskjöld's insistence on strict neutrality in the Katangese affair, agreeing that with the withdrawal of the Belgian troops, the situation had become an internal one and was therefore off-limits to UN involvement.

The situation calmed, at least temporarily. Lumumba said he was satisfied with the Security Council debate, but he continued to insist that UN aid to Congo not be conditional on any unilateral demands on his government. He agreed that Soviet intervention was not necessary, but he continued to insist that black UN troops replace white ones. Meanwhile, the

Soviet Union redoubled its criticism of the United Nations' actions in the Congo, accusing both Bunche and Hammarskjöld of being "pro-American" and threatening to intervene if Belgian troops did not leave the country immediately.

While the UN presence had temporarily defused the crisis in Katanga, a new secessionist movement took hold in the neighboring province of Kasai in late August. Under Albert Kalonji, the Baluba ethnic leader and head of the conservative wing of the MNC, an independent "mining" state had been declared in the mineral-rich province. Tshombe of Katanga and several other provincial governors expressed their support for Kalonji, and there was increasing talk of an anti-Lumumba federation. Congo seemed to be breaking apart under the centrifugal forces of ethnicity, the personal ambitions of local leaders, and the claims of local interest groups to the mineral wealth of their provinces. But when forces dispatched by Lumumba sent Kalonji fleeing from his base in Kasai, Tshombe expressed disgust at the latter's timidity and refused to send Katangese troops to defend him.

Lumumba was more conciliatory toward the United Nations. When a group of Canadian troops were attacked at Leopoldville airport, the Congolese premier issued a plea to the citizenry, telling them to welcome those whites who had come to the country to aid in its development and security. For his efforts, Lumumba was rewarded with an agreement hammered out between Hammarskjöld and Brussels that secured the complete withdrawal of Belgian troops by September 9.

Fall of Lumumba

Ironically, the Belgian departure—one of the few things the various factions in the capital agreed upon—spurred further disputes. Claiming that Lumumba had "plunged the nation into fratricidal warfare," Congolese president Kasavubu removed Lumumba from office. Lumumba responded with the claim that Kasavubu was no longer head of state and thus his order was invalid. As tensions mounted, UN forces fanned out across the capital city of Leopoldville but could not stop Congolese police from firing on demonstrators who were marching on Lumumba's house, demanding he obey Kasavubu.

As both Kasavubu and Lumumba rallied their forces—largely broken down along rival ethnic lines—tensions mounted. Kasavubu had his police arrest Lumumba, but the latter's own forces liberated him from jail a few hours later. Backed by his troops, Lumumba made a triumphal tour of the city and won "special powers" from the Congolese parliament to restore order.

Meanwhile, the international situation was heating up. After it was discovered that both the Belgians and the Soviets were shipping arms to their respective sides in the Katangese conflict—that is, to Tshombe and Lumumba—the United Nations ordered the closure of the province's airports. The Soviets then demanded that the United Nations desist, and some of the African contingents in the UN force withdrew in protest. The United Nations reopened the airports a week later, though not before the United States had issued a warning to the Soviets to stop shipping arms. Backed by a UN General Assembly resolution, Hammarskjöld finally secured a cease-fire in the Kasai and Katanga provinces, though the United Nations remained deadlocked by the United States and the Soviet Union over whether and how to continue its peacekeeping and aid activities in the Congo, as well as whether it should accept the credentials of the Kasavubu or Lumumba delegation. It ultimately decided to deny both parties a seat.

Unable to make up its mind, the United Nations soon found itself outpaced by events in Leopoldville, for, on September 14, 1960, a military junta under the command of the Congolese chief of staff, Joseph Mobutu, took power. Though maintaining that both Lumumba and Kasavubu would retain their offices, he quickly had the former placed under house arrest. Mobutu then ordered all Soviet personnel out of the country and recalled government troops from Kasai and Katanga. The new Congolese strongman also announced the establishment of a nonpartisan caretaker government, known as the College of High Commissioners, to hold power until the various disputes in the country had been resolved, a move Kasavubu agreed to.

On October 11, Mobutu issued an order to imprison Lumumba, but the United Nations refused to allow it to be carried out. Two weeks later, Kasavubu officially dissolved the Lumumba government and signed a constitutional decree legalizing Mobutu's College. At the same time, Mobutu announced an accord with Tshombe that declared Katanga part of the Congolese state but agreed to a further decentralization of power.

Despite these seemingly decisive moves, Mobutu was still having trouble securing his own position in the capital and the provinces. When Congolese troops began to riot over lack of pay, it became obvious that Mobutu was not in effective command. Criticizing the total breakdown in law and order, the United Nations announced it was willing to assume control of the situation in the capital but did not make any moves in this direction. In fact, despite a harsh report about Mobutu by Hammarskjöld's personal representative in the Congo, the General Assembly agreed to seat the pro-Mobutu delegation of Kasavubu on November 22.

Whether it was aware of it or not, the General Assembly's decision reflected the balance of power in the Congo itself. On November 28, Lumumba had eluded the troops around his house and slipped out of the city, heading for supporters in the provinces. But he was captured by Mobutu's forces in Kasai on December 1 and returned to the capital. Charging the former premier with inciting an army rebellion—Mobutu believed Lumumba was behind the earlier troop riots—the new head of state refused to allow the Red Cross or the United Nations to see Lumumba in prison.

Meanwhile, Lumumba's forces were rallying in Orientale province in the northeast. They established yet another rebel government in the provincial capital of Stanleyville (now Kisangani) and invaded Katanga and Kivu provinces along the border with Rwanda in December 1960 and January 1961, respectively. The invasion of Kivu took place partly under the leadership of Laurent Kabila, who would overthrow the Mobutu government, but not until 1997, more than thirty-five years later. Heavy fighting between pro-Tshombe and pro-Lumumba troops forced the United Nations to withdraw from the region.

On January 18, Lumumba was transferred from a prison in Leopoldville to one in Katanga, a provocative move, given the war situation there and the Katangese hostility to the former premier. After UN troops witnessed Lumumba being beaten in Elizabethville, Hammarskjöld demanded that he be returned to the capital. He was not. Instead, the government announced his death on February 12, 1961, in Katanga. Officials there insisted he was killed while trying to escape, but a UN report later determined that Lumumba was handed over to Tshombe's forces for execution. The Soviets claimed that the transfer was actually orchestrated by the U.S. Central Intelligence Agency (CIA), which was actively supporting Tshombe's forces, though the agency denied any involvement. The pro-Lumumba government in Stanleyville was now headed by Antoine Gizenga, the former leader of a party allied to Lumumba's wing of the MNC.

More Violence

The slaying set off demonstrations around the developing world and in the socialist bloc, including attacks on Belgian embassies in Cairo, Rome, and even Moscow. They also sparked a new round of violence in the Congo, prompting the United Nations to issue an order authorizing the use of force in order to disarm Congolese and rebel forces, as well as a request by Hammarskjöld to supplement the 18,000-man force with more troops. These actions, in turn, led to protests by both the socialist bloc countries and officials of the Mobutu government, both sides seeing the UN actions as being aimed at their respective positions.

At the end of February 1961, the various anti-Lumumbist parties—including Tshombe in Katanga, Kalonji in Kasai, and the new Congolese Premier Joseph Ileo—issued a declaration announcing their intention to form a common front against "the danger of a UN trusteeship, Communist tyranny, and a Korean-style war" in the country. In early March, fighting broke out between Congolese forces and a UN contingent of Sudanese troops. Meanwhile, the various anti-Lumumbist forces were meeting in Madagascar, where they hammered out plans for a Congolese federation of quasi-independent states, a move rejected by Gizenga.

Concerned about the complete breakdown of a central government, the United Nations issued a report on March 21, warning that the Congo was "on the verge of catastrophe" and appealing for more funds from member states to bolster the peacekeeping forces. Hammarskjöld also released a report that the Katanga regime was recruiting European mercenaries, with the help of the Belgian government. To prevent this and restore order to the country generally, UN officials sat down with Kasavubu in mid-April. The two sides signed an agreement calling for the withdrawal of all foreign political and military personnel from the country.

But the agreement was only as good as the United Nations' and Congolese government's capacity to enforce it. On April 24, Mobutu took a step in that direction by arresting Tshombe while he was attending a conference with other provincial officials in Coquilhatville (now Mbandaka), capital of Equateur province. Freed two months later, Tshombe agreed to send representatives to the Congolese national assembly and to integrate his forces in the central government's army. While Tshombe was in jail, Gizenga, too, pledged his allegiance to the regime in Leopoldville and ordered his forces to honor a cease-fire. Then, in August, Gizenga formally disbanded the pro-Lumumbist government in Stanleyville.

Despite early promises, however, Tshombe refused to integrate his forces with the Congolese army. In early September, the United Nations launched a highly controversial assault on Katanga, controversial because it was the first aggressive military action ever undertaken by the organization. Hammarskjöld justified the attack on the grounds that it would help ensure the unity and tranquility of the Congolese state, in line with resolutions passed by the vast majority of the United Nations' member states.

In mid-September, Hammarskjöld agreed to fly to Katanga to work out a truce with Tshombe, but he was killed when his airplane crashed in northern Rhodesia (now Zambia). UN officials persisted, however, working out a joint UN-Katangese occupation agreement for Elizabethville, an agreement that the Congolese government condemned in no uncertain terms. On October 30, the Congolese army invaded the province, aiming, the government's order said, "to liquidate the Katanga secession." The force, however, was driven back by the rebels.

Meanwhile, new trouble was brewing in the eastern provinces of the country. Like Tshombe, Gizenga reneged on his agreement to support the government. Leaving the capital for Stanleyville, he instigated a mutiny among pro-Lumumbist troops of the Congolese army. In January, however, government troops were dispatched and, after a brief firefight with Lumumbist forces, succeeded in arresting Gizenga. This move quieted the situation there until January 1964, when a new rebellion had to be quelled. The pro-Lumumbist forces were finally forced to retreat into the countryside, where they remained a destabilizing force for several decades, living off earnings from smuggling.

Fighting, however, intensified in Katanga, with both UN and Congolese forces alternately assaulting Tshombe's troops. During the summer of 1962, Hammarskjöld's successor as secretary-general, U Thant, ordered economic sanctions imposed on Katanga and new UN assaults. These measures ultimately destroyed the Katangese rebel movement and forced Tshombe into exile in early 1963. Despite the UN victory, however, the situation remained tense in the breakaway province.

To win the allegiance of the Katangese, Kasavubu invited Tshombe to form an interim government in Leopoldville in July 1964. But the president soon grew tired of Tshombe's resistance to giving up Katangese autonomy and dismissed the former rebel from the government, despite the latter's party having overwhelmingly won the legislative elections in the spring of 1965. The Katangese rebellion did not disappear forever, however. Supported by the anti-Mobutu Angolan government, exiled Katangese rebels invaded Katanga province, now known as Shaba, in 1976 but were quickly crushed.

With a parliamentary deadlock and growing unrest in the capital, the army once again intervened in November 1965. Mobutu dismissed Kasavubu, assumed full executive powers, and declared himself head of the Second Republic. Moving quickly to consolidate his position, Mobutu outlawed all political parties in 1966 for at least five years and then established his own party, the Mouvement Populaire de la Revolution (MPR), which soon took over all administrative posts in the country. To prevent further rebellions, Mobutu changed the Congolese federal government, establishing a more centralized rule by appointing loyal supporters as governors. He then consolidated his hold over the country, ruling it as a virtual one-man state until his ouster by forces under the command of former Lumumbist Laurent Kabila in 1997.

James Ciment

See also: Cold War Confrontations; Anticolonialism; Coups; Ethnic and Religious Conflicts; Congo, Democratic Republic of: Kabila Uprising, 1996–1997.

Bibliography

Dayal, Rajeshwar. *Mission for Hammarskjöld: The Congo Crisis.* Princeton, NJ: Princeton University Press, 1976.

Epstein, Howard, ed. *Revolt in the Congo: 1960–1964.* New York: Facts on File, 1965.

Hoskyns, Catherine. *The Congo: A Chronology of Events, January–December 1961.* London: Oxford University Press, The Royal Institute of International Affairs, 1962.

Kanza, Thomas R. *Conflict in the Congo: The Rise and Fall of Lumumba.* Harmondsworth, UK: Penguin, 1972.

Lefever, Ernest. *Crisis in the Congo: A United Nations Force in Action.* Washington, DC: Brookings Institution, 1965.

Martelli, George. *Experiment in World Government: An Account of the United Nations Operation in the Congo, 1960–1964.* London: Johnson, 1966.

Schatzberg, Michael G. *The Dialectics of Oppression in Zaire.* Bloomington: Indiana University Press, 1988.

CONGO, DEMOCRATIC REPUBLIC OF:
Kabila Uprising, 1996–1997

TYPE OF CONFLICT: Coups; Ethnic and Religious
PARTICIPANTS: Angola; Rwanda; Uganda; Zimbabwe

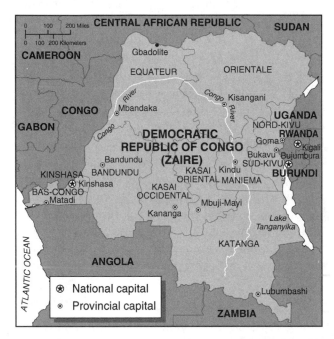

The Democratic Republic of Congo (DRC)* was freed from nearly a hundred years of Belgian colonial rule in June 1960. Immediately, a brutal civil war broke out in this vast land of diverse ethnic groups and semiautonomous provinces. Belgian troops remained, and UN troops were flown in. The left-wing government of Patrice Lumumba, elected in the first national elections, was overthrown, and Lumumba was allegedly ordered killed by Katangese separatist leader Moise Tshombe. By 1964, the Katangese separatist movement was crushed by a combination of UN forces and Congolese troops under the command

of Army Chief of Staff Joseph Mobutu (later Mobutu Sese Seko). Tshombe was forced into exile and died in 1969.

Mobutu meanwhile declared himself head of the country's Second Republic in 1965. The parliament ordered itself into suspension, and Mobutu then banned all political parties for five years. In 1966, he created his own party, called the Mouvement Populaire de la Revolution (MPR), and began consolidating state power in his own hands. To prevent rebellions in the sprawling and poorly connected country, Mobutu appointed his own supporters to the positions of provincial governors. He also ordered the execution of ministers from former governments whose loyalty he suspected. Student rebellions against the increasingly authoritarian government were crushed, and labor's right to strike was annulled.

In June 1967, a new constitution was approved by a general referendum. While the new document called for a bicameral legislature and two legally authorized political parties, Mobutu ignored it. Opposition figures were arrested, forced into exile, or assigned to diplomatic posts overseas. By the time presidential and legislative elections were held in 1970, there were no significant opposition candidates willing to campaign. Mobutu was duly elected as president, being the only candidate running, while the legislators were chosen from a slate of handpicked MPR candidates. The constitution was then amended to make all institutions of government, including the judiciary, part of the MPR, and all citizens were automatically enrolled

*The Democratic Republic of Congo (DRC) has changed names several times in its history. Dubbed the Republic of the Congo upon independence, its name was changed to the Democratic Republic of the Congo in 1964, the Republic of Zaire in 1971, and back to the DRC in 1997. Adding to the confusion, its neighbor to the west—the former French Congo—is now officially known as the Republic of Congo. To simplify things, the name Congo—or the initials DRC—will be used throughout this entry. The Republic of Congo will be referred to as Congo-Brazzaville, after its capital.

KEY DATES

1966	Joseph Mobutu (later Mobutu Sese Seko) bans all political parties and assumes absolute power.
1966–1996	During thirty years in power, Mobutu and his supporters pillage the national economy, growing rich while the nation's infrastructure collapses.
1991	In the wake of massive protests, Mobutu legalizes political parties and calls for national elections; nevertheless, he clings to power.
1994	Following the genocide of Tutsi in Rwanda, a Tutsi rebel group seizes power in Rwanda, sending hundreds of thousands of Hutu refugees, including leaders of the genocide, into eastern Congo.
1996	To destroy Hutu forces that are conducting raids across the border into Rwanda, Rwandan forces, backed by ally Uganda, march into eastern Zaire, fighting alongside anti-Mobutu rebel leader Laurent Kabila.
1996–1997	Kabila's forces sweep westward, meeting little resistance from the poorly equipped and motivated Congolese army; on April 8, 1997, Mobutu declares a state of emergency; on May 16, Mobutu flees the country, and four days later Kabila takes power in the capital Kinshasa.
2001	Kabila is assassinated by his bodyguards; his son Joseph is sworn into office as president four days later.

as members. As part of his policy of *authenticité*, Mobutu renamed the country Zaire, the capital Kinshasa, and himself Mobutu Sese Seko Kuku Ngbendu Wa Za Banga (translation: "great lion king who makes all his enemies run before him in fear").

From the 1960s onward, Mobutu offered his territory as a base for the rebel National Liberation Front of Angola (FNLA, its Portuguese acronym), fighting against Portuguese colonialists in Angola. When Lisbon agreed to pull out of the colony in 1974, Mobutu allowed both the People's Republic of China and the United States to use airfields in his country to transship arms to the FNLA, now fighting the Soviet-backed Popular Movement for the Liberation of Angola (MPLA), another rebel group about to assume power in Luanda. When the FNLA began losing, Mobutu sent in his own troops, but they, too, were driven back.

With the MPLA in power, Mobutu made his peace with the new Angolan government in March 1977, agreeing to a joint exchange: Angolan refugees in Zaire would be repatriated in exchange for Katangese rebels still hiding out in Angola. Fearful of retribution, the Katangese invaded their home province of Katanga, now renamed Shaba. Mobutu asked France and Morocco for assistance. Troops were sent in and brutally crushed the rebel movement. In doing so, they sparked enormous resentment in the province, resulting in the Second Shaba War of 1978. Again, French paratroopers helped Mobutu crush the rebels.

Aside from these foreign escapades, Mobutu spent the 1970s uncovering a number of real and fictitious plots against him, including within the military. He executed a number of the real and supposed coup-makers. At the same time, Mobutu began to develop his characteristic style of rule. Referred to by some political scientists as a "kleptocracy"—that is, a government based on theft—Mobutu's regime allowed the numerous international mining firms enormous license to expatriate profits so long as they paid sufficiently large bribes to Mobutu and his followers. By the time of his downfall, it is estimated that Mobutu had skimmed off between $4 billion and $20 billion, much of which he secreted in Swiss and other offshore bank accounts.

Other funds were spent on grandiose prestige projects, such as the government complex in Kinshasa. To secure his hold on power, Mobutu doled out much of the money destined for the provinces to his native Equateur province in the northwest part of the country. Indeed, his ancestral hometown of Gbadolite became a kind of second capital, with lavish palaces, fine roads, and other amenities virtually unknown in the rest of the country. The ranks of government were filled with people from his own ethnic group, as well as numerous members of his extended family. These favorites lived in great luxury, spending conspicuously on themselves in the midst of the country's great poverty.

To his critics, this poverty exemplified the problems of Mobutuism. Blessed with enormous mineral wealth and vast expanses of rich farmland, Zaire descended into deeper and deeper economic distress. Indeed, the gross national product of the country was far lower in 1990 than it had been at independence in 1960. Moreover, Mobutu administered his country with a kind of malicious neglect. What little transportation infrastructure had been bequeathed to the country by the Belgians was allowed to deteriorate in the tropical climate. Mobutu simply did not believe in highways or railways; their absence, he once said, prevented rebel movements from growing too big or marching on the capital.

Mobutu had other, even more effective, means for maintaining a tight grip on power. First, he constantly shifted his army commanders from one part of the country to another, to keep them from developing a rapport with local opposition forces that might lead to a coup. More importantly, Mobutu was assiduous in maintaining close ties with the United States and even—albeit clandestinely—with the apartheid regime in South Africa. Fearful of Soviet and Cuban penetration in neighboring Angola, the United States provided Mobutu's regime with arms and military aid in lavish quantities as a bulwark against Communism. Mobutu returned the favor by allowing the United States to arm the rebel leader Jonas Savimbi in his ongoing war against the leftist MPLA government in Angola during the late 1980s and early 1990s.

Growing Political Opposition

Still, despite these advantages, Mobutu began to face a growing opposition movement both inside the country and in exile, largely in the Congo's former metropolis of Belgium. In 1980, Mobutu reorganized the government as a part of what he declared was an anticorruption campaign, but which his critics said was yet another purge of potential opponents. Two years later, a small group of opposition politicians tried to organize a second party, the Union pour la Democratie et le Progrès Social (UDPS). Mobutu imprisoned thirteen of its leaders—an act which, in turn, sparked the formation of yet another opposition coalition, le Front Congolais pour le Rétablissement de la Démocratie (FCD).

Following a critical report on Mobutu's government by the human rights group Amnesty International in 1983, Mobutu offered amnesty to his many political opponents in exile. Some returned, but many remained out of the country, where they continued to plot against the regime in Kinshasa. In 1984, violence broke out in the country in the form of a series of mysterious bomb explosions in the capital and a brief rebel invasion of Shaba. By the late 1980s, the opposition movement had begun to coalesce around the figure of Etienne Tshisekedi, former secretary-general of the MPR and minister of the interior. Arrested by Mobutu, he was charged with inciting riots that had led to thirty-seven deaths in 1989.

This did not stop the UDPS from organizing a series of opposition rallies in the capital. In response to these demonstrations and under increasing pressure from Washington for his antidemocratic practices, Mobutu responded with a series of governmental reforms and the announcement of the inauguration of the Third Republic. He promised elections and a devolution of power to a transitional government. These reforms, however, did not stop the street demonstrations, nor did they prevent the United States from cutting off military and economic aid to Mobutu's government in 1990. With the war in Angola winding down—at least temporarily—and with waning fears of the collapsing Soviet Union, Washington was less beholden to the anticommunist Mobutu.

Massive student protests in 1990 and a general strike in February 1991 increased the pressure on Mobutu, who announced the restoration of multiparty democracy and the inauguration of yet another transitional government in March. Most of the now legalized major parties, however, boycotted it, calling instead for Mobutu's resignation. In August, the opposition parties organized a conference in Kinshasa to discuss ways to oust Mobutu. When massive demonstrations in support of the conference were attacked by police, the situation deteriorated into rioting and looting throughout the capital, prompting the dispatch of French and Belgian troops, ostensibly on a peace-restoring mission. Critics of Mobutu said the Europeans had come to defend the regime.

Under continuing pressure at home and abroad, Mobutu agreed to organize yet another national conference on democratization in April 1992. The conference declared itself the government and appointed Tshisikedi as prime minister, while maintaining Mobutu as head of state. In December 1992, the national conference turned itself into a parliament known as the High Council of the Republic (HCR), which followed with a warrant for Mobutu's arrest on charges of treason. The two rival governments were unable to resolve their differences through the mid-1990s, and it seemed that Mobutu would remain in power by cleverly playing rival politicians and ethnic groups against one another.

Fall of Mobutu and Rise of Kabila

In the midst of the perennial political crises in the capital, new troubles were developing for the Mobutu regime in the far eastern province of Kivu. In the summer of 1994, the decades-old conflict between the Tutsi minority and the Hutu majority in neighboring Rwanda exploded into a genocide in which hundreds of thousands of Tutsi were massacred by the Hutu. When Tutsi rebels, based in Uganda, invaded Rwanda to halt the killing, hundreds of thousands of Hutu— including many of the leaders of the genocide—fled to refugee camps inside the Congolese border, fearing Tutsi retribution. Under UN protections, former members of the Hutu army, militia, and government began to organize the masses of Hutu refugees, refusing to allow them to return to Rwanda.

Beginning in mid-1996, the Hutu leaders in the camps began to try to carve a section out of Kivu province as a base for launching attacks against the Tutsi-dominated government now in power in Rwanda. Supported by elements of the Congolese army, the Hutu began to expel thousands of the Tutsi, who had lived in Kivu for many years. Some had fled there after the Hutu took power in Rwanda in the 1960s, but others had lived there for generations. No matter how long they had been there, the Tutsi of eastern Congo, known popularly as the Banyamulenge, had been in a long-running dispute with the Mobutu government, which had refused to grant them Congolese citizenship for decades. The governor of Kivu province, allegedly under pressure from the Hutu militia leaders, ordered all of the Tutsi to leave the province within a week, in early October 1996. Though he quickly repealed the order, the local Tutsi had already risen up to defend themselves.

With covert aid from the Tutsi government in Rwanda and its ally the Ugandan government of Yoweru Museveni, the Tutsi militias soon made rapid advances against the poorly trained Congolese army, many of whose enlisted men hadn't been paid in months and chose to either loot civilians or flee, rather than fight. What at first seemed to be a regional uprising, familiar in Congolese history, soon turned into a national military campaign to oust the dictator Mobutu from the country.

The key player in all this was a local strongman named Laurent Kabila. A former minister in the leftist, post-independence Congolese government of Patrice Lumumba, Kabila had fled to the far eastern reaches of the Congo after the fall of Lumumba's government and the rise to power of Mobutu. While maintaining the pretense of being a rebel leader, Kabila in fact had long been running a local criminal syndicate involved in smuggling goods, including weapons, across the Rwandan-Congolese border.

But Kabila proved an able commander and coalition leader. As he led his army southward and westward into the Congo, he persuaded the leaders of the old secessionist movements in Shaba and Kasai provinces to join his forces, which he had dubbed the Alliance des Forces Démocratiques pour la Libération du Congo-Zaire (AFDL). By early November, AFDL forces had captured much of the eastern part of the country, as the Congolese army melted in front of them.

At this point violence broke out in the capital. With Mobutu fatally ill with liver cancer and staying at one of his villas in the south of France in order

A soldier of Laurent Kabila's rebel alliance destroys a portrait of ousted Zairean President Mobutu Sese Seko at one of the former leader's Kinshasa residences during the May 1997 military coup. *(Pascal Guyot/AFP/Getty Images)*

to receive medical treatment, the opposition government ordered the expulsion of all Tutsi from the capital while turning a blind eye to popular attacks on Tutsi residents, many of whom now fled to Brazzaville, across the river in the Republic of Congo. Mobutu flew back to Kinshasa in December, banned all demonstrations and strikes, and ordered a counteroffensive against Kabila. Though aided by Serbian and other foreign mercenaries, the offensive failed as the AFDL continued its relentless march across the country, hampered less by the Congolese army than by the near total lack of serviceable roads.

By early April 1997, most of the major provincial capitals in the southern and eastern parts of the country, including Lubumbashi in Katanga and Kisangani in Orientale, Congo's second- and third-largest cities respectively, had fallen to the rebels with barely any resistance from government forces, many of whom, in fact, joined ranks with the rebels. Disgusted with Mobutu's corrupt, dictatorial, and incompetent gov-

ernment, local peoples cheered on Kabila's forces, especially when they showed far greater restraint than the government forces by neither looting property nor attacking civilians.

On April 8, Mobutu declared a national state of emergency, but that did not prevent opposition leaders from organizing a two-day, widely observed general strike in the capital less than a week later. Besieged at home and abandoned abroad, Mobutu still seemed determined to hold onto power, preferring to die in office than go into exile. When South African President Nelson Mandela organized and mediated a conference between Kabila and Mobutu aboard a South African ship off the west coast of the Congo in early May, Mobutu, despite intense international pressure, refused to sign either a cease-fire or a transfer of power. A final Mobutu-orchestrated effort to establish yet another opposition government, with the dictator still standing as head of state, was rejected by the rebels, now close to Kinshasa and unconditional victory.

On May 16, Mobutu fled the country, first to Togo and then on to Morocco. Members of his family and entourage escaped to Brazzaville, though not before Mobutu's son allegedly killed Chief of Staff Mahele Bokungu, whom he suspected of negotiating a peaceful transfer of power to Kabila to avoid a battle in the capital. In the Katanga provincial capital of Lubumbashi, Kabila declared an end to the Zairean state, returning the country to its original pre-Mobutu name, the Democratic Republic of Congo. On May 20, the new head of state arrived in the capital, to cheering throngs. Three days later, he announced the formation of a new government, dominated by members of his AFDL, but also including representatives from other opposition parties.

This conciliatory gesture, however, did not necessarily represent where Kabila intended to take the country. Within the week, he had banned all political parties and all public demonstrations, going so far as to use his forces to break up an opposition rally of Tshisekedi supporters. By the end of the month, Kabila had been sworn into power and had issued an interim constitution that granted him sweeping powers. Opposition politicians began to be harassed, and Tshisekedi was held in detention for a night.

Antidemocratic moves such as these prompted concerns in both the Congo and the international community that Kabila intended to replace the Mobutu dictatorship with one of his own, though these fears did not stop international mining company representatives from descending on the new government to obtain new concessions. Adding to the concerns were reports of massacres of Hutu refugees who had fled into Zaire in front of the AFDC army earlier in the year. While Kabila allowed a UN inspection team to search for evidence of such massacres, allegedly by AFDC troops, he hampered their efforts at every turn, or so the UN investigators complained. In April 1998, the United Nations, fearing for the investigators' safety and frustrated by the obstacles the Kabila government put in their way, pulled them out of the country.

James Ciment

See also: Invasions and Border Disputes; Ethnic and Religious Conflicts; Congo, Democratic Republic of the: Post-Independence Wars, 1960–1965; Rwanda: Civil War and Genocide Since 1991.

Bibliography

Berkeley, Bill. "An African Horror Story." *Atlantic Monthly*, August 1993, pp. 20–25.

Gourevitch, Philip. "Continental Shift." *New Yorker*, August 4, 1997, pp. 42–55.

Parker, Frank J. "From Mobutu to Kabila: An Improvement?" *America*, November 8, 1997, pp. 18–21.

Rosenblum, Peter. "Endgame in Zaire." *Current History* (May 1997): 200–05.

Schatzberg, Michael. *The Dialectics of Oppression in Zaire.* Bloomington: Indiana University Press, 1988.

———. *Mobutu or Chaos? The United States and Zaire, 1960–1990.* Lanham, MD: University Press of America, 1991.

Young, Crawford. *The Rise and Decline of the Zairean State.* Madison: University of Wisconsin Press, 1985.

CONGO, DEMOCRATIC REPUBLIC OF:
Invasions and Internal Strife, 1998–

TYPE OF CONFLICT: Invasions and Border Disputes; Ethnic and Religious
PARTICIPANTS: Angola; Burundi; Namibia; Rwanda; Sudan; Uganda; Zimbabwe

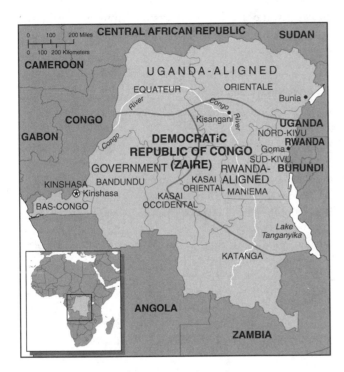

The Democratic Republic of Congo* became the site of a multilateral war soon after the rebel leader Laurent Kabila, with backing from Rwanda and Uganda, overthrew the decades-long dictatorship of Mobutu Sese Seko in 1997. Kabila's uprising is often referred to as the First Congo War, and the conflict that began in 1998—the subject of this article—is called the Second Congo War.

This second war pitted rebel groups against the government and each other, and involved no fewer than seven neighboring and nearby states: Angola, Namibia, Rwanda, Burundi, Sudan, Uganda, and Zimbabwe. Triggered by ethnic hatred, govern-

ment repression, retaliation for human rights abuses, and national rivalries, the war became something of a free-for-all, with various parties profiteering from the conflict by exploiting natural resources within the areas they controlled. An estimated 4 million people died in the succeeding eight years, some from the conflict itself but most from war-induced famine. It was the costliest conflict in African history and the deadliest in the world since the Vietnam War of the 1960s and 1970s. Because of its staggering death toll and the participation of so many nations, some observers have come to call it Africa's "first world war."

Background

From the early 1960s until 1997, Mobutu ruled over what was called a "kleptocracy" in the Congo, a government by theft. Mobutu and his followers made fortunes by selling off the nation's enormous mineral wealth to foreign corporations, while pocketing huge bribes. Little was reinvested in the country, and the Congo's infrastructure, already dilapidated when former colonial ruler Belgium withdrew in 1960, deteriorated even further. Indeed, Mobutu made it a point of letting the transportation system decline so that various opponents in the far-flung reaches of the vast nation could not unite against him and march on Kinshasa, the capital. Mobutu maintained himself in power through a combination of repression, cooptation, and manipulation of opposition groups.

Meanwhile, in 1994, long-running ethnic animosities in neighboring Rwanda exploded in genocide, as the majority Hutu massacred hundreds of thousands

* The Democratic Republic of Congo (DRC) has changed names several times in its history. Dubbed the Republic of the Congo upon independence, it changed its name to the Democratic Republic of the Congo in 1964, the Republic of Zaire in 1971, and to the Democratic Republic of Congo (with no "the") in 1997. For simplicity, it is referred to as Congo or DRC throughout this article.

KEY DATES

1994 In the wake of the genocide of Tutsi by Hutu in neighboring Rwanda, thousands of Hutu refugees, including leaders of the genocide, flee to the Democratic Republic of Congo (DRC).

1997 Long-time Congolese dictator Mobutu Sese Seko is overthrown in a Rwandan-backed rebellion led by Laurent Kabila.

1998 Rwanda and Rwanda-backed rebels turn on Laurent Kabila and launch an offensive aimed at overthrowing his government; with the aid of Angola and Zimbabwe, Kabila turns back the offensive, and the conflict descends into a stalemate.

1999 Splits form within the ranks of the Rwandan-backed rebel group Rassemblement Congolais pour la Démocratie (Rally for Congolese Democracy, RCD); fighting intensifies in the conflict between Hema and Lendu peoples in the Ituri region of the DRC; the UN sends 5,500 peacekeepers to the DRC in November.

2001 President Laurent Kabila is assassinated in January and replaced by his son Joseph.

2002 Peace treaties are signed between the Congolese government and foreign governments involved in the conflict, as well as with the rebel groups they support.

2004 Coup attempts by the military are put down by the Kabila government; the UN attacks rebels who have killed its peacekeepers.

2005 The Congolese vote overwhelmingly to pass a new constitution.

2006 Joseph Kabila is reelected president.

of minority Tutsi. This triggered an invasion of Rwanda by the Uganda-based Tutsi rebels of the Rwandan Patriotic Front (RPF), which overthrew the Hutu regime in Rwanda. Hundreds of thousands of Hutu refugees, including many of the organizers of the genocide, fled into eastern Congo as refugees.

In 1996, Hutu leaders in the refugee camps of the eastern Congo pressured the government of the Congo states of Nord-Kivu and Sud-Kivu (North Kivu and South Kivu) to order all Tutsi to leave. Most of the Tutsi in the region were natives known as the Banyamulenge. At the same time, Hutu based in Rwanda continued to carry out raids against Tutsi in the eastern Congo. These events triggered a rebellion by Tutsi militias in the Kivu provinces, backed by the new Tutsi regime in Rwanda and by its ally Uganda. The rebellion was led by Laurent Kabila, a longtime

opponent of Mobutu. Kabila's forces soon swept across the eastern Congo, as the poorly trained and equipped Congo army collapsed before them. On May 16, 1996, dictator Mobutu Sese Seko fled the country. Four days later, Kabila entered Kinshasa and assumed power.

At first Kabila proved conciliatory, establishing a government embracing many of the groups long opposed to Mobutu. But those democratic moves proved short-lived, as Kabila soon banned all political parties and issued an interim constitution giving himself sweeping powers. Reports also soon emerged of massacres of Hutu refugees by the Congo's armed forces. When the United Nations sent investigators, they were harassed by the Kabila administration. Fearing for the investigators' safety, the international organization pulled them out in April 1998.

Second Congo War

Meanwhile, in the early months of 1998, ethnic tensions were boiling over in the Kivu provinces between Hutu and Tutsi. Hutu rebels were fighting a low-intensity conflict with Banyamulenge (Tutsi) troops affiliated with Kabila and the Tutsi-led army of Rwanda. Angry at the lack of support they were receiving from Kabila, the Banyamulenge troops mutinied against the government, and the Rwanda government put pressure on the Kabila government to crush Hutu militants. With Tutsi rebels now aligned against his Tutsi government, Kabila had lost his main supporters in the east. Complaining that Rwandan Tutsi had too much power within his government, he responded by firing his chief of staff, James Kabare (a native of Rwanda), and other supporters of the eastern rebels.

The loss of position and influence in the government in Kinshasa concerned the Banyamulenge. In August, they established a new rebel group known as Rassemblement Congolais pour la Démocratie (Rally for Congolese Democracy [RCD]), headed by longtime politician and scholar Ernest Wamba da Wamba. They soon captured the city of Goma, the capital of Nord-Kivu, and began marching on the capital at Kinshasa, as Kabila had done earlier. The government claimed that the RCD was backed by Rwanda. Rwanda denied the claim, but many outside observers agreed that Rwanda was providing assistance to the RCD.

In one daring move, RCD rebels hijacked a plane and flew to the government military base at Kitona at the far western edge of the Congo on the Atlantic coast. There they persuaded the government troops to mutiny and march toward Kinshasa. On the way, the RCD and the mutineers seized a major hydroelectric facility that provided power to Kinshasa. It appeared that Kabila's regime was about to fall to an irresistible force, much as Mobutu's had fallen earlier.

Kabila was able to halt the RCD's advance, however, after receiving troops and materiel from Angola and Zimbabwe. Angola, in the midst of its own civil war, had supported Kabila's toppling of the Mobutu regime because Mobutu was providing sanctuary and supply lines for rebels against the Angolan government. Namibia, a longtime ally of the government in Angola, also sent help. Zimbabwe's dictator, Robert Mugabe, announced that he supported Kabila's government as a show of solidarity with a democratic regime under rebel threat, but many believed that he was hoping to gain access to some of the Congo's vast mineral wealth.

By 1999, the rebels had gained control of the eastern third of the Congo. When it became clear that there would be no easy march into Kinshasa, however, the anti-Kabila forces began to come apart. In May 1999, RCD organizer Ernest Wamba dia Wamba broke away from the group. Wamba had always maintained that his movement was aiming not just to replace Kabila but also to democratize the Congo. He finally concluded, however, that the RCD was becoming a vehicle for Rwandan Tutsi to seize control of the Congo through Banyamulenge surrogates. Because Wamba's breakaway group was formed in the eastern Congolese city of Kisangani, it became known as the RCD-Kisangani, or RCD-K, and was supported by Uganda. The latter had become increasingly alarmed at the efforts of the new Tutsi government in Rwanda to manipulate and control the Congo. Shortly after the RCD-K was formed, fighting broke out between Uganda and the RCD-K on one side and Rwanda and the RCD on the other. In a battle at Kisangani, the Ugandan and RCD-K forces were routed and forced to retreat to the town of Bunia, near the Uganda border.

Bunia is the main city of the Ituri region in Congo's vast Orientale province. Here the RCD-K got caught up in an entirely separate conflict between farming Lendu and pastoralist Hema ethnic groups. The RCD-K backed a member of the Hema people to serve as governor of a new "province" called Ituri. This caused Lenda groups to form militias and attack the Hema. Soon thousands were dead and hundreds of thousands displaced in the Ituri region. The RCD-K moved to calm the situation by replacing the Hema governor with a more neutral person in late 1999, but fighting started up again in 2001.

Meanwhile, the RCD-K was splitting over internal differences. In 2000, a new group called the RCD-Mouvement de Liberation (RCD-ML), dominated by Hema people, emerged to challenge Wamba's RCD-K. Both groups were opposed by the Mouvement pour la Liberation de Congo, or MLC, a Ugandan-based group. In addition, Sudan, long a supporter of rebel forces in Uganda, also got involved by sending support for Congolese government troops, which were fighting both the Ugandan- and Rwandan-backed rebels.

Nature of the Conflict

As this already simplified description makes clear, the Second Congo War was a complex affair with many different sides supported by at least half a dozen foreign countries. Moreover, the conflict ranged widely across much of eastern Congo and even into Congo's Atlantic region, some 1,000 miles to the west.

The presence of foreign troops was often overplayed in outside accounts of the conflict. In fact, these forces usually stayed close to the bases they created around supply points like towns and airstrips. Not wanting to deploy too many troops or use too much of their weaponry, the regular troops did not occupy territory. Instead, they concentrated on providing support and supplies to militias that roamed widely across the landscape, living off what they could capture or steal. With little oversight, these militias engaged in brutal human rights violations, including murder, rape, and forced conscription.

Much of the conflict was financed by the plundering of resources. Indeed, the main reason there was so much fighting in Orientale province is that it is the Congo's main diamond-mining area. Other regions offer valuable metals, including cobalt and gold, or timber. All of these plentiful natural resources were plundered by militia groups or foreign armies, working through shady middlemen who provided contacts with major multinational mining and timber corporations. Some of the wealth generated was used to supply troops, but much of it went into the pockets of militia leaders and army officers from Uganda, Rwanda, and elsewhere. The same processes work on both sides. Zimbabwe, a supporter of the Kabila government, also made arrangements to harvest its share of resources, according to a UN investigation in April 2001.

Because the militias operated autonomously and were not fully answerable to any government or party, peace negotiations were especially difficult to carry out. Even if foreign governments and official Congo parties agreed at conferences in distant cities, the militias on the ground were often ignorant of what had been decided or refused to abide by decisions that had been made.

Peace Efforts

By 1999, Congo had been officially carved up into three major regions. The northeast was controlled by Ugandan troops and the militias they supported, most notably the MLC. The eastern part of the country was under the control of Rwandan forces and members of the original RCD militia. Western Congo and the capital of Kinshasa were under the authority of the Congolese government, backed by Angola, Namibia, and Zimbabwe.

In July 1999, representatives of the Congo government met with representatives from Angola, Namibia, Rwanda, Uganda, and Zimbabwe in Lusaka, Zambia, and signed a cease-fire agreement. A month later MLC forces in the northeast agreed to the cease-fire, but the RCD in the east refused. Under the provisions of the agreement, all parties were to track down and disarm all armed groups in the Congo, especially Hutu groups connected to the 1994 Rwandan genocide. The UN Security Council put its stamp of approval on the agreement and sent ninety liaison personnel to work with the signers of the Lusaka cease-fire. As noted above, however, tensions between Uganda and Rwanda and the rebel groups they supported soon flared up in Orientale province.

In response, the UN decided to beef up its presence. In November 1999, the United Nations Organization Mission in the Democratic Republic of Congo (MONUC, its French acronym) was established with over 5,500 troops. While large by UN standards, the force was tiny given the size of the problem. An immense country, the Congo covers 900,000 square miles, an area equivalent to the entire United States east of the Mississippi River, and has nearly 60 million people. Fighting continued between government forces and militias connected to Uganda and Rwanda throughout 2000. Peace efforts by the African Union and the South African Development Community also failed to halt the fighting.

In January 2001, Laurent Kabila was assassinated by one of his bodyguards. At first this seemed yet another setback to peace efforts, as various sides speculated on who ordered the assassination. Most observers finally concluded that Kabila was killed by opponents within his own ranks, concerned that Kabila had no intention of sharing power. At the discreet urging of Angola and Zimbabwe, the Congolese parliament selected Kabila's twenty-nine-year-old son Joseph to head the government. Joseph then kept on most of his father's cabinet.

In 2002, the peace process began to move forward, spurred by two factors. One was the surprisingly effective leadership of Joseph Kabila, whose government was able to secure the western part of the country, eradicating militia forces there and helping to stabilize the economy. Meanwhile, in the eastern part of the country, both the RCD and the Banyamulenge militia were growing tired of fighting and of Rwandan control. In the Sun City agreements of April 19, 2002—named after the South African resort where they were signed—the MLC and the government agreed to stop fighting. They could not reach a power-sharing deal, but the agreement brought a reduction of fighting in the northeast, where the MLC predominated.

Over the next eight months, several more agreements were signed, including ones between Uganda and the Congo and Rwanda and the Congo. The signings culminated in the Global and All-Inclusive Agreement of December 17, 2002, signed by the government and all of the major rebel groups, including the MLC and the various subdivisions of the RCD. The agreement called for a transitional power-sharing government and presidential elections within two years. The agreement marked the formal end of the Second Congo War.

The year 2003 saw major progress in implementing the various accords signed in 2002. In April, President Kabila approved the transitional constitution, allowing for the formation of an interim government pending formal elections. In the following month the last Ugandan troops left the country, followed in June by deployment of a French-led, UN-mandated rapid reaction force. That same month, Kabila named a transitional government, bringing in representatives of all the major rebel groups, and, in August, an interim parliament met for the first time.

The following years were less hopeful. While the government was able to put down two coup attempts by elements of the military, its troops became embroiled in fighting with renegade RCD militia groups. Meanwhile, UN forces were being caught up in the conflict. In early 2005, nine Bangladeshi peacekeepers were killed, causing the UN force to go on the offensive for the first time in decades, killing some 50 militia members connected to renegade RCD groups. There was also the threat of renewed foreign involvement. Rwanda denied any involvement in the attacks by RCD members, but many observers doubted their word. Meanwhile, Uganda warned that it would send troops back into Congo unless the Congolese government could halt cross-border raids by the Lord's Resistance Army, a particularly brutal rebel group committing human rights abuses in Uganda.

Still, in December 2005, Congolese voters went to the polls, as provided in the Global and All-Inclusive Agreement, only a year later than originally planned. They overwhelmingly approved a new constitution written and passed by an interim parliament. Presidential elections were scheduled for June

2006. While it took several weeks to tabulate the vote in the far-flung country, Joseph Kabila emerged the victor.

Costs of War

A survey by the International Rescue Committee, a non-governmental organization that works with refugees, put the death toll in the Second Congo War at between 3.4 and 4.4 million, out of a population of about 60 million. An estimated 80–90 percent of the deaths resulted from disease and malnutrition connected to the conflict. Amnesty International put the number of rapes at 40,000. Meanwhile, the war sent roughly 2 million persons fleeing to Burundi, Rwanda, Tanzania, and Uganda. Environmental groups, including the World Wildlife Fund for Nature, reported that the conflict had decimated a number of rare species, most notably the mountain gorilla.

Perhaps the most serious casualty of the conflict was peace itself. While Africa had been plagued by innumerable conflicts after independence came to much of the continent in the early 1960s, most of the fighting remained within single countries, usually between government and rebel groups. Brutal as these conflicts were, they rarely drew in outside players. Most African governments took the position that the internal conflicts of their neighbors were no business of theirs. The Second Congo War broke with that pattern, and some Africa experts feared it would remove traditional constraints on interference by outside powers in internal conflicts. Thus, the Second Congo War may have been Africa's "first world war" but perhaps not its last.

James Ciment

See also: Invasions and Border Disputes; Ethnic and Religious Conflicts; Congo, Democratic Republic of: Kabila Uprising, 1996–1997; Rwanda: Civil War and Genocide Since 1991.

Bibliography

Berkeley, Bill. *The Graves Are Not Yet Full: Race, Tribe, and Power in the Heart of Africa.* New York: Basic Books, 2001.

Clark, John F. *The African Stakes in the Congo War.* New York: Palgrave Macmillan, 2002.

Edgerton, Robert G. *The Troubled Heart of Africa: A History of the Congo.* New York: St. Martin's Press, 2002.

Gondola, C. Didier. *The History of Congo.* Westport, CT: Greenwood Press, 2002.

Human Rights Watch. *Curse of Gold: Democratic Republic of Congo.* New York: Human Rights Watch, 2005.

CONGO, REPUBLIC OF: Civil Conflict, 1997

TYPE OF CONFLICT: Coup; Ethnic and Religious Conflict

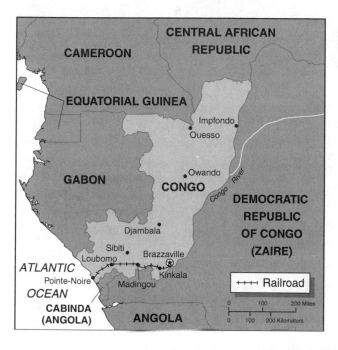

Always overshadowed by events in its much larger and similarly named neighbor, the Republic of Congo* has had a very different history, one marred more by instability and violence than the one-man dictatorial rule that predominated in the Democratic Republic of Congo across the Congo River.

The instability finally exploded into all-out civil conflict in the mid-1990s when two major party factions battled in the streets of Brazzaville, the capital, and elsewhere. Much of the fighting has pitted northerners against southerners in a struggle for political power in the capital and control over revenues from the lucrative oil fields along the coast.

Historical Background

Originally known as the French Congo, Congo-Brazzaville was freed from direct European rule in August 1960. Following a series of military coups

from the left and the right through the 1960s and 1970s, interspersed with brief periods of civilian rule, the country was turned over to a provisional committee of the leftist Parti Congolais du Travail (Congolese Labor Party [PCT]) in 1979. The committee in turn made its own president, Colonel Denis Sassou-Nguesso, president of the country. Though a self-proclaimed Marxist-Leninist, Sassou-Nguesso, a member of Edou tribe of northern Congo, opened the country up to more Western investment, particularly in its oil fields just off the Atlantic coast.

Despite a collapsing economy, ethnic rivalries within the ruling PCT, and a failed coup attempt, Sassou-Nguesso kept his hold on both the chairmanship of the party and the presidency of the republic. Following a one-party election in 1989, the government moved to liberalize the economy by reducing the public sector and fostering privatization, much of this activity under the impetus of the International Monetary Fund (IMF). The following year, a PCT congress, reflecting the changes in the socialist bloc countries to which it was allied, agreed to multiparty elections and a reduction of its own role as the primary political institution. A number of political prisoners, in jail since the mid-1980s, were released, and the army was ordered to disassociate itself from both the PCT and the country's political establishment.

At the end of 1991, a special council of the republic prepared a draft constitution calling for a bicameral legislature, a president, and an independent judiciary. Shortly thereafter, however, Sassou-Nguesso and his prime minister restructured the military, dismissing from its ranks political opponents and members of rival ethnic groups. An army mutiny led to a brief bout of street fighting in the capital, which was resolved by appointing a new defense minister more popular with the army. In March, the

*Originally known as the French Congo, the country is now known as Republic of Congo. It should not be confused with the Democratic Republic of Congo, known, until 1997, as Zaire. To avoid confusion, the popular usage for the Republic of Congo—Congo-Brazzaville, after its capital—will be used throughout this entry.

KEY DATES

1960	Congo-Brazzaville wins its independence from France.
1979	The leftist government led by the Congolese Labor Party (PCT, its French acronym) takes power, with Colonel Denis Sassou-Nguesso as president.
1989	Following victory in the one-party election, the PCT government moves to liberalize the economy along market lines.
1992–1993	Following adoption of the new constitution, opposition party Pan-African Union for Democratic Socialism (UPADS) wins national elections, and Pascal Lissouba becomes president.
1993–1995	In the wake of disputed elections, conflict breaks out between the government and militias connected to the opposition PCT.
1995	Efforts at integrating militias into the military fail, and fighting breaks out briefly in the north of the country in 1996.
1997	Fighting breaks out once again when the government refuses to heed the opposition's call to move elections forward from August to the early part of the year.
1999	The Government and the militias sign a peace agreement in Zambia.
2002	Sassou-Nguesso wins national elections and once again becomes president of the country.
2005	Sassou-Nguesso's government survives a coup attempt.

electorate overwhelmingly ratified the constitution, and legislative and presidential elections were scheduled for June and July 1992. The voting went against the PCT, which won just 18 of 125 contested seats. The majority went to Union Panafricaine pour la Démocratie Sociale (UPADS), and its candidate, Pascal Lissouba, a former prime minister, was elected president. Because UPADS did not have an absolute majority in the assembly, it formed a coalition with the PCT. Sassou-Nguesso then retired to his home in the north of the country, taking a well-armed militia with him for protection and, some charged, as a power base for a possible return to power.

Upon taking office, Lissouba began to act on his campaign promises to further liberalize the economy and devolve power from the central government to the provinces. But when he failed to appoint as many of the PCT members to government posts as the PCT said he had promised, the PCT pulled out of the governing alliance, leaving Lissouba without a parliamentary majority. He then dissolved the national assembly, prompting mass demonstrations in the capital. The army chief of staff ordered that a transitional government—a coalition of UPADS and PCT members—be formed. In May 1993, legislative elections gave a majority to UPADS and its allies, while the PCT became a part of the major opposition coalition.

Questions about the legitimacy of the vote and maneuverings within the opposition coalition produced a new political crisis when the opposition demanded new elections and held mass demonstrations to force the issue. Violence between militias identified with the various parties and ethnic groups broke out in the capital in June and July, leading Lissouba to declare a state of emergency. Following an order from the country's Supreme Court—declaring that irregularities in the balloting had occurred—and mediation by France, the Organization of African Unity (OAU), and the president of neighboring Gabon, new elections were organized, which once again led to a majority vote for the UPADS coalition.

And once again, militia fighting broke out, followed by an international report challenging the legitimacy of the latest round of voting. By November 1993, the PCT coalition, led by Sassou-Nguesso, was once again mounting antigovernment protests and strikes, prompting Lissouba to charge that foreign countries—specifically, Mobutu Sese Seko's Zaire—were encouraging and supporting the opposition. As sporadic violence continued through 1994, the government announced its intention of bringing members of the opposition into the ruling coalition. In early 1995, the head of the army said that some 2,000 of the estimated 3,000 members of the rival militias would be incorporated into the country's military, though this goal failed to take place on time.

At the end of 1995, a new plan was announced to integrate the militias into the military. But when the Forces Démocratiques Unies (FDU)—the new name for the Sassou-Nguesso's PCT coalition—charged that the army was favoring progovernment militias in the integration process, some 200 FDU militia members briefly fomented a rebellion in a northern Congo-Brazzaville town in March 1996.

Though some 4,000 militia members had been integrated into the military by the end of 1996, the process was marred by a series of mutinies and protests. When militiamen seized the Congo-Ocean, the country's main rail link between the capital and Pointe-Noire, its most important port, the Lissouba government caved in to their demands, incorporating them into the military at the rank of sergeant. Opposition politicians, accusing the government of favoritism and even fomenting the rebellion itself, forced Lissouba to once again shuffle the military high command.

Conflict Breaks Out

In February 1997, nineteen opposition parties, including the FDU, demanded that the government move the elections forward from July and August. They also insisted that, to avoid the violence of 1993–1994, it

disarm civilians, establish an independent electoral commission, and deploy a multinational peacekeeping force. Lissouba turned these requests down. In March, however, he agreed that a multinational force should be stationed in Brazzaville to protect foreign nationals if violence should spill over from Congo (Zaire) where rebel leader Laurent Kabila was about to capture the capital of Kinshasa, just across the Congo River from Brazzaville. Kabila's forces entered Kinshasa peaceably, and most of the peacekeepers left Brazzaville, leaving only a French force of 300.

In May, skirmishes broke out between rival militias supporting the government and various opposition groups in the northern towns of Owando and Oyo. When Sassou-Nguesso moved back to the capital at the end of the month and declared himself a presidential candidate, Lissouba sent troops to arrest him, but Sassou-Nguesso's militia fought them off. Barricades were then set up, and the capital became divided into three armed and hostile zones: one controlled by Lissouba's forces, one by Sassou-Nguesso, and a third representing Bernard Kolela, another aspirant for power. Numerous cease-fires arranged by the OAU, Gabon, and Kolela failed to hold. Massacres of civilians were reported, while the French force—bolstered by new troops—evacuated foreign nationals to Gabon and to U.S. warships off the coast. By the end of July, some 3,000 people had died in the fighting.

For months, the city remained divided, with no force able to gain the edge, but in the north, Sassou-Nguesso's troops had consolidated their control. In addition, the war was threatening to spread to neighboring Congo, especially after artillery shells landed in Kinshasa in October, killing twenty-five people. Kabila, who backed Lissouba's government, sent troops across the river, ostensibly to protect his own citizens but also to help Lissouba. Meanwhile, the French government, still smarting from Lissouba's decision to end the French oil company Elf's monopoly on oil extraction in the country, was allegedly helping Sassou-Nguesso's forces, as was a 1,500-man contingent of Angolan forces, long allied to Sassou-Nguesso for supporting them in their conflict with rebel forces in that country.

By the end of October 1997, the fighting had come to an end, with the victory of Sassou-Nguesso and his reinstatement as president. Lissouba fled across the river to Kinshasa, and his prime minister, Bernard Kolelas, left for Mali and then France. Meantime,

A young member of the Congolese rebel force known as the "ninja" or "Japanese" (for their fast combat skills) waits to hear whether he will be able to join the regular army of the Sassou-Nguesso regime in October 1997. International organizations launched a campaign to ban children's participation in war. *(Jean-Philippe Ksiazek/AFP/Getty Images)*

refugees began to filter back into Brazzaville. A U.S.-mediated agreement saw the pullout of troops from Angola, Congo (Zaire), and France.

Peace Agreements and Renewed Fighting

In 1999, the government and rebel forces signed a peace deal in Zambia, calling for demilitarization of all political parties and the integration of rebel fighters into the nation's army and police. By 2001, some 15,000 militia had disarmed and exchanged their weapons for cash payments. As for Lissouba, he was convicted in absentia of treason and corruption, and sentenced to thirty years in prison. In 2002, voters supported a referendum calling for a new constitution, with expanded executive powers, and elected Sassou-Nguesso to the presidency. Sassou-Nguesso ran unopposed after his main rivals were banned from the contest.

But Sassou-Nguesso's consolidation of power set off new fighting in the region around the capital, where supporters of former prime minister Kolelas engaged Congolese troops in bitter conflicts. Led by renegade priest Pastor Ntumi, the rebels, known as "ninjas" after the Japanese warriors depicted in popular Asian films, feared domination by northern Edou supporters of Sassou-Nguesso. Several hundred persons were killed in the fighting that lasted into early 2003. In March, however, Ntumi and the government signed an accord ending the fighting and guaranteeing that the rights of southerners would be protected. After the 2003 accord, Congo-Brazzaville remained largely at peace, but tensions between northerners and southerners remained. In 2006, Sassou-Nguesso was elected to head the African Union.

James Ciment

See also: Coups; Ethnic and Religious Conflicts; Congo, Democratic Republic of: Kabila Uprising, 1996–1997.

Bibliography

Amphas, Mbow M. *Political Transformations of the Congo.* Durham, NC: Pentland Press, 2000.

Decalo, Samuel. *Historical Dictionary of Congo.* Lanham, MD: Scarecrow Press, 1996.

Economist Intelligence Unit. *Country Profile: Congo.* London: Economist Intelligence Unit, 2005.

Johnson, Douglas. "End of French Africa." *Spectator* 278/8812 June 21, 1997, 14–15.

United Nations. "Peacewatch: Republic of the Congo." *UN Chronicle* 34, no. 3 (1997): 50.

DJIBOUTI: Civil Conflict, 1991–2000

TYPE OF CONFLICT: Ethnic and Religious
PARTICIPANTS: Ethiopia; France

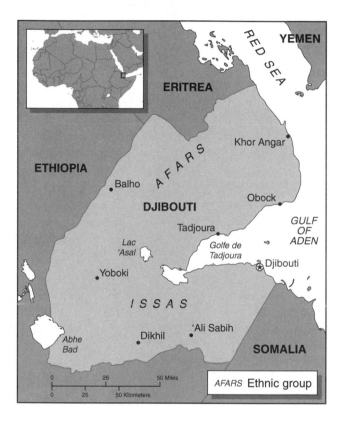

AFARS Ethnic group

Djibouti is a small African nation situated on the southwestern shore of the Red Sea, surrounded by Eritrea to the north, Ethiopia to the west, and Somalia to the south. With little industry, a desert climate, and few resources, the economy is largely based on trade and providing port services to various navies in the strategic Horn of Africa region. The annual per capita income is around $1,500.

A Sunni Muslim country of about 675,000 people, Djibouti is divided into two main ethnic groups, the Issa (roughly 60 percent of the population) and the Afar (about 35 percent). (The remaining 5 percent largely consist of persons of Arab and European descent.) The Issa are related to the neighboring Somalis, and the Afar to the Amharic

people of Ethiopia. The country's official languages are Arabic and French, but most of the citizens speak either Somali or Amharic as their primary language.

Djibouti was occupied by France in the late nineteenth century and was known as French Somaliland by the beginning of the twentieth century. While much of France's African empire became independent in the early 1960s, the people of Djibouti voted in 1958 and 1967 to remain a French colony. In 1967 the country was named the Territory of Afars and Issas. As France moved to grant independence to Djibouti in the mid-1970s, there were fears that the two ethnic groups in the country would become pawns of their larger neighbors in the strategic Horn of Africa region. Ethiopia (backed by the Soviet Union) and Somalia (backed by the United States) were at war over the Ogaden region of Ethiopia, which was claimed by both countries. In fact, Djibouti's leaders proved adept at keeping their country out of the conflict and, in 1988, hosted a peace conference that resulted in a series of accords ending tense relations between Somalia and Ethiopia.

In its first decade or so of independence, Djibouti's leaders also proved able to prevent conflict between the two main ethnic groups—the Issas, who favored neighboring Somalia, and the Afars, who identified with Ethiopia. During the 1980s, power was shared between an Issa president, Hassan Gouled Aptidon, and an Afar prime minister, Barkat Gourad Hamadou, while various government ministries were headed by members of the two different ethnic groups through carefully determined quotas.

This careful ethnic balancing in the government was more appearance than reality, however. While the heads of ministries were both Issas and Afars, the Issas dominated both the civil service and the security forces. During the 1970s and 1980s Afars lost more and more positions in the civil service and military. In

KEY DATES

1967 Residents of Djibouti vote for second time to remain part of France.

1977 Djibouti becomes independent of France.

1981 President Hassan Gouled Aptidon, a member of the dominant Issa ethnic group, bans all opposition parties.

1991 Fighting breaks out between the Aptidon government and Afar rebels organized into the Front for the Restoration of Unity and Democracy (FRUD).

1994 While most FRUD rebels demobilize and are integrated into the military, a radical wing of FRUD continues to fight the government.

1999 Aptidon steps down from the presidency, and a coalition of the ruling People's Progress Assembly and FRUD wins the elections in April.

1981, the president moved to ban all opposition parties, leaving his own, the People's Progress Assembly (RPP, its French acronym), as the only legal party. It, too, was dominated by the Issas.

Economic problems were adding to the country's ethnic tensions. Under the French, the capital city of the county, also known as Djibouti, had been essentially off-limits to migrants from the impoverished and drought-stricken countryside. The poor who did migrate to the capital settled in shantytowns outside the city limits. After independence, thousands more flocked to the capital, and the shantytowns were incorporated into the city proper. By the 1980s, more than half the country's population lived in the capital, where they faced high living costs and high rates of unemployment. The mass migration into the city also led to the establishment of neighborhoods with distinctive ethnic casts. Afars charged that the government favored Issa districts in providing much-needed services. Meanwhile, government efforts to develop rural areas were complicated when refugees from Ethiopia and Somalia poured into Djibouti's countryside.

By the end of the 1980s, tensions between the Afars and Issas had reached the boiling point. Dissatisfied Afars formed the Front for the Restoration of Unity and Democracy (FRUD) to demand multiparty democracy and a more equitable distribution of government positions and services. In 1991, fighting broke out between government forces and FRUD guerrillas. FRUD soon gained control over the north-ern and western portions of the country bordering Ethiopia and Eritrea. France sent in troops to quell the fighting in 1992, and the Afars offered a unilateral cease-fire. The government of President Hassan Gouled Aptidon, however, refused to honor the peace and launched a counteroffensive in July. Much of the rebel-held territory was retaken, and many FRUD leaders were captured and imprisoned, including FRUD leader Ali Aref Bourhan.

Facing military setbacks, the FRUD leadership split over negotiations with the government. The more moderate wing signed an accord with the government in December 1994. Much of the military wing of FRUD demobilized, and its former members were integrated into the nation's security forces. Several FRUD officials became government ministers. Meanwhile, the radical wing of the party (known as FRUD-Renaissance) was attacked in a series of government raids in the late 1990s. The organization was largely eliminated as a serious military threat, finally signing a peace accord with the government in 2000.

Meanwhile, in February 1999, the authoritarian Aptidon stepped down from the presidency, and a coalition of the RPP and FRUD won the elections in April. Their candidate—Aptidon's nephew and aide, Ismael Omar Guelleh—became president. While nominally a multiparty democracy, Djibouti was cited for human rights violations by several international monitoring groups. The United States maintained cordial relations with Djibouti, which it considered a strategic ally in the fight against terrorism.

James Ciment

See also: Ethnic and Religious Conflicts; Ethiopia: War with Somalia, 1977–1978; Ethiopia: Civil War, 1978–1991; Somalia: Civil War Since 1991.

Bibliography

Alwan, Daoud A., and Yohanis Mibrathu. *Historical Dictionary of Djibouti.* Lanham, MD: Scarecrow Press, 2000.

Morrow, James. *Djibouti.* Philadelphia: Mason Crest Publishers, 2004.

Tholomier, Robert. *Djibouti, Pawn of the Horn of Africa.* Metuchen, NJ: Scarecrow Press, 1981.

ERITREA: War for Independence, 1958–1991

TYPE OF CONFLICT: Ethnic and Religious
PARTICIPANT: Ethiopia

Eritrea's ethnic and religious makeup is complex, which made the road to independence a winding one. The original inhabitants of Eritrea were a mixed group of Cushitic and Semitic peoples who had moved into the region some 3,000 years ago. In the fourth century C.E., the coastal areas were converted to Christianity, which then spread to the inland hills and from there to the Ethiopian Empire beyond. In the seventh century, Muslim invaders and merchants brought Islam to the coastal regions of Eritrea. By the twentieth century, Eritrea was approximately evenly divided between the Muslims of the coastal towns and the plains and the Christians who lived in the highlands closer to Ethiopia.

Ethnically the Eritreans were divided between the Tigrinay-speaking Tigray of the highlands (who were almost entirely Christian) and the Muslim peoples of the lowlands, of whom the Tigre are the largest group. (Tigrinay and Tigre are linguistically related but mutually unintelligible.)

Politically, the Eritreans were dominated by outsiders until the twentieth century and had little sense of self-identity as a unique or unified nation. In early modern times, the area was fought over by the Turks, who wished to control the coastal areas, and the Ethiopian Empire, which was constantly trying to expand its influence toward the sea. Starting in the 1860s, the Italians gradually took over the whole of Eritrea, both the Muslim coast and the Christian highlands.

It was the Italian conquest, completed in 1889, which gave Eritrea its first experience of being a separate and united province. The creation of Eritrea was artificial—there was no homogeneous Eritrean nation that shared a common culture or religion. Its ethnic composition, however, was no more mixed than that of neighboring Ethiopia, and the Italian conquest, by imposing a common government for all of Eritrea, gave the area the beginnings of a national consciousness, one that might be shared by both Muslims and Christians.

Eritrea and Ethiopia

World War II swept the Italians out of Eritrea and put the British in temporary control of the country. Emperor Haile Selassie of Ethiopia took the opportunity to demand that Eritrea be united with Ethiopia, as, he claimed, it had always been. Although this was a patent falsehood, the United Nations was willing to support Selassie's claims out of a combination of sympathy (Ethiopia had also suffered under an Italian occupation), geopolitical realism (Eritrea did not seem large enough to be a viable state, and

KEY DATES

1952   British occupiers turn Eritrea over to Ethiopia but with the condition that Eritrea would have autonomy.

1958   Eritrean exiles form the Eritrean Liberation Movement (ELM) to fight for Eritrean independence from Ethiopia.

1962   An Ethiopian-controlled Eritrean legislature votes to merge Eritrea into Ethiopia, with no autonomous rights; ELM is destroyed in a government crackdown but has already been superseded by the Eritrean Liberation Front (ELF) in 1961.

1974   The imperial reign of Haile Selassie falls to the Communist Dergue, led by Mengistu Haile Mariam; the new government intensifies the fight against a new coalition of Eritrean independence forces, the Eritrean People's Liberation Front (EPLF).

1988   The EPLF wins a major battle against Ethiopian forces near the Eritrean town of Afabet.

1991   An increasingly victorious EPLF joins forces with an Ethiopian rebel group, the Tigre People's Liberation Front (TPLF), to bring down the Mengistu regime; the last Ethiopian soldiers leave Eritrea.

1993   In a UN-sponsored referendum, Eritreans vote overwhelmingly for independence, and the country becomes independent on May 3.

landlocked Ethiopia needed its seaports), and indifference (the United Nations had other issues of greater import to distract it in the late 1940s). Moreover, the Ethiopians had the support of most of the Christian Tigray in Eritrea, who felt a connection to Ethiopia because of religion and the fact that the Ethiopian province of Tigre was also dominated by ethnic Tigray.

There were Eritreans who objected to union with Ethiopia. First among them were the Muslims of the coast, but some Christians also questioned whether they would truly be better off under Selassie's autocratic rule. The United Nations committee that decided Eritrea's fate put forward a compromise plan (as a concession to pressure from Arab member states in the UN) in which Eritrea would retain some local autonomy but would be united with Ethiopia in a federal union. This did not satisfy the Muslims, but most Christians—some of whom were beginning to question the benefits of full unity—accepted it as a fair compromise.

Selassie, however, had no intention of living up to his side of the bargain. From the moment the British turned Eritrea over to Ethiopia in 1952, Selassie and his ministers worked to undermine Eritrean autonomy. Amharic, the language of Ethiopia's ruling ethnic group, was decreed to be the language of Eritrea; political parties were made illegal; and the government undercut or ignored the role of the Eritrean legislature. Outbreaks of labor unrest were crushed by Ethiopian troops. Finally, in 1962, the Eritrean legislature voted to merge Eritrea into Ethiopia, where it would have the same status as any other province. The election had been rigged—there was strong evidence of bribery—but Selassie had succeeded in turning Eritrea into an integral part of Ethiopia.

Eritrean Resistance

Even before Ethiopia had consummated its absorption of Eritrea, the Eritreans began to resist their conquerors. In 1958, a group of Eritrean exiles formed the Eritrean Liberation Movement (ELM) under the leadership of Hamid Idris Awate. An imperial crackdown had crushed the ELM by 1962; however, it had already been superseded by a new and more aggressive group, the Eritrean Liberation Front (ELF). The ELF, founded in 1960, dedicated itself to removing the Ethiopians through armed struggle.

The ELF began as a Muslim organization—for this reason it received small amounts of military aid from Sudan, Syria, and Iraq—but it soon began to gain followers from among the Eritrean Christians. Although the Christians shared religious ties with the Ethiopian establishment, they resented the prominence of the Amhara ethnic group in the upper levels of Ethiopia's government and disliked the lack of freedom that existed under Selassie's regime. The eleven years of British rule (1941–1952) had given all Eritreans a taste for greater freedom.

In 1961, the ELF began hit-and-run raids on government outposts in Eritrea. By 1966 its guerrillas controlled large parts of the Eritrean countryside. In 1967, Ethiopia embarked on a brutal campaign against the ELF. More than a hundred villages suspected of supporting the movement were attacked and burned. Perhaps as many as 30,000 Eritreans, mostly Muslims, were turned into refugees. Ethiopia combined this offensive with a diplomatic agreement with Sudan to restrict the ELF's access to outside support. Ethiopia promised to stop permitting Israel to transport aid through its territory to the South Sudanese Anya-Nya rebels if, in return, Sudan ceased providing aid and cross-border refuges to the ELF.

The 1967 campaign slowed the ELF down but did not eliminate it. After 1969, supplies were smuggled across the Red Sea from friendly Yemen, largely bankrolled by Muammar Qaddafi's new Libyan government. The ELF was revitalized and continued its attacks, some of which included hijackings and attempted hijackings of Ethiopian Airlines' planes. By the early 1970s, the Eritrean countryside was again the scene of guerrilla ambushes of government troops, assassinations of government officials, and attempts to interfere with the roads connecting the coastal cities to the rest of Ethiopia.

Selassie's government responded with increased repression and more military attacks on pro-guerrilla villages. Martial law was put into effect throughout the province. These techniques did reduce the ELF's effectiveness, but they also helped to inspire sympathy, along with anger at the Ethiopian army's brutality—when villages were bombed, the innocent died alongside the guilty.

Birth of the EPLF

From 1970 to 1974, the Eritrean resistance movement went through a civil war that temporarily limited its effectiveness in its struggle against Ethiopian control. The causes of the internal conflict are obscure, but it seems that elements in the front-line ELF felt that the leadership, which was based in Cairo, was out of touch with the realities of the Eritrean struggle. Many of them objected to the leadership's strong Muslim orientation, which alienated the large numbers of Christians who were joining the organization.

In 1970, a Muslim leader, Osman Salah Sabbe, who shared the general discontent broke away from the ELF to form the Popular Liberation Forces (PLF). This faction soon joined with other dissident factions to form the ELF-PLF. This breakup led to a civil war between the ELF-PLF and the old ELF. The struggle had ideological and religious overtones—the ELF had a stronger Muslim presence, while the ELF-PLF was more Marxist in outlook—but was also about regional and personality conflicts. By 1974 the fighting between the two groups had died down, and the new ELF-PLF had emerged as the more powerful faction. In the process, it had renamed itself the Eritrean People's Liberation Front (EPLF).

The new EPLF would become the main revolutionary organization of Eritrea (the ELF continued to operate, but most of its supporters gradually defected to the more successful EPLF). It was a more tightly disciplined organization than its predecessor and was better able to garner support among both Christians and Muslims—the EPLF declared that religious affiliation was irrelevant to the struggle against Ethiopia. The EPLF announced that it was fighting to create a socialist and Eritrean nationalist state.

The War's Second Phase

The Ethiopian revolution, which began in 1974, gave the EPLF an opportunity to expand its support in Eritrea while Ethiopia's army was distracted by political turmoil. There was also some hope among

EPLF leaders that the revolution might lead to a negotiated settlement. Part of the cause of the Ethiopian revolution was the army's dissatisfaction with the way in which Selassie was conducing the Eritrean war. As a result, there was a faction within the Ethiopian revolutionary committee (known as the Dergue, the Amharic word for "committee") that believed in reaching an agreement with the Eritrean revolutionaries.

While the Ethiopians were engaged in their internal power struggles, the EPLF was able to gain recruits and control over large sections of Eritrea, including most of its towns. This easy expansion was halted by a massive 1978 campaign of the Ethiopian army. Ethiopia's new ruler, Mengistu Haile Mariam—who led the Dergue faction that had never favored letting Eritrea go free—had gained the support of the Soviet Union, and the post-1977 Ethiopian army was far better equipped than Selassie's troops had been. At the start of the campaign, Mengistu was able to march a 100,000-man army into Eritrea. With this massive, well-equipped force, he was soon able to force the EPLF back into its rural hideouts.

The Ethiopians were helped in their war by a final clash between the EPLF and the ELF. The fight ended with the ELF retreating to its bases in the Sudan, where it would gradually disintegrate. The internecine warfare, however, had damaged the EPLF—by the end of 1978, it probably had fewer than 15,000 soldiers under arms.

The only base that the weakened guerrillas were able to hold was the town of Nakfa, in the northern mountains. The EPLF constructed a twenty-five-mile-long line of trenches and bunkers around the town that held out against every Ethiopian army assault. Nakfa became a symbol of Eritrean resistance. Assaults continued through 1982, when Mengistu mobilized a huge 120,000-man attack force in an attempt to take the redoubt. This assault, the sixth, also failed; 40,000 Ethiopian soldiers were killed in the process.

In the rest of Eritrea, particularly in the coastal and southern plains, the Ethiopian army was able to dominate the towns and, during the day, the roads. But at night the EPLF could operate, carrying out raids against airfields, army bases, and local police stations. Ethiopian control was only maintained through a massive troop presence.

In the north, the EPLF forces in Nakfa continued to hold out, a remarkable achievement for a guerrilla

Rebel forces of the Eritrean People's Liberation Front conduct military drills in 1988. They gained control of the province in May 1991, and Eritrean independence was formally declared two years later. *(Michael Springer/Getty Images News)*

group that Ethiopian authorities contemptuously referred to as "hill bandits." Control of Nakfa gave the EPLF a base from which it could rebuild its strength and launch raids against Ethiopian-held towns. Nakfa also became a center of Eritrean civilization. The supposed hill bandits built underground schools, hospitals, pharmaceutical production centers, and even movie theaters. The mountains around Nakfa were honeycombed with bunkers, both military and civilian.

Although the Ethiopians always had more troops—Ethiopia had more than ten times the population of Eritrea—and better equipment, the Eritreans around Nakfa had the advantage of operating in rough, mountainous terrain, which they knew far better than their opponents did. Ethiopia's Soviet-built jets and helicopters were relatively useless in the rough terrain of northern Eritrea. They did, however, badly reduce the EPLF's effectiveness in the open coastal plains.

The EPLF received most of its military supplies from Arab countries, who smuggled them in over the Sudanese border, or from the seacoast on the occasions when the Eritreans managed to seize a coastal village or two. Even though the EPLF was fighting against a Soviet-backed government, the movement's Marxist orientation alienated the United States and its allies and so kept them from offering support. The EPLF's more reliable patrons were Saudi Arabia, Syria, and Iraq.

Victory

By 1986, the Ethiopian army had effectively conceded its inability to conquer Nakfa. Instead, it concentrated on maintaining its control of the towns in the Eritrean lowlands. From 1986, the EPLF, led by its low-profile commander, Isseyas Afewerki, gradually expanded its area of operations to include most of Eritrea outside the capital of Asmara and the major coastal towns of Mitsiwa and Aseb. In March 1988, the EPLF won a fight against an entire Ethiopian army corps at the town of Afabet, killing and capturing thousands of Ethiopian soldiers after a messy pitched battle.

The following year, 1989, saw increasing cooperation between the EPLF and the Tigre People's Liberation Front (TPLF), based in Tigre province, adjacent to Eritrea. The two groups joined in attacks on both sides of the border. The Soviet Union's 1989 decision to greatly reduce military aid shipments to Ethiopia put Mengistu's regime under increasing pressure. (Gorbachev had initiated one reduction in Soviet aid after coming to power in 1985.) Ethiopia agreed to hold peace talks with the EPLF. The late 1989 talks achieved little, but they demonstrated the weakness of a regime that had previously refused to consider the EPLF as anything but robbers and bandits.

On February 10, 1990, the EPLF captured the port of Mitsiwa, which put the entire north of Eritrea, except for the capital, under Eritrean control. The following year they marched south against the port of Aseb, while also contributing troops to the general uprising against Mengistu's regime that was taking place in Ethiopia itself. In May 1991, the EPLF finally captured the capital of Asmara. The last Ethiopian soldiers in Eritrea surrendered on May 25, 1991. In Ethiopia, Mengistu had already fled for Zimbabwe a few days earlier. The world's longest guerrilla war had ended.

Analysis

The Eritreans' defeat of Ethiopia, which brought down two separate governments, was an amazing military and political feat. That the EPLF succeeded rested on its ability to unite most Eritreans under its banner, whether Christian or Muslim, Tigray or Tigre. It is still unclear how the EPLF was able to unite a disparate set of peoples into one nation when similar attempts by other African nations had been only dismal failures.

The Eritrean national consciousness was begun under the rule of the Italian colonizers. The Italian administrators helped to give a sense of cohesion to an area that had previously been separated by its ethnic and religious divisions. The eleven-year period of British administration gave this newly united territory an appreciation of democratic and liberal institutions, including elective assemblies and a free press.

Ethiopia's move into Eritrea in 1952 was feared by the Muslim population but largely accepted by the Christians. The Ethiopian government's behavior—arrogant, antidemocratic, and ethnically biased in favor of Amharic speakers—convinced many Eritrean Christians that they had more in common with their Muslim neighbors than they did with their coreligionists from Ethiopia. The result was the rise of the ELF and the EPLF.

Finally, the EPLF's success owed something to brilliant leadership. With only limited outside support from the Islamic world—many Arab nations distrusted a movement that included Christians as equal partners—the EPLF was able to fight off a vastly superior army while maintaining the loyalty of its own people. The success of the EPLF inspired rebel movements elsewhere in Ethiopia, which in turn led to the final downfall of the Mengistu regime.

The Future

In the aftermath of the EPLF's victory, Eritrea's future remained unclear but hopeful. Under the leadership of its chairman, Afewerki, the EPLF transformed itself into a civilian organization, the People's Front for Democracy and Justice (PFDJ). In 1991 it had renounced its original hard-line Marxist ideology, embracing the idea of a mixed economy. Local elections were held in March 1997. As of May 1998, the PFDJ and President Afewerki, who was elected in 1993, still dominated Eritrea's government, but they both seemed to be moving in the direction of creating full democratic institutions. In the meantime, Eritrea's economy was being put back together, becoming one of the fastest growing in Africa.

Regionally, the victory of the EPLF ended the many years of war in the Horn of Africa. With Ethiopia and Eritrea on good terms, the region seemed set on the road to stability.

Finally, Eritrea's victory had the regional effect of benefiting the South Sudanese fighters in that country's long civil war. Eritrea, Ethiopia, and Uganda all offered their support to John Garang's Sudanese People's Liberation Army (SPLA), greatly improving its chances of success against the fundamentalist Islamic regime in Khartoum. But Eritrea's promising democratic start turned sour in the late 1990s. In 1998, the country went to war with Ethiopia over a disputed border. The short but bloody conflict left roughly 20,000 Eritrean dead. It also led to crackdowns by the Afewerki government against opposition parties and the press, both of whom questioned the government's conduct of the war. Afewerki also indefinitely postponed discussions on a new constitution and national elections.

Carl Skutsch

See also: People's Wars; Ethnic and Religious Conflicts; Eritrea: Border War with Ethiopia, 1998–2000; Ethiopia: Revolution, 1974–1978; Ethiopia: War with Somalia, 1977–1978; Ethiopia: Civil War, 1978–1991.

Bibliography

Connell, Dan. *Against All Odds: A Chronicle of the Eritrean Revolution.* Lawrenceville, NJ: Red Sea Press, 1997.

Iyob, Ruth. *The Eritrean Struggle for Independence.* New York: Cambridge University Press, 1995.

Marcus, Harold G. *A History of Ethiopia.* Berkeley: University of California Press, 1994.

ERITREA: Border War with Ethiopia, 1998–2000

TYPE OF CONFLICT: Border Dispute

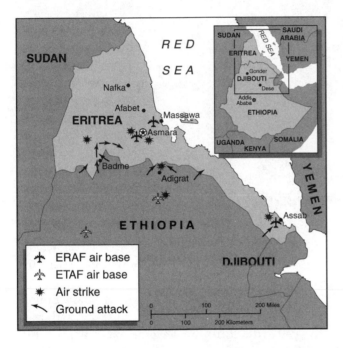

The 1998–2000 border war between Ethiopia and Eritrea, a former Ethiopian province, would see two of Africa's poorest nations spend millions of dollars in military expenditures to fight one another. It would end with tens of thousands of people dead and hundreds of thousands more displaced and homeless. The war exacerbated economic and social crises originally caused by the thirty-year guerrilla war (1963–1993) that culminated in Eritrean independence. That struggle was Africa's longest war in the twentieth century.

Causes

The cause of the conflict lay in the colonial history of the two countries. The Eritrean government based its claim to the disputed territory on an agreement signed between Italy's fascist government and the Ethiopian monarchy during the 1930s. Eritrea had been an Italian colony since the 1890s, and Italian dictator Benito Mussolini used it as a staging ground for his 1936 invasion of Ethiopia. Both Eritrea and Ethiopia were liberated by the British early in World War II. After the war, they remained under British control.

In 1952, Ethiopia regained its independence. At the insistence of Ethiopian emperor Haile Selassie, Eritrea became a part of Ethiopia but received semi-autonomous status. In 1962, Haile Selassie ended Eritrea's special status and made it one of Ethiopia's provinces. This set off a thirty-year period of war and conflict.

The United States supported Haile Selassie for decades, seeing him as a faithful anticommunist ally during the Cold War. The emperor granted the United States unrestricted access to a military base and, in return, received substantial military aid, which he used both against Eritrean separatists and against guerrilla forces in other provinces. The U.S. military base afforded the United States a useful post for monitoring the shipping lanes off Eritrea's shores that connected the Persian Gulf oil fields with the Red Sea and the Suez Canal, allowing oil to be shipped to the Mediterranean and Western Europe.

The armed struggle for independence in Eritrea was led for two decades by the Eritrean People's Liberation Front (EPLF), a nominally Marxist group. In January 1974, the EPLF dealt Haile Selassie's army a devastating setback in a battle at Asmara. The battle weakened the resolve of the Ethiopian army and also revealed the declining power of Haile Selassie himself; later that year, he was overthrown in a military coup. The disorders in Ethiopia gave Eritrea further opportunity to campaign for its independence.

During the 1980s, Ethiopia formed an alliance with the Soviet Union and claimed to be creating a

KEY DATES

1962   The Ethiopian government abolishes the federation with Eritrea and establishes full central government control over the territory, setting off a thirty-year-long civil war.

1974   The Eritrean People's Liberation Front (EPLF) defeats the Ethiopian army in a major battle; the defeat contributes to the fall of the royal government of Haile Selassie and its replacement by a Marxist government.

1991   The EPLF wins control of Eritrea, leading to full independence in 1993.

1997   Growing economic and political tensions between the two countries lead Eritrea to stop using Ethiopian currency.

1998   A tense standoff on the border between the two countries' armies breaks out into warfare.

2000   A major offensive by the Ethiopian army breaks through Eritrean lines in May; in December, the two countries sign onto the Algiers Accord, ending the conflict; in two years of fighting, more than 140,000 soldiers, mostly on the Ethiopian side, have been killed, and 750,000 Eritrean civilians have been displaced from their homes.

Marxist state. The U.S. administration of President Ronald Reagan withdrew support from Ethiopia and began to favor Eritrea's war for independence. The EPLF gained control of an increasing area in Eritrea. Finally, in May 1991, the EPLF captured Asmara, the Eritrean capital and the last Ethiopian stronghold. Ethiopian troops withdrew before May ended. Secretary-General Issaias Afworki of the People's Front for Democracy and Justice (PFDJ) announced the establishment of the Provisional Government of Eritrea. Meanwhile, in Ethiopia itself, the Tigrayan People's Liberation Front, an alliance of opposition groups, toppled the country's ruling dictatorship and installed their leader, Meles Zenawi, as Ethiopia's head of state. In 1993, Eritreans voted overwhelmingly in favor of independence from Ethiopia. Eritrea became an independent state on May 24, 1993.

Immediately the newly formed government was forced to deal with the economic difficulties facing a small, poor country in which more than two-thirds of the population was engaged in subsistence agriculture, hundreds of thousands of peasants had been displaced by years of constant warfare, and most of the country's industrial and communications infrastructure had been destroyed.

Disagreement between Eritrea and Ethiopia soon emerged over matters of currency and trade. In 1997 the Eritrean government stopped using the Ethiopian currency, the birr, and instead created its own currency, the nakfa. The government of Ethiopia responded by demanding that all trade between the two countries be carried out in dollars. Even during Eritrea's war for independence, Ethiopia had been its primary trading partner, accounting for approximately two-thirds of Eritrean trade, including much of its food. After independence, Ethiopia increased restrictions on trade, and the newly independent country faced severe food shortages.

By the same token, Ethiopia had also lost much in the Eritrean war. Eritrea controlled all of the coastline that Ethiopia had once claimed as its own. Now all of Ethiopia's trade had to pass through another country on its way to market. After independence, the Eritrean government demanded that Ethiopia pay increased rates for the use of port facilities.

As if disagreements on currency and access to port facilities were not enough, the agreements ending the war for Eritrean independence left the exact borders between the two countries undefined. Several border areas soon came under dispute as both countries laid claim to a number of regions, most notably Badme, Tsorona-Zalambessa, and Bure. As tensions mounted, the two nations undertook a buildup of armed forces on their respective sides of the contested border.

War

On May 6, 1998, the tense standoff gave way to war when Eritrean troops advanced into a disputed region along the border with the northern Ethiopian province of Tigray. Under the pretext that several Eritrean officials had been killed by Ethiopians, the Eritreans invaded the area near Badme (previously controlled by Ethiopia) and engaged local militia and security forces. The military conflict escalated quickly, with each side increasing troop numbers to more than 100,000 and launching artillery and air attacks against the other.

Ethiopia launched a full assault against Eritrea, including air strikes on the Eritrean capital, Asmara. In response, in June 1998, Eritrea bombed the northern Ethiopian towns of Adigrat and Mek'ele, killing dozens of civilians. In November, Eritrean forces launched an artillery assault on Adrigat in Ethiopia, killing more civilians.

In June 1998, both sides agreed to cease the air raids. Within months, however, air assaults had resumed. That month, Ethiopia attacked Badme, seeking to take it from Eritrean control. In some of the heaviest fighting of the war, the Ethiopians employed artillery, tanks, and air raids in a strong push to take the town, but the Eritrean forces refused to withdraw despite suffering heavy casualties.

As both sides amassed large-scale forces along the border, the battle shifted to a kind of trench warfare that had not been seen since World War I. More than 300,000 troops dug in along a 500-mile front. The pitched battles caused high casualties; in addition, tens of thousands of civilians fled the war zones, creating enormous refugee crises in both countries.

Ethiopian soldiers cheer a strategic victory in the border war with Eritrea in May 2000. A buffer zone patrolled by UN peacekeeping forces was eventually established, but not before both sides suffered heavy casualties. *(Alexander Joe/AFP/Getty Images)*

To make matters worse, Ethiopia drove nearly 80,000 Eritreans and Ethiopians of Eritrean background out of their country and into Eritrea.

Fighting eventually spread to Somalia, where the Oromo Liberation Front, another insurgent group seeking independence from Ethiopia, was based. Eritrea began supporting the group, and Ethiopia responded by supporting the Eritrean Islamic Jihad, a rebel group in Eritrea. Ethiopia also established relations with the Islamic regime in Sudan to support the Eritrean Islamic Salvation, which also opposed the Eritrean government and carried out several terrorist attacks along Eritrea's border with Sudan.

The Organization of African Unity (OAU) spent months trying to get Ethiopia and Eritrea to agree on a peace plan that called for mutual troop withdrawals, international observers to monitor the ceasefire, and a commission to establish the border between the two countries. If one country agreed to the proposal, however, the other side withdrew its approval.

In May 2000, a major Ethiopian offensive broke through Eritrean lines, capturing a key town within Eritrean territory and cutting off the main supply route for Eritrean troops on the western front. By the end of the month, Ethiopian troops occupied almost a quarter of Eritrean territory. The occupation and subsequent loss of much of its infrastructure left Eritrea with little choice but to accept an Ethiopian cease-fire offer.

Negotiations and Legacy

On December 12, 2000, the two countries accepted the terms of the Algiers Agreement to end the war. The agreement established a process of binding arbitration for settling disputes between the countries and established a fifteen-mile-wide temporary security zone to be patrolled by United Nations peacekeeping forces. The agreement also established a Boundary Commission, which determined a new official boundary between the two countries.

In a move that would prove controversial and potentially inflammatory, the Boundary Commission awarded Badme, formerly controlled by Ethiopia, to Eritrea. For years afterward, Ethiopia threatened further military action to reclaim Badme, raising fears that the countries might once again find themselves at war with each other.

The impact of the border war on local populations in both countries was enormous. Eritrea lost approximately 19,000 soldiers, while Ethiopia lost almost 123,000. The conflict also left more than 750,000 Eritreans homeless as refugees.

Jeffrey A. Shantz

See also: Invasions and Border Disputes; Eritrea: War for Independence, 1958–1991.

Bibliography

Gilkes, Patrick, and Martin Plaut. *War in the Horn: The Conflicts Between Eritrea and Ethiopia.* London: Royal Institute of International Affairs, 1999.

Pool, David. *From Guerrillas to Government: The Eritrean People's Liberation Front.* Athens: Ohio University Press, 2001.

Wrong, Michela. *I Didn't Do It for You: How the World Betrayed a Small African Nation.* New York: HarperCollins, 2005.

ETHIOPIA: Revolution, 1974–1978

TYPE OF CONFLICT: Coup
PARTICIPANT: Soviet Union

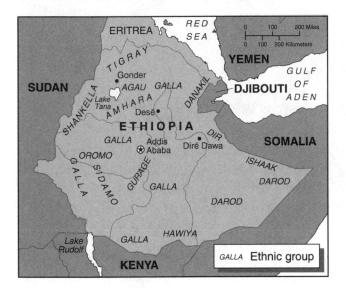

Ethiopia had been a civilized state for at least 2,000 years before the turmoil that removed Haile Selassie, its last emperor. Selassie had begun his reign as a popular monarch, and for much of the world he became a symbol of courage in adversity. His later years, however, were marked by incompetence that eventually led to his overthrow.

Historical Background

Selassie had ruled the country since 1930. In the early years of his reign he had been a modernizing monarch, building roads, schools, hospitals, and a more efficient central government. Tax revenues had flowed into the previously poor kingdom. This progress was halted when Italy, ruled by fascist dictator Benito Mussolini, invaded Ethiopia in 1935. Selassie was forced to flee into exile in May 1936. The following month he made a famous speech before the League of Nations begging for justice, but the organization did not respond.

During World War II, Italy allied itself with Nazi Germany, which soon overran much of Western Europe. The British attacked Ethiopia in 1941, however, and Selassie was able to return to his country with the British army. Defeating the unenthusiastic Italian army, the British entered Addis Ababa in May 1941, and Selassie gathered up the reins of government.

Although Selassie was still regarded with respect, his ability to control the country remained limited. Ethiopia was divided among dozens of different ethnic groups and two major religions (Ethiopian Orthodox Christianity and Islam) and was dominated by a wealthy class of landholders and provincial nobles who resisted sacrificing their prerogatives to the power of the throne.

In the 1950s and 1960s, Selassie made some limited attempts to modernize Ethiopia's economy, but he was unwilling to profoundly alter Ethiopia's social or economic systems. When rich landlords resisted his attempts to alter the tax system to take some of the tax burden off the poor peasants, he backed down and allowed the landlords to retain their privileges. Selassie's policies had the unfortunate effect of alienating both sides: The landlords were annoyed that he had even tried to reduce their economic power, while progressives in Ethiopia were angry to see no changes in its archaic structures.

Selassie also did little to modernize the country's government. In 1955 he decreed a new constitution that provided for an elected parliament, but he allowed it no power. He also did nothing to reduce the dominance of the Christian Amharic people in local and national government. The Amhara had been Ethiopia's traditional ruling class (Selassie was an Amhara), but they made up only 25 percent of the population. Other ethnic groups, particularly the Oromo, who made up 40 percent of the population, and the Tigray, who constituted 14 percent, resented the Amhara's privileged position.

KEY DATES

1955	Responding to unrest, Emperor Haile Selassie decrees a new constitution, providing for an elected parliament, but he allows it no power.
1962	Selassie ignores demands for autonomy of the Ethiopian province of Eritrea, increasing armed resistance in the province.
1974	On January 12, the army brigade mutinies, citing its own poor treatment and the government's failure to respond to famine in Wollo and Tigre provinces; in February, Selassie promises reforms but is slow to enact them; in June, a group of junior officers forms the Coordinating Committee of the Armed Forces, Police, and Territorial Army, known as the Dergue, which is Amharic for "committee."
1974–1977	Internal struggle within the Dergue ends with a victory by Major Mengistu Haile Mariam; by November of 1977, Mengistu has executed the last of his major rivals within the Dergue.
1991	Unable to quell revolts in Tigre and Eritrea, and with Tigrean forces surrounding the capital of Addis Ababa, Mengistu flees the country.

Growing Dissatisfaction

By 1960 unhappiness with Selassie's methods had increased, particularly among the educated classes. Selassie's attempts to modernize Ethiopia's educational system gave more students the opportunity to attend a university, but these students, seduced by Western ideas about freedom and democracy, resented that he limited modernization to economic areas and was unwilling to allow greater political freedom or to reduce the power of the traditional Ethiopian nobility. (Selassie did wish to reduce the nobility's power, but only in order to increase his own.)

On December 13, 1960, a group of disgruntled officers led a coup attempt against Selassie while he was out of the country. They were supported by student demonstrations but were quickly ousted once the emperor returned. The failure of the coup showed that Selassie still retained authority over most of the traditional forces in Ethiopia. That there had been a coup at all, however, revealed to the world and to many Ethiopians that there was also widespread dissatisfaction. The failed coup also

showed that the greatest resistance to Selassie's regime lay with the students and the military. The army's officers were divided between an older generation, which felt a personal loyalty to the emperor, and a younger, better-educated generation, which was frustrated with Ethiopia's backward economy and society.

After 1960, Ethiopia also faced growing regional resistance to Selassie's centralization plans. Selassie wished all of Ethiopia's regions to be fully under the control of a strong centralized state, but this ambition went against a strong tradition of regional autonomy in Ethiopian history. Many regions chafed under Selassie's policies, none more so than Eritrea.

Eritrea, which had been semi-independent under the Italians and the British, was forced into a federal union with Ethiopia in 1952. Selassie gradually subverted the Eritreans' federal assembly and, in 1962, turned the territory into a mere province of Ethiopia. Eritreans fought against Ethiopian control. In 1960 they founded the Eritrean Liberation Front (ELF). The ELF led an armed resistance to Ethiopia, which forced Selassie to commit a large portion of his armed forces to hunting Eritrean guerrillas.

The Eritrean resistance was the most serious regional unrest facing Ethiopia during Selassie's regime, but the army also faced low-level resistance from the Somali, the Tigray, and the Oromo. The regions occupied by these peoples required further commitments of troops. The lack of success in these ongoing struggles disturbed the army, which blamed its failure on corruption and incompetence within Selassie's government.

Selassie also had to deal with growing resistance by the landed nobility. A 1966 plan to create a modern tax system led to a revolt in Gojam that required military intervention. Other provinces resisted the new system, and Selassie was obliged to rescind the changes, lowering his prestige in the process.

Criticized by progressives for not changing fast enough, and by traditional-minded landlords for trying to change too much, and facing constant unrest by Ethiopia's many ethnic minorities, Selassie had less and less control over his country in the early 1970s. His rule was further handicapped by his own advanced age and growing obstinacy. The progressive monarch of the 1930s had become a stubborn reactionary by 1974. Ethiopia's government stagnated amid growing corruption.

Open Unrest

On January 12, 1974, an army brigade at Negele rose up in mutiny. The soldiers were upset at their own poor treatment as well as at the government's seeming inability to deal with a famine that had begun in 1972—200,000 had died in Wollo and Tigre provinces. Units around the country joined the Negele brigade in its mutiny. In January the soldiers were joined by striking workers and students who demanded changes in the government ranging from better pay to more effective famine relief. Finally, many Ethiopians began to demand a complete overhaul of the government itself.

In late February, Selassie responded by promising reforms and appointing a new prime minister, Endalkatchew Medonnen—Medonnen replaced Selassie's longtime favorite Akilu Habte Wold. There was no real change, however, and the new government began to clamp down on the military, arresting officers it considered unreliable.

In June, a group of young junior officers frustrated with the glacial pace of change, organized

themselves into a Coordinating Committee of the Armed Forces, Police, and Territorial Army. The Dergue, as the group came to be known ("Dergue" is the Amharic word for "committee"), declared themselves dedicated to a general ideal of a better Ethiopia. Operating within the chaos that was taking over Ethiopia, the Dergue was able to claim for itself the right to dictate policy to the government. These 120 men, ranging in rank from sergeant to major, slowly became Ethiopia's new rulers.

The Dergue's Creeping Coup

At first, the old government continued to function. The Dergue pledged its loyalty to Selassie, and Medonnen remained Ethiopia's prime minister. But the Dergue made demands and, because the army seemed to support it, the emperor and his ministers felt obliged to cooperate. Each successful demand increased the Dergue's confidence and lowered the prestige of the regime. Selassie steadily lost what support he still had, and the Dergue became the organization that all parties felt obliged to obey.

In a process that was described as a "creeping coup," the Dergue ordered senior officers arrested for corruption, forced Selassie to replace his ministers, and gradually removed the entire structure upon which the emperor's power rested. Throughout the creeping coup the Dergue kept itself behind the scenes as much as possible. Its chairman, Major Mengistu Haile Mariam, and vice chairman, Major Atnafu Abate, did their best to avoid public notice. It seems likely that the Dergue's members feared that revealing their identities would make them vulnerable to assassination or suppression.

At first it appeared that the Dergue did not plan to replace the government and that they simply wanted to force it to reform. By August 1974, however, with the emperor obeying all their demands, it appeared their ambitions had grown. They decided that Selassie himself had to be removed from power.

In August the Dergue forced Selassie to replace Medonnen with a more reform-minded prime minister, and also made him choose General Aman Michael Andom as the new defense minister (Andom was considered sympathetic by the Dergue). Finally, in September, the Dergue accused the emperor of covering up the Wollo famine (which was true). Angry crowds demanded Selassie's arrest. On September 12, Selassie was driven away in a blue Volkswagen, emperor no more; he died in custody the following year.

Major Mengistu Haile Mariam, who played a key role in the 1974 revolution that ousted Ethiopia's Emperor Haile Selassie, emerged as head of the Military Administrative Council (Dergue) in 1977 and served as the nation's president from 1987 to 1991. *(AFP/Getty Images)*

On September 15, the Dergue changed itself into the Provisional Military Administrative Council (PMAC) and made General Aman its chairman.

Power Struggle

From 1974 to 1977 the Dergue was engaged in a struggle for power within its own ranks. At the same time, the Dergue was fighting against the attempts of Eritrea to break away. It also had to suppress popular movements within Ethiopia itself, which were demanding an end to military rule. When the struggle ended, Mengistu, chairman of the Dergue, emerged as the sole victor in this bloody civil war.

The first victim to fall was General Aman. Aman was trying to negotiate a peaceful settlement to the Eritrean war (he was an Eritrean), and many Dergue members rejected any plan that might give Eritrea its independence. On November 23, 1974 (a day that would be remembered as "Bloody Sunday"), troops loyal to the Dergue attempted to arrest Aman. The general resisted with the help of his personal body-

guard, but after a firefight, in which the Dergue was forced to call in tanks, Aman was killed, along with two Dergue members who had supported him. The Dergue then went on to kill fifty-nine prisoners already in custody, including former prime minister Medonnen.

The Dergue then appointed another general, Tafari Banti, to be the new head of the PMAC, but real power remained with Mengistu and his colleagues.

In December 1974, the Dergue called for Ethiopia to become a socialist state. In April 1976, Mengistu elaborated on the Dergue's idea of socialism with the publication of a Program for the National Democratic Revolution (PNDR). The PNDR promised steady progress toward socialism under the leadership of workers, peasants, and other anti-traditionalist classes, but in practice the Dergue continued to keep all power in its own hands. It was Stalinism with a Marxist face.

Although many Ethiopians on the left, particularly university students, had initially supported the Dergue, they grew increasingly angry at the Dergue's refusal—despite its leftist rhetoric—to share power with the people. The government nationalized farms and factories, but did so completely from above, allowing little worker or farmer participation in the process.

The most important Ethiopian socialist party, the Ethiopian People's Revolutionary Party (EPRP), had at first worked with the Dergue, but in February 1977, it decided that the military rulers would never willingly share power and so declared war on the Dergue. For more than a year the EPRP and the Dergue engaged in an urban guerrilla war of assassination and counterassassination. Squads of EPRP gunmen spent their nights stalking military leaders, while the military gave weapons to private militias who hunted EPRP members during the day. The streets of Addis Ababa echoed with gunfire and grenade blasts. Tens of thousands of students who were suspected of having EPRP loyalties were imprisoned; many were tortured and others were never seen again. A number of Dergue members were killed by the EPRP, but Mengistu succeeded in crushing the movement by the end of 1978. At least 10,000 EPRP members and sympathizers, mostly students, died in this war of Marxist military government versus Marxist revolutionary party.

Before the final defeat of the EPRP, Mengistu had already eliminated his last competitors within the Dergue. In late December 1976, Tafari Banti, the official head of the PMAC, and Major Atnafu Abate, a longtime Dergue leader, had attempted to maneuver Mengistu into a less powerful position within the Dergue hierarchy. At first they seemed to have succeeded in reducing his power base, but in a February 3, 1977, shootout, supporters of Mengistu cornered Tafari at the Grand Palace in Addis Ababa and killed him, along with six other Dergue members. In November, Mengistu ordered his last rival, Atnafu, executed.

Epilogue

Mengistu was now the sole leader of Ethiopia's revolution. Although he continued to speak in Marxist terms, it was clear that his brand of Communism was solely directed toward maintaining himself in power. He created a commission in 1979 whose job it was to build a new Marxist party in Ethiopia. The result was the September 1984 birth of the Workers Party of Ethiopia (WPE). However, the WPE had little popular support and was clearly a tool designed to keep Mengistu in power. In 1987, Mengistu ordered the name of his country changed to the People's Democratic Republic of Ethiopia.

For Ethiopia, Mengistu's rule was disastrous. He forced all areas of the economy into a top-down state-controlled system that emulated Soviet-style Communism, but he did so at a time when even the Soviet Union itself was recognizing the failure of its own command economy. His land distribution programs, combined with the creation of peasant agricultural associations, led to declining harvests and a massive famine in 1984. Nationalization of the industrial and financial sectors of the economy proved to be equally unsuccessful. And the indiscriminately waged war against the EPRP had killed or forced out of the country thousands of Ethiopia's best and brightest minds (many of the students targeted by Mengistu in the anti-EPRP war had only peripheral connections to the outlawed group).

In foreign policy, Mengistu's victory had the effect of bringing Ethiopia within the Soviet Union's system of alliances. The Soviet government began supplying large quantities of arms to the Ethiopians (an overnight switch from their previous policy of supporting Ethiopia's neighbor and archenemy Somalia). In 1989, however, Soviet reform leader Mikhail Gorbachev ended Soviet support for the Ethiopian dictator.

Mengistu also continued the previous regime's policy of suppressing Ethiopia's various ethnic secessionist groups. It was these groups that were the cause of his eventual downfall. Ethnic armies in Eritrea drained Ethiopia's resources and weakened Mengistu's authority. Then in May 1991 an army of ethnic Tigray was able to march on Addis Ababa and force Mengistu to flee.

It was the end of the Ethiopian revolution begun seventeen years earlier.

Analysis

Ethiopia collapsed because Haile Selassie's regime was too rigid to deal with the conflicting demands of a new generation that desired modernization and change, and because Ethiopia's traditional elites resisted all change that might reduce their economic power over the poor peasantry. The government was unable to satisfy the desire of ethnic minorities, particularly the Eritreans, to achieve either autonomy or independence.

Once Selassie had lost the support of most areas within Ethiopian society, it took only a spark to bring down his regime. The 1974 spark was probably the general dissatisfaction of most Ethiopians with the government's handling of the 1972–1974 famine.

The success of Mengistu and the Dergue in replacing Selassie was based upon the general disunity of the country and on Mengistu's own political acumen. Mengistu allied himself with popular generals, and when he no longer needed them, he eliminated them. Likewise, the EPRP was a useful ally while Mengistu and the Dergue were busy tearing down the economic structures that supported Ethiopia's traditional elites, but once they had succeeded, the EPRP was no longer needed and was removed in a bloody civil struggle. When the dust cleared, only Mengistu was left standing. And Ethiopia was forced to suffer fourteen years of Mengistu's dictatorial policies.

Carl Skutsch

See also: Cold War Confrontations; Coups; Eritrea: War for Independence, 1958–1991; Ethiopia: War with Somalia, 1977–1978; Ethiopia: Civil War, 1978–1991.

Bibliography

Keller, Edmond J. *Revolutionary Ethiopia: From Empire to People's Republic.* Bloomington: Indiana University Press, 1988.

Marcus, Harold G. *A History of Ethiopia.* Berkeley: University of California Press, 1994.

Tiruneh, Andargachew. *The Ethiopian Revolution, 1974–1987.* New York: Cambridge University Press, 1993.

ETHIOPIA: War with Somalia, 1977–1978

TYPE OF CONFLICT: Invasions and Border Disputes
PARTICIPANT: Somalia

When the Ethiopian empire expanded its borders in the late nineteenth century, it laid claim to an eastern region called the Ogaden. Unfortunately for future peace, the Ogaden was mostly inhabited by nomadic Somali tribesmen who had no desire to be absorbed into the Ethiopian state.

Unlike Ethiopia, Somalia has a largely uniform culture. Most of its population are ethnic Somalis who speak the same language and share Islam as their religion. Two-thirds of Somalis are nomadic or semi-nomadic, driving their herds of sheep, goats, cattle, and camels back and forth across the terrain, moving from one fertile region to another.

The Ogaden lies in the middle of many Somalis' migratory patterns. Somali clans were accustomed to moving from the Hawd to the Ogaden depending on the time of year. In the process, however, they were crossing into territory claimed by Ethiopia. It was this clash of ethnic and political realities that would lead to the 1977 war between Ethiopia and Somalia.

Historical Background

When the Ethiopian Emperor Menelik laid claim to the Ogaden in 1890, the Somalis had no independent government. A people made up of wandering tribesmen, they had never been united into one nation—although their shared language and culture gave a strong structure on which a sense of nationalism could be built. In 1890, the Somalis were ruled by two colonial powers. In the north, the British had established a British Somaliland Protectorate; in the south, the Italians had moved their troops into the main ports and declared the area to be Italian Somaliland.

So, when Menelik announced that Ogaden should be Ethiopian territory, it was Europeans, not Somalis, who negotiated the province's fate with him. The British only wanted to maintain their control over the coast and so had no objection to Ethiopian control of the interior. The Italians, dreaming of empire, objected more strongly, but a brief Italian-Ethiopian war (1895–1896) put an end to those dreams and gave Ethiopia control over the Ogaden. The rest of the Somali people, under British, French, and Italian control, could do nothing to alter the situation.

When World War II began in 1939, Italy was allied with Nazi Germany, and Great Britain was a key nation of the Allied Powers assembled to defeat them. The war quickly came to Somalia and put the Somalis on the road to independence. In 1940, an Italian army conquered British Somaliland, and Italy united all its territories in the region into one province, Italian East Africa. The Somalis, for the first time, were under a single government. In 1941, the British counterattacked and threw the Italians out of Africa, but kept Somalia. The British encouraged the Somalis in the creation of their first modern political organization, the Somali Youth League (SYL). The SYL agitated for a united Somalia, which would encompass all territories where Somalis lived,

KEY DATES

1960	Somali-backed guerrillas of the Western Somali Liberation Front (WSLF) conduct a low-level conflict in the Ogaden region against Ethiopian government forces.
1969	General Mohammed Siad Barre leads a military coup in Somalia.
1974	Marxist forces under Mengistu Haile Mariam overthrow the reign of Emperor Haile Selassie and take power in Addis Ababa.
1977	Somali regulars begin to provide support for the WSLF; in July, Somali tanks roll into Ogaden.
1978	Ethiopian forces, backed by Cuban advisers, take the upper hand in the conflict, driving the Somali army out of Ogaden.
1980–1983	Ogaden guerrillas are pursued by Ethiopian forces into Somalia, causing tension between the two countries.
1991	Regimes in both Ethiopia and Somalia collapse.

including former British Somaliland, Italian Somaliland, and the contested Ogaden region.

Haile Selassie, Ethiopia's emperor, contested Somalia's claim to the Ogaden, insisting that the region was Ethiopian land. Unlike the SYL, Selassie had the ear of the United Nations, which ruled in Selassie's favor in 1948. Britain bowed to the decision and withdrew its forces from the Ogaden. When Ethiopian administrators arrived, SYL activists attempted to keep them out, leading to bloodshed. But without international support and their own independence as a nation, the Somalis could do little to stop the Ethiopian takeover.

In 1960, the Somalis had a reversal in fortune. Italy, which had regained temporary control of Italian Somaliland, gave it independence in 1959. Britain followed suit in British Somaliland in June 1960. The leading parties in the two new nations immediately agreed to merge, and on July 1, 1960, the Somali Republic was born.

From the beginning, Somali politicians announced their intention of recovering lands they believed belonged to Somalia and were inhabited by people of Somali descent. These lands included northern Kenya, French Somaliland (after independence renamed Djibouti), and the Ogaden. The new government did not have the economic or military might to confront Ethiopia directly, but it did support an Ogaden Somali guerrilla movement, the Western Somali Liberation Front (WSLF).

From 1960 to 1977 the trouble caused by the WSLF was minor but irritating. Guerrillas moved back and forth across the border, using Somalia as a refuge and attacking Ethiopians in Ogaden. Sometimes Ethiopian forces pursued the guerrillas into Somalia itself. In 1961 and 1964 there were minor border skirmishes between regular Somali and Ethiopian troops. The better equipped Ethiopian army emerged victorious.

Siad Barre and War

In 1969, after a civilian political crisis, the Somali military staged a coup and declared General Mohammed Siad Barre to be Somalia's new leader. Siad Barre embraced an ideology of revolutionary Communism. Posters went up around Somalia praising "Comrade Marx, Comrade Lenin, and Comrade Siad."

While Siad Barre's devotion to Communism seemed to stem primarily from its usefulness as a tool for totalitarian control of his country, it also gained him the friendship of the Soviet Union. The Soviets considered an ally in Somalia a counterbalance to the pro-American Ethiopian government. The Soviets helped their new ally by pouring economic and military aid into Somalia. Siad Barre was able to build his army up to a strength of 23,000, equipped with 200 Soviet-built tanks (including sophisticated T-54s), 300 armored personnel carriers, and 50 MiG fighter-bombers. The Ethiopians had more troops, but fewer tanks and less sophisticated aircraft.

When a 1974 revolution sent Ethiopia spiraling into chaos, Siad Barre saw the event as an opportunity to reopen Somali claims on the Ogaden. In 1975, the dormant WSLF was revived and encouraged to cross back into the Ogaden, attacking Ethiopian troops. In June 1977, Somali regulars began to provide surreptitious aid to the guerrillas. Finally, in July 1977, Somali tanks rolled across the border in an attempt to seize the Ogaden before the Ethiopian government could react.

At first the Somalis had some success. The Ethiopian government was still distracted by its own internal problems, and its troops were not as well equipped as the Soviet-supplied Somalis. In July, the Somalis seized the provincial village of Dagahbur. By September they had captured Jijiga, along with some 60 percent of the Ogaden. They then began to move on the only remaining sizable town in the Ogaden, Harer.

At that point, a reversal of alliances led to a reversal of fortune on the battlefield. Since the beginning of the 1974 Ethiopian revolution, the Soviet Union had hoped to replace the Americans and make themselves Ethiopia's main patron. In late 1976 their efforts had begun to pay off with the signing of aid treaties between the two nations. At first the Soviets had tried to balance their Somali and Ethiopian friendships, but the July 1977 invasion made it impossible. Four months later, the Soviets decided to back the Ethiopians (with a population six times that of Somalia, it was a much better prize) and began a massive airlift of supplies to the Ethiopian army—$1 billion worth delivered over five months—along with large numbers of Cuban advisers and 17,000 Cuban ground troops.

Betrayed, Siad Barre expelled his Soviet advisers and began searching for other friends and other sources of military aid, but the most likely sources, the United States and its allies, refused to supply him with any aid as long as his troops remained inside Ethiopia's official borders. The Americans would not tolerate any African border readjustments based on ethnic self-determination, because they feared that any such adjustment would send the continent into a series of chaotic border wars, for most African borders had been drawn by Europeans with little regard for ethnic realities.

Over the 1977–1978 winter, the balance of forces shifted from the advancing Somalis to the defending Ethiopians. When the WSLF and the Somali army attacked in January 1978, they were repulsed by the Ethiopian army with the help of Cuban troops and the new Soviet supplies. In February, Ethiopia launched a counterattack with a 50,000-man force spearheaded by new tank units and backed up by helicopter-transported assault troops. The Somalis had fewer than 20,000 regulars backed by 10,000 WSLF guerrillas. The Ethiopians and Cubans outnumbered the Somalis by more than 2 to 1, and their equipment was now also better. The Somali army collapsed and fled in disorder back across the Somali border. On March 9, Siad Barre announced that all Somali forces were back in Somalia, and he declared an end to the fighting.

The WSLF continued to harass the Ethiopian army. As a result, Ethiopian tanks pursued the guerrillas across the border into Somalia in 1980 and 1983. Tensions between Somalia and Ethiopia remained high; nevertheless, after 1978 Siad Barre ended his attempts to gain the Ogaden by force.

Analysis

On the basis of popular sovereignty, Somalia's claim to the Ogaden was quite reasonable. To the extent that any sizable population lived there, it was a Somali population. But Selassie and Ethiopia were able to take advantage of European lack of interest to extend the borders of their nation to surround the entire Ogaden. In the confusion following the 1974 Ethiopian revolution, Somalia saw its chance to redress this perceived wrong and gained Soviet sponsorship. It could not imagine that in the middle of the conflict, the Soviets would change sides and support the Ethiopians. The transfer of Soviet support was the critical factor that kept Somalia from retaking the Ogaden.

One result of the 1977–1978 war was a shift in East African power relationships. After the Soviet Union took up support of Ethiopia, the United States began offering help to Somalia. In Cold War terms, the Soviet Union, gaining the friendship of larger and richer Ethiopia, was the winner.

For the African nations, however, the result was less clear. The war would add to instability in both countries. Ethiopia's leader, Mengistu Haile Mariam, and Somalia's Siad Barre both faced continued internal turmoil (sometimes supported by each other). Both leaders would fall from power in 1991.

Carl Skutsch

See also: Cold War Confrontations; Invasions and Border Disputes; Ethiopia: Revolution, 1974–1978; Ethiopia: Civil War, 1978–1991.

Bibliography

Farer, Tom. *War Clouds on the Horn of Africa.* New York: Carnegie Endowment for International Peace, 1979.

Lewis, Ioan. *A Modern History of Somalia.* Boulder, CO: Westview Press, 1988.

Marcus, Harold G. *A History of Ethiopia.* Berkeley: University of California Press, 1994.

ETHIOPIA: Civil War, 1978–1991

TYPE OF CONFLICT: Ethnic and Religious
PARTICIPANT: Eritrea

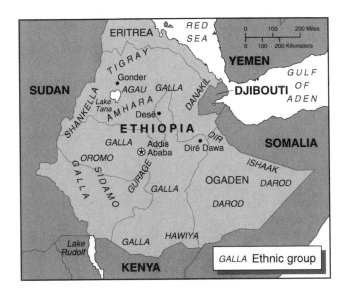

GALLA **Ethnic group**

The Ethiopian civil war began in 1974 when a civil-military uprising led to the ouster of the Emperor Haile Selassie's regime. From that moment on, rival forces within Ethiopia did not cease their struggle for power. Even during the brief period from about 1978 through 1982, when Mengistu Haile Mariam appeared to have complete control over the country, he still faced serious military threats in the northern Eritrean and Tigray provinces. These threats, combined with other uprisings, would overwhelm his regime.

Mengistu rose to power as part of a military junta known as the Dergue ("Dergue" is the Amharic world for "committee"). Once the Dergue had removed the emperor from his throne, they faced four threats to their hold on power. The first was internal, a radical Marxist movement known as the Ethiopian People's Revolutionary Party (EPRP). (The Dergue also claimed to be Marxists, but the EPRP doubted their ideological purity.) The second and third threats were the Somali and Eritrean separatist movements in the north and east. In both provinces, local ethnic groups objected to Ethiopian control over their territories. The final threat came from within the Dergue itself:

Its members, unable to agree on who was to wield power, would eventually fall into a vicious internal struggle for power.

By 1978, Mengistu, the Dergue's chairman, had seemingly resolved all these threats to the Dergue's position in Ethiopia. The EPRP was defeated in a messy civil war during 1977 and 1978. Thousands of students, the EPRP's main base of support, were killed or forced into exile. The Somali and Eritrean rebels were defeated in 1978 with the help of military support provided by the Soviet Union. The Dergue itself was badly bloodied in all these struggles—particularly those with the EPRP, which had waged an assassination campaign against Dergue members. Those prominent Dergue members who remained were eliminated by Mengistu himself in 1977. The Dergue became a tool through which Mengistu exercised control over the country. The end of 1978 saw Mengistu apparently in firm control of almost all of Ethiopia.

A Soviet Client

The key factor in Mengistu's success, beyond his own personal ruthlessness, was the support provided by the Soviet Union. Before the 1974 revolution, Ethiopia had been a friend of the United States and its allies, and at first it seemed possible that Mengistu and the Dergue might, despite their Marxist rhetoric, stay within the American orbit. But the Soviets had assiduously courted Mengistu, and in 1976 they had signed a deal to provide his regime with $365 million in military aid.

Late in 1977 the relationship was solidified when the Soviet Union decided to back Ethiopia rather than Somalia in the 1977–1978 Ethiopian-Somalian war. Before 1977, Somalia had been the Soviet Union's favored client in the region, but responding to Mengistu's desperate request for assistance, the Soviets ended their support of the Siad Barre regime and poured massive amounts of military equipment into Ethiopia. It was

KEY DATES

1958   The independence struggle by liberation forces in the Ethiopian province of Eritrea begins.

1974   The reign of Emperor Haile Selassie is overthrown in a military coup led by the Coordinating Committee of the Armed Forces, Police, and Territorial Army, known as the Dergue, which is Amharic for "committee."

1978   Dergue leader Mengistu Haile Mariam eliminates rivals and consolidates power in his own hands.

Ethiopia triumphs over Somalia in a brief war over the contested Ogaden region of Ethiopia.

1988   Independence forces in the Ethiopian province of Eritrea score a major military victory over the Ethiopian army; liberation forces in Oromo and Tigre provinces begin recruiting large armies.

1991   With Tigrean forces surrounding the capital of Addis Ababa, Mengistu flees to Zimbabwe.

this aid—including 600 tanks and 300 armored personnel carriers—that allowed the Ethiopians to defeat Somalia's attempt to seize the Ogaden province.

With the Ogaden front stabilized, Mengistu was able to transfer his newly reequipped army to the Eritrean front and defeat the rebels there. In these efforts he was also assisted by Cuban soldiers and Soviet advisers.

In November 1978, the Soviets and Mengistu signed a twenty-year Treaty of Friendship and Cooperation. The Soviet Union promised full backing to Mengistu's attempts to suppress all dissent within Ethiopia. Without such support, Mengistu's regime might not have lasted past 1979. In return for the substantial expense of supporting Mengistu, the Soviet Union gained a loyal ally adjacent to the strategically important Horn of Africa, which all shipments going to and from the Suez Canal pass. The Soviets also used Ethiopia as an airbase from which they had easy access to the Persian Gulf and North Africa.

Problems Within Ethiopia

The causes of Mengistu's 1991 fall were rooted in two problems: economic dissatisfaction and ethnic unrest.

Mengistu, an avowed Marxist, tried to impose on Ethiopia a Soviet-style command economy, controlling all sectors of Ethiopian society and industry. He created an artificial puppet political party, the Workers Party of Ethiopia (WPE), whose popularity was minimal but which served the purpose of providing an instrument with which he could implement his economic and political decrees.

Farmers were forced to subdivide their land into twenty-five-acre plots, each of which would be farmed by a separate peasant family, regardless of their effectiveness or energy. The peasant farms were grouped together in peasant agricultural associations, whose policies were guided by the WPE, and independent farmers were forced to move into village collectives. The result of these ideological plans was a 1984 famine, which led to humanitarian donations of food from the wealthy nations of the world.

Mengistu's industrial policy was no more successful. Ethiopia's state-controlled industries had stagnant growth, and Ethiopia's economy suffered. The influx of Soviet aid helped only slightly—most of the Soviet aid was military, not consumer or industrial, in nature. The generally poor economy helped to fuel resentment among all Ethiopians. But the ethnic groups in the outlying provinces felt that they suffered disproportionately from Mengistu's failed policies.

Mengistu's original decision to call for Soviet support had been caused by the Ogaden and Eritrean separatist crises, but in reality all of Ethiopia was an ethnic problem for Mengistu. Ethiopia's population was divided into a dozen major ethnic groups. The most prominent were the Amhara, who were Ethiopia's traditional ruling class. Out of a population of about 30 million in 1975, approximately 25 percent were Amhara. Ethiopia also contained Tigray (14 percent of the population), Oromo (40 percent), Sidamo speakers (7 percent), Tigre speakers (3 percent), Somalis (3 percent), and a mix of other, smaller ethnic groupings. Both Amhara and Tigray were predominantly Christian, but most of the remainder were Muslim or worshiped animist gods. The population broke down thus: Christians, 45 percent; Muslims, 45 percent; and animist, 10 percent.

In this complex ethnic and religious mixture, there had traditionally been much resentment by all ethnic groups directed at the dominance of the Amhara and the Ethiopian Orthodox Church. Even the Tigray, who were mostly Orthodox Christians, resented that the Amhara tended to receive all the best government jobs and monopolize the lion's share of the country's wealth. Ethiopia's 1974 revolution claimed to have ended ethnic favoritism, but other ethnicities believed that the Amhara continued to have a preponderance of power.

It was these ethnic resentments that would eventually coalesce into the rebellions that defeated Mengistu's regime.

The Ogaden

The Ogaden had been the initial reason for Mengistu's request for Soviet help and would remain a problem for Ethiopia throughout the 1980s. The Ogaden was an arid province in eastern Ethiopia inhabited primarily by Somali tribesmen. Most Somalis lived along the Indian Ocean coast, but many Somalis—two-thirds of whom lived a nomadic life—traditionally wandered back and forth from the coastal regions to the Ogaden, looking for grazing land for their flocks. Ethiopia's conquest of the Ogaden in the 1890s had divided the Somalis' grazing grounds into two parts. For decades afterward, the Somalis paid little attention to the arbitrary border—border guards were nonexistent—but, in 1960, the creation of an independent Somali Republic among the Indian Ocean Somali led to rising tensions between Somalia and Ethiopia.

Somalia claimed to represent all Somalis and argued that the Ogaden should rightfully belong to Somalia. The Somali government supported a guerrilla group, the Western Somali Liberation Front (WSLF), which led attacks against Ethiopian outposts. Growing friction between Somalia, the WSLF, and Ethiopia led to the 1977–1978 Ethiopian-Somalian War.

With Soviet help—and Cuban troops—the Somalis were badly defeated, but unrest in the Ogaden did not stop. The WSLF, sometimes surreptitiously aided by Somali army regulars, continued to harass the Ethiopian army throughout the 1980s. There were also two major skirmishes between Ethiopian and Somali army units in 1980 and 1983. As a result, Mengistu was forced to maintain a large army within the Ogaden, which was both economically damaging and militarily a problem (troops in the Ogaden were unavailable to deal with troubles elsewhere in Ethiopia).

Eritrea

The most serious military problem faced by Mengistu was an inheritance from imperial Ethiopia. Eritrea had been in revolt since 1962 when Ethiopia absorbed the small federal state into the empire. In past centuries, the Ethiopian empire had occasionally controlled Eritrea, but its people had no desire to be ruled from Addis Ababa. About half the population were ethnic Tigray Christians, while the other half were Muslims from a variety of ethnic groups, mostly Tigre.

Originally, Eritrea's Christians had welcomed union with Ethiopia, but the Emperor Selassie's heavy-handed methods convinced them to join forces with their Muslim neighbors and rise up in rebellion against Ethiopian control.

By the time Mengistu came to power, the Eritrean People's Liberation Front (EPLF) controlled most of the countryside and many of the towns within Eritrea. After Mengistu defeated the Somalians, he switched his new Soviet-equipped army to the Eritrean front and, in 1978, almost completely cleared the province of rebels.

The rebels survived, however, in their fortress stronghold of Nakfa. Repeated campaigns, using more than 100,000 troops and backed by Soviet-supplied jets and tanks, were unable to dislodge the Eritreans from their mountain fortress. In the early 1980s, the EPLF was even able to mount occasional counterattacks against the Ethiopian invaders.

Of all the problems faced by Mengistu's regime, the chronically unresolved Eritrean war was probably the most damaging. The Eritrean front forced Mengistu to station most of the Ethiopian army within or near Eritrea, making other areas more vulnerable to unrest. And his failure to defeat tiny Eritrea, with a population of about 3 million, badly hurt his regime's prestige. Eritrea's successes provided encouragement for other groups within Ethiopia.

The Tigray and the Oromo

The Tigray had long resented Amharic dominance in Ethiopia. As Orthodox Christians, they believed that they had the right to share power with the Amhara elite, but although their political and economic position was substantially better than that of other ethnicities, they still considered themselves slighted within the Ethiopian empire. Their discontent led to a 1943 uprising that was brutally suppressed by Haile Selassie.

The rise of Mengistu and the Dergue brought Tigrayan resentments to the fore again. An attempt by the Dergue to replace the traditional Tigrayan leaders of Tigray province led to an open revolt. Supported by the EPLF (Tigray and Eritrea are adjacent to one another), the Tigray established the Tigray People's Liberation Front (TPLF) in 1975. The TPLF (which absorbed members from the defeated EPRP) was dedicated to overthrowing Mengistu by armed force.

Gradually the number of armed fighters in the TPLF rose. By 1989, they had an army of 20,000 guerrilla soldiers. Mengistu staged numerous campaigns against the TPLF, but he was handicapped by the need to keep large numbers of troops in Ogaden and Eritrea.

The Oromo, although the largest ethnic group within Ethiopia, had been late to develop a strong national consciousness. Many upper-class Oromo had learned Amharic and tried to fit into the Amhara elite, albeit with only limited success. However, by the 1970s, the Oromo had also become infected with the desire to free themselves from Addis Ababa's control.

In 1973, Oromo militants established the Oromo Liberation Front (OLF) and embarked on a campaign to achieve greater independence for the Oromo. Despite the large numbers of Oromo in Ethiopia, the OLF could only mobilize a small guerrilla army. By 1988, the OLF had been able to improve its position and recruit a larger army. Some of the credit belonged to the TPLF and EPLF, which had provided the OLF with weapons and military advisers. While the OLF was never as dangerous to Mengistu as its Tigray and Eritrean brethren, it created one more region where Mengistu was forced to commit his badly stretched army.

Mengistu's Fall

The turning point in Mengistu's fortunes came with a change in regime in the Soviet Union. In 1985, Mikhail Gorbachev became the Soviet Union's new reform leader and ended the virtually unlimited aid that had previously been offered to Ethiopia. Gorbachev wished to end the Cold War confrontations with the United States. Soviet military aid declined precipitously, from more than $1 billion to less than $300 million. Furthermore, Gorbachev put pressure on Mengistu to reach a negotiated settlement, warning that future Soviet support was not guaranteed.

With decreasing Soviet arms shipments, Mengistu found it difficult to maintain Ethiopia's position in its many internal wars. Particularly troublesome was the reduction in the number of Soviet and Cuban advisers stationed in the country; Ethiopia relied on these advisers to maintain its sophisticated Soviet-built tanks and aircraft. After 1985, the Ethiopian army became increasingly ineffective. And in 1989, the Soviets began to completely phase out all military aid. By 1991, there were no Soviets or Cubans left to help Mengistu stay in power.

The effects of the Soviet reduction in aid were felt immediately. In Eritrea, the EPLF became increasingly bold, moving out from its northern mountain strongholds to harass the Ethiopian army throughout Eritrea. In March 1988, the EPLF was strong enough to destroy an entire Ethiopian army corps in a pitched battle at Afabet. This victory allowed them to gain control over all but a few major Eritrean towns. The victory also made it possible for the EPLF to provide greater support to the TPLF. In a February 1989 battle, the Tigrayans, with help from EPLF units, were able to destroy another large Ethiopian force at the town of Inda Silase. Mengistu was forced to withdraw his army from most of Tigray.

The TPLF began to expand its operations into neighboring Gonder, Welo, and Shewa regions. In January 1989, the TPLF allied itself with a smaller Amhara organization, the Ethiopian People's Democratic Movement (EPDM), which it had originally helped to create. The alliance was called the Ethiopian People's Revolutionary Democratic Front (EPRDF). The EPRDF, which remained dominated by the Tigrayans of the TPLF, helped to sponsor other revolutionary movements, including the Oromo People's Democratic Organization (OPDO) and the Ethiopian Democratic Officers' Revolutionary Movement. These new rebel organizations, although accused by the government of being mere offshoots of the Tigrayan movement, were able to greatly increase the strength and area of the Mengistu opposition.

Mengistu's growing weakness triggered a May 1989 military coup against his government by officers frustrated with his failures to end Ethiopia's turmoil. Mengistu successfully put down the coup, executing twelve generals in the process, but his regime suffered increased criticism, even from Dergue loyalists. Mengistu opened negotiations with the TPLF and the EPLF, but was unable to come to any agreement, largely because the two movements saw victory within their grasp and saw no need to make any concessions to a Mengistu regime.

By 1990, EPRDF forces were only 100 miles from Addis Ababa, and the EPLF had, in February, succeeded in seizing the port of Mitsiwa, cutting Ethiopia's ties to the sea. Almost the entire north was in rebel hands. In desperation, Mengistu declared an end to Ethiopian Marxism, ending the redistribution program that had forced peasants into villages. His popularity did not rise; the peasants simply moved back into their old farms, ignoring, or sometimes attacking, local government administrators. Mengistu's local bureaucracy began to fall apart.

On May 21, 1991, with his armies throwing down their arms in the face of the advancing rebels, Mengistu fled to Zimbabwe. On May 28, the EPRDF moved into Addis Ababa and took over the reins of government. Ethiopia's civil war was over.

Rebel forces of the EPRDF arrive in seized Russian tanks at the government palace in Addis Ababa during the fall of the Mengistu regime in 1991. *(Françoise De Mulder/Roger Viollet/Getty Images)*

Epilogue

The Eritreans were the key catalyst that brought down the Mengistu regime. It was the draining Eritrean war that damaged Mengistu's army and prestige and allowed the Tigrayans to create their own successful resistance movement. Caught between these internal wars, Mengistu's regime was unable to take the shock of the post-1985 withdrawal of Soviet support. Without Soviet aid, Mengistu's armies steadily retreated until the inevitable collapse in 1991. The rebels' success was facilitated by the TPLF's decision to sponsor other ethnic liberation movements, and then coordinate the creation of the EPRDF coalition.

The EPRDF originally had a Marxist program, like its creator the TPLF, but in 1991 it announced a new moderate and democratic program that was open to creating a free market economy in post–civil war Ethiopia. Politically, the EPRDF accepted the idea of a free Eritrea, and after May 1991, Eritrea was for all practical purposes an independent state. The EPRDF also supported greater autonomy for the various Ethiopian ethnicities. A new map for Ethiopia was drawn up dividing the country into nine provinces—Tigray, Afar, Amhara, Oromiya, Somali, Benshangul-Bumuz, Southern Peoples, Gambela, and Harar—and one federal city, Addis Ababa.

Despite the EPRDF's success, there remained substantial opposition to its policies. Many groups accused the Tigrayan-dominated organization of setting up puppet parties in the various provinces in order to maintain itself in control. The OLF, in particular, waged a low-level guerrilla insurgency against the new Ethiopian government after 1992.

Elections held in 1995 resulted in an EPRDF victory and the selection of Meles Zenawi, the EPRDF's chairman, as Ethiopia's new prime minister. Although foreign observers called the elections free and fair, they were marred by the lack of opposition party participation; many opposition parties had boycotted the elections, protesting what they called unfair domination of government and media by the EPRDF. Meles Zenawi was reelected prime minister in 2000 and 2005.

Although Ethiopia was more peaceful than it had been for decades, ethnic tensions continued to smolder, and the EPRDF continued its iron-fist-in-a-velvet-glove domination of Ethiopia's government. Calm was disturbed once again in 1998 when Ethiopia and Eritrea went to war over a border dispute. Continued strife had the unfortunate result of diminishing investment from overseas, which Ethiopia desperately needed to improve the lives of its millions of citizens.

Carl Skutsch

See also: Cold War Confrontations; Eritrea: War for Independence, 1958–1991; Ethiopia: Revolution, 1974–1978; Ethiopia: War with Somalia, 1977–1978.

Bibliography

Araia, Ghelawdewos. *Ethiopia: The Political Economy of Transition.* Lanham, MD: University Press of America, 1995.

Marcus, Harold G. *A History of Ethiopia.* Berkeley: University of California Press, 1994.

Prouty, Chris. *Historical Dictionary of Ethiopia and Eritrea.* Lanham, MD: Scarecrow Press, 1994.

GHANA: Rawlings Coups, 1979–1981

TYPE OF CONFLICT: Coups

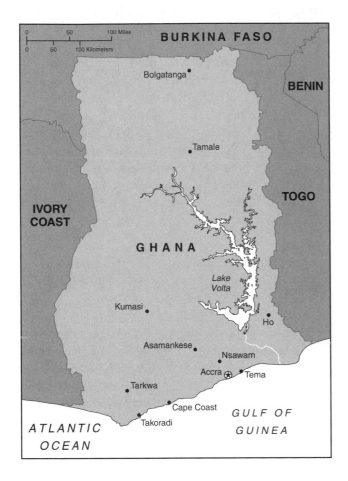

The first Europeans to arrive on the coast of what is now Ghana were the Portuguese, who established forts there to preserve their monopoly over the gold trade. (Ghana's colonial name was the Gold Coast.) By the 1600s, the Protestant sea powers had taken over control of the coastal trade. This led to a shift in strength among the African peoples of the area, as power shifted from the kingdoms of the northern savannah to those of the coast. At the end of the century arose the Akan state of Akwamu, followed thereafter by the powerful Ashante kingdom, which encompassed what is now Ghana and surrounding areas.

By the mid-nineteenth century, the British had assumed a protectorate over the non-Ashante peoples of the coast. Continued Ashante attacks on British and non-Ashante settlements resulted in a successful punitive expedition by the British and their African allies against the Ashante capital at Kumasi in 1874. Thereafter, the Gold Coast was formally declared a British colony. Still, it took another quarter of a century to fully defeat the Ashante and establish British administration over the whole territory of what is now Ghana. From the 1920s, the British began to develop an export economy, based on cocoa, timber, and manganese. By bringing together large numbers of persons from different ethnic groups in these industries, the British incidentally established the beginnings of a Ghanaian nationalism.

By the late 1940s, an independence movement was beginning to form among the professional classes of Accra, the capital. In 1949, Kwame Nkrumah broke away from the main independence organization—the United Gold Coast Convention—to form his own, more radical Convention People's Party (CPP). Though briefly imprisoned by the British in 1950, Nkrumah was elected prime minister of a quasi-independent government in 1951. Continued agitation by Nkrumah and the CPP forced the British to speed up their plans for departure, leading to the independent British Commonwealth state of the Gold Coast on March 6, 1957, the first European colony in sub-Saharan Africa to obtain its freedom.

Ghana witnessed political turmoil from its very birth. In 1957, opponents of Nkrumah's socialist and pan-Africanist vision for the new country formed the United Party (UP) but were jailed under emergency powers assumed by the CPP government. Following a referendum in 1958, the Gold Coast broke from the Commonwealth and declared itself the Republic of Ghana. In 1964, Nkrumah officially declared Ghana a "socialist single-party state."

KEY DATES

1957	Ghana, then known as the Gold Coast, becomes the first of Europe's sub-Saharan colonies to gain independent black majority rule, under the leadership of radical pan-Africanist Kwame Nkrumah.
1966	The military overthrows Nkrumah in the country's first coup.
1976	The military government agrees to a referendum on a new government, in which the military, police authorities, and civilians would share power.
1978	A bare majority of 55 percent of Ghanaians vote in favor of the referendum, with national elections set for June 1979.
1979	Political parties are unbanned in January; in May, a group of young military officers led by Flight Lieutenant Jerry Rawlings launches an unsuccessful coup and are arrested; quickly freed, they launch a successful coup on June 4; their takeover is greeted positively by much of the public; Rawlings allows national elections to proceed.
1979–1981	Political strife continues; Rawlings launches a third and final coup on December 31 of 1981.
1992	Military rule ends with national elections; Rawlings wins election for the presidency with 60 percent of the vote in a poll that observers from the British Commonwealth declared "free and fair."

But economic mismanagement and official corruption led to a military coup in February 1966. Under the National Liberation Council, plans were announced for investigations into the corruption of the CPP and a quick restoration of civilian rule. Still, it was three years before a ban on political parties was lifted. In August, the Progress Party (PP)—under the leadership of Kofi Busia, the party's founder—swept the national elections.

Like its predecessor, the PP and Busia proved unable to deal with the severe economic problems of the country and were also accused of corruption, leading to yet another military coup in 1972. A National Redemption Council was established to govern the country, and political parties were again banned. With some improvements being made in the economy—largely due to rising prices for Ghanaian raw materials—the military government announced

the formation of a "union government" (UNIGOV) in 1976, in which power would be shared by the armed forces, the police, and civilian leaders. Despite widespread opposition, the plan was then put to a referendum in March 1978 where it was approved by 55 percent of the voters, though most observers of the poll agreed the results had been manipulated by the government. Still, plans for national elections in June 1979 went forward, despite widespread arrests of UNIGOV opponents.

The Rawlings Coups

When the ban on political parties was lifted in January 1979, the campaign for the June elections got into full swing. Before the vote could occur, however, a group of young military officers—headed by Flight Lieutenant Jerry Rawlings—attempted an unsuccessful coup in May. Briefly imprisoned and then released, the group quickly re-formed and launched a successful coup, taking power on June 4 to national acclaim. Within a few days, the officers had established the Armed Forces Revolutionary Council (AFRC), headed by Rawlings. They also launched an anticorruption investigation into the affairs of past governments, which led to a number of executions.

Still, Rawlings denied that he was seeking permanent power and insisted on carrying out the elections in June. The winner, Hilla Limann of the People's National Party, took office as scheduled, and Rawlings stepped aside. Disputes among the various other parties in the ruling coalition, however, led to political strife during 1979 and 1980, as government efforts to revive the economy in the face of yet another slump in resource prices did not produce the expected results. Instead, as the price of food escalated, strikes and rioting broke out. Most people in Ghana believed it was only a matter of time before the still-popular Rawlings took power again. He did with his third coup on December 31, 1981.

Restoration of Democracy

This time, Rawlings had no intention of returning the government to civilian rule any time soon. He abolished the constitution, jailed or put under house arrest many members of the former government—including Limann—and set himself up as chairman of the ruling Provisional National Defence Council (PNDC). Still, Rawlings promulgated a plan to democratize the country, beginning with its local governments and armed forces. Unfortunately, this move led to a breakdown of authority in the army and several unsuccessful coup attempts. By 1990, Rawlings was forced to assume command of the military to prevent further army threats to his power. Meanwhile, efforts to reform the universities and unions soon led to demonstrations and strikes, as these institutions that had supported Rawlings turned against him.

Under both domestic and foreign pressure to return Ghana to democracy, Rawlings announced a plan for the reestablishment of constitutional rule by the end of 1991. Despite protests that the committee assembled to draw up the new constitution was dominated by pro-government appointees, the PNDC announced national elections for November 1992. With several popular measures to his credit—including an increase in government salaries and a minimum wage—Rawlings won the presidency with nearly 60 percent of the vote. Observers from the British Commonwealth declared the election "free and fair."

In the following years Rawlings's government helped bring stability to the country. Nevertheless, serious problems remained. First, under pressure from international lending agencies, the government was forced to institute unpopular austerity plans that resulted in increases in food and fuel prices. Second, ethnic tensions broke out in the northern part of the country, where fighting between the economically dominant Nanumba and the dispossessed Konkomba led to the deaths of nearly 500 persons before government troops could restore order. Moreover, a lengthy drought in the 1990s caused severe water and power shortages, as the hydroelectric projects on which Ghana relied operated well below capacity. Still, the Rawlings government received a positive public relations boost when President Bill Clinton made Accra his first destination on his 1998 African tour, where he praised Rawlings's commitment to democracy.

Rawlings stepped down from the presidency in 2000, and John Kufuor was elected to the post. This was the first peaceful transfer of power in Ghana since its independence. Kufuor was reelected in 2004.

James Ciment

See also: Coups.

Bibliography

Herbst, Jeffrey Ira. *The Politics of Reform in Ghana, 1982–1991.* Berkeley: University of California Press, 1993.

Petchenkine, Youry. *Ghana: In Search of Stability, 1957–1992.* Westport, CT: Praeger, 1993.

Shillington, Kevin. *Ghana and the Rawlings Factor.* New York: St. Martin's Press, 1992.

GUINEA-BISSAU: War of National Liberation, 1962–1974

TYPE OF CONFLICT: Anticolonialism
PARTICIPANT: Portugal

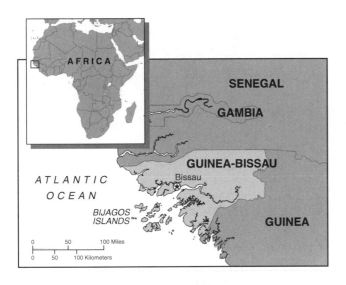

Initially colonized by Portugal in the 1500s, Guinea-Bissau—known before independence as Portuguese Guinea—was fully incorporated into the Portuguese Empire in 1886, following an agreement between Lisbon and France, the colonizers of Senegal and French Guinea, the two colonies that surrounded Portuguese Guinea. Largely neglected by its governing country, Portuguese Guinea's seven major ethnic groups were mostly involved in subsistence agriculture, as well as a modicum of commercial farming and trade. Unlike Mozambique and Angola, Portugal's larger colonies in southern Africa, Portuguese Guinea never saw a large influx of white settlers, even during the boom years of World War II and the postwar era. Because of that, Portuguese Guinea also had few of the mixed-race *assimilados* who would come to lead the independence movements in those other colonies.

Historical Background

The man who would lead the independence movement until his death in 1973, Amilcar Cabral, was born in Portuguese Guinea in 1924, the son of a schoolteacher and the operator of a small hotel. After completing his primary and secondary education in the Portuguese colony of Cape Verde Islands, Cabral won a scholarship to study agronomy at an institute in Lisbon, graduating near the top of his class in 1952. Like other Lusophone African intellectuals studying in Portugal, Cabral gravitated toward the anti-imperialist Portuguese Communist Party, which was banned and had to function underground during the rule of Portuguese dictator António de Oliveira Salazar. But the future revolutionary did not like the party's doctrine that revolution should come in capitalist countries before their colonies were given independence. Though adhering to the economic agenda of socialism, Cabral increasingly became pan-Africanist in his political outlook.

During his student days in Lisbon, Cabral became a leading exponent of a movement known as re-Africanization, in which the trappings of European civilization would be discarded and replaced with African traditions. In a 1953 article, he called for intellectuals to put their education to work in the liberation of their fellow Africans. That same year, he returned to Portuguese Guinea with his family and took a job as an accountant in a Portuguese-owned manufacturing firm. Even as he became involved in nationalist politics, he was commissioned by the governor of the colony to do an agricultural survey. His travels around the country illustrated a problem he had begun to think about in Lisbon—that is, the gulf between the educated colonial elite and the masses

KEY DATES

1500s Portugal takes control of the region that would become Guinea-Bissau, as a center of trade, including that in slaves.

1956 Left-wing pan-Africanist Amilcar Cabral and several others form the African Party for the Independence of Guinea and Cape Verde (PAIGC, its Portuguese acronym), calling for the independence of the colonies.

1960 Under pressure from Portuguese forces, PAIGC moves its headquarters to neighboring Guinea.

1962 PAIGC begins to engage Portuguese forces in conflict.

1973 Cabral is assassinated by PAIGC defectors recruited by the Portuguese government to kidnap the rebel leader.

1974 In the so-called "Carnation Revolution" in April, left-wing military officers in Portugal overthrow the right-wing dictatorship and announce their intention to free all of Portugal's African colonies; Guinea-Bissau becomes independent on September 10.

of Africans. At the same time, he became aware of the ways colonialism sapped the strength of African agriculture by gearing it to the needs of the mother country.

In 1955, Cabral left Portuguese Guinea to work in Angola, where he made contacts with nationalists there. He also made frequent trips home. During one of these, in September 1956, Cabral and five other anticolonial militants founded the Partido Africano da Independencia da Guine e Cabo Verde (PAIGC). While Cabral spent much of the rest of the decade in Angola, Portuguese Guinea saw increasing labor unrest, especially among stevedores and other workers in the administrative capital of Bissau. Under increasing pressure from the Portuguese security forces, the PAIGC decided to change tactics. At a secret meeting in September 1959, attended by Cabral, it abandoned its emphasis on organizing urban workers and shifted to rural agitation. This rural organizing was brutally suppressed in a series of massacres by Portuguese security forces. Meanwhile, after a number of arrests and raids, the PAIGC moved its headquarters to Conakry, capital of the newly independent neighboring country of Guinea, in May 1960.

Armed Conflict

After winning the support of Guinea's president Sekou Touré, Cabral and the PAIGC began to mobilize Portuguese-Guinean exiles and prepare for armed conflict. Beginning in mid-1962, the PAIGC decided it was ready and engaged in a series of small hit-and-run raids from camps inside Guinea. In September, the decision was made to launch a major guerrilla campaign from inside the colony. Concentrating their efforts in areas where political mobilization had already been achieved, PAIGC guerrillas inflicted heavy losses on the Portuguese military. Portugal responded by increasing its military force from 1,000 to 13,000 men by the following year.

At the same time, Portugal decided to institute a number of political reforms in the colony. In 1963, it limited the broad executive powers of the governor. It also established a legislative assembly—most of whose eleven members were chosen by traditional leaders and Europeans—with authority over indigenous peoples. And while Lisbon offered citizenship and voting rights to the educated African elite, the vast majority of colonials could not vote. These moves did little to placate the PAIGC.

In 1964, the PAIGC leaders met in a congress to discuss the difficulties facing the struggle. At the top of their agenda were three problems. One concerned militarism. Though the guerrilla force was increasingly successful in its campaigns against the Portuguese army, it was also committing abuses against the indigenous peoples. Cabral immediately instituted serious punishments for violators of its rules, including the execution of a number of combatants. A second problem centered on localism. To help integrate combatants and civilians, the PAIGC had tried to send guerrillas to their native areas. But this attempt led many of them to abandon the nationalist cause once they had rid their region of the Portuguese. Finally, the PAIGC faced the problem of traditional customs' interfering with the nationalist cause. Too many of its political and military cadres, the party leaders believed, were caught up in old practices and customs that impeded their efforts to raise the nationalist consciousness of the indigenous people.

Still, the 1964 congress was largely successful in reforming the practices of party members, and through the rest of the decade, the PAIGC concentrated on mobilizing and organizing the masses in the areas liberated from the Portuguese, as well as carrying the war to the rest of the colony. By 1969, their success could be measured by the fact that the Portuguese military was largely confined to the major cities and a string of fortified camps, despite the fact that there were more than 40,000 Portuguese soldiers now in the colony. The Portuguese were forced to fight the war from the air, with helicopter-borne attacks on so-called free-fire zones. By 1973, however, the PAIGC had acquired the weapons necessary to checkmate Portuguese air superiority.

At the same time, as Portugal realized it could not win the struggle by military means alone, it attempted to improve living conditions in the cities and other areas under its control. A number of schools and hospitals were built. New housing was developed, and food became cheaper and more available. So, too, the PAIGC instituted numerous economic, social, and political reforms in the liberated zones. The PAIGC established schools and clinics, while devolving political authority onto a series of local councils and courts.

With the war going against them, the Portuguese decided to try a desperate gamble. In 1972, the Portuguese military forces hatched a plan to kidnap Cabral and the other PAIGC leaders. Knowing that many Portuguese Guineans in the PAIGC were upset about the domination of Cape Verdeans in the party's leadership, the Portuguese recruited a number of defectors to carry out their plan. But in January 1973, the leader of the cabal proved trigger-happy—instead of kidnapping Cabral, he assassinated him.

The plan backfired in other ways as well. The new leaders of the PAIGC, less interested in political mobilization in liberated areas, decided to break the military deadlock by launching a major colony-wide campaign to drive out the Portuguese for good. On September 24, 1973, the PAIGC—now under the leadership of Cabral's brother Luiz—unilaterally declared Guinea-Bissau independent. These attacks were more than the Portuguese military command (also faced with crises in Angola and Mozambique) could handle. In Portugal, longtime dictator Antonio Salazar had died in 1968 and been succeeded by Marcello Caetano, who lacked the support of the older leader. In April 1974, a group of Portuguese military officers overthrew the dictator Caetano. In August, Portugal withdrew its forces from Guinea-Bissau and recognized its independence on September 10.

From 1974 to 1980, both Guinea-Bissau and Cape Verde were ruled by the PAIGC under separate constitutions, with an eye to future unification. These hopes were dashed when Guinea-Bissau Prime Minister João Bernardo Vieira led a military coup in 1980. Though committing himself to the principles of the PAIGC, Vieira began to move Guinea-Bissau toward a market economy, even as he kept a tight rein on its politics. In the country's first multiparty elections in 1994, Vieira won by a narrow margin. He was driven from office in 1998 but would return to win another election as president in 2005.

James Ciment

See also: Anticolonialism; Angola: War of National Liberation, 1961–1974; Guinea-Bissau: Civil War, 1998–2000; Mozambique: War of National Liberation, 1961–1974.

Bibliography

Chabal, Patrick. *Amilcar Cabral: Revolutionary Leadership and People's War.* New York: Cambridge University Press, 1983.

Chaliand, Gérard. *Armed Struggle in Africa: With the Guerrillas in Portuguese Guinea.* New York: Monthly Review Press, 1969.

Davidson, Basil. *The Liberation of Guiné: Aspects of an African Revolution.* Harmondsworth, UK: Penguin, 1969.

GUINEA-BISSAU: Civil War, 1998–2000

TYPE OF CONFLICT: Coup
PARTICIPANTS: Guinea-Bissau; Senegal; ECOWAS

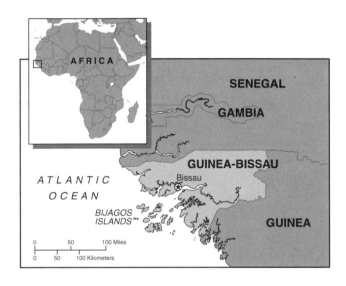

Guinea-Bissau is a small, ethnically diverse country on the western coast of Africa, one of the smallest and poorest countries in West Africa. It has been notable historically for a fairly bloody history, including a messy separation from the Portuguese in the 1960s and 1970s and continuing political strife that led to a civil war in 1998 and 1999.

Background

Although the Portuguese claimed Guinea in 1446, they only subdued the coastal portions of the country and did little to develop their new possession beyond using the Guinean city of Cacheu as a major slave-trading center. Bissau was founded as a military post and slave-trading city in 1765. When the slave trade declined in the nineteenth century, Bissau became a commercial center. Although the Portuguese lost much of their African territory to the French, including Guinea, they held on to Guinea-Bissau. (Guinea is known locally as Guinea-Conakry to distinguish it from its neighbor to the northwest, Guinea-Bissau.) The Portuguese only subdued the Guinean interior after years of fighting, and it was only in 1936 that they

finally conquered the people of the Bijagos Islands. In 1941, the administrative center of Portuguese Guinea moved to Bissau. The colony of Portuguese Guinea became an overseas province of Portugal in 1952.

In 1956, left-wing, pan-Africanist revolutionaries Amilcar Cabral and Raphael Barbosa secretly organized the African Party for the Independence of Guinea and Cape Verde (PAIGC, its Portuguese acronym). An armed rebellion against the Portuguese began in 1961. Despite the presence of almost 35,000 Portuguese troops, PAIGC controlled much of rural Guinea-Bissau by 1968. Cabral was assassinated by native agents of the Portuguese government in 1973. Following his death, PAIGC declared the independence of Guinea-Bissau on September 24, 1973, and in the wake of Portugal's April 1974 revolution, Lisbon granted independence to Guinea-Bissau on September 10, 1974. Luis Cabral, half-brother of Amilcar, became president but was overthrown in a bloodless coup in 1980 by prime minister and former armed forces commander Joao Bernardo Vieira. There were attempted coups against the Vieira government in 1983, 1985, and 1993, prompted by the Vieira's government's penchant for cronyism and corruptions, and for its inability to deal with the nation's endemic poverty. Coup leaders complained that PAIGC insiders and veterans were monopolizing government jobs and contracting. In 1986, coup organizer First Vice President Paulo Correia and five others were executed for treason following a lengthy trial. Nevertheless, local and international pressure forced the Vieira government to allow for reforms. In 1994, Guinea-Bissau held its first multiparty legislative and presidential elections with Vieira remaining in power.

Coup and Civil War

An army uprising led by General Ansumane Mane against the Vieira government on June 7, 1998, triggered a civil war. Most of the 6,000-strong army and

KEY DATES

1956   Radical pan-Africanists organize the African Party for the Independence of Guinea and Cape Verde (PAIGC, its Portuguese acronym) to fight for independence from Portugal.

1961   Fighting breaks out between PAIGC and Portuguese colonial forces.

1974   Following a leftist coup in Portugal in April, Guinea-Bissau wins its independence in September, with Luis Cabral as president.

1980   The Cabral government is overthrown in a military coup led by armed forces commander Joao Bernardo Vieira.

1994   After three attempted coups in 1983, 1985, and 1993, the government holds multiparty elections for the first time, with Vieira remaining in the presidency.

1998   An army uprising against the Vieira government triggers civil war.

1999   After several aborted cease-fires, peace returns when Vieira gives up power and multiparty elections are held.

1.1 million civilian population supported Mane. Vieira had become widely disliked for reportedly selling out Guinea-Bissau to foreign interests. Vieira brought Guinea-Bissau into the franc zone by joining the Economic Community of West African States (ECOWAS). As a result, the Central Bank of Guinea Bissau, which had controlled the national currency, lost its financial powers to the Central Bank of West African States (BCEAO, its French acronym). The BCEAO, based in Senegal, issued the CFA franc, which replaced the Guinea peso. (CFA is the French acronym of the Financial Cooperative of Central Africa.) BCEAO controls the CFA franc for the seven countries in the union: Benin, Burkina-Faso, Ivory Coast, Mali, Niger, Senegal, and Togo. Future financial and monetary decisions for Guinea-Bissau would thereafter be taken at the conference of franc zone heads of state and of France, which guarantees the stability of the CFA franc. Guinea-Bissau, one of the poorest countries in the world, also owed Portugal $2.5 million, which had to be paid back before it joined ECOWAS.

Both Senegal and Guinea sent troops to support Vieira, the former because the Guinea-Bissau junta headed by Mane was reportedly smuggling arms across the Senegalese border to assist secessionists in the Senegalese region of Casamance and the junta headed by Mane. This foreign support kept Vieira in power, but it was not strong enough to restore peace. Soldiers from ECOWAS intervened, as did the Community of Portuguese Speaking Countries (CPLP), and a cease-fire agreement was signed on Aug. 24, 1998.

Fighting resumed in October 1998 when the rebels accused the government of breaking the truce by receiving a consignment of military equipment for the troops loyal to Vieira. A new peace agreement was signed at Abuja, Nigeria, on Nov. 1, 1998, guaranteeing that Vieira would remain in office, but Mane's supporters would receive government positions. Eventually, four out of nine ministries in the newly appointed government went to the rebels. However, both sides remained armed, and, before ECOWAS peacekeeping forces could fully deploy, fighting broke out in February 1999. It is not known whether fighting occurred by accident or whether a group, probably not interested in the peace process, provoked this renewed fighting. After a few days of fighting, a new truce was signed. The Senegalese and Guinean soldiers left in March 1999, after 600 ECOWAS peacekeepers from Gambia, Mali, Niger, Benin, and Togo were deployed.

General Ansumane Mane (left) meets with other military commanders after toppling Guinea-Bissau's President Joao Bernardo Vieira in May 1999. Mane was killed in another coup attempt, against newly elected President Kumba Yala, the following year. *(Tiago Petinga/AFP/Getty Images)*

Elections were set for November 28, 1999. However, neither side disarmed, and both sides continued to hold entrenched positions in Bissau. The formation of a joint government did not ensure trust between the factions of Mane and Vieira. On May 8, 1999, fighting resumed when Vieira refused to reduce his 600-strong presidential guard to 30 soldiers. Within hours, Mane's forces occupied all of Bissau and forced the surrender of the presidential guard. With rebel forces controlling most of the country, the capital had been the last government stronghold. The attack killed more than 70 people. Vieira first sought safety at the French Cultural Center, but the building was surrounded by local troops and an angry mob. To avoid further loss of life, the Portuguese ambassador drove to the French building and rescued Vieira, who then took refuge in the Portuguese embassy. The presidential palace, the French embassy, and the French Cultural Center were subsequently burned by Mane's supporters. Malam Bacai Sanha, president of

the National Assembly, became interim president with the joint government still in office.

End of Fighting

ECOWAS condemned the coup. However, fighting came to an end because Vieira gave up resistance since he had no soldiers or base of support. Guinea-Bissau's civil war came to a close with very few reports of the massacres and systematic torture that often accompany civil wars. Free elections were held in November. Kumba Yala, who had lost to Vieira in 1994, won the presidency. His party, Partido Para a Renovaaao Social (PRS), subsequently took control of the government and ended twenty-six years of PAIGC governance. Since Yala came to power, human rights abuses at the hands of military personnel have continued in Guinea-Bissau. Human rights activists, journalists, and ordinary citizens have been beaten and arrested.

Prior to the civil war, Guinea-Bissau had one of the poorest economies in Africa, and it was one of the most foreign-aid–dependent nations in the world. The fighting disrupted both the economy and shipments of aid. Trade slowed, banks were shut for more than a year, and Bissau harbor was largely unused because of the fighting. Most of the country's infrastructure lay in ruins. Guineans expected full recovery to prewar standards to take decades. With the end of the fighting, the International Monetary Fund, the European Union, the World Bank, and the United States donated funds to reconstruct the economy, rebuild roads, improve the electricity grid, and demobilize 26,000 soldiers. Non-governmental organizations also helped Guinea-Bissau, with groups such as Humanitarian Aid digging up unexploded shells and marking minefields.

Caryn E. Neumann

See also: Ethnic and Religious Conflicts; Guinea-Bissau: War of National Liberation, 1962–1974.

Bibliography

Forrest, Joshua B. *Guinea-Bissau: Power, Conflict, and Renewal in a West African Nation.* Boulder, CO: Westview Press, 1992.

Lobban, Richard, and Joshua Forrest. *Historical Dictionary of the Republic of Guinea-Bissau.* London: Scarecrow Press, 1988.

Mwakikagile, Godfrey. *Military Coups in West Africa Since the Sixties.* Huntington, NY: Nova Science Publishers, 2001.

IVORY COAST: Civil Disorder Since 1999

TYPE OF CONFLICT: Ethnic and Religious
PARTICIPANTS: Burkina Faso; France

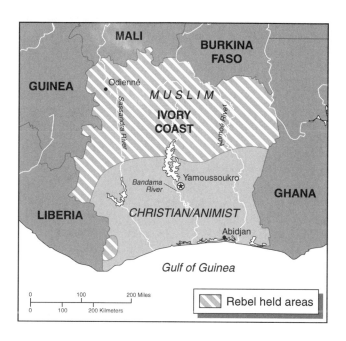

Once lauded as a rare success story in a region plagued by corruption, coups d'état, military rule, and civil war, Ivory Coast in recent years has succumbed to the maladies that have plagued its West African neighbors since independence came to all of these countries nearly a half-century ago. The death of long-serving President Félix Houphouët-Boigny in December 1993 ushered in a period of instability that his less charismatic successors have proven unable to surmount. Simmering religious and ethnic disputes, combined with rigged elections, petty political squabbling, and grave economic dislocation, provoked a civil war in 2002 that left the country divided into a Muslim north and mainly Christian south. Forces from France, Ivory Coast's former colonial ruler, later bolstered by UN forces, helped establish a fragile cease-fire, but a peace deal between rebel forces and the government in 2003 was not fully implemented.

Houphouët-Boigny Era, 1960–1993

Felix Houphouët-Boigny, known to admiring Westerners as the "Sage of Africa" or "Grand Old Man of Africa" for his firm yet moderate leadership, served as Ivory Coast's president from its independence in 1960 to his death in 1993, leaving an indelible mark on the country. Houphouët-Boigny's rule was benign by most accounts—religious and ethnic strife was noticeably absent—but political opposition was illegal until 1990, and he was repeatedly reelected in stage-managed balloting. He made tentative moves to open the political system in his last three years in office, but Ivorians were still unprepared for the shift to an open democratic system after his death.

Houphouët-Boigny had chosen to avoid the socialistic experimentation that appealed to governments in so many newly independent African countries. Instead, the Ivorian president maintained close economic and political ties with the West, particularly with France. As a result, the economy—based chiefly on cocoa and coffee production—became the star performer in the region during the 1960s and early 1970s. After that, the Ivory Coast went into a slow but steady economic decline, due partly to decreased prices for its exports but also to Houphouët-Boigny's faltering health and failure to provide leadership in the economically troubled period. State-controlled industries proved too rigid to counteract falling cocoa and coffee prices, leading to a currency devaluation and an economic recession following his death.

Post-Houphouët-Boigny Politics, 1993–2002

The presidency of Henri Konan Bédié, Houphouët-Boigny's hand-picked successor in 1993, was charac-

KEY DATES

1960	Ivory Coast wins its independence from France.
1993	Félix Houphouët-Boigny, the pro-French, pro-capitalist leader of Ivory Coast since its independence, dies.
1993–1999	Henri Konan Bédié, Houphouët-Boigny's hand-picked successor, stirs up popular sentiment against foreign immigrants to bolster support for his flagging regime.
1999	Bédié is overthrown in a bloodless coup on Christmas Eve by former chief of the army Robert Guei.
2000	In elections marred by violence, Laurent Gbagbo wins the presidency.
2002	Demobilized soldiers mutiny in the commercial capital of Abidjan in September; by the end of year, armed bands have divided the country into two halves along ethnic and religious lines.
2003	Government and rebel forces sign a cease-fire accord in May.
2004	UN peacekeepers arrive in March to bolster French forces already in the country; a comprehensive peace accord between rebels and the government is signed in South Africa.
2005	In October, Gbagbo postpones elections but claims his decision does not violate the accord signed in South Africa.

terized by rampant corruption and political repression. Bédié attempted to boost flagging support for his regime by stirring up xenophobia against Muslim northerners, mostly migrants from neighboring Burkina Faso, who differed linguistically and culturally from residents of the predominantly Christian south. Under Houphouët-Boigny's rule, immigrants from other West African countries had been welcome to settle in Ivory Coast, do the hard labor on cocoa and coffee plantations, and share in some of the country's wealth. By the mid-1990s, roughly 40 percent of Ivory Coast's 15 million people were foreign born. Ironically, even the xenophobic Bédié himself was rumored to be of foreign descent.

Bédié made a calculated break from his predecessor's policy of tolerance. He championed a vision of *Ivoirité* ("Ivorianness") that would limit land ownership to native Ivorians and exclude immigrants from voting. Discord grew so intense in the country

that Bédié was driven from power and forced to flee by former army general Robert Guei in December 1999. The international community condemned the revolt, but residents of Abidjan, the country's commercial and administrative capital, rejoiced in the streets at the overthrow of the unpopular Bédié.

Guei's rule began on a promising note, but he quickly disappointed many of his backers. He presented himself as a caretaker figure capable of ushering in a democratic restoration, and it appeared that he would bring a peaceful transfer of power to a newly elected government. For example, Guei also invited Alassane Ouattara to join his government of national reconciliation. Outattara, a Muslim from the north, had been Bédié's chief political rival, and several members of his party had been jailed in November 1999 after being convicted in show trials. It seemed that Guei was shifting away from the exclusionary policies of the Bédié regime.

Relations between the two soon soured, however, and Guei dismissed Ouattara's followers from the government. He also amended the constitution to prohibit anyone who had previously held a foreign nationality from running for the presidency—a deliberate bid to prevent Ouattara from taking power. This decision harkened back to the worst of the Bédié administration and left only one significant contender to run against Guei, Laurent Gbagbo.

Gbagbo, a leftist history professor who had been forced into exile in the early 1980s for opposing the closed political system of the Houphouët-Boigny regime, seemed capable of creating a return to normalcy. Once again, however, Ivorians were disappointed. Though it was Bédié who let the ethnic genie out of the bottle, Gbagbo seemed unwilling to put it back in. Political allegiances divided along ethnic lines during the campaign leading to the 2000 election. Politicians of all stripes used xenophobia as a means of rallying support behind them.

Gbagbo emerged victorious in October 2000, but Guei refused to recognize the result. However, the outgoing president was soon forced to flee in the face of a revolt by Ivorians, who accused him of electoral tampering. Gbagbo was proclaimed president later in the month, but Ouattara now called for a new election in which he would be permitted to run. In parliamentary elections in December, Gbagbo's Ivorian Popular Front (FPI) gained more seats than any other party. At the same time, fighting broke out between Gbagbo's mostly Christian backers in the south and Ouattara's Muslim supporters in the north.

The fierce rivalry between Gbagbo and Ouattara was complicated when former presidents Bédié and Guei made political comebacks, clouding Ivory Coast's already murky political landscape. In January 2001, an attempted coup failed, but opposition newspapers openly called for a revolution throughout the year. All the while, the four men at the head of Ivorian politics squabbled bitterly, refusing to compromise for the sake of meaningful national reconciliation.

Civil War and Abortive Attempts at Power-Sharing

The tenuous peace finally collapsed on September 19, 2002, as soldiers angered by orders to demobilize mutinied in Abidjan. During the following weeks, at least 270 people were killed, including the interior minister and former president Guei. Rebels from the Ivory Coast Patriotic Movement quickly took control of the northern half of the country. Only a rapid French military intervention halted the rebels before they could capture Abidjan and chase Gbagbo from power.

By late 2002, armed bands had effectively divided Ivory Coast along ethnic and religious lines. Gbagbo took a hard line on the insurgents, accusing them of being "traitors aided by a foreign rogue state" and "terrorists." He also accused neighboring Burkina Faso of instigating the revolt in Ivory Coast. Paramilitary gendarmes supported by the government launched a campaign of persecution against migrant workers. Torching their homes became a favorite form of harassment.

At first, the rebel movement (now called the New Forces) lacked leadership and a platform beyond a general desire to remove Gbagbo from power and end southern Christian domination. Still, fighting raged into 2003 as outside parties, including France and the United Nations, attempted to broker a peace deal. Gbagbo eventually backed down from his hard-line position and agreed to a power-sharing government.

The new government took power in March 2003 under consensus prime minister Seydou Diarra. It was to include nine members from rebel ranks. The armed forces of the two sides signed a full cease-fire in May, ending eight months of fighting, and in July a formal end to hostilities was announced. Ivorians were hopeful. By September, however, the northerners were accusing Gbagbo of failing to honor the peace agreement, and their representatives withdrew from the national unity government.

UN peacekeepers arrived in March 2004 to bolster the French force already on the ground. Soon afterward, an anti-Gbagbo rally in Abidjan provoked a violent government response. A UN report alleged that Gbagbo's troops had killed at least 120 people, many by torture or summary execution. The opposition charged Gbagbo with deliberately flaunting the terms of the peace agreement, and a return to open warfare seemed imminent.

Hostilities resumed in November 2004, when the Ivorian air force bombed rebel positions in the north. France, which had staked its reputation on upholding the cease-fire, lost nine of its soldiers in the government attacks. It responded to prevent the war from escalating, destroying the Ivorian air force (a

Rivals in the tangled politics of the Ivory Coast—(left to right) opposition leader Alassane Ouattara, former president Henri Konan Bédié, President Laurent Gbagbo, and former junta leader Robert Guei—meet in January 2002 to seek an end to ethnic unrest. The fighting raged on. *(Georges Gobet/AFP/Getty Images)*

pair of Soviet-built aircraft and a few helicopters), then moved to capture the international airport in Abidjan and flew in reinforcements. Gbagbo supporters began violent protests across the south, objecting to French interference. Many charged that France was needlessly complicating a local dispute, but other observers believed that French actions had forestalled another bloody civil war.

Return to Peace

It was clear that France could not hold the line indefinitely and that the government and opposition would have to return to the negotiating table. At this point, South Africa stepped into the process, convening peace negotiations in Pretoria. A com-

prehensive peace deal, the Pretoria Accord, was agreed to in April 2004. Under its terms, the UN was to monitor the next presidential election, the country's Independent Electoral Commission was to include more members of the opposition, the national reconciliation government would be reconstituted with opposition participation, and President Gbagbo would disband the southern militias that were persecuting migrants and northerners. Future disputes, including those over which candidates can run for office, were to be resolved by the sponsor of the deal, South African President Thabo Mbeki.

Before new presidential elections could be held in October 2005, however, President Gbagbo postponed them, invoking a law that he claimed allowed him to retain power. In December, peace negotiators named economist Charles Konan Banny prime minister. He took on the difficult task of disarming governmental militias and rebels as well as organizing upcoming elections. It was not clear that the nation would easily resolve its political and ethnic differences. If it failed, the Ivory Coast, once a beacon of peace and prosperity in a troubled region, seemed destined to sink further into the ethnic and religious fighting, and the economic troubles triggered by such conflict.

Sean J. McLaughlin

See also: Ethnic and Religious Conflicts; Liberia: Anti-Taylor Uprising, 1998–2003.

Bibliography

Konate, Siendou A. "The Politics of Identity and Violence in Còte d'Ivoire." *West Africa Review*, no. 5 (2004).

Meredith, Martin. *The Fate of Africa: From the Hopes of Freedom to the Heart of Despair: A History of Fifty Years of Independence.* New York: Public Affairs, 2005.

Mundt, Robert J. *Historical Dictionary of Côte d'Ivoire (the Ivory Coast).* Lanham, MD: Scarecrow Press, 1995.

KENYA: Mau Mau Uprising, 1952–1956

TYPE OF CONFLICT: Anticolonial
PARTICIPANT: United Kingdom

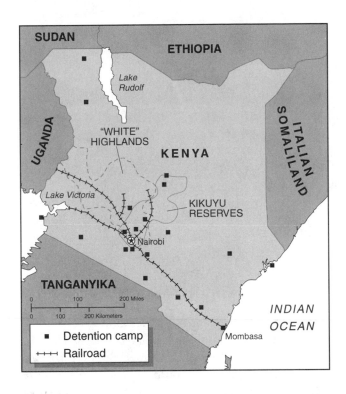

After Britain succeeded in conquering Kenya in 1900, it embarked upon a program of encouraging substantial English colonization of the country. From 1901 onward, thousands of English settlers, many of them from South Africa, came to Kenya seeking their fortune as large-scale farmers. They were joined by a large number of Indian immigrants, who came either to help build the railroads or as merchants eager to serve Kenya's growing economy. Most of the Europeans settled in the Kenyan highlands around Nairobi, which was a city designed by the British to be Kenya's capital.

This influx of foreigners disturbed many Kenyans, particularly when the British government gave the Europeans land that had once belonged to Africans, or attempted to have forced-labor laws passed (the European settlers were frustrated by the Kenyans' unwillingness to work long hours on their coffee and tea plantations).

By the 1920s, Kenyans had begun to organize political resistance to the Europeans. The most prominent of these groups was the Young Kikuyu Association (YKA), founded in 1921. The Kikuyu, making up 25 percent of the population, were Kenya's largest ethnic group and lived directly adjacent to the area of greatest English colonization. Living next door to Nairobi gave them opportunities for education that raised their level of political sophistication. Living beside the English also meant that the Kikuyu were the group most likely to suffer from settler arrogance, land grabbing, or attempts at imposing forced labor.

The young Kikuyu men in the YKA were upset that Africans had no say in Kenya's governance. Kenya had been transformed from a protectorate into a colony in 1920, and Europeans were given the right to elect representatives to the legislative council of the new colony. Even the Indian immigrants were given minority representation in 1927, but the Africans were only represented informally by a single white missionary.

Growth of the Mau Mau

In 1944, a broader-based movement was organized around the Kenya African Union (KAU), which included members of all ethnic groups, although the Kikuyu were still the dominant group. In 1947, Jomo Kenyatta, a Kikuyu and former member of the YKA, was chosen to be president of the KAU. Kenyatta traveled the country gathering support for his goal of making Kenya an African country run by Africans.

Kenyatta found a receptive audience. Many Kenyans had fought for the British during World War II and resented coming home to a country where they still had few economic opportunities and fewer political rights. They felt it unfair that 40,000 Europeans and 100,000 Indians should have more wealth and power than Kenya's 5 million Africans. They were also angered by British attempts to change their

KEY DATES

1901   English colonists begin to settle in Kenyan highlands, displacing native Kikuyu farmers.

1921   Anticolonial Kikuyu organize the Young Kikuyu Association (YKA).

1944   A broader anticolonial movement emerges with the founding of the Kenya African Union (KAU).

1950   Kikuyu begin organizing an underground anticolonial militant organization known as the Mau Mau.

1952   Mau Mau begin raids on white Kenyan farms; the government declares a state of emergency.

1953   The British begin a massive military campaign against Mau Mau militants; Jomo Kenyatta, head of KAU and future president of independent Kenya, is sentenced to six years imprisonment for inciting a Mau Mau uprising.

1956   British colonial authorities declare the defeat of the Mau Mau movement.

1963   Kenya wins its independence from Britain on December 12.

culture—including attacks by missionaries on the Kikuyu practice of female circumcision.

In 1950, the Kikuyu began to organize a secret organization known as the Mau Mau. The origin of the name is unclear, but the Mau Mau were dedicated to throwing the English settlers out of Kenya. New initiates to the secret society were made to swear ritual oaths dedicating themselves to the cause of Kenyan independence. Sometimes Kikuyu were intimidated into swearing the oaths. Having taken the oath, most felt tied to the cause. To tradition-minded Kikuyu, the oaths were terrible and binding, dedicating them to a lifelong commitment to the Mau Mau. Better-educated Kikuyu were less susceptible to such mystical beliefs but joined the Mau Mau because they believed in its goals. The British authorities banned the Mau Mau in late 1950, but the secret society continued to grow.

Mau Mau Revolt

Rumors of Mau Mau activity were widespread by mid-1952. English settlers demanded action on the part of the government but were ignored. Prominent Kikuyu chiefs who argued against joining the Mau Mau were being killed. It seemed possible that the entire Kikuyu nation would be converted to Mau Mau and that the movement might then spread to other Kenyan ethnic groups.

Finally, in October 1952, the government declared a state of emergency and ordered 183 known members of Mau Mau arrested, including Kenyatta. Kenyatta always denied leading the Mau Mau movement, but it was clear that he was deeply sympathetic to, if not directly involved in, its goals. In 1953, Kenyatta was found guilty of inciting the Mau Mau and sentenced to six years in prison.

Despite the jailing of their supposed leaders, the Mau Mau continued to strike in late 1952 and early 1953. Most of their targets were Kikuyu who refused to join their cause, but they also murdered some English settlers in a brutal fashion, using knives and machetes to hack the victims to death. Europeans in Kenya responded by marching through downtown Nairobi and demanding firm government action. The British at first were helpless in the face of these attacks, as the Mau Mau operated in small bands of guerrillas and would fade into the thick forest at the first sign of heavily armed troops.

Mau Mau activity increased after March 1953, with entire villages of non–Mau Mau Kikuyu attacked and burned to the ground. Although the Europeans continued to demand more government action, throughout the Mau Mau rising, it was the Kikuyu loyal to Britain who suffered the greatest number of casualties.

British Sweeps and Detention Camps

In June 1953, the British began to organize an effective campaign against the Mau Mau. First, they worked to strengthen the Kikuyu Home Guard, giving its units weapons so they could protect their own villages. At the same time the British targeted areas where there were believed to be high concentrations of Mau Mau sympathizers. Troops were sent on sweeps through the forests and villages looking for Mau Mau followers. In open areas the soldiers had the right to

stop and question any suspicious-looking persons; in the forest they could shoot to kill without warning.

The British had 10,000 regular troops at their disposal, divided evenly between British battalions and the King's African Rifle (KAR) battalions (the KAR battalions consisted of black troops led by white officers). They also could use some 21,000 Kenyan police and 25,000 Kikuyu Home Guards, although the latter were reserved almost entirely for defensive purposes.

Opposing them, the Mau Mau had an estimated 12,000 militants, supported by some 30,000 followers who provided safe havens and helped to keep them supplied. Only about 2,000 of the Mau Mau had modern rifles; the rest used knives, spears, and homemade gunpowder weapons.

Despite the Mau Mau's poor equipment, the terrain in which they operated made it extremely difficult for the British to defeat them. Thick forests, rugged hills, fast rivers—all made movement by regular troops difficult. The irregular soldiers of the Mau Mau, however, knew the region well and could move more quickly through it than their opponents. The

British colonial forces in Kenya set up detention camps for those suspected of Mau Mau activities in the early 1950s. Eventually more than 100,000 Kiyuku were taken prisoner. *(Terrence Spencer/Time Life Pictures/Getty Images)*

possibilities for ambush in the thick woods helped to compensate for the Mau Mau's lack of modern rifles.

Nevertheless, the British slowly beat down the Mau Mau resistance. Sweeps rounded up tens of thousands of Kikuyu. Those who were suspected of Mau Mau activities were put in detention camps. Eventually more than 100,000 Kikuyu would spend at least some time in the camps.

Many other Kikuyu were forced to relocate into villages, which caused some difficulty. Most Kikuyu operated small farms; in Kikuyu tradition, centralized villages were the exception rather than the rule. But the small farms were isolated and vulnerable, and their scattered nature made it impossible for the British security forces to determine which were loyal and which were supporters of the Mau Mau. Although it was resented by the Kikuyu, the campaign to house Kikuyu in villages made it easier for the British and the Kikuyu Home Guard to defend against Mau Mau attacks; loyal Kikuyu were encouraged to dig ditches filled with stakes around their villages.

Some Mau Mau bases were in especially hard-to-reach areas. In particular, the bases in the central forest and in the rough woods around Mount Kenya were very hard for British troops to reach quickly. The British compensated for this difficulty by using aircraft to bomb the more inaccessible Mau Mau camps.

Mau Mau Defeated

In April 1954, having successfully cleared most of the countryside, the British targeted Nairobi itself. About 65,000 Kikuyu lived in Nairobi, making up about one-third of the population. The British army, in an operation code-named "Anvil," sealed off the city and went from house to house looking for Mau Mau. They detained more than 30,000, of whom they decided 16,000 were active or passive Mau Mau supporters. These were added to the growing numbers in the detention camps.

Operation Anvil broke the back of the Mau Mau resistance. Much of the Mau Mau's support had come from the Kikuyu of Nairobi, and without access to those resources, the units in the forest began to lose hope. The general population of Kikuyu also became more willing to help in operations against the Mau Mau guerrillas.

The British were able to use brainwashing techniques on some captured Mau Mau, changing them from opponents into collaborators. These turncoat Mau Mau were then used to help hunt down their fellows, leading special fast-moving tracker teams into the Kenyan woods. Those Mau Mau who could not be talked into surrendering could be caught or killed.

By 1956, most of the Mau Mau had been caught. The most prominent Mau Mau leader, Dedan Kimathi, was captured and executed in October of that year. Kenya was once more firmly under British control.

Aftermath

During the war 10,500 Mau Mau died, and another 75,000 Mau Mau and alleged supporters were arrested and detained. The Mau Mau had succeeded in killing 1,800 African civilians, along with 58 European and Indian civilians; the British army had lost 63 British soldiers and 534 Africans.

The Mau Mau rebellion failed because it had been poorly equipped and extremely disorganized, and because its operations were characterized by brutal methods that repelled those it was supposed to attract. But it still took the British four years—and £55 million ($250 million)—to defeat the uprising. And they only succeeded after they had placed a large percentage of young Kikuyu males into detention camps. The uprising had made it clear to Britain that holding on to Kenya was not viable in the long term. Kenyan nationalism had only been slowed, not defeated.

In 1957, the British allowed Africans to be elected to Kenya's legislature, although only in limited numbers. In 1961, Africans won a majority of seats in a newly created legislative council. Kenyatta was freed by the British in late 1961 and became Kenya's first prime minister. On December 12, 1963, Kenya became completely independent.

Carl Skutsch

See also: Anticolonialism.

Bibliography

Kershaw, Greet. *Mau Mau from Below.* Athens: Ohio University Press, 1997.
Ochieng, William R. *A History of Kenya.* Nairobi, Kenya: Macmillan, 1985.

LIBERIA: Doe Coup, 1980

TYPE OF CONFLICT: Coups

Liberia is Africa's oldest republic, founded by freed slaves and free blacks from the United States in the mid-nineteenth century. From the first colony in 1822 through independence in 1847 and up to the American Civil War and emancipation in the 1860s, some 20,000 descendants of North American slaves settled in what is now Liberia. They were joined by some 5,000 to 10,000 "recaptureds," Africans seized from illegal slaving ships after the trans-Atlantic trade was outlawed by the British and Americans in the first decade of the nineteenth century. In the latter years of the century, the Americos—as the North Americans were called—and the recaptureds were joined by several thousand West Indians. Together, these groups formed the class that ruled Liberia during much of the nineteenth and twentieth centuries.

Unlike African colonies ruled by Europeans, Liberia had no racial barriers. Many of the indigenous peoples—particularly the offspring of important personages among the country's sixteen ethnic groups—were formally adopted by Americo families and assimilated into what Liberians called "civilized life."

Thus, the Americos, who never represented more than 2 to 3 percent of the population, were able to constantly reinvigorate their numbers.

Most of the Americos lived in the coastal settlements, where they engaged in commerce, selling the products of the Liberian countryside—including timber, coffee, cotton, gold, and diamonds—on the world market. At the same time, they zealously defended their hard-won independence against the encroachment of the aggressive European powers that surrounded them. Still, by the early twentieth century, the country was in serious financial trouble, deeply in debt to European bankers.

Between the 1920s and the 1940s, the Americos tried several schemes for rescuing their country from the British receivership in which it had been placed in the early 1900s. One plan involved working with Marcus Garvey, a Jamaican-born African American leader from Harlem who wanted to establish settlements for American blacks in Liberia. But the relationship was a rocky one. The conservative Americo elite became concerned that Garvey's plans to lead a decolonization movement from its base in Liberia would invite the wrath of European imperialists. When Garvey was convicted of mail fraud in the United States and deported to Jamaica, the plan collapsed.

A second scheme involved the exportation of indigenous laborers to the cocoa and sugar islands of Fernando Po, then a Spanish colony off the coast of Nigeria (and now a part of Equatorial Guinea). But the plan smacked too much of forced labor and even slavery and was shut down after a League of Nations investigation in the late 1920s. Finally, the only successful plan to put Liberia on the road to financial security involved rubber. By the 1920s, the United States was the world's largest rubber consumer—largely for tires for the new automobile industry—but it had no supplies of its own and was paying exorbitant prices to the British-controlled rubber cartel of Southeast Asia. In the

KEY DATES

1847 Liberia becomes Africa's first independent republic, led by former slaves and free blacks who have emigrated from the United States.

1971 Long-time president William Tubman dies and is replaced by Vice President William Tolbert.

1979 Mass rioting breaks out across the country in response to a rise in the price of rice, the staple food of most Liberian poor.

1980 A small group of military men under the leadership of Master Sergeant Samuel Doe invade the executive mansion and murder Tolbert; Doe becomes the leader of Liberia.

1990 In the wake of an invasion by rebel forces, Doe is trapped in Monrovia and murdered by rebel leader Prince Johnson on September 9.

mid-1920s, Harvey Firestone—head of the tire company that bore his name—decided Liberia was the ideal place to set up the world's largest rubber plantation.

By the beginning of World War II, the Liberian economy was beginning to get back on its feet. Rich sources of iron ore were discovered and exploited, just in time for the huge demands of the postwar global capitalist boom of the 1950s and 1960s. At the same time, there rose to power in 1944 a new and dynamic president of Liberia, William V.S. Tubman. Tubman was determined to open up Liberia to world trade. He was also a master politician. Over the course of his long tenure as president—from 1944 until his death in 1971—Tubman dramatically expanded the Liberian economy while incorporating the vast indigenous population into the political system for the first time.

In some ways, this was the golden age in Liberian history. A rudimentary transportation system was constructed; the capital, Monrovia, was modernized; schools and hospitals were built—all on the revenues generated by the burgeoning rubber and iron industries. But there was a downside to this period as well. Tubman would brook no opposition and used his several security forces to crush any signs of dissent. While maintaining the appearance of electoral politics, Tubman's True Whig party—which had been in power continuously since the late 1800s—won every campaign by a landslide.

Growing Unrest

During the 1970s a downturn in the world's economy undermined the demand for Liberian iron and rubber. Tubman's successor—the long-serving vice president, William Tolbert—inherited a declining economy, as well as a population with rising expectations. Many of the new graduates from the indigenous groups expected to be rewarded with good-paying jobs in the upper echelons of the Liberian government and business community. But as the pie shrank, the ruling Americos more jealously guarded their perquisites.

Protest movements grew, both among the newly educated indigenous population in Liberia and among the many Liberians studying at American universities. The Movement for Justice in Africa (MOJA) and the Progressive Alliance of Liberia (PAL) borrowed heavily from political currents in both America and Africa. They blended civil rights rhetoric with African nationalism, demanding a more inclusive political order and an end to the corruption of the Tolbert administration. By the mid-1970s, they began to agitate both among the student and intellectual population of Monrovia and in the military.

The Liberian military was ripe for change. Since its founding as the Liberian Frontier Force in 1909, the Armed Forces of Liberia (AFL) had been ruled by an officer corps of elite Americos, though with a sprinkling of Africans largely assimilated into Americo customs and ideology. As the army expanded during the Tubman years, a number of more radical African nationalist officers rose in the ranks. Still, the institution remained highly segregated and exploitative. Enlisted men—mostly recruited from the poorest and most isolated ethnic groups in the country, including the Krahn—were routinely required to work as servants in officers' homes. Moreover, the enlisted men lived in dismal conditions, often little more than shacks set up by the sides of roads.

By the late 1970s, both the AFL and Liberian society generally were in a state of turmoil. With government revenues falling due to the continuing slump in the demand for Liberian raw materials, Tolbert decided to remove the subsidies on the basic foodstuff of the country—rice. As prices for this staple soared, the leaders of PAL and MOJA agitated the populace, pointing out to them that it was the Tolbert family, which controlled much of the rice trade, that was most likely to benefit from the price increases. In July 1979, a PAL-organized demonstration against the government degenerated into rioting and looting. The army was called out, and it shot down hundreds of demonstrators and conducted looting of its own. Tolbert, who had a reputation for vacillation, assumed emergency powers, but then resumed rice subsidies. He also agreed to allow PAL to organize a legal political party to launch a challenge in the upcoming presidential and congressional elections.

The Doe Coup

The elections never took place. Instead, a group of noncommissioned officers of indigenous origins began to make plans for a coup that would topple the Tolbert administration. To lend their efforts credibility, they recruited Thomas Quiwonkpa, the highest-ranking indigenous officer in the Liberian army and a popular and well-respected leader in society. But unforeseen circumstances changed the scenario at the last minute. Hearing word of trouble, Tolbert decided to spend his nights in April 1980 at the executive mansion in Monrovia rather than at his preferred estate in the suburbs, unbeknownst to the coup-planners. Thus, Quiwonkpa was sent to arrest Tolbert at his estate while Master Sergeant Samuel Doe, a relatively uneducated Krahn man and the highest-ranking noncommissioned officer in the army, was sent to seize the mansion.

Instead, Doe found Tolbert and had him murdered in his bed. Within a few hours, the news went out that Doe and his seventeen fellow occupiers of the mansion had seized control of the Liberian government. The news was met with jubilation throughout the country. After 133 years of Americo rule, a native African was leading the country for the first time. The following day, Doe executed eleven members of Tolbert's cabinet on a Monrovia beach, but he still won over many of the intellectuals from PAL and MOJA to his cause. Over the course of a ten-year reign, however, the new government would prove to be even more repressive and incompetent than any Americo administration. By 1990 it had alienated most of its supporters, as well as the mass of Liberians. The Doe administration prepared the way for a disastrous civil war that would destroy the country in the course of the 1990s.

James Ciment

See also: Coups; Liberia: Civil War, 1989–1997.

Bibliography

Boley, G.E. Saigbe. *Liberia, the Rise and Fall of the First Republic.* New York: St. Martin's Press, 1984.

Dunn, Elwood. *Liberia: A National Polity in Transition.* Metuchen, NJ: Scarecrow Press, 1988.

LIBERIA: Civil War, 1989–1997

TYPE OF CONFLICT: Ethnic and Religious; Cold War Confrontation
PARTICIPANT: Economic Community of West African States (ECOWAS)

After 133 years of rule by the descendants of American slaves—known in Liberia as Americos—Africa's oldest republic fell to a coup by indigenous soldiers in April 1980. The leader of the coup, Master Sergeant Samuel Doe, was a poorly educated member of the Krahn ethnic group, one of the poorest and most isolated of Liberia's sixteen indigenous peoples. Doe was an ambitious man and a quick study. He soon gathered around him many of the reformist intellectuals at the University of Liberia who had led the protests against the last Americo regime in the 1970s. Indeed, the head of these reformers—Professor Amos Sawyer—once taught Doe in a night school Sawyer had set up for working people and soldiers in Monrovia. Doe picked Sawyer to head up a commission to draft a new constitution for the country.

At the same time, Doe introduced the People's Redemption Council (PRC). The council, largely composed of military personnel, was chaired by Doe himself and ran the country alongside the Council of Ministers, which included a majority of civilians. But this coalition collapsed within a couple of years.

Many of the reformers hoped that the Doe administration would allow them to carry out their radical plans for a redistribution of resources to the countryside and the establishment of genuine democratic rule. As it became clear that they were being marginalized by Doe's fellow soldiers, some of the more idealistic reformers left the government, while others began to partake of the corruption themselves.

Meanwhile, the Doe regime struggled to win international recognition. After being refused the seat of William Tolbert, the last Americo president and Doe's predecessor in the executive mansion, at the Organization of African Unity summit in 1980, Doe was forced to pledge that there would be no more summary executions of members of the previous government. But it was his efforts to curry favor with the West that won his government the biggest benefits. Tolbert had followed a policy of strict neutrality between East and West and had joined with other nonaligned nations. He allowed the Soviets to open an embassy for the first time in Monrovia and he ousted the Israelis.

Doe turned this policy around, welcoming back the Israelis and cozying up to the Americans. During his administration—largely coinciding with the Reagan years—Doe received nearly $500 million in aid, more than Liberia had received from the United States in its previous 130 years, making it—next to Israel—the largest recipient of U.S. aid per capita during the 1980s. Doe used most of the money to build up and improve the army. He recruited large numbers of new soldiers—mostly from his own Krahn group—and lavished new barracks, uniforms, and weapons on them, winning their undying allegiance. In return, the United States won the use of Liberian territory as a listening post for the South Atlantic, a way station for the shipment of arms to anticommunist rebels in Angola, and a site for the Voice of America's African transmission tower.

KEY DATES

1980 After 133 years under the rule of Americo-Liberians, the descendants of slaves and free blacks from the United States, the regime is overthrown in a violent coup led by Master Sergeant Samuel Doe.

1989 Rebel leader Charles Taylor, head of the National Patriotic Front of Liberia (NPFL), invades the country on Christmas Eve.

1990 Doe is murdered by another rebel leader, Prince Johnson, on September 9; as the NPFL and other rebel groups close in on the capital Monrovia, Economic Community of West African State Monitoring Group (ECOMOG) peacekeepers are sent in to keep the warring factions apart in October.

1996 In wake of the failure to reach a cease-fire, NPFL forces launch an offensive in April to seize Monrovia from government and ECOMOG forces; the city is heavily damaged; various rebel groups agree to demobilization efforts in late 1996 and early 1997.

1997 Charles Taylor wins the presidency in internationally monitored elections.

2003 After six years of rule, Taylor is overthrown in a rebel uprising and flees to exile in Nigeria.

By the mid-1980s, the excesses of the Doe administration were becoming an embarrassment for the Reagan White House. The Liberian leader was executing opponents and unleashing his security forces on the populace to crush all dissent. Moreover, as the more educated reformers left his government or began to engage in the widespread corruption themselves, the government's capacity to run the country deteriorated. Doe attempted several desultory efforts to clean up the corruption, but he was too dependent on the ministers involved to remove them. He was, however, more intent on shoring up his own base in the military, dismissing his fellow plotter, the popular and competent General Thomas Quiwonkpa, in 1983.

Meanwhile, the United States began pressuring Doe to hold elections under the constitution that had been ratified by nearly 80 percent of the voters in 1983. While it was not much different from the old constitution, it did get rid of property qualifications for voting and banned the hated hut tax, the flat property tax paid by every head of household. In 1984, Doe dissolved the PRC, replaced it with an interim national assembly, also under his chairmanship, and established the National Democratic Party of Liberia (NDPL) as his own electoral vehicle. Elections were scheduled for October 1985, with several reformist parties competing against the NDPL. As predicted, Doe stole the elections, or at least that's what most people in Liberia believed. But the United States backed the results, saying that the small margin of victory—Doe took just 50.9 percent of the vote—proved their legitimacy. Of course, under the American-inspired winner-take-all system, 51 percent was as good as 99 percent.

Believing that there was only one way to rid the country of the increasingly hated dictator, now the elected president, a group of reformist-minded civilians and military officers led by Quiwonkpa attempted a coup. Initially successful in seizing key points, the coup planners convinced the populace they had won, leading many opponents to come out openly against Doe. But in vicious fighting between the coup forces and the Israeli-trained elite pro-Doe brigades, the dictator won the day. Doe then unleashed his military forces against the conspirators and their supporters. Since Quiwonkpa came from the Gio and Mano ethnic areas of Liberia, many of his supporters also came from those two groups, both of which had had rivalries with the nearby Krahn for decades. Thousands were massacred in the Gio and Mano areas, planting animosities that would later be used to topple Doe.

Charles Taylor Invades

The final Doe years were marked by increasing repression, corruption, incompetence, and regional political maneuvering, all of which contributed to the new president's downfall and the collapse of his so-called Second Liberian Republic. The regional element was a key in Doe's demise. Tolbert, the president Doe had assassinated, had been a close ally of Félix Houphouët-Boigny, neighboring Ivory Coast's long-serving, conservative president. Indeed, Tolbert's son was married to Houphouët-Boigny's daughter. Thus, there was no love lost between Houphouët-Boigny and Doe. As the Liberian leader became more erratic and repressive in the late 1980s, Houphouët-Boigny offered his territory as a base for anti-Doe forces, including those headed by Charles Taylor.

A descendent of the Americo elite and an American-educated economist, Taylor served in the early Doe administration as head of the General Services Administration—the agency responsible for government supplies. He was dismissed from his post in 1983, charged with embezzling nearly $1 million. After fleeing to the United States, he was jailed in Massachusetts, at the request of the Doe administration, for possible extradition. But he escaped first and fled to Mexico, and then West Africa, allegedly showing up in both Libya and Burkina Faso before setting up operations in the Ivory Coast.

On Christmas Eve 1989, Taylor led his force—consisting of several hundred men and known as the National Patriotic Front of Liberia (NPFL)—into the Mano and Gio areas of Liberia, where he knew anti-Doe sentiment ran highest. Within a few weeks, his army had swelled to several thousand, equipped with weapons supposedly received from Libya, via Burkina Faso and the Ivory Coast. Over the next several months, Taylor's forces overwhelmed the AFL and controlled most of the countryside, though bitter fighting along ethnic lines—between the Mano and Gio on the one

hand and the Krahn on the other—resulted in several hundred deaths. By May, he had Monrovia surrounded, and in July, he launched what he hoped would be the final offensive against Doe, announcing that he would honor a cease-fire only if the president resigned.

ECOMOG Intervention

Several events prevented Taylor's victory that summer. First, a breakaway faction—known as the Independent National Patriotic Front of Liberia (INPFL) and headed by a former Taylor lieutenant named Prince Johnson—engaged in fighting with NPFL forces. More important in blocking Taylor, however, was the introduction of the Economic Community of West African States (ECOWAS) forces in the fall. ECOWAS had been set up largely by the Nigerians in 1975 and soon emerged as both an economic grouping and a mutual security force. In August 1990, ECOWAS convened a conference to iron out differences between the INPFL and NPFL and find a way to ease Doe from power.

But the Nigerian-led conference failed to achieve its aims. Taylor, rightly suspecting that Nigeria stood opposed to him because of his alliance with Nigeria's main rival, the Ivory Coast, refused to attend. Nevertheless Doe offered to resign in September under ECOWAS protection. Not wanting Doe to fall into the hands of Taylor, ECOWAS turned him over to Taylor's rival, Prince Johnson, for protection. Johnson, an unbalanced individual by most accounts, did not help Doe get out of the country, as he had promised ECOWAS. Instead, he had the former president dismembered and killed, recording the grisly event for posterity on videotape.

In October, ECOWAS forces—known as the ECOWAS Monitoring Group (ECOMOG)—launched its first offensive, ostensibly to divide the warring factions but also to keep Taylor out of the capital. An Interim Government of National Unity (IGNU) was then established, with Amos Sawyer (formerly Doe's mentor) as president. IGNU controlled little of the country outside of Monrovia. Following a series of failed cease-fires during 1991, a new group emerged in the conflict. While the INPFL faded, Doe's former supporters rallied to the United Liberation Movement of Liberia for Democracy (ULIMO), which had established a base in the southwestern part of the country, adjacent to the Sierra Leone border. Indeed, Taylor accused the Sierra Leone government of

Liberian rebel leader Charles Taylor (center) celebrates a key victory in the countryside in July 1990. Taylor's forces surrounded the capital of Monrovia, but a multinational peacekeeping force kept him from taking over the country. He was finally elected president in 1997. *(Pascal Guyot/AFP/Getty Images)*

supporting ULIMO, and he consequently aided rebels in that country.

After the summer monsoon season, the NPFL launched a new offensive against ECOMOG forces in the suburbs of Monrovia. During the attack, NPFL guerrillas murdered five American nuns, earning the group Washington's condemnation. The attack led ECOMOG to abandon whatever pretense of neutrality it had maintained. It began to launch attacks openly on NPFL forces, including aerial attacks on supply routes near the Ivory Coast border. In November 1992, the United Nations announced an arms embargo against all factions in Liberia except ECOMOG. But the ban had little effect, as the NPFL became more sophisticated in its ability to plunder national resources in exchange for arms. Thus, major battles came to be fought around the Firestone Rubber plantation in the interior and near the port of Buchanan, Liberia's second-largest city, in early 1993.

At the same time, fighting intensified in the western part of the country as ULIMO went on the

offensive against NPFL positions there. But by this time, ULIMO itself had split into two factions. ULIMO-J, headed by Roosevelt Johnson, was largely composed of Krahn men and had loose ties to the remnants of the AFL. Its main bases were along the Sierra Leone border. ULIMO-K, led by Alhaji Kromah, was made up of Mandingos, an Islamic minority widely resented in Liberia for their aloofness and commercial acumen.

With the various forces fighting fiercely for control of the country's natural resources—in order to barter for weapons—civilian deaths climbed. In June, more than 600 refugees, largely Krahn, were massacred at the Harbel Rubber Plantation, allegedly by Taylor's forces. The UN Security Council then issued a declaration that it would isolate any faction that refused to abide by the accords signed by the various parties in the Ivory Coast the previous year. The threat appeared to work. In July, a conference of all the warring factions was held in Geneva, and the accord they reached was signed in Cotonou, Benin, in

July. The Cotonou agreement called for a thirty-five-member transitional parliament, consisting of representatives of all the warring factions, with the NPFL receiving the most.

The cease-fire called for in the accords failed to hold, after being violated by at least two factions—the NPFL and the inappropriately named Liberian Peace Council (LPC), a collection of Krahn men and former AFL soldiers from the center of the country led by George Boley, a former member of ULIMO. Meanwhile, at year's end, fighting intensified between ULIMO-J forces and a new regional faction known as the Lofa Defense Force (LDF). Still, there were some hopeful signs. In December, augmented ECOMOG forces and the first contingent of a UN monitoring team arrived to begin disarming the various factions under the Cotonou Accords. But their efforts were hampered by intense fighting between ULIMO factions in the western part of the country. By April of 1994, fewer than 1,500 of the estimated 60,000 combatants had been demobilized.

Even the capital of Monrovia was not spared violence. In September 1994, dissident members of the AFL—led by General Charles Julu—seized the Executive Mansion, trying to oust Wilson Sankawulo, Sawyer's successor as head of IGNU and a man seen as a Taylor protégé. The attackers were eventually removed from the mansion by ECOMOG forces. In November, yet another conference—this time sponsored by Ghanaian President Jerry Rawlings—tried to bring the warring factions together. But this attempt failed when the NPFL launched a new offensive in December from its base in Gbarnga, in central Liberia. Still, a new cease-fire was arranged in early 1995. This one held for a time, despite skirmishing among the various groups, allowing Nigeria to reduce its troop contingent from 10,000 to 6,000.

Under the Ghana agreement, a transition council was to be set up to rule the country until elections could be held. But Taylor's insistence that he chair the council jeopardized the arrangements. Meanwhile, new fighting broke out in February 1995, as Taylor tried to take control of the port of Buchanan from LPC forces. Even as another peace conference was being set up in the Nigerian capital of Abuja in May, new massacres and new fighting were reported in the Buchanan area. Taylor refused to attend the conference, suspecting the Nigerians of wanting to kidnap him, but he did agree to allow ECOMOG forces to begin demining the main highway between Monrovia and his head-

quarters in Gbarnga and to set up defensive positions around the Bong iron mines near the border with Guinea. These later arrangements failed to occur when fighting broke out in July between the NPFL on one side and ECOMOG and Guinean troops on the other.

The fighting around the Bong mines was indicative of some of the underlying causes of the war's persistence. Many of ECOMOG's officer corps saw the conflict as an opportunity to make their own personal fortunes selling off Liberian resources. Indeed, much of the fighting in the war occurred around the mines, rubber plantations, and gold and diamond fields scattered across the interior of Liberia. But by 1995, both the NPFL and ECOMOG found themselves in a stalemate. While Taylor still controlled much of the interior—where the resources were located—ECOMOG and various anti-NPFL factions—which Taylor accused of being surrogates for the Nigerians—held the ports, where the goods could be transported out of the country.

In late 1995, it was reported that Taylor secretly flew to Nigeria to cut a bargain with Nigerian leader Sani Abacha, whereby the two sides would work out a plan for smuggling out contraband goods. Whether the deal succeeded or not, it failed to end the fighting. Frustrated by his inability to take power and end the war, Taylor decided on a last offensive against the capital of Monrovia. On April 6, 1996, he launched his 30,000-man force against the city. Penetrating the outskirts and even making it into the center of the city, the NPFL forces met fierce resistance from ULIMO-J and AFL fighters.

In the course of the fighting, the city—which had once been a refuge from the fighting and had seen its population swell to over a million—was largely destroyed. Fighters from the various factions, often egged on by ECOMOG, which acted as a fence for the looted goods, plundered the city. Tens of thousands of refugees then poured out of Monrovia by ship, some making it to the nearby Guinean capital of Conakry, while others were forced to wander the West African coast for weeks before finally being permitted to disembark in Ghana.

Return to Peace and Elections

The intensive fighting of April 6 shocked all the participants, as well as the international community, which saw extensive destruction of its aid headquarters and embassies. (The prompt dispatch of heavily armed Navy SEALS and marines prevented a similar fate for the U.S. Embassy, which became a refuge for the remaining foreigners in Liberia.)

At this point, all sides seemed exhausted by the conflict. ECOWAS decided to appoint Victor Malu, a Nigerian general with a reputation for honesty and toughness, to head the ECOMOG forces in August 1996. Malu immediately announced a demobilization schedule, whereby all forces would be required to turn in their weapons by February 1, 1997, or face being charged as criminals. To the surprise of all concerned, Malu's plan worked. After dispatching forces throughout the country, he was able to bring in most of the weapons and soldiers, though many caches remained hidden in the bush in case the new cease-fire and peace plan, worked out in Abuja that summer, failed to hold.

But hold it did. Moreover, ECOMOG announced that elections for president and congress would be held in May. All warring factions could participate as long as they reorganized as political parties; their leaders could run for office if they resigned from the interim council. With the exception of Roosevelt Johnson—who announced his retirement from politics—all the participants complied.

Because of logistical problems, however, the elections had to be delayed until July. The two front-runners were Taylor and Ellen Johnson-Sirleaf, an economist who had spent most of the war years as a UN official in New York. Everybody expected Taylor to win, given his willingness to spend some of the fortune he had accumulated during the war on his campaign. Taylor and his National Patriotic Party (NPP) did sweep the polls, electing the former NPFL leader by more than 5 to 1 over his nearest opponent and giving the NPP a majority of congressional seats. Most Liberians hoped that by electing the most powerful of the warlords, they could assure themselves a peaceful future, and, indeed, Taylor emphasized reconciliation as the main tenet of his administration.

James Ciment

See also: Ethnic and Religious Conflicts; Liberia: Doe Coup, 1980; Liberia: Anti-Taylor Uprising, 1998–2003; Sierra Leone: Civil Conflict, 1990–Present.

Bibliography

Africa Watch. *Easy Prey: Child Soldiers in Liberia.* New York: Human Rights Watch, 1994.

Dolo, Emmanuel. *Democracy versus Dictatorship: The Quest for Freedom and Justice in Africa's Oldest Republic—Liberia.* Lanham, MD: University Press of America, 1996.

Dunn, Elwood. *Liberia: A National Polity in Transition.* Metuchen, NJ: Scarecrow Press, 1988.

Osaghae, Eghosa. *Ethnicity, Class and the Struggle for State Power in Liberia.* Dakar, Senegal: CODESRIA, 1996.

LIBERIA: Anti-Taylor Uprising, 1998–2003

TYPE OF CONFLICT: Ethnic and Religious
PARTICIPANTS: ECOWAS; Guinea; Ivory Coast; Sierra Leone

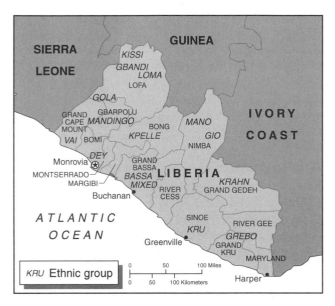

On August 4, 1997, Charles Taylor became president of Liberia. As leader of the National Patriotic Front of Liberia (NPFL), Taylor had launched a rebellion against President Samuel Doe in late 1989. Although Doe was killed in 1990 by a rival rebel leader, Taylor continued his armed efforts to seize power in Africa's oldest republic, thwarted by other rebel groups and a Nigerian-dominated peacekeeping force from the Economic Community of West African States (ECOWAS; the force was called the ECOWAS Monitoring Group, or ECOMOG). Finally, a peace accord reached in late 1996 called for elections the following year.

Many in Liberia were wary of Taylor. Though Doe was reviled, the rebellion that Taylor had launched in 1989 resulted in the deaths of roughly 200,000 people, nearly one out of every ten Liberians, the displacement of half the country, and the wholesale destruction of city and countryside alike. As the internationally monitored elections approached in the summer of 1997, Liberians could be heard singing: "He [Taylor] killed my ma, he killed m' pa, I gonna vote for that man," a chant cynically taken up by Taylor's own campaign. But as Liberia's freewheeling press noted, Taylor

had a gun to the Liberian electorate's head—they could vote for him or risk a new outbreak of war. Liberia's voters took the hint, overwhelmingly electing for president a man who once fled the country under suspicion of embezzling a million dollars in government funds.

Taylor's administration started off hopefully. In a country where corruption was endemic, Taylor promised a housecleaning of government ministries. In a country where the infrastructure had been utterly destroyed (the capital Monrovia had been without running water and electricity for most of the 1990s), Taylor emphasized reconstruction. And, most importantly, in a country where leaders, including Taylor himself, had cynically pitted members of one ethnic group against another, the new president vowed to make national reconciliation a top priority.

All promises soon put aside, Taylor's administration quickly proved to be one of the most corrupt and self-serving in the country's history, according to both Liberian and international critics. Taylor had already reaped huge profits from the civil war he launched in 1989, engaging in illicit timber sales and diamond smuggling. Once in office, he presided over the theft of the nation's resources for the personal gain of his closest followers and himself. He invested little in rebuilding the country's ruined infrastructure. Meanwhile, both unemployment and illiteracy in Liberia continued to hover at around 75 percent. Monrovia continued to survive without electricity or running water through his tenure and beyond. As for reconciliation, Taylor surrounded himself with loyal supporters from the Gio and Mano tribes, antagonizing many of the nation's other fourteen official ethnic groups.

Liberians United for Reconciliation and Democracy

All of these factors contributed to the uprising that broke out in 1999, led by an armed resistance group

208

KEY DATES

1980	Military coup by Master Sergeant Samuel Doe ends the 133-year rule of Americo-Liberians, the descendants of free blacks and freed slaves from North America who founded the country.
1990	In the wake of the invasion by rebel forces led by Charles Taylor, Doe is killed by a rival rebel leader.
1996	The first Liberian civil war ends with a cease-fire enforced by the Economic Community of West African States Monitoring Group (ECOMOG).
1997	Taylor is elected president in internationally monitored elections.
1999	A rebel group called Liberians United for Reconciliation and Democracy (LURD) launches attacks against Taylor's government, which it accuses of corruption and repression.
2003	LURD and a second rebel group, known as the Movement for Democracy in Liberia (MODEL), launch a major offensive against the Liberian capital of Monrovia in July, forcing Taylor into Nigerian exile.
2003–2004	A UN peacekeeping force arrives in the country and conducts the demobilization of rebel armies.
2005	Ellen Johnson-Sirleaf is elected president, becoming the first elected female head of state in modern African history.

known as Liberians United for Reconciliation and Democracy (LURD). The group was dominated by Mandingoes and Lomas (both groups members of a rebel group that opposed Taylor's NPFL during the long civil war) and Krahns (who had been loyal supporters of former president Doe). LURD criticized Taylor for his failure to achieve the goals he set out in his inaugural speech: clean government, reconstruction, and reconciliation.

In the end, however, Taylor's interference in the affairs of neighboring states ultimately proved his undoing. He began by supporting the brutal Revolutionary United Front (RUF) rebels in Sierra Leone, known for hacking off the limbs of civilians as a form of terrorist intimidation. Taylor and his cronies offered RUF weapons in exchange for diamonds from Sierra Leone's diamond-mining region, one of the richest in the world. RUF's attacks in Sierra Leone sent thousands of its citizens into exile in neighbor-

ing Guinea, where they in turn were accused of supporting Guinean rebels. Guinea also accused Taylor of launching raids into its territory in pursuit of Liberian dissidents. Guinea was already accommodating thousands of Liberian refugees from the 1989–1996 civil war. Most were members of the Mandingo, Loma, and Krahn tribes, who feared retribution from Taylor's government even as they suffered from raids carried out by Guinean authorities on their refugee camps. At the same time, according to experts on West African politics, Guinea helped organize and support LURD's insurgency in Liberia to make up for Taylor's support for the rebels of RUF in Guinea.

Taylor was also suspected of interfering with Ivory Coast, Liberia's neighbor to the east. A coup in late 1999 plunged the formerly peaceful and prosperous country into civil war, as rebel groups in the northern and western parts of the country challenged the leadership in the commercial capital of Abidjan. Many of the rebels were foreigners—including some Liberians—who had been attracted to Ivory Coast because of its stability and economic opportunity but had been denied citizenship by the xenophobic Ivory Coast government. Its president, Laurent Gbagbo, believed that Taylor was supporting the rebels.

When a new anti-Taylor organization known as the Movement for Democracy in Liberia (MODEL) was founded in early 2003 in Liberia's Krahn-dominated southeast, Gbagbo's government allegedly began supplying it with arms, allowing it to use bases inside the Ivory Coast. Some experts even argue that MODEL was organized by Gbagbo's government.

Vicious as Taylor had been as a rebel leader and as president, both LURD and MODEL were also accused by aid workers and international observers of repeated human rights abuses, including murder, mass rape, and the forcible recruitment of civilians for both fighting and basic labor. Still, LURD and MODEL soon succeeded in gaining control of most of Liberia, putting themselves in a position to share in the looting of the country's resources, most notably its rainforest timber and iron ore. MODEL captured the city of Buchanan, Liberia's second largest port, in early 2003. By mid-2003, the insurgents controlled roughly 80 percent of Liberia's territory, leaving Taylor with control only of the capital, Monrovia, and its environs. In June 2003, the same month that a UN-backed tribunal investigating atrocities in Sierra Leone indicted Taylor for war crimes in that country, LURD issued an ultimatum to Taylor—resign and leave the country or face a final assault on Monrovia.

Taylor was being pressed from all quarters. ECOWAS was conducting on-again, off-again peace negotiations in Accra, Ghana, urging the Taylor government and rebel groups to end the fighting. Neighboring states kept up their complaints about Taylor's meddling in their affairs, finding support from the United Nations and the United States.

Taylor Bows Out

On July 6, Taylor succumbed to the pressure. He agreed to accept an offer of asylum from Nigeria, but there was one catch: Taylor himself would decide when to step down as Liberia's president. LURD leaders, whose forces surrounded the capital and held the port area, launched an offensive on the already battered capital that sent thousands of new refugees fleeing for safety. The United States sent warships to Liberian waters to rescue Americans and other foreigners in the capital. Taylor's troops were able to withstand the rebel attack, but it was clear the president's days were numbered. On August 11, Taylor fled to Nigeria, replaced by his vice president, Moses Blah, in a ceremony attended by dignitaries who included the presidents of South Africa, Mozambique, and Ghana. Leaders of both LURD and MODEL proclaimed the war over.

Still, problems remained. Some 40,000 rebel soldiers, many of them teenagers, had yet to be demobilized. Meeting in Ghana, representatives of LURD, MODEL and Liberia's political parties, women's organizations, religious groups, and others met to hammer out plans for demobilization of rebel fighters and their integration into civilian life. Meanwhile, seeing Liberia as the linchpin of efforts to end fighting across West Africa, the UN organized the largest peacekeeping mission in its history. In February 2004, 15,000 UN troops were fully deployed. By October, the UN claimed that the rebel groups had largely demobilized. Many groups may have hidden weapons in rural areas, however, in case Taylor, who still had many supporters in the country, was plotting a return from Nigerian exile.

Liberian political parties and the interim government began making plans for national elections, to be held in October 2005. While there were nearly a dozen candidates, two quickly emerged as frontrunners: international soccer star George Weah, whose support came largely from Liberia's younger voters, and former World Bank economist Ellen Johnson-Sirleaf, who had finished a distant second to Taylor in the 1997 elections. In 2005, Weah finished first, followed by Johnson-Sirleaf. Because Weah failed to win at least 50 percent of the vote, a runoff was scheduled for November 8. In that election Johnson-Sirleaf received backing from the supporters of the other losing candidates and defeated George Weah. While some Weah supporters protested the decision, claiming voting irregularities, international observers pronounced the election free, fair, and transparent. On January 16, 2006, Johnson-Sirleaf was inaugurated president, the first elected woman leader in modern African history.

Among her first acts in office was an extradition

request to the government of Nigeria. Johnson-Sirleaf wanted Taylor arrested and sent to the International Criminal Court in Sierra Leone, where most of Taylor's alleged war crimes and crimes against humanity had been committed. Nigerian President Olesegun Obasanjo had consistently maintained that he would not extradite Taylor until a democratically elected government in Liberia asked him to. In March 2006, Taylor was arrested while trying to flee Nigeria, and sent to Sierra Leone. But a new issue arose at this point: where he should be tried. Some in West Africa argued that he should face trial in Sierra Leone, so that witnesses could more easily testify against him and so that the victims of his alleged crimes could play a role in trying him. Others feared that his presence in the region—where he still enjoyed much support—could destabilize the fragile peace in both Sierra Leone and Liberia. The government of The Netherlands, where the permanent International Criminal Court is based, said it would not allow a trial there unless another country agreed to take Taylor afterward, whether he was found guilty or not. In June 2006, Britain—the former colonial power in Sierra Leone—agreed to the Dutch request, and Taylor was flown to The Hague to face trial.

James Ciment

See also: Ethnic and Religious Conflicts; Liberia: Civil War, 1989–1997; Sierra Leone: Civil Conflict, 1990–Present.

Bibliography

Levitt, Jeremy I. *The Evolution of Deadly Conflict in Liberia: From "Paternaltarianism" to State Collapse.* Durham, NC: Carolina Academic Press, 2005.

Moran, Mary H. *Liberia: The Violence of Democracy.* Philadelphia: University of Pennsylvania, 2005.

Pham, John-Peter. *Liberia: Portrait of a Failed State.* New York: Reed Press, 2004.

Sawyer, Amos. *Beyond Plunder: Toward Democratic Governance in Liberia.* Boulder, CO: Lynne Rienner, 2005.

Yoder, John C. *Popular Culture, Civil Society, and State Crisis in Liberia.* Lewiston, NY: E. Mellen Press, 2003.

MADAGASCAR: Independence Movement and Coups, 1947–2002

TYPE OF CONFLICT: Anticolonialism; Coups
PARTICIPANT: France

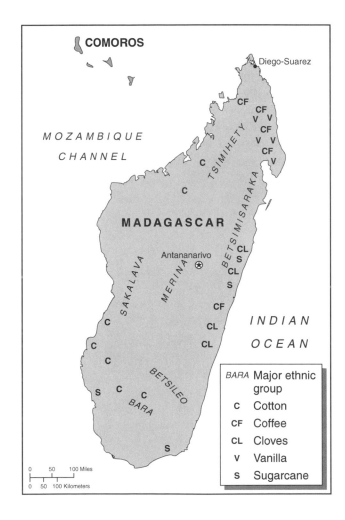

BARA — Major ethnic group
c — Cotton
CF — Coffee
CL — Cloves
v — Vanilla
s — Sugarcane

The Republic of Madagascar is an island of 226,658 square miles. It is 980 miles long and, at its widest point, 360 miles across, and lies in the Indian Ocean about 300 miles off the southeast coast of Africa. It has a population of about 11 million. Despite the island's proximity to Africa, the people are of Malayo-Indonesian stock, with some African and Arab admixture, particularly on the coasts. The capi-

tal, Antananarivo, a city of about half a million people, is on the high central plateau at an elevation of over 4,000 feet.

Traditional agriculture is well developed, and Madagascar is able to feed its people. Rice, maize, yams, cassava, and small livestock and poultry are abundant. For cash crops farmers rely on coffee, cloves, vanilla, rice, peppers, tobacco, and peanuts. Landholding is essentially equitable since a plantation system never existed in Madagascar to any great extent.

The society is a traditional one with a complex and sophisticated culture that has been able to absorb and exploit European innovations without surrendering its core values. One feature is a highly developed and important cult of dead ancestors, although Christianity, both Protestant and Roman Catholic, is practiced by a large majority. Malagasy is the official language, but French is widely spoken as well.

Historical Background

The people of Madagascar apparently arrived by sea from present-day Indonesia early in the Middle Ages, an astonishing open sea voyage of about 3,500 miles. Contact with the outside world began when Arab slave traders arrived in the late Middle Ages. The Portuguese and the Dutch showed up in the sixteenth century. An English colony of several hundred people was established in 1644, but only twelve survived constant attacks from the local defenders. The colony was abandoned within two years. A contemporary and even more ambitious French settlement met the same fate, but both attempts laid the basis for nineteenth-century English and French imperial claims.

During the Napoleonic wars the island assumed strategic significance for both the British and the

KEY DATES

1896   The French parliament declares Madagascar a French colony.

1947   Unknown rebel groups lead an assault on French installations and the homes of French settlers.

1960   Madagascar wins its independence from France.

1972   The government of Philibert Tsiranana is overthrown in a military coup.

1975   Military officers create the Supreme Revolutionary Council to rule the country, with Commander Didier Ratsiraka as president.

2001   Ratsiraka runs for reelection against Marc Ravalomanana, mayor of the capital Antananarivo; the government announces that results are inconclusive and that a runoff would be required.

2002   Ravalomanana cites alleged fraud in the election and unilaterally declares himself president on February 22; Ratsiraka declares martial law and flees the capital; in April the nation's high court declares Ravalomanana the winner in elections; facing international condemnation, Ratsiraka flees the country in July.

2003   The former head of the armed forces is charged with attempting a coup against Ravalomanana in February; in August, Ratsiraka is sentenced in absentia to ten years' imprisonment for embezzling government funds.

French. This renewed interest came at the same time the Merina kingdom with its capital at Tananarive (now known as Antananarivo) was establishing its authority over the whole island. Even after the European peace, the British and the French continued their competition. Both sent military instructors to the Merina king, Radama, who was determined to establish his rule over the coastal regions. The French, for their part, tended, at least initially, to support the coastal opponents of Radama. Religion (Protestant versus Catholic) and technology were other areas of competition. The London Missionary Society was first in the field; French Jesuits followed in the 1840s and 1850s. First British and then French craftsmen and engineers became influential. The rivalry was suspended during the Crimean War, in which Britain and France were allies.

After the death of the last Merina king, Radama II, in 1862, a succession of "prime ministers" controlled the series of queens who succeeded him.

These prime ministers managed to play England and France off against each other, at the same time modernizing the society and the economy as rapidly as possible in what proved a vain attempt to head off annexation by one or another of the two foreign powers. In 1890, Great Britain officially recognized a French protectorate in Madagascar in exchange for French recognition of the British protectorate over Zanzibar. In 1894, France invaded, forcing Queen Ranavalona III to sign a treaty under which a French resident had all effective powers of government on October 1. Within months, the *menalamba* movement, the Uprising of the Red Shawls, inspired by the belief that abandoning the traditional religion had caused the foreign conquest, began attacking all Europeans, especially missionaries and churches.

On August 6, 1896, the French parliament declared Madagascar a French colony and sent General Joseph Henri Gallieni there to be governor, with full military and civil authority. His first actions were to order the executions of leading Merina government officials and exile of the queen. Fighting continued sporadically until 1905 and killed as many as 100,000 Malagasy, but after that French rule was essentially uncontested for sixty-three years.

Colonial Era

In many ways French colonial administration in Madagascar was beneficial. An excellent primary and vocational and technical educational system was established, and medical services were far superior to those in most European colonies. Numerous locals entered the professions, becoming medical doctors and teachers. Malagasy who spoke French and fulfilled certain educational qualifications were made French citizens with full rights. There were about 8,000 of them by 1947. The biggest local grievance was the system of forced labor under which much of the rural population had to work fifty days a year on roads and other public improvements. Basically, this was a continuation of the Merina kingdom system, but it was still widely resented.

World War II and After

After the fall of France to German armies in May 1940, Madagascar came under control of France's Vichy government, which collaborated with its German captors. As part of the international struggle, the British landed an amphibious force at Diego-Suarez (on the northern tip of Madagascar) on May 5, 1942, and secured the surrender of the Vichy French garrison in September. Two months later, authority on the island was given to the Free French government-in-exile, but British and South African troops remained until 1946. In 1944, General Charles de Gaulle, leader of the Free French, made the famous Brazzaville Declaration, promising that all inhabitants of French territories would become French citizens. At the end of the war, the French government established the French Union, which gave representation in the French parliament to its overseas territories, the former colonies.

Except for the British invasion, Madagascar was not an active theater during the war. However, the war did result in reimposition of forced labor and in what was even less popular with the small farmers, establishment of quotas for delivery of rice and other basics, as well as price controls. Resentment of these

conditions was exploited by Dr. Joseph Ravoahangy and another doctor, Joseph Raseta, who were among the two Malagasy elected to the French Constituent Assembly in 1945. In Paris, the two doctors met the young intellectual Jacques Rabemananjara, who had spent the war years in France, and formed the first true Madagascar political party, the Democratic Movement for Malagasy Renewal (MDRM, its French acronym), with Raseta as party president.

In October 1946, Madagascar became a territory of France, with all of its inhabitants French citizens and with forced labor abolished. In addition, by French decree, Madagascar, unique among French territories, was divided into five provinces, each to have its own assembly and budget. Moreover, French authorities in Madagascar sponsored a new party to compete with the MDRM, the Party of the Dispossessed Malagasy (PADESM), in an attempt to pit the non-Merina groups against the Merina-dominated MDRM. Whatever the intent, the French attempt failed politically. In the November 1946 elections for the French parliament, Ravoahangy and Raseta were handily reelected and joined by a third MDRM candidate, Rabemananjara.

1947 Rebellion

As Madagascar prepared for the first meeting of its national assembly on March 30, the MDRM at home had become confident of controlling politics on the island. MDRM and PADESM partisans clashed in the streets. Nevertheless, Ravoahangy and his colleagues in Paris sent a telegram to local MDRM leaders urging them to "maintain . . . *sang-froid*" and not to react to provocations designed to "sabotage peaceful policies."

On the night of March 29, 1947, simultaneous assaults by hitherto unknown groups took place against French installations and the homes of French settlers throughout the island. Once the initial assaults had been repulsed, the rebellion, which had spread all over the island, became guerrilla warfare between the heavily armed French and the rebels, mostly equipped with spears and axes. Imposition of martial law and mass arrests caused thousands of civilians to flee into the forests.

On April 19, 1947, the French high commissioner in Madagascar, Marcel de Coppet, declared the MDRM solely responsible. MDRM leaders Ravoahangy, Raseta, and Rabemananjara had their parliamentary immunity lifted and were arrested. Even

A French military convoy departs on a reconnaissance mission in Madagascar during the native rebellion in 1947. Tens of thousands were killed before the violence ended late the following year. *(AFP/Getty Images)*

before they were tried, military tribunals had tried and executed numerous supposed leaders of the revolt, including its "generalissimo," Samuel Rakotondrabe. The MDRM had already been officially repressed, and when, in the fall of 1948, Ravoahangy and Raseta were sentenced to death, and Rabemananjara and seven other MDRM leaders to life imprisonment, the party was effectively destroyed. By December 1, 1948, when the emergency was declared over, officially 11,000 had been killed, and as many as 80,000 may have died of starvation.

There has never been a satisfactory explanation of the 1947 rebellion. It is generally accepted that the MDRM leaders were not involved. Some argue that *agents provocateurs* had infiltrated MDRM and used the revolt to discredit it. Another theory is that extreme MDRM elements opposed any grant of independence, insisting that true liberation had to come through violence. This theory, however, presupposes some ideological debate, which the party records do not reveal. Others believe, with some reason, that the rebellion was planned and directed by witch doctors and magicians, leaders of the most primitive ele-

ments in Malagasy society, who hated and feared the Europeanized Malagasy as much as or more than they did the French.

Independence and After

After the crushing of the rebellion and suppression of the MDRM, there was essentially no visible political activity in Madagascar until 1954. French Premier Pierre Mendes-France, who had just ended the French war in France's former colony of Indochina and granted autonomy to Tunisia, was eager to wind up the French empire. New elections to the French parliament were scheduled for January 1956. Elected to represent the west coast of Madagascar was a schoolteacher, Philibert Tsiranana, who had organized the Social Democratic Party (PSD). Events moved quickly thereafter. On June 28, France passed the Loi Cadre, establishing internal autonomy for all former colonies, with elections to the national assembly of each former colony to be on the basis of universal suffrage with no separate status for European electors. Tsiranana declared he looked forward to Madagascar's becoming to France like a member of the British Commonwealth to England. On April 2, 1960, a Franco-Madagascar treaty was signed, and on June 26, Madagascar "recovered," as its spokesman said, its independence.

Tsiranana and the PSD—both the man and the party were nationalist but ideologically conservative—easily dominated the political scene. Tsiranana's main political foe, Norbert Zafimahova, head of the Union of Social Democrats of Madagascar (USDM), differed in ideology from Tsiranana only in wanting a stronger role for the provincial assemblies. There was no vocal left-wing or third-world political movement visible. Tsiranana was easily reelected in 1965. All observers of Madagascar at the end of the 1960s remarked on the island nation's calm, so different from that of most former colonies.

After 1967, however, there was an economic downturn. Increasing complaints were heard about Tsiranana's authoritarianism. The crime rate, always high, grew worse. In the south, riots turned into armed demonstrations. In 1972 there was a military coup, and Tsiranana turned over the government to the army chief of staff, General Gabriel Ramanantsoa, who managed to keep control until the elections of 1973, which returned the PSD to power. However, this move angered radicals within the military hierarchy, and in early 1975, Ramanantsoa resigned in favor of another military officer, Colonel Richard Ratsimandrava. Within a week Ratsimandrava was assassinated, and General Gilles Andriamahazo took power, declared martial law, and suspended all political parties. He, in turn, was succeeded in June by a naval officer, Commander Didier Ratsiraka, who made himself chairman of the Supreme Revolutionary Council (SRC).

In December 1975 the SRC proclaimed the Democratic Republic of Madagascar. Only a single political party was allowed—the National Front for the Defense of the Malagasy Socialist Revolution (FNDR). Ratsiraka became president for a term of seven years, proclaiming as his policy "the creation of a socialist republic under divine protection by the year 2000." Madagascar withdrew from the French Community and the franc zone, and established diplomatic relations with the USSR and the People's Republic of China. The most dramatic of Ratsiraka's acts was the 1975 pogrom against the Comoros Island community in Madagascar. Some 1,400 were slaughtered, and another 16,000 fled back to the Comoros.

Civil and Regional Conflict

Despite the left-wing rhetoric and foreign policy, Ratsiraka's government began to move to the right in the late 1980s. Its relations with France became warmer, and plans for nationalization and other socialist economic policies were abandoned in favor of market reforms, in the hope of winning the backing of international financial institutions. Political unrest, socialist experimentation, and environmental problems had had a negative impact on the economy.

The shift to market reforms did little to repair the economy, however, even after France forgave Madagascar's debt of nearly a billion dollars. Responding to domestic opposition and international pressure, Ratsiraka agreed to share power with the prodemocracy leader Albert Zafy. In elections the following year, Zafy became president. While Madagascar was returning to democracy, its economy remained in dire straits. International lending agencies and donor countries continued to press the Zafy government to cut the budget deficit, reduce the bloated civil service, and cut subsidies. As Zafy implemented the reforms, unemployment and poverty grew, leading to political unrest. In 1996, parliament moved to impeach him but, before they could, he was defeated in national elections by Ratsiraka.

Madagascar was also riven by sectional unrest. While the Malagasy-speaking people make up the vast majority of the population (roughly 95 percent), they are divided by regions. The three major ones are the east coast, the west coast, and the plateau region between. The people of the plateau, known as the Merina, or "elevated people," dominated the island's politics both before and after the French, fostering jealousy and unrest in the other provinces, known as *faritany*. For years, people in the outlying faritany have demanded a decentralized governmental system that would allow more autonomy for provincial governments. This centrifugal political force had been kept in check by Ratsiraka, who enjoyed popularity in the outlying provinces.

The twin crises of economic distress and regionalism came together to produce a series of political crises in the early 2000s. In December 2001, Ratsiraka ran for election against Marc Ravalomanana, mayor of the capital Antananarivo in the plateau region. When the government announced that the results were inconclusive and a runoff would be required, supporters of Ravalomanana claimed fraud and, on February 22, 2002, their candidate unilaterally declared himself president.

Mass demonstrations by supporters of the two rival claimants for the presidency had been held throughout the crisis and turned violent by mid-February. After Ravalomanana assumed the presidency, Ratsiraka fled the violence in the capital and set up a rival government in the east coast city of Toamasina, where he declared martial law. The move did little to stop the fighting. Clashes among protesters and between protesters and soldiers rocked the capital, which was blockaded by Ratsiraka supporters, leading to shortages of food and fuel. By April, dozens had been killed when the violence spread to the northern half of the country as Ravalomanana's soldiers tried to quell disturbances in the region, which was dominated by Ratsikara supporters.

That same month, the two claimants signed an accord in Senegal calling for a recount of December's vote. On April 29, the nation's High Constitutional Court officially declared Ravalomanana the winner with 51.5 percent of the vote to Raksimana's 35.9 percent. But Ratsiraka and much of the government in Toamasina refused to abide by the ruling, and the governor of Toamasina declared his province independent, claiming that three more of the nation's six provinces were willing to form a confederation independent of Antananarivo. Fighting continued through June as international reporters claimed that Ratsiraka's government was fomenting clashes between his coastal supporters and the people of the central highlands.

On June 26, 2002, U.S. Ambassador to Madagascar Wanda Nesbitt passed a letter to Ravalomanana telling him that the administration of George W. Bush was recognizing him as the legitimate president of the country. Most countries in Europe soon followed suit. France, which had long supported Ratsiraka, refused to go along the Ravalomanana government. The French government, caught up in its own elections, vowed not to take sides in the conflict and would abide by the Organization of African Unity's decision on whether to intervene and how to intervene. That organization, which had supported many long-time dictators on the mainland, had sided with Ratsiraka in the dispute but had not become directly involved in the conflict. By late June, however, the new French government of Jacques Chirac decided to break with past policies and drop support of Ratsiraka. Realizing that he was isolated internationally, Ratsiraka fled to the Seychelles in July and then to France, claiming he left his country to avoid a "bloodbath."

After Ratsiraka's departure in 2002, Madagascar's government remained in control of the country, but not without political intrigue and natural disaster. In February 2003, the former head of the armed forces was charged with attempting a coup against Ravalomana, and in August 2002, Ratsiraka was sentenced in absentia to ten years' hard labor for embezzling government funds. Former prime minister Tantely Andrianariov was sentenced to twelve years' hard labor for abuse of office. In 2004, Madagascar was devastated by two major cyclones, leading international lending institutions to forgive about half of its $4 billion foreign debt. In 2005, Madagascar became the first country to receive U.S. aid under a new Bush administration program to reward countries that promoted democratic and market economy reforms.

David MacMichael and James Ciment

See also: Anticolonialism; Coups; Ethnic and Religious Conflicts.

Bibliography

Brown, Mervyn. *A History of Madagascar.* Princeton, NJ: Markus Wiener, 2000.

Cornwell, Richard. "Madagascar: Stumbling at the First Hurdle?" *Institute for Security Studies,* Paper 68, April 2003.

Ellis, Stephen. *The Rising of the Red Shawls: A Revolt in Madagascar, 1895–1899.* New York: Cambridge University Press, 1985.

Feeley-Harnik, Gillian. *A Green Estate: Restoring Independence in Madagascar.* Washington, DC: Smithsonian Institution Press, 1991.

Heseltine, Nigel. *Madagascar.* New York: Praeger, 1971.

Stratton, Arthur. *The Great Red Island.* New York: Scribner's, 1964.

MALI: Ethnic and Political Conflict, 1968–1996

TYPE OF CONFLICT: Ethnic and Religious; Coups
PARTICIPANT: Congo (Zaire)

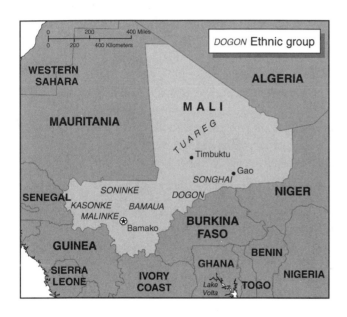

The territory that is now Mali was the center of several of Western Africa's greatest empires, including the Ghana from the fourth to eleventh centuries C.E., the Mali from the twelfth to the fifteenth centuries, and the Songhai, which followed the Mali and was then defeated by the Moroccan kingdom at the end of the sixteenth century. The Moroccans then occupied the great trading cities of Gao and Timbuktu, destroying all political and intellectual centers. These events came at a time when increased European contact on the coast was reorienting African trade in that direction.

The French began to arrive in the region in the mid-nineteenth century, establishing their first outpost in what is now Mali in 1855, following a series of wars between various clans in the region. At first welcomed by Segou Tukolor's kingdom—which had arisen earlier in the century—as a protection against the British, the French soon began to expand their holdings, first through diplomacy and then by military expedition. In the 1890s, the French led a series of raids against Segou Tukolor and Samory Toure, the Muslim leader. By 1899, all hostile clans and kingdoms had been fully pacified, and the French set up their own administration in what they called French Sudan.

Political parties were first established in the territory in 1946, when a legislature was established. The dominant party was the Sudanese Union-African Democratic Assembly (US-RDA, its French acronym), headed by the charismatic Marxist Modibo Keita. In 1958, the territory was renamed the Sudanese Republic and was incorporated as an autonomous state within the French Community. Following a failed attempt at confederation with Senegal in 1959, the independent Republic of Mali came into being on September 22, 1960.

Political and Ethnic Tensions

Under the leadership of the US-RDA, Mali tried to chart a course independent of France, dropping out of the franc zone in 1962. But the economic costs of this move eventually forced the government to seek reentry, a move that angered radicals within the party. When a militant wing began to purge the government of pro-French elements, the army stepped in, seizing power in November 1968. The Military Committee for National Liberation (CMLN) was established with Lieutenant Moussa Traore—one of the coup leaders—as its chair. While Traore promised a return to civilian rule, continued economic hardship and a six-year drought caused delays.

In 1974, the government instituted a new constitution, calling for a return to elections after a five-year transition period. Throughout the 1980s, the

218

KEY DATES

1960   Mali wins its independence from France.

1968   The army seizes power in the country's first coup.

1974   The government issues a new constitution calling for national elections within five years.

1980s   Government austerity measures, urged by international lending institutions, provoke widespread protest.

1991   After issuing warnings to protesters for years, troops open fire on student demonstrators in March, killing over 100 persons; by the second half of the year, fighting breaks out between Tuareg guerrillas and government forces.

1992   Algeria mediates a truce between Tuareg rebels of the Unified Movement and Fronts of the Azaouad (MFUA, its French acronym) and the Malian government.

1996   3,000 former MFUA fighters turn in their weapons and register with the government.

government tried to introduce economic austerity measures, at the urging of major international lending institutions like the World Bank and the International Monetary Fund. These measures set off antigovernment protests by the end of the decade, just as the government was attempting a transition to democracy. Warnings to the protesters went unheeded for several months in 1991. In March, troops opened fire on student protesters in the capital of Bamako, killing more than 100 persons and injuring some 700 others. Nevertheless, elections were scheduled for March 1992, leading to the victory of the Alliance for Democracy in Mali (ADEMA), headed by an academic named Alpha Oumar Konare. Democracy continued in Mali in subsequent years as the ADEMA won yet another victory at the polls in 1997.

Meanwhile, ethnic tensions were building in the northern part of the country around the ancient cities of Gao and Timbuktu. Following the end of yet another prolonged drought in 1990, large numbers of Tuaregs began to return to the country after years in Algeria and Libya. Light-skinned and fiercely independent nomads, the Tuaregs had a tradition of resistance to government control that went back to the

French regime and before. The Tuaregs resented the fact that the ethnic groups of the south controlled the government. The government suspected that the Tuaregs were planning to form a breakaway republic of their own. By the latter half of 1991, fighting had broken out between the Tuaregs and government troops, as well as between the Tuaregs and the majority ethnic group in the north, the Songhai.

Algeria made efforts to mediate the crisis, which led to a pact between the Tuaregs and Bamako in March 1992. Under the agreement, the Unified Movement and Fronts of the Azaouad (MFUA), as the Tuaregs call their region of Mali, were guaranteed administrative posts in the government, while some of their fighters would be incorporated into the national army. Still, sporadic attacks against the Songhai, resented for their efforts to keep the nomadic Tuaregs out of their lands, continued. A further agreement in May 1994 called for the full integration of MFUA and Tuareg fighters into the Malian government and armed forces.

Even after the agreement, clashes and acts of banditry increased, and tensions grew between Tuareg fighters and regular members of the Malian armed forces. At the same time, a Songhai defense force had emerged in the north, and it conducted periodic attacks on Tuaregs. Despite more Algerian efforts to mediate the crisis, Tuareg anger rose as its leaders and civilians were targeted by the Songhai and the army for assassination.

In early 1995, President Konare made an appeal to Tuareg and Songhai leaders to end the hostilities and implement the national reconciliation pacts reached in 1992 and 1994. The appeal seemed to work. The government's "normalization" plan for the north included the restoration of local civilian government in the region and the establishment of a number of health clinics, schools, and utilities. By February 1996, some 3,000 former MFUA fighters had registered with the government and turned in their weapons. In March, a ceremonial burning of the weapons was conducted in Timbuktu, as a way to symbolize the new harmonious relations between the Tuaregs and the government. During this period of reconciliation, virtually all of the 100,000 or so Tuareg and Songhai refugees in surrounding states returned to Mali.

James Ciment

See also: Ethnic and Religious Conflicts; Niger: Ethnic and Political Conflict Since 1990.

Bibliography

Drisdell, Rheal. *Mali: A Prospect of Peace?* Oxford, UK: Oxfam UK and Ireland, 1997.

Economist Intelligence Unit. *Country Profile: Guinea, Mali, Mauritania.* London: Economic Intelligence Unit, 1986–1992.

MAURITANIA: Coups Since 1978

TYPE OF CONFLICT: Coups
PARTICIPANTS: Spain; Western Sahara

Mauritania is a mainly desert nation that straddles black and Arab Africa. The country has significant deposits of iron ore and began exporting oil from off-shore rigs in 2006. Politically, Mauritania has experienced numerous coups and countercoups since gaining independence from France in 1960.

In 1975, Mauritania joined with Morocco in an effort to annex and divide Sahara (now Western Sahara), whose people were engaged in a liberation struggle against Spanish control. Mauritania had coveted the region since its independence, but its involvement in military action to occupy Sahara was ill fated. Sahara's Polisario Front proved stronger than the Mauritanian army and ultimately occupied part of Mauritania itself, causing social and economic turmoil. Conflicting calls for withdrawal and more fighting brought mass political demonstrations, street fighting, and ultimately a popular uprising against the Mauritanian government.

1970s and 1980s

Beginning in 1978, Mauritania experienced five coups in little more than six years. In 1978, military commander Mustapha Ould Salek ended the reign of the country's first post-independence president, Ould Daddah. In January 1980, Salek was removed and replaced by Ould Haidalla, who recognized the Polisario movement in Sahara, ending Mauritania's military actions there. Ould Haidalla lacked support in Mauritania, however, and after four years of tenuous rule was replaced in another army coup. Maaouya Ould Taya was installed as president.

Ould Taya proved to be the most durable leader of Mauritania since Ould Daddah. He survived a coup attempt by the Forces de Liberation Africaine de Mauritanie (FLAM), an organization of black African nationalists, at the end of 1987. By April 1989, violent conflicts within Mauritania between African Mauritanians and Arabs and Berbers contributed to the eruption of a violent border dispute with Senegal. The conflict had a disastrous impact on both countries. Thousands of Mauritanians fled into Senegal, where they struggled to survive for years.

In 1992, Ould Taya's administration returned a form of electoral politics to Mauritania, but the first elected president was Ould Taya himself; he was reelected in 1997. As he prepared to run for yet another term in 2003, another coup attempt resulted in several days of street fighting in the capital, and the insurgents captured several government buildings. The government put down the uprising, however, and in November, Taya was reelected.

Heydalla, Taya's main challenger in the 2003 voting, rejected the results and was arrested for plotting a coup. He was convicted and sentenced to a five-year suspended jail term and a prohibition against running in future elections.

KEY DATES

1960	Mauritania wins its independence from France.
1975	Mauritania joins with Morocco in annexing and occupying Western Sahara, after the withdrawal of colonial Spanish troops.
1978–1984	Mauritania experiences five military coups.
1989	Internal conflicts between black African and Arab and Berber Mauritanians spark a border conflict with Senegal.
2003	A coup attempt against the government of Maaouya Ould Taya fails, sparking street fighting in the capital.
2005	Ould Taya is overthrown in a military coup.

Finally, in August 2005, Ould Taya was overthrown by army officers who named security chief Ely Ould Mohammed Vall as the country's new leader. The bloodless coup took place while Taya was attending the funeral of King Fahd in Saudia Arabia. Taya took up residence in the Republic of Niger, but claimed to be president of Mauritania and ordered the armed forces to protect his right to the office.

Taya had become widely unpopular in Mauritania, and the military plotters paid no attention to his orders. Immediately following the announcement of the coup, hundreds of people took to the streets in Mauritania's capital, Nouakchott, to express their support for the Military Council. Even Taya's Social Democratic Republican Party (PRDS) issued a statement backing the council.

Taya had turned the country increasingly toward the West and against radical Islamist groups. In 1999, he had established full diplomatic relations with Israel, and after the 2001 attacks on the United States, he expressed support for the U.S. war on terror. Taya often accused his opponents of being allied to insurgent groups in Algeria rumored to have connections with the international terrorist organization al-Qaeda.

In predominantly Muslim Mauritania, Taya's moves had been strongly condemned by Islamist leaders and contributed to his downfall. After the coup, the new military government reversed Taya's diplomatic direction. Within days of its takeover, the Military Council released twenty-one Islamic activists who had been imprisoned by Taya for their supposed connection to terrorist organizations. On the other hand, the international community condemned the coup. Disapproving statements were issued by Nigeria, the African Union, the European Union, and the United Nations. The United States explicitly called for a return to the established government of President Taya.

It was clear even to outsiders, however, that Taya's regime in Mauritania had created many difficulties. Economic and political mismanagement had left the country with major problems, including famine. Its vital agricultural and mining sectors were near ruin. Taya had also drawn widespread criticism for persecuting the Black Sonninkes, a small minority, most of whom were forced to flee the country. Taya's actions against this group had led the United States to suspend aid to Mauritania in 1993.

The Military Council named Colonel Ely Ould Mohamed Vall as president of the council. Vall, 55, had participated in the 1984 coup that brought Taya to power and had served as national security chief and a member of Taya's inner circle for more than two decades.

In the weeks following the coup, the council sought to build on the support it had received at home and to answer international critics. It promised to hold a referendum on amendments to the constitution within a year and to call legislative elections within two years. A civilian prime minister, Sidi Mohamed Ould Boubacar, was selected by the council to head a caretaker government. The council also promised opposition leaders that no council member or anyone serving in the caretaker government would stand as a candidate in the new elections.

Jeffrey A. Shantz

See also: Coups; Western Sahara: Polisario-Moroccan War, 1975–1991.

Bibliography

Amnesty International. *Mauritania, 1986–1989: Background to a Crisis, Three Years of Political Imprisonment, Torture, and Unfair Trials.* New York: Amnesty International, 1989.

Fleischman, Janet. *Mauritania's Campaign of Terror: State-Sponsored Repression of Black Africans.* New York: Human Rights Watch/Africa, 1994.

Park, Thomas K., Mamadou Baro, and Tidane Ngaido. *Conflicts over Land: The Crisis of Nationalism of Mauritania.* Madison: Land Tenure Center, University of Wisconsin, 1991.

Pazzanita, Anthony G. *Historical Dictionary of Mauritania.* Lanham, MD: Scarecrow Press, 1996.

MOZAMBIQUE: War of National Liberation, 1961–1974

TYPE OF CONFLICT: Anticolonialism
PARTICIPANT: Portugal

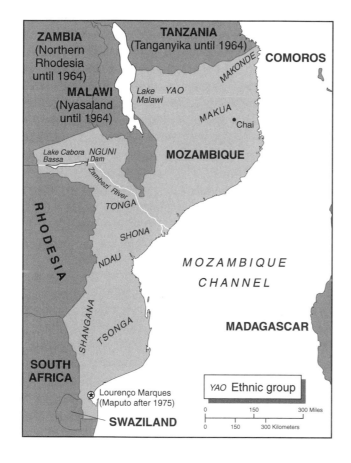

Precolonial Mozambique was roughly divided into three regions, each with its own dominant ethnic group. The sparsely populated north was inhabited by the Lomwe- and Makua-speaking peoples, who largely lived off subsistence agriculture. The agriculturally rich Zambezi valley was populated by the Shona, who often traded their agricultural surplus with trading cities along the coast. The southern highlands were inhabited by the cattle-herding Tsonga. When the Portuguese arrived in the late fifteenth century, some of the Tsonga, descendants of the great Zimbabwe

Empire of the eleventh to fourteenth centuries, formed the Mutapa kingdom, though most of the Mutapa's domains were located in what is now Zimbabwe. A number of Arab trading settlements existed along the coast, part of a vast archipelago that girded the Indian Ocean.

Beginning in the early fifteenth century, Portuguese mariners painstakingly made their way down the Atlantic coast of Africa, seeking an all-sea route to India and East Asia. By the last decade of the century, they had rounded Cape Horn, and in 1498 they first set foot in what is now Mozambique. Utilizing their superior navigational skills and weaponry, the Portuguese quickly ousted the Arab traders from the coastal and island settlements of eastern Africa—occupying the towns at Sofala, Pemba, and Moçambique, the latter lending its name to the future colony. From these posts, the Portuguese took control of one end of an interior African trading system that saw European-manufactured goods heading inland, and gold and ivory moving toward the sea.

Still, until the twentieth century, Portuguese colonization remained minimal, confined to the coastal settlements and a thin presence along the banks of the Zambezi. As late as the opening of World War II, there were just 27,000 Portuguese living in Mozambique. While their physical presence was minimal, the Portuguese cultural impact was profound. Like the Spanish of the New World, the Portuguese colonists intermingled and intermarried with indigenous peoples, producing a small but very influential Creole population of Afro-Portuguese, known as *muzungu*, a word also used to define whites.

Indeed, it was the Afro-Portuguese who conducted most of the interior trade and policing. They led the caravans into the interior and served as officers in the military created to protect that trade. They

KEY DATES

1500s	Portuguese traders begin to occupy Mozambique.
1932	António de Oliveira Salazar takes power in Portugal; he will rule over the country as dictator until his death in 1968.
1960–1964	Many British and French colonies in sub-Saharan Africa win their independence.
1962	Exiled Mozambican nationalists and leftists organize the Liberation Front of Mozambique (known popularly as Frelimo) in Tanzania.
1964	Frelimo launches its first attack on Portuguese troops.
1974	Left-wing anti-imperialist officers overthrow the Portuguese dictatorship in Lisbon and call for liberation of the country's colonies in Asia and Africa.
1975	As Mozambican independence approaches, tens of thousands of Portuguese colonists flee the territory, leaving Mozambique with few trained administrators or technicians.

also served as teachers and religious officials in Mozambique and became planters on the large estates, or *prazos*, of the Zambezi valley. It was largely through these Creoles that the Portuguese maintained what little control they had over Mozambique during the first three centuries of colonization.

Culturally, however, the Afro-Portuguese were more African than Portuguese. Though many spoke Portuguese and some converted to Catholicism, most retained their traditional African customs and ways of life. They were largely African in appearance, and most assumed the roles of traditional African leaders, especially those who ran the *prazos*. Economically, too, they followed African ways, practicing African forms of land use, inheritance, and reciprocal obligation that satisfied their fellow Africans and their ancestors.

The presence of the Afro-Portuguese was laced with paradoxes as well. While they were partly agents of Portuguese cultural transmission, their existence prevented a deeper colonial penetration. Not only did they perform tasks for the Portuguese traders of the coast, they fiercely resisted any efforts by those traders to establish direct links with the interior. In the mid-twentieth century, the Creoles would lead the nationalist cause as well.

Among the trades they engaged in was slavery, though this business came rather late to Mozambique. Located on the Indian Ocean, the colony was poorly situated to provide human cargo for the great transatlantic slave trade of the sixteenth through early nineteenth centuries. Only in the late 1700s and early 1800s was a market for slaves opened up on the French sugar islands of the southern Indian Ocean. About 10,000 slaves had been exported from Mozambique by the time the trade was shut down in the mid-nineteenth century.

Portuguese Control

The pattern of limited colonial presence in Mozambique became a problem for Lisbon in the late nineteenth century, as other more powerful European countries began to cast a covetous eye on southern Africa. The discovery of diamonds and then gold in what is now the Transvaal district of South Africa—immediately adjacent to southern Mozambique—saw a massive inrush of European miners and the establishment of Boer and then British dominance on Mozambique's southwestern frontier. Meanwhile, the Belgians and Germans were establishing a presence in central and eastern Africa.

This imperial scramble for Africa portended trouble for the various European countries. Thus, in the 1880s, the various governments sat down at a conference in Berlin to divide up the continent among themselves. Of concern were African resources, existing European settlements, and, perhaps most importantly, the avoidance of imperial wars. While the great powers of Europe had little respect for Portuguese power, they recognized that Lisbon's presence in Africa served as a buffer between the colonies of more powerful players. Thus, Portugal was allowed to maintain its hold over Mozambique, which separated German-controlled Tanganyika (now Tanzania) from British-controlled South Africa.

At the same time, since no Africans were consulted at the conference, the resulting colonial borders bore no resemblance to the natural or human geography of precolonial Africa. Various ethnic groups were lumped into a single colony, or a single people were divided into several colonies. The final boundaries of Mozambique proved as ill-considered as boundaries elsewhere on the continent.

The Portuguese had made some desultory efforts to populate the interior of Mozambique. During the nineteenth century they had settled prisoners there, but these colonies failed, as most of the settlers disliked the harsh conditions and migrated to the coastal settlements. Still fearful that other Europeans might take advantage of the fact that much of Mozambique was still ruled by Africans or African-appearing Creoles, Lisbon instituted a series of laws designed to establish more administrative control over the region. The feudalist political power of the *prazos* was curtailed, even as they were given more economic leeway. To spur colonial settlement and investment, the *prazos* were turned into freehold properties. But the impoverished people of Portugal were in no position to take up the opportunities. Instead, many of the *prazos* came to be incorporated into French and British plantation systems. This intrusion was resented by both Afro-Portuguese and African leaders, and it led to several decades of violence around the turn of the century.

To solve the problem, the Portuguese passed a law in 1907 setting aside areas for African communities only. By implication, however, this left large swaths of land open to colonial settlement. Once again, the Portuguese attempted a colonization project, this time for the impoverished farmers of the overcrowded metropolis. Again, the experiment failed abysmally. The more entrepreneurial members of this class were emigrating to the more pleasant and productive climes of Brazil, leaving the most impoverished and uneducated for Mozambique. Moreover, without a proper transportation infrastructure, commercial farming remained impracticable. Again, the settlement policy proved a drain on the Portuguese treasury, as many of the farmers had to be heavily subsidized to remain on the land. Most fled to the coastal settlements.

As the colonists drifted to the cities, they came into direct competition for jobs and housing with the existing Afro-Portuguese population, which had previously occupied most of the middling commercial and administrative posts. The competition between the Europeans and the Afro-Portuguese soon turned on the color question. By the early twentieth century, Lisbon and its administration in Mozambique were passing laws that made it increasingly difficult for Creoles to find government employment. These laws set higher and higher educational standards for available positions, even as funding for African schooling remained almost nonexistent. Only the largely Protestant missions in the colony offered schooling for a significant number of Africans. Yet, at the same time, practically illiterate Portuguese colonists were given jobs that better-educated Creoles could not obtain. Meanwhile, citizenship was restricted to only the wealthiest and most assimilated Afro-Portuguese.

Not surprisingly, it was among the *asimilados* that the earliest signs of Mozambican nationalism were seen, though the movements of the early twentieth century were oriented toward racial equality within a colonial framework rather than toward independence. Part of the reason for this was the Portuguese conception of "luso-tropicalism," an idea that implied a special role for the Portuguese in Africa. Unlike other Europeans, the thinking went, the Portuguese were not racist, a fact witnessed by the extensive intermixing of Portuguese and Africans. Thus, the Portuguese mission in Africa was to extend Portuguese culture in exchange for African loyalty and labor—and to accomplish this without the harsh racial edicts of other European colonies.

The hypocrisy behind this policy was obvious, as the Portuguese began to exploit Mozambique more effectively in the early twentieth century. Unlike other European colonizers, the Portuguese had neither the capital to invest nor the manufacturing capacity to market. Thus, Mozambique was not an outlet for surplus capital but a source of it. If colonists could not be recruited to that end, then the Portuguese would more effectively exploit African labor. This took several forms. First, taxes were raised on peasant farmers in the colony, and these taxes now had to be paid in cash, not kind. Thus, farmers were forced to labor part of the year on the plantations.

Second, taxes were imposed on migrant workers laboring in South African mines. This source of income was particularly lucrative, since taxes could amount to nearly half of all wages, and these were collected by the more efficient British administration and passed along to the Portuguese. This labor experience in South Africa would have important repercussions for the independence struggle in Mozambique, serving as a unifying nationalist experience for the thousands of Mozambicans who discovered a common identity as exploited mine workers. Finally, vaguely worded vagrancy laws were passed that basically allowed for imprisonment and forced labor of people who were not actually working at the moment they were encountered by security forces.

Two events in mid-twentieth-century Europe sped up this process of more effective exploitation of Mozambique. First was the rise to power of the dictator Antonio de Oliveira Salazar in Lisbon. A former economist, Salazar set up an elaborate bureaucracy to micromanage the economy both at home and in Mozambique. He hoped to create a closed Portuguese colonial system that would allow Mozambican raw materials and capital to fuel industrialization in Portugal. His efforts were aided by World War II. Neutral in the conflict, Portugal and its colonies were well situated to sell critical tropical products to both sides in the war. As labor laws were more strictly enforced—to ensure output—government revenues tripled and the production of key products soared.

The anomalies of Portuguese colonialism became even more apparent in the post–World War II period. While other European powers were preparing to leave their colonies in sub-Saharan Africa in the 1950s, the Portuguese were not only resisting the trend but also encouraging further settlement. As the postwar capitalist boom created seemingly endless demand for tropical products, thousands of Portuguese colonists poured in to take advantage of well-paying jobs, since most of the basic unskilled labor was performed by Africans. Still, for many of the middling occupations and semi-skilled tasks, the new colonists were able—with the help of racist employer attitudes and discriminatory laws—to muscle aside both *asimilados* and Africans. Between 1945 and 1974, the Portuguese

and European population in Mozambique grew from 50,000 to 200,000 persons.

At the same time, the colony also began to develop a modest industrial infrastructure to process some of its raw materials and agricultural products. By 1974, the colony boasted the eighth-largest industrial capacity in Africa. Increasingly, the Portuguese treasury was becoming dependent on remittances from its colonies. However, because the Portuguese economy was so weak, neocolonialism was not an option. Whereas the French and, to a lesser extent, the British believed they could continue to control the economies of their former colonies, the Portuguese government and financial community felt that they would be thrust aside by greater economic powers if their colonies became independent.

This newfound income was only part of the reason the Portuguese refused to give up their colonies in Africa, including Mozambique. The ideology of Salazarism also played a role, as did the political power of the growing colonial population. Salazar's colonial policy was based on the idea that Portugal had a special role to play in the world, as a link between the cultures of Europe and the southern hemisphere. Moreover, the government hoped to reconcile the contradictions of Western Europe's poorest society by providing a safety valve in colonial emigration.

The political element in the equation came to the fore in 1961, when Portugal—hoping to take international pressure off itself for keeping its colonies—declared the colonies part of Portugal itself, extending the vote to white colonists and assimilated Africans. By this measure, they turned colonial issues into internal ones, thus outside the purview of the United Nations. But as the colonists came to vote for parliament, they became a coherent and determined voice for continued colonization.

Resistance and Rebellion

By the late 1950s, resistance to colonial exploitation was growing in both rural and urban areas. There were several wildcat strikes by African workers in Mozambican ports, followed in 1960 by a massive protest of peasant farmers—angry about the low prices paid for their crops at government-controlled marketing boards—in the northern town of Mueda. When the army moved in and shot down some 500 demonstrators, the news sparked a new determination by the *asimilado* elite to push for independence, rather than equality within a Portuguese system. Moreover, it demonstrated to these potential nationalists that unarmed resistance was pointless. The fact that the revolt and suppression took place in the north meant that that region would become the most solid base of support for the anticolonial resistance.

In 1962, a group of educated *asimilados*, in exile in Tanzania after being forced out of the colony by Portugal's International and State Defense Police (PIDE), met to organize the Liberation Front of Mozambique (known popularly as Frelimo). While most of the founders—including leader Eduardo Mondlane—were from the elite and had been educated abroad, others, such as Mozambique's first president, Samora Machel, were more humble in origin and products of local missionary schooling. At first, the Frelimo leadership was hesitant to launch an armed resistance, but they were persuaded that they must use violence by the rise of quasi-organized anticolonial banditry inside Mozambique and by the urging of Tanzanian president Julius Nyerere.

On September 25, 1964, Frelimo launched its first attack against the Portuguese military, at Chai in the northern part of the country. The effort to set off a massive urban uprising later in the year, however, was thwarted by a mass PIDE raid in which 1,500 Frelimo members and sympathizers were arrested in the capital. From that point on, Frelimo's guerrilla activities were confined to the more remote northern and central sectors of the colony.

The Portuguese military launched a ruthless campaign against both the guerrillas and the civilian population, which was often forced into resettlement camps where it could not help the guerrillas. Even so, the Portuguese commanders were hard-pressed to defeat Frelimo. They were fighting simultaneous conflicts in Mozambique, Angola, and Guinea-Bissau, and did not have the resources, despite support from their North Atlantic Treaty Organization (NATO) allies, including the United States. While Americans condemned colonialism in public, they did not want to offend a strongly anticommunist government in

Portuguese troops pass through a Mozambican village during the campaign against colonial rule in 1973. Mozambique's war of independence began in the early 1960s and culminated in the formal transfer of power on June 25, 1975. *(David Hume Kennerly/Getty Images)*

Lisbon, which was also allowing U.S. forces to use the Azore Islands in the Atlantic.

As the Portuguese army began to adopt counterinsurgency tactics in the late 1960s, Frelimo changed its strategy as well, shifting to a "soft" policy of political education and the provision of social services in liberated areas. They also moved more heavily into the economically strategic Zambezi River valley, hoping to disrupt commerce and farming. Still, the government held the upper hand through much of the late 1960s and early 1970s. It was defeated, however, in a major offensive in 1972, aided by Rhodesian and South African forces, when Frelimo guerrillas outflanked the colonial forces and headed into the southern part of the country, threatening critical rail lines and the massive Cabora Bassa dam, which was nearing completion at that time. For the next two years, the war remained stalemated.

Independence

Portugal's many ongoing colonial wars were beginning to bankrupt its economy and were sparking unrest among the population at home. On the night of April 24, 1974, a group of leftist army officers—calling themselves the Armed Forces Movement (MFA)—initiated a bloodless coup that overthrew the dictatorship of Marcello Caetano, who had ruled since Salazar's death in 1968. Under the leadership of Commander-in-Chief General Antonio de Spinola—recruited by the MFA for his impeccable conservative credentials and high reputation—the new Portuguese government hoped to work out some kind of associative relationship between the country and its colonies.

In the summer of 1974, however, the more radical elements in the MFA came to the fore, forcing Spinola to retire in September and assuming direct control of the government. Among their first decisions was the immediate and total abandonment of the Portuguese empire. While this precipitous retreat would cause enormous difficulties in Angola—where three different rebel groups competed for power—the transition to Frelimo rule went relatively smoothly in Mozambique, except for one thing.

As the date for formal independence—July 1975—approached, the frustrations and fears of the white colonists neared fever pitch. They planned their own declaration of independence and appealed to South Africa and Rhodesia for support. When South Africa's Pretoria turned them down, they were forced to abandon their plans. Though Frelimo promised equality for all citizens regardless of color in an independent Mozambique, the fear and anger of the now abandoned colonists ran too deep.

By independence some 180,000 of the 200,000 Portuguese in the former colony had fled the country, spitefully destroying much of the country's infrastructure before they left. The departure of these white settlers eliminated a potential fifth column within the new country, but it also cost the new country nearly all of its technicians and administrators. The crucial port and railway sector alone lost 7,000 skilled workers. Equally important, some of the embittered exiles would come to support reactionary rebel forces intent on overthrowing the Frelimo government and destroying Mozambique in the process.

James Ciment

See also: Anticolonialism; Angola: War of National Liberation, 1961–1974; Guinea-Bissau: War of National Liberation, 1962–1974.

Bibliography

Birmingham, David. *Frontline Nationalism in Angola and Mozambique.* Trenton, NJ: Africa World Press, 1992.

Ciment, James. *Angola and Mozambique: Postcolonial Wars in Southern Africa.* New York: Facts on File, 1997.

Khadiagala, Gilbert. *Allies in Adversity: The Frontline States in Southern African Security.* Athens: Ohio University Press, 1994.

Newitt, Malyn. *A History of Mozambique.* Bloomington: Indiana University Press, 1995.

Seidman, Ann. *The Roots of Crisis in Southern Africa.* Trenton, NJ: Africa World Press, 1985.

MOZAMBIQUE: Renamo War, 1976–1992

TYPE OF CONFLICT: Terrorism and International Incidents; Ethnic and Religious
PARTICIPANTS: Rhodesia (Zimbabwe); South Africa

The Liberation Front of Mozambique (known as Frelimo, its Portuguese acronym) fought a decade-long war against Portuguese colonists and the Portuguese military from 1964 to 1974. Though the guerrilla force had made some headway, particularly in the more remote central and northern regions of the country, it had been unable to defeat the Portuguese militarily. The war's drain on the Portuguese treasury and the unrest it was causing among the Portuguese people led to a coup against the right-wing dictatorship in Lisbon. Among the first decisions made by the leftist coup leaders was to rid Portugal of its overseas possessions as quickly as possible.

In Angola, this divestment led to war, as three competing rebel groups fought to win control of the new government. Mozambique was more fortunate, at least at first. With no real opposition, Frelimo was able to assume power immediately, without a fight. The only major setback was the flight of 90 percent of the white colonial population, which included most of the new country's technicians and administrators. Adding to Mozambique's good fortune was the quality of Frelimo leadership. The country's first president—Samora Machel, who had taken charge of Frelimo after the assassination of the organization's founder, Eduardo Mondlane, in 1969—came from an impoverished peasant family and understood many of the concerns of this sector of the population, to which the vast majority of Mozambicans belonged.

Under both Mondlane and Machel's leadership, Frelimo had emphasized a solid working relationship between guerrilla fighter—now government representative—and peasant. In liberated zones during the war, Frelimo established health, education, and other programs, winning the confidence of much of the population. Once in power, the government committed much of its revenues to health and education. Indeed, its emphasis on low-tech, primary-care clinics earned the commendation of the World Health Organization, which used it as an example in other countries. The social indexes in the first years of Frelimo rule were excellent: 95 percent of children vaccinated within three years of independence and a fourfold increase in the number of students graduating from primary and secondary schools.

At the same time, Frelimo attempted the much more daunting task of redirecting an economy built for the needs of a distant imperial government. Mozambique as a colony had been a great generator of revenue for Portugal. Tens of thousands of migrant Mozambican laborers in the South African mines were heavily taxed, while peasant farmers were forced to sell their surpluses at government-controlled

KEY DATES

1965 White settlers in neighboring Rhodesia unilaterally declare independence from Britain, establishing white minority rule in the country.

1975 Thousands of Portuguese settlers flee Mozambique as the country wins independence under the rule of Liberation Front of Mozambique (Frelimo, its popular name) rebels; the Frelimo government vows to aid various black guerrillas armies fighting white minority rule in Rhodesia.

1976 Rhodesian Central Intelligence Organizations set up training camps for the Mozambique National Resistance, an anti-Frelimo guerrilla group.

1980 As black majority rule comes to Rhodesia (now Zimbabwe), support for Renamo shifts to apartheid South Africa.

1984 Frelimo and South Africa negotiate an agreement whereby South Africa promises to stop supporting Renamo and Frelimo agrees to end its help to the anti-apartheid African National Congress (ANC).

1986 Mozambican president Samora Machel dies in a mysterious plane crash in South Africa.

1990 The South African government legalizes the ANC and frees ANC leader Nelson Mandela from prison.

1992 Mediated by a Catholic peace group, Frelimo and Renamo negotiate a peace agreement demobilizing Renamo and allowing it to participate as a political party in Mozambican elections.

1994 Frelimo easily defeats Renamo in national elections.

marketing boards that paid well below competitive prices. Frelimo was determined to change all that.

Borrowing from the socialist bloc countries and Algeria—the models of progressive third-world development at the time—Frelimo instituted a program of rapid industrialization that would produce both the basic goods necessary for the agricultural economy and consumer goods to offset imports. To increase productivity in the countryside, the vast acreage abandoned by the Portuguese settlers was turned into state farms and cooperatives. Peasants were either moved onto these new farms or herded into new consolidated villages. The intention was a benign one. The government believed that large estates were more efficient producers and that bigger villages allowed for better provision of social services.

Frelimo also attempted to break the power of the local leadership hierarchies, which Frelimo officials believed was a product of Portuguese rule. There was

some truth in this. The Portuguese had used and manipulated the more amenable local chiefs to guarantee order and production among the peasants. These chiefs were given the title *regulos* and virtually total sway over local peoples. Some of the regulos earned a comfortable living from lands that they forced the local peasants to work. Frelimo saw the regulos as the main obstacle to its economic, political, and social reforms, and it was determined to eliminate them. Thus, the government sent its own administrators into rural areas to displace the regulos. Within a few years, most of the local leadership network had been destroyed and replaced by a bureaucratic administration answerable to the Frelimo government in the capital, Maputo.

Each of these policies—from the economic to the political—had inherent flaws. First, the model of rapid industrialization proved too ambitious, draining precious financial resources on impractical economic projects. More significantly, much of the peasantry was deeply opposed to the consolidation of villages and the establishment of government-controlled estates. They resented being forced to move from their ancestral villages and to work in teams on large estates. Though the policy made rational sense, it failed to take into consideration ancient custom, not a surprising oversight given the urban-based origins of most Frelimo officials.

Finally, the efforts to destroy the regulos and the Catholic Church were also resented to a degree. While many regulos and priests were corrupt, still others did their best to shield their villagers from the harshest effects of colonial exploitation. That they worked with the Portuguese made them suspect in Frelimo eyes but did not necessarily condemn them in the peasants' opinion. In fact, many of the regulos would have won local elections against Frelimo officials if these had been allowed to take place. But Frelimo officials believed in the Leninist notion of a vanguard party and saw elections as a Western import with little usefulness for an African revolutionary society.

Finally, Frelimo's foreign policy—while well intentioned—also undermined its efforts to transform and improve the lives of Mozambicans. While Mozambique as a Portuguese colony had served as the major sea outlet for landlocked Rhodesia and the nearby Transvaal district of South Africa—generating large revenues in the process—that role dried up after independence. First, South Africa began to shift its rail traffic to its own ports. As for Rhodesia, the Frelimo government assiduously honored the international sanctions against that illegal, white minority regime, allowing no Rhodesian goods to travel through Mozambican ports. In fact, Frelimo's solidarity with the guerrillas fighting the government in Rhodesia would set off the devastating civil war Frelimo fought against the Mozambique National Resistance (Renamo) through the early 1990s.

Rhodesia and the Birth of Renamo

Renamo's origins date back to the first years of Mozambican independence. In 1976, the Rhodesian Central Intelligence Organization (CIO) came up with a plan designed to undermine Mozambican support for the black guerrilla movements fighting against the white-minority regime. They would establish their own Mozambican guerrilla force that would not only hunt down anti-Rhodesian guerrillas in Mozambique but also disrupt the country economically. Many former Portuguese colonists from Mozambique who now lived in Rhodesia were strong supporters of the plan. These exiles offered money and expertise. Speaking the local languages, they helped to locate and recruit likely candidates for the organization.

Soon the organization had hundreds of supporters in Mozambique, including many displaced regulos and some dissatisfied Frelimo renegades, upset that their newly won power did not translate into wealth. (Frelimo officials all the way up to Machel himself were renowned for their frugality.) Among the renegades were André Matsangaissa and Afonso Dhlakama, both future heads of Renamo. They had been arrested by their former Frelimo compatriots for petty crimes and sent to reeducation camps, which is where Rhodesian recruiters found many of their converts. By late 1976, the Rhodesian CIO had set up training camps in Rhodesia, with an emphasis on economic sabotage. As far as the CIO was concerned, there need be no ideological basis for the organization, other than that it be anti-Frelimo. Later, Dhlakama would offer a free enterprise, multiparty democracy ideology for his organization.

Under Rhodesia's tutelage, Renamo's impact was largely felt in central Mozambique, in the agriculturally rich Zambezi River valley. Because the region had little experience with the liberated zones of Frelimo activism during the anticolonial war, there was less allegiance to the Frelimo government. Moreover, this was the area where the first heavy mobilization for estate labor was conducted, and resentment of the government ran higher. But Renamo's strategy, learned from the Rhodesians, of burning villages, plundering agricultural cooperatives, and destroying shops, clinics, and schools was not intended to win support or recruits, other than those eager for a life of banditry. Instead, it was designed to instill terror by demonstrating to the peasantry that the Frelimo government could not and would not protect them.

At first, the Mozambican army was largely ineffective against the Renamo attacks. Frelimo had demobilized, since it believed that the only threat to the country's freedom would come from South Africa and that no army Mozambique could field would stand a chance against the mighty South African Defense Force (SADF). Instead, Frelimo hoped to defend itself by winning friends in powerful places outside the region, in both the West and East.

By the late 1970s, the Frelimo government had come to recognize the extent of the Renamo threat. It began to draft many of the leaders and soldiers of its war against the Portuguese in the 1960s and early 1970s. Renamo's efforts to push its destructive campaign to the coast, thereby cutting Mozambique in half, failed. André Matsangaissa, the organization's first leader (though largely a figurehead), was killed in this offensive. Fighting then broke out at Renamo headquarters in the remote Gorongosa Mountains of central Mozambique between several aspirants for power. The winner was Dhlakama.

At the same time, the war between the white minority government in Rhodesia and the guerrilla forces there was heading toward a negotiated settlement. In 1980, the white minority government gave way. In universal elections Robert Mugabe, leader of the largest Zimbabwean guerrilla army and a close ally of Frelimo, was elected and formed the first majority black government. Mugabe and his party changed the name of Rhodesia (for the early British capitalist Cecil Rhodes) to Zimbabwe. The government immediately ended its support for Renamo.

It appeared that the loss of support from Rhodesia/Zimbabwe would condemn Renamo to defeat, but that was not to be. The South African government, seeing an opportunity to destabilize a major supporter of the anti-apartheid African National Congress (ANC) in South Africa, took up the role of Renamo's mentor and benefactor. With its immense resources, the South African government was able to turn the resistance movement into a major force for the disruption and destruction of Mozambique's economy and society during the 1980s.

South Africa and the Growth of Renamo

By the late 1970s, South Africa's leaders had realized that continued guerrilla warfare in Rhodesia was a greater threat to their own apartheid system than the possibility of a conservative black majority regime. By supporting the British-mediated peace efforts, South Africa hoped to install a compliant regime to its north, much like that in pro–South African Malawi. This shift toward support of negotiations helped persuade the recalcitrant Ian Smith regime in Rhodesia to accept black majority rule.

Both Rhodesia and South Africa were shocked when Mugabe, the most radical of the guerrilla leaders, won the presidency in 1980. They were not without resources, however. Even before Mugabe took office, Renamo and Rhodesian officials had been in touch with the powerful South African Defense Forces (SADF). Under arch-conservative prime minister P.W. Botha, South Africa had been supplying small shipments of arms to Renamo. Now plans were put in place for South Africa to pick up the slack if Rhodesia's support collapsed.

Support for Renamo was not universal among South African military officials; some advocated direct intervention by the SADF in Mozambique. Emboldened by the election of conservative Ronald Reagan—whom they saw as an ally—as U.S. president, the Botha government launched a raid on the suburbs of Maputo, Mozambique's capital, in January 1981. The immediate target was the offices of the anti-apartheid ANC, but the larger aim was to show Maputo the costs of aiding the black South African resistance organization. In that, the raid was a failure. President Machel lashed out at South Africa and insisted his government would continue its wholehearted backing of the ANC. Seeing the international outcry about the raid, South Africa's SADF decided on a new tactic—supporting Renamo heavily.

Renamo's Rhodesian instructors were integrated into the SADF's Special Forces units, arms shipments were increased, military training facilities were set up at South African bases, and a Renamo radio station was set up on South African soil. The SADF believed that Renamo attacks could achieve many purposes beyond neutralizing the ANC's infrastructure in Mozambique. Destabilizing Mozambique's economy would be a useful warning to any other African country considering support for the anti-apartheid struggle. Destabilization would demonstrate to the world that the blacks of southern Africa were incapable of carrying on in the absence of white leadership.

Within a year of the change in strategy, the impact could be felt in the Mozambican countryside. In 1982, Renamo forces moved southward from their stronghold in central Mozambique. The purpose of this offensive was to wreak economic havoc and sow terror among the populace. Renamo targeted both major economic projects and social service facilities. Mozambique's rail system—a critical part of its economy and potentially a major source of foreign earnings when it began transporting the goods of landlocked Zimbabwe—was knocked out of commission. The Portuguese hydroelectric dam at Cabora Bassa, though never directly attacked, was rendered useless by the destruction of power lines.

Meanwhile, softer targets were attacked as well. According to a 1985 United Nations International Children's Emergency Fund (UNICEF) report, Renamo had destroyed some 1,800 schools, affecting more than 300,000 students, and had ruined 25 percent of the country's newly created health clinics. Moreover, Renamo became well versed in the art of terror. It made a practice of mutilating civilians, as a warning to others not to support the government. It also forcibly recruited both soldiers and porters, some as young as ten years old. To win their allegiance, Renamo leaders in the field were known to force their potential recruits to kill family members and friends, thereby bonding them to the organization through trauma. Meanwhile, some farmers were forced to grow crops for Renamo forces while others saw their crops seized just before harvest. Looting was a major occupation of Renamo fighters as well. When they attacked villages or government facilities, they stripped away anything of value and destroyed what was left. The valuables were smuggled across the border to Malawi, where they could be sold on the black market.

By the mid-1980s, Renamo had divided Mozambique into three zones. In the areas of direct control, Renamo resettled peasants around its bases, reestablishing a rudimentary barter economy and setting up a few clinics and schools. Life was relatively stable here. Much of this territory was Ndau-speaking, as were most of Renamo's guerrillas and Dhlakama, their leader. Still, Renamo never really took on the role of an ethnic-based fighting force. Ethnicity was never part of its rhetoric, and there were many non-Ndau persons in the upper echelons of the organization.

The second zone was known as the "area of taxation." These were no-man's lands, where neither Frelimo nor Renamo held sway. Subject to constant raiding by Renamo, the civilians were forced to surrender their property and crops as a form of "taxes." Finally, there were the so-called areas of destruction. These were territories generally under Frelimo control. Here the object was to instill terror and undermine the authority of the government. Here, too, was where most of the worst Renamo atrocities took place.

Frelimo, too, was responsible for civilian deaths, but this was largely through omission rather than commission. Having once again failed to recognize the new and enlarged threat of a South African–backed Renamo, the Mozambican army was slow to extend its protection to the countryside, allowing the insurgents to conduct several years of destruction and terror without a response. It also failed to mobilize the peasantry to defend themselves, fearing that untrained militia would be no match for Renamo and might surrender themselves and their weapons. In addition, some of Frelimo's more precipitous political and economic policies to drag the countryside into the modern era were highly unpopular with peasants and may have served to push some of them into the arms of Renamo.

By the mid-1980s, then, Mozambique was caught up in a multifaceted catastrophe of war, compounded by prolonged drought and financial collapse. In 1984, the government was forced to go to the International Monetary Fund (IMF) for help. The IMF imposed strict conditions, forcing Frelimo to abandon some of its more successful programs in the countryside, including subsidizing the prices paid to peasant farmers for their surplus crops.

Still, Machel and the Frelimo leadership recognized that improving the economy hinged on ending the war. Thus, in 1983, the president of Mozambique went on the diplomatic offensive, winning the support of even arch-conservatives Margaret Thatcher of Britain and Ronald Reagan of the United States to put pressure on Pretoria to stop its war against Mozambique. Thus, the war in the country never escalated into a Cold War confrontation, as the contemporaneous conflict in Angola had. Indeed, both Reagan and Thatcher even tried to offer aid to the government, though both were unable to win the approval of their respective legislatures.

With this international effort, Machel was able to get South Africa to the negotiating table in 1984. At the border town of Nkomati, the two sides worked out a simple agreement whereby Frelimo would cut its support for the ANC while Pretoria would stop helping Renamo. Since the ANC had already been ordered out of Mozambique, it appeared that Frelimo had won the better bargain. But events turned out otherwise. Within a year, a raid on Renamo's headquarters unearthed secret files detailing that the South African military had no intention of honoring the Nkomati Accords. South Africa vehemently denied the charges, saying that it had merely expanded its supply operations in the six months leading up to signing the accords.

Natives in Mozambique celebrate the signing of a 1992 cease-fire by President Joaquim Chissano and Renamo guerrilla leader Afonso Dhlakama, ending sixteen years of civil war. *(Alexander Joe/AFP/Getty Images)*

This violation of the spirit of the accords—if not the letter—resulted in yet more Renamo raids and destruction in the late 1980s. The continuing warfare, drought, IMF-imposed austerity, and the mysterious death of Machel in 1986—in a plane crash over South African territory—had devastated Mozambique by the end of the decade. In 1990, it won two dubious distinctions: it was the poorest country in the world and the most aid-dependent.

Move Toward Peace

In August 1988, the Mozambican Catholic Church—which officially had stayed out of the contest between Frelimo and Renamo—offered to host preliminary negotiations. But suspicions on both sides ran high. Largely cut off from the outside world (except for South Africa) and with its leadership generally uneducated, Renamo was fearful that it would be taken advantage of by the more sophisticated Frelimo representatives. Moreover, because of its isolation, it believed—quite rightly—that much of the international community was opposed to it. For its part, Frelimo did not want to give Renamo the respectability

that negotiations implied. Even after it had sat down with the insurgents, it continued to publicly refer to them as "bandits" and "terrorists." Only when conservative Kenyan President Daniel arap Moi, a nominal Renamo supporter, came on board as a mediator—along with the pro-Frelimo Mugabe of Zimbabwe—did Renamo agree to talk.

But the Kenyan and Zimbabwean leaders soon proved too controversial to mediate the dispute. Frelimo pointed out that Moi offered training facilities to Renamo guerrillas, while Renamo noted that Zimbabwean troops were helping Frelimo defend the critical railways connecting that landlocked country to Mozambican ports. By the end of 1989, the talks had broken down, though they were soon revived under the good offices of the Sant'Edigio religious community in Rome, a Christian brotherhood that specialized in peace talks and had helped end a war in Lebanon.

In July 1990, the negotiations began again. While there were many sticking points, the main obstacle to a treaty came from Renamo's inability or unwillingness to negotiate in good faith. Internally divided between accepting a peaceful solution and continuing the war, it constantly reopened issues that had already been decided in previous sessions. In fact, Renamo's leaders were concerned about its ability to survive after the war and to turn itself into a legitimate political party. They were also worried that their own personal safety could not be ensured if they moved to the capital to campaign.

Once again the seeds of a solution came from outside Mozambique. In 1989, F.W. de Klerk became president of South Africa. He soon spoke in favor of building a multiracial state, legalized the African National Congress (ANC), and freed its leader, Nelson Mandela, from jail. De Klerk ended support of Renamo's activities in Mozambique, and its leaders had little choice but to negotiate. Finally, after ten long sessions, the two sides reached an agreement in October 1992. Provisions included a UN-directed demobilization of Renamo guerrillas and government troops, as well as their integration into civilian life. A new 30,000-man army would be set up with equal numbers of Renamo and Frelimo troops. Elections for the presidency and parliament would be held under UN auspices within one year.

The agreement came not a moment too soon. The costs of the war had been immense. UNICEF estimated that the war had directly or indirectly cost the lives of some 1 million Mozambicans—roughly 1 citizen in 16—including 500,000 children who had died of hunger and disease caused by Renamo's destabilization tactics. At least one-third of the population were living as refugees in nearby countries or were internally displaced within Mozambique at war's end. Financially, the conflict was estimated to have cost the Mozambican government and people some $15 billion in direct and indirect losses, roughly ten times the country's annual gross national product. Moreover, some 3,000 schools and rural shops, 1,500 heavy vehicles (both truck and railroad), and 1,000 health clinics had been destroyed.

Postwar Era

While the Sant'Edigio accords called for a strict timetable for demobilization and elections, the United Nations allowed the time frame to be stretched out. Events in nearby Angola cast a sobering shadow over the effort in Mozambique, when the rebel leader Jonas Savimbi restarted the war there after losing what he considered to be an unfair election. Because the United Nations had failed to properly demobilize Savimbi's forces, the war in Angola continued for another two years. Determined not to make the same mistake again, the United Nations offered a much bigger contingent of blue helmets and more money for the Mozambican effort. And it allowed both the demobilization and the electioneering schedule to fit facts in the field rather than a bureaucratic timetable.

Fearful for their safety, Renamo's leaders and its soldiers were hesitant to move to the Mozambican capital to demobilize and organize as a political party. The two processes moved at an excruciatingly slow pace. Gradually, however, the United Nations was able to set up nearly fifty demobilization camps throughout the country, hampered in part by the reluctance of member states to send troops for the UN force. The demobilization process was finally near completion by early 1994.

During the rest of that year, both parties—along with several other minor ones—ran for office throughout the country. But the campaign was a desultory affair, with little enthusiasm and largely negative attacks. Ultimately, the October 1994 elections—in which some 90 percent of the electorate voted, despite a last-minute boycott call by Dhlakama and his Renamo party—offered something to both sides. The government party won a plurality of the vote, while its presidential candidate Joaquim Chissano—already in power since the death of Machel in 1986—won by a landslide. Frelimo controlled a slim majority of the 129 seats in the national assembly.

Renamo, meanwhile, won a substantial minority of the votes, proving its contention that it did indeed have support among the Mozambican people. But this assertion was questioned by Frelimo officials and many outside observers, who noted that virtually all the votes for Renamo came in areas that were under its control and hinted that the former guerrilla organization had used coercion and/or fraud.

While the elections decided who would govern Mozambique, they did not settle how it would be ruled. At both the national and the local levels, disputes between the two major parties quickly emerged. When Frelimo parliamentarians pushed a hard-liner of their own for speaker in December, the Renamo delegates walked out, hinting that only a power-sharing arrangement would bring them back. Meanwhile, in those provinces where Renamo had once held sway, there was general intimidation of government officials from Frelimo. At one point, former Renamo soldiers even blockaded highways, both to collect revenue and to protest the government's unwillingness to provide them with the money they had been promised as a condition of demobilization.

Renamo's fears and insecurities were downplayed by Frelimo officials, which still considered the group little more than terrorists who had blackmailed their way into government. There was talk of a conspiracy between Renamo officials and unreconstructed regulos from the colonial era. Renamo even tried to convince its former international backers in white South Africa and Portugal that it would be forced to go back to fighting if it did not get new financial support. Few took the threat very seriously.

Meanwhile, Mozambique continued to reel from the economic effects of the war. Under the IMF sanctions, the government embarked on a privatization campaign that led to corruption, as many Frelimo officials—once known for their revolutionary-inspired frugality—took advantage of the changes to make personal fortunes. At the same time, to raise revenues, the government invited in white South African investors and farmers, which raised protests among many in Mozambique who blamed former apartheid supporters for their suffering. Natural disasters, including massive flooding in 1996, led to epidemics and losses of farmland.

On the positive side, most of the Mozambican refugees returned, and the landmine problem—it was estimated that there were some 2 million unmapped mines at war's end—turned out not to be as extensive as originally feared. The government also invited international firms to begin exploration of potential gas and oil fields along the country's 1,500-mile coast. Most importantly, and in stark contrast to Angola, there was no return to warfare.

James Ciment

See also: Ethnic and Religious Conflicts; Mozambique: War of National Liberation, 1961–1974; South Africa: Anti-Apartheid Struggle, 1948–1994; Zimbabwe: Struggle for Majority Rule, 1965–1980.

Bibliography

Birmingham, David. *Frontline Nationalism in Angola and Mozambique.* Trenton, NJ: Africa World Press, 1992.

Chan, Stephen, ed. *Exporting Apartheid: Foreign Policies in Southern Africa, 1978–1988.* New York: St. Martin's Press, 1990.

Ciment, James. *Angola and Mozambique: Postcolonial Wars in Southern Africa.* New York: Facts on File, 1997.

Finnegan, William. *A Complicated War: The Harrowing of Mozambique.* Berkeley: University of California Press, 1992.

Hanlon, Joseph. *Mozambique: Who Calls the Shots?* Bloomington: Indiana University Press, 1991.

Magaia, Lina. *Dumba Nengue: Run for Your Life: Peasant Tales of Tragedy in Mozambique.* Trenton, NJ: Africa World Press, 1988.

Saul, John. *Recolonization and Resistance in Southern Africa in the 1990s.* Trenton, NJ: Africa World Press, 1993.

NAMIBIA: War of National Liberation, 1966–1990

TYPE OF CONFLICT: Anticolonialism
PARTICIPANT: South Africa

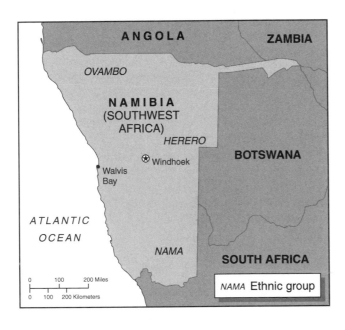

Namibia was first inhabited by the San (who are also, though pejoratively, known as Bushmen), but these original people were gradually pushed farther into the Kalahari Desert as more technologically advanced groups such as the Nama, Herero, and Ovambo moved into the greener parts of the country. There was little European contact or settlement in the region until Germany was granted sovereignty over what was then called Southwest Africa in 1890. As German settlers moved in, they were met by Herero-led resistance. The resulting war led to a mass genocide, when about 90 percent of the Herero were massacred and the Nama were placed in concentration camps. During World War I, Namibia was taken from the Germans by South African forces. The League of Nations made the region a Class C mandate—that is, one with no prospects for independence—and awarded it to Britain, though it would be administered by South African authorities.

Over the next fifty or so years, the country was increasingly woven into the South African economy and political system, as Afrikaner ranchers, diamond companies, and railroads moved in. European enclaves in the administrative capital of Windhoek and the port of Walvis Bay flourished, especially after World War II, while black Namibians lost much of their land and were forced to work for the Europeans for poverty-level wages.

Beginning in 1947, however, black Namibians began to petition the United Nations against South African rule. In a series of International Court of Justice decisions, the international community sided with the Namibians, declaring the League of Nations mandate null and void in 1966 and establishing a de jure UN trusteeship. South Africa ignored all such rulings. At the same time, the United Nations supported the cause of Namibian independence through publicity campaigns, negotiations, and even training of officials in preparation for independence. In Namibia itself, the cause of national independence—though not necessarily armed struggle—was centered in the local churches, while more militant efforts were concentrated in the growing trade union movement, even though trade unions were banned in Namibia under South African law until the mid-1980s.

By the late 1950s, leadership of the movement was shifting away from the traditional chiefs and allied church groups to a younger generation of more politically oriented men and women. In 1958, an organization known as the Ovamboland People's Organization was founded. It quickly expanded beyond a single ethnic group and became the South West Africa People's Organization (SWAPO) in 1960, largely through the organizing done by Ovambo contract laborers who worked throughout the colony and developed a territory-wide national communications and mobilization capacity.

KEY DATES

1890 Germany wins control over Southwest Africa, the future Namibia.

1915 South Africa seizes Southwest Africa from Germany in World War I.

1920 South Africa is granted a League of Nations mandate over Southwest Africa.

1947 Black Namibian nationalists begin petitioning the UN for independence from South Africa.

1958 Ovampoland People's Organization is formed to push for Namibian independence; to avoid ethnic differences, it changes its name to Southwest African People's Organization (SWAPO) in 1962.

1966 The UN negates South Africa's mandate for Southwest Africa; SWAPO launches its first attacks on South African military forces in the territory.

1988 A major defeat of the South African army in the Angolan civil war resuscitates negotiations with SWAPO over Southwest Africa's future status.

1989 The UN Transition Assistance Group (UNTAG) arrives in Southwest Africa to run the SWAPO demobilization and independence referendum; the South African military massacres SWAPO-affiliated guerrillas when they show up at the voter registration and demobilization center.

1990 Namibia becomes officially independent on March 21.

1994 Majority rule comes to South Africa with the election of African National Congress leader Nelson Mandela.

Meanwhile, beginning in the 1960s, the South African government had begun its policy of creating homeland areas for the black ethnic groups within the territory. Namibia, in effect, became the laboratory for South Africa's efforts to relocate and manage such groups. When the South African government forced the removal of black Namibians from the Old Location neighborhood in Windhoek to a homeland at Katatura, it pushed SWAPO toward armed struggle. The group's direction was further confirmed when the government in Pretoria ignored the United Nations' revocation of South Africa's mandate in the region.

The War

In 1966, the year of the United Nations' decision to revoke the South African mandate, armed conflict began in the territory. SWAPO began raids from bases across the border in Zambia. Until the 1970s, however, these forays were largely ineffective and presented virtually no security problems for South Africa. Two events—one internal and the other external—increased the scope and seriousness of the armed struggle.

The first was a general strike of black Namibian workers in 1971–1972, which helped galvanize the territory, producing a nationalist identity and solidarity among various ethnic groups for the first time. After the strikes, the administration of the liberal John Vorster made serious efforts to rectify the situation in Namibia. It began to expand social services to the black population and to incorporate more Africans into the civil service. These conciliatory gestures led in turn to the Turnhalle conference in 1975–1976, which resulted in publication of an independence plan for the territory. However, the constitution proposed by South Africa satisfied neither Namibian nationalists nor the international community, since it effectively denied black majority rule. It was rejected by both SWAPO and the United Nations. In 1978, Prime Minister Vorster was driven from office and replaced by P.W. Botha, a racial hard-liner.

The second event leading to the expansion of the nationalist struggle in Namibia was the success of neighboring Angola, a longtime Portuguese territory, in achieving independence. The new black majority government there permitted SWAPO to use its territory as a base. Even as SWAPO went through a series of crises and divisions of its own in the late 1970s, it was becoming a serious military drain on the South African Defense Forces (SADF). By 1986, some 2,500 South African soldiers had been killed in the fighting in Namibia, along with an estimated 10,000 SWAPO guerrillas and black civilians.

SWAPO's use of bases in Angola enraged the SADF, and it conducted major operations in Angolan border territories in the early and mid-1980s. The attacks were aimed not only at disrupting SWAPO but also at toppling Angola's leftist, anti-apartheid regime. Although the invasions set back SWAPO military efforts and caused enormous death and destruction in Angola, they were repelled by the Angolan army, supported by thousands of Cuban troops and Soviet-supplied weapons. In 1988, a major defeat of another SADF invasion force by an Angolan-Cuban army forced South Africa to retreat permanently from Angola and to begin cutting off aid to rebel movements attempting to overthrow the government there.

Meanwhile, several other factors were contributing to South Africa's problems in the region. First, international economic sanctions were beginning to have their effect on the entire South African economy, reducing the government's revenues and ability to support the kind of military effort necessary to overcome SWAPO resistance. Overfishing in the waters off Namibia and an extended drought undermined two of the colony's major industries, fishing and agriculture, leading to a serious decline in the economy of Namibia that was felt even by the white residents.

SWAPO leader Sam Nujoma (on horseback) attends a political rally before the November 1989 balloting in which a Namibian assembly was chosen and Nujoma was elected president. Namibia officially became independent on March 21, 1990. *(Trevor Samson/AFP/Getty Images)*

Negotiations and Independence

The economic decline and the 1988 defeat in Angola revived negotiations on the future status of Namibia. To avoid seeing its Angolan invasion force of 6,000 captured by Cubans and Angolans, South Africa was forced to make major concessions. It then sat down at U.S.-mediated talks to arrange a multilateral deal with Angola and the Cubans. In exchange for the Cubans' withdrawal from Angola, Pretoria agreed to withdraw its troops from Namibia and to accept a UN-supervised election that would lead to independence shortly thereafter.

Hopeful as this development seemed, there was still one final outrage in the Namibian conflict. Following the arrival of the UN Transition Assistance Group (UNTAG) in April 1989, a South African force massacred a contingent of guerrillas allied to SWAPO when they showed up at a voter registration and demobilization center. The South African government claimed it was the act of out-of-control commanders angry at the settlement. SWAPO agreed to put the incident behind them, and UNTAG soon gained control of the registration process in virtually all parts of the country.

SWAPO swept to victory in the 1989 elections, with 60 percent of the seats in the national assembly and its longtime leader Sam Nujoma chosen as the country's first president. Independence followed officially on March 21, 1990, when the South African flag was lowered over Windhoek. (South Africa did, however, keep control of the strategic port at Walvis Bay.)

The relatively easy reconciliation process between black and white Namibians, the latter being allowed to stay in the country and granted full civil rights, saw the new country through a peaceful decade with a rising level of prosperity, particularly for its black citizens. But there have been costs. The government agreed to keep on 15,000 "unnecessary" white civil servants and to grant full amnesty to all individuals who committed war crimes during the conflict.

In the early 1990s, the South African administration of F.W. de Klerk agreed to hand Walvis Bay over to Namibian sovereignty, a move that was effected in 1994. Disagreements over the border between the two countries were also settled at this time, and relations between Pretoria and Windhoek warmed considerably after the election of Nelson Mandela and his African National Congress party in 1994. The SWAPO-led government also enjoyed warm relations with its longtime ally, Angola.

James Ciment

See also: Anticolonialism; Angola: First War with UNITA, 1975–1992; South Africa: Anti-Apartheid Struggle, 1948–1994.

Bibliography

Chan, Stephen, and Vivienne Jabri, eds. *Mediation in Southern Africa*. New York: Macmillan, 1993.

Kaela, Laurent. *The Question of Namibia*. New York: St. Martin's Press, 1996.

Singham, A.W., and Shirley Hune. *Namibian Independence: A Global Responsibility*. Westport, CT: Lawrence and Hill, 1986.

NIGER: Ethnic and Political Conflict Since 1990

TYPE OF CONFLICT: Ethnic and Religious; Coups

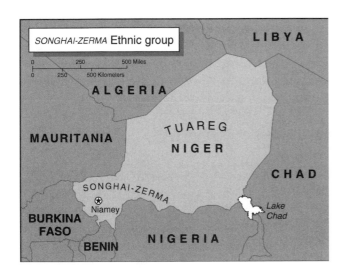

For at least 1,000 years, the territory that now makes up Niger has been divided between the darker-skinned, more sedentary agriculturalists of the south and the lighter-skinned, nomadic Tuareg pastoralists of the Saharan north. The agriculturalists, in turn, are divided into three general ethnic groups: the Songhai-Zerma in the west, the Hausa in the center, and the Kanuri in the east. The Hausa have always been the most numerous and constitute about half of the country's population today, though the vast majority of this large ethnic group lives in neighboring Nigeria.

Largely isolated and composed of the peripheral populations whose cores were elsewhere, the territory that is now Niger did not excite European imperialist ambition until the last year of the nineteenth century, when a French expedition was nearly wiped out by attacks from local groups. Over the next twenty years the French were able to quell several Tuareg revolts and establish civilian administration by the end of World War I. Under the French, cash-crop agriculture spread, particularly among the Hausa. There was also a marked increase in population and a spread of Islam.

The French tended to promote the Songhai-Zerma peoples over others in the territory. As Paris began to prepare Niger for independence, it was largely members of this group that formed the first political parties. In 1958, France held the first referendum in Niger, asking the citizens if they would like to remain a part of the French Community. Despite efforts by the left-wing Djibo Bakary to turn this offer down in favor of full independence, the people of Niger agreed. Two years later, they were granted full independence. The country was then ruled by Bakary's successor, a fellow Songhai-Zerma named Hamai Diori, as a single-party dictatorship until 1974.

Coups and Political Tensions

Diori's government was overthrown by a coup led by Lieutenant Colonel Seyni Kountche. The coup's participants quickly formed the Supreme Military Council (CMS) to run the government. The regime of Kountche and, after his death in 1987, Chief of Staff Colonel Ali Saibou was marked by economic difficulties, rising political tensions, and demands for democratic reforms, and ethnic tensions in the northern and eastern parts of the country.

The political tensions in the capital peaked in the early 1990s, when students and workers in the crucial uranium-mining industry held protests and went on strike. Saibou responded with an announcement that the military would withdraw from politics and would establish a national conference to lay out plans for a return to democracy. When the conference insisted on a halt in payments to international creditors, the International Monetary Fund and the World Bank suspended new loans. This action further heightened the economic crisis and led to a mutiny among unpaid soldiers in February 1992. The government

242

KEY DATES

1960   Niger wins its independence from France after nearly a century of colonial rule.

1974   A military coup overthrows the dictatorship of Hamai Diori.

1991   Backed by Libya, Tuareg rebels form the Liberation Front of Air Azaouad (FLAA, its French acronym) and launch guerrilla war against the Niger government.

1992   Elections lead to a new constitution and the accession of civilian government.

1993   The government and FLAA sign a cease-fire accord, but fighting soon resumes and continues through 1995.

1994   Ethnic tensions lead to fighting in the Lake Chad region.

1996   The military overthrows the civilian government in a coup.

eventually conceded to demands for back payments and the release of several officers arrested for the killing of Tuareg civilians.

Still, the transition to democracy continued. In December 1992, nearly 90 percent of the country's voters approved a new constitution. National elections—held in February 1993—saw the victory of a six-party coalition called the Alliance for the Forces of Change (AFC), headed by Mahamane Ousmane, an orthodox Muslim and the first Hausa to head the country. Unfortunately, continuing protests, strikes, and demonstrations—set off by internationally demanded austerity measures—led to another military coup in January 1996, leading to the formation of the military-dominated Council of National Salvation (CSN), chaired by Colonel Ibrahim Bare Mainassara. Promising a quick return to civilian rule, Mainassara himself ran for president in July 1996, winning the office by a slim majority in elections that the opposition said were rigged. Continuing labor unrest and student protests marked the Mainassara administration. Moreover, the government's failure to return Niger to democracy jeopardized its relations with the West. Following the suspicious 1996 elections, the United States cut off all economic and military assistance to the Mainassara administration, while France merely expressed concern. Meanwhile, Mainassara tried to shore up his relations in the region through frequent visits to neighboring capitals.

Ethnic Tensions

Following a prolonged drought that afflicted the region during most of the 1980s, large numbers of Tuareg nomads began to return to Niger from Libya and Algeria. By 1990 and 1991, unrest among this group was growing, including an attack on a prison in northeastern Niger where several dozen Tuaregs were being held for having protested the government's failure to aid the refugees in their return. The raid was quelled with great brutality by the Niger armed forces, leading to further tensions, though forty-four Tuaregs were acquitted of involvement in the prison attack in April 1991.

Throughout 1991 and 1992, the Tuaregs, under the leadership of the Liberation Front of Air and Azaouad (FLAA, named after the Tuareg regions of the country), and government forces engaged in a series of attacks and counterattacks. The Tuaregs complained that they were being ruthlessly suppressed by the army, while the government said the Tuaregs were fighting to establish an independent state in the northern part of Niger. This charge was denied by FLAA leader Rissa Ag Boula, who said the organization simply wanted an autonomous region within a federated Niger.

By early 1993, however, the government and the FLAA were reaching an accord on ending the fighting during secret discussions in Paris. Though sporadic violence continued, the cease-fire agreed upon in April seemed to hold. But when the FLAA began to move away from the agreement—citing government violations, including the imprisonment of several dozen Tuaregs—pro-government elements in the organization formed the Tamoust Liberation Front (FLT) and signed an extension of the cease-fire. The FLAA refused, however, and renewed fighting between the government and FLAA guerrillas continued through the rest of the year. Still, by mid-1995, an accord had been reached, setting out a tentative plan for the administrative reorganization of the country into federated districts. Fighting between the FLAA and the government died down, only to flare up again when yet another Boula-led antigovernment Tuareg organization—the Organization of Armed Resistance (ORA)—accused the government of inadequacy in helping to integrate former Tuareg fighters back into Niger society.

Meanwhile, there were reports of ethnic unrest in southern and eastern Niger in late 1994 and early 1995, largely in the Lake Chad region, as fighting between nomadic and sedentary groups broke out over grazing rights. The land dispute quickly acquired political overtones when the nomads of the region formed the Democratic Renovation Front (FDR), an organization demanding autonomy in the southeast. The fighting among local peoples and between the FDR and the government was exacerbated by the huge number of refugees and weapons that had spilled over the border from Chad, then engaged in its own internal conflicts.

In 1999, citizens of Niger approved a new constitution, and later that year Mamadou Tandja was elected president. His five-year term was generally peaceful, and he was reelected in December 2004.

James Ciment

See also: Ethnic and Religious Conflicts; Mali: Ethnic and Political Conflict, 1968–1996.

Bibliography

Baier, Stephen. *An Economic History of Central Niger.* New York: Oxford University Press, 1980.

Charlick, Robert. *Niger: Personal Rule and Survival in the Sahel.* Boulder, CO: Westview Press, 1991.

Economist Intelligence Unit. *Country Profile: Niger, Burkina Faso.* London: Economic Intelligence Unit, 1986–1987.

NIGERIA: Biafra War, 1967–1970

TYPE OF CONFLICT: Ethnic and Religious

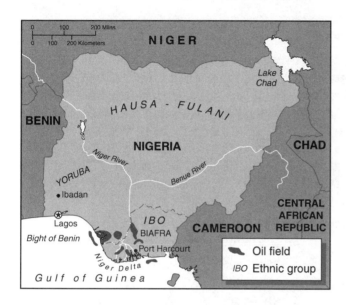

The Biafra War represented the first great ethnic conflict of post-independence Africa, serving as a tragic harbinger of things to come. Angry at their marginalization under a northern-led military government, the Ibos of southeastern Nigeria rose up in rebellion in early 1967, attempting to establish the independent Ibo state of Biafra. Though initially successful in defending their homeland, Ibo forces were eventually overwhelmed by the Nigerian army, which attempted to starve the rebels into submission by establishing a blockade around the territory they controlled. The strategy worked, but the costs were enormous. The name "Biafra" became synonymous with hunger, suffering, and Africa's remorseless ethnic warfare.

Causes of the War

Nigeria, the most populous country in sub-Saharan Africa with about 130 million people, is divided into some 200 different ethnic groups, though three dominate: the animist and Christian Yorubas in the west, the animist and Christian Ibos in the south, and the Muslim Hausa-Fulanis in the north. Together, the "big three" account for approximately two-thirds of the country's population. Because of its dominance of the north, the most populous region in the country, the Hausa-Fulanis controlled the largest political party in Nigeria when the country won its independence from Great Britain in October 1960.

In 1963, the government drew up a new constitution providing more autonomy to individual states, but deep ethnic conflicts persisted. The first elections in independent Nigeria, held in 1964 and 1965, reflected the animosities among the various peoples that made up Nigeria. Leaders in eastern states organized boycotts, and election violence erupted in the west. The result of the vote was a coalition government in the capital of Lagos. Because of continuing violence, the state government in the west was placed under federal control until peace could be restored.

When Nigerian leaders hosted the meeting of the British Commonwealth heads of state in Lagos in 1966, Nigeria seemed a picture of peace and prosperity. There was talk of this country leading Africa into the age of modern industrialism and democracy. But internally, severe problems remained. Corruption was endemic, encouraged by recent changes that gave the president power to appoint most important federal officers without consulting the legislature. Many feared that the president would choose loyalists from his own ethnic group, increasing traditional rivalries. At the same time, Nigerian citizens had already seen a marked decline in the freedoms they enjoyed in the first years of independence—including the right to assemble and the right to have an uncensored press.

The most serious troubles could only be glimpsed in the provincial homelands of Nigeria's major ethnic groups. Already a movement was growing in the north to declare an independent country to be known as the Tiv. Even more troubling, however, was the situation among the Ibo people of the south. For several generations, many had left their traditional region and settled in other parts of the country. Many were successful, but most failed—or were denied the right—to assimilate into the general population.

KEY DATES

1960	Nigeria wins its independence from Great Britain after more than a century of colonial rule.
1963	The country draws up a federal-style constitution devolving some powers from the central government to the states.
1964–1965	Local and national elections reflect growing regional and ethnic divisions within the country.
1966	A military coup puts Ibo officers in power in Nigeria in January; this causes rioting in northern Hausa areas, forcing Ibos to flee that region for their homeland in the southeast; second military coup in July puts Hausa officers in charge of the country; an ad hoc committee of officers opts to keep the country together, but to devolve more powers to states; its meeting is boycotted by the Ibo military leader; rioting in the southeast leads to the killing of northerners in September; rioting triggers violence in the north against the Ibos.
1967	Ibo leaders in the southeast announce the secession of their region, which they call Biafra, on May 30; Nigerian forces launch an offensive against oil facilities held by Biafra in July.
1967–1970	Several outside efforts at mediating the civil war fail; as Nigerian forces surround Biafra and cut off the region from the outside world, an estimated 1/2 to 2 million Biafran civilians die.
1970	Southeast leaders formally surrender to the Nigerian government, ending the Biafra War; an estimated 100,000 soldiers on both sides died in the fighting.

The divisions within the population were reflected in the military. The Ibos dominated the officer corps, while most of the enlisted men were recruited from the middle belt of provinces. Neither officers nor men were well disposed to the northern Hausa-Fulani people or their Northern People's Congress (NPC), even though it was the party of Nigeria's president, Tafawa Balewa.

In January 1966, the predominantly Ibo officers launched a bloody coup in which President Balewa was killed, together with ministers for the northern and western regions. Within twenty-four hours, the surviving ministers requested the army's Ibo commander-in-chief, Major General Johnson Aguiyi-Ironsi, to form a new government. Ironsi immediately formed the Supreme Military Council (SMC), suspended the con-

stitution, and imposed martial law. He substituted military men, mostly of Ibo origin, for the civilian governors in the various regions of the country.

Anti-Ibo rioting broke out across the country and lasted throughout the winter and spring months. In May, protests gripped the cities in the north as Hausa-Fulani expressed their dissatisfaction with Ibo rule. They felt that Ibo leaders were taking traditional powers away from the individual states to increase Ibo dominance. Soldiers were sent in, and a number of the protesters were shot down. At the end of July, northern troops in the capital rose up and overthrew the government, killing Ironsi and massacring Ibo officers.

As a conciliatory move, the northern officers chose General Yakubu Gowon—a northerner, but a Christian rather than a Muslim—to head the interim government. Gowon tried his best to restore military discipline and revive the federal system by granting further autonomy to regional governments. These conciliatory gestures eased tensions in some regions, but were not enough to pacify the angry and frightened Ibo. Ibo living in many parts of Nigeria had closed up their homes and traveled back to the south, in fear for their safety and their lives.

Meanwhile, in Lagos, Gowon established an ad hoc committee to discuss the future of the country. On the table was one basic question: whether to dissolve the Nigerian union and allow the formation of new countries or to keep the country together but federalize the government further, devolving most powers to the states. Advisers from the capital and from western Nigeria succeeded in urging unity. At the same time, they urged that past grievances be addressed, tensions lowered, and differences among the regions reconciled. Significantly, they did not approve loosening the rules of confederation, and they ruled out the right of states to secede from Nigeria.

Easterners on the committee were angry with the outcome. They had held out for the right of their region to secede. Worse, the meeting was boycotted altogether by the military governor of the southern region, Lieutenant Colonel Chukwuemeka Odumegwu-Ojukwu, who was under pressure from leading Ibo politicians and military officers to declare the Ibos' secession from the Nigerian confederation. In late September 1966, rioting broke out in the Ibo region. Many northerners who lived in the south were killed, and most other northerners soon fled the region.

As the stories of the killings spread, Ibos living in the north were targeted for massacre by northern troops. Officially, some 7,000 were killed, though Ojukwu later claimed the figure was as high as 30,000. Most Ibos felt that the government did too little to stop the rioting. The government responded with evidence that Ibo terrorists were planning a bombing campaign in Lagos, though this allegation was never proved.

Secession and Preparations for War

The Gowon government attempted to make up for its failure by supplying the southern state government with some $2.5 million to help pay for the resettlement of Ibo refugees. Little of this money, however, reached the refugees. The government claimed that Ojukwu's government had used the funds to purchase arms from abroad. The allegation was a serious one, for it would indicate that the eastern government had been preparing for secession long before it announced its plans.

To ease the growing tensions, a conference was held in nearby Ghana in January 1967. At the meeting, the Ibo leader Ojukwu accused the government in Lagos of preparing for a major police action in Ibo lands, pointing to recent arms purchases by the government in Europe. The government replied that the purchases had been made, but only for routine policing purposes. Even as both sides talked of peace, ominous events were occurring back in Nigeria.

One of the longstanding complaints of the Ibo people was that the region did not receive its fair share of the oil revenues generated from its territory. Nigeria was the largest producer of oil in Africa, and its clean-burning fuel obtained the highest prices in the international crude oil market. To make their point, Ibos seized railroad tank cars and disrupted the Shell Oil facilities at Port Harcourt. At the same time, they demanded that tax revenues raised in the south be collected by the Ibo government for its own use. The Nigerian government responded with an offer of a bigger share of federal revenues, including those from oil, but refused to concede on tax collection. Their offer was rejected by Ibo leaders.

On May 27, 1967, Gowon announced the formation of a new interim government for Nigeria and, more controversially, a plan for redistricting the country. While leaving the old west and midwest states largely intact, the plan divided the northern and southern states into six and three states, respectively. Each would be governed by a military governor—appointed by the central government—for the duration of the national emergency, after which civilian rule would be established.

The plan was immediately rejected by Ojukwu and other Ibo leaders in the south, who saw it as a method for undermining their authority, diluting Ibo political power, and maintaining central government control over the region. Their demands that the plan be scuttled were ignored by the government. On May 30, Ojukwu and other Ibo leaders formally seceded from Nigeria, declaring the formation of an independent Republic of Biafra, the name based on medieval and early modern-era references to the region.

The Biafra War

The Gowon government pronounced the eastern region in a state of rebellion and said that Nigeria would crush the rebellion, by force of arms if necessary. Severe economic sanctions were imposed and all telecommunications to the region were cut. Ojukwu and all other officers in the new Biafran government were stripped of their ranks and positions and charged with treason and other crimes against the Nigerian state. At the same time, Gowon also requested that all foreign governments stay out of the conflict.

Almost immediately, the new government of Biafra tried to seize control of the oil facilities in its territory, but it did permit Shell to retain its share of profits under earlier agreements it had made with the Nigerian government. In response, the Nigerian government demanded that all tankers taking on oil at Port Harcourt in Ibo territory call at Lagos first, where they would receive naval clearance. Ultimately, the oil companies—including Shell—ignored Ibo demands and continued to pay revenues into the central treasury in Lagos.

Meanwhile, both sides began recruiting and conscripting soldiers for the coming battle and arranging to purchase arms. The Ibo rebels ran guns from the nearby Portuguese and Spanish colonies of São Tomé, Princípe, and Fernando Po (now Equatorial Guinea). For the first several weeks, each side could do little against the other. The rainy season had begun, and the few roads that entered the Ibo region were virtually impassable. The Ibo forces soon captured the one railroad line and the single bridge across the Niger River. The only thing federal troops could do was establish a naval quarantine around Biafra, but they were limited even here by their inability to control the Niger River. Both sides also conducted air raids, but they had so few planes that the raids caused little damage.

In July, a Nigerian amphibious force succeeded in taking the oil port on Bonny Island, recently developed by Shell off the shore of Ibo territory. Later that month, Nigerian troops flanked the Biafran forces around Lagos and marched into Ibo territory from the north and west. In response, Ojukwo launched an Ibo offensive against Nigeria itself, crossing the Niger River and invading the state of Benue. Supported by those Ibo officers and men who remained in the army, the Biafran force then moved on Nigeria's second-largest city, Ibadan. By early August, the rebel forces were in the suburbs of Lagos itself.

Gowon responded with a general call for support from the Nigerian people, making a special appeal to the Yoruba, who were centered around Lagos. Suspicious of northerners (most of whom were Muslims), the Yoruba were reluctant to turn on their fellow Christians in the south. But the threat of invasion of their own lands by Ibo forces convinced Yoruba leaders to back the government. This decision helped turn the tide. Through September and October, federal troops slowly drove the invaders out of the western and midwestern territories of the country, inflicting a major loss on them near the city of Enugu on October 1.

By the end of October 1967, the fighting had died down. But the costs to the Biafran forces had been immense. Ojukwo's invasion had been launched in the hope that a decisive victory would end the war quickly and lead to a peace settlement that would allow Biafra to remain independent. When the invasion failed, Biafran leaders found that they had used up most of their weapons and ammunition and lost thousands of their best troops. Now they would be forced to fight a defensive war.

Despite their successes, the federal forces found it difficult to take the initiative. Their desire to push the war into the southeast bogged down in a host of problems. Their supply lines were stretched thin, the transportation infrastructure was limited, and they were fighting on the enemy's home territory, which meant they were subject to guerrilla-style raids that sapped their morale and strength. The army tried to secure the roads and airfields but often lost control of them. Thus, through much of late 1967 and early 1968, the conflict degenerated into a bloody war of attrition.

Finally, in June 1968, federal troops captured the critical port and oil-shipping city of Port Harcourt. This victory effectively cut off the Ibo rebels from access to the sea and put major oil-producing assets in federal hands. International observers believed that the war was all but over. It wasn't. New shipments of armored transports and artillery to Biafra forced the government to halt its occupation of Ibo land. And as the rebel enclave shrank, the Ibos' job of defending it became somewhat easier. Still, the federal troops pressed on, using their increasing capacity for air attacks. They captured most of the major cities in the south by the end of 1968. By early 1969, they had surrounded the heart of Ibo land.

Now the shrinking Biafran enclave was hard put to bring in enough food to sustain its people. Nigerian troops made it a point to destroy whatever acreage they

Nigerian troops enter Port Harcourt in the secessionist state of Biafra after routing rebel troops there in 1968. Up to two million Biafrans, many of them Ibo suffering from starvation, died in the civil war. *(Evening Standard/Getty Images)*

found under cultivation and to seize all food stores. As the blockade became more efficient, hunger turned into malnutrition and famine. Television and newspaper photos soon conveyed to the world the image of starving Biafran civilians. Appeals by foreign governments and organizations poured into the government in Lagos, but Gowon continued his strategy of starving the rebels out.

Late in 1969, the Biafran forces were all but defeated. Further Nigerian offenses had cut them off from one another and from supplies of military equipment and food. On January 10, 1970, Ojukwo fled the country, handing over authority to Major General Philip Effiong. Five days later, Effiong flew to Lagos and formally surrendered. It is estimated that some 100,000 soldiers on both sides died in the conflict. But the real tragedy concerned civilian losses. Experts estimated that at least 500,000 and perhaps as many as 2 million civilians in the war zone died, most from starvation caused by the federal blockade.

Negotiations and Aftermath

There had been a number of attempts to resolve the conflict peacefully even as it was going on. In May 1968, a British Commonwealth–sponsored peace conference was held in Kampala, Uganda, with the chief justices of Nigeria and Biafra (the Biafran representative had formerly been the chief justice of the eastern region) in attendance. The two sides agreed that a cease-fire must precede any talks concerning Ibo grievances, but the talks collapsed over the question of disarming. Predictably, the government insisted that Biafran forces lay down their arms and renounce armed conflict before a ceasefire could occur. The rebels rejected the proposal outright and added denunciations of federal army atrocities. The government countered with charges of attacks by Ibo soldiers on non-Ibo minorities in rebel-held territories.

When the rebels proposed an immediate unconditional cease-fire at Organization of African Unity (OAU)–sponsored talks in Niamey, Niger, in August 1968, the federal government refused, saying that this demand presumed equal sovereignty on both sides. Still, it was agreed to resume the talks in April 1969 in Addis Ababa. But a proposal insisting on the Ibos' right to maintain an independent army even if it rejoined a much more loosely confederated Nigeria was rejected by Lagos, which now felt that the war was turning in its favor. Intervention by the pope in August also failed to resolve the differences between the two sides and represented the last serious effort to end the war through negotiations.

The twelve-state plan initiated by Gowon in 1967 and put into effect in 1968 remained in force after the war. In January 1970, the East Central State, which had once been the heartland of Biafra, was reintegrated into the Nigerian state, on Lagos's terms. There were, however, some attempts at reconciliation. A number of Biafran officers and government officials were reincorporated into the Nigerian army and bureaucracy. At the same time, some of the complaints about a lack of spending in the east were redressed. Several large infrastructure projects were begun, in part to take advantage of rising world oil prices following the Organization of Petroleum Exporting Countries (OPEC) boycott in 1973–1974.

In 1975, Nigeria helped to organize the Economic Community of West African States (ECOWAS). The organization was largely an economic one at first, but it soon took on mutual defense and peacekeeping responsibilities. Internally, however, Nigeria remained torn by conflict. A national census held in 1973, meant to apportion political power and federal funding, was protested by the Ibos and Yorubas of the south, who disagreed with its findings that the population in the north had doubled since independence while that in the south had shrunk slightly.

Moreover, the country was having a difficult time returning to civilian rule. While Gowon had promised elections in 1976, he announced an indefinite postponement of the transition in October 1974. A year later, he was overthrown in a bloodless coup by northern Brigadier General Murtala Ramat Muhammed, who immediately purged the government of most Gowon-appointed officials and announced preparations for a return to civilian rule in 1976. Muhammed himself was overthrown by military supporters of Gowon in February 1976. As a compromise measure with the anti-Gowon forces, power was instead transferred to Muhammed's deputy, Lieutenant General Olusegun Obasanjo. Obasanjo presented a new constitution in 1978, which installed numerous checks and balances between the government's three branches. It also stated that in presidential elections, the winner must receive at least 25 percent of the votes in at least twelve of the fifteen states. The first elections under the new constitution were held in 1979.

James Ciment

See also: Ethnic and Religious Conflicts; Nigeria: Coups and Ethnic Unrest Since 1966.

Bibliography

Collis, William Robert. *Nigeria in Conflict*. London: Secker and Warburg, 1970.

De St. Jorre, John. *The Brothers' War: Biafra and Nigeria*. Boston: Houghton Mifflin, 1972.

———. *The Nigerian Civil War*. London: Hodder and Stoughton, 1972.

Ekwe-Ekwe, Herbert. *The Biafra War: Nigeria and the Aftermath*. Lewiston, NY: E. Mellen Press, 1990.

Niven, Cecil Rex. *The War of Nigerian Unity, 1967–1970*. Totowa, NJ: Rowman and Littlefield, 1971.

Nwankwo, Arthur Agwuncha. *The Making of a Nation: Biafra*. London: C. Hurst, 1969.

Saro-Wiwa, Ken. *On a Darkling Plain: An Account of the Nigerian Civil War*. London: Saros, 1989.

Stremlau, John. *The International Politics of the Nigerian Civil War, 1967–1970*. Princeton, NJ: Princeton University Press, 1977.

NIGERIA: Coups and Ethnic Unrest Since 1966

TYPE OF CONFLICT: Coups; Ethnic and Religious Conflict

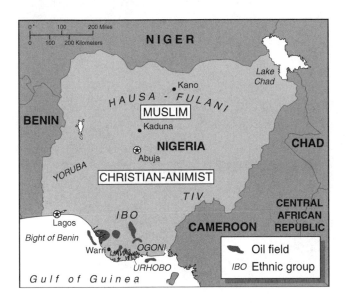

Torn by ethnic and geographic divisions, the Federal Republic of Nigeria was ruled by military regimes for more than twenty-five of its first forty years after achieving independence from Britain in 1960. The pattern of military coups followed a relatively predictable pattern, with northern Muslim Hausas seizing power to prevent domination by southern, often Yoruba, politicians. The south of the country is where most of the people live. It is also where all the oil, Nigeria's most valuable export, lies.

During its first six years of independence, Nigeria was torn by political infighting, marked by uprisings in the southwest among the Yoruba and repeated efforts to find a constitutional solution to its deep regional, ethnic, and religious divisions. Although the Hausa and the Yoruba peoples were the dominant groups in Nigeria, the Ibo group in the southeast brought on the country's first major conflict. The Ibo dominated the officer corps of the Nigerian military at the time, and in January 1966, Major General Johnson Aguiyi-Ironsi, an Ibo, overthrew the government and seized power.

Protests from other Nigerian ethnic groups soon turned into to rioting, particularly in the north. Thousands of Ibo who lived in other parts of the country fled back to their homeland in the southeast. There they organized a movement supporting the secession of Ibo people to establish a new, independent state, to be called Biafra. In July 1966, Aguiyi-Ironsi was killed in a countercoup led by a northern lieutenant colonel named Yakubu Gowon. In May 1967, war broke out as the federal troops tried to crush the separatist effort in the southeast. The resulting Biafran civil war lasted for three years and resulted in hundreds of thousands of military deaths. The victory by the central government likely prevented the splintering of the newly independent state.

Coups of the 1970s

At the end of the Biafran War in 1970, Gowon attempted to reconcile the defeated Biafran separatists with the remainder of Nigeria. In the following years, he incorporated many former Ibo leaders into the Nigerian government. At the same time, he embarked on a plan to construct a stronger central government and promote economic development. Internationally, the Gowon government presided over the creation of the Economic Community of West African States (ECOWAS) in an effort to strengthen the economy and security of West Africa through cooperation. Gowon often promised to return civilian rule to Nigeria, but he kept putting off the date.

In July 1975, while attending a meeting of the Organization of African Unity (OAU) in Uganda, Gowon was overthrown in a bloodless coup by northern Brigadier General Murtala Ramat Muhammed. Muhammed immediately purged most Gowon-appointed officials and announced preparations for a

KEY DATES

1960	Nigeria wins its independence from Britain.
1966	Nigeria experiences its first military coup.
1967–1970	Ibo separatists in the southeast of the country declare independence as the Republic of Biafra but are then defeated by the Nigerian military, as up to 2 million people die of starvation due to a Nigerian blockade of the rebel-held territories.
1975	Yakubu Gowon, leader of the 1966 coup, is himself overthrown in a bloodless military coup.
1982	Uprisings in the Muslim north of the country lead to rioting and a military crackdown there.
1983	Civilian leader Alhaji Shehu Shagari is overthrown in a military coup led by Major General Muhammadu Buhari.
1985	The Buhari regime is overthrown in a coup led by Major General Ibrahim Babangida.
1993	As wealthy Yoruba publisher Moshood Kashimawo Olawale Abiola leads in national elections for president, the military intervenes and Army Chief of Staff Sani Abacha seizes power.
1995	The Abacha government executes playwright Ken Saro-Wiwa and other Ogoni rebels in the face of international protests.
1998	Abacha dies of a heart attack and is replaced by Chief of Staff Abdulsalam Abubakar, who promises a return to elections and civilian rule.
1999	General Olusegun Obasanjo, the only military leader to voluntarily give up power, is elected president.
2004	Conflict between Muslims and Christians in Plateau State produces 800,000 internally displaced persons (IDPs).

return to civilian rule in 1976. These plans met with widespread approval, but not from the military supporters of Gowon, who overthrew Muhammed in February 1976. The insurgents and the outgoing government agreed to transfer power to Muhammed's deputy, Lieutenant General Olusegun Obasanjo, who established a commission to write a new Nigerian constitution. He also promised to end the practice of earlier rulers who had constantly changed borders between Nigeria's states as a means of limiting the powers of regions and ethnic groups.

Return to Civilian Rule

The constitutional commission drew up a national charter resembling that of the United States. The constitution provided for a relatively strong executive and carefully balanced powers between the federal government and the states. It also sought to prevent dominance by any single ethnic or regional group by requiring that a presidential candidate receive a solid portion of the vote in the majority of states in order to be elected.

Five major parties competed in the parliamentary elections in July 1979 and in the presidential elections in August. The National Party of Nigeria (NPN) received a solid plurality of the vote with roughly 35 percent in both elections. On October 1, the military handed over power to the civilian president, Alhaji Shehu Shagari, a northern-based politician. It had been thirteen years since Nigeria had last been ruled by an elected government. Unfortunately, Shagari took office at a time when oil prices were collapsing, bringing dire consequences for the Nigerian economy and undermining his ambitious development plans.

Regional leaders complained that the new constitution gave the federal government too much power at the expense of the states and that it gave Shagari and his followers the chance to grow rich at the country's expense. Uprisings in the north in 1982 led to rioting and a military crackdown in which hundreds of dissidents were killed. Shagari became so unpopular that when he was reelected to a second term in August and September 1983, most Nigerians believed that the voting had been rigged.

Rise of Babangida

On New Year's Eve 1983, Shagari was overthrown in yet another bloodless military coup, this time led by Major General Muhammadu Buhari, a former military governor from the north. Buhari immediately moved to ban political parties and arrest members of the former government on charges of corruption. The people of Nigeria applauded. Then the corruption trials were delayed and deals were worked out to release many detainees. Sensing that Buhari had made a deal of his own with the old corrupt government, Nigerians became angry. Yet again, the military intervened. In August 1985, it overthrew the Buhari regime in a bloodless coup headed by Major General Ibrahim Babangida, the military chief of staff and a northerner. Babangida's deputy in the coup was Major General Sani Abacha, chief of the army staff.

In October 1985, Babangida declared a state of national economic emergency and assumed extensive executive powers as head of the Armed Forces Ruling Council (AFRC). Babangida suspended negotiations with the International Monetary Fund (IMF) on Nigeria's economic policies, a move widely approved. Nevertheless, the army attempted another coup in December. This time, the government suppressed the

revolt and soon executed thirteen of the conspirators. At the same time, Babangida also announced that the army would transfer power to a civilian government within five years, by October 1990.

In 1987, renewed ethnic and religious fighting broke out in the country. The Babangida regime announced that the return to civilian rule would be delayed until 1992. The government did set up a program for political education, however, as a first step toward ending the dictatorship. In May 1989, Babangida took other steps toward a return to civilian rule. He reduced the number of AFRC members and legalized political parties. But unrest continued, particularly in the southern and western parts of the country, where people believed they were underrepresented in the federal government. During 1990, the government announced an "open ballot" system to prevent electoral fraud.

Still, numerous challenges remained for the Babangida government, including an initially disastrous military intervention in the Liberian civil war—under the aegis of ECOWAS—and renewed ethnic conflict in the southeast. In October 1990, the Movement for the Survival of the Ogoni People (MOSOP) was founded. MOSOP demanded a fairer share of the oil revenues coming from Ogoni people's lands and protested the extensive environmental destruction that industry had wrought in their region. Meanwhile, rioting between Christians and Muslims broke out in the north.

Despite these problems, the electoral process continued. In October 1991, primary elections for governors and state assemblies were held, and in December the federal capital was officially transferred from coastal Lagos to the more centrally located Abuja. Despite rioting over a rise in fuel prices, elections for the national assembly took place in July 1992. The Social Democratic Party (SDP) received a majority in both the upper and lower houses. A month later, primary elections for presidential candidates were marred by violence and confusion, leading Babangida to announce a postponement of the final vote from December 1992 elections to June 1993. Many Nigerians feared the military was planning to hold onto power despite its promises to the contrary.

The elections did occur on the new schedule, in June 1993. Voter turnout was low, and the electorate chose SDP candidate Moshood Kashimawo Olawale Abiola, a wealthy Yoruba publisher. Even as the returns were coming in, however, there were ominous signs. The military announced a delay in reporting election results. An independent commission was assembled to look into the problems, and it declared Abiola the winner. Even so, on June 23, the Babangida government announced that the results of the election were invalid.

In July, the Babangida's government seized many of Abiola's publishing holdings and announced the formation of an "interim national government." Under pressure from his former protégé, Abacha, Babangida resigned and transferred power to businessman Ernest Shonenkan. Supporters of Abiola rioted in the streets, demanding that power be turned over to him. In November, the high court in Lagos ruled in favor of Abiola and declared the interim government was illegal. Before their decision could be enforced, however, Shonenkan resigned on November 17 and handed power to Abacha.

Abacha Regime

Within twenty-four hours of taking power, Abacha dissolved the interim government, replaced all elected state governors with military administrators, and prohibited all political activity. He announced the formation of the Provisional Ruling Council (PRC), composed of senior military officials and promilitary civilians. Abacha still maintained that he was committed to bringing civilian rule, but in June 1994, when Abiola had himself symbolically inaugurated as president on the one-year anniversary of his election, Abacha had him arrested and imprisoned. Abiola's supporters demonstrated in Nigeria, and formal protests against his arrest were made by the United States, Britain, and other governments.

In July, the writer Wole Soyinka, the best known and most admired Nigerian outside his own country, brought a suit against the Nigerian government challenging the legitimacy of the Abacha government. The country's highest court ruled that Abiola's detention was illegal, but he remained in prison. Such challenges from civilian politicians and political groups continued through 1995. Abacha addressed them by dissolving the groups involved, even while he claimed that he favored a return to civilian rule. After several alleged coup attempts were reported, Abacha cracked down further on the opposition, arresting its leaders, both military and civilian.

The Abacha regime also moved against MOSOP, arresting a number of Ogoni leaders, including Ken

Sani Abacha, the military dictator of Nigeria, reviews security forces in 1996 as his regime became more repressive. With the political opposition mounting, Abacha succumbed to a heart attack in June 1998. *(Issouf Sanogo/AFP/Getty Images)*

Saro-Wiwa, a playwright and popular opposition figure, on charges of treason for demonstrating against the government and Shell Oil for the environmental damage to the Ogonis' lands. In October 1995, Saro-Wiwa and eight other Ogoni activists were sentenced to death, attracting international condemnation and appeals for clemency. Abacha ignored the protests, and the nine Ogoni leaders were executed in November, sparking national and international outrage and limited sanctions against the government.

While the Abacha regime continued to institute various programs for a return to civilian rule, most Nigerian politicians believed these were little more than delaying tactics. In June 1996, Abiola's wife, Kudirat, a prominent opposition figure in her own right, was gunned down by unidentified assailants on a street in Lagos. Opposition figures said it was her constant agitation for her husband's release that led to her murder, and they accused the government of complicity in the killing.

By 1997, Nigeria was in an almost constant state of crisis. The corrupt Abacha regime was bankrupting the country, rolling back virtually all the economic gains made since independence. In addition, it was fomenting ethnic unrest in a bid to stay in power. Local and international human rights organizations cited the Abacha regime as one of the greatest violators of human rights in Africa and indeed the world. But Abacha, increasingly a recluse in Abuja, conducted further crackdowns, issuing a decree in April by which he empowered himself to replace all local mayors with his own appointees.

Plans announcing elections for early 1998 were denounced as shams by political opponents and international critics, especially since they would be limited to candidates nominated by a few government-approved parties. Nigerians also suspected that Abacha himself was planning to become a civilian candidate in the elections. Later, Abacha delayed the elections still again.

In June 1998, all speculation about Abacha ended when he died of a sudden heart attack. At first, hopes rose that Abacha's death might lead to an opening up of Nigerian politics, but Abacha's chief of staff, Major General Abdulsalam Abubakar, quickly announced his succession to power. Abubakar did move to release a few political prisoners, but Abiola, the last elected president, was not among them. Opposition leaders demanded that Abubakar release Abiola and either turn power over to him or announce a legitimate schedule for free and fair elections. Then, only a month after Abacha's death, Abiola died in prison.

Democracy Under Obasanjo

Abubakar proved more willing to end the long stretch of military rule than his critics had imagined. Regional and local elections brought to the fore former General Olusegun Obasanjo's Popular Democratic Party, and his main rival, the Alliance for Democracy, which primarily represented the Yoruba ethnic group. Sani Abacha's All Peoples Party won in only one of Nigeria's thirty-six states. In the general elections of March 1999, Obasanjo won the presidency.

The successful return to democracy after sixteen years of autocracy immediately improved Nigeria's international image and won for it increases in foreign aid and IMF cooperation. Obasanjo immediately sought administrative reforms, adjustments to Nigeria's investment policies, a purge of thirty senior military officers, and reclamation of fortunes stolen from the national treasury.

In 1979, Obasanjo was the only Nigerian military leader voluntarily to relinquish power to a civilian government. He was a member of the Yoruba people and maintained strong support among Yorubas in the north (most of them Muslims). Obasanjo himself, however, grew up in southern Nigeria and was a Christian, which gave him some ties to southern Christians. Despite his long ties with the military, Obasanjo took steps to reduce the influence of northern Muslim officers in the army. Obasanjo himself had been imprisoned by the military regime of Sani Abacha in 1995, so he had personal experience with the brutality of military rule.

After stabilizing the central government, Obasanjo faced many other daunting problems. Corruption remained widespread, limiting the ability of public and private organizations to accomplish things quickly and efficiently. Local militias—now well armed by the flood of small arms in the region—continued to threaten Nigeria with regional warfare. Perhaps most difficult was Nigeria's reliance on oil to fund government activities and development efforts. A drop in oil prices could ruin the country's economy in a matter of weeks or months.

Despite Obasanjo's weak support in the legislature and his inability to end persistent mass poverty, he was elected to a second four-year term in April 2003. Perhaps more encouraging, he managed to avoid intervention by the military, which had overthrown so many elected governments in the past.

Ethnic and Religious Conflict

Throughout his first two terms, Obasanjo faced constant ethnic and religious disorder. The region with the worst ethnic tension was the oil-rich and environmentally devastated Niger Delta in the south. There was constant conflict over the distribution of the oil wealth, little of which reached the hundred ethnolinguistic communities located there. The region's abjectly poor people often flared up against neighboring groups and the central government. They also mounted attacks against the oil companies and their wells, kidnapping oil workers and forcing production shutdowns. Much of the communal violence was carried out by armed youth gangs belonging to such ethnic groups as the Ijaw. In one such dispute in May

1999 involving the relocation of a local administrative center in the town of Warri, nearly 200 persons were killed. Directly or indirectly, these disputes were often over access to the region's immense oil wealth.

Other incidents were caused primarily by ethnic conflict. In December 1999, the Ijaw and the Ilaje communities clashed in the city of Lagos. By March 2000, hundreds had died. In this case, Obasanjo intervened and set up a committee to coordinate a truce. In another incident, in June 2001, 40,000 people fled when fighting broke out between Azara and Tiv people in the state of Nasarawa.

Yet another source of tension was religion. About 36 percent of Nigerians are Christian, and 48 percent, predominantly from the North, are Muslim. The remainder practice various animist faiths. For decades, Nigeria was able to sidestep religious violence because most of the active political parties represented both Christians and Muslims. Two major parties in particular, the All Nigeria's People's Party (ANPP) and the People's Democratic Party (PDP), succeeded in finding common ground between the Muslim north and Christian south.

Muslim-Christian tensions did arise after Obasanjo's election. In December 1999, Muslim extremists damaged eighteen Christian churches in Ilorin. Further attacks targeted Christian Ibos in the northern city of Kaduna in February 2000, leaving at least 500 dead and displacing thousands of others. Violence elsewhere along the Christian-Muslim divide killed thousands more. Some of the tensions in northern Nigeria were caused by attempts of devoted Muslims to introduce Sharia (laws based specifically on the Koran and other Islamic texts). Sharia prescribes extreme punishments for common offenses—stoning for adultery, amputation of a hand for theft, and so on. The resistance of Christians and others to the new codes often erupted in violence.

Although Obasanjo was himself Christian, he relied on the Muslim north for much of his political support. He did succeed, however, in reaching an agreement with the Muslim states of the north to limit the scope of Sharia.

Religious Violence in the Plateau State

Nevertheless, religious conflict worsened in Nigeria. In the Plateau State, Muslim extremists attacked and killed 48 Christian churchgoers in early 2004. In April, Christian Tarok and Muslim Fulani militants fought each other in the district of Shendam, leaving at least 20 dead. Increased police and military presence did not end the violence. In May, Christian militias killed 600 in Yelwa, and Muslim retaliation inflicted further fatalities. Hundreds of thousands were driven from their homes in search of a safe haven with co-religionists.

Another dimension of the Muslim-Christian violence was the emergence of small, well-funded, and well-organized terrorist groups often associated with pan-Islamic goals. As part of an attempt to put a restraint on the preaching of factional hatred, particularly against the Christians, the Plateau authorities banned the Council of Ulamma, an extremist Muslim group. Although Obasanjo was fearful of alienating his Muslim electoral base, he was compelled by events to intervene and stop the violence. In May 2004, Obasanjo declared a state of emergency, removed the Plateau legislature, and replaced the governor with a former army general. Cash rewards and an amnesty were offered to people who turned in small arms, and it was made illegal to accumulate weapons. The military set up a cordon-and-search operation to secure the undeclared weapons caches. The Plateau was largely stabilized by November 2004, and power was transferred back to the elected governor. Nevertheless, it was likely that large caches of weapons remained hidden. Meanwhile, violence erupted elsewhere, albeit on a smaller scale.

James Ciment and Julian Schofield

See also: Coups; Ethnic and Religious Conflicts; Nigeria: Biafra War, 1967–1970.

Bibliography

Diamond, Larry. *Class, Ethnicity, and Democracy in Nigeria: The Failure of the First Republic.* Syracuse, NY: Syracuse University Press, 1988.

Diamond, Larry, Anthony Kirk-Greene, and Oyeleye Oyediran, eds. *Transition Without End: Nigerian Politics and Civil Society Under Babangida.* Boulder, CO: Lynne Rienner, 1997.

Dudley, Billy. *An Introduction to Nigerian Government and Politics.* Bloomington: Indiana University Press, 1982.

Ike, Okonta, and Douglas Oronto. *Where Vultures Feast: Shell, Human Rights, and Oil in the Niger Delta.* New York: Sierra Club, 2001.

International Institute for Strategic Studies. *Strategic Survey 1999–2005.* London: International Institute for Strategic Studies, 2000–2005.

Joseph, Richard A. *Democracy and Prebendal Politics in Nigeria:*

The Rise and Fall of the Second Republic. New York: Cambridge University Press, 1987.

Maier, Karl. *This House Has Fallen: Nigeria in Crisis.* Scranton, PA: Perseus, 2002.

McLean, George, Robert Magliola, and Joseph Abah, eds. *Democracy and Values in Global Times—With Nigeria as a Case Study.* Washington, DC: Council for Research in Values and Philosophy, 2004.

Ndaeyo Uko. *Romancing the Gun: The Press as Promoter of Military Rule.* Trenton, NJ: Africa World Press, 2004.

Soyinka, Wole. *The Open Sore of a Continent: A Personal Narrative of the Nigerian Crisis.* New York: Oxford University Press, 1996.

RWANDA: Civil War and Genocide Since 1991

TYPE OF CONFLICT: Ethnic and Religious
PARTICIPANTS: Congo (Zaire); Uganda

Like many other African civil wars in recent decades, the civil war in Rwanda had its roots both in precolonial history and in misguided or maliciously guided colonial policies. The tiny country of Rwanda (some 10,000 square miles) is naturally a kind of Eden. Situated about a mile high on the equator, it is both well watered and beautiful. The altitude keeps it relatively cool and also keeps at bay certain pests dangerous to humans and animals—specifically, the malaria-carrying mosquito and the cattle-killing tsetse fly.

Historical Background

This idyllic setting has drawn people from across sub-Saharan Africa for thousands of years. Scholars speculate that of the six to seven different sociocultural groups inhabiting Rwanda, the first inhabitants were the Twa—also known as Pygmies—who have dwelled in the extensive upland rain forests that have covered the northern Great Lakes region of Central and East Africa since prehistoric times. These people were followed by Bantu-speaking Hutu, a largely agricultural people who settled in the region more than a thousand years ago, and the Tutsi, a largely pastoral people who moved into the area perhaps 500 years ago. By modern times, Hutu accounted for about 84 percent of the population, and the Tutsi 15 percent. The Twa had been largely displaced by the newcomers, accounting for less than 1 percent of the total.

Partly because precolonial Rwanda was such a crowded and intensively farmed place, it developed a uniquely centralized and ordered form of government. At the center of political life was the king, who was believed to have divine origins, and his court. Beneath the king was an elaborate political structure of chiefs and subchiefs who had a number of duties, including the regulation of economic and political affairs, the collection of tribute and taxes, and recruitment and training for the army.

The Rwandans developed a feudal social and economic order in which the cattle-owning warrior class of Tutsi acted as lords and the agricultural Hutu served as serfs. Still, these labels can be misleading. Many Hutu served in the king's army and were rewarded with cattle, while most Tutsi were just as poor as their Hutu neighbors and tilled the fields beside them. Indeed, there was a certain amount of upward and downward mobility. In the years just before the arrival of Europeans, however, the Banyinginya dynasty was confining the Hutu to more feudal obligations and providing them with less freedom to move upward. Indeed, moves were made to ban Hutu from owning cattle altogether.

Colonial Rwanda

When European colonial powers were dividing up African territories, Rwanda fell to Germany in 1890.

258

KEY DATES

1918	Belgians take over the colony of Rwanda from the defeated Germans; over the next forty-four years, Belgians will favor minority Tutsi over majority Hutu, creating resentment among the latter group.
1962	Rwanda wins independence from Belgium with the Hutu party in power; thousands of Tutsi flee violence in the country.
1990	Militants of the Rwandan Patriotic Front (RPF), mainly Tutsi exiles in Uganda, launch an invasion of Rwanda, in an effort to overthrow the repressive Hutu government of General Juvenal Habyarimana.
1990–1992	With the help of France, the Rwandan army expands to 50,000 troops to fight off the RPF.
1992	The Habyarimana government and the RPF sign a peace accord in Tanzania, but continuing violence in Rwanda prevents its implementation.
1993	Fighting in neighboring Burundi leads to massacres of both Tutsi and Hutu in that Tutsi-led country; 300,000 Burundian Hutu refugees pour into Rwanda, inflaming Hutu feelings against Tutsi.
1994	In April, Habyarimana flies to Tanzania to explain to African leaders why the peace accord has not been implemented; on his return on April 6, his plane is shot down over the Rwandan capital of Kigali; Hutu extremists immediately blame Tutsi militants and call on Hutu people to massacre Tutsi; between early April and early June, Hutu—urged on by extremist politicians—massacre an estimated 800,000 Tutsi and their Hutu sympathizers in the worst genocide in world history since the Cambodian genocide of the 1970s; while the whole world does almost nothing to stop the killings, the massacres only come to an end when RPF forces enter Kigali; hundreds of thousands of Hutu—including many leaders of the genocide—flee the country, mostly to Zaire (now the Democratic Republic of Congo).
1998	In an effort to prevent a Hutu revival and to stop cross-border raids by Hutu militants, the Tutsi-led Rwandan government invades Congo, setting off a rebellion that overthrows the government of that country.
2001	The government of Rwanda institutes a traditional system of popular participatory justice to deal with a massive backlog of cases against those who participated in the genocide.

Early German visitors took note of the extensive and intensive farming, made possible by the benign climate and topography. They also studied the large population and identified the leading ethnic or social groups. They observed that the Tutsi and the Hutu seemed to be quite distinct and recognizable physical types and noticed the elaborate social order that had been created.

Following racial beliefs then widely held in Europe and North America, German colonial leaders concluded that the Rwandan social order was based entirely on race. Because many Tutsi leaders were tall and thin and had aquiline features (more like Europeans), the Europeans judged them to be superior to the Hutu, whose body shapes and features were less European. Colonial powers were much slower to recognize the widespread intermingling and intermarriage between Tutsi and Hutu or their shared Bantu-type language.

During World War I, Belgium (already a colonial power in Africa) drove German authorities out of Rwanda and took charge. At the end of the war, Belgium was given official responsibility for the colony. Based on the same racial assumptions as the Germans made earlier, the Belgian administration saw the Tutsi leaders as far more intelligent than the Hutu and gave them far more extensive power, putting the full power of the colonial regime behind them and absolving them from any need for consultation with village leaders (including the Hutu). Indeed, the old order, in which Hutu chiefs managed the lands and Tutsi chiefs the herds, was replaced by one directed by a single chief administrator, invariably a Tutsi.

Not surprisingly, the Tutsi used this power to gain advantage by seizing Hutu property. When farming enterprises were commercialized and woven into the imperialist economy, the Hutu were turned into a kind of rural proletariat. In other enterprises, they were kept down by the old feudal practices more thoroughly codified and rigidly enforced. This treatment left the Hutu increasingly frustrated and angry.

Gradually, both the Hutu and the Tutsi began to accept the Belgians' distorted and simplified gloss on their own history, culture, and social order. The Tutsi came to believe that they were, in fact, superior, with a natural right to rule over the Hutu, while the Hutu came to believe they were indeed a peaceful, agricultural people who had been conquered by the stronger and more aggressive Tutsi. Even so, the seeds of resentment between the groups had been planted.

Independence

After World War II, the Tutsi elite, wealthier and more educated than the vast majority of Hutu, were much better situated to comprehend the political ideas sweeping Africa. They understood that African independence was coming in the not-too-distant future, but they also understood that their superior position in Rwanda could be jeopardized if the country became a broad-based democracy, since Hutu voters would make an overwhelming majority. In the 1950s, as the Belgians began to prepare for independence by giving greater local powers to Africans, the Tutsi elite manipulated the system to ensure themselves a dominant position in an independent government.

The Roman Catholic Church, which had become a powerful force in Rwanda, had begun with the same admiration for the Tutsi felt by colonial leaders, but gradually it was changing its allegiance. As the Tutsi increasingly challenged European clerics for control of the Church, those clerics began to recognize the injustice being done to the Hutu. Indeed, the Church had long represented the only path to education, better economic position, and higher status for aspiring Hutu. By the mid-1950s, the Church had nurtured a Hutu counterelite that challenged Tutsi economic dominance and the right of the Tutsi elite to inherit the colonial administration upon independence.

This development produced a Tutsi backlash, and competition between the two groups became increasingly bitter as they fought over the symbolic trappings of power. More substantial developments were also occurring in the political arena on the eve of independence. In June 1957, Grégoire Kayibanda founded the country's first political party, the MuHutu Social Movement (MSM), largely based in the central and northern parts of the country. The group later became the MSM/Party of the Movement and of Hutu Emancipation and was known as PARMEHUTU for short. Only months later, another Hutu, businessman Joseph Gitera, formed the Association for the Social Promotion of the Masses (APROSOMA), which soon became the party of Hutu from the southern region.

Meanwhile, the Tutsi were organizing political parties as well. The more conservative elements established the strongly monarchical, anti-Belgian Rwandese National Union (UNAR), while liberals founded the Rwandese Democratic Assembly (RADER). The latter group advocated social equality and cooperation between Hutu and Tutsi, but few Hutu joined it, distrusting its Tutsi majority.

Rhetoric between these parties reached a fever pitch by late 1959, and tension in the country increased to the breaking point. A Hutu subchief was attacked by the Tutsi group UNAR, and fighting broke out between Hutu and Tutsi in various parts of the country. Some 300 people were killed, and many Tutsi homes were destroyed. Meanwhile the struggle intensified between the Hutu and Tutsi elites. The Hutu demanded that the colonial Belgian regime establish a broad-based government with majority rule before independence was declared. The Tutsi demanded immediate independence, saving questions about the permanent government for later discussion.

The Belgians increasingly backed the Hutu and began to replace Tutsi chiefs with Hutu leaders. There were several reasons for doing so. First, their relations with the Tutsi had become more and more confrontational, as the Tutsi demanded to be given the preference they had enjoyed for decades. Second, government and business interests came to believe that the Hutu would be more pliable rulers, allowing Belgians to continue managing the country's economic affairs. Finally, in the intense cold-war atmosphere of the time, the Tutsi elite, who were vocally anticolonialist, had attracted the support of Communist regimes, which persuaded the Belgians and other Western powers that the Hutu might be less dangerous. Thus the Tutsi, who were more reactionary than Marxist, were perceived as allies by leftist governments and as enemies by the colonial powers.

Despite the growing state of insecurity, the Belgians organized local elections in June and July 1960 in preparation for independence. Relying on the large Hutu majority, PARMEHUTU won overwhelmingly. This victory allowed the Belgian administration to announce that the "social revolution" was complete, since the majority Hutu were taking control of the country. In fact, the new Hutu elite were already encouraging attacks on impoverished Tutsi in the countryside.

The international reaction to Rwanda's elections was not positive. Both the United Nations and the Communist bloc feared that Hutu rule would allow the Belgians to continue to call the shots in Rwanda. Thus they supported the more radically anticolonialist UNAR Tutsi party to lead the country. A conference to reconcile the Hutu and Tutsi was held in Belgium but made little progress. Grégoire Kayibanda of PARMEHUTU announced a "legal coup,"

asserting that Rwanda had established its independence. As the violence continued, legislative elections were held. Another PARMEHUTU landslide gave it control of the legislature. Tutsi began emigrating to neighboring countries in large numbers. In the midst of this anarchic and violent situation, independence was formally declared on July 1, 1962. Since the last king had died without an heir, the new country became a republic under the presidency of Kayibanda of the PARMEHUTU Party.

Kayibanda and Habyarimana Regimes

Rwanda in the Kayibanda years (1962–1973) was a rather strange place. The president ruled much as the kings of old had, appointing favorites to administer the various regions but also relying on elaborate alliances with local chiefs to ensure social peace. There was much talk of egalitarian social and ethnic order, but the country was run by a secretive clique of Hutu elites, the Akazu, who monopolized much of the country's limited commercial potential. At the same time, having been saved by the Belgians, the Hutu government of Kayibanda did not enthusiastically join in the general African trend toward anticolonial leftist politics.

Meanwhile, the rise to power of PARMEHUTU and the continuing Hutu violence against Tutsi led to a massive emigration. In a continuous stream between 1959 and 1964, some 336,000 "official" refugees had fled. The largest number, about 200,000 traveled to Burundi in the South. (Like Rwanda, Burundi was a Belgian colony divided between a Hutu majority and a Tutsi minority.) More than 100,000 fled north and east to the former British colonies of Uganda and Tanganyika (now Tanzania). Many more Tutsi may have fled without official recognition. Some estimates of total emigration run as high as 775,000, about half of the Tutsi population of Rwanda. The Tutsi refugees from Rwanda were known for three things. First, they gained success in their adopted countries, thanks to their education and entrepreneurial instincts. Second, they maintained an almost mythic connection to their homeland, which, over decades, parents would pass on to their children. The exiles in Uganda dropped French as their second language and adopted English, yet they never lost their sense of belonging to Rwanda. Third, the refugee Tutsi continued to launch ineffective attacks against Rwanda. The first of these came even before independence, in the form of raids from Uganda that more resembled looting expeditions than guerrilla warfare. A more substantial but poorly organized invasion from Burundi nearly reached the capital, Kigali, but was driven back by the Rwandan army.

A more formidable force developed in Uganda when the brutal Idi Amin ruled that country. In 1980, the Rwandan refugees in Uganda formed the militant Rwandese Alliance for National Unity (RANU), which demanded the right to return to a safe and secure Rwanda. When Amin was overthrown, Uganda's new dictator, Milton Obote, drove RANU out of Uganda. Even so, many of the militants stayed behind, joining up with an anti-Obote guerrilla group, the National Resistance Army (NRA), headed by former defense minister Yuweri Museveni. As the Rwandan exiles gained battlefield experience, they came to dominate the officer corps of the Ugandan resistance movement. In early 1986 Museveni captured the capital, Kampala, and overthrew the old regime. More Rwandans were recruited for the new national army of Uganda.

Though appreciative of the Rwandans' help, Museveni was also worried about their dominance in the army. The Rwandans began planning a radical solution to their exile. At a congress in 1987, RANU changed its name to the Rwandese Patriotic Front (RPF) and dedicated itself to returning to Rwanda, by the use of force if necessary.

Meanwhile in Kigali, the cliquish, secretive, and reactionary regime of Kayibanda had been overthrown. In July 1973, General Juvénal Habyarimana took charge after a relatively bloodless military coup. At first, the new regime was popular, and Habyarimana achieved a degree of social peace. While Tutsi remained marginalized—with virtually no representation in government or the military—the popular and official violence against them largely stopped.

At the same time, however, Habyarimana made it clear that he intended to rule Rwanda in the fashion of the old monarchy. In 1974, he organized the National Revolutionary Movement for Development (MNRD) and banned all political parties from the country. Indeed, he tried to ban politics altogether, declaring the MNRD to be a social movement. The new president also imposed a rigid and repressive bureaucratic structure that required people to register before moving or traveling. It was also socially conservative, arresting hundreds of Tutsi girlfriends and mistresses of European residents.

The country did progress economically, however, joining both French-speaking and English-speaking organizations in Africa. By the late 1980s it had won hundreds of millions of dollars in foreign aid. To outsiders, then, Rwanda appeared to be a peaceful, well-ordered, and increasingly prosperous African country. But beneath the surface, things were not so peaceful. Security forces ruthlessly crushed any sign of opposition to the regime. Nor was the economic growth secure. While the vast majority of Rwandan peasants got by on subsistence farming, the commercial elites lived off earnings generated from the country's two main exports, coffee and tin, both of which saw a downward spiral in world prices during the 1980s. Indeed, as the prices declined, political instability increased. In 1980 there was a failed coup.

In 1988, Colonel Stanislas Muyuya, a potential successor to Habyarimana, was murdered. This event reflected deep divisions within the Hutu elite. Like the Rwandan royal courts of old, various clans, representing various regions of the country, maneuvered for access to the ruler. The murder of Muyuya set off serious infighting in the capital just at a time when falling commodity prices necessitated a 40 percent cut in social spending. Already overburdened by taxes and forced labor recruitment for government projects, the peasantry grew increasingly unruly, especially as overcrowding led to demands for land reform (which would ruin some commercial elites). When domestic and foreign journalists reported on the growing tensions, they were arrested or thrown out of the country.

RPF Invasion and French Intervention

The Tutsi exiles in Uganda were only too aware that unrest was growing in their country. Militants in the RPF decided that the situation represented a great opportunity to seize power, or a share of power, in Kigali. Conscious of these developments, the Habyarimana regime decided to try to repatriate some Tutsi peacefully. The RPF saw this move as a threat to its plans, and on October 1, 1990, some 2,500 guerrillas of the Rwandese Patriotic Army—the military branch of the RPF—crossed the Ugandan border into Rwanda. After some initial successes, the well-equipped guerrilla operation bogged down, immeasurably set back by the accidental death of its commander, Major General Fred Rwigyema.

Within a week, both the French—who had become increasingly involved in Rwanda's politics and economy—and the Belgians sent in troops. But their small numbers and their official noncombat status left much to be desired as far as the Rwandan government was concerned. To win more support, Habyarimana staged a fake attack on the capital. The ruse worked, and the French sent in more troops. The scheme played on French fears—they had always insisted on tight political and economic control of the colonies they managed. They were especially eager to maintain some control in Africa, the one region in the world where they continued to dominate. They saw their main challengers as the British and Americans. The Tutsi of the invading RPF spoke English, and to the French this represented the threat that English speakers might one day dominate in Rwanda, where French had long ruled as the official language. While France sent in more troops to defend this postcolonial colony, Belgium sent more troops for a more practical reason—to protect the substantial community of Belgian expatriates in the country.

Habyarimana used the staged attack on Kigali not only to gain French support, but also to justify further action against the Tutsi. The regime arrested hundreds of Tutsi political activists. At the same time, it vastly expanded its army, which succeeded in driving the RPF out of the country and back into Uganda by the end of 1990. By mid-1992, the Rwandan army had increased from a relatively well-disciplined and well-trained force of about 5,000 to some 50,000. The French, Egyptians, and South Africans supplied arms. The force represented an important deterrent to invasion, but it proved dangerous and undisciplined. If payment to the troops was late, they often looted and pillaged both Hutu and Tutsi property.

For the next several years, the RPF regrouped its forces in Uganda under its new commander, Major General Paul Kagame. It recruited émigré soldiers from Uganda and other countries. The relatively high level of education among these recruits meant that the larger RPF—numbering some 25,000 by 1994—was better disciplined and better trained. Funding was provided by the international community of Tutsi expatriates from Rwanda, many of whom had done well financially. Though reorganizing itself, the RPF also continued its raids, including a successful one on a Rwandan prison that freed a number of Tutsi militants.

Attempts at Democracy and Peace

Despite its efforts to round up Tutsi militants, the Habyarimana regime sought to ease tensions by moves to liberalize. In November 1991, the president announced several reforms. For Hutu opponents, he offered multiparty elections and a new constitution. For the Tutsi, he promised an end to ethnic references on identity cards and all other official papers.

In the wake of this speech, many political organizations were formed. The largest and most important was a new incarnation of the PARMEHUTU, which had been banned after the 1973 coup. Others included a radical Hutu nationalist party, Coalition for the Defense of the Republic (CDR), the more liberal Social Democratic Party, the Liberal Party, and the church-based Christian Democratic Party. Meanwhile, the president's own National Revolutionary Movement for Development (MRND) added a second "D" to its name standing for "and Democracy."

The new political parties quickly realized that they were meant to adorn Rwanda, not rule it. That is to say, their existence allowed the Habyarimana regime to show the world it was democratic without actually surrendering any power. A joint statement by the opposition parties complained that Habyarimana's MRNDD party had a monopoly on the government-owned media and often used goons to break up opposition rallies.

Unfortunately, the violence was not confined to political hooliganism. As the country moved hesitantly toward democracy, it remained in a high state of tension. Although it had just turned back an invasion by the RPF, it still faced a crisis atmosphere as fighting between the army and the guerrillas continued along the border. Hard-line elements within the ruling MRNDD used this climate to organize Hutu voters to combat Tutsi infiltration. Spreading rumors of Tutsi massacres of Hutu at political rallies, they set off a number of massacres of the Tutsi. Fearful of the hard-liners' growing political power and popularity, the government failed to prosecute those who were inciting violence.

Still, opposition to the regime grew. After a mass rally of some 50,000 people in the capital, Habyarimana agreed to a multiparty cabinet in January 1992. As the new cabinet worked to lower ethnic tensions and open up the government, the MRNDD hard-liners were sending a different message, charging the

Habyarimana administration with weakness in the face of Tutsi threats and labeling the opposition parties as "fifth columns" for the RPF.

Habyarimana was desperately seeking a way to resolve the growing political tensions and low-level civil conflict in the country. The strife was bankrupting his regime, undermining the country's economy, and potentially creating a revolutionary situation. Spiraling foreign debt forced the government to enact International Monetary Fund reforms that required the firing of thousands of civil servants and major cuts in food and fuel subsidies needed by the average Rwandan peasant and worker. By this time, most of the operating budget for Rwanda was coming directly from foreign aid.

On August 17, 1992, the president announced on national radio that he had signed a cease-fire agreement with the RPF in Arusha, Tanzania. But as the negotiations for a repatriation of Tutsi continued in Arusha, the Hutu militants in the MRNDD and the CDR complained that the government was selling the country out to the Tutsi. More insidiously, they were beginning to organize a number of alternative institutions—including Hutu militias, known traditionally as the *interhamwe*, and death squads recruited from the army—designed to scare the opposition parties into submission, end the Arusha negotiations, and force the president to launch an all-out war with the RPF.

The militants were also increasing their political organizing throughout the country. At rallies and over their own radio stations, they charged the government with selling out the country. Using the old myths of Tutsi dominance perpetuated by the Belgians, militants warned their fellow Hutu that the Tutsi had infiltrated the government and were using the Arusha negotiations to reestablish their dominance over the Hutu population. They described Tutsi massacres of Hutu in RPF-controlled territory and a regime that turned Hutu into slaves. In January 1993, they organized violent demonstrations in the northwest part of the country. The MRNDD and CDR militants massacred some 300 Tutsi civilians over a period of about a week.

The RPF retaliated in February, invading the region and driving some 300,000 Hutu refugees before them. The RPF targeted those they believed had organized the earlier atrocities but killed numerous innocent civilians and government workers in the process. The attack alienated Hutu liberals in the capital and sparked a harsh response from Paris, leading to the dispatch of 300 more troops to Rwanda. The presence of the French troops dissuaded the RPF from marching on the capital.

Despite the setback, negotiations in Arusha continued. While a plan for repatriating refugees was worked out, the thornier question of how many Tutsi to integrate into the national army remained unsolved. Though Habyarimana faced increasing opposition from both Hutu militants and liberals at home and increasing demands from RPF negotiators, the president signed the Arusha Accord in August 1993, paving the way for Tutsi repatriation, a new coalition government, and an integrated national army. It was a complicated agreement, with many parts, and would require goodwill on the part of all parties, a commodity in short supply in Rwanda. Aside from the many difficulties of integrating the Tutsi back into Rwandan life and society, the accord also called for the presence of a multinational peacekeeping force. In September, the United Nations agreed to establish its Assistance Mission to Rwanda (UNAMIR) with a complement of 2,500 well-armed troops.

While Rwanda waited for their arrival, tensions mounted. Preparing for a new political order, the hard-liners—now supported by a new organization, Hutu Power—began to organize for a showdown with the new coalition government, settling personal scores with opponents and setting up a clandestine network of militias and political groups. Hutu Power as a movement claimed that the Tutsi were an alien race to Rwanda and, based on their outsider status, ought to be eliminated. Amid this political turmoil came a shock from the outside: the assassination of neighboring Burundi's first democratically elected Hutu president by Tutsi militants in October 1993. With its army still in Tutsi hands, Burundi descended into anarchy and mass killings, as soldiers massacred civilians, and Hutu militias and civilians murdered Tutsi. Over the next several weeks, some 50,000 Burundians were killed, about 60 percent Tutsi and 40 percent Hutu. Equally significant, the massacres sent some 300,000 Burundian Hutu refugees into Rwanda.

The assassination and the arrival of traumatized Hutu civilians fed the propaganda of the militant Rwandan Hutu and hardened their conviction that the Arusha Accord meant disaster for themselves and their country. It also put fear into the more liberal Hutu opposition. Burned once by the RPF invasion

A Rwandan soldier inspects the wreckage of the plane, shot down in an April 1994 missile attack, in which President Juvenal Habyarimana was killed. The incident sparked an outbreak of genocide that took the lives of up to 1 million Tutsi and moderate Hutu. *(Scott Peterson/Getty Images News)*

in February, they now saw yet another danger of coalition-building with Tutsi, a fear enhanced by the RPF's lack of enthusiasm in condemning the assassination conducted by fellow Tutsi in Burundi.

In the midst of this growing tension, the various components of the Arusha Accord were being put into place. In November, UNAMIR peacekeepers began to replace French paratroopers. The following month, several RPF leaders flew to Kigali to take up their positions in the new cabinet. Meanwhile, demonstrations and murders rocked the capital, as militant Hutu assassinated liberal politicians, and liberal parties retaliated with attacks on the CDR. The violence prevented Habyarimana from implementing the Arusha Accord, and so he flew back to the Tanzanian city in early April to explain his difficulties to the impatient heads of states of neighboring African states. After a series of lectures, Habyarimana—along with the new Burundian president, Cyprien Ntaryamira—boarded his jet to return to Kigali, where he planned to lend it to Ntaryamira

to fly back to the Burundian capital. Flying into Kigali airport, however, the plane was struck by two missiles and crashed, killing everyone aboard.

Genocide and War

While controversy surrounds the assassination, most Rwanda observers now agree, despite the lack of an official investigation, that the missiles were launched by Hutu militants who had two reasons for doing so. One was obvious: to eliminate the moderate Habyarimana and destroy the Arusha peace process. The other was to launch the genocide. Indeed, within minutes of the attack, Hutu-controlled radio, in particular Radio Télévision Libre de Mille Collines (RTLM), was broadcasting inflammatory reports about a Tutsi-inspired assassination of Habyarimana. Moreover, the Hutu militia and extremist elements in the army immediately began rounding up all potential opponents, including both Tutsi and liberal Hutu. Militia roadblocks went up around the city.

To eliminate the foreign presence in the country—which they believed might present an obstacle to their plans—Hutu militants murdered ten Belgian members of the UNAMIR force. The strategy worked. Belgium, the European country most likely to intervene against the militants, immediately pulled out the rest of its troops. And UNAMIR, lacking even a mandate to use force to defend itself, pulled back into its compound. These actions were taken despite the warnings the UN had received from UNAMIR's commander, Roméo Dallaire, three months earlier, that massacres were occurring, and it looked as if they would spread and intensify. Meanwhile, across Rwanda, the Hutu underground went into action, organizing brigades of civilians and setting them on their Tutsi neighbors. Radio broadcasts spoke of the duty of all Hutu to defend their country by destroying the *inyenzi*, "cockroaches"—the term they applied to the Tutsi.

Hutu propaganda broadcasts contradicted themselves. On the one hand, they sought to dehumanize the Tutsi by referring to them as insects, making it easier for Hutu peasants—long used to taking orders from a powerful and all-intrusive bureaucracy—to commit countless massacres that beggar the imagination. At the same time, the radio broadcasts insisted that the Tutsi were a dangerous and powerful group, who were secretly organizing to destroy the Hutu people. Together this potent brew of contempt and fear led thousands of ordinary Hutu into an orgy of carnage against their friends, their neighbors, and—given the tradition of Hutu-Tutsi intermarriage—their own kin. Most of the killing was done with simple tools, like machetes and clubs. Hutu peasants, organized and led by members of the militias and soldiers from the army, killed an estimated 800,000 Tutsi civilians and Hutu sympathizers, about 11 percent of the country's population, between April 6 and early June 1994.

Another shocking aspect of this genocide was the deep involvement of the Catholic Church. Rwanda was the most Catholic country in Africa, and many fled to churches seeking protection, only to find that priests were either actively or passively complicit with the genocide. This disaster was not mindless killing on the part of uneducated peasants alone: physicians in hospitals also took part, murdering their Tutsi patients in their beds. With the exception of the genocide in Cambodia under the Khmer Rouge, this carnage represented the worst act of genocide since the Holocaust of World War II.

Like the Holocaust, the Rwandan genocide occurred during a war that the organizers of the genocide were losing. Just two days after the assassination of Habyarimana, the RPF launched a new offensive deep into the country, with some of its troops arriving in the capital by April 11, where for the next three months they battled with elements of the Hutu army and militias for control. Not only did the RPF attack the Hutu army; when they encountered UNAMIR troops at the airport, the RPF attacked them, claiming they could not distinguish UN peacekeepers from Hutu troops.

Meanwhile, the outside world failed to act. The administration of U.S. President Bill Clinton, stung by the loss of U.S. troops in Somalia a year before, equivocated on the question of genocide, fearing that any admission that genocide was taking place would require America's intervention as a signatory of a 1948 international accord on genocide. And while both the United Nations and the Organization of African Unity (OAU, now the African Union) recognized the genocide for what it was, the former continued to insist that it was being conducted by both Hutu and Tutsi when, in fact, it was an entirely Hutu affair.

Ironically, the Rwandan genocide was financed primarily with foreign aid, particularly funds from the World Bank and International Monetary Fund Structural Adjustment programs, though neither institution was aware of what was being done with the money. It is estimated that $134 million in aid was spent on genocide preparation in Rwanda—with some $4.6 million spent on weapons alone. A number of experts believe that such spending allowed the distribution of one new machete to every three Hutu males. The poverty in Rwanda, whose government was so strongly supported by international aid, is another possible cause of the genocide. Scholars suggest that overpopulation may have been one motivation for the murder of Tutsi. Indeed, after their deaths, their land and houses were frequently claimed with eagerness by their Hutu neighbors.

The presence of France, the only country to get deeply involved, made things even worse for the Tutsi of Rwanda. Still seeing their interest in defending French-speaking Africans (the Rwandan army) from English-speaking invaders (the RPF), the French determined to save the Rwandan Hutu by establishing a line that essentially trapped the Tutsi of the RPF and allowed Hutu extremists to continue their massacres. Dallaire, commander of the UN peacekeepers, later charged that the French troops could have been used to prevent the genocidal attacks of the Hutu.

Aftermath and Legacy

By mid-June the capital of Kigali had fallen to RPF troops, who set up an interim government in July with a Hutu as president, despite the fact that most of the city's Hutu inhabitants had fled and most of the Tutsi were dead. Indeed, under the goading of Hutu extremists and fearful of Tutsi reprisals, some 2 million Hutu refugees, many of whom had participated in the genocide, poured across the country's borders, dropping their weapons as they fled. Most went to Zaire (now Democratic Republic of Congo) and some to Tanzania. This was the largest sudden mass movement of refugees in African history and overwhelmed the nongovernmental organizations (NGOs), such as the Red Cross, that were trying to provide food and medical care. There was little water, shelter, or food. Cholera broke out in the camps, killing thousands more. The murderers of just a few weeks before now hid among the refugees, receiving foreign aid and assistance.

Over the next two years, as the new Tutsi-dominated government of Rwanda tried to reestablish a semblance of order and redevelopment in the country, huge numbers of Hutu refugees remained in the camps in Tanzania and Zaire, cared for by the United Nations and other NGOs. Inside the camps, the Hutu militia organizers took charge. Supported by the masses of Hutu peasants, the organizers threatened violence to protect themselves from being turned over to Rwandan or international authorities. In addition, they began organizing a rebel movement to invade Rwanda, take over the government again, and finish the task of eliminating the Tutsi population once and for all.

These Hutu militant plans were dashed when long-time Tutsi expatriates began to demand the leaders' removal from the camps. In Zaire, the Tutsi, together with Zairian rebels, forced the closure of the camps in late 1996, sending hundreds of thousands of refugees back into Rwanda. The Tanzanian government soon followed suit. Some Hutu refugees escaped and traveled deeper into Zaire, to the Kivu province, pursued by the combined forces of Rwandan Tutsi and Zairian revolutionaries. In effect, both the Hutu and the Tutsi of Rwanda were exporting their bitter controversy to another and much larger country where an oncoming civil war would cause even more death and destruction.

Like the Holocaust before it, the Rwandan genocide, along with the "ethnic cleansing" in the former Yugoslavia, prompted the international community to create a court system to prosecute those who commit crimes against humanity. The International Criminal Tribunal for Rwanda (ICTR) was established under United Nations auspices at the end of 1994, issuing a list of 200 persons considered to be prime movers of the genocide. The list included members of the Akazu, the small circle of Hutu power elite, and Agathe Hayarimana, the wife of the slain president.

In the tribunal's first years, progress was slow. The first conviction came in 1998 and was followed by former prime minister Kambanda's admission of guilt. Beginning in 1999, the court's pace picked up. More than twenty-five trials were completed by 2005, and the tribunal hopes to complete sixty-five to seventy-five cases.

In Rwanda, the government under the RPF's Paul Kagame faced great difficulties in reconciling its citizens and rebuilding the country's society. Since a majority of Hutu Rwandans may have participated in the genocide, Tutsi and other survivors remained fearful. The United Nations and nongovernmental organizations sought to help by dividing citizens into such groups as "returnee," "victim," and "survivor." In 2001, the government began implementation of a traditional participatory justice system, known as "gacaca," to address the enormous backlog of cases. Democratic local elections were held for the first time in 1999, and, despite sweeping political reforms, the country continued its struggle to attract investment and to increase agricultural production. One striking indicator of the long way left to go for true reconciliation is that Rwandan schools no longer teach history, fearing that examination of the country's painful past would only continue to tear society apart.

Ten years after the genocide in Rwanda, the world was still trying to clarify the lessons of the grim disaster. Among them were the failure of international organizations and powerful nations to intervene during the long months of slaughter; the complicity of former colonial governments in current African problems; and the deep difficulty of mounting effective humanitarian interventions in the face of longstanding feuds between ethnic and cultural enemies. The killing in Rwanda has made world powers and organizations more willing to identify emerging conflicts as "genocide" but still has not led to the development of effective means of intervention to end or prevent future conflicts.

James Ciment and Erika Quinn

See also: Ethnic and Religious Conflicts; Burundi: Ethnic Strife Since 1962; Congo, Democratic Republic of: Kabila Uprising, 1996–1997; Congo, Democratic Republic of: Invasions and Internal Strife, 1998.

Bibliography

African Rights Organization. *Rwanda, Killing the Evidence: Murder, Attacks, Arrests, and Intimidation of Survivors and Witnesses.* London: African Rights, 1996.

Dallaire, Roméo. *Shake Hands with the Devil: The Failure of Humanity in Rwanda.* New York: Carroll and Graf, 2003.

Destexhe, Alain. *Rwanda and Genocide in the Twentieth Century.* New York: New York University Press, 1995.

Gourevitch, Philip. *We Wish to Inform You That Tomorrow We Will Be Killed with Our Families.* New York: Farrar, Straus, and Giroux, 1998.

Keane, Fergal. *Season of Blood: A Rwandan Journey.* New York: Viking, 1995.

Mamdani, Mahmood. *When Victims Become Killers: Colonialism, Nativism, and Genocide in Rwanda.* Princeton, NJ: Princeton University Press, 2001.

McCullum, Hugh. *The Angels Have Left Us: The Rwanda Tragedy and the Churches.* Geneva: WCC Publications, 1995.

Minear, Larry. *Soldiers to the Rescue: Humanitarian Lessons from Rwanda.* Paris: Development Centre, Organisation for Economic Cooperation and Development, 1996.

Peress, Gilles. *The Silence.* New York: Scalo, 1995.

Prunier, Gérard. *The Rwanda Crisis: History of a Genocide.* New York: Columbia University Press, 1995.

Scherrer, Christian P. *Genocide and Crisis in Central Africa: Conflict Roots, Mass Violence, and Regional War.* Westport, CT: Praeger, 2002.

Vassall-Adams, Guy. *Rwanda: An Agenda for International Action.* Oxford: Oxfam Publications, 1994.

SIERRA LEONE: Civil Conflict, 1990–Present

TYPE OF CONFLICT: Ethnic and Religious; Coups
PARTICIPANTS: Economic Community of West African States (ECOWAS); Liberia

Like its Liberian neighbor to the east, Sierra Leone was founded as a haven for freed slaves and, later, "recaptureds"—slaves freed from ships by the British navy after Parliament declared the international slave trade illegal in 1807. Unlike the case in Liberia, however, the population of freed slaves in Sierra Leone was never large enough to form an independent ruling class. Thus, coastal Sierra Leone remained a colony of the British government until 1961. A British protectorate over the interior of the country was established in 1896.

In 1951, Britain granted a constitution to the country that allowed for free elections. On April 27, 1961, Sierra Leone won its independence from Britain, with Milton Margai of the Sierra Leone People's Party (SLPP) as its first prime minister and with the opposition All People's Congress (APC) holding the majority of seats in the legislature. Following several attempted coups and mutinies, a republic was declared in 1971, with APC head Siaka Stevens as president. A declining economy in the 1970s led to political unrest and a new constitution in 1978

declaring the country a one-party state of the APC. Upon completion of his term in 1985, Stevens was replaced as president by the head of the armed forces, Joseph Saidu Momoh.

Unable to reverse the economic decline, Momoh's government faced a growing wave of strikes and political protests, as well as charges of corruption among government officials. In response, Momoh declared a state of emergency in November 1987, curtailing nearly all political activity and imposing harsh penalties for corruption. Still, protests calling for political reform continued to mount in the late 1980s and early 1990s, forcing Momoh to accept a new multiparty constitution in 1991, which was passed by 60 percent of the voters. Rising political unrest led to a military coup in April 1992 under the leadership of Captain Valentine Strasser.

Rise of the RUF and Liberian Civil War

While the Momoh government was collapsing and Strasser was making his plans for a coup d'état in the capital of Freetown, trouble was brewing in the provinces. Foday Sankoh, a political radical from the capital who had been involved in various protests and coup attempts, had organized a mysterious guerrilla movement called the Revolutionary United Front (RUF) and was establishing political cells throughout the country. Claiming to follow the precepts of Cambodia's brutal leader Pol Pot and a mystical nineteenth-century Sierra Leonean rebel named Bai Bureh, the RUF largely confined itself during the 1980s to small raids on army outposts and smuggling of gems from Sierra Leone's small diamond fields.

Civil war in neighboring Liberia provided Sankoh the opportunity to expand his struggle to overthrow the Momoh government, which he said was corrupt and ideologically bankrupt. Liberian rebel leader Charles

269

KEY DATES

1961	Sierra Leone wins its independence from Britain.
1985	Army head Joseph Saidu Momoh becomes president.
1987	Strikes and political protests lead Momoh to declare a state of emergency.
1991	Continuing protests force Momah to accept a new multiparty constitution; Nigerian and Guinean troops help the Sierra Leone government launch a counterattack against the newly formed rebel group, the Revolutionary United Front (RUF).
1992	A military coup, led by Captain Valentine Strasser, topples the government.
1995	RUF leaders refuse to negotiate with the government until all foreign forces leave the country.
1996	Ahmed Tejan Kabbah wins the presidency in March elections; in November, Kabbah and Foday Sankoh, head of the RUF, sign a peace agreement.
1997	Despite the fact that all foreign troops have left the country, the RUF violates the agreement and launches new attacks; Kabbah is overthrown in a military coup in May.
1998–1999	Fighting continues as first the Nigerians and then the RUF launch major offensives.
1999	On July 7, representatives from the government and the RUF sign the Lome Accord, ending the conflict and calling for the RUF's demobilization and incorporation into the political process; nevertheless, fighting contnues.
2002	After new peace agreements, fighting in Sierra Leone comes to an end.
2003	Sankoh dies of heart failure; Liberian president Charles Taylor, who supported the RUF, is ejected from power and forced to seek exile in Nigeria.

Taylor and his National Patriotic Liberation Front (NPFL) were fighting a West African peacekeeping force called the Economic Community of West African States Cease-fire Monitoring Group (ECOMOG), which was headed by Nigeria and included a contingent of Sierra Leonean soldiers. In 1990 and 1991, Taylor invaded Sierra Leone, hoping to force the government to abandon its support for ECOMOG and give him a share of its income from diamond smuggling. In his battle against the government, Taylor offered military aid to the RUF.

Together, the Liberian NPFL and Sierra Leone's RUF launched attacks on Sierra Leonean government troops. Then in November 1991, ECOMOG and the Sierra Leone government launched a counterattack against the rebels. Meanwhile, ECOMOG was cooperating with another rebel group in Liberia—the United Liberation Movement (ULIMO)—in its battle against Taylor's NPFL. Following failed peace talks between the Sierra Leone government, now headed by Strasser, and various Liberian factions in January 1992, government forces, aided by Guineans, went on the offensive against the RUF and gradually won the upper hand. In Liberia, ULIMO forces were gaining control of the provinces bordering Sierra Leone, increasingly isolating the RUF, which was caught between ULIMO and the forces of the Sierra Leone government.

In desperation, the RUF took two British relief workers hostage, claiming that Great Britain was arming the government. The British, who had cut off relations with Sierra Leone following the Strasser coup in April 1992, denied the allegations. In January 1995, the RUF gained control of two mining companies, seizing a number of foreign nationals as hostages. Adding to the chaos was the emergence of bands of renegade soldiers. Known colloquially as "sobels," a combination of the words *soldier* and *rebel*, the renegades often fought for the army during the day and became rebels at night. Because they frequently went unpaid, they tended to engage in banditry, smuggling, rape, and murder.

By February 1995, Sankoh began making peace overtures to the government. The fighting and general chaos had displaced some 900,000 Sierra Leonean civilians—about 300,000 to neighboring Liberia and Guinea and 600,000 to the capital, Freetown. But hopes for peace collapsed when the RUF demanded that all foreign troops leave the country before the beginning of negotiations. Besides forces from neighboring Guinea, the Sierra Leone government was depending on mercenaries from South Africa and Gurkha troops from Nepal to recapture territory and mining companies held by the rebels. By June, the government had reclaimed most of the mining territory. The RUF released all foreign nationals to the Red Cross by April, and in October it requested civilian mediation; the government refused. In response, Sankoh ordered all relief agencies to leave the territory he controlled, amid reports of numerous atrocities against civilians.

Meanwhile, the Strasser government in Freetown was making hesitant moves toward democracy. After defeating an attempted overthrow in October 1995, Strasser announced legislative elections for February 1996. Before they could take place, however, Strasser

was ousted in a bloodless coup led by his chief of staff, Maada Bio. The new government allowed the election to go ahead as scheduled, despite continuing political violence and RUF efforts to disrupt the voting. The Sierra Leone People's Party won a plurality, and in second-round voting in March, Ahmed Tejan Kabbah was elected president.

Kabbah moved to end the rebellion by the RUF, demanding that the rebels lay down their arms or face a renewed government offensive. In November 1996, Kabbah and Sankoh signed a peace agreement providing that the RUF would disarm and become a legal political party, while the government agreed to remove of all foreign troops from the country and replace them with foreign observers. By February 1997, all foreign troops had indeed left the country, but no sooner had they left than the RUF began violating the agreement.

In March, members of the political wing of the RUF removed Sankoh as leader, accusing him of opposing the peace agreement and fomenting unrest within the RUF. Sankoh was placed under house arrest in Nigeria. His remaining supporters sought to win his release by kidnapping the RUF members who had voted for his ouster and Nigeria's ambassador to Sierra Leone. Neither Nigeria nor the Kabbah government would negotiate with the RUF kidnappers.

Koroma Coup

In May 1997, President Kabbah was overthrown in yet another military coup. Claiming they were taking power in order to move talks with the RUF forward, the new junta, led by Major Johnny Paul Koroma, was condemned by the international community, which immediately slapped heavy sanctions on Sierra Leone. The Nigerian government demanded that Koroma relinquish power and restore the government of Kabbah. It also sent more troops to its base in Freetown. Supported by two naval gunboats, the Nigerians launched an attack against the Koroma regime in June but were driven back by a combined force of the Sierra Leonean army and rebels from the RUF, now formed into a security force known as the People's Army. Koroma's government was also facing resistance in the provinces from the Kamajors, traditional Sierra Leonean guerrillas who continued to support Kabbah.

Despite being isolated by the international community and besieged by Nigerian troops, the Koroma government tried to consolidate its power by establishing a twenty-member ruling council and a cabinet of secretaries. Still, Koroma's government was unable to win acceptance by its fellow African states. In August 1997, ECOWAS (Economic Community of West African States) voted to tighten the sanctions against Sierra Leone, prohibiting shipment of virtually all essential items except food and medicine. Fighting between the Kamajors and Nigeria on one side and Koroma's forces and the People's Army on the other continued throughout the rest of 1997.

In January 1998, the Nigerians mounted yet another offensive, backed by jet fighters and naval craft. This assault finally ousted the Koroma government on February 12, forcing its leaders to flee to Guinea. A month later, Kabbah was restored to power at an official ceremony in Freetown. International and African sanctions against Sierra Leone were lifted, but Nigerian troops remained in the country.

In late 1998 and early 1999, the RUF launched a new offensive in an effort to capture Freetown. ECOWAS forces drove RUF forces from the capital and halted the offensive, but there had been thousands of casualties. Sankoh and the RUF leadership were forced to ask for terms toward a peace settlement.

Ending the Conflict

Beginning in May 1999, members of Sierra Leone's government met with the leadership of the RUF in the city of Lomé, Togo, to begin peace negotiations with the support of the international community, including ECOWAS and the United Nations, which established the UN Mission in Sierra Leone (UNAMSIL). On July 7, 1999, the Lomé Accord was announced, declaring an end to the nearly decade-old conflict between the Sierra Leone government and the RUF and providing a framework within which peace could be restored.

A cease-fire would be monitored by ECOWAS and UNAMSIL, together with representatives of the government and the RUF. Once again, the RUF was to disarm and transform itself into a political party, allowing its members to hold office and help govern the country. The accord further provided for the establishment of a "commission for the consolidation of peace," or CCP, whose duty would be to oversee the peace process and verify that all parties adhered to its provisions. The CCP was to incorporate several different committees and national commissions, including the Committee for Humanitarian Assistance to help the

thousands affected by the war, as well as the Truth and Reconciliation Commission to create a record of violations of human rights and humanitarian law and promote reconciliation. A separate commission was established to help manage Sierra Leone's strategic resources, the most important being diamonds and gold.

Finally, the Lomé Accord offered full amnesty and pardon to the RUF combatants, including commander Foday Sankoh, even though many had committed horrible atrocities. The accord also provided for many details in managing the peace. They established a fixed date for elections and arranged for the withdrawal of mercenaries and the return of refugees and prisoners to their homes.

The accord proved difficult to enforce. In the early months of 2000, RUF forces were already violating the cease-fire, and they compounded their offenses by killing demonstrators who were protesting the violations. These actions resulted in the repeal of some of the articles of the Lomé Accord, including the ones offering Sankoh and other RUF members amnesty as well as allowing them to hold government positions. Sankoh was arrested, and a number of RUF members were removed from office.

A new cease-fire agreement was signed in November 2000 in Abuja, Nigeria. The agreement reaffirmed the Lomé Accord but failed to end the resurging conflict. A second agreement, signed in Abuja in May 2001, proved more successful in upholding the terms of the original Lomé Accord. Over the course of the next year, the government of Kabbah further consolidated its power, helping to restore the rule of law throughout large parts of Sierra Leone. This development was assisted by the demobilization and disarming of thousands of former combatants. On January 18, 2002, President Kabbah gave a speech in the town of Lungi, where he made a "declaration of peace in Sierra Leone."

Postwar Sierra Leone

Four months after declaring the civil war to be at an end, Kabbah's party, the SLPP, won a major victory in general elections. At the same time, the RUF, which was again allowed to run its own candidates, failed to win any seats in the new government. Soon after, foreign troops began disembarking from the country, though the UN mission was extended until the end of 2005.

After the war's end, Sierra Leone made a number of efforts to bring closure to the conflict. Perhaps most important was the establishment of a "special court agreement" between Sierra Leone and the UN, which was to try war criminals who bore the greatest responsibility for war crimes since 1996. These UN-backed courts provided some closure, but many of the main participants of the conflict evaded justice, including RUF commander Sankoh, who died from heart failure in 2003 while in custody and awaiting trial. Charles Taylor, whose support helped to establish the RUF as an effective fighting force, resigned as president of Liberia in 2003, following pressure from both the UN and the United States. Taylor went into exile in Nigeria, which refused to extradite him for trial on his role in the civil war. In 2006, Taylor was moved from his exile in Nigeria to face a war crimes tribunal in Sierra Leone. Several months later, he was once again moved to The Hague for trial at the international criminal court.

Analysis

The civil conflict that tore Sierra Leone apart ended in 2002. It is estimated that over 50,000 Sierra Leoneans died in the conflict, with many tens of thousands more suffering permanent injuries from the war. Millions also were left homeless and forced to seek refuge in neighboring countries, where they were not always welcomed. On the positive side, the disarmament of the country was swift, and rapid assistance from the UN, World Bank, and other international organizations allowed Sierra Leone to begin the long process of rebuilding.

James Ciment and Daniel F. Cuthbertson

See also: Ethnic and Religious Conflicts; Liberia: Civil War, 1989–1997; Liberia: Anti-Taylor Uprising, 1998–2003.

Bibliography

Berger, Daniel. *In the Land of Magic Soldiers: A Story of White and Black in West Africa.* New York: Farrar, Straus and Giroux, 2003.

Keen, David. *Conflict & Collusion in Sierra Leone.* New York: Palgrave, 2005.

Kpundeh, Sahr John. *Politics and Corruption in Africa: A Case Study of Sierra Leone.* Lanham, MD: University Press of America, 1995.

Kup, Alexander Peter. *Sierra Leone: A Concise History.* New York: St. Martin's Press, 1975.

Richards, Paul. *Fighting for the Rain Forest: War, Youth and Resources in Sierra Leone.* Portsmouth, NH: Heinemann, 1996.

SOMALIA: Civil War Since 1991

TYPE OF CONFLICT: Cold War Confrontation; Ethnic and Religious
PARTICIPANTS: Ethiopia; United Nations; United States

The Somali civil war, one of the most protracted in Africa, offers a series of paradoxes for students of contemporary African history. First, the nation of Somalia comprises a largely homogeneous ethnic group, sharing faith, language, and culture, which seemed to make a bitter civil war less likely. Second, it was one of the most commercially and technologically backward of African states, yet the regime of Mohammed Siad Barre from 1969 to 1991 was one of the continent's most totalitarian systems. Finally, even though the country seemed to have little value to East or West at the end of the Cold War in the 1990s, it drew the international community into its intractable disputes. Still, the Somali civil war was bloody and destructive—and one of its chief victims was the Somali state itself, which was still seeking to become

a viable political entity fifteen years after the fall of Barre.

Historical Background

The Somalis are a distinct ethnic group of some 7 million people who have inhabited the Horn of Africa for centuries. Long connected by trading routes to Arabia, the Somalis converted to Islam soon after Muhammad founded the religion. Indeed, the Islamic connections of the Somali people are represented in both the ancient tradition of tracing their ancestry to the Prophet Muhammad and their modern membership in the Arab League. This Islamic heritage was reinforced by the strong Somali role in the religious wars against Christian Ethiopia in the Middle Ages.

For much of their history, the Somalis have been divided into six major clans, distributed in distinct geographic zones and identified with particular pastoral or agricultural practices. While the Somalis never established statehood, they remained a strongly united people and effectively formed a nation. Since they were scattered across a huge, inhospitable territory, political unification proved difficult, but students of history still find it unaccountable that the closely related Somali peoples fell into such bitter internecine fighting.

Somalia attracted the attention of European imperialists in the late nineteenth century because of its strategic position, with a long coastline running along the Gulf of Aden and the Indian Ocean. The British, who controlled Aden (in present-day Yemen), just to the north, hoped to prevent the French from gaining a foothold in the region. Thus, the British maneuvered to ensure that southern Somalia fell into the hands of its ally, Italy. The French succeeded in gaining control of Djibouti, just to Somalia's northwest and extended their influence in that region. Britain itself seized what is now northern Somalia. At the same time, the Somalis were under siege from the west, where they

KEY DATES

1960 The UN trusteeship of Somalia and British-administered Northern Somaliland are united to form independent Somalia.

1978 The Ethiopian army crushes pro-Somali rebels in the Ogaden region of Ethiopia.

1991 Armed resistance from the United Somali Congress (USC) forces longtime dictator Siad Barre to flee the country; in the wake of his ouster, warfare among various clans breaks out across Somalia; members of the Isaq clan in northern Somalia declare their independence from the rest of Somalia.

1992 Clan fighting and drought lead to famine in large parts of Somalia; in December, 30,000 UN troops, including American soldiers, move into Somalia to prevent clan attacks on aid workers trying to feed hungry Somalis.

1993 U.S. forces begin to fight various clan leaders that have attacked UN troops; in July, a U.S. attack on clan leader Mohammed Farrah Aidid's headquarters kills seventy-three Somali elders by accident; nineteen U.S. soldiers are killed in another raid in search of Aidid in October.

1994 UN troops pull out of Somalia in March.

1996 Aidid is killed in a skirmish; while many hope this might lead to peace, he is succeeded by his son Hussein Muhammed, who vows to fight on.

2004 Leading Somalis, meeting in Kenya, form the Transitional Federal Government in hopes of bringing an end to clan fighting in Somalia.

shared a long and isolated desert border with Ethiopia. Seeking to expand, the Ethiopians gained control of Ogaden, home to many Somalis.

Each of the powers occupying parts of traditional Somalia—Italy, France, Britain, and Ethiopia—established alliances with Somali clans, beginning the splintering that would factionalize Somalia after independence. The region was divided into five different jurisdictions: one each under the Italian, French, and Ethiopian flags, and two under British control. Efforts by Muslim forces to drive the imperialists out in the early 1900s failed, leaving the Europeans and Ethiopians even more entrenched. In the 1930s, the Italian government of Benito Mussolini used Italian Somaliland as a base for the successful invasion of Ethiopia, forming a short-lived Italian East African empire. With the defeat of Italy by Allied forces in World War II, Italian Somaliland was ceded to the British.

Following the war, Britain proposed a united Somaliland under UN trusteeship, but the plan was rejected and the country remained partitioned among France, Britain, and Ethiopia. The Italians also returned to administer part of the region in 1950. During these years, the Somalis, encouraged by the British, futilely sought the return of Ethiopian-occupied western Somaliland and the Ogaden region.

Pan-Somali Nationalism

In 1960, the various colonial regions of Somalia were united in the newly independent state of Somalia. At first, the leadership of Somalia struggled to overcome the colonial legacy of being administered by several distinct political, judicial, and linguistic systems. Differences were especially great between clans in the north and south. In 1961, officers from a northern faction of the army rose up in an unsuccessful coup against the government, which was dominated by southerners.

Still, the common linguistic and ethnic bonds of the Somali people eventually led to an uneasy integration of the northern and southern administrations. What prevented a more effective administration was clan loyalty. With regional administrations controlled by different clan networks, personality and personal connections tended to matter more than competence in the appointment of government employees. To solve the problem of clan identification, the government instituted a neat but largely superficial solution: All references to clan identity had to be prefaced with an "ex-," thereby consigning clans to history by a manipulation of language.

The only topic on which most Somalis agreed was unification of the Somali homeland. They especially wanted the territories just outside their borders that were occupied by Somali-speaking peoples. These included northern Kenya (controlled by Britain), Djibouti (controlled by France), and western Somalia and Ogaden (controlled by Ethiopia). The first target was northern Kenya. When Britain refused to acknowledge the wishes of the Somali majority there and handed the territory over to newly independent Kenya in 1963, a low-intensity guerrilla war—known by Kenyan authorities as the *shifta*, or "bandit war"— broke out, lasting some four years. Though it disrupted the region, it never seriously threatened Kenyan sovereignty.

Meanwhile, a more serious Somali uprising had broken out in Ogaden. Somalia appealed to Western powers for help in its fight against Ethiopia but was turned down. It then approached the Soviet Union and succeeded in gaining sympathy and limited assistance. This relationship between Mogadishu and Moscow would bear fruit in later years.

After seven years of low-intensity conflict with Kenya and Ethiopia, a new Somali government under Muhammed Egal took office in 1969. It sought to ease relations with its neighbors, cutting off aid to the rebels and attempting to unify the Somali nation by diplomatic means. But Egal's softer approach inflamed Somali nationalists, as did his manipulation of Somalia's last nominally free national elections and his increasingly autocratic rule. On October 15, 1969, the president was assassinated. A week later the Somali military took over in a bloodless coup.

Somali Revolution

The officers who revolted were sick of the corruption, nepotism, and incompetence of the earlier regimes. But the new government soon went a step further than the mere administrative reforms initially envisioned by the officers. Under the increasingly tight control of coup leader and army commander Mohammed Siad Barre—now head of state and president of the Supreme Revolutionary Council (SRC)— Somali society was turned upside down. Among other changes, Barre established the death penalty for serious crimes rather than the traditional tribal blood payment, hoping to break down clan loyalties and forge a more united national identity.

In 1970, on the first anniversary of the coup, Siad Barre announced more far-reaching measures under a program he called "scientific socialism," patterned after similar models in the Eastern bloc. With the army growing ever more dependent on Russian aid and advisors, the government instituted national propaganda campaigns against tribalism and corruption. The word *jaalle*, or "comrade," was substituted for the complex set of forms of address in traditional Somali usage. Street children and orphans were gathered into Revolutionary Youth Centers, and vigilante squads were set up in every village and neighborhood to defend the principles of the revolution.

Increasingly, the state grew more totalitarian. A national cult resembling those in Stalinist Russia or latter-day North Korea was propagated by the Ministry of Information and National Guidance around the figure of Siad Barre, who was often portrayed in murals and billboards alongside Lenin. The new form of address for Siad Barre became "Father of the Nation." The office of the presidency was extended to include virtually all government agencies and independent organizations. A National Security Service and National Security Courts dealt with political opponents. The country was divided into fifteen new regions that had nothing to do with the old clan boundaries, while the old clan leaders were retitled "peacemakers" and woven, at least theoretically, into the state bureaucracy.

The effort to destroy old political loyalties and instill a new nationalism was matched by economic and cultural reforms. The Siad Barre government nationalized what little industry the country had and made farmers and herdsmen sell their commodities to government purchasing boards. (This was difficult to enforce among the pastoralists, since they could simply herd their animals to market in neighboring countries.) In its efforts to settle northern nomads, in order to increase productivity and establish more effective political control, the government was aided by a drought that forced many herdsmen to settle in government camps in the south of the country, where they were taught to fish and farm.

Renewed Pan-Somali Nationalism

Siad Barre focused on domestic issues of economic reform and political control during his first five years in power. In 1974 events outside the country forced him to focus his attention on foreign affairs. During that year, the longstanding monarchy of Haile Selassie in Ethiopia fell to a military coup of left-wing officers. In the confusion that followed, the Eritrean people of northern Ethiopia rose up in revolt to achieve an independent homeland. Somali nationalists in eastern Ethiopia rose up, hoping to unite with their brethren in Somalia. By 1976, the Western Somali Liberation Front had driven the demoralized Ethiopian army out of much of Ogaden.

The new socialist government of Colonel Mengistu Haile Mariam in Ethiopia sought military help from the Soviet Union to battle its restive minority populations. The United States had cut off assistance to Ethiopia as it became increasingly socialist. Within a year, a major change had occurred in the Horn of Africa. The Soviets abandoned Somalia, which it had been aiding, and took the side of Ethiopia. The United States moved tentatively to fill the aid gap in Somalia and retain some influence in the region.

With Russian aid, Ethiopia crushed the Ogaden rebellion in 1978. Nearly a million Somali refugees crossed the border into Somalia. Half were housed in government-run camps, while the other half were absorbed by their Somalian families and clans. By 1980, approximately one out of every four Somalis was a refugee.

Somalia's defeat in Ogaden also produced unrest in its military, leading to a coup attempt in April 1978 by military officers from the Dayod clan, a traditional rival of Siad Barre's Marrehan clan. The coup failed, but its leaders formed an antigovernment guerrilla force called the Somali Salvation Democratic Front (SSDF) across the border in Ethiopia.

With Ethiopian aid, they made some progress against the Siad Barre government.

Even though Russian aid to Ethiopia had helped cause a massive refugee problem for Somalia, the Russians' departure from Somalia in 1978 was welcomed by the Somali people, who realized that Soviet advisers contributed to the more repressive aspects of the Siad Barre regime. After the Soviet departure, Siad Barre announced a return to democracy and the freeing of some 3,000 political prisoners. Much of this declaration, however, was merely rhetoric. In elections held in 1979, Siad Barre manipulated the system to ensure the overwhelming victory of the government party.

With the loss of Russian support, Siad Barre felt vulnerable to his enemies at home. To strengthen his hold on power, he developed closer ties with particular clan leaders. He moved to appoint members of three specific clans—his own (Marrehan) and those of his mother (Ogaden) and son-in-law (Dulbahante)—to all key government posts. The ruling party increasingly became associated with these clans. Through the party network of security officials and spies, these three clans began to impose their will over all other clans throughout the country.

Famine and Civil War

The 1980s were a terrible time for the Horn of Africa. A prolonged drought led to large-scale refugee movements and the need for massive international food aid. The suffering, as well as the increasingly militaristic rule of the Siad Barre regime, led to yet another guerrilla uprising in Somalia in the early and mid-1980s. The Isaq clan of the north formed the Somali National Movement (SNM) to express its deep resentment against the domination of southerners in the national government. To crush the movement, the government employed political repression and harsh economic measures, including withholding food aid to the northern region. Despite these measures, armed opposition to the Siad Barre regime was growing.

In April 1988, Siad Barre and Ethiopia's Mengistu finally signed a peace treaty in which they agreed to stop supporting rebel movements in each other's territory. Siad Barre stopped supporting Somalis attempting to liberate western Somalia from Ethiopia, and Mengistu ended his help to Siad Barre's Somali enemies in the north. This loss of support goaded the SNM to launch a bold attack on military installations

A clan fighter loyal to the joint forces of the United Somali Congress and Somali Patriotic Movement displays a truck-borne missile system amid fighting in the southern part of the country in May 1992. *(Alexander Joe/AFP/Getty Images)*

throughout northern Somalia, leading to an all-out civil war between the regime and the Isaq clan that would last until 1991.

In southern Ethiopia, Ogaden Somalis who had lost their support from the Somali government gave up their fight against Ethiopia and crossed the border back into Somalia. There, many were recruited to serve in militias in northern Somalia, while others settled in lands and towns abandoned by the Isaq, taking over their property. Siad Barre struck back by recruiting other northern clans to fight the SNM, calling on their sense of clan solidarity. Thus the slowly collapsing Siad Barre regime used old divisions and animosities to keep itself in power.

Siad Barre continued to court the Ogaden refugee population, but the increasing barbarity of his pacification efforts alienated this key group. Many accepted a deal from Ethiopia's Mengistu that allowed them to return to new autonomous areas within the Ogaden. Angry at their second-class treatment by Somali officers, the Ogaden Somalis formed yet another rebel group, the Somali Patriotic Movement.

This group then joined other opposition groups in a loose confederation called the United Somali Congress (USC).

The USC was dominated by the Hawiye branch of the Somali family of peoples. One Hawiye clan lived in and around the Somali capital, Mogadishu. Another, from the north, was led by Mohammed Farrah Aidid, a former general and diplomat in Siad Barre's government. Desperate to end the multiple uprisings, Siad Barre called upon his Dayod clan to massacre the Hawiye opposition in Mogadishu. This warlike act sparked a new round of bitter interclan fighting and brought the northern forces of Aidid to Mogadishu. On January 26, 1991, Siad Barre was forced to flee Mogadishu, taking refuge in his clan's home base in Gedo, northwest of the capital. He took with him the last semblance of a central government for Somalia.

In Gedo, Siad Barre formed the Somali National Front (SNF), based on his own clan and its allies, to return himself to power. His recruiters told stories of the Hawiye's indiscriminate revenge killings of

Dayod clansmen, but it was too late to be effective. In April, the rebel USC defeated Siad Barre's followers, driving tens of thousands of new refugees into Kenya and Ethiopia.

With Siad Barre gone, the Abgal group, under a prominent Mogadishu trader named Ali Mahdi, established an interim government. But this move created suspicions among Aidid's group, sparking renewed fighting in the capital between the two groups for six months. Finally, a USC party congress in July elected Aidid chairman and permitted Mahdi to stay on as interim president. Tensions persisted nevertheless and, by September, had flared up into heavy street fighting, leaving the capital divided between the Abgal and Aidid-run clans.

Even during the fighting, the Abgal government was sending emissaries to powerful countries abroad, attempting to win recognition and support. In addition, Abgal leaders began talks with the northern Isaq clan and its organization. Misunderstanding and jealousies between regions and clans continued to disrupt the talks, however, and the Isaq organization remained cool to the idea of joining the interim government.

Instead of joining an alliance with southerners, the Isaqs were successfully allying themselves with other clans in the northwest, an alliance based on their mutual distrust and hatred of southerners and the memories of the atrocities that Siad Barre had committed against the peoples of the northwest. At a conference in May 1991, the Isaqs and others in the area declared their region—formerly British Somaliland—independent of the south. Somalia was breaking apart along the old imperialist boundaries that Britain and Italy had set a hundred years earlier. It had two interim governments that refused to recognize each other, both of which were actively seeking international recognition. Neither group would gain that recognition. Mahdi's "government" represented only the capital of Mogadishu (and sometimes only a few key neighborhoods of that city). By contrast, the Isaqs' SNM controlled much of the country, at least on paper, but they did not have access to the remaining shreds of government administration in the capital.

Throughout 1992, then, the country remained divided along clan lines, based on divisions that had been deepened by Siad Barre's covert use of clan loyalties to reinforce his power. As they gained access to improved weapons, the clans sought first for revenge

against enemy clans. Increasingly fearful and enraged, they launched invasions of other clans' territories and organized to defend their own territories against attack. The year was marked by some of the most vicious fighting in the war. Mogadishu was being destroyed in the sustained street fighting between the various factions. The commercial and industrial sectors of the economy were in ruins, and even agriculture was being affected. The standard of living for ordinary Somalis, already at a low ebb, began to spiral downward again. Hunger and starvation were spreading throughout the south. Moreover, the fighting had driven the United Nations and virtually all international aid agencies out of the country, compounding the suffering. And when the effort was made to bring in supplies through the Mogadishu airport, the goods were looted by various factions, sparking resentment outside the city and a belief that the international community supported the Hawiye.

International Intervention— and Withdrawal

With the intense suffering of Somali civilians gaining increasing attention in the world's media, the international community began to respond. After failed UN mediation, U.S. President George H.W. Bush, recently defeated for reelection, decided to send U.S. troops to Somalia in December under the operational name "Restore Hope." The 30,000-man force—known officially as the Unified Task Force (UNITAF), then the United Nations Operation in Somalia (UNOSOM), and drawn from first-world (largely the United States), Islamic, and African countries—was given the mission of securing peace, mediating between the clans, and ensuring the safe and effective delivery of food aid to the civilian population of the country.

At first, UNOSOM seemed effective in cooling the fighting near Mogadishu and ensuring food deliveries, but it soon got caught up in the clan struggles. In attempting to mediate disputes, it accepted warlords and their representatives as serious negotiators. Many of these leaders proved to be more interested in using the talks to improve the position of their clan and blaming violence on others than in bringing an end to the conflict. UNOSOM commanders began to interpret the hostilities as direct attacks on them. Then Aidid's forces did attack UNOSOM troops and killed twenty-three Pakistani soldiers to prevent delivery of arms and food to their opponents in the city. UNOSOM immediately set out to capture Aidid. In July, a U.S. helicopter raid on a building suspected of being Aidid's Mogadishu headquarters accidentally killed seventy-three Somali elders holding a peace conference, increasing the animosities between UNOSOM and Aidid's forces.

The United States and UNOSOM received warnings from Somalis and international experts to call off their search for Aidid and end the spiraling violence. Yet, they persisted in their efforts. On October 3, UNOSOM forces engaged in an all-night battle with Aidid's men, leading to the death of nineteen UNOSOM soldiers. When television news showed Somali forces dragging the body of a dead U.S. Marine through the streets of Mogadishu, public support in the United States for the mission to Somalia ended. American and European countries soon announced that they would withdraw in March 1994. U.S. military leaders felt humiliated by the incident and bitter that the Somalis seemed unable to negotiate in good faith. The United Nations was forced to revise its mandate in Somalia. Disgusted by the continuing quagmire, the UN also withdrew in March.

The withdrawal seemed to spur Aidid and Mahdi to reach an agreement over the crucial question of access to the port and airport in Mogadishu, but this agreement also was quickly violated by both sides. After a conference of pro-Aidid groups in southern Somalia elected Aidid "president" of yet another interim government, conflict quickly reemerged between Aidid and opposition groups. Aidid captured the southern port of Baidoa, but renewed fighting broke out in Mogadishu at the end of 1995 and lasted into the summer. In August 1996, Aidid died in a skirmish, and many were hopeful that his death might lead to an end to the fighting. It did not. His son, Hussein Muhammed Aidid, was elected to replace his father and vowed to continue the armed struggle. Following a failed October cease-fire, fighting continued throughout the country into early 1997.

Meanwhile, renewed efforts to find a peaceful solution to the conflict proceeded. In December 1996, the leaders of more than twenty-five Somali factions—with the notable exception of Aidid's—met in Ethiopia, where they hammered out a resolution calling for a forty-one-member National Salvation Council (NSF), with nine members from each of the four major clans and a total of five from the smaller ones. Hussein Ai-

did, however, rejected the council, insisting he was the rightfully elected president of Somalia.

Still, the NSF tried to find a way to end the fighting. When information was obtained pointing to an illicit trade between European Union countries and various clans—whereby Somalia's banana crop was exchanged for weapons—the NSF won an EU decision to halt the imports of Somali fruit. The NSF also gained financial aid for a national reconciliation conference, which was held early in 1997 in Ethiopia.

While the NSF was seeking international help, Aidid and Mahdi were attempting to resolve the differences between their groups. In January 1997, the two met and agreed to the rules established by the October 1996 cease-fire, which included halting the fighting, removing roadblocks, ending inflammatory propaganda broadcasts, helping the delivery of food aid, and permitting the free movement of people throughout the capital. Still, Aidid refused to accept a power-sharing agreement reached at the Ethiopian national reconciliation conference.

It is estimated that tens of thousands of Somalis died in these years of fighting, while hundreds of thousands succumbed to the starvation and disease the war helped to create. The conflict left the country shattered, not only politically and economically but also culturally and socially. In the early 2000s, approximately 2 million Somali refugees were scattered around the globe, most of them in the neighboring countries of Kenya, Ethiopia, and Djibouti. In addition, roughly 50 percent of the population within the country were considered by the UN to be internally displaced people (IDP), most of them living in and around the capital, Mogadishu. Although the era of major open battles ended in the mid-1990s, a low-intensity conflict among clans persisted in the capital and other regions.

Efforts to End the Conflict

The political efforts to end the conflict continued. In 2004 leading Somalis met in Kenya and established the Somali Transitional Federal Government (TFG). Colonel Abdullah Yusuf Ahmed was elected interim president, although he was opposed by many factions. Many Somalis were skeptical about Yusuf Ahmed's leadership, seeing him as a potential stalking horse for the government of neighboring Ethiopia, which had designs on Somali territory. The TFG, with its base in the Kenyan capital, Nairobi, hoped to return to

Somalia to become the resident government. But during months of waiting, it became detached from the everyday life of Somalia. Yusuf Ahmed seemed aware of his government's unpopularity, as he requested that the African Union send troops to protect its move to Jawhar, a city just outside the old capital of Mogadishu.

Meanwhile, the TGF made it a top priority to unify the clans under a single government. This meant bringing self-governing territories such as Somaliland, autonomous since 1991, and Puntland, under its own leadership since 1998, into the national polity. (Both regional governments were relatively stable, but neither was recognized internationally.) TGF plans called for unifying the government, disarming roughly 50,000 clan-based militiamen, establishing a judicial system, and rebuilding the economy with foreign aid.

Establishing a new basis of national leadership was essential to the process, experts said. In the long civil war, the authority of traditional clan elders was undermined; a new political elite called the shots and told the clan elders what to do. In addition, there was a need to build a stronger civil society, with an emphasis on creating new educational institutions and allowing small businesses to take the lead in recreating the country's shattered economy. The Somali Leadership Foundation (FALSAN) was one of the major actors in this sector. Finally, there was the matter of the Islamist movement. Organizations and parties such as Al Ittihaad Al Islami, and Islah, rose above clan-based loyalties and demonstrated a far greater sense of social responsibility than other parties. They played a major role in establishing civil society in the capital. However, the Islamists were denied opportunities to participate in the peace meetings. To succeed, observers argued, the TGF had to find a way of integrating them into the political process.

International efforts to resolve the Somalian civil conflict intensified in the early 2000s. The Intergovernmental Authority on Development (IGAD) gathered all East African nations in an effort to resolve conflicts in the region. IGAD considered not only the conditions inside Somalia, but also the effects of the long struggle on neighboring states. The body's primary fields of focus were conflict prevention, infrastructure development, food security, and environment protection.

In June 2006, militias loyal to the religious and political organization Union of Islamic Courts took control of Mogadishu. This raised international concerns that an extremist government, such as the former Taliban in Afghanistan, was seizing power in the country, which might foster a haven for Islamist terrorists.

James Ciment and Emin Poljarevic

See also: Ethnic and Religious Conflicts; Ethiopia: War with Somalia, 1977–1978; Ethiopia: Civil War, 1978–1991.

Bibliography

Abraham, Knife. *Somalia Calling: The Crisis of Statehood and Quest for Peace.* Addis Ababa, EIIPD, 2002.

Africa Watch. *Somalia: A Government at War with Its Own People: Testimonies About the Killings and the Conflict in the North.* New York: Africa Watch Committee, 1990.

Fox, Mary-Jane. *Political Culture in Somalia: Tracing Paths to Peace and Conflict.* Uppsala, Sweden. Uppsala University, 2000.

Ghalib, Jama Mohamed. *The Cost of Dictatorship: The Somalian Experience.* New York: L. Barber, 1994.

Laitin, David D. *Somalia: Nation in Search of a State.* Boulder, CO: Westview, 1987.

Lewis, I.M. *A Modern History of Somalia: Nation and State in the Horn of Africa.* Boulder, CO: Westview Press, 1988.

Lyons, Terrence. *Somalia: State Collapse, Multilateral Intervention, and Strategies for Political Reconstruction.* Washington, DC: Brookings Institution, 1995.

Makinda, Sam. *Seeking Peace from Chaos: Humanitarian Intervention in Somalia.* Boulder, CO: Lynne Rienner, 1993.

Sahnoun, Mohamed. *Somalia: The Missed Opportunities.* Washington, DC: Institute of Peace Press, 1994.

Samatar, Ahmed I. *Socialist Somalia: Rhetoric and Reality.* Atlantic Highlands, NJ: Zed Books, 1988.

SOUTH AFRICA: Anti-Apartheid Struggle, 1948–1994

TYPE OF CONFLICT: Ethnic and Religious; Anticolonialism

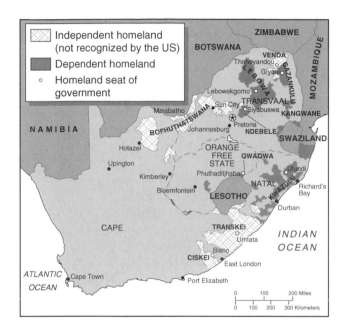

Independent homeland (not recognized by the US)
Dependent homeland
○ Homeland seat of government

The African and multiracial struggle against the apartheid, or official racial segregation, system of South Africa represents one of the longest, bitterest, but ultimately most successful liberation movements of the post–World War II era. Utilizing guerrilla attacks, bombings, mass demonstrations, and strikes, the outlawed African National Congress (ANC) and its anti-apartheid allies in the labor and religious spheres eventually forced the ruling National Party to legalize black opposition organizations, free anti-apartheid leaders such as Nelson Mandela, dismantle apartheid legislation, and permit full and universal suffrage in open and free elections. Along the way, the ANC was supported by a growing international movement of sanctions, often inspired by solidarity demonstrations among people of goodwill throughout the world.

The struggle was not an easy one. The ruling white National Party utilized brutal tactics to suppress the movement. As noted above, these steps included

banning anti-apartheid organizations and the imprisonment of anti-apartheid leaders. But it also involved massive repression and violence directed against the rank and file of the anti-apartheid movement, as well as against ordinary blacks in South Africa. The South African government organized and sustained its own black organizations that engaged in bitter ethnic fighting with ANC supporters. In defense of apartheid, the South African government also launched invasions of and supported rebel armies in neighboring black-ruled states, forcing them to cut their ties to the ANC.

Historical Background

One of the cradles of humanity, the area that is now South Africa has been inhabited by humans and their ancestors for more than a million years. In historic times, the region was settled by a number of ethnic groups. These include the Xhosa-speaking peoples around the western Cape, the Venda- and Tswana-speaking peoples in the central and northern parts of the country, and the Zulu speakers in the northeast.

The first Europeans to arrive in the region were the Dutch, who established provisioning stations for Dutch East India Company ships making the long journey around Africa to the East Indies. Further settlements of Dutch, French, German, and British settlers added to the population of the Cape colony through the eighteenth century, leading to its official incorporation into the British Empire in 1806 and rising enmity between the British Crown and the descendants of the original Dutch settlers, known as Boers or, later, Afrikaners. With the banning of slavery in the empire in 1834, the Boers—who spoke a dialect of Dutch called Afrikaans—emigrated to the interior in what they call the "great trek," attacking the native Africans and seizing their lands in the

KEY DATES

1912   The African National Congress (ANC) is founded to fight discrimination against native Africans in South Africa.

1948   The Afrikaner-dominated National Party (NP) takes power in elections on a platform of formal separation, or apartheid, of South African blacks, whites, Asians, and mixed race, or colored, persons.

1955   Africans, Asians, colored persons, and whites meet to write the Freedom Charter, calling for a nonracial democracy in South Africa.

1960   Seventy African anti-apartheid protesters are shot down by police in Sharpeville; the ANC is banned.

1964   ANC leader Nelson Mandela and other ANC officials are sentenced to life in prison.

1976   Protesting government efforts to impose the Afrikaner language in African schools, students in Soweto protest in the streets; dozens are killed by police.

1990   Responding to more than a decade of mass demonstrations and an international movement to economically isolate South Africa, the NP government legalizes the ANC and releases Mandela and other ANC leaders from prison.

1994   Mandela is elected president, and the ANC wins a majority of seats in parliament in South Africa's first elections open to citizens of all races.

process. While Britain annexed Natal province (now KwaZulu-Natal), they permitted the formation of two independent Boer republics—the Orange Free State (now Free State) and the Transvaal (now Gauteng)—but only for a time.

The discovery of diamonds and then gold in the Transvaal, beginning in the 1860s, led to a massive realignment of South Africa's political and economic landscape. Waves of miners from around the world poured into the region, leading to the imposition of white rule over the remaining African-controlled areas, but only after a bitter struggle with the Zulu nation. The growing wealth and power of the Transvaal inspired imperial ambitions, and the British occupied the Boer republics. The Boers rose up in a rebellion to preserve their independence, but were ultimately defeated after three years of guerrilla-style warfare from 1899 to 1902. In 1910, the Union of South Africa was declared an independent dominion under the British Crown.

At the same time, the various British-owned mining companies in South Africa—increasingly powerful as they consolidated their control over the rich deposits of gold and diamonds—imported East Indians and recruited black Africans to do the heavy labor in the mines and to build the transportation and manufacturing infrastructure necessary to the industry. Unique in Africa, then, South Africa early on saw the formation of an urban black proletariat.

Independent South Africa

The Union Constitution of 1910 offered the franchise to white males only, though the so-called "coloreds," or mixed-race persons, around the Cape colony were included. The white electorate was divided into two main groups: the Afrikaners and the English. The much more numerous Afrikaners were led by Boer general Jan Smuts and Louis Botha. They organized the South Africa Party (SAP), though an anti-imperialist, anti-mining group broke off in 1912 to form the National Party (NP) under the leadership of J.B.M. Hertzog. At the same time, the disenfranchised African elites, under the chairmanship of Pixley Seme, formed the African Native National Congress, soon renamed the African National Congress (ANC).

The first independent South African legislation to control the African population was the Land Act of 1913, denying the right of Africans to purchase land outside of their native reserves. The intent of the law was to force Africans to serve as migrant laborers in the mines. World War I, which began a year after the act was passed, represented a major watershed in South African history for several reasons. First, it led to South African control of the former German colony of Southwest Africa (now Namibia). Second, the war resulted in the formation of the secret Broederbond society of Afrikaner leaders, who established political cells in virtually every major institution of South African life and eventually paved the way for Afrikaner control of the South African government.

Finally, and most importantly, the war resulted in a new wave of urbanization as Africans poured in to work in the mines and industries. The squalid living conditions in the ghettos of South African cities led to a huge number of deaths from the influenza pandemic after the war. And the influx renewed fears of African domination among the white population. In 1923, the government passed its second major piece of racial legislation: the Natives (Urban Areas) Act, making it illegal for Africans to live in most urban areas.

The inflow of African miners also led to a decision by mine owners to replace highly paid white workers with blacks. This move led to a strike by poor Afrikaner workers, which was suppressed by government troops. The Labour Party, in an alliance with the NP, won the parliamentary elections of 1924. The new majority formulated the so-called civilized labor policy, whereby blacks were barred from virtually all skilled and semiskilled jobs. In 1936, the National Party and the South African Party reunited to form the United Party (UP) and gained a parliamentary majority. It passed another Land Act, excluding coloreds from owning land outside certain areas (but still allowing them to vote). The unification of the two Afrikaner parties also led its most conservative members to break away and form the "purified" NP, led by the Broederbond.

During World War II, this party would support Nazi Germany.

Like World War I, World War II accelerated South African urbanization and industrialization, as the country was forced to manufacture products no longer available from Europe and America. Thousands of black workers poured into factories, as the restrictions of the "civilized labor" policy were eased. The need for black labor also reinvigorated the African National Congress, which had been hard hit by the Great Depression of the 1930s. Now the ANC demanded universal suffrage and helped organize African trade unions. Prime Minister Smuts rejected its democratic reforms—and used the military to crush a black mine workers' strike in 1946—but his United Party accepted the need for some reforms, allowing some of the black workers into skilled positions. Smuts's "liberal" stance and a depressed agricultural sector brought new support to the right-wing, racist National Party, which narrowly won the 1948 elections and introduced the system that would come to be known as apartheid.

Apartheid

Apartheid was not merely, as it name suggests, a system of racial segregation, but a series of laws intended to guarantee the white minority in South Africa economic dominance, political control, and social supremacy. At first, there was little attempt to justify the apartheid system. Among the Afrikaners who dominated the government that imposed it, there was a general belief that Africans and other races were simply inferior to whites both biologically and culturally, incapable of running their own affairs and in need of white leadership and white-maintained law and order.

As the rest of black Africa won its independence in the 1950s and 1960s, however, a new antiracist consciousness spread through the industrialized world. This development forced South African whites to develop a rationale for their system of racial separation. They argued that the different cultures of South Africa required separation for them to reach their fullest potential. For example, the government took steps to enable Africans to develop along "their own lines" in the native reserves assigned to them, though this was often interpreted to mean archaic, preindustrial tribal lines, no longer appropriate for a modern society. The government handpicked chiefs to govern these areas, giving them extraordinarily broad powers that undermined traditional forms of African democracy.

From 1948 to 1959, a series of interrelated laws were passed that restructured South African society to fit the ideals of apartheid. Among the first of these laws was the Population Registration Act, which classified all South Africans into various racial groups—white, black, or colored (a class that included East Indians, other Asians, and people of mixed parentage). This was the keystone for all subsequent apartheid legislation, which was based on these classifications. Thereafter, the government passed the Immorality Act, banning all sexual relations between the races and forbidding interracial marriage. Another law designed to separate social intermingling was the Separate Amenities Act, which sanctioned separate public and private facilities for the different races and specifically stated that these need not be of equal quality.

Similarly, the government passed the Bantu Education Act, "Bantu" being a pejorative word, in the South African context, for black Africans. Under this legislation, control over black education was shifted from the Ministry of Education, which had tried to promote somewhat equal educational opportunities, to the Ministry for Native Affairs, which saw its mission as keeping blacks under control.

Equally significant were the laws designed to regulate black movement and labor. Legislation was enacted that further restricted black access to skilled jobs. Urban segregation was enforced through the Group Areas Act, which required different races to live in different districts of metropolitan areas and towns. Pass laws were instituted that required blacks to present identification showing that they were permitted to be in a given white area, usually for work purposes only. The many violations that this act inevitably produced provided prison labor that subsidized South Africa's agriculture industry.

At the same time that these restrictive laws were being passed, legislation was also being enacted that curtailed political activity not just by blacks but by opposition forces of all races, including whites. Under the Suppression of Communism Act, the powerful South African Communist Party was banned, along with many other opposition organizations under the loosely worded law. The act took away the voting rights of people in the colored class in the Cape Province. This result effectively reduced the power of the more moderate United Party, which colored voters had long supported.

Resistance and Repression

In response to this repressive legislation, the ANC—allied with the South African Indian Congress (SAIC)—began a campaign of mass civil disobedience, with members purposely violating segregation laws. At the same time, a coalition of black, colored, and liberal white forces met in 1955 to hammer out the Freedom Charter, calling for a nonracial South Africa. These moves sparked drastic retaliation by the government, which put most of the opposition leaders on trial for treason. Though acquitted after some five years on trial, their indictments deprived the anti-apartheid movement of its leadership at a critical moment in South African history. In 1960, South Africa declared itself a republic and applied for membership in the British Commonwealth, but it was rejected after strong protests from black African states that were already members of the Commonwealth.

During that same year, repression of anti-apartheid activism turned extremely violent. At a rally in the Johannesburg township of Sharpeville in March, police opened fire on unarmed demonstrators, leaving sixty-seven dead and hundreds wounded. After the massacre, members of the international community began to discuss ostracizing South Africa and imposing sanctions. Inside the country, the government responded to the growing unrest by banning the ANC and its more radical sister organization, the Pan African Congress (PAC). Under the leadership of Nelson Mandela, the ANC formed a military wing, the *Unkhonto we Sizwe* (Spear of the Nation, or SN), and the PAC founded Poqo. Together, they launched a campaign of sabotage against white property and government facilities, making a point of avoiding violence against persons. With the help of the U.S. Central Intelligence Agency, the South African government was able to capture Mandela and other ANC leaders, who were put on trial and sentenced to life imprisonment. Others fled the country to continue the struggle from abroad.

To counter pressure from the world community, the South African government developed a plan that it believed would pass muster under international law. In 1963, it began to "decolonize" South Africa by establishing "independent" homelands for Africans. Under this plan, South Africa's regulations on black mobility and segregation would fall under the internationally recognized right of all governments to regulate the movement of "foreigners" in their territory. In 1963, Transkei—or Bantustan, as it was often called—became the first such homeland with its own government. Six others followed in the early 1970s: Ciskei, Bophuthatswana, Lebowa, Venda, Gazankulu, Qwaqwa, and KwaZulu. Though containing traditional territories of the various ethnic groups, the Bantustans were much smaller than the traditional territories, usually including only the poorest agricultural land. The South African government also developed industry around the periphery of the homelands to make use of low-paid African laborers, who would be required to return to the homeland each night.

To further enhance the policy of making non-Bantustan South Africa a fully white country, new and stricter controls were placed on blacks living in urban areas. Increasingly, black workers were required to leave their families in the homelands while working in the cities. Living in rundown and overcrowded workers' barracks, they could see their families only occasionally. The homelands thus began to serve as warehouses for surplus labor.

By the 1970s, the market for migrant labor was declining, as modernization eliminated the need for much low-skilled labor. The homelands grew increasingly impoverished, and more blacks violated the laws to live in urban areas. Meanwhile, blacks with the right to live in the urban townships began to demand skilled and better-paying jobs, especially since there was a shortage of white labor. In 1973, these various pressures resulted in a massive wave of African labor strikes, which paralyzed South African mines and factories. While the government of John Vorster accepted some of the black demands, it also granted full "independence" to several of the homelands. These states were then turned over to handpicked tribal leaders willing to do Pretoria's bidding. However, none of these so-called independent nations was ever recognized by a single foreign government.

Another crisis facing the apartheid government in the mid-1970s concerned developing conflicts on its borders. In 1975, Portugal abruptly pulled out of its southern African colonies of Angola and Mozambique. Mozambique shared a long border with South Africa, and Angola bordered its illegal colony of Namibia. Suddenly both were governed by socialist and strongly anti-apartheid regimes. To keep these governments from supporting the exiled African National Congress—and to prove that black Africans were incapable of self-government—the South African military launched invasions and supported rebel movements in both countries to undermine their economies and destabilize their governments. Eventually defeated in Angola in the late 1980s, the South African military was forced to withdraw. Faced with an independence movement in Namibia, the South Africans also agreed in 1988 to grant Namibia its independence by 1990.

Resistance and Repression Intensifies

The Soweto uprising, the largest black racial clash in South African history up to that time, began as a walkout by black students in Soweto, a huge impoverished black township about fifteen miles from Johannesburg. The students were protesting the requirement that they learn the Afrikaans language. Police met the marching children and opened fire without warning, killing 172 and injuring 439. Within hours, demonstrations spread across the entire country, prompting more crackdowns by police over the next year. Hundreds of demonstrators who had not been killed or arrested fled South Africa and joined the liberation organizations in exile. Most joined the African National Congress, which became the most powerful organization representing South Africa's black population.

Prime Minister Vorster responded to the widespread unrest with a plan to divide the resistance movement along racial lines. Since no homelands could be developed for coloreds—since they had no traditional territory in South Africa—the Vorster government proposed the formation of a new parliament with separate houses for coloreds and Asians. In the 1977 elections, the arch-conservative National Party (NP) won the whites-only election overwhelmingly, but was challenged for the first time by a liberal opposition party, the Progressive Federal Party. The plan for a legislature with three houses was soon sunk by hard-liners in the NP.

The following year Vorster was eased out of office as a result of a corruption scandal. The new prime minister was P.W. Botha, who began easing some of the apartheid system's restrictions. Certain job restrictions were lifted, and more trade union activities were permitted. New laws allowed blacks

In the aftermath of the Soweto uprising of June 1976, major anti-apartheid demonstrations were held in Cape Town (seen here) and throughout South Africa. The police responded with a harsh crackdown, escalating the violence. *(AFP/Getty Images)*

to obtain long-term leases on their homes. Blacks with rights to be in urban areas were allowed to move freely from one town to another, and the laws against interracial sex and marriage were repealed. As had happened earlier, these modest reforms sparked a secession by hard-liners in the National Party and the formation of the Conservative Party of South Africa (CPSA). With the ultra-conservatives gone from the ruling party, Botha was able to institute the three-house legislature, which went into effect in 1984.

As it turned out, the plan to provide token representation for blacks and coloreds backfired. In August 1983, various multiracial, anti-apartheid organizations gathered to form the United Democratic Front (UDF) in opposing the three-house plan. They pointed out that huge numbers of blacks had been subtracted from the South African total by making them citizens of the so-called independent homelands. In low-turnout elections in 1984, colored voters overwhelmingly voted against the plan. At the same time, a new wave of township rebellions spread across the country in opposition to the plan. The demonstrators were supported by the newly formed Congress of South African Trade Unions (COSATU),

representing black trade unionists, which launched a series of solidarity strikes that paralyzed the country.

Township violence escalated again in 1985, following yet another police massacre of black protesters, this time memorializing the twenty-fifth anniversary of the Sharpeville massacre. Twenty blacks were killed when police opened fire in Uitenhage, a township outside Port Elizabeth. Protests and demonstrations were met by police violence across the country, leading to the imposition of a state of emergency in July. The emergency allowed increased police powers, but the government was losing control of the black townships to "comrades," who killed or terrorized the many police informers and collaborators living in their midst.

In Natal province, one black group took up arms against the African National Congress. The Zulu-supported Inkatha movement, under Chief Mangosuthu Buthelezi, a minister in the government of the KwaZulu homeland, led the attack. At first, outsiders saw this as ethnic-based violence between the Zulu people and the Xhosa, who supported the ANC. The ANC insisted that the black-versus-black violence was largely instigated by the government. Years later, when police files were opened during "truth" hearings, the ANC claims were corroborated.

By 1987, the combination of a massive army presence and a large expenditure of government funds for housing and social service in the black townships quieted the situation. In other parts of the world, however, the actions of the South African government continued to cause outrage. Under pressure from student and worker demonstrations in Europe and the United States, governments began applying economic sanctions to South Africa. The conservative administrations of President Ronald Reagan in the United States and Prime Minister Margaret Thatcher in Britain tried to resist sanctions but were gradually persuaded to go along.

Supporters of sanctions also targeted international corporations doing business in South Africa. Many companies decided they could not take the bad publicity and began withdrawing from their South African operations, often selling them to South African interests. Even though South Africa had long prided itself on its self-reliance, the country soon discovered that its economy suffered when foreign investment and business with other countries began to dry up and a large number of its experienced managers began to leave. The South African currency, the rand, collapsed.

The country's growing economic problems had a polarizing effect on politics. The liberal wing of the National Party, under Prime Minister Botha, was beginning to move toward negotiations that might lead to government participation with cooperative black leaders such as Buthelezi. By this time, however, blacks in South Africa had united behind the African National Congress and its long-imprisoned leader, Nelson Mandela. Trade unions and black church leaders such as Bishop Desmond Tutu were solidly behind the ANC. Equally important in thwarting Botha's plans was the lurch toward the right among a large part of the Afrikaner population. The Afrikaanse Weerstandsbeweging—a right-wing paramilitary organization launched by Eugene TerreBlanche in 1977—was growing in popularity and recruiting heavily among the country's various security forces. And in the all-white parliamentary elections of 1987, the arch-conservative CPSA became the main opposition party. In such a polarized environment, it seemed that South Africa might erupt in unimaginable violence.

Apartheid Abandoned

There were some on both sides who were already at work trying to prevent a violent outcome. As early as 1987, influential members of the Afrikaner elite were secretly meeting with leaders of the ANC (technically breaking the law). These meetings were being encouraged quietly by elements in the Botha administration. By 1989, however, Botha had had enough and announced his resignation from the presidency, citing ill health as the reason. Before leaving office, he met with Nelson Mandela, the ANC leader, at the Robbins Island prison off the coast of Cape Town. Even though Mandela had been in jail for more than twenty-five years, Botha acknowledged that both Mandela and the ANC would have a role in negotiating the end of the apartheid regime. In August elections, F.W. de Klerk was elected president, and the National Party retained a clear but diminished majority in parliament.

The full crisis was reached in 1989. The economy was deteriorating rapidly. International isolation and opprobrium were reaching a fever pitch. Indeed, new administrations in London and Washington—though still conservative—were joining in the efforts to pressure Pretoria. Black protesters and organizations had made it clear that no compromise measures such as the three-house parliament would be acceptable. Africans from the impoverished homelands were pouring into the townships in such numbers that the security forces could no longer contain them.

The ANC also faced problems—including continued opposition from Inkatha and the loss of support from collapsing socialist-bloc governments in Eastern Europe and the Soviet Union. Yet it was clearly recognized by the international community as the only legitimate negotiating partner, a realization that was increasingly dawning on de Klerk and the mainstream NP leadership. In September, the Bush administration announced that if Mandela was not freed within six months, the U.S. government would go along with strict UN sanctions against South Africa.

Speaking before the three houses of parliament on February 2, 1990, de Klerk announced that he was releasing Mandela and ending the legal ban on the African National Congress and other anti-apartheid parties, including the South African Communist Party (SACP). He also announced that it was the government's intention to open negotiations that would lead to equality for all South African citizens and universal suffrage. On February 11, in front of the international press corps, Mandela walked to freedom after twenty-seven years in prison. ANC exiles began to return to the country.

The joyous moment was shadowed by several looming problems for the ANC, which was internally divided between radicals, who demanded a social and economic revolution for the country, and conservatives, who insisted that the capitalist system in South Africa be retained in the post-apartheid era. Moreover, the ANC would have a difficult time imposing discipline on the "young comrades" in the townships who had come of age in a time of violent opposition to apartheid and retained a commitment to street confrontation. The ANC also faced challenges to its authority from Inkatha—still being provided heavy covert support by the government—as well as from the black nationalist PAC.

ANC-Government Negotiations and Renewed Violence

In May 1990, as some of the more egregious segregation restrictions of the apartheid regime were reversed, the ANC met in negotiations with the de Klerk administration. The ANC agreed to end its guerrilla operations but refused to accede to the government's plan for a multiparty conference to draw up a new constitution in which each party would represent a race and have an equal voice. The possibility of a peaceful transition to a post-apartheid era was further threatened by violence between ANC and Inkatha supporters that was spreading beyond Natal to other sections of the country.

Although the government faced increasingly vocal and violent opposition from hard-line white groups, it eliminated the last remaining apartheid legislation during 1991, including the Group Areas Act and the so-called pass laws restricting black movement. The National Party even invited blacks to join it. As the restrictions fell, the international community began to lift its sanctions, despite ANC pleas to hold off until free and universal elections were held. Meanwhile, the ANC had effected a rapprochement with the PAC at a conference in April.

Still, the violence between the ANC and Inkatha continued to escalate, despite meetings between Mandela and Buthelezi. The ANC threatened to walk out of the negotiations unless the government did more to stop the violence. Suspicions remained among ANC and PAC supporters that certain elements within the security forces were still aiding Inkatha. For example, eyewitnesses to a massacre of women and children in Biopatong, Natal, by Inkatha fighters in June 1992 reported seeing the fighters arrive in police vehicles.

After a request by Mandela in July, the UN Security Council sent an investigative commission to look into the South African security forces' complicity in the ANC-Inkatha violence. Their findings confirmed Mandela's fears and led to the dispatch of peacekeepers to South Africa. At the same time, the ANC and its allies organized mass actions—including a two-day general strike—demanding that the government negotiate in good faith and end Inkatha violence. When police in the homeland of Ciskei fired on ANC marchers, killing 28 and wounding 200 others, Mandela demanded the dismantling of homeland governments and an end to their spurious independence.

In November, the ANC and the de Klerk government announced the formation of an interim government, headed by a joint commission of ANC and NP members. This collaboration angered many in both organizations. Outsiders were also alarmed, fearing that an agreement on a new constitution was imminent. The fear was sustained by both Inkatha and white conservatives, who believed that the constitutional reforms would favor the two main parties. A group of officials from Inkatha and the various homelands organized the Concerned South Africans Group in April 1993, aimed at pressuring the negotiators to enhance the power of regional governments over the federal one.

Violence also greeted the impending announcement of a constitution, as a series of terrorist bombings against white civilians—allegedly by members of the Azanian People's Liberation Army, the new military wing of the PAC—rocked the country. Then, as the forum negotiating the coming elections announced April 27, 1994, as the date for the country's first nonracial poll, 2,000 armed white commandos occupied the conference center. The commandos surrendered peacefully after several days, but ANC officials accused the security forces of laxity, if not complicity. Not so peaceful was the continuing conflict with Inkatha. In August, Inkatha forces near Johannesburg attacked a migrant workers' hostel, killing 100 persons, largely ANC supporters.

In November, the forum offered details of the interim constitution. New provinces with new names were included, and the homelands disappeared as political entities. Plans for the legislative and executive branches were drawn up with an eye to the various regions and races of the country. A central parliament with 400 members would be drawn, half from national and half from regional lists of candidates. There would be one president and two vice presidents, the latter apportioned to parties obtaining at least 20 percent of the vote. This was done to placate the National Party and its white members. Any party with 5 percent of the vote would be entitled to a cabinet member. Meanwhile, it was left up to the assembly to draw up a permanent constitution within two years of its election.

Both the ANC and the NP had difficulties lining up support among their respective racial communities, though the ANC had the harder time of it. De Klerk was able to persuade right-wing groups to go along with the new constitution by promising them a possible future province of their own in a majority-ruled South Africa. Meanwhile, Buthelezi and Inkatha, though initially agreeing to register for the elections as the Inkatha Freedom Party (IFP), soon pulled out and threatened a boycott. These actions came at a time when fighting between the ANC and Inkatha was intensifying. In March, a state of emergency was declared in Natal, and troops were sent in, but the violence continued. An alliance between Inkatha and white right-wing forces—potentially plunging the country into civil war—now seemed possible.

The possibility ended, however, after right-wing forces tried but failed to bolster the Bophuthatswana homeland government, which was besieged by protesters. The humiliating retreat of Afrikaner extremists in the face of black resistance fighters deflated the right-wing cause, just as the collapse of the homeland government further isolated Buthelezi. Still, Buthelezi persisted with his threats to boycott the elections up to the last minute, changing his mind only when he won several concessions concerning the sovereignty of the Zulu monarch—largely a figurehead for Inkatha. Buthelezi's announcement on April 21 that he would participate in the April 24 elections immediately ended much of the violence in Natal and ensured that the election went off smoothly.

Elections and ANC Government

The elections produced the predicted ANC landslide, though the party fell just short of the two-thirds majority necessary to write the new constitution unilaterally. The only other party winning at least 20 percent of the vote was the NP, which entitled de Klerk to serve as vice president in the next administration. Inkatha, which took just 10 percent of the vote nationally, won a slight majority in Natal. The two main parties on the far right and black nationalist left—the Afrikaner Volksfront and the PAC—failed to receive the 5 percent necessary to earn a cabinet position. On May 9, the first truly multiracial national assembly in South African history overwhelmingly elected Mandela as the country's first black president.

The new ANC government faced a host of problems, both foreign and domestic. Recognizing South Africa's history of interference in the internal affairs of neighboring states, it tried to stay out of conflicts in African countries, though Mandela was called in to mediate in various crises, including the Congo crisis of 1997. At home, the government walked a fine line, providing much-needed social and economic improvements in the lives of black South Africans without causing the flight of white citizens and their capital. To assure the international business community that South Africa remained a safe place to invest, Mandela appointed whites from the banking and business community to run the economy. The discrepancies in wealth between the two communities—as well as the absence of apartheid-era restrictions—led to an explosion of crime, though most victims were black.

Political reforms went more smoothly. A draft for the permanent constitution was completed by June 1996, leading the NP to drop out of its coalition with the ANC to become an official opposition party, while the Inkatha Freedom Party remained part of the ruling coalition. Meanwhile, the aging Mandela—whose steady hand and universally acclaimed integrity did so much to ensure a peaceful transition to black majority rule—turned over the day-to-day running of the government and leadership of the ANC to Thabo Mbeki in 1997.

The new government also walked a fine line between punishing those guilty of apartheid-era crimes and trying to turn over a new leaf in South African history. In 1995, the national assembly established a seventeen-member Truth and Reconciliation Commission, headed by Archbishop Desmond Tutu. Under the rules of the commission, victims and perpetrators of violence were permitted to testify, the latter receiving amnesty for full disclosure of their human rights violations and crimes.

The commission was criticized by many—especcially victims of apartheid oppression and the family members of those killed by police—who saw the perpetrators exonerated. Supporters argued that the commission was the only practical way to expose the crimes of the era, since it did not require long, expensive, and potentially divisive court proceedings.

James Ciment

See also: People's Wars; Ethnic and Religious Conflicts; Angola: First War with UNITA, 1975–1992; Mozambique: Renamo War, 1976–1992; Namibia: War of National Liberation, 1966–1990; Zimbabwe: Struggle for Majority Rule, 1965–1980.

Bibliography

Crankshaw, Owen. *Race, Class and the Changing Division of Labour Under Apartheid.* New York: Routledge, 1997.

Gutteridge, William Frank. *South Africa: From Apartheid to National Unity, 1981–1994.* Brookfield, VT: Dartmouth, 1995.

Juckes, Tim J. *Opposition in South Africa: The Leadership of Z.K. Matthews, Nelson Mandela, and Stephen Biko.* Westport, CT: Praeger, 1995.

Kanfer, Stefan. *The Last Empire: South Africa, Diamonds, and De Beers from Cecil Rhodes to the Oppenheimers.* New York: Farrar, Straus and Giroux, 1993.

Le May, G.H.L. *The Afrikaners: An Historical Interpretation.* Cambridge, MA: Blackwell, 1995.

Lester, Alan. *From Colonization to Democracy: A New Historical Geography of South Africa.* New York: Tauris Academic Studies, 1996.

Marx, Anthony W. *Lessons of Struggle: South African Internal Opposition, 1960–1990.* New York: Oxford University Press, 1992.

Murray, Martin J. *South Africa, Time of Agony, Time of Destiny: The Upsurge of Popular Protest.* London: Verso, 1987.

———. *Revolution Deferred: The Painful Birth of Post-Apartheid South Africa.* New York: Verso, 1994.

Thompson, Leonard Monteath. *A History of South Africa.* New Haven, CT: Yale University Press, 1995.

SUDAN: Civil Wars in South, 1955–1972; 1983–2005

TYPE OF CONFLICT: Ethnic and Religious
PARTICIPANTS: Chad; Eritrea; Ethiopia; Uganda

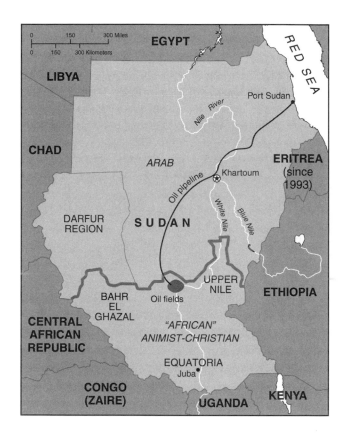

Sudan's civil wars, which have raged intermittently for nearly fifty years, have been the result of the complex religious and ethnic subdivisions that exist within Sudanese society. By the twentieth century, the Sudanese were divided among nineteen major ethnic groups, spoke dozens of different languages, and followed three different religious traditions.

The central divisions within Sudan have been between the Muslim Arab north and the Christian and animist African south. (Animism is the worship of traditional local gods and spirits.) The dividing line between the two groups was rather arbitrary. When Arab attackers brought Islam to the region in the

fifteenth century, the process of conquest and conversion also involved intermarriage and cultural cross-fertilization. The result was that the "Arabs" of the north were of many different ethnic backgrounds, from Semitic to Nilotic, and often looked no different than the "Africans" of the south. "Arab" was as much a cultural and linguistic category as an ethnic one. Many northerners adopted Arabic as their language and Islam as their religion, and therefore called themselves Arabs. (Other northerners were Muslims but did not consider themselves Arabs.)

In the south, the African peoples kept the animist religion of their ancestors. In the nineteenth century, the arrival of Christian missionaries added a third religious tradition to Sudan's mix. (A form of Christianity had existed in Sudan many centuries before the Europeans arrived but had died out by the eighteenth century.) The missionaries had more success in the south, which became divided between animists and Christians, with a small number of Muslims.

The relationship between north and south Sudan was traditionally hostile. The Arabs of the north sent soldiers, slavers, and bureaucrats to oppress the peoples of the south. The Africans felt that the Arab elites in Khartoum, Sudan's capital, were contemptuous toward the cultures of the south and treated them as second-class citizens.

Although this view of north-south relations was not completely accurate on either side—the Arabs and the Africans had a complex history, and the Arabs were not always its villains—it was accepted by many southerners, encouraging suspicion and distrust.

In 1899, Sudan was conquered by an Anglo-Egyptian army and made a part of the British Empire. Although Sudan was officially the joint conquest of the Egyptians and British, it was the British who actually ruled the country. The British administered

KEY DATES

1956 Sudan wins its independence from joint British-Egyptian rule.

1962 Southern Sudanese exiles form the Sudan African National Union, while rebels within the south of Sudan form the Anya-Nya ("Venom of the Viper") rebel movement, which launches its first attack on Sudanese government targets the following year.

1970 Efforts to end infighting among southerners lead southern rebels to form the unified Southern Sudan Liberation Movement.

1972 The Government of Sudan (GOS) and rebel leaders sign the Addis Ababa Agreement on February 28, ending the first phase of the southern Sudanese civil war.

1983 When the GOS tries to impose Islamic law in the country, southern army units rebel; GOS sends Colonel John Garang, a southerner, to put down the rebellion, but he joins it instead.

1989 A military coup puts a hard-line Islamic government in power in Khartoum.

1991 Rebel movement in the south splits along tribal lines.

2001 A separate conflict breaks out between rebels and GOS forces, along with government-supported militias, in the western Sudan region of Darfur.

2002 A cease-fire is declared in southern Sudan, as the two sides meet to discuss a permanent peace agreement.

2005 A final peace and power-sharing agreement is signed between southern rebels and the government on January 9; Garang dies in a helicopter crash on July 30.

north and south Sudan as two separate regions, an approach that many Arabs felt was part of a British colonial policy of divide and conquer. While this belief was partially true, the British division of Sudan also recognized that southerners had not always benefited from northern dominance. Whatever the motivations, the result was to further divide north from south.

In the 1930s, a growing nationalist movement in the country began to demand Sudanese independence. In 1953, the British set up a timetable to grant self-rule. Self-government began that same year, and full independence came in 1956. The British also gave in to the demands of the Arab north that, upon independence, north and south Sudan would be ruled as one

country. It was this unified Sudan that became an independent nation on January 1, 1956. But many in the south were unhappy with the outcome.

Revolt in the South

The decision to merge north and south Sudan alienated many southerners. The Muslim north not only was economically better off, it had three times the population of the south. Southerners were afraid that their rights and culture would be ignored by a government that was sure to be dominated by the Arabs of Khartoum.

The initial appointments of the new government confirmed southern fears. As hundreds of low-level

British officials left the country, they were replaced by northerners, with only four posts given to southerners. Khartoum justified this discrimination by arguing that the south had too small an educated class to fill very many government positions. While there was some truth to this contention, it did not prevent the southerners from feeling resentment.

Motivated by their fear of northern power, southern politicians demanded that Sudan adopt a federal form of government that would give the south a degree of autonomy. In 1955, some of these politicians were arrested and jailed on doubtful charges, prompting the formation of southern mobs in July and August to protest Khartoum's behavior. In small skirmishes, rioting civilians were shot and killed. In August 1955, the Equatoria Corps of the Sudanese army (consisting mostly of southerners) rose up in a mutiny.

In the first few days of fighting, southern troops and mobs attacked northern merchants, officials, their wives, and sometimes even their children. Several hundred northerners were killed in these riots, which were a response to rumors that the northerners were planning massacres in the south. When northern troops were sent south to restore order, the southern mutineers fled into the bush with their weapons.

Northern Repression

The unrest in the south simmered from 1955 to 1958. Khartoum attempted to reimpose control over the three southern provinces that were dominated by non-Muslim Africans (Bahr el Ghazal, Upper Nile, and Equatoria) but was met with passive resistance by the population, accompanied by occasional outbreaks of violence. Rebel resistance was scattered and uncoordinated. Many southerners who thought that a political solution was possible did not support armed resistance.

This mood changed with the 1958 coup d'état of General Ibrahim Abboud. Whereas the previous Sudanese government had tried to combine repression with overtures to cooperative southern leaders, Abboud set out to destroy the low-level resistance with harsh measures. Sudanese army units were encouraged to attack villages that were suspected of being sympathetic to the rebels. Southern politicians were silenced, and many were forced to flee the country to avoid arrest.

Abboud's regime also introduced to Sudan a stricter observance of Islam, which he imposed on both the north and the south. In the south, Arabs replaced Christian missionary teachers, and Arabic became the official language rather than English. Christian churches were burned, and Friday, rather than Sunday, was made the official day of rest. These policies increased the southerners' animosity toward the government. Although most southern Sudanese were animists, the substantial minority of Christians were often the primary target of government repression so they were at the forefront of the resistance.

Anya-Nya

In 1962, a group of exiled Sudanese southerners created a political movement that eventually took the name Sudan African National Union (SANU). At the same time, resistance inside the country coalesced around a strike by secondary-school students against discrimination by Arab teachers from the north. Many students, along with many non-Arab teachers, fled the persecution that followed the strike and helped to become the nucleus of a new rebel movement: the Anya-Nya.

Anya-Nya translates as "venom of the Gabon viper," and the newly organized southern fighters intended to be as dangerous as poisonous snakes. In 1963, the Anya-Nya opened up an offensive that succeeded in temporarily capturing government outposts in Upper Nile and Equatoria provinces. At first the rebels were mostly armed with spears and machetes, along with a few captured rifles. But in 1965, they acquired weapons from Congolese who were fleeing a failed rebellion in the Congo (later renamed Zaire). The Anya-Nya also probably received secret support from Israel, which disliked the Arab-world orientation of Sudan's government. (Khartoum had sent troops to fight against Israel in the 1967 Six Days' War.) The Israelis supplied the Anya-Nya with weapons and also hired European mercenaries who could train the southerners in their use.

The amount of support given to the southerners was minuscule compared to the military aid that the government in Khartoum received from Egypt and the Soviet Union. Egypt contributed at least 5,000 troops to its fellow Arab state, while the Soviets provided sophisticated tanks and aircraft, including MiG jets and attack helicopters. The Soviet decision to help Khartoum fit in with the general Soviet

With foreign support, the Sudanese rebel organization known as *Anya-Nya,* or "viper venom," gained control of the southern countryside by the late 1960s. Attacks by both government and guerrilla forces were reported to be extremely brutal. *(John Downing/Getty Images)*

policy of supporting Arab states against Israel and its Western allies.

The war in the south was characterized by massacre and counter-massacre. Although southern reports of northern atrocities may have been exaggerated, outside journalists and aid workers confirmed that the army's attacks were carried out with great brutality. Even when there were no orders to attack southern villages, it was clear that northern troops, often unable to find an enemy who hid in the rough countryside, took out their frustrations on the civilian population. The Anya-Nya fought back with massacres of their own; when northern outposts were taken, northern civilians would often be killed. During the repressive Abboud administration (1958–1964), such attacks became government policy—Abboud wanted to Islamicize and Arabize the south. Villages that refused to cooperate were often bombed by government planes. An estimated 500,000 died during the seventeen years of fighting, most of them civilians. Hundreds of thousands more were forced to flee their homes, some going

to refugee camps in neighboring Congo, Uganda, and Ethiopia. Abboud's Arabization policies were an attempt at cultural genocide.

Politically, the southern Sudanese were handicapped by their lack of a unified organization. Tribal and political differences among southerners led to the creation, disbanding, and re-creation of a plethora of political organizations, including the SANU, the Anzania Liberation Front, and a southern Sudan provisional government. These groups often refused to cooperate with each other. In the field, the Anya-Nya were theoretically united, but in practice they fought as small, uncoordinated units. Their troops dominated the countryside of the south, while the government held the major towns.

In 1970, this chaos among the insurgents was ended when the various southern opposition groups agreed to form the Southern Sudan Liberation Movement, with the Anya-Nya as their military arm. General Joseph Lagu, a longtime fighter in the Anya-Nya, was put in charge of both organizations. This reorganization made the southerners more effective fighters; it also made it easier to carry out negotiations with the north.

Peace Interval

The drawn-out war in the south helped to undercut Abboud's power in the north, and he was overthrown in a 1964 civilian uprising. The change in administration led to a brief pause in the fighting, but the new civilian-led government was equally unwilling to compromise with southern rebels. The fighting resumed. The new government did not attack southern civilians as a matter of policy, but government soldiers continued to occasionally attack opposition villages. The government also expelled all Christian missionaries, whom many northerners held responsible for originally stirring up anti-Arab sentiments among southerners.

In 1969, a group of military officers, tired of Sudan's stagnant economy and frustrated by the lack of success in the war, led a coup against the civilian government. The leader of the military coup was Colonel Gaafar Mohammed Nimeiri, a relative moderate. Nimeiri continued the war against the south, but he believed that some kind of compromise would eventually be necessary, and so he also attempted to open negotiations with southern leaders. General Lagu's rise to power in the south made negotiations possible. The south now had one spokesman with whom Nimeiri could discuss terms. The two sides met for peace talks in 1971.

The result of these talks was the Addis Ababa Agreement, signed on February 28, 1972. Nimeiri agreed to merge the three provinces of the south into one regional state, which would be allowed limited autonomy. The south was given its own legislature, and religious freedom was to be permitted. Nimeiri's government was as Islamic in outlook as its predecessors, but it was willing to be tolerant toward southern beliefs. This peace lasted until 1983.

Turn to Islam and the Second Civil War

The peace between north and south held during the 1970s, but relations between the two regions began to cool after 1980. Southerners worried about Sudan's 1980 alliance with Egypt, which seemed to move the country closer to the Arab world. The early 1980s also saw an increase in the influence of the National Islamic Front (NIF) and the Muslim Brotherhood, both led by Hassan al-Turabi; during the 1970s and 1980s, the NIF infiltrated its members into Sudan's bureaucracy and military.

In 1983, reacting to the growing power of these Islamic organizations, Nimeiri appointed Turabi attorney general of Sudan, and concurred when Turabi ruled that in the future, Sharia (Islamic law) would be the basis of Sudanese law. This decision was especially worrisome for the non-Muslim south; among other harsh penalties, Sharia called for amputating the hands of petty thieves.

Already disturbed, the south was outraged by Nimeiri's June 1983 decree that redivided the southern region into its original three provinces. Nimeiri claimed that he only wished to reduce the power of the Dinka (the south's largest ethnic group), but southerners, particularly the Dinka, saw this move as an attempt to repeal the Addis Ababa Agreement.

In May 1983, two army garrisons in the south, angry about Nimeiri's Islamic policies (and worried that they might be transferred to the north), mutinied in protest. When the government sent Colonel John Garang, a Dinka, south to put down the mutiny, he joined it. Garang had been born into a Christian family and had spent time in the United States (he graduated from Grinnell College and earned a Ph.D. in economics at the University of Iowa), and he was not happy with the Islamic direction of the Nimeiri government. Instead of putting down the mutineers, he encouraged other units in the region to rise up against the government, then took control of the rebels and led them into the bush, beginning a new guerrilla war against the government. To prosecute the war, Garang created a political organization, the Sudanese People's Liberation Movement (SPLM), and a military wing, the Sudanese People's Liberation Army (SPLA).

In many ways, the second Sudanese civil war resembled the first. Again the southerners dominated the countryside, and again the northerners controlled the towns. However, unlike the Anya-Nya, which had had a broad base of support, Garang's army was grounded in ethnic and personal loyalties. Because Garang was a Dinka, most of the top jobs in the SPLA were occupied by Dinkas. Garang also demanded a level of personal loyalty that disturbed his more idealistic followers. Southerners who opposed his methods might find themselves imprisoned in a pit for months. The treatment meted out to the civilian population by the SPLA was harsh. Garang's troops often acted like an occupying army, acquiring their supplies by theft and killing those who objected. Despite Garang's authoritarian behavior, most southerners stayed loyal to his cause. To them, the threat of the north required the south to unite behind one leader, even if they disliked his methods.

Islamic Fundamentalism

Throughout the 1980s, the hard-line Islamists gained in power and influence. There was a temporary abatement in this trend in 1985, when Nimeiri was overthrown—the SPLA even opened up negotiations with the new government—but a 1989 military coup put a new pro-Islamist government into power.

The new government was led by the Revolutionary Command Council for National Salvation (RCC-NS), whose leader was General Omar Hassan Ahmad al-Bashir. Much of the support for the new regime, however, came from Turabi and his National Islamic Front. Many observers considered Turabi and his Islamists to be the real powers in Sudan. Turabi's goal was to bring all of Sudan, including the south, into line with his fundamentalist Islamic views. Al-Bashir and Turabi broke off negotiations with the SPLA and launched a full-scale offensive against the southern rebels.

The attacks on the south were carried out with a ruthlessness that the war had not seen before. Planes bombed rebel villages, while government-supported Arab militias (called "popular defense forces") raided African villages in southern Sudan. International aid agencies accused the government of carrying out a war of genocide against the African south. Certainly much of the south was depopulated, with hundreds of thousands fleeing across Sudan's borders or north to the relative safety of Khartoum. Those who reached Khartoum were not harmed; the Sudanese government was clearly bent not on killing all southerners, but on destroying their ability to resist as a culture. Khartoum's goal was the Islamization of the entire south.

International Support

The new Sudanese government soon managed to alienate much of the world, including many Arab states, by its extreme fundamentalist Islamic policies. The United States and others accused Sudan of supporting Islamic terrorist groups around the world. It was accused of being connected to both the 1993 bombing of New York's World Trade Center and the 1995 attempt to assassinate Egyptian leader Hosni Mubarak. Sudan also maintained close ties with Iraq and Libya, two states that were pariahs in the eyes of much of the world. Because of the international animosity the Sudanese government had inspired, Garang and the SPLA received substantial amounts of foreign military support.

The countries providing this support included Ethiopia, Kenya, Uganda, and Eritrea. Ethiopia, an ally of the Soviet Union, had been the most important supporter in the 1980s, providing arms and equipment to Garang's SPLA, which portrayed itself as a Marxist-Leninist movement. It maintained large training camps in southern Ethiopia. In 1991, however, the regime of Mengistu Haile Mariam collapsed. At that point, Uganda and Eritrea became the primary supporters of the SPLA. Both nations aided the rebel movement in Sudan because the Khartoum regime was supporting Islamic rebels inside their borders. In addition, all of Sudan's southern neighbors were black African states that sympathized with the plight of the African Sudanese. The SPLA may also have received covert military aid from the United States and Israel. The press reported rumors that special U.S. Army detachments carried out clandestine operations in Sudan.

Internal Fissures and the Widening Civil War

One of the key handicaps for the south was its divided aspect. There were five major ethnic groups—Dinka, Nuer, Shilluk, Bari, and Azande—and traditional ethnic hostilities among them complicated efforts to join forces against the north. This tendency was exacerbated by Garang's policy of favoring his own Dinka people.

In 1991, frustration with Garang's dictatorial leadership style led Riek Machar, an ethnic Nuer, to break away and form his own SPLA United (SPLA-U) faction, in which a number of further splits led to the establishment of a new group, the Southern Sudanese Independence Movement (SSIM). On the surface, the motivation for the breakup was policy disagreement—Machar wanted to create an independent south Sudan, while Garang favored remaining in Sudan as a secular autonomous province. Much of the animosity between the two, however, seemed to be fueled by personal rivalry and competition for power.

Whatever its causes, the intra-SPLA conflict was a disaster for the south. Garang and Machar spent as much of their effort attacking each other and raiding villages suspected of supporting the opposition as they did the government. Other, lesser leaders broke away from the SPLA and formed their own guerrilla bands. The government in Khartoum took advantage of this conflict, occasionally providing support to Machar and the SSIM. In 1996–1997, the SPLA-U and SSIM signed a political agreement with the government in which they gave up their demand for independence. On his part, Garang had managed by 1997 to mend some of the breaks in the SPLA, and many of his former opponents had rejoined his army.

Omar Hassan al-Bashir's government in Khartoum had its own problems. Within Khartoum's Arab society, many Muslims opposed the rigidity of the government and the power of Turabi and the NIF. The NIF was reported to have persecuted Muslim sects that differed with the official Muslim ideology of Sudan. Outside greater Khartoum, other regions resented the government's behavior. The western state of Darfur was predominantly Muslim, but many of its people were black Africans, not Arabs, and some of them voiced dissatisfaction with the way the central government treated them.

These strains had the potential of undercutting Khartoum's war efforts in the south. In February 1992, a coalition of northern opposition parties led by the Democratic Unionist Party, the Umma Party, and the SPLM created the National Democratic Alliance (NDA) as an antigovernment umbrella group. It called for a multiparty democracy and the preservation of cultural and ethnic diversity in Sudan. In 1995 the NDA members agreed on the secular character of future government and on a referendum on self-determination for the south. In October 1996, a joint NDA military command under John Garang was established. These developments opened a northeastern front in the civil war, transforming what had been a predominantly ethnic and religious conflict into a center-periphery conflict. While the SPLA remained suspicious about the long-term goals of their new allies, in 1997 the NDA successfully coordinated military operations in areas along the borders with Ethiopia and Eritrea. There were even rumors about preparations for a joint NDA march on Khartoum.

Stalemate and Cease-fire

By 1998, the war in south Sudan was a continuing stalemate in which neither side appeared capable of mounting a decisive military effort. Government forces conducted indiscriminate aerial bombardments and used helicopter gunships to attack insurgents, supply bases, and civilian targets, with particularly devastating effects. In 1999, those same forces carried out sixty-five aerial attacks on civil targets, mostly in Bahr El Ghazal, Eastern Equatoria, and the Southern Blue Nile regions; in 2000, the number of such attacks grew to 132, and in 2001 to 195. The Islamic government controlled the major cities of the Nile River valley, although it was tightly besieged by insurgents. The rebels dominated the villages and smaller towns of the countryside. Garang and the SPLA were estimated to have about 25,000 hard-core fighters, with tens of thousands more who joined the fighting when it threatened their own districts. The SPLM had established some government functions in the areas it controlled, setting up an administration, collecting taxes, creating a judicial system, and training a police force. Under pressure from his supporters in Eritrea and Uganda, Garang had altered his dictatorial leadership style, allowing public criticism of his policies and sharing power with members of other tribes (although Dinkas still tended to dominate the higher ranks of the SPLA).

Perhaps for these reasons, or because of increased foreign aid, Garang was able to recover from the splits that damaged his movement after 1991. By 1998, the SPLA had regained control of most of Equatoria and had the provincial capital of Juba almost completely cut off from the north. His improved circumstances and well-equipped fighting force, which had evolved into a conventional army, gave him a better chance of being able to seize most of the south. In addition, political support from the United States had become more open. In January 1998, Garang and other rebel leaders met with U.S. Secretary of State Madeleine Albright in Uganda. Washington still denied providing military aid, but Garang's 1998 offensives were backed by heavy artillery and Russian-made tanks. These were obviously not built in south Sudan.

The war had also turned southern Sudan into one large refugee camp, according to international monitors. Millions of villagers had fled government attacks or been forced to leave by fighting between rebel factions. The refugee crisis was aggravated by widespread food shortages. The United Nations set up a special relief effort to help the starving population in the south. On average, the UN delivered (mainly by air drops) about 70, 000 tons of food supplies per year.

The grim irony of the Sudanese war was that, because of the shortage of competent local pilots, the UN hired Russian airmen to carry out the risky food drops in war-torn areas. Meanwhile, the government also hired Russians to bomb the same areas. A few, it was rumored in the media, performed both jobs in turn. Some of the southern refugees moved north to Khartoum, filling shantytowns around the city; others spilled into neighboring countries, taking the conflict with them. Khartoum was accused of supporting Islamic rebels in Uganda and Eritrea.

Steps Toward Peace

As early as 1993, the antagonists in the long war were seeking a political solution. The military stalemate continued, and the south was overwhelmed by a humanitarian crisis in which hundreds of thousands of refugees were at risk of death by starvation or disease. Sudan's neighbors, fearing that the conflict could spread, took a strong role in seeking a comprehensive peace agreement. Eritrea, Ethiopia, Uganda, and Kenya collaborated within the regional association—the Intergovernmental Authority on Development (IGAD), which includes also Sudan and Somalia—to promote the peace initiative based on a settlement of the relationship between mosque and state in Sudan, power sharing between the government and the opposition, and resource sharing between Khartoum and the provinces.

The southerners, who made up only 25 percent of Sudan's population, still faced formidable problems. Fortunately, they could achieve many of their goals without invading the north or overthrowing the Sudanese government. Even the SPLA was ready for a political settlement. At first, the Khartoum government tried to maneuver, signing agreements with some rebel factions in a framework it called "peace from within." After significant battle losses to the SPLA in 1997, however, the regime agreed to a more comprehensive framework for ending the war. This plan included the separation of mosque and state in Sudan and self-determination for the southern region,

as proposed by the IGAD. The government hoped that by making peace it could improve the country's relations with other nations in the region. In December 1999, Sudan and Uganda also signed an accord agreeing not to provide support to rebel forces in each other's countries.

The IGAD mediation efforts were strongly supported by the United States and Great Britain. These countries, as well as Italy and Norway, formed an international observer group to help find a peaceful solution. In September 2001, President George W. Bush appointed former senator John Danforth as his envoy to Sudan to explore a prospective U.S. role in the peace process. The widespread U.S. perception of the Sudanese civil war as religious (Islamists vs. Christians) and ethnic (Arabs vs. black Africans) prompted an informal and unlikely alliance of the religious right and the Congressional Black Caucus in support of an active American role in seeking a settlement.

In January 2002 a tentative cease-fire agreement between the parties was negotiated under U.S. mediation, although sporadic fighting continued for the first half of the year. Particularly fierce fighting occurred in the oil-rich Western Upper Nile region on the contested border between north and south, where government forces tried to grab as many oil fields as they could.

Following further negotiations, a preliminary peace agreement was concluded between the SPLA and Sudanese government on July 20, 2002, in Machakos, Kenya. The agreement provided a framework for future talks on ending the conflict: a six-year interim period preceding a referendum on southern self-determination and the exemption of the south from Islamic law. On July 27, 2002, Omar al-Bashir and John Garang met for the first time in Kampala, Uganda. In talks that ran through 2004, the parties agreed on a complete cessation of hostilities, a power-sharing arrangement, and economic cooperation. The comprehensive agreement was signed in Naivisha, Kenya, on May 26, 2004.

Peace and the Future

The final peace accord between the Sudanese government and the SPLM marked the end of Africa's longest civil war and one of the most devastating wars in its history. It was signed on January 9, 2005, in Nairobi, Kenya. The document confirmed all political provisions agreed by the parties in the 2002–2004 talks. Additionally, it called for national elections within four years, the drafting of a new constitution within six years, the creation of a transitional, power-sharing government in Khartoum, making Garang first vice president of the country, and a 70–30 north-south member ratio in a new national assembly. The agreement also stipulated a 50–50 split of oil profits between the north and south. As first vice president, Garang was to head a separate administration for the south; the SPLA would keep its forces in the south and withdraw from the east, while the government would withdraw from the south in two-and-a-half years. A UN peacekeeping force of 10,000 was to be deployed in Sudan to oversee the agreement. The African Union also agreed to provide up to 4,000 peacekeeping troops. Thus ended a war that had lasted more than two decades, claimed some 2 million lives by combat, starvation, and disease, and led to the dislocation of 4 million people.

Prospects for peace in Sudan were overshadowed after 2003 by still another internal war, this one in the country's western Darfur region. By 2006, additional hundreds of thousands had died, and the conflict threatened to engulf neighboring Chad as well. As for the south, the ruined region remained one of the poorest in the world. There was no electricity and not a single stretch of paved road across an area the size of France and Germany combined. The south remained unstable and deeply divided along ethnic lines and by tribal, political, and personal loyalties. In late 2004, there was a failed revolt against Garang by some SPLA officers who favored immediate and complete independence for the south.

Western media often portrayed the Sudanese conflict as one of a Christian David in the south fighting an oppressive Muslim Goliath in the north. Although there was an element of truth to this characterization, it ignored the complexity of the conflict, which was fueled by not only historic and religious issues but also by the ambitions of Sudanese leaders and the actions of outside forces.

The prospects for peace in Sudan were dealt yet another serious blow with the death of John Garang in a helicopter crash on July 30, 2005. His entrance into Khartoum months earlier had attracted a crowd of more than 1 million, and his death was mourned throughout the south. It also touched off a new wave of violence, as southerners in Khartoum, suspecting foul play, began riots in which some 130 people were killed.

Carl Skutsch and Peter Jacob Rainow

See also: Ethnic and Religious Conflicts; Sudan: Conflict in Darfur Since 2002; Uganda: Civil Conflict Since 1980.

Bibliography

Abdel-Rahim, M., et al. *Sudan Since Independence.* Brookfield, VT: Gower, 1986.

Eprile, Cecil. *War and Peace in the Sudan, 1955–1972.* Newton Abbot, UK: David and Charles, 1974.

Hold, Peter Malcom, and Michele W. Daly. *A History of the Sudan from the Coming of Islam to the Present Day.* New York: Longman, 1988.

Johnson, Douglas Hamilton. *The Root Cases of Sudan's Civil Wars.* Bloomington: Indiana University Press, 2003.

Jok, Madok Jok. *War and Slavery in Sudan.* Philadelphia: University of Pennsylvania Press, 2001.

O'Balance, Edgar. *Sudan Civil War and Terrorism, 1956–1999.* New York: St. Martin's Press, 2000.

Voll, John Obert. *Historical Dictionary of the Sudan.* Lanham, MD: Scarecrow Press, 1992.

Woodward, Peter. *Sudan 1898–1989: The Unstable State.* Boulder, CO: Lynne Rienner, 1990.

SUDAN: Conflict in Darfur Since 2002

TYPE OF CONFLICT: Ethnic and Religious
PARTICIPANTS: African Union

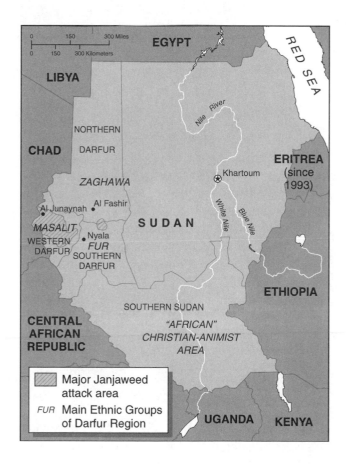

Sudan is geographically the largest nation in Africa. Approximately one-fourth the size of the United States, it shares borders with nine countries: Chad, Libya, Egypt, Eritrea, Ethiopia, Kenya, Uganda, Democratic Republic of the Congo, and the Central African Republic. Its population of nearly 40 million people is among the most diverse in Africa, representing some 130 languages and dialects. According to the U.S. Central Intelligence Agency (CIA), about 52 percent of the population may be classified as non-Arab. The non-Arab population is often referred to as "black Africans." This term can be misleading, however, as all Sudanese are dark-skinned. The vast majority of the population (some 75 percent) is Muslim, though 20 percent practice indigenous religions, and 5 percent, mainly in the southern region, are Christian. Most Sudanese (68 percent) live in rural areas, while 32 percent are urban dwellers, and about 7 percent are nomadic. Sudan is also one of the poorest nations in the world; it ranks 139 out of 177 nations on the UN Human Development Index.

Since achieving independence from the United Kingdom and Egypt in 1956, Sudan has been wracked by civil war and despotic governments for all but approximately ten years. President Omar Hassan al-Bashir took power in June 1989, when, along with other military officers, he carried out a coup d'état against the democratically elected government of Sadiqu Al-Mahdi. A former paratrooper, Bashir had fought with Egypt against Israel in the 1973 war. On his return to Sudan, he served as the commander of numerous assaults on the Sudanese People's Liberation Army (SPLA), fighting an independence struggle in the south in the early 1980s. As for the reason behind the coup, al-Bashir asserted that his purpose was to "save the country from rotten political parties."

In collaboration with Hassan al-Turabi, the fundamentalist leader of the National Islamic Front (NIF), al-Bashir made Sudan an "Islamic state." In doing so, al-Turabi dissolved parliament, placed a ban on all political parties, and closed down all media outlets except that of the government of Sudan. However, suspicious of the ever-increasing power of al-Turabi, al-Bashir in December 1999 issued a state of emergency and kicked al-Turabi out of the government. In a rigged election, in which most of the opposition party members were fearful of running, Bashir easily won the presidency. Shortly thereafter, the military arrested al-Turabi. Accused of planning a coup and, later, interfering with government matters, al-Turabi has been imprisoned off and on since 2000.

KEY DATES

1956   Sudan wins its independence from joint British-Egyptian rule.

1983   Civil war breaks out in the south of the country between rebels of the Sudanese Liberation Army (SLA) and the government of Sudan.

1989   General Omar Hassan al-Bashir takes power in a military coup; he governs in collaboration with National Islamic front leader Hassan al-Turabi.

1991   Arab militias begin attacking non-Arab villagers in the Darfur region in western Sudan.

1999   Al-Bashir forces al-Turabi out of power and declares a state of emergency.

2001   Two non-Arab rebel groups begin fighting the Arab-dominated government in the Darfur region.

2003   Various rebel groups join forces to form the Darfur Liberation Front (DLF); government forces and Arab militias known as Janjaweed engage in widespread attacks on non-Arab villagers in Darfur.

2004   The U.S. House of Representatives declares that government and janjaweed attacks in Darfur constitute genocide; the African Union begins its deployment of peacekeepers to the region.

2005   The UN Commission of Inquiry concludes that crimes against humanity are being perpetrated in Darfur by the government of Sudan and the janjaweed it supports; a peace agreement is signed between southern Sudanese rebels and the government of Sudan.

A civil war between the Khartoum-based government forces and rebels in the south, the Sudanese People's Liberation Army/Movement (SPLA/M), lasted from 1983 to 2005, constituting the longest-running conflict in Africa. The resulting violence cost the lives of about 4 million people. As many as 4 million others were forcibly displaced from their homes.

After the al-Qaeda terror attacks of September 11, 2001, the United States began cultivating relations with Sudan as a potential ally in the war against terrorism. (Osama bin Laden lived in Sudan for several years and used the country as a base, but had been expelled by the Sudanese government in 1996). The United States led an effort, with the United Kingdom and Norway, to promote negotiations to end the north-south conflict. After a series of talks during 2002 and 2003, a Comprehensive Peace Agreement (CPA) was signed in Nairobi on January 9, 2005. The CPA provided for the sharing of power between the government of Sudan and leaders of the SPLA/M and determined that the main rebel leader, John Garang, would become first vice president of Sudan. Another important provision of the CPA called for the sharing of revenues from oil, which had begun to be pumped from the south in 1999, between the north and the south. Six years after the signing of the CPA, the south would be permitted to hold a referendum for self-determination and independence. A shadow was cast over the prospects for lasting peace when John Garang was killed in an unexplained helicopter crash on July 30, 2005.

Emergence of Genocidal Conflict

Although Darfur—a region in northwestern Sudan sharing borders with Libya, Chad, and the Central African Republic—was not directly involved in the north-south civil war, festering problems in that region were to lead to an ongoing conflict there that has been labeled "genocide" by the government of the United States, other nations, and a number of nongovernmental organizations (NGOs).

Prior to the conflict, Darfur was home to approximately 6 million people, virtually all of them Muslim. Darfur shares the ethnic diversity of Sudan, containing between forty and ninety ethnic groups or tribes, depending on how one defines what constitutes an ethnic group. Darfur is one of the most underdeveloped and isolated regions of Sudan, with very few roads, schools, or hospitals. It is also an area that has often been wracked by conflict.

According to some observers, the seeds of the conflict in Darfur were sown in the 1980s, when fighting in neighboring Chad's civil war spilled into western Darfur. More specifically, while Darfur was comprised of people who were largely Muslim, roughly 40 percent were not Arab and felt closer ethnic ties to groups in Chad. This aggravated traditional tensions between the non-Arab Fur and Zaghawa ethnic groups. Further, many Fur felt that Khartoum not only encouraged but also supported their enemies, a feeling that sparked Fur attacks on government installations in Darfur. Adding to the unrest was the ongoing drought and near famine that began to plague the Darfur region in the mid-1980s, and the fact that Khartoum virtually ignored the plight of the Darfurians.

While much of the region is dry, burning desert (except during a short rainy season), there are areas where crops are cultivated and cattle grazed. The productive land is occupied, in the main, by sedentary farmers and cattle owners, who have tended to be black African. At certain times of the year, however, the farmland has traditionally been used by semi-nomadic Arab peoples for grazing their cattle and camels, which in turn fertilized and renewed the soil for subsequent growing seasons. Disputes among the two groups were traditionally settled by local leaders of the African and Arab tribal groups. This symbiotic relationship, however, began to disintegrate during the 1970s and 1980s, when drought and spreading desertification intensified competition for increasingly scarce resources.

The drought also affected other countries in the region, and nomads from Chad and Libya migrated to Darfur in search of grazing land, which put further pressure on the available resources. At the same time, weapons began to flow into Darfur from neighboring countries, as well as from the civil war raging in the south of Sudan. Tensions between non-Arabs and Arabs were also aggravated by the political ideology of Arab supremacy that emanated from Khartoum during the early 1980s.

These factors, along with the fact that Khartoum put little or no money into the infrastructure of Darfur (such as roads, schools, water systems), angered various tribal groups (including the Fur, Masalit, and Zaghawa). This anger continued to simmer and grew increasingly volatile as the drought and famine took an ever-greater toll on residents.

By the 1990s, traditional dispute resolution approaches proved inadequate, and non-Arabs and Arabs alike began to form local armed self-defense units to protect land and animals. As early as 1991, armed Arab militias formed and engaged in attacks against non-Arab villages and settlements. In August 1995, for example, Arab raiders attacked and burned the non-Arab village of Mejmeri in west Darfur, stealing 40,000 cattle and massacring 23 civilians. By late 1998, more than 100,000 non-Arab Masalit had fled to Chad to escape the violent attacks.

Adding to this mix of issues was the general notion held by many Darfurians that, while the conflict in the south was being attended to and resulting in shared governance and shared resources, Darfur continued to be neglected and ignored. The commixture of all these factors induced the formation of rebel groups and attacks on the Sudanese government.

In 2001 and 2002, before the conflict became widely known to the outside world, a rebel movement began to form among non-Arabs in Darfur, largely drawn from the self-defense forces that had been formed previously. Two main rebel groups emerged—the Sudanese People's Liberation Army/Movement (SPLA/M) and the Justice and Equality Movement (JEM)—both of which, in addition to wanting to provide local security for non-Arabs, protested against the economic and political marginalization of Darfur and claimed to speak on behalf of all Darfurians, both Arab and non-Arab. Members of both rebel groups came primarily (but by no means exclusively) from three non-Arab tribes—the Fur, Masalit, and Zaghawa—that had been attacked by Arab militias. Leaders of both groups closely observed the ongoing peace negotiations between the government and the southern rebels and realized that armed insurrection eventually led to concessions by the government, including power sharing and access to economic resources.

As is often the case, the history of the diverse rebel groups is a messy affair. In February 2003, various rebels formed the Darfur Liberation Front, which declared its opposition to the government of Sudan. Not a month later, in mid-March, the Darfur Liberation Front changed its name to the Sudan Liberation Movement and the Sudan Liberation Army (SLM/SLA). While the Darfur Liberation Front called for the secession of Darfur from Sudan, the SLA's secretary general, Mini Arkoi Minawi, asserted that its aim was to "create a united, democratic Sudan."

The other major rebel group, the Justice and Equality Movement (JEM), was said to be supported by Sudanese opposition leader Hassan al-Turabi, who once served as the speaker of Sudan's parliament and was considered the main ideologue of Sudan's Islamist revolution. In May 2000, he was unceremoniously kicked out of the government and imprisoned.

The first rebel attack involving Fur, Masalit, and Zaghawa forces against a government military base is generally believed to have taken place on February 25, 2002. Alarmed by the violence spreading in Darfur, but with its military forces stretched thin by the north-south civil war, the Sudanese government recruited, trained, and equipped Arab militias to suppress the rebellion in the province. According to Gerard Prunier, a veteran journalist of African civil wars, the so-called Janjaweed (meaning, variously, "hordes," "ruffians," or "men or devils on horseback") had been used by the Sudanese leadership since the late 1980s to supplement government troops in the fight against southern rebels.

Members of the Justice and Equality Movement, a rebel group in the western Sudanese province of Darfur, travel to base camp in May 2004. Fighting escalated between government-backed Arab "Janjaweed" militia and largely non-Arab rebel factions in the province. *(Daniel Pepper/Getty Images News)*

On May 1, 2002, a group of Fur politicians complained to Sudanese president al-Bashir that 181 villages had been attacked by Arab militias, with hundreds of people killed and thousands of animals stolen. In early 2003, a series of attacks by rebels forces against government installations and troops caused humiliation, alarm, and anger in Khartoum. On April 25, 2003, which some experts have called a critical turning point in the war, the SLA and JEM forces struck the government air force base at Al Fashir. The rebels killed at least 75 people at the base, destroyed several airplanes and bombers, and captured the base commander. Then in May, the SLA attacked a Sudanese battalion and killed 500 soldiers. Other successful attacks followed. According to Western journalists in mid-2003, the rebels were winning most of the encounters, and the government feared it would lose the province.

In response to rebel victories, government leaders put the Darfur crisis in the hands of its powerful Military Intelligence agency, which directed government soldiers and the Janjaweed militias to expand the counterinsurgency campaign from rebel forces to civilians from the three main tribes—Fur, Masalit, and Zagahawa—from which the rebels came. The man heading up the Sudanese intelligence agency was Major General Salah Abdallah Gosh, who, according to a United Nations document leaked in February 2006, was one of seventeen individuals whom the UN was considering for possible prosecution for his involvement in the Darfur conflict.

The escalating violence led to hundreds of thousands of deaths and millions of people forcibly displaced from their homes and forced to eke out an existence in camps within Darfur or, if they were lucky, across the border in neighboring Chad. Tribal leaders targeted by the government and Janjaweed asserted, time and again, that, as journalist John Pike quoted them, "the depopulation of villages and consequent changes in land ownership are part of a government strategy to change the whole democracy of the region of Darfur."

Beginning in early 2003, the Janjaweed and government troops engaged in widespread and systematic attacks against non-Arab villages in Darfur, slaughtering men, raping women, abducting or killing children, looting household goods and animals, and burning the villages to the ground. The initial attacks were often carried out in the early hours of the morning, thereby catching the victims off-guard. Many,

if not most, of the ground attacks were preceded by aerial bombardment from Antonov bombers, government military aircraft. Apparently running out of ordnance at times, the government reportedly resorted to dropping heavy pieces of metal, including old appliances. A few survivors reported that a yellow, wet substance was dropped on them from the planes, and that it caused great sickness among the people. The bombings were generally followed by attacks by hundreds of Janjaweed racing into the village on horseback and camels, followed close behind by four-wheeled vehicles, many with mounted guns.

As of early 2006, tens of thousands of Darfurians had been forced into internally displaced person (IDP) camps in the region; others had made their way to refugee camps in Chad, not knowing whether their loved ones had survived. Some young women were reportedly kidnapped and forced to become concubines of the Janjaweed and soldiers.

Not content with terrorizing the population, chasing them off, and looting their villages, the government troops and Janjaweed would frequently follow black Africans into the hills and mountains, shoot the men, and rape the women and girls. Wells, critical to human life and essential livestock, were poisoned by tossing in dead bodies. As many as 2,000 black African villages had been destroyed by early 2006. Close to 2 million people were residing in poorly equipped IDP camps, which were attacked at will.

Although the government of Sudan repeatedly denied sponsoring or supporting the Janjaweed, the 2005 UN Commission of Inquiry in Darfur found that "the large majority of attacks on villages conducted by the [Janjaweed] militia have been undertaken with the acquiescence of State officials."

International Awareness

By late 2003, the world began to take notice of the escalating carnage in Darfur, as hundreds of thousands of civilians were forcibly displaced from their homes and villages. In December, Jan Egeland, UN undersecretary for humanitarian affairs, asserted that the Darfur crisis was possibly the "worst in the world today." In the same month, Tom Vraalsen, the UN security general's special envoy for humanitarian affairs for Sudan, claimed that the situation in Darfur was "nothing less than the organized destruction of sedentary African agriculturalists—the Fur, the Masalit, and the Zaghawa."

In 2004, the government and citizens of the United States, which was engaged in wars in Afghanistan and Iraq, began to express alarm over the situation in Darfur. On June 16, members of the U.S. House of Representatives and Senate issued a warning to Sudan to desist from its violent actions or face financial sanctions or legal consequences. On June 24, the House unanimously declared that the situation in Darfur constituted genocide. A week later, Secretary of State Colin Powell visited an IDP camp in the province and a refugee camp in Chad. UN Secretary General Kofi Annan also made a personal visit.

In July and August 2004, the United States—in a joint effort of the U.S. State Department, the Coalition of International Justice (CIJ), and the U.S. Agency for International Aid (USAID)—sent a team of investigators, the Atrocities Documentation Team (ADT), to conduct interviews with Sudanese refugees from Darfur and collect evidence to ascertain whether genocide had been perpetrated by the Sudanese government and Janjaweed on the black population. Upon analyzing the data, the U.S. government declared that genocide indeed had been perpetrated in Darfur.

The United States referred the matter to the UN Security Council. The Commission of Inquiry (COI), established by Security Council Resolution 1564 on September 18, 2004, conducted in-depth investigations in Khartoum, Darfur, Chad, Ethiopia, and Eritrea from November 2004 through January 2005. The commission declared that crimes against humanity had been perpetrated in Darfur. Although it did not come to a finding of genocide, further investigations might reveal that genocidal activity in fact had been committed. In its report, the COI stated, "The pillaging and destruction of villages, being conducted on a systematic as well as widespread basis in a discriminatory fashion, appears to have been directed to bring about the destruction of the livelihoods and means of survival of these populations."

Failed Peace Talks, Limited International Intervention

The rebel groups (SPLA/M and JEM) and government of Sudan began a series of peace talks in mid-2004, the chief results of which have been recrimination and walkouts. Making the process even more difficult was the splintering of rebel groups, with each new off-shoot claiming a place at the peace talks. Meanwhile, the government, the Janjaweed, and the rebels continued to battle one another viciously.

The African Union deployed peacekeeping troops to Darfur in 2004, but the number proved too small to make a difference. The initial force was just 150 soldiers, followed by another three hundred. The total eventually reached about 7,000, but most analysts believed that at least two or three times that number was needed to quell the violence. Moreover, the peacekeepers were undertrained, underarmed, and working under a mandate that did not allow them to engage in battle. Instead, they were allowed only to protect the human rights monitors on the ground and to act in self-defense. The AU, meanwhile, insisted that Darfur is an "African problem" that must be solved by African nations, and it refused to allow the UN to send in troops to assist with the effort. Recognizing that it was severely outmanned and outgunned, however, the AU did begin to consider suggestions that UN troops ought to be deployed in Darfur. As of March 2006, the UN, along with various nations, was exploring the possibility of replacing African Union troops with a more robust international peacekeeping force. The Sudanese government, of course, balked at the suggestion, and the conflict raged on.

Samuel Totten and Eric Markusen

See also: Ethnic and Religious Conflicts; Sudan: Civil War in South, 1955–1972; 1983–2005.

Bibliography

De Waal, Alex, and Alexander De Waal. *Famine That Kills: Darfur, Sudan.* New York: Oxford University Press, 2005.

Flint, Julie, and Alex de Waal. *Darfur: A Short History of a Long War.* New York: Zed Books, 2005.

Power, Samantha. *"A Problem from Hell": America and the Age of Genocide.* New York: Basic Books, 2002.

Prunier, Gerard. *Darfur: The Ambiguous Genocide.* Ithaca, NY: Cornell University Press, 2005.

United Nations. *UN Commission of Inquiry: Darfur Conflict.* New York: United Nations, 2005.

U.S. State Department. "Documenting Atrocities in Darfur." State Publication 11182. Washington, DC, September 9, 2004.

TOGO: Coups and Political Unrest, 1963–1990s

TYPE OF CONFLICT: Coups; Ethnic and Religious

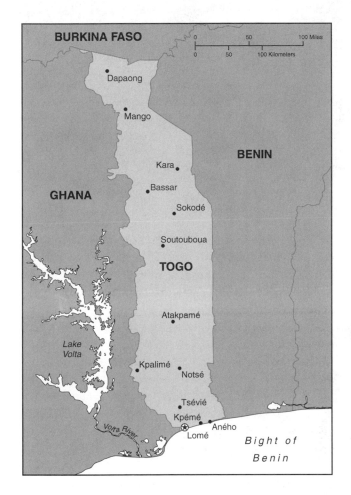

Until the establishment of a German protectorate in the 1880s, the territory of what is now Togo served as a buffer zone between the often-warring Asante and Dahomey states. In 1914, Togo was seized by British and French colonial troops in neighboring Gold Coast and Dahomey, now Benin. Following World War I, the colony was divided into French- and British-administered zones under a League of Nations mandate. This partition divided the Ewe people.

Following World War II, the British and French governments placed their spheres under a UN trusteeship. The Ewe's pleas to have their territory united were refused since much of their territory lay in the British colony of the Gold Coast. Following a plebiscite in 1957, however, the British sphere was incorporated into the newly independent state of Ghana, while the French territory became an independent nation within the French Community.

Politics during the last years of French control and the early years of independence were dominated by one family. The two major parties—the United Togolese Committee and the Togolese Progress Party—were headed by brothers-in-law Nicolas Grunitzky and Sylvanus Olympio, respectively. Grunitzky won the first election for prime minister in 1956, while Olympio succeeded him in the 1958 elections, on a platform of Ewe unification.

The Olympio regime, however, became increasingly authoritarian during the first years of independence, forcing Grunitzky and other opponents into jail or exile. Olympio was overthrown and killed in the first military coup in postcolonial Africa, in 1963. The coup leader, Sergeant Etienne Eyadéma, asked Grunitzky to return from exile to become head of state. Grunitzky's efforts to achieve constitutional multiparty democracy failed, however, and Eyadéma assumed full power in 1967.

Eyadéma's Rule

Over the course of the next ten years, Eyadéma attempted to create a one-party state around the Togolese People's Assembly (RPT). Numerous attempts to overthrow him, however, including an alleged mercenary invasion headed by several sons of Olympio, kept the nation in a state of political turmoil

KEY DATES

1960	Togo wins its independence from France.
1963	President Sylvanus Olympio is overthrown and killed in a military coup led by Sergeant Etienne Eyadéma, who calls on former opposition leader Nicolas Grunitzky to form a new government.
1967	After Grunitzky fails to establish a multiparty democracy, Eyadema assumes full power.
1985	First multiparty elections are held under the 1980 constitution.
1986	An effort to seize the government in a coup is thwarted; the government blames foreign governments for the coup attempt and seals the borders.
1990	Opposition parties denounce government efforts to restore democracy as a sham.
1991–1997	Prodemocracy protests against Eyadéma rule grow in size and intensity.

throughout most of the 1970s. During those years, Eyadéma kept firm control over the politics of the country, while the main opposition group—the Togolese Movement for Democracy (MTD)—remained in exile in Ghana.

In March 1985, the first general elections were held under the 1980 constitution, though the RPT was the only party permitted to field candidates for office. Two months later, however, other parties were permitted to form. Nevertheless, this reform came too late to prevent more political unrest, including a series of bomb attacks in the capital of Lomé. The government blamed the MTD and Ghanaian authorities, who responded with charges that the RPT had used the bomb attacks as a pretext for political repression, including the arrests of a number of MTD activists.

In September 1986, some nineteen persons were detained after an attempt to seize the main army barracks in Lomé, the RPT headquarters, and the national radio station. More than a dozen persons, including six civilians, were killed in the attack. The RPT once again blamed foreign governments for the attempted coup, including Ghana and Burkina Faso. The borders of the country were sealed, and some 600 French and Zairean troops were flown in to protect

the government. Several opposition leaders, including Gilchrist Olympio, son of the former president, were sentenced to death in absentia.

Efforts to restore constitutional rule in 1990 were denounced by the opposition as a sham, leading to student boycotts and clashes between protesters and troops. Continuing demonstrations led to the closing of all schools in April 1991, a government announcement of a general amnesty, and the legalization of political parties. The news, however, was overshadowed by the discovery of twenty-six bodies in a Lomé lagoon, which the opposition claimed were those of protesters killed by security forces.

Continuing Political and Ethnic Unrest

In August 1991, a national conference—with a rehabilitated Gilchrist Olympio in attendance—was convened to offer constitutional and political reforms and to find a way of cooling tensions between the Ewe and Kabiye ethnic groups, the former largely in the opposition and the latter generally supporting the government. When the conference voted to suspend most of Eyadéma's powers, however, the head of state canceled the meetings and established an interim government under the control of the High Council of the Republic (HCR). Eyadéma then agreed to relinquish control of the government, though he remained head of the military.

This arrangement was a recipe for further political discord. Loyal to Eyadéma, the army seized control of the state broadcasting services in Lomé on October 1, after the government had failed to pay their salaries. The troops demanded the resignation of the HCR, but Eyadéma ordered them to return to their barracks. Some five people were killed in the unrest. A week later, the presidential guards, under the command of Eyadéma's half-brother, attempted to arrest the prime minister and head of the HCR, Joseph Kokou Koffigoh. This move resulted in more deaths and the arrests of Eyadéma's half-brother and several other officers.

Unrest between Eyadéma and Koffigoh supporters continued throughout the fall of 1991, as a committee attempted to draft a new constitution. In November, troops were called out to put down the protests and impose a curfew on the capital, but outbreaks of violence continued into the early part of 1992. In early May, an assassination attempt against Olympio was blamed on the army, resulting in a two-day general strike in Lomé. Continued unrest prevented the scheduling of elections for the rest of the year and into 1993. In March, an attack on the military camp in Lomé, where Eyadéma kept his residence, was blamed on supporters of Olympio. In April, an announcement of June elections for president was made, but the poll was delayed after a series of bomb attacks on both government and opposition targets in May. New elections were scheduled for January 1994, but another armed attack on Eyadéma's

military base—again blamed on Olympio and the Ghana government—forced their postponement until February.

The elections resulted in the victory of a coalition of opposition parties but did not resolve the political violence plaguing the country. In October came an attack on the Togolese Office of Phosphates, the government agency that administered the country's main industry. Continued unrest marred the transition to democracy, especially after the opposition coalition fell apart through defections to the party of Eyadéma. This led to a rally of some 100,000 supporters of the opposition in the capital in May 1997, at which Eyadéma was accused of manipulating the political system. Eyadéma ran for reelection in 1998 and won, but there were reports that thousands were killed in postelection violence.

Eyedéma was expected to retire in 2003, but he decided to run still again. He died in 2003 after thirty-eight years in power in Togo. The military installed his son, Faure Gnassingbe, causing violent protests by opposition parties. Soon afterward, Gnassinbe was elected to the presidency to succeed his father.

James Ciment

See also: Coups.

Bibliography

Economist Intelligence Unit. Country Report: Togo, Niger, Benin, Burkina Faso. London: Economic Intelligence Unit, 1986–1996.

Greene, Sandra. *Gender, Ethnicity, and Social Change on the Upper Slave Coast: A History of the Anlo-Ewe.* Portsmouth, NH: Heinemann, 1996.

Verdon, Michel. *The Abutia Ewe of West Africa: A Chiefdom That Never Was.* New York: Mouton, 1983.

UGANDA: Anti-Amin Struggle, 1971–1979

TYPE OF CONFLICT: Coups
PARTICIPANT: Tanzania

Like other countries in the Great Lakes region of East Africa, Uganda is a mélange of ethnic groups, largely divided between Nilotic-Sudanese people in the north and Bantu-speakers in the south. Also like the other small Great Lakes states of Rwanda and Burundi, densely populated Uganda was ruled by a centralized monarchy during the immediate precolonial period—the royal house of Buganda, with a king, a council of ministers, and a parliament. Dominated by the Buganda people of the southern half of the country, Uganda's population had extensive contacts with the outside world, primarily for purposes of trade.

The first British explorers arrived in Uganda in the 1860s, searching for the source of the Nile. A decade later, missionaries both Protestant and Catholic followed and succeeded in converting many Ugandans to Christianity. Rallying around their new faith, two contending political factions led the country into a brief civil war in 1892, largely over the issue of naming a successor to the throne. The fighting led the British to impose a protectorate over the country in 1894. Challenged by the Bunyoro kingdom to the north, the British sided with the Buganda, extending both colonial rule and the Bugandan monarchy to the north of the country.

The British also utilized the Christianized Buganda as their administrative agents and security force throughout the Muslim and animist areas of the country, inflaming ethnic divisions within the country that persist to this day. At the same time, under an agreement signed between the Buganda monarchy and the British government, new forms of land ownership were instituted. Before the arrival of the Europeans, the Buganda monarchy had held all lands in trust for the people, but the new dispensation created private ownership, and much of the land fell into the hands of the Buganda elite. The British also established an educational system that disproportionately benefited the Buganda.

Despite these benefits, it was the Buganda who first began to agitate for more power within the colonial system and then for independence. In the 1930s and 1940s, Buganda workers and peasants began to organize unions, leading to demonstrations against both British and royal rule and, increasingly, calls for independence. These demands caused concern among the leaders of other ethnic groups, who feared that an independent Uganda would be largely controlled by the Buganda. Indeed, the first two political parties in the country—the Uganda National Congress (UNC), founded in 1952, and the Democratic Party (DP), established two years later—were Buganda-controlled, though both included members of other ethnic groups. Thus began a lasting conceit among the Buganda that the interests of their ethnic

KEY DATES

1962 Uganda wins its independence from Great Britain, with Milton Obote as president.

1966 With the national assembly demanding an investigation into corruption in the Obote administration, the president declares a state of emergency and postpones elections until 1971.

1971 Army second-in-command Idi Amin, one of the figures targeted for corruption investigation in 1966, seizes power while Obote is out of the country.

1972 Amin orders all 45,000 Asian residents of Uganda to leave the country; as this group represents much of the business class of the country, the economy is devastated as a result; former members of the military, led by former officers David Oyite-Ojok and Yuweri Museveni, form an anti-Amin guerrilla army and invade the country from Tanzania.

1978 To counteract Tanzanian support for the rebels, Amin invades Tanzania.

1979 The Tanzanian army and the Uganda National Liberation Army (UNLA) invade the country in January; they quickly defeat the demoralized Ugandan army and force Amin into exile in Saudi Arabia; it is estimated that between 300,000 and 500,000 persons were killed by Amin's forces during the eight-year dictatorship.

group coincided with the interests of the country at large.

The rise of the Buganda independence movement sparked political organizing in the largely non-Buganda north of the country. There, Milton Obote helped to organize the Uganda People's Union in 1958, which later merged with renegades from the UNC to form the Uganda People's Congress (UPC). Still, the Buganda were not entirely united. Divided between Protestant and Catholic wings, the Buganda split over the question of whether to secede and form their own independent country. When the secession plan failed, the opposition Buganda group formed the Kabaka Yekka (KY), which sought to ensure the continued presence and power of the royal house within a federated state. To achieve this goal, it united with the UPC, and together the coalition swept to power in the pre-independence elections of April 1962, with Obote serving as the new country's first prime minister.

Obote Regime

The ruling UPC-KY alliance faced a number of major internal problems during the early years of independence, most revolving around the question of central versus local government power. Moreover, agitation among the Bunyoro to win back two districts lost to the Buganda after the 1892 civil war led to a plebiscite in which the local residents voted to return the districts to Bunyoro County in 1964, a decision ignored by the government. Meanwhile, the UPC was increasing its control over all district councils and legislatures outside of Buganda. Despite these local successes, the UPC was facing political problems in the capital. Its KY partners dropped out of the coalition, and the UPC grew increasingly divided over economic policies, with Obote attempting to nationalize much of the commercial and industrial sector.

In April 1966, the national assembly approved a motion demanding an investigation into a gold-smuggling operation conducted by two of Obote's top officials, one of whom was the army's second-in-command, Idi Amin. Obote used the tense situation to launch a preemptive coup, arresting a number of ministers, suspending the constitution, and granting himself all executive powers. A month later, after elements of the armed forces loyal to the royal house demanded autonomy for the Buganda, the rest of the army, under Amin's command, seized the royal palace—the king had fled the country—and Obote declared a state of emergency, postponing elections until 1971.

During these years, Uganda slipped increasingly into a state of repressive dictatorship. Relying on Amin's forces, Obote arrested anyone who challenged his rule. But Amin was not entirely reliable. A northerner, he was sympathetic to the rebels in Sudan—related to his own ethnic group—who were fighting for autonomy. When Obote demanded that Amin stop funneling arms to the Sudanese rebels in 1969, Amin attempted a coup but was forced to flee to a base in his home district. There, he plotted his return to power, and when Obote left the country on a diplomatic mission in January 1971, Amin seized power.

Amin's Dictatorship

Both the people of Uganda and the international community welcomed the coup, the former because it promised national unity and the latter because Obote was seen as too dictatorial. But Amin soon showed his true colors. An uneducated man who had risen in the ranks of the colonial army through his skills as a boxer, Amin immediately purged the army and police of Obote supporters by massacring them. Suspending all political activity and most civil rights, Amin dissolved the national assembly and ruled by fiat. Military courts were given expanded jurisdiction over all citizens, and several new security agencies were established to keep an eye on any possible dissent or challenge to Amin's rule. Though Amin was already responsible for hundreds of murders, it was his decision to expel Uganda's substantial Asian community that earned him international condemnation and a severing of diplomatic and commercial relations with Britain, then Uganda's number-one trading partner.

Like other East African countries, Uganda had had a large population of Asians—largely from India—since the turn of the century, when they were brought in as labor to build the colonial railroads.

President Idi Amin ruled Uganda ruthlessly from 1971 to 1979. The armed forces and national police attacked civilians and looted indiscriminately. An estimated half-million Ugandans died from violence during his eight years of dictatorship. *(Keystone/Getty Images)*

Many then moved into small business, succeeding because they were often favored by the British and because, as a tightly knit community, they provided capital to one another. In the process, they had earned a certain degree of resentment from the African community. Uganda had seen anti-Asian riots in the 1940s, but both the British colonial administration and the Obote regime recognized the Indian community's importance and so offered a degree of protection.

But Amin, unfamiliar with the crucial economic role they played, accepted the populist notion that they were parasites, feeding off the African people. Following his August announcement that all non-citizen Asians—later expanded to all Asians—must leave his country, troops and police took over businesses and other Asian property, often at gunpoint or for pennies on the dollar. Harassed and even murdered as they tried to leave the country, all but 4,000 Asians fled the country, most to Britain. In the hands of cronies and military officers, the businesses were plundered and soon disappeared. The Ugandan economy went into a tailspin and would not revive until the late 1980s.

Meanwhile, Amin conducted a reign of terror and folly. He murdered virtually any figure in the country who represented a challenge to his rule, including politicians, religious officials, businesspersons, and intellectuals. The police and military were given carte blanche to attack individuals and loot property, which they did with zeal. Despite these ill-gotten gains made possible by Amin, the dictator faced several army challenges to his rule, mostly from ethnic groups that he had attacked early in his regime. When the Anglican archbishop and several ministers criticized the massacres of Langi and Acholi peoples, Amin ordered their assassinations. All in all, it is estimated that some 500,000 Ugandans died from violence during the eight years of dictatorship. But it was Amin's comically misguided foreign policy ventures that spelled his doom.

In September 1972, former members of Obote's military and security forces—now organized into a guerrilla army under the command of David Oyite-Ojok and Yuweri Museveni, both former military officers—invaded the country from neighboring Tanzania, intending to overthrow the Amin regime. Amin, supplied with weapons by the Soviet Union and Libya—for which he had paid with the property stolen from the exiled Asian community, sent his air force to bomb Tanzanian towns, provoking Tanzanian president Julius Nyerere to sever diplomatic relations and begin organizing a coalition of East African heads of state to oppose Amin. Amin also managed to offend the United States by making scandalous charges against President Jimmy Carter and threatening the American ambassador and his family. The United States cut off relations with Uganda as well.

Uganda's diplomatic isolation soon had detrimental effects on its economy. Much of the commercial and industrial sector was in ruins. Most of the commercial agricultural plantations had closed down. What little international trade Uganda still engaged in was mostly conducted by smugglers. Unemployment in the cities skyrocketed, and people began to grow hungry in a country that once had been a food exporter. Having purged his government of any and all competent administrators, Amin now surrounded himself with sycophants who catered to his every paranoid fantasy. His regime soon reached new levels of depravity as Amin took personal charge of the torture and murder of supposed opponents, going so far as to store their body parts in huge refrigerators in his compound, where he would examine them and show them off to visitors.

The morass the country was sinking into was evident even to formerly loyal officers in the military. Soon Amin's many enemies were hatching clandestine plots to overthrow him; popular unrest grew. In response, Amin cooked up a desperate and fantastical plan to divert the army and public's attention from the troubles he had inflicted on the country. In October 1978, Amin launched an invasion of Tanzania, with the aim of seizing the Kagera area, which would give landlocked Uganda access to the Indian Ocean. The invasion was easily turned back by the Tanzanian army, but Tanzanian president Nyerere was infuriated. He came to the conclusion that Amin had to go.

Lining up his fellow East African heads of state and encouraging Ugandan exiles to form a united anti-Amin front, Nyerere made his move in January 1979. Meeting little resistance from the demoralized Ugandan army and their 1,500 Libyan allies, the Tanzanian army and the new Uganda National Liberation Army (UNLA) quickly rolled across the country and captured the capital, Kampala, in April. Amin fled the country for Saudi Arabia, where he lived until his death in 2003.

Aftermath

Even before Kampala was taken, the political parties of the early years of independence began to organize an interim government. In early March, they organized a conference, establishing a new political party—the Uganda National Liberation Front (UNLF)—and a thirty-member national consultative committee to serve as a temporary legislature. Obote, responding to Nyerere's suggestion that he would antagonize delegates, agreed not to participate, and a former academic named Yusufu Lule was picked to run the national executive committee and serve as president until general elections could be held. After attempting to reorganize the executive committee, however, the consultative committee ousted Lule in favor of former attorney general Godfrey Binaisa.

Meanwhile, post-Amin Uganda was descending into anarchy. Relations between Tanzanian soldiers and guerrillas of the UNLA deteriorated as the latter began to fight amongst themselves along ethnic lines, often at the instigation of the many untrained recruits brought into the army during its reconquest of Uganda. Moreover, many of the new troops began to engage in the same kind of looting of property and violence against civilians that marked the Amin regime. In late 1979, Obote convinced Binaisa to dismiss both Oyite-Ojok and Museveni from their respective positions of chief of staff and defense minister, resulting in an army mutiny that placed the two back in power.

A year later, in December 1980, the promised general elections were held, with all of the old parties participating. While the Democratic Party was prevented from registering its candidates because of supposed technical violations of the electoral law, the Uganda People's Conference (Obote's old party) split into a mainstream faction, headed by Obote, and a radical group under Museveni. In the end, the mainstream UPC faction swept the elections, returning Obote to the presidency after some nine years in exile.

James Ciment

See also: Coups; Uganda: Civil Conflict Since 1980.

Bibliography

Hansen, Holger Bernt, and Michael Twaddle, eds. *Uganda Now: Between Decay and Development.* Athens: Ohio University Press, 1988.

Kasfir, Nelson. *The Shrinking Political Arena: Participation and Ethnicity in African Politics, with a Case Study of Uganda.* Berkeley: University of California Press, 1976.

Kyemba, Henry. *A State of Blood: The Inside Story of Idi Amin.* New York: Ace Books, 1977.

Mamdani, Mahmood. *Politics and Class Formation in Uganda.* New York: Monthly Review Press, 1976.

Mazrui, Ali Al'Amin. *Soldiers and Kinsmen in Uganda: The Making of a Military Ethnocracy.* Beverly Hills, CA: Sage, 1975.

Mittelman, James H. *Ideology and Politics in Uganda: From Obote to Amin.* Ithaca, NY: Cornell University Press, 1975.

UGANDA: Civil Conflict Since 1980

TYPE OF CONFLICT: Religious and Ethnic; Coups
PARTICIPANT: Rwanda

After former dictator Milton Obote was elected its president in 1980, Uganda settled into several years of tension and low-level violence. The former dictator, Idi Amin, who had been ousted from power by Ugandan rebels and the Tanzanian army in 1979, had left a legacy of corruption and rule by terror that was difficult to eradicate. Obote's security forces, though not as extensive or violent as those under Amin, engaged in many of the same oppressive and destructive tactics, acting as a law unto themselves.

Meanwhile, several small guerrilla groups opposed Obote and his United People's Congress (UPC). The groups included the Uganda National Rescue Front (UNRF), former Amin supporters operating out of the former dictator's home district in the west; the Ugandan Freedom Movement (UFM); and the National Resistance Army (NRA), led by former defense minister and radical UPC politician Yuweri Museveni, operating out of the Luwero Triangle north of the capital.

Obote was a northerner whose coalition included southern Buganda people (precolonial rulers of Uganda) in addition to the Acholi and Langi of the north. He was disliked by the radical and disaffected Buganda. The opposition also won the support of the Banyarwanda Tutsi, exiles from Rwanda who were fleeing from an anti-Tutsi Hutu government. To counter the increasingly powerful NRA, Obote and his Uganda National Liberation Army (UNLA) launched massive raids on Luwero. The attacks succeeded in driving tens of thousands of civilians into refugee camps; thousands of others became NRA supporters.

Obote also faced serious economic problems. After spending the International Monetary Fund loans it received upon coming to power in 1980, the government found itself unable to provide the subsidies for basic food and fuel. Further loans were not forthcoming because investigations conducted by the U.S. Congress and Amnesty International in 1984 found the UPC government guilty of gross violations of human rights and the deaths of tens of thousands of Ugandan citizens. While not as flamboyant as Amin, Obote was proving himself a dictator of the worst kind.

Museveni Takes Power

Meanwhile, ethnic divisions in the army were coming to a head. In 1985, the two largest groups—the Acholi and the Langi—began to fire upon each other within the Kampala barracks. The Acholi left the barracks and marched northward, where they joined forces with the UNRF, even though their traditional rivals, the West Nile people, dominated the latter. Together, the two forces returned to Kampala, forcing Obote to flee to Kenya and later to Zambia. But even as the new Acholi-dominated government, headed by Tito Okello, tried to assert its control over

315

KEY DATES

1979	Dictator Idi Amin is overthrown in an invasion by the Tanzanian Army and guerrillas of the Uganda National Liberation Army (UNLA).
1980	Former dictator Milton Obote is elected president; several factions of parties defeated in the election form small guerrilla groups in opposition to the ruling Uganda People's Congress (UPC).
1985	Ethnic divisions within the national army lead to violence in the Kampala barracks; Obote is overthrown in a military coup.
1986	Yuweri Museveni, head of the National Resistance Army (NRA) guerrilla organization, seizes power.
1991	Museveni dispatches the NRA to destroy various guerrilla forces in the north of the country.
1994	Uganda-based Tutsi rebels invade neighboring Rwanda and end the Hutu genocide of Tutsi in that country.
1996	Museveni is overwhelmingly elected president.
1999	Uganda and Sudan sign an agreement whereby each side promises to stop aiding or providing sanctuary for rebel movements in the other country.
2003–2004	The Ugandan army conducts a major offensive against rebels of the Lord's Resistance Army (LRA), but the group's attacks on refugee camps continue.

the country, it faced the same challenge that Obote had—the NRA, which had expanded its territory to include much of the south and west of the country.

At the end of 1985, the Okello government agreed to meet with Museveni, head of the NRA, to arrange a cease-fire and a possible power-sharing arrangement. In fact, Okello was using the talks as a cover for disarming his West Nile allies, who were threatening a coup d'état. The West Nile people fled to their homeland in the northwest, destroying everything in their path. Museveni, realizing that the power-sharing agreement with Okello was meaningless, broke off the talks and returned to the NRA in the southwest to plan an offensive to take the capital. He attacked and drove Okello out of power in January 1986.

Museveni invited civilians into his government and promised an administration of national reconcili-

ation. He established a commission to investigate the abuses of the Amin, Obote, and Okello regimes; the report they issued was horrifying. As many as 800,000 Ugandans had been killed by the violence that had torn apart the country since Obote's original coup in 1966. Museveni dismissed 2,500 police officers who were suspected of committing human rights violations and created a nationwide network of resistance committees, made up of local civilians. The committees were charged with preventing official abuses and corruption and protecting villages against guerrilla and bandit attacks.

Continuing Violence

Guerilla threats were especially challenging in the early years of the Museveni administration. Various guerrilla armies—including loyalists of the former Amin and Obote regimes—were wreaking havoc throughout the north of the country. Often nothing more than lawless bands, they looted property, raped women, and forced peasants to work for them. Often they assassinated officials, teachers, and anyone else they perceived as working for the Museveni government. Among the strangest of these groups was the Holy Spirit Movement, led by a charismatic cult leader named Alice Lakwena and manned by Acholi peasants. Virtually unarmed, they attacked the NRA with machetes and spears. Not surprisingly, they were easily overcome by the army, which killed several thousand. The survivors fled to neighboring Kenya, where they organized themselves as the Lord's Resistance Army (LRA).

A more serious challenge were the remnants of the antigovernment guerrillas operating in the north and northwest of the country. In April 1991, the NRA launched a sweep of the area, hoping to wipe out the guerrilla armies. By July, the army reported having killed 1,500 and arresting 1,000 more, though human rights organizations cited the army for abuses against civilians. Though facing guerrilla challenges, as well as several coup plots within his own army, Museveni was also making conciliatory gestures. To appease the opposition, he offered cabinet positions and other favors. To gain support from the international community, he formally invited the Asian Ugandans—brutally expelled by Amin in 1972—to come back to Uganda and, where possible, recoup the property that had been seized from them.

Gradually Museveni introduced more stability and prosperity than Uganda had seen since the early years of independence. Though he claimed that political parties antagonize ethnic divisions, he slowly allowed the introduction of opposition parties. His efforts were rewarded by the Ugandan people, who elected him president in 1996 with nearly three-quarters of the vote, and by the international community. International lending agencies, governments, and nongovernmental organizations, pleased by the progress he had made in reestablishing a degree of democracy and reviving the economy, offered financial and other forms of help. Less satisfactory to outsiders—particularly the French—was the support he offered the Banyarwanda Tutsi exiles from Rwanda in their attacks on the French-supported Hutu government there in the 1980s. In 1994, however, Museveni helped the Tutsi launch the invasion that

helped end the slaughter of Tutsis by Hutu forces. In 1997, the Museveni government supported the military campaign of Laurent Kabila in the Congo to oust Mobutu Sese Seko from power. The next year, Museveni supported the campaign to remove Kabila himself.

One remaining challenge for the Museveni government was the Lord's Resistance Army. Having moved from Kenya to southern Sudan, it reputedly received arms and assistance from the Islamist government there. The Sudanese were said to provide the assistance to counter Uganda's supposed support of black Christian rebels in Sudan. Whatever the truth of these assertions, the LRA mounted major attacks on villages in northwestern Uganda during 1995 and 1996, killing, torturing, raping, and abducting civilians (for training as guerrilla fighters), while also virtually enslaving numerous children. The LRA was mystical and secretive, claiming to seek the establishment of a government founded on the Bible's Ten Commandments, yet it lacked any real political agenda. It proved difficult to negotiate with and difficult to eradicate by force. While the Ugandan army conducted extensive sweeps of the northwest, the LRA continued to launch attacks on civilians and military outposts. Some 10,000 people were killed in the fighting, and the unrest in the region led to food shortages among a population of some 230,000 Ugandan refugees.

In 1999, Uganda and Sudan signed an agreement by which Sudan agreed to stop funding the LRA and Uganda agreed to end support for the Sudan People's Liberation Army (SPLA). The agreement reduced the level of LRA attacks, but the group remained a threat to Ugandan civilians in the north and west. In early 2003, there was hope that peace talks would resume. Later that year, Ugandan troops conduced another massive roundup of LRA rebels, resulting in the rescue of over 7,000 abductees and the killing or arrest of 1,700 rebels, according to the Ugandan Defense Ministry. These intermittent roundups were setbacks for future LRA terror campaigns, but the group continued its attacks. It also seems likely that the LRA continues to receive supplies and assistance from groups outside Uganda.

Uganda in the Twenty-first Century

By the early 2000s, Uganda had 27 million inhabitants. Approximately one-third were Catholic, another third Protestant, and the balance split nearly evenly between Muslims and those holding indigenous beliefs. The Buganda people remained the largest ethnic group, representing approximately 17 percent of the population; the remaining population represented more than two dozen ethnic groups. With so many ethnic groups, one alone often controls the government, security organizations, and much of the economy. This is often unacceptable to other ethnic groups and leads to conflict along ethnic lines. When these rivalries persist, they pose a challenge to peace and stability in the region. Often conflicts spill over into neighboring countries, since larger ethnic groups commonly straddle borders.

Thus, the continuing challenge for Uganda continued to be addressing the diversity and inequality between different ethnic groups. To complicate matters, the Museveni government was often accused of nepotism and corruption. Ministers were censored in Parliament on charges of influence peddling and corruption. The World Bank mission to Uganda in 1998 revealed widespread secrecy, insider dealings, and corruption, even at the highest levels of government. Cases of large-scale embezzlement were common, including the theft of donor funds disbursed to the ministries of health and education and to the Ugandan Electoral Commission.

Despite Uganda's vast natural resources, its people remained in the grip of poverty, squalor, and destitution. UN Secretary-General Kofi Annan frequently lashed out at corrupt African leaders, noting that the UN Security Council spends the majority of its time working on issues related to Africa. In Uganda, the Political Organizations Bill, passed by Parliament in 2001, aimed to remove restrictions on political parties and open up more space for new reform-minded movements. President Museveni's government opposed these measures and further consolidated its position. In the March 2001 presidential election, Museveni captured 69.3 percent of the vote, and his opponent, Colonel Kizza Besigye, went into self-imposed exile. Besigye's wife, Winnie Byanyima, an outspoken opposition member of Parliament, remained in her government post during the elections, but soon afterward she was dismissed for speaking out against government corruption. Later she was charged with illegally possessing a handgun.

Although additional political reforms aimed at reducing ethnic conflict were being considered by a Constitutional Review Commission (CRC), the government remained opposed to empowering real opposition parties. In general, the Museveni era brought some stability and economic improvement to the country. As long as effective political opposition is forbidden, however, the situation in Uganda will remain tense.

James Ciment and Luke Nichter

See also: Ethnic and Religious Conflicts; Sudan: Civil War in South, 1955–1972; 1983–2005; Uganda: Anti-Amin Struggle, 1971–1979.

Bibliography

Ayittey, George B.N. *Africa Unchained: The Blueprint for Africa's Future.* New York: Palgrave-Macmillan, 2005.

Bastian, Sunil, and Robin Luckham, eds. *Can Democracy Be Designed? The Politics of Institutional Choice in Conflict-Torn Societies.* New York: St. Martin's Press, 2003.

Hansen, Bernt Holder, and Michael Twaddle, eds. *From Chaos to Order: The Politics of Constitutionmaking in Uganda.* London: J. Currey, 1995.

WESTERN SAHARA: Polisario-Moroccan War, 1975–1991

TYPE OF CONFLICT: Anticolonialism; Invasions and Border Disputes
PARTICIPANTS: Morocco; Mauritania

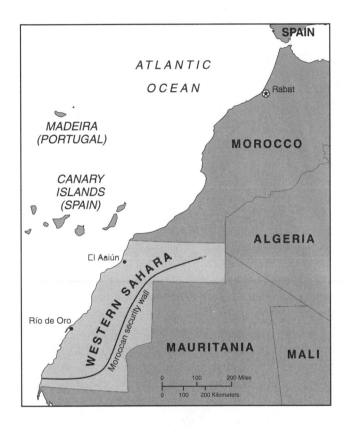

Western Sahara (formerly Spanish Sahara) is located at the extreme western edge of the Sahara Desert. One of the harshest environments on earth, it averages only about two inches of rain per year. Much of its territory is gravel desert with sparse vegetation. It borders Morocco in the north, Algeria in the northeast, and Mauritania to the south and east. Its long Atlantic coastline is rocky, lined with sandbars, and largely bereft of natural harbors. Along the coast is a narrow belt of sand dunes about ten to twenty miles wide. Much of the interior is windswept gravel plains.

The Western Sahara has two major regions. In the north is the Saguia El-Hamra region of the Saguia El-Hamra (the "Red River") valley. It is the only important river in the country, but it flows only in the wet season. Western Sahara's southern region is known as the Río de Oro.

From time immemorial, the territory of the Western Sahara has been inhabited by nomadic ethnic groups. Because of the harshness of the desert climate, the population is thin and widely dispersed over some 100,000 square miles of territory. The native people are Arabs, Berbers, Tuaregs, Reguibat, Delim, and Izarguen. The people today are collectively referred to as Saharawis. While all are Muslim and under leaders who claim descent from the prophet Muhammad, no supratribal government had ever established authority in the region, though an elaborate caste system rates some groups as higher in status than others. These castes contain various groups of nomads within them, each group related by complicated kinship ties to a ruling family. The tribes remain independent of each other and engage in generations-long blood feuds.

Historical Background

The Spanish established their first settlement in the region at Río de Oro Bay in 1884 but were unable to pacify the interior of the region until the 1930s. As late as the early 1950s, the Spanish presence was minimal: a few villages and several hundred settlers. But the discovery of vast phosphate deposits—critical in the production of chemical fertilizers—in the latter years of the decade changed all that. In 1962, the Spanish established their first major phosphate-processing plant in the Western Sahara, and by the early 1970s, the territory had become the sixth largest producer of the mineral in the world. Within these same years, some 20,000 Spanish workers and administrators settled in the region.

KEY DATES

1884	Spain takes over control of the region that will become the Western Sahara.
1958	Numerous Saharawis, or people of the Western Sahara, are forced to flee to Morocco after their uprising against Spanish rule is put down.
1973	Saharawi nationalists, exiled in Morocco, form the Polisario Front to fight for Western Saharan independence from Spain.
1974	Spain announces it will offer the Saharawi a referendum on independence in 1975.
1975	Citing prior claims to the mineral-rich territory, Morocco and Mauritania launch an invasion of the Western Sahara; in response to the invasion, the Polisario announces the formation of the Saharawi Arab Democratic Republic and the formation of the Saharawi Popular Liberation Army (SPLA).
1978	Backed by Algeria, guerrillas of the SPLA launch an invasion of Mauritania, forcing that country to give up its claims to territory in the Western Sahara.
1978–1982	The SPLA establishes control over 90 percent of the territory of the Western Sahara.
1991	UN Secretary-General Javier Pérez de Cuéllar negotiates a cease-fire between the SPLA and Morocco, but the fighting continues.
2000	Talks are held between Polisario and Morocco in London and Berlin.
2003	International energy corporations begin exploring for oil in the Western Sahara.
2005	The Algerian president declares that the Western Sahara conflict can only be resolved through the mediation of the UN.

These developments, along with several prolonged droughts, encouraged thousands of Saharawis to settle on the outskirts of Spanish settlements in the 1960s, where they were given some access to education and paid employment. By 1974, roughly half the population was living in towns. The Spanish also offered limited self-rule in a territorial assembly.

While Spain occupied the Western Sahara from 1884 to 1975, two neighboring African countries—Morocco to the north and Mauritania to the east and south—have had claims on the territory since their own independence. Morocco's independence from France in 1958 inspired the first anticolonial guerrilla movement in Western Sahara, known as the Saharawi wing of Morocco's Army of Liberation. But this force was quickly subdued by a Spanish-French expeditionary force. With the support of Algeria—Morocco's chief rival for political dominance in northwestern Africa—Mauritania claimed the right to rule through an ethnic affinity with the Saharawi people.

Meanwhile, both the United Nations and the Organization of African Unity (OAU) began pushing for self-determination of the Saharawi nation in the mid-1960s. Spain agreed, but threw up delay after delay, arguing that the nomadic nature of the inhabitants made self-government difficult to establish. Finally, in August 1974, as the Francisco Franco regime entered its final, senescent days, Madrid announced it would offer the Saharawi a referendum on independence sometime during the first half of 1975. To maintain its control over the mineral resources of the territory, Spain began grooming a compliant new leader for Western Sahara, Kahlihenna Ould Rachid and his Partido de la Unión Nacional Saharaui (PUNS). The announcement angered Morocco's King Hassan, who believed he had a tacit understanding with the Spanish that the territory would be turned over to his government rather than being given independence. His threats forced Spain to announce yet another delay in the referendum.

Saharawi Nationalism

Developing a national consciousness out of a collection of dispersed and mutually antagonistic nomadic groups was not an easy task. Two factors, however, were key. First, Spain and Morocco—both hoping to develop a pliable local elite who could run the territory for them—permitted hundreds of children of tribal leaders to receive an education at schools and universities in the two countries. Many more Saharawis, forced to migrate to Morocco after the failed uprising of 1958, also became educated. But, as is often the case, these educated elites came to serve as the core of a Saharawi nationalist movement.

While studying in Morocco, a group of Saharawi students began organizing around a refugee student named El-Ouali Mustapha Sayed. At first, they allied themselves with Moroccan opposition parties, hoping they could pressure the king to push for independence for the Western Sahara. But after anti-Spanish

Commandos of the Polisario Front independence group in Western Sahara scramble to take positions near the front line with Morocco in June 1988. As of the mid-2000s, the conflict over sovereignty defied resolution. *(AFP/Getty Images)*

demonstrations were broken up by Moroccan police, Sayed and other Saharawi leaders decided that the struggle had to be based in the Western Sahara. In May 1973, these leaders organized the Polisario Front (a Spanish acronym for the Popular Liberation of Sahara and Río de Oro) on the border of Western Sahara and Mauritania.

The second event contributing to a development of a Saharawi nationalism, one that permeated the masses as well as the elites, was the Mauritanian-Moroccan invasion of 1975. While the former country merely sent in troops to occupy a strip along its northern border with Western Sahara, Morocco launched its so-called Green March, whereby some 350,000 civilians marched across the sands in a "peaceful" occupation, with the clear indication that Morocco was there to stay. Pressured by this stunt, Spain negotiated with Hassan. Then, having worked out a deal to retain economic rights, Madrid reversed itself in November 1975, allowing troops from Morocco and Mauritania to occupy the Western Sahara upon its departure.

In response to the occupation, the Polisario declared the establishment of the Saharawi Arab Democratic Republic (SADR) and launched the Saharawi Popular Liberation Army (SPLA). Armed by its Algerian allies, the SPLA launched an invasion of Mauritania, quickly overwhelming that country's tiny military and forcing its government in Nouakchott to give up its claims on Western Sahara and pull out its remaining troops in 1978.

War Between the Polisario and Morocco

Morocco—with one of the largest and most modern armies in northern Africa—proved much harder to dislodge. Still, from 1978 to 1982, the SPLA was able to establish control over about nine-tenths of the territory of Western Sahara, launch guerrilla attacks that paralyzed the phosphate mining industry, and drive Moroccan troops from most of their posts. In response, Morocco decided to change tactics. It began construction of huge defensive sand berms—augmented by minefields, heavy armaments, and electronic sensing equipment—around much of the settled and economically crucial parts of the territory.

The strategy worked, after a fashion. The SPLA found it extremely difficult to establish permanent control over territories inside these defenses, and the phosphate industry not only returned to production but actually expanded under Moroccan protection. At the same time, the cost of these defenses—which include some 150,000 troops—is staggering, offsetting much of the profits from the mining industry. Indeed, the conflict settled into a war of attrition through much of the 1980s. The Polisario was unable to stop the mining operations or drive the Moroccans out, but it continued to breach the defenses almost at will, inflicting heavy casualties on Moroccan units. Meanwhile, the SADR supplemented its battlefield efforts in the diplomatic arena, where it won the recognition of most African states as well as twenty-five more in the rest of the world.

Negotiations and Elections

By the late 1980s, however, both sides were indicating that they might be willing to find a negotiated solution. The Moroccans were tired of the war, and, because of increased instability in Algeria, the Polisario has lost much of the support it received from its main ally. In 1988 and again in 1991, UN Secretary-General Javier Pérez de Cuéllar worked to win an agreement from both sides, calling for the gradual withdrawal of Moroccan troops and the demobilization of SPLA fighters under UN auspices. These moves would precede a referendum in which the residents of the territory would be offered three choices: continued Moroccan rule, full independence, or a compromise federated status with Morocco. Despite sporadic fighting and violations of the cease-fire arranged in 1991, progress toward a peaceful settlement has proceeded.

The main sticking point, however, was the election or, more specifically, registration for the election. While the UN mission in the territory based the voter rolls on a 1974 Spanish census, Morocco has continued to claim that some 400,000 people are eligible to vote, more than half of whom have been living in Morocco for over two decades. The Polisario, knowing that many of these refugees will vote for continued Moroccan sovereignty, insists on a smaller and tighter registration list.

Events Since 2000

The official Arabic name for Western Sahara used by the Polisario is al-Jumhuriya as-Sahrawiya ad-Dimuqratiya al-'Arabiya (Democratic Arab Republic of Sahara). In 2000 talks were held in London and Berlin between the Polisario and Morocco, in response to UN Security Council Resolution 1309. Both Morocco and the Polisario were intransigent, however, and no progress was made in resolving the conflict.

Tension mounted, with a referendum on independence delayed as a result. In April 2001 Morocco proposed the "Third Option," a ten-year transition period for studying a way to implement a self-determination referendum. Mohamed Abdelaziz, the leader of the Polisario, renewed its declaration that the conflict could only be resolved by respecting the right of the Saharawi to self-determination.

In recent decades, the leadership of the Polisario has become more skilled at diplomacy and public relations, as they have sought to present their case in a growing number of public forums. The Polisario Front proposed its own peace plan (June 4, 2001), which was essentially a renewal of its call for a referendum leading to independence for Western Sahara. It accepted the UN secretary-general's special envoy, former U.S. Secretary of State James Baker, as a mediator, but his efforts produced little in the way of agreement.

In 2002, both the Organization for African Unity (now the African Union) and Spain renewed their positions that the solution to the conflict lay in self-determination. However, in November the king of Morocco, Mohamed VI, rejected the United Nations Settlement Plan for Western Sahara. The king said that autonomy was possible but not independence. France supported Morocco in this position.

In 2003 and 2004, Kerr-McGee and other oil companies began exploring Western Sahara for oil, but the deal was opposed by a coalition of more than twenty activist groups spread across four continents. Activists in Norway were able to pressure the state-owned oil company to dissolve its ties with Kerr-McGree. These groups sided with Western Sahara, viewing the Moroccan occupation as illegal; thus, any oil deals Morocco makes for exploration in Western Sahara are also illegal.

The struggle continued in 2005, with the Polisario charging Morocco with engaging in human rights abuses because of harsh treatment of its supporters at the hands of Moroccan police. Amnesty International also accused Morocco of mistreating civil society activists who were working for Western Saharan independence.

As of the mid-2000s, no resolution of the conflict appeared imminent. Because of the very small Saharawi population, the weight of numbers and of power seemed to favor Morocco in the long term.

James Ciment and Andrew J. Waskey

See also: People's Wars; Invasions and Border Disputes; Mauritania: Coups Since 1978.

Bibliography

Hodges, Tony. *Western Sahara: The Roots of a Desert War.* Westport, CT: L. Hill, 1983.

Jensen, Erik. *Western Sahara: Anatomy of a Stalemate.* Boulder, CO: Lynne Rienner, 2004.

Kamil, Leo. *Fueling the Fire: U.S. Policy and the Western Sahara Conflict.* Trenton, NJ: Red Sea Press, 1987.

Shelly, Toby. *Endgame in the Western Sahara: What Future for Africa's Last Colony?* New York: Zed Books, 2004.

Thobhani, Akbarali. *Western Sahara Since 1975 Under Moroccan Administration: Social, Economic and Political Transformation.* Lewiston, NY: Lampeter, 2002.

Volman, Daniel, and Yahia Zoubir, eds. *International Dimensions of the Western Sahara Conflict.* Westport, CT: Praeger, 1993.

ZIMBABWE: Struggle for Majority Rule, 1965–1980

TYPE OF CONFLICT: Anticolonialism

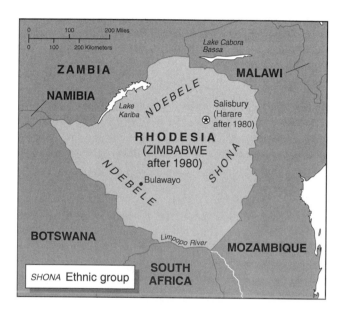

The first civilizations in what is now Zimbabwe date back roughly a thousand years to the building of the stone city of Great Zimbabwe. Under the authority of their kings, the people of Zimbabwe engaged in iron making, cattle raising, and trade that extended to both the southwestern and southeastern coasts of Africa. By the second half of the fifteenth century, Great Zimbabwe had been abruptly abandoned, probably because of climatic change; long-lasting droughts are a frequent occurrence in the region. Great Zimbabwe's extensive territories were divided between several different civilizations, including the Mutapa, Ndebele, and Torwa kingdoms, the latter giving way to the Rozwi dynasty around 1700. The Mutapa, Ndebele, and Rozwi kingdoms continued until well into the nineteenth century and the arrival of large numbers of white settlers from South Africa. The predominant ethnic groups during this period and down to the present are the Shona, Ndebele, and Tonga.

Until the arrival of British and Boer settlers in the late nineteenth century, the peoples of Zimbabwe had little contact with the outside world, though they conducted trade with the coastal settlements on the Indian Ocean, first with the Arabs and then, after the 1500s, with the Portuguese. Indeed, Portuguese settlement of coastal southwest and southeast South Africa (now Angola and Mozambique, respectively) led to the creation of a mixed caste of Afro-Portuguese *asimilados*, who acted as middlemen between the cattle-raising kingdoms of highland Zimbabwe and port cities on the Atlantic and Indian Oceans. But, by and large, European settlement in southern Africa remained confined to a few coastal settlements and the Cape Colony of Boers, descendants of early Dutch settlers, until the late nineteenth century.

Europeans largely stayed out for several reasons. First, the climate along the coasts was not particularly conducive to European settlement, with malaria taking its toll on humans and the tsetse fly making livestock raising impossible. Moreover, the presence of well-organized and well-defended African kingdoms in the region discouraged all but the most intrepid explorers. Yet, early explorers like David Livingstone and Henry Stanley did penetrate the region, reporting that the interior of southern Africa was much different from the coasts, with the highlands offering a benign climate free of the malarial mosquito and the tsetse fly.

White Settlement

The most dramatic event in modern southern African history, however, had to do with a different kind of finding. The discoveries first of diamonds and then of gold in the 1870s and 1880s in the Transvaal region of South Africa vastly accelerated settlement south of the Limpopo River, which now divides

KEY DATES

1963 Divisions within the African nationalist opposition to colonial rule lead to the formation of two competing black resistance groups, the Zimbabwe African People's Union (ZAPU) and the Zimbabwe African National Union (ZANU).

1964 Britain grants independence to Zambia, the former Northern Rhodesia.

1965 Fearing Britain will turn over power to the black majority, the minority white population of Rhodesia (formerly Southern Rhodesia) unilaterally declares the country independent, with themselves in power.

1974 The victory of black nationalists over Portuguese colonists in neighboring Mozambique gives a major boost to ZANU forces, which establish bases there.

1976 ZANU and ZAPU form an uneasy alliance, leading to intensification of the struggle against the white minority regime.

1979 Negotiations between the white minority regime and ZANU/ZAPU representatives lead to a cease-fire and agreement for nonracial national elections to be held in 1980.

1980 Nonracial elections lead to the victory of ZANU leader Robert Mugabe as president of the newly renamed Zimbabwe.

South Africa and Zimbabwe. As mining concession hunters poured into Ndebele lands, the British high commissioner for the Cape colony declared what is now present-day Zimbabwe a British sphere of influence.

In 1888, Cecil Rhodes, organizer of the De Beers diamond conglomerate and future prime minister of the Cape, sent his agents to the Ndebele king to secure exclusive mining rights for his British South Africa Company. At the same time, he received a royal charter to administer a vast area north of the Limpopo, later divided into Northern and Southern Rhodesia (which ultimately became Zambia and Zimbabwe). Local rulers agreed to allow this administration, as long as it applied largely to non-Africans.

In 1890, Rhodes sent a "pioneer column" into Shona territory. Three years later, he provoked and won a war against the Ndebele. But when the initial goal of discovering more gold deposits failed, the settlers were granted extensive farmlands, which soon passed into the hands of speculators. A combined Ndebele-Shona revolt in 1896, brutally put down by the British, represented the last major African challenge to British rule until after World War II.

In the meantime, white colonists continued to pour into the colony as news spread of its agricultural potential and benign climate. In 1923, the British government took over administration of what was now referred to as Southern Rhodesia from Rhodes's British South Africa Company, allowing white settlers a large margin of autonomous rule, but virtually no political power to blacks. In 1930, the foundations of Southern Rhodesia's segregated and white-supremacist society were laid with the passage of the Land Apportionments Act. Under this law, the colony was divided into two territories, one set aside for each race. The territory for whites was far larger and more fertile than the one for blacks. Statutes were also passed that restricted black access to education, jobs, and agricultural commerce, so that they could not compete with white workers and farmers. Like South Africa, Rhodesia enacted pass laws, which limited blacks to working as migrant laborers in the white areas.

The period immediately following World War II represented a time of great economic growth in Rhodesia and renewed black agitation. By 1960, Rhodesia's population of 200,000 whites and 4,000,000 blacks was becoming increasingly urbanized, as the colony developed an industrial economy second on the continent only to South Africa. Needing a better-trained workforce, the government expanded educational opportunities for blacks. But the economic prosperity was very unequally shared, producing a wave of strikes and rural protests throughout the late 1950s and early 1960s, just at the time other sub-Saharan countries were winning their independence.

The British responded with a plan to create a Central African Federation out of what is now Zimbabwe, Zambia, and Malawi, in which both races would govern equally. But the two latter countries, which had never been heavily settled by whites, rejected the plan, forcing London to break up the federation and grant Malawi and Zambia independence in 1964. The move terrified the white settlers in Rhodesia, who feared they would be handed over to a black government.

Under the white-supremacist Rhodesian Front party, the colonists demanded independence from Britain under a minority-rule constitution. When Britain refused, the Front elected the intransigent Ian Smith as prime minister. In November 1965, Smith and the Front carried out their long-threatened Universal Declaration of Independence from Britain. Though shunned by the international community, Rhodesia prospered over the next decade, protected by the white minority regime in South Africa and by the Portuguese presence in Mozambique.

Struggle for Majority Rule

During the ferment of the late 1950s, several major black political organizations demanding majority rule were formed in Rhodesia. Largely confined to urban areas, they were infiltrated by security agents of the white colonial regime. In 1963, the African nationalist opposition experienced internal divisions, which led to the formation of two competing organizations: the Zimbabwe African People's Union (ZAPU) and the Zimbabwe African National Union (ZANU). The former, led by Joshua Nkomo and popular among the Ndebele people, was the more conservative of the two organizations, advocating a power-sharing relationship with whites in the country. Based in Zambia, it received assistance from the Soviet Union and several East European countries and launched guerrilla raids inside Rhodesia, hoping to spark a confrontation between the black majority states in the region and Rhodesia and force the latter to accept a power-sharing agreement.

ZANU was the more radical organization, demanding black majority rule for Zimbabwe. Headed first by the Reverend Ndabaningi Sithole and, after 1975, by Robert Mugabe, ZANU's strength lay in the Shona community of eastern Zimbabwe. It operated from bases inside Portuguese Mozambique in zones controlled by its ally, the Mozambique Liberation Front (known by its Portuguese abbreviation, Frelimo). ZANU received aid from China in its attempts to infiltrate Rhodesia and mobilize the poor blacks against the white regime. ZANU was immensely bolstered in 1974, when Mozambique became independent, and Frelimo took power the following year.

Indeed, the independence of Mozambique under the radical Frelimo represented a watershed in the history of the Zimbabwe struggle. Under Portuguese rule, Mozambique had largely provided convenient ports for shipment of Rhodesian goods and had ignored international pressure to close the ports and rail lines to isolate Rhodesia. Mozambique's colonial military forces had worked closely with those in Rhodesia against both Frelimo and ZANU guerrillas. The new Frelimo government, on the other hand, imposed the full weight of economic sanctions against the white minority government in Rhodesia and gave its full support to the ZANU guerrillas. In response, the Rhodesian Central Intelligence Organization created the Mozambique National Resistance (Renamo) to destabilize the Frelimo government with the help of disaffected Mozambicans (including many of Portuguese descent). (Renamo would develop into one of the most destructive and vicious guerrilla movements in all of Africa and would outlast the white minority government in Rhodesia that had created it.)

Still, efforts were made to find a negotiated settlement in the mid-1970s. Fearful of the rise of pro-Communist regimes in southern Africa, both the United States and Britain hoped to prevent the radical forces of ZANU from taking over in Rhodesia. The white regime in South Africa, too, became a close ally of the Rhodesian government. Even Kenneth

Kaunda, leader of the conservative black regime in Zambia, was worried about radicalism in the region (and among his own people).

Rhodesia's Ian Smith proved a difficult leader to support, however. After several years of fruitless talks, the guerrilla war resumed with a new intensity in 1976. The insurgent forces gained strength when ZANU and ZAPU formed an uneasy alliance called the Patriotic Front (PF) and began to receive support from the so-called frontline states of black Africa: Angola, Mozambique, Botswana, Tanzania, and Zambia. Between 1972 and 1979, the combined forces of the PF grew from a few hundred guerrillas to more than 10,000. Meanwhile, the Rhodesian Security Forces (RSF)—divided into a quasi-military police force to guard the cities and areas of white settlement and an army trained in bush warfare—numbered about 100,000 well-equipped soldiers and reservists by 1979, most of whom by then were black.

The war between the RSF and the PF took on the character of a classic guerrilla struggle. Using its superior firepower and air resources—largely provided by South Africa—the RSF conducted search-and-destroy missions against PF guerrillas. Strong as it was, however, the RSF was hampered by growing rivalries in its own organization and the development of private militias in Rhodesia that became laws unto themselves, conducting looting operations and brutally attacking black villages. Among these militias were some made up of black warriors, who claimed to fight under the banner of Bishop Abel Murozewa, Smith's closest ally in the African community, but were really little more than criminal gangs. Foreign mercenaries—hired by wealthy white farmers to protect their persons and their property—also made an appearance as law and order began disintegrating in the late 1970s.

For its part, the PF tried to avoid direct encounters with the better-armed RSF, preferring instead to conduct hit-and-run attacks on isolated outposts and acts of sabotage and assassination against white settlers, before fading back into Mozambique. They also conducted a low-level bombing campaign in the capital, Salisbury (now Harare), and other white-controlled cities. By 1979, the PF had established control over large sections of eastern Zimbabwe, where they conducted political mobilization campaigns among the masses of peasants. The war had essentially become a stalemate between two roughly equivalent forces.

Negotiations

As the struggle between black and white forces intensified, outside groups were attempting to achieve a negotiated settlement. South Africa led the way. Prime Minister John Vorster believed that the Smith regime was losing the war and failing to find creative solutions to the problem of black majority rule. Vorster feared that an intransigent white minority regime in Rhodesia might help bring on its own defeat, resulting in the rise to power of a radical black regime, much like that in Mozambique and Angola. Vorster and his hard-line successor, P.W. Botha, did not want Rhodesia's skilled security apparatus and army falling into radical black hands. Instead, Pretoria wanted to see a negotiated settlement in which the black majority would be represented by a manageable black leader who would acquiesce in continuing white domination.

Calling on the United States—which, in 1976, still maintained close relations with South Africa—Vorster persuaded Secretary of State Henry Kissinger to come to Africa and mediate. After consultations with the British, who still considered themselves responsible for the Rhodesian situation, Kissinger tried to persuade the Smith regime to accept black majority rule, and to get the frontline states' leaders to realize the difference between immediate majority rule and immediate black power. Kissinger tried to fudge the difference but failed to convince black African leaders to go along. The Kissinger negotiations and similar Anglo-American initiatives in 1977 failed to find a negotiated solution that would satisfy black aspirations for power and white demands for continued dominance.

Still, Kissinger did reach a deal with Smith in which Smith would ceremonially step down and allow a black prime minister to take his place. In March 1978, Smith reached an agreement with the conservative black leader Bishop Able Murozewa, and on June 1, 1979, Murozewa became the first black prime minister of the new state of Zimbabwe-Rhodesia. But the facade of black rule was not convincing. The PF and most of the international community refused to take seriously a "black majority government" in which whites held all key ministerial posts, only a handful of blacks served as military officers, land reform was not carried out, and most of the segregation laws remained on the books.

Time was running out for the white regime. With much of its budget devoted to defense, falling prices for its major mineral exports, and stiffening international sanctions, Rhodesia was going bankrupt even as it descended into anarchy. The administration was unable to end the war, lift the international sanctions, or improve the lives of ordinary blacks in the country. Meanwhile, the guerrilla forces of the PF, now secure in their liberated territories, still proved unable to deliver the knockout blow to the white-controlled regime.

During the summer of 1979, the various parties to the conflict—under pressure from their respective allies—agreed that a negotiated settlement was in everyone's interest. The frontline states—increasingly under attack by Rhodesian forces pursuing Zimbabwe guerrillas—pushed the PF to the negotiating table. Meanwhile, hoping to involve the PF in the talks without guaranteeing them control of a new government, Britain and South Africa worked to push the Murozewa government to accept a deal in which a prime-minister-type system—rather than an executive-dominated one—would continue in a new government that would guarantee the white community a disproportionate (though not majority) voice in the legislature. This plan, it was hoped, would prevent the rise of a powerful and radical black regime in Zimbabwe.

Under the chairmanship of the British foreign minister, peace talks began at Lancaster House in London on September 10. After fourteen weeks, an agreement was signed in a form largely reflecting British and South African wishes. A cease-fire was immediately declared and plans for the demobilization of guerrilla forces put into action. Lord Soames, a senior British diplomat, replaced the Murozewa regime and directed the transition in preparation for democratic elections including all of Zimbabwe's black and white citizens in February 1980.

As the largest guerrilla movement in control of the most territory, ZANU decided to run its candidates under a banner separate from ZAPU. Several other parties—including Murozewa's and Smith's—

Black nationalist guerrillas loyal to the Zimbabwe African National Union of Robert Mugabe cheer a victory in the field in early 1980. Black majority rule came in April, with Mugabe installed as prime minister of the new republic. *(Pierre Haski/AFP/Getty Images)*

also contested the election. While white Rhodesians, South Africans, and the British hoped that anti-ZANU forces would win and form a coalition government, they were surprised and disappointed by the results. ZANU won 63 percent of the vote and 57 of the 100 seats in parliament. (Of the latter figure, twenty had been guaranteed to the white community.) On April 18, 1980, the new black majority state of Zimbabwe was officially declared, with ZANU leader Robert Mugabe as prime minister.

Zimbabwe Under Majority Rule

The new governing coalition of ZANU and ZAPU faced a host of problems, the trickiest of which was land reform. For most Zimbabwean peasants, the struggle of the last twenty years had largely been about winning back the lands they believed had been stolen from them by white farmers. But due to restrictions of the Lancaster House accords, continuing drought in the region, and the need to maintain the foreign earnings brought to the country by white-controlled commercial farming, Mugabe's government hesitated. Other problems included ethnic tensions between the ruling Shona people and other black groups in Zimbabwe, leading to a break-up of the ZANU and ZAPU coalition and a turn to banditry by some of the demobilized guerrilla forces that had served under ZAPU. International problems also continued. Across one border, in Mozambique, the war between Frelimo and Renamo continued, and across another border, the struggle against the apartheid system in South Africa intensified.

To deal with these problems, the Mugabe government adopted a more authoritarian style of rule. In 1987, it eliminated the seats reserved for whites and enacted constitutional changes that turned the presidency—once ceremonial—into a powerful executive branch. But the key question of land reform continued to bedevil the government. Efforts in 1997

to distribute the large estates of white landowners to black small-scale farmers produced a storm of controversy inside the country and led to a deterioration in value of the Zimbabwean currency abroad. The resulting inflation set off food riots in several cities, including the capital. As the economy continued its downward spiral, thousands of Zimbabweans emigrated in search of better conditions.

Only Robert Mugabe remained seemingly unchanged. He gained still another re-election in 2002 in an election widely believed to be rigged. In 2005 elections, his party gained a two-thirds majority in the parliament. Twenty-five years after independence, Mugabe was among the longest-serving political leaders in Africa.

James Ciment

See also: People's Wars; Ethnic and Religious Conflicts; Mozambique: Renamo War, 1976–1992; South Africa: Anti-Apartheid Struggle, 1948–1994.

Bibliography

Astrow, André. *Zimbabwe: A Revolution That Lost Its Way?* Totowa, NJ: Zed Press, 1983.

Caute, David. *Under the Skin: The Death of White Rhodesia.* London: Allen Lane, 1983.

Chidoda, A.M. *Understanding ZANU and the Armed Struggle to Liberate Zimbabwe.* Toronto: Norman Bethune Institute, 1977.

Flower, Ken. *Serving Secretly: An Intelligence Chief on Record: Rhodesia into Zimbabwe, 1964 to 1981.* London: J. Murray, 1987.

Gann, Lewis H. *The Struggle for Zimbabwe: Battle in the Bush.* New York: Praeger, 1981.

Godwin, Peter. *"Rhodesians Never Die": The Impact of War and Political Change on White Rhodesia, 1970–1980.* New York: Oxford University Press, 1993.

Mungazi, Dickson A. *Colonial Policy and Conflict in Zimbabwe: A Study of Cultures in Collision, 1890–1979.* New York: Crane Russak, 1992.

Verrier, Anthony. *The Road to Zimbabwe, 1890–1980.* London: J. Cape, 1986.

ZIMBABWE: Anti-Mugabe Struggle

TYPE OF CONFLICT: Popular Uprising

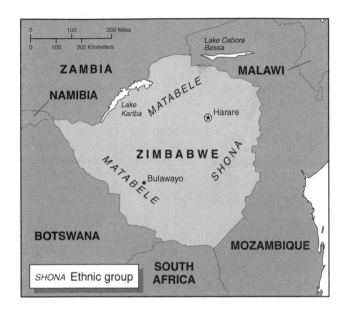

SHONA Ethnic group

Zimbabwe, a land-locked country in southern Africa, is known for its scenic beauty and the historic ruins of a native civilization dating to the twelfth century. It also gained notoriety in the postwar era for violent clashes between white colonizers and native Africans and for later violent conflicts among its African peoples. Zimbabwe has an area of about 150,000 square miles and a population approaching 13 million.

Until 1965, Zimbabwe was known as Southern Rhodesia and was a colony of Britain. In negotiations leading toward independence, the British government urged Rhodesian leaders to allow full voting rights for the colony's black majority. The white minority, which controlled much of the valuable farmland and the colony's main businesses, resisted. Finally, under Ian Smith, the white minority issued a Unilateral Declaration of Independence, establishing the white minority state of Rhodesia, resembling white-ruled South Africa, with which it shared a border.

For the next fifteen years, black nationalists fought a guerrilla war to bring majority rule to Rhodesia. One of the leaders of the insurgency was the Zimbabwe National Union (ZANU), led by Robert Mugabe. In 1979, the white minority government and the black guerrilla movements signed a British-brokered treaty calling for a democratic vote. The following year, Mugabe was elected president, and the country was renamed Zimbabwe.

Mugabe's administration began with great promise for economic and social success. By the mid-1990s, however, much of the promise had evaporated, as the country sank into a severe economic depression and experienced widespread human rights violations. As Mugabe continued to use violence to impose his less than effective policies, opposition grew, bringing increased violence and economic dislocation. Students, trade unionists, and homeless people mounted widespread protests and were in turn suppressed by government forces.

Early Conflicts

Opposition to Mugabe emerged soon after he assumed power in 1980. During the following year, the government discovered large stores of arms and ammunition built up by the Patriotic Front-Zimbabwe African People's Union (PF-ZAPU), an opposition party led by Joshua Nkomo, one of the leaders in the liberation struggle against white minority rule. Mugabe charged PF-ZAPU of plotting to overthrow his government, and Nkomo and his closest associates were removed from the presidential cabinet.

In response, Nkomo and PF-ZAPU launched a political protest campaign against the government. It had its center in Matabeleland in the southwest part of the country, home of the Ndebele people, who represented a minority (about 15 percent) of Zimbabwe's population and were devoted followers of Nkomo and his party. The protests included violent attacks on government personnel and property, armed theft and economic disruption, and harassment of Mugabe's ZANU party members. In addition to insisting that Nkomo and his associates be returned to the cabinet, PF-ZAPU members demanded that the government

KEY DATES

1980 After years of fighting, the white minority government of Rhodesia is replaced by a black majority government, with Zimbabwe African National Union leader Robert Mugabe as president; the country is renamed Zimbabwe.

1983 The government launches a military campaign in Matabeleland, center of political opposition to the Mugabe government.

1987 The leader of the opposition Zimbabwe African People's Union (ZAPU), Joshua Nkomo, signs an agreement to merge his party with ZANU, ending the conflict with the government.

1996 Civil servants strike against the government to protest economic policies that strike leaders say are bankrupting the country and impoverishing its people.

1999 Opposition groups form the Movement for Democratic Change (MDC).

2000 A referendum granting government officials immunity from prosecution and sanctioning seizure of white-owned farms fails at the polls; in response, the government launches a crackdown against opposition groups.

2005 With poverty spreading and unemployment estimated at almost 80 percent, the government launches Operation Murambatsvina ("Sweep Out the Trash"), targeting informal shanty towns around the capital of Harare.

return farms and other properties it had taken from PF-ZAPU members.

Mugabe was a member of the majority Shona people, who made up more than 80 percent of the country's population. Their homeland was in the north and east of the country, where the capital, Harare, is located. Mugabe encouraged a continuing conflict between the Ndebele and the Shona, though before he came to power, there had been little conflict between the two groups. In fact, they had cooperated in the long struggle for majority rule after 1965.

In 1983 and 1984, the government declared a curfew in parts of Matabelaland and launched a military campaign against dissidents. The so-called pacification campaign, Gukuruhundi ("Strong Wind"), was in fact marked by widespread violence and human rights abuses, including at least 20,000 civilian deaths. The conflict was resolved when Nkomo agreed to merge his PF-ZAPU party into ZANU in

1987. The enlarged party took the name Zimbabwe National Union-Patriotic Front (ZANU-PF).

Economic Crisis

In January 1992, Mugabe's government announced a five-year economic plan designed to liberalize the economy and reduce the huge budget deficit. Among the broad cuts to public spending were major reductions in the funding of education, including the elimination of free post-secondary education. In response, massive student demonstrations were held, resulting in the expulsion of 10,000 students from the University of Zimbabwe. The expulsions brought on even larger demonstrations, which in turn were put down severely by police. As the economy worsened and unemployment rose to disastrous levels, the Zimbabwean Congress of Trade Unions became a second supporter of mass protest. It declared a general strike, which gained widespread support but was unsuccessful in forcing changes in government policies.

In August 1996, civil servants went on strike over economic losses that had caused wages to fall by approximately 40 percent in four years. The job action eventually won wage gains of 20 percent, a dramatic increase over government proposals of 9 percent. Still, rapidly growing unemployment, to more than 45 percent, sparked new opposition movements and increased tension throughout the society. In January 1998, price increases on staple goods set off days of rioting as thousands of residents raided shops and businesses in Harare's suburbs. The army was eventually called in to regain control. In 1999, after the death of Joshua Nkomo and with social and economic conditions continuing to deteriorate, opposition to Mugabe and his one-party government escalated.

In 2000, the government offered a referendum that would grant government officials immunity from prosecution and would sanction the government seizure of remaining white-owned farms. Voters defeated the referendum, causing another violent clampdown on opposition groups. The "no" vote on the referendum reflected widespread anger against a network of Zimbabwean army veterans who had been forcibly expropriating farmland previously owned by white farmers. The program had brought death or violence not only to white farmers but also to black farmworkers and opposition activists. Critics charged that the veterans land expropriation campaign was an attempt by the government to divert attention from the failure of earlier land redistribution projects. They pointed out that the government controlled approximately 2 million acres of farmland that had been promised to small farmers for resettlement but never delivered. Instead, it had been given to Mugabe's allies and supporters.

The main public opposition to the Mugabe government came from the Ndebele-based Movement for Democratic Change (MDC), which ran candidates against the government's candidates beginning in September 1999. Mugabe's ZANU-PF accused MDC of being a front for Western interests, especially the British. Mugabe publicly referred to MDC members as traitors, and in 2005 his government passed legislation to prevent party members from traveling abroad to meet with supporters in other countries.

Among the strongest opposition groups was the 200,000-member Zimbabwe National Students Union (ZINASU), which repeatedly held mass political rallies in defiance of the government's Public Order and Security Act. Under that measure, Zimbabweans were required to apply for police permission for any meeting of three or more people to discuss politics. Despite government surveillance and violent police repression, ZINASU demonstrated openly against government policies on behalf of the poor. In fact, ZINASU advocated more radical policies than the MDC did, urging that Zimbabwe adopt a kind of internationalist socialism.

By 2005, unemployment in Zimbabwe stood at almost 80 percent. As the official economy ground to a halt, millions of Zimbabweans became dependent on the unofficial economy, in which barter took the place of money. Tens of thousands of Zimbabweans fled the country for both economic and political reasons, most heading to neighboring South Africa. Meanwhile, international observers urged the South African government of Thabo Mbeki to take a harder line against Mugabe. Mbeki replied that quiet diplomacy rather than tougher measures was more likely to bring needed reforms to Zimbabwe.

In early 2005, the Mugabe government launched Operation Murambatsvina ("Sweep Out the Trash"), a massive project to demolish the shantytowns surrounding Harare. By the end of the year, more than 1 million people had lost their homes or jobs as a result of the campaign and had become internal refugees. More than 22,000 poor people who survived on illegal trade were arrested and their goods confiscated. UN-Habitat, the United Nations agency for human settlements, declared the campaign a violation of international law; opposition groups contended that it specifically targeted people who voted against the ruling party in March 31 parliamentary elections. Police also rounded up homeless people and beggars and put them on forced labor farms. Opponents of the government suggested that the underlying aim of Operation Murambatsvina was precisely to take away people's livelihoods and force them into state labor. Eventually the humanitarian crisis grew so large that the government allowed relief agencies into the camps to avoid thousands of deaths from disease and starvation.

Meanwhile, Operation Murambatsvina met with stiff resistance. Residents of the townships outside Harare put up barricades and fought pitched battles with police. Organizations such as Women of Zimbabwe Arise (WOZA) and the Zimbabwe Congress of Trades Unions (ZCTU) organized peaceful demonstrations and mass protests. In response, Senior Assistant Police Commissioner Edmore Veterai ordered his officers to treat the campaign as a war and to respond with violence.

Amid the political strife and economic despair, Zimbabweans could not help looking to the future. While it seemed unlikely that Mugabe's hold on power would soon be shaken, he had turned eighty years old in 2004, and the people began to ask what would come of their troubled homeland when he was no longer on the scene.

Jeffrey A. Shantz

See also: Ethnic and Religious Conflicts; Zimbabwe: Struggle for Majority Rule, 1965–1980.

Bibliography

Hill, Geoff. *What Happens After Mugabe?* Cape Town: Zebra Press, 2005.

Raftopoulos, Brian, and Tyrone Savage, eds. *Zimbabwe: Injustice and Political Reconciliation.* Cape Town: Institute for Justice and Reconciliation, 2004.

INDEX

General Index

Salazar, Antonio de Oliveria, 1:78, 227; 2:590; 4:1198
Salek, Mustapha Ould, 1:221
Salih, Ali Abdullah, 4:1077, 1198
Salinas de Gortari, Carlos, 2:460–462
Sallal, Abdullah as-, 4:1075, 1076, 1198
Saloth Sar. *See* Pol Pot
SALT. *See* Strategic Arms Limitation Talks
Samakuva, Isaias, 1:96
Samoyoa, Salvador, 2:418
Samper, Ernesto, 2:377–378; 4:1198
Sampson, Nicos, 3:783
San Andres Accords, 2:464
Sanaa (Yemen), 4:1076
Sanchéz Cerro, Luis, 2:494
Sandinista National Liberation Front, 2:468–472; 4:1209
Sandinista People's Army, 2:479–480
Sandino, Agusto, 2:468
Sandline International, 4:1096
Sands, Bobby, 3:838
Sandy's, Duncan, 2:444
Sangkum Reastr Niyum, 2:527
Sanguinetti, Julian, 2:516
Sanha, Malam Bacai, 1:188
Sankara, Thomas, 1:98–99; 4:1198
Sankawulo, Wilson, 1:206
Sankoh, Foday, 1:269, 271–273; 4:1198
Santa Cruz massacre, 2:593
Sant'Edigio Accords, 1:235
SANU. *See* Sudan African National Union
Sanusiyah, 4:1053
SAOs. *See* Serbian Autonomous Regions
SAP. *See* South Africa Party
Sarajevo (Bosnia), 3:767–769, 771
Sarekat Dagang Islam (Indonesia), 2:599
Sarekat Islam (Indonesia), 2:599
Sarin, 4:1183
Sarkij, Elias, 4:1047
Sarkis, Ilyas, 4:1048
Saro-Wiwa, Ken, 1:254; 4:1198
Sassou Nguesso, Denis, 1:147–151; 4:1107, 1198
Satanic Verses, The, 4:1154–1155
Satellites, Sputnik, 2:568
Saudi Arabia
    arms trade, 1:68
    foreign policy and relations
        Afghanistan, 3:689
        Iraq, 4:985
        Kuwait, 4:986
        Taliban, 3:696
        United States, 4:987
        Yemen, 4:1075–1076
    Osama bin Laden. *See* Bin Laden, Osama
    support of Muslim militants, 1:60
    terrorist attacks, 2:509
    U.S. in, 1:60
SAVAK. *See* Organization of Information and Security of Iran
Savimbi, Jonas, 1:38, 78, 88, 91, 94; 4:1198
    death of, 1:96
    first war in Angola, 1:87–88
    formation of UNITA, 1:80
    loss of election, 1:93–94
    second war in Angola, 1:95

Savimbi, Jonas *(continued)*
    See also Union for the Total Independence of Angola
Saw Maung, 2:648
Sawyer, Amos, 1:202, 204
Sayed, El-Ouali Mustapha, 1:321
Schaufelberger, Albert, 2:419
Schneider, Rene, 2:370
School of the Americas, 2:464, 483, 486–487
School uniforms, 2:111
Schwartzkopf, Norman, 4:1198
Scientific socialism, 1:276
Scud missiles, 4:988
SDA. *See* Party of Democratic Action
SDLP. *See* Social Democratic and Labour Party
SDP. *See* Social Democratic Party
SDS. *See* Serbian Democratic Party
Sea agreements, 4:1184
SEATO. *See* Southeast Asia Treaty Organization
Secessions
    Abkhazia and South Ossetia from Georgia, 3:803
    Chechnya from Russia, 3:871
    Croatia from Yugoslavia, 3:777
    Darfur from Sudan, 1:304
    Georgia from Soviet Union, 3:802
    Ibo from Nigeria, 1:247
    Kosovo movement, 3:878–880
    Macedonia from Yugoslavia, 3:854
    See also Separatist movements
Secret Armed Organization, 3:923, 925
SED. *See* Socialist Unity Party
Sekber Golkar, 2:608
Selassie, Haile, 1:155–156, 161, 165, 166
    bio, 4:1198
    claim of Ogaden, 1:171
    fall of, 1:169
    growing dissatisfaction with, 1:166–167
    Pan-Africanism, 4:1104
Seme, Pixley, 1:284
Sen, Hun, 4:1198
Senanayake, Don Stephen, 3:747
Sendero Luminoso. *See* Shining Path
Sendic, Raul, 2:514, 515, 516; 4:1198
Sengal, 1:221
Separate Amenities Act, 1:285
Separatist movements
    Cabinda (Angola), 1:83–85
    Canada, 2:364–368
    Comoros, 1:125–127
    India, 3:734–736
    Indonesia, 2:609–612; 4:1085–1087
    Patani, 3:664–666; 4:1208
    Solomon Islands, 4:1098–1100
    Thailand, 3:664–666
    See also Secessions
September 11, 1:60, 61; 2:508; 3:699, 713; 4:1148
September 30 Movement, 2:606–607
Serbia, 1:44, 52, 56; 3:857, 876–880
    key dates, 3:877
Serbian Autonomous Regions, 3:766
Serbian Democratic Party, 3:766
Serbs
    Croatian, 3:776–777
    Kosovar, 3:878

Seregni Mosquera, Liber, 2:515, 516
Serrano, Jorge, 2:440
Seven Years' War, 2:364
Seventeenth parallel, 3:673
SFLP. *See* Sri Lanka Freedom Party
Shaat al-Arab waterway, 4:978, 985
Shaba. *See* Katanga province
Shagari, Alhaji Shehu, 1:253
Shamir, Yitzhak, 4:1198
Shan State Army-South, 2:651
Shankhill Butchers, 3:838
Shara, Farouk al-, 4:1137
Sharia. *See* Islamic law
Sharif, Nawaz, 3:713
Sharon, Ariel, 4:1013–1014, 1029–1030, 1198
    Al-Aqsa mosque, 4:1067, 1069
Sharpeville massacre, 1:285
Shastri, Lal Bahadur, 3:718, 720
Shatila, 4:1209
Shehabi, Yusuf, 4:1039
Shehada, Salah, 4:1071
Shell Oil, 1:247, 248, 254
Shevardnadze, Eduard, 3:801–804; 4:1198
Shia (branch of Islam), 4:963–964, 1210
Shi'a muslims, Taliban attack on, 3:696–697
Shi'a Wahdat, 3:695
Shiism, 3:954–955
Shi'ite Ismaili Muslim, 1:56
Shining Path, 2:496–499; 4:1210
Shonenkan, Ernest, 1:254
Shtykov, Terentyi, 2:624, 625
Shukeiry, Ahmed, 4:1008
Shuttle diplomacy, 4:1023–1024, 1045
SI. *See* Sarekat Islam
Siad Barre, Mohammed, 1:38, 171–172, 276–279; 4:1198
Sicarii (Jewish sect), 1:56
Sicilian Mafia. *See* Italian Mafia
Sierra Leone
    Charles Taylor, 1:204–205, 209, 211, 270
    coups, 1:269–273
    elections, 1:271
    ethnic and religious conflicts, 1:269–273
    historical background, 1:269
    independence, 1:269
    key dates, 1:270
    peacekeeping efforts, 1:271, 272; 4:1124–1125
    post-war, 1:272–273
    rise of RUF, 1:269–271
Sierra Leone People's Party, 1:269, 271
Sihamoni, Norodom, 2:535
Sihanouk, Norodom, 2:525–527, 532, 535, 537; 4:1198
Sik, Ota, 3:794–795
Sikh uprising, 3:731–733
Sikhs, 3:707, 731–733
Siles Zuazo, Hernan, 2:355–356
Simla conference, 3:710, 728
Simmel effect, 1:40
Simon Bolívar Guerrilla Coordinator, 2:377
Sinai War, 3:944–945
Sindicatos, 2:356
Sindono, Michele, 3:846–847